LINCOLN CHRISTIAN UNIVERSITY
P9-DEA-143

This is That

Personal Experiences
Sermons and
Writings

of

Aimee Semple McPherson
EVANGELIST

Echo Park Evangelistic Association, Inc.
1100 Glendale Boulevard :: Los Angeles, California

YOUR SISTER IN THE KING'S GLAD SERVICE

Aimee Semple McPherson.

THIS IS THAT

Acts 2:16-18.

THIS IS THAT which was spoken by the Prophet Joel: "And it shall come to pass in the last days, saith God, I will pour out of my Spirit upon all flesh; and your sons and daughters shall prophesy . . . and upon my servants and my handmaidens I will pour out, in those days, of My Spirit; and they shall prophesy."

COPIES OF THIS BOOK
MAY BE OBTAINED FROM

ECHO PARK EVANGELISTIC ASSOCIATION, INC.

1100 Glendale Boulevard

LOS ANGELES, CAL.

ILLUSTRATIONS

Contents

PART I.

PERSONAL TESTIMONY

CONTENTS—Continued

PART II.

SOME SERMONS AND WRITINGS OF AIMEE SEMPLE McPHERSON

CONTENTS—Concluded

THE LITTLE GREY HOME IN THE WEST

Known to the world as "The House that God Built"—now opened as "The Bungalow Church of the Four-Square Gospel"

Preface

"We cannot but speak those things which we have seen and heard," (Acts 4:20) said the Apostle Peter when called before Annas, the High Priest.

"None of these things move me, neither count I my life dear unto myself, so that I might finish my course with joy, and the ministry, which I have received of the Lord Jesus, to testify the Gospel of the Grace of God," (Acts 20:24) declared the Apostle Paul when standing before the elders at Ephesus.

There are tears in my eyes and a holy awe in my heart, as I look back over the past fifteen years of ministry and consider the loving kindness and the tender mercies of the Lord Jesus Christ unto this, his unworthy handmaiden.

Hallelujah! Glory, glory to His name! To think that He ever could have loved me and have called me from a life of carelessness and frivolity unto His own dear service! To think that He could have permitted me to be a cup-bearer for the King! A worm within His dear Hand, with which He might thrash a mountain! An empty pitcher with which He might water His lilies! A yielded channel through whom He might pour streams of blessing upon a thirsty desert! A poor, but a willing mouthpiece through whom the story of the Saviour's Love might be preached unto hundreds of thousands in Canada, Ireland, England, China, Australia, and the United States of America! To think that He ever could have permitted me to lead tens of thousands of penitent sinners to the Fountain of Blood opened in the House of David for sin and uncleanness.

Hallelujah! All of the glory, the honor and the praise belongeth unto Him both now and forever!

The very memory of His goodness, His patience, and His dealings set my heart to singing and my lips to shouting the glory of His matchless Name!

The recounting of His mercies, His leadings and His gentle ministrations flood my soul with unutterable joy and sweep me out into the midst of a sea of infinite love, all a-wonder that He could have cared for one so unworthy as I and have called me to Himself!

> "I stand all amazed in the presence
> Of Jesus, the Nazarene;
> And wonder how He could love me,
> A sinner condemned unclean.

Oh, how marvelous! oh, how wonderful!
And my song shall ever be
Oh, how marvelous! oh, how wonderful,
Is my Saviour's love for me!''

When, several years ago, I took in hand to set forth in order a declaration of those things which the Lord had done for me, the task was undertaken under the most unfavorable circumstances. I was at that time traveling from city to city, and from state to state, writing the story page by page, often in the midnight hours when a revival service was closed and the crowds had gone to their homes, and were fast asleep.

As I thought of His great goodness to me and lived the meetings over again, I would write a while and cry a while; and write a while and smile a while. I pray this testimony may be as great a blessing to those who read as to the one who wrote.

Remember, as you peruse these pages, that the Lord is no respecter of persons. That what He did for one so unworthy as I, he waits to do for all!

The first edition and the second edition met such a great demand on the American continent, in Europe and in the islands of the sea that they were soon exhausted. This third edition has been enlarged in personal testimony, having added the story of two and a half years of the best revival campaigns which we have ever been privileged to conduct. In order not to enlarge the size or the price of the book, some other writings have been removed and may be found under separate cover by those who desire.

As this book, containing personal testimony and writings, goes forth to the world, we are continuing the Lord's work in the great Angelus Temple at Echo Park, Los Angeles, California. During the first six months, since the Temple opened, between seven and eight thousand men and women have been converted; some one thousand five hundred have been baptized in water; hundreds have been healed and filled with the Holy Spirit. And, humbly, under the precious blood of Jesus Christ, our battle-cry is "Onward Christian Soldiers."

Pray for us, Beloved, as we will pray for you and for the saints everywhere. Though the reader and the writer may never meet in this present life, this book goes from my hand and heart with the earnest prayer and hope that we shall all rise together to meet the Lord in the clouds of glory, when He shall appear.

THE AUTHOR.

Part I—Personal Testimony

CHAPTER I.

MY MOTHER.

"The word of the Lord came unto me, saying,
Before I formed thee . . . I knew thee; and before thou camest forth . . . I sanctified thee and I ordained thee a prophet unto the nations. Then said I, Ah! Lord God! behold, I cannot speak; for I am a child. But the Lord said unto me, Say not, I am a child; for thou shalt go to all that I shall send thee, and whatsoever I command thee thou shalt speak. Be not afraid of their faces; for I am with thee to deliver thee. Then the Lord put forth His hand, and touched my mouth, and said unto me, Behold, I have put My Words in thy mouth." Jer. 1:(4-9).

WHEN I was a girl seventeen years of age, the Lord spoke these words plainly into my startled ears, as I was alone in my bedroom praying one day. It was a solemn time when He ordained me there to preach the Gospel. At first it seemed too astounding and impossible to be true that the Lord would ever call such a simple, unworthy little country girl as I to go out and preach the Gospel but the call and ordination were so real that, although later set apart and ordained by the saints of God, the memory of my little bedroom, flooded with the glory of God as He spoke those words, has always been to me my real ordination.

It is because the words, "Before I formed thee I knew thee, and before thou camest forth I sanctified thee," are so true in my life that I must begin my testimony by taking you back some twenty years before I was born. Our lives are like a great loom, weaving many threads together, and the first threads of my life are inseparably woven about my dear Mother: it is with her, therefore, that the story of my life really begins.

Returning from school at the age of twelve, she read excitedly of a strange "Army" who were announced to bombard the town and take prisoners for the King. Prevailing upon her mother to risk the danger, they stood in a downpour of rain, awaiting the advent of the army. Presently the word was passed—

"Here they come!"

But where were they? Could this be all? Three strangers, cloaked in quiet blue, stepped forth into the square, and knelt in silent prayer.

The humility, seriousness and sweetness of it swept over her heart. She realized the tender drawing of the Holy Spirit, and before a word had been spoken she knew that these were God's people and her people. As they sang—

"We are bound for the land of the pure and the holy,
The home of the happy, the kingdom of love.
Ye wanderers from God, in the broad road of folly,
O! say—will you go to the Eden above?"

Her heart, melting in love and adoration, answered — "I will go."

Her mother had talked much of the mighty power of God manifested in the early Methodist church, and here in the Army she found it again, and it was nothing uncommon to see men and women slain as in the church of John Wesley's day. Her heart was filled with a desire to win other souls for Jesus; the love of Christ constrained her to His glad service, and the all-absorbing purpose of her soul was to prepare in obedience to the divine call.

* * *

Soon came the illness and death of her mother, who had talked to her solemnly of the time soon coming when the little girl should be left alone in the world, telling her that she would commend her to the tender care of God and the Captain's wife, who had been her spiritual mother. She did not waver for an instant in answering the call to the ranks of the Army and after quickly packing her simple belongings, my mother left all, friends and home, and native land, to follow Jesus.

The period of service which followed her arrival at the Army quarters in the distant town, brought blessed help and inspiration. The godly life of her leaders, and the prayers of the Captain, who frequently spent whole nights on his face before God in intercession for precious souls, the hours spent in visiting the sick and sinful—the trudging five miles to assist in "Outpost" duties, the "War Cry" selling, and meetings, all helped comprise the routine of life.

But again fell the shadows — this time an illness which necessitated an extended change of scene and work; this meant a painful goodby to her comrades, and a visit to a country farm.

Then it was, while weak in body, depressed in spirit, and mourning over the loss of a mother's sympathetic hand, that she married, hoping to be able to continue her work for God, but amidst the strenuous and unaccustomed duties of heavy farm work, she was compelled to acknowledge that she was caught in the devil's net, and helpless as far as active service was concerned, and must largely devote herself to the manifold cares of life and home.

Even so environed, she stood true to her Lord, setting up a family altar, and helping with meetings in the homes of the neighborhood, often driving or walking the six miles to the nearest corps, and counted it the one bright hour of her day, even when weary and worn with heavy toil and care. Yet, realizing ever that she had failed the Lord, who had redeemed and set her apart for His glorious purpose, life grew more and more dreary; her spirit grieved sore, with no ray of hope to rectify herself toward God, and the souls she had been called to win.

Ah! Many who read this experience will know how to enter into her feelings, for alas, many grow faint and falter by the wayside, or seek to find an easier pathway, only to discover themselves outside the paths of obedience and blessing.

My Mother's pathway, in these days, was hedged about with difficulties. Shorn of her usefulness, fettered by circumstances, she truly did grind in the prison house; but, strange as it may seem, during all the time that her body was fettered, her soul was turning Heavenward. Each hour the longing became more intense to go on with the work for which God had ordained her, and for which purpose she had left home and friends and separated herself unto the Lord. Finally it absorbed her every thought in waking, and became her one dream in repose—*she must* make good her belated pledge. She must "come back" to the glorious calling of the Cross.

HOPE'S ONE RAY.

One day, after reading over and over the story of Hannah, she went to her room, and closing the door, kneeled by her bed, and prayed unto the Lord, and vowed a vow, saying—

"Oh, Lord, You called me to preach the Gospel, but somehow I have failed You and cannot go, but if You will only hear my prayer, as You heard Hannah's prayer of old, and give me a little baby girl, I will give her unreservedly into your service, that she may preach the word I should have preached, fill the place I should have filled, and live the life I should have lived in Thy service. O Lord, hear and answer me; give me the witness that Thou hast heard me, O Lord, for Thine own Name's sake. Amen."

Turning to the window, she swept back the curtains and gazed wistfully up at the dark clouds shrouding the face of the sky and shutting out the sunshine beyond.

Suddenly there came a rift in the clouds, and a ray of sunlight illumined yonder hilltop, moved quickly down the slope of the hill, reached the valley, the orchard, the house itself, and fell full upon the white, anxious face with its tear-reddened eyes, framed in the window, lighting it with divine radiance, hope and courage, and swept on into the room, flooding it with golden glory.

To the longing little heart of my Mother, as she kneeled at the window, it seemed that surely here was the divine witness from above—the sealing of her vow unto God.

Again she read and reread the story of Hannah, and the child she had dedicated unto the Lord. She sat on, gazing far away—dreaming of the future years. Over the distant hills the sun was fast sinking, transforming the sombre sky into a glorious mirage of hope, flaming with crimson, purple and gold.

O Hope! dazzling, radiant Hope!— What a change thou bringest to the hopeless; brightening the darkened paths, and cheering the lonely way.

SCENE OF CHAPTERS II AND III
"There was a B-a-b-y in the quiet old farm house"
HOME OF MY EARLY PENTECOSTAL EXPERIENCES
AND WEDDING

SISTER McPHERSON WITH HER TWO CHILDREN
ROBERTA SEMPLE AND ROLF McPHERSON

CHAPTER II.

THE BABY.

"For this child I prayed; and the Lord gave me my petition, which I asked of Him. Therefore also I have lent him unto the Lord; as long as he liveth he shall be lent unto the Lord." I Sam. 1:27, 28.

"Hush, my babe,
  Lie still and slumber,
Holy angels guard thy bed.
  Heavenly blessings without number,
Gently falling on thy head."

THERE was a B-A-B-Y in the house!—a tiny, insignificant little thing; not good for much of anything but sleeping, and crying, and sucking a soft little pink thumb,—and it seems that I was that baby.

Mother was rocking the warm little bundle, so carefully wrapped in the big embroidered shawl, and singing softly the childtime lullaby—

"Hush, my babe—"

The little head was nodding, nodding, n-o-d-d-i-n-g—,

"Lie still and sl—"

Tired eyes were drooping, d-r-o-o-p-i-n-g—.

"Holy angels guard thy b—"

The tiny fingers were slowly relaxing their clasp,

"Heavenly blessings, without num—"

Another final little pat and—the baby was asleep.

Outside the dining-room windows the autumn leaves were again drifting lightly to the earth. The late October sunshine was again slanting through the gorgeous foliage of the big maple and locusts that stood as sentries by our door. Fall breezes, rustling through the leaves, shook the branches and sent a veritable shower of gay colored leaves cascading through the air and tapping lightly at the window-pane, as though inviting memory to soar as lightly as they back to the fall, when last these same trees had shaken off their coat of many colors—back to the day in her room, when she had prayed for the little daughter that should take her place and preach the good tidings of great joy.

Never, for a moment, in the days that followed, had she

doubted God—was He not faithful who had promised? Piece by piece the wardrobe had been finished and hidden away cautiously under lock and key. Sitting there, folding the baby in her arms, in memory she again tip-toed lightly up the stairs, and after locking her door, with greatest delight unfolded and lovingly fingered, garment by garment, the wardrobe that was to be for the little girl. Had she not asked God for a "daughter" that would fill her place in His service? Even the morning the little pink-faced, brown-eyed stranger had announced its arrival with no uncertain tones, making the quiet old farmhouse ring and echo, my little Mother had not doubted, but asked confidently—

"Where is *she?* Bring *her* here."

Then her thoughts swept beyond the past and the present, and soared far away into the future—dreaming of the years that were to come, when this wee creature with the turned-up nose, and the "ten tiny fingers and toes," would be preaching the Gospel of Jesus Christ, the Son of God.

Caressing the little fingers, she dreamed of the day when these same little hands, grown stronger, would hold a Bible, and wield the sword of the Word, when these little feet would follow the Lamb "whithersoever He leadeth"—when these little lips would preach the Word. Ah—

"Faith, mighty faith, the promise sees,
And looks to that alone.
Laughs at impossibilities,
And cries—'It shall be done'."

The great torrent of love and desire for personal service, which had hitherto flooded my Mother's soul, was now turned into a new channel—the one absorbing, all-important business of her life became the bringing up of the baby in the way she should go. This training, Mother felt, could not begin too early in life, and therefore, when I arrived at the age of three weeks, she announced to the horrified nurse, and the astonished household-in-general, her firm determination to take the baby to a "Jubilee" at the five-mile distant corps.

Much well-meant advice to—

"Keep that child at home by the fire," followed my Mother to the door. Some declared that the baby would surely have pneumonia. Aunt Maria, who "knew all about babies," shook her head, and told how they managed their baby at her house, protesting to the last—

"You'll kill that Baby! You don't know anything about a baby. Anyone who does not know how to take better care of a baby than that shouldn't have one." (But alas! Aunt Maria's baby, whose natural body they nurtured so carefully, and kept cuddled by the fire, soon took the much-feared cold and died.)

Mother tells me that from the very first meeting I was warmly welcomed—occupied the front seat—and contributed, without request, my full share to the music and interest of the evening.

At six weeks of age I was promoted to the platform. It was my solemn dedication service in the Salvation Army—the hour for which my Mother had longed and prayed—the hour of her dreams and hopes—the hour wherein she publicly consecrated this visible answer to prayer—her little daughter—to the service of the Lord.

Thus in my infancy, my precious Mother fulfilled her vow unto the Lord, who had looked upon the affliction of His handmaid, remembered her, and given unto her the child for which she prayed.

"On Him who watches over all,
I cast my weight of care,
Assured He hears me when I pray,
And always answers prayer.

Sometimes I wait full many a year
Sometimes 'tis then and there,
His answering message I can hear;
God always answers prayer.

Sometimes afar He bids me 'go'—
But He'll go with me there;
If He says 'stay', I'm glad 'tis so;
Love always answers prayer.

Tomorrow, perhaps—it may be today,
But whether 'tis 'Yea',
Or whether 'tis 'Nay',
God always answers prayer."

CHAPTER III.

CHILDHOOD DAYS.

(A chapter written for the children—big folks and wise folks should not read, but pass on to Chapter IV.)

* * *

"Train up a child in the way he should go; and when he is old, he will not depart from it." Prov. 22:6.

* * *

"Gentle Jesus, meek and mild,
Look upon this little child;
Pity my simplicity,
Suffer me to come to Thee.
Fain I would to Thee be brought,
Gracious Lord, forbid it not.
Find a little child a place."

GOD bless Papa, God bless Mamma, God bless everybody, all over the world, and make little Aimee a good girl, for Jesus' sake, Amen."—

So ended each happy, childhood day, with prayers and kisses, and Bible stories. My own childhood days being so blessed with Christian influence and Bible teaching, it has always seemed to me that the home without a Godly praying Mother had been deprived of the greatest of all earthly blessings; that home has been robbed of the greatest of all earthly jewels. The child of that home has suffered an irreparable loss, never to be regained.

On the other hand, the poorest home—the humblest cottage in the dell, that contains a godly Mother—who day by day dispenses her prayers, tears and smiles, her words of reproof and encouragement, her patience and love, her sunshine, and the lilt of a song—that home, though poor as this world counts poverty, is as a casket that contains a priceless jewel.

If anyone should ask me which of my childhood memories I hold most dear, I should skip over the beloved wee lambies, the big Newfoundland dog, the bossies, the colts, the downy little goslings and chickens, my white doves, and numerous other childish treasures of my heart, and should tell of that hallowed twilight hour when, clasped tightly in my Mother's arms, we rocked to and fro in the big old comfy rocker, as she told me the most wonderful Bible stories and sang hymns of the Saviour's love.

There was the story of Daniel in the lion's den, ever dear to the heart of a child—the three Hebrew children in the fiery furnace—Joseph with his coat of many colors—Moses and Aaron with the children of Israel—the life and sacrifice of Jesus, the beauty of that wonderful place called heaven, which He had gone to prepare. All these and many others were as bright, golden threads woven through my childish training. At the age of five there were very few stories in the Bible I could not rise and tell when asked to do so. So much for an early Christian training.

Did any of you little children ever see the picture of the guardian angel watching over and protecting the tiny boy and girl that ran along plucking flowers at the edge of a great precipice? In the same miraculous way our dear Jesus watched over and protected me—that happened again and again.

There was the time I climbed into the big old bucket that hung over the deep, black well with its rows and rows of moss-covered stones that formed its wall—down, down, down as far as my inquisitive eyes could see, as I peered over the square, boarded enclosure which stood just on a level with my chin when I stood on tip-top-toe. Sometimes, when the sun was just right, and the bucket was resting on its little shelf just inside the well, I could see another little girl down there, and when I called a friendly little—

"Hello!" to her, she would always echo back— "'Lo!" Reaching across the board enclosure that guarded the mouth of the well was the windlass with the crank that turned the roller and let down such yards and yards of big rope, and then drew up the great bucket brimming full of icy water.

The big handle had given me many hard, warning whacks when I was experimenting with it, and Mother had warned me again and again not to go near the well; but one day when she was having company, I slipped down out of my chair at the table, away from her protecting care, and watchful eyes, and toddled straight to the well which held such mystery and interest.

What fun it would be to get hold of the swinging rope, get into the bucket and go down to visit the little girl I had seen reflected in the water! I had just climbed up on a box, leaned over, and was scrambling into the bucket, when Mother missed me. The silence pervading the air arousing her apprehensions, she flew to the door just in time to see the skirt of a pink dress and a little pair of feet disappearing as I crept over. The handle jarred loose from its holder and was beginning to turn when she caught it and snatched me from the mouth of the well into her arms.

The well was boarded up higher after that, and soon a windmill was put in. There was no more chance to play with the bucket, but surely the Father who watches over all had protected and spared my life. Bless His name.

When you read the next chapter you will see how I slipped from my heavenly Father's table in just the same way, and leaned far out over the yawning black well of sin, and was just being allured into its depths, and the handle was beginning to turn, when Jesus rescued me and snatched me up into His arms and safety.

Then there was the time Mother had sent me out behind the barn to gather a pail of chips for the kitchen fire. This was one of my daily chores. My Father was a bridge contractor and builder, and there were always such piles of chips where he had been hewing the great timbers.

This particular evening I had on a little white dress with red moons in it, of which I was very proud. The bull, who, with the other cattle, was returning from the fields and gathering about the watering trough, evidently did not like those fine red moons in my dress. He had always been so gentle and harmless that danger from that source was never expected.

I was just at the corner of the barn, opposite a big pile of lumber, and had my bucket almost filled with chips. Frightened at the menacing way in which he advanced, I threw a chip at him and told him to "Go away." Without halting, however, he came on—in a business-like, determined way I did not like.

Towering over me, he hit me with his forehead, and every time that I would get up he would bunt me so hard that I would fall down again in the muddy barnyard. Fortunately my Father had sawed his horns off sometime previous, but it was only the mercy of God that kept him from pawing me under his great, angry feet, and that gave me the presence of mind to crawl into and through the hollow place that ran under the pile of lumber, clear to the other end, thus escaping as he waited my reappearance.

I seemed perfectly numb; my mouth was filled with dirt and blood but tightly in my hands I clasped that bucket of chips. Mamma had sent me after chips, and chips I was going to take to Mamma.

Mother heard the sound of my crying but thought I was singing. (This did not speak very well for my singing). However, she caught a sight of me through the window, and in a moment was by my side, and when she gathered me up in her arms I was still clinging to the pail of chips, and it was not until she got me to the well and began to bathe me with cold water that I fainted away in her arms, releasing my hold upon them.

Being called upon to endure hardness as a good soldier, and to bring back precious souls for Jesus, no matter how hard the conflict, the Lord has put that within me which causes me to go through, refusing defeat, refusing even to be discouraged, and I often think of the little girl in the bedraggled, red-mooned dress, who brought home the bucket of chips; and someway I know that just as my Mother gathered me with the marks of combat, chips and all into her arms, He will meet me at the end of life's little day and gather me with my tight-clasped, precious burden, into His arms.

Riding the horses on my Father's farm was one of my greatest delights. Here again the Lord watched over me. One time when I was riding a high-mettled horse whom even the menfolks hardly risked themselves with, but who had succumbed condescendingly to my coaxings of sugar and pettings, he became frightened at the rattling of the wire fence, from which I sprang to his back, and began a mad gallop across the fields before I had well gotten my equilibrium.

He was running toward a barbed-wire fence. I knew that if he reached this fence it would ruin the horse, one which my Father valued highly, and decided to cling to his long, flowing mane and spring as he sprang, alighting on my feet, believing that he would slow down immediately. This I had done at other times, but now, unfortunately, I landed on an anthill, which turned my ankle and sprained it badly, severing some of the cords. But my life was spared, praise God, and in spite of crutches and pain I passed the examinations at the head of my class, and came in second for the scholarship offered the one making the highest grades in the collegiate entrance examination.

During the early years of my life my Mother was Junior Sergeant-Major in the Salvation Army (in other words, Superintendent of the Sunday School), and had a great flock of young people under her care. It was often a great effort for her to go to the five-mile distant corps where her work lay. When roads were poor or horse and carriage was not to be had, she would walk; and when roads were good, many's the time (when I was the age of five and six and seven), she carried me on the handle-bars of her bicycle, over hills and dust to the meeting, and kept up her Christian work.

These meetings were to me a great delight. It was a special joy to bring other little children to the penitent form to be prayed for. Very proud was I also of my Mother's imposing title. It seemed very grand and important to me, and not satisfied to await the next meeting at the barracks, I would often convert the big bedroom upstairs into a meeting house. Carrying chairs from other parts of the house thither and lining them up in rows I would conduct a meeting myself, and Mother, listening outside the door, would hear me solemnly announce—

"Now, Sergeant-Major will lead in prayer." With this I would kneel and pray.

"Now, the Sergeant-Major will sing a solo." Here followed the best imitation I knew how to produce of one of her sweet songs.

"Now, the Sergeant-Major will lead the testimony meeting" —"Read the Word," and finally all the chairs were solemnly requested to bow their heads while the Sergeant-Major closed in prayer.

And so you see God had His hand upon me, and the desires of my heart, and the aspirations of my mind in these early days. It seemed indeed true that as a child of prayer He had in loving compassion known me, and in tender mercy called me for a purpose. Oh, Hallelujah!

At the Young People's rallies it was customary for the children to wear white sashes with colored mottoes embroidered upon them, and whilst upon the other children's sashes would be such words as "Jesus Saves" or "God Is Love," etc., the one my Mother had worked for me read—"God's Little Child." And so did she hold me, for the fulfillment of her prayer,—through tempest and trial, sorrow and discouragement, that she might claim the promise and bring up the child in the way it should go, that when it was old it should not depart from it.

Tell me, little girls and boys who read this chapter, does your Mamma know Jesus? Does she pray for you that you may be a worker for Him some day, and have you given Him your heart while it is tender and you are in the beginning of Life?

CHAPTER IV.

GIRLHOOD.

"Foolishness is bound in the heart of a child." Prov. 22:15.

THEN came the days of study in the little white schoolhouse that stood on the corner a mile from our home. I was the only Salvationist child there, the other scholars being church members. At first they teased me about the Army with their shouting, their marching and their drum, for they were still a despised people in those days. I finally won over the hearts of the children, however, when I invented a drum from a round cheese box and with a ruler for a drum-stick and a "Blood and Fire" banner made from a red tablecloth we marched round the school and played "Army".

Everything went well until it was learned that I had some little talent for elocution. The distance to the barracks being great, and the churches seeming much more popular, I began going to the Methodist church, where my father had formerly been a choir leader. Once invited to take part in their entertainments, I was soon received in other churches and appearing on the programs the country round. We received great help and teaching along the lines of elocution, dialogues and plays by the church instructors in this art. After competing with others in the W. C. T. U. work, a silver and later a gold medal was awarded me.

Except for the temperance work, however, very few of the selections or plays were anything but comic. Upon asking preachers whether they would prefer something sacred they would invariably answer:

"Oh, give us something humorous; something comical to make the people laugh. That last Irish recitation was grand. Give us something like that."

As I recited, the audience would laugh and clap and laugh again until the tears came to their eyes, and I was very popular indeed with the churches in those days,—a great deal more so than I am now, mayhap.

As years went by I passed from grammar school to high, and became still more interested in the entertainments of the church. There were the oyster suppers, the strawberry festivals, the Christmas trees, and always the concerts to follow, for which tickets were sold—"to help God pay His debts and help support the church," I supposed then. But I have learned now that our God is so richly able to supply the funds for His work that He need not resort to any such methods.

The praise and applause of the people was very alluring to some of us younger ones, and we often talked together of going on the stage, arguing that the church was giving us a good training on this line and that anyway there was not much difference whether a play or a concert was given in the church or at the theatre.

My next step on the downward path was when I began reading novels from the Sunday School library (for a novel is a novel whether in a paper or a cloth-bound cover). And when I had devoured them I learned where more could be obtained.

The next luring of the tempter came when I was asked by a member of the choir as to whether I had been to the moving-picture theatre that week. I told her:

"No," that I had never seen any motion pictures outside of the church. She looked at me in such a condescending, pitying way that my pride was stung and I decided to go. I did not tell my Mother, however, and felt very guilty in entering until I saw several church members and a Sunday School teacher there; then I felt better (it surely must be all right if they were there), and settled down to enjoy the pictures.

Athletic, and fond of out-door sports, next in line came costume skating carnivals and then my first "college ball"—I was now well advanced in the high school. When I brought home the engraved invitation card, Mother flatly refused her permission for me to go and it took a great deal of pleading and coaxing to gain an unwilling consent. My dress and slippers were purchased and I went to my first dance radiantly happy on the exterior, but a little heavy and conscience-stricken on the interior, for I knew that Mother was sad and praying alone at home.

It seemed to be a very proper affair, however. My first dancing partner was the Presbyterian preacher. Other good (?) church members were there—surely Mother must be mistaken or a little old-fashioned in her ideas. How lovely it all seemed, the orchestra, the flowers, the attention paid me, the fine clothes, and the well-appointed luncheon!

Ah, sin, with what dazzling beauty, with what refinement and velvet dost thou cover thy claws! How alluring are the fair promises with which thou enticest the feet of youth! How cunning are the devices of the enemy! How smoothly and craftily he lays his plans and weaves the net which he draws ever tighter and tighter, illumining the future and its prospects with rose colors and fair painted promises, the fruit of which, once plucked, crumbles into gray ashes in the hand of him who runneth after it.

My future and educational prospects looked promising. No effort or labor was counted too great upon the part of my parents to send me to school, and indeed it was no little matter for them—ten miles must be covered each day, five in the morning and five at night, on the train or with horse and carriage, despite country roads, with their mud or rain or snow.

There was introduced into our class room at this time, a text-book entitled "High School Physical Geography," which delved into the problems of earth formation, rock strata, etc., and learnedly described the origin of life and the process of evolution. There were quotations from Darwin and other authorities on these weighty subjects. Explaining the origin of life upon this planet, it taught us that from the sea, with its slime, seaweed and fungus growth, insect life appeared. From insect life came animal life, and through continuous processes of evolution at last man appeared, who, of course, was higher than the monkeys or any other creature.

How these theories or teachings impressed other students I cannot say, but they had a remarkable effect upon me.

"Man?—a process of evolution?

—Why, then God had not created him at all, as the Bible said He did—preachers were true when they said there were errors and mistakes in the Bible." On and on raced the thoughts in my young mind until I reached the point:

"Well, then, if the Bible is mistaken in one place it is very apt to be mistaken in others. Its information is not reliable, and I guess there's no God at all, and that's why Christians act so pious in church on Sundays and do as they please through the week."

"No, I guess there *is* no God." Even the existence of the big moon and the twinkling stars had been explained by science. The sun, once a great mass of molten lava, had acquired a whirling motion and thrown off all these other planets, earth, moon and stars. Nothing about God, just science and a logical outcome of conditions now revealed by wise astronomers who had studied it all out through great telescopes (which had cost fabulous sums of money and taken many years to invent); and therefore they knew all about it.

This book raised so many questions in my mind that I delved deeper into other infidelistic theories. So interested did I become that I wrote an article to the "Family Herald and Weekly Star," published at Montreal, then Canada's leading paper. My inquiries were answered by Archbishop Hamilton and many others. Arguments both for and against the book and its teachings were brought out.

Is it any wonder that our pulpits are filled with infidels and higher critics today?

Out of the letters that poured in for months from England, New Zealand, Australia, and all parts of America, as well as from my own land, each containing a different explanation, not one said:

"Child, the Bible is true. Take the simple Word of God and believe it just as it reads."

The more I read and observed the lives of Christians, the more skeptical of the reality of God I became. (How I could ever have doubted is today a puzzle and a shame to me). The devil must have blinded my eyes for a time to the genuine Christians about me. All that I could see was empty profession. I saw men singing in the choir or sitting in the pews on Sunday and attending all sorts of worldly functions during the week. I began reading my Bible, to see whether it contradicted itself and how it compared with the books which I had read. Oh, I must know the truth—was there anything in religion?

Every time I had an opportunity I questioned and cross-questioned each Christian that I could get hold of. But I did not seem to get far. My first attempt was made upon my Mother. I had been thinking earnestly upon the subject, and just as she was coming up the steep cellar steps with a pan of milk in her hands, I met her with the question:

"Mother, how do you know there is a God?"

Poor dear, she was so surprised that she nearly fell backwards, down the steps. She explained things the best she knew how, bringing forth Scriptures, and pointing to creation with all its wonders as proving the handiwork of a Creator.

Each attempt at explanation I met with the learned words of those books and the superior (?) twentieth-century wisdom of my seventeen summers—books and wisdom which left mothers and Bibles far behind. Her arguments seemed to shrink to nothing, and her eyes opened with astonishment as she sat down suddenly on the kitchen chair, unable to get a word in edgeways.

My next attempt was made upon the minister when he came to our house to tea. Mother was out in the kitchen preparing the proverbial ministerial chicken dinner, but I had business in the parlor, ostensibly displaying the family album, but in reality endeavoring to probe him with the questions upon my mind.

"Does the Lord ever perform any miracles or heal any sick folks now?" I asked.

"Why no, child, the day of miracles is over," was his surprised reply. "People are expected to use the intelligence and wisdom the Lord has given them along medical and surgical lines—these are really miraculous, you know."

"But doesn't it say, over here in James 5:14, if any are sick among you to *'let him call for the elders of the church; and let them pray over him, anointing him with oil in the name of the Lord: And the prayer of faith shall save the sick, and they shall recover?'* "

"And is there not a scripture that says, *'Jesus Christ is the same yesterday, and today, and forever'?* and *'He that believeth on Me, the works that I do shall he do also; and greater works than these shall he do; because I go unto my Father'?*

"How do you reconcile the fact that the Lord no longer does such miraculous things, with these scriptures?"

My questions were evaded, and I was made to feel that I was but a mere child, and therefore could not understand these matters. They were never explained to my satisfaction.

Alarmed over my attitude and questions, my Mother asked me to join some church. When I made excuses she offered to take me to all the different churches, asking me to study the teachings of each of them and to join the one that seemed best. I replied that I felt I was doing enough church work now, with the entertainments and concerts, and added, in a self-righteous way, that I thought I was just as good as any of the others—I didn't see any particular difference in our lives, whether I was a member of the church or not did not matter.

"Well, let us go to the Salvation Army special meetings to-night. It is a long time since we have been there together."

Poor Mother! Will I ever forget her face when she found they were having an entertainment there that night, and the first selection rendered after we entered was:

"High diddle, diddle,
The cat and the fiddle,
The cow jumped over the moon!"

acted out by one of the local officers, amid the applause of the laughing audience. He was dressed to represent a colored minstrel.

Later we attended the special services being conducted by the Brigadier, his wife and daughter, who invited me very sweetly to give my heart to Jesus. I argued with her that there was no God, nothing in the Bible. She seemed to get into deep waters and went for her mother, who also begged me to come to the altar. Then they sent for the father, and before long I was the center of a group, my Mother on the outskirts, listening with blushing face while I set forth, in my ignorance, my opinion regarding evolution.

Oh, dear Jesus, how could I ever have doubted You when You have been so good, so merciful and so true to me all the days of my life!

Mother cried bitterly all the long drive home, and all the reproach she laid upon me was:

"Oh, Aimee, I never dreamed that I should bring up a daughter who would talk as you have before those people tonight! After all my years as a Christian, after my prayers and my work in that corps, *you* of all people, to talk like this! Oh, where have I failed? Oh! OH!! O-H!!!"

Conscience-stricken, and shamed before her grief, I fled to my room, as soon as we arrived, to think things over. I certainly loved my Mother; to cause her grief and sorrow was the last thing in this wide world which I wished to do—"and yet—and yet."

Not pausing to light the lamp, I went over to my bedroom window, threw it open wide and sat down on the floor with my elbows on the window-sill, my chin propped on my hands, and gazed reflectively up at the starry floors of heaven and at the great white silvery moon sailing majestically toward me from the eastern sky, before I finished my broken sentence—"I wonder if there really is a God? Who is right? What is the truth?"

The white mantle of snow which covered the fields and the trees, glistened in the clear, frosty air, and—

My! how big that moon looked up there, and how ten million stars seemed to wink and blink and twinkle! I drew a comforter round me and sat on and on, unmindful of the cold, looking up at the milky way, the big dipper, and other familiar luminaries.

—Surely, there m-u-s-t be a God up there back of them all. They seemed to breathe and emanate from His very presence and nearness.

At school we had studied the planets and how each rotated and revolved upon its own axis, and in its own orbit without friction or confusion. It was all so big, so high, so above the reach and ken of mortal man—surely a DIVINE hand must hold and control this wonderful solar system—

Why! how near God seemed—right now!

Suddenly, without stopping to think, I threw both arms impulsively out of the window and, reaching toward heaven, cried:

"Oh God!—If there be a God—reveal Yourself to me!"

The cry came from my very heart. In reality, a whisper was all that came from my lips—but just that whisper from an honest, longing heart, was enough to echo through the stars and reach the Father's throne. Up there, He whose ear is ever open to the cries of His little children, heard me and answered. Bless His Name.

Oh, if every doubter and professed infidel would just breathe that one sincere prayer to God, He would reveal Himself to them as He did to me, for He is no respecter of persons. Hallelujah!

CHAPTER V.

SALVATION AND THE BAPTISM OF THE HOLY SPIRIT.

"And it shall come to pass, that before they call, I will answer; and while they are yet speaking, I will hear." Isa. 65:24.

OUR prayer-answering God who sitteth upon the throne, whose ear is ever open to our cry, and whose heart is touched by our infirmities, was already answering the cry of this poor, unworthy child. He had set on foot a chain of events which was to lead not only to the salvation and baptism of my own soul, but which was to lead me out into His vineyard and make me a worker in His dear service.

It was just a few days after my prayer at the open window of my bedroom that (my Father having come into school for me) we were driving along Main Street on the way home, eagerly talking over and planning my parts in the grand Christmas affairs and concerts in the various churches and halls then looming above us. How pretty the store windows were in their Christmas dress of green and red and tinsel!

But look! Over there on the left hand side of the street there was a new sign on a window, which we had not seen before. It advertised a "Holy Ghost Revival" with old time "Pentecostal Power," and announced meetings every night and all day Sunday.

Turning to my father, I said:

"Daddy, I would like to go to that meeting tomorrow night. I believe this is the place, that I have heard about, where the congregation says "Amen" right out loud, and where sometimes the power of God falls upon the people, as it used to fall upon the old time Methodists. It would be loads of fun to go and see them."

"All right, daughter, we can go tomorrow night before your rehearsal in the town hall," he replied.

And thus it was that the next evening found us in the back seat, (where we could see all) in the little Mission which had recently been opened for the revival.

The congregation seemed to be largely composed of the middle classes. None of the wealthy or well known citizens of the town were there. Dressed as I was in worldly attire with my foolish little heart filled with unbelief and egotism, I felt just a little bit above the status of those round about me and looked on with an amused air as they sang, shouted, testified and prayed.

True to the reports which I had heard they had an "Amen Corner" with a Hallelujah echo. Bright testimonies and earnest zeal left not a dull moment. There was something strange about these people, they seemed to be so in earnest.

Then a tall young man, six feet two inches in height rose to his feet on the platform and taking his Bible in his hand opened it and began to read. His was a frank, kindly face, with Irish blue eyes that had the light of heaven in them, chestnut brown hair, with one rebellious brown curl which would insist in falling down close to his eye no matter how often he brushed it back.

Without a moment's hesitation he opened his Bible at the second chapter of Acts and read the 38th and 39th verses. (There is one thing about these Holy Ghost meetings where the Power of Pentecost is preached, one cannot attend them very long without learning that there is a second chapter to the Book of Acts. I learned this in my first meeting.)

The evangelist—Robert Semple—began his discourse with the first word of his text:

"Repent." Oh, how he did repeat that word—Repent! REPENT!! R-E-P-E-N-T!!! over and over again. How I did wish he would stop and say some other. It seemed to pierce like an arrow through my heart, for he was preaching under divine inspiration and in power and demonstration of the Holy Spirit. He really spoke as though he believed there was a Jesus and a Holy Spirit, not some vague, mythical, intangible shadow, something away off yonder in the clouds, but a real, living, vital, tangible, moving reality dwelling in our hearts and lives—making us His temple—causing us to walk in Godliness, holiness and adoration in His presence.

There were no announcements of oyster suppers or Christmas entertainments or sewing circles made—no appeal for money. Not even a collection was taken. It was just God, God, God from one end to the other, and his words seemed to rain down upon me, and every one of them hurt some particular part of my spirit and life until I could not tell where I was hurt the worst.

"Repent!" The evangelist went on to say that if the love of the world was in us the love of the Father was not there: theatres, moving pictures, dancing, novels, fancy-dress skating rinks (why, it just looked as if somebody had told him I was there, so vividly did he picture my own life and walk), worldly and rag-time music, etc., he condemned wholesale, and declared that all the people who were wrapped up in this sort of thing were of the devil, and were on their way to hell, and that unless they repented and that right speedily, renouncing the world, the flesh and the devil, they would be lost—eternally damned forever.

I did not do any more laughing, I assure you. I sat up straight in my seat. With eyes and ears wide open I drank in every word he said. After he had finished with the word "Repent," and explained what true salvation meant—the death, burial and resurrection that we would know as we were identified with our Lord, he began to preach on the next verse—

"And ye shall receive the gift of the Holy Ghost. For the promise is unto you, and to your children, and to all that are afar off, even as many as the Lord our God shall call."

Here he began to preach the baptism of the Holy Spirit, declaring that the message of salvation and the incoming of the Spirit should be preached side by side and hand in hand, and that for a Christian to live without the baptism of the Holy Spirit was to live in an abnormal condition not in accordance with God's wishes. He told how the Holy Spirit was received in Bible days and how the recipients of the Spirit had spoken in other tongues—languages they had never learned—as the Spirit gave them utterance.

Suddenly, in the midst of his sermon, the Evangelist closed his eyes and with radiant face began to speak in a language that was not his own—but the words of the Holy Spirit.

To me it was the voice of God thundering into my soul awful words of conviction and condemnation, and though the message was spoken in tongues it seemed as though God had said to me—

"YOU are a poor, lost, miserable, hell-deserving sinner!" I want to say right here that I *knew* this was God speaking by His Spirit through the lips of clay. There is a verse in the 14th chapter of I Corinthians which says the speaking in tongues is a sign to the unbeliever. This was certainly true in my case. From the moment I heard that young man speak with tongues to this day I have never doubted for the shadow of a second that there was a God, and that He had shown me my true condition as a poor, lost, miserable, hell-deserving sinner.

No one had ever spoken to me like this before. I had been petted, loved and perhaps a little spoiled: told how smart and good I was. But thank God that He tells the truth. He does not varnish us nor pat us on the back or give us any little sugar-coated pills, but shows us just where we stand, vile and sinful and undone, outside of Jesus and His precious blood.

All my amusement and haughty pride had gone. My very soul had been stripped before God—there was a God, and I was not ready to meet Him. Oh, how could I have looked down upon these dear people and felt that I was better than they? Why, I was not even worthy to black their shoes. They were saints and I was a sinner.

We had to slip out early, before the service was over, and how I got through the rehearsal I cannot say, but one thing I knew, and that is that during the next seventy-two hours I lived through the most miserable three days I had ever known up to that time.

Conviction! Oh! I could scarcely eat or rest or sleep. Study was out of the question. "Poor, lost, miserable, hell-deserving sinner" rang in my ears over and over again. I could see those closed eyes and that outstretched hand that pointed to my shrinking, sinful soul that was bared before the eyes of my Maker.

I began enumerating the many things which I would have to give up in order to become a Christian—there was the dancing. I was willing to part with that,—the novels, the theatre, my worldly instrumental music. I asked myself about each of them and found that I did not count them dear as compared with the joy of salvation and knowing my sins forgiven.

There was just one thing, however, that I found myself unwilling and seemingly unable to do. I knew that I could not be a Christian and recite those foolish Irish recitations and go through those plays and dialogues. A child of God must be holy and consecrated, with a conversation covered with the blood of Jesus. My Bible said that even for one idle word (let alone foolish words), we should have to give an account before the judgment throne of God. Yet it was too late now to cancel my promises for Christmas, too late to get others to fill my place. Evidently there was nothing to do but wait until after Christmas in order to become a Christian.

But how could I wait? I was desperately afraid. I trembled with conviction. It seemed as though every moment which I lived outside of God and without repentance toward Him was lived in the most awful peril and gravest danger of being cast into hell without mercy. Oh, that every sinner who reads these words might feel the same awful conviction upon his soul!

The second and third day I fell to praying something like this:

"Oh, God, I do want to be a Christian. I want to ever love and serve You. I want to confess my sin and be washed in the blood of Jesus Christ. But oh, please just let me live until after Christmas, and then I will give my heart to You. Have mercy on me, Lord. Oh, don't, don't let me die until after Christmas."

Many people smile now as I testify of that awful terror that seized upon my soul, but the eternal welfare of my soul was at stake—for me it was going to be life or death, heaven or hell forever.

At the end of the third day, while driving home from school, I could stand it no longer. The lowering skies above, the trees, the fields, the very road beneath me seemed to look down upon me with displeasure, and I could see written everywhere—

"Poor, lost, miserable, hell-deserving sinner!"

Utterly at the end of myself—not stopping to think what preachers or entertainment committees or anyone else would think—I threw up my hands, and all alone in that country road, I screamed aloud toward the heavens:

"Oh, Lord God, be merciful to me, a sinner!" Immediately the most wonderful change took place in my soul. Darkness passed away and light entered. The sky was filled with brightness, the trees, the fields, and the little snow birds flitting to and fro were praising the Lord and smiling upon me.

So conscious was I of the pardoning blood of Jesus that I seemed to feel it flowing over me. I discovered that my face was bathed in tears, which dropped on my hands as I held the reins. And without effort or apparent thought on my part I was singing that old, familiar hymn:

"Take my life and let it be
Consecrated, Lord, to Thee;
Take my moments and my days,
Let them flow in ceaseless praise."

I was singing brokenly between my sobs:

"Take my life and let it be
Consecrated, Lord, to Thee."

My whole soul was flowing out toward God, my Father.

"M-Y F-A-T-H-E-R!" Oh, glory to Jesus! I had a heavenly Father! No more need for fear, but His love and kindness and protection were now for me.

When I came to the part in the song that said

"Take my hands and let them move
At the impulse of Thy love"

I knew there would be no more worldly music for me, and it has been hymns from that time forth. And when I sang—

"Take my feet and let them be
Swift and beautiful for Thee"

I knew that did not mean at the dance hall nor the skating rink. Bless the Lord.

"Take my lips and let them sing
Always, only, for my King."

No more foolish recitations and rag-time songs.

"Oh, Jesus, I love Thee,
I know Thou art mine;
For Thee all the follies
Of sin I resign."

Song after song burst from my lips. I shouted aloud and praised God all the way home. I had been redeemed!

Needless to say I did not take part in the entertainments, and many in our town thought me fanatical and very foolish. Nevertheless the succeeding days were brimful of joy and happiness. How dearly I loved God's Word! I wanted it under my pillow when I went to sleep, and in my hands when my eyes opened in the morning. At school, where I used to have a novel hidden away inside of my Algebra and Geometry, there was now a little New Testament, and I was studying each passage that referred to the baptism of the Holy Spirit.

Of all the promises in which I found comfort there was none, I believe, that compared with the simple promises of Matthew 7: 7 to 11.

"Ask, and it shall be given you; seek, and ye shall find; knock, and it shall be opened unto you:

"For everyone that asketh receiveth and he that seeketh findeth; and to him that knocketh it shall be opened." Here He assured me that if I asked bread He would not give me a stone, also that He was more willing to give me the Holy Spirit than earthly parents were to give good gifts to their children.

I would get about so far with my reading, and oh, the Bible seemed to me all so new, so living and speaking, (and it was God speaking to me), that unable to wait another moment, I would excuse myself from the room, go down to the basement, fall upon my knees and begin to pray:

"Oh, Lord, baptize me with the Holy Spirit. Lord, you said the promise was unto even as many as were afar off, even as many as the Lord our God should call. Now, Lord, you've called me, the promise is unto me; fill me just now."

The girls found me thus praying and did not know what to make of me so utterly was I changed. No more putting glue in teacher's chair or helping to lock him in the gymnasium, or practicing dance steps in the corridors at noon hour. A wonderful change had taken place—all old things had passed away and all things had become new. I had been born again and was a new creature in Christ Jesus.

Each day the hunger for the baptism of the Holy Spirit became stronger and stronger, more and more intense until, no longer contented to stay in school, my mind no longer on my studies, I would slip away to the tarrying meetings where the dear saints met to pray for those who were seeking the baptism of the Holy Spirit.

What wonderful hours those were! What a revelation to my soul! It was as though heaven had come down to earth. So much of the time was I away from school that I began to fall behind in my studies for the first time, and although the final examinations were near, I could not make myself take any interest in Algebra or Geometry or Chemistry, or anything but the baptism of the Holy Spirit and preparing to meet my soon-coming Savior in the air.

Then came the day when the principal of the High School sent a letter to my Mother which told her that unless I paid more attention to my studies I was certainly going to fail.

And to make matters worse, the same day one of the S. A. officers came to call upon Mother, saying:

"We really are surprised and think you do wrong in letting your daughter go to that Mission. You being connected with the work for so many years, it sets a bad example to other people for you to allow her to be in any way associated with them."

When I went home that night Mother was waiting for me. She gave me a very serious talking to, and wound up by issuing the ultimatum:

"Now, if I ever hear of your leaving school and going down

to that Mission again, or to the tarrying meetings, I will have to keep you home altogether. I will not have you talked about in this way."

I went to school on the train the next morning as the roads were banked high with snow, and all the way in I was looking out of the window at the falling flakes of snow and praying for the Lord to fix it all some way so that I should be able to knock until He opened or else to baptize me at once.

Walking from the train to High School it was necessary to pass both the Mission and the Sister's home where I often went to tarry for the baptism. As I went past the latter I looked longingly at the windows, hoping that she might be there and that I could speak to her from the sidewalk without going in and thus disobeying Mother's command, but not a sign of her did I see.

I walked slowly past, looking sadly and hungrily back all the way; then finally came to a halt on the sidewalk and said to myself:

"Well, here now, Jesus is coming soon and you know it is more important for you to receive the Holy Spirit than to pass all the examinations in the world. You need the Holy Spirit —oil in your vessel with your lamp—in order to be ready for His appearing.

"As you have to make a choice between going to school and seeking the baptism I guess you won't go to school at all today, but will just go back to the sister's house and make a whole day of seeking the baptism."

With this I turned and walked quickly back to the house, rang the door bell and went in. I told the sister my dilemma, and she said quietly:

"Let's tell Father all about it." So we got down and began to pray. She asked the Lord in her prayer either to baptize me then and there or to arrange it some way that I could stay until I received my baptism.

The Lord heard this prayer, and outside the window the snow which had been falling in light flakes, began to come down like a blinding blizzard. My heavenly Father sent out His angels to stir up some of those big, old, fleecy clouds of His, and down came the snow and—

causing the window-panes to rattle, and one of our old-fashioned Canadian blizzards was on.

The entire day was spent in prayer and at night on going to the depot to see about my train home, the ticket agent said, through the window:

"Sorry, Miss, but the train is not running tonight. The roads are blocked with snow. We are not able to get through." Oh, Hallelujah! I was not sorry a bit.

Then the thought came—"This will not do you much good, for you will have to call Mother on the telephone and she will ask you to go to her friend's home to stay, and warn you not to go near the Mission." But when I went to the telephone and gave the number, Central said:

"Sorry, wires all down on account of the storm." This time I did shout "Glory" and ran almost all the way back to the sister's home.

The storm increased, and as fast as the men endeavored to open a pathway, the Lord filled it in with mountains of white snow, until at last all thought of getting through while the storm lasted was abandoned.

Oh, how earnestly I sought the baptism of the Spirit. Sometimes when people come to the altar now and sit themselves down in a comfortable position, prop their heads up on one hand, and begin to ask God in a languid, indifferent way for the Spirit, it seems to me that they do not know what real seeking is.

Time was precious, for while man was working so hard to shovel out the snow, and God had His big clouds all working to shovel it in, I must do my part in seeking with all my heart.

Friday I waited before the Lord until midnight. Saturday morning, rising at the break of day, before anyone was astir in the house, and going into the parlor, I kneeled down by the big Morris chair in the corner, with a real determination in my heart.

My Bible had told me *"the kingdom of heaven suffereth violence, and the violent take it by force."* Matt. 11:12. I read the parable again of the man who had knocked for bread and found that it was not because he was his friend, but because of his importunity, that the good man within the house had risen up and given him as many loaves as he had need of. Now Jesus *was* my friend; He had bidden me knock, and assured me that He *would* open unto me. He had invited me to ask, promising that I should receive, and that the empty He would not turn hungry away. I began to seek in desperate earnest, and remember saying:

"Oh, Lord, I am so hungry for your Holy Spirit. You have told me that in the day when I seek with my whole heart you will be found of me. Now, Lord, I am going to stay right here until you pour out upon me the promise of the Holy Spirit for whom you commanded me to tarry, if I die of starvation. I am so hungry for Him I can't wait another day. I will not eat another meal until you baptize me."

You ask if I was not afraid of getting a wrong spirit, or being hypnotized, as my parents feared. There was no such fear in my heart. I trusted my heavenly Father implicitly according to Luke 11:11, wherein He assured me that if I asked for bread He would not give me a stone. I knew that my Lord was not bestowing serpents and scorpions on His blood-washed children when they asked for bread. Had He not said, if your earthly fathers know how to bestow good gifts upon their children, *"how much more shall your heavenly Father give the Holy Spirit to them that ask Him?"* Lu. 11:13.

After praying thus earnestly,—storming heaven, as it were, with my pleadings for the Holy Spirit, a quietness seemed to steal over me, the holy presence of the Lord to envelop me. The Voice of the Lord spoke tenderly:

"Now, child, cease your strivings and your begging; just begin to praise Me, and in simple, child-like faith, receive ye the Holy Ghost."

Oh, it was not hard to praise Him. He had become so near and so inexpressibly dear to my heart. Hallelujah! Without effort on my part I began to say:

"Glory to Jesus! Glory to Jesus!! GLORY TO JESUS!!!" Each time that I said "Glory to Jesus!" it seemed to come from a deeper place in my being than the last, and in a deeper voice, until great waves of "Glory to Jesus" were rolling from my toes up; such adoration and praise I had never known possible.

All at once my hands and arms began to tremble gently at

first, then more and more, until my whole body was atremble with the power of the Holy Spirit. I did not consider this at all strange, as I knew how the batteries we experimented with in the laboratory at collge hummed and shook and trembled under the power of electricity, and there was the Third Person of the Trinity coming into my body in all His fulness, making me His dwelling, "the temple of the Holy Ghost." Was it any wonder that this poor human frame of mine should quake beneath the mighty movings of His power?

How happy I was, Oh, how happy! happy just to feel His wonderful power taking control of my being. Oh, Glory! That sacred hour is so sweet to me, the remembrance of its sacredness thrills me as I write.

Almost without my notice my body slipped gently to the floor, and I was lying under the power of God, but felt as though caught up and floating uopn the billowy clouds of glory. Do not understand by this that I was unconscious of my surroundings, for I was not, but Jesus was more real and near than the things of earth round about me. The desire to praise and worship and adore Him flamed up within my soul. He was so wonderful, so glorious, and this poor tongue of mine so utterly incapable of finding words with which to praise Him.

My lungs began to fill and heave under the power as the Comforter came in. The cords of my throat began to twitch —my chin began to quiver, and then to shake violently, but Oh, so sweetly! My tongue began to move up and down and sideways in my mouth. Unintelligible sounds as of stammering lips and another tongue, spoken of in Isaiah 28:11, began to issue from my lips. This stammering of different syllables, then words, then connected sentences, was continued for some time as the Spirit was teaching me to yield to Him. Then suddenly, out of my innermost being flowed rivers of praise in other tongues as the Spirit gave utterance (Acts 2:4), and Oh, I knew that He was praising Jesus with glorious language, clothing Him with honor and glory which I felt but never could have put into words.

How wonderful that I, even I, away down here in 1908, was speaking in an unknown tongue, just as the believers had in Bible days at Ephesus and Caesarea, and that now He had come of whom Jesus had said—*"He will glorify Me."*

I shouted and sang and laughed and talked in tongues until it seemed that I was too full to hold another bit of blessing lest I should burst with the glory. The Word of God was true. The promise was really to them that were afar off, even as many as the Lord our God should call. The Comforter had come, lifting my soul in ecstatic praises to Jesus in a language I had never learned. I remember having said:

"Oh, Lord, can you not take me right on up to heaven now? I am so near anyway. Do I have to go back to that old world again?

"Hypnotism," you say? If so, it is a remarkably long spell and an exceedingly delightful one which has lasted for fourteen years, making me love Jesus with all my heart and long for His appearing. Besides this you must take into consideration that there was no one in the room to hypnotize me. I was all alone when I was saved, and all alone when I received the baptism of the Holy Spirit.

"Demon power"—"all of the devil," someone may say. If so the devil must have recently gotten soundly converted, for that which entered into my soul makes me to love and obey my Lord and Savior Jesus Christ, to exalt the blood and honor the Holy Ghost.

"Excitement," you say? Never! It has stood the test too long, dear unbeliever. In sickness, in sorrow, even in the gates of death He has proved Himself to be the Comforter whom Jesus said He would send.

Hearing me speaking in the tongues and praising the Lord, the dear Sister of the home in which I stayed, came down stairs and into the parlor, weeping and praising the Lord with me. Soon Brother Semple and other saints gathered in. What shouting and rejoicing! Oh, hallelujah! And yet with all the joy and glory, there was a stillness and a solemn hush pervading my whole being.

Walking down the street, I kept saying to myself:

"Now you must walk very softly and carefully, with unshod feet, in the presence of the King lest you grieve this tender, gentle dove who has come into your being to make you His temple and to abide with you forever."

The next day was Sunday. The storm had cleared away; the sun was shining down in'its melting warmth. Attending the morning services at the Mission, we partook of the Lord's Supper, and as we meditated upon His wonderful love, His blood that was shed for us, His body that was broken on the tree, it was more than I could bear.

Oh, who can describe that exceeding weight of glory as He revealed Himself, my crucified Savior, my resurrected Lord, my coming King!

School-mates and friends were standing up to look over the seats to see what had happened to me, but I was lost again with Jesus, whom my soul loved.

A friend of our family left the meeting, and going to the telephone called my Mother. (The wires which had been down during the storm, unknown to me, had been repaired). He said:

"You had better come into town and see to your daughter, for she is again disobeying your orders. She is at those meetings, shouting more than any of them."

Poor Mother! She was frantic to think her daughter should so far forget her dignity and disgrace herself in such a manner. She called me to the phone and I heard her dear voice saying:

"What in the world is this I hear about you? What does this all mean?"

I tried to answer, but the Holy Spirit began speaking through me again.

"What's that?" she demanded. I tried to explain. Then came her voice stern and forbidding:

"You just wait till I get there, my lady; I will attend to you."

(Just to relieve the tension of your mind, I will run a little ahead of my story and tell you that since then my dear Mother has also received the Baptism of the Holy Spirit just as they did in Bible days).

Returning to the sister's home, I sat down at the organ, awaiting in some trepidation and fear, I confess, the coming of my Mother. To keep my courage up I sang over and over that old, familiar hymn:

"I will never leave thee nor forsake thee;
In my hands I'll hold thee;
In my arms I'll fold thee;
I am thy Redeemer; I will care for thee!"

What would Mother say? Would she understand? Why, it had not been so very long since the power of God used to come down in the dear old Salvation Army. Had I not heard her tell how Brother Kitchen (whom they used to call "the Kitchen that God lived in") had shaken as he kneeled in prayer, until he had gone clear across the platform and had lain stretched out under the power at the other side? Had I not heard my Father tell how the old-time Methodist Church used to have this same power? Praying God for strength and wisdom, I sang on—

"E'en though the night
Be dark within the valley,
Just beyond is shining,
An eternal light."

Six o'clock arrived—so did Mother! I heard the jingle of the sleigh-bells suddenly stop in response to my Mother's "whoa!" Then an imperious ring of the bell shivered the tense silence within the house. Slipping down from the organ stool I caught my coat and hat in my hand as I hastened to the door. Mother met me, and with:

"My lady, you come right out and get in here this minute," lost no time in bundling me into the cutter. The Sister and Brother both tried to get a word in edgeways, to reason with and explain to her, but she would hear none of it, and in a moment we were off.

All the way home Mother scolded and cried and almost broke her heart over her daughter who had, as she supposed, been cast under some dire spell by those "awful" people. Oh, praise the Lord! No matter what the devil called them he had to admit that they were holy anyway, and that's more than he could have said of many professing denominations, now, isn't it?

Being an only child, loved and petted, it needed only a word of scolding or remonstrance to bring the tears, but now, when she was scolding me more severely and saying more harsh things than she ever had in my life, for some mysterious reason I couldn't shed a tear. I felt duty bound to squeeze out a few tears, out of respect to her feelings, but I could not do it to help myself. All I could do was sing and sing and sing—all the way—

"Joys are flowing like a river.
Since the Comforter has come;
He abides with me forever,
Makes the trusting heart His home."

The Spirit within rose up and filled me with joy unspeakable and full of glory. Poor Mother would turn to me and say:

"Oh, Aimee! do stop that singing. I can't understand how you can sing; you know your Mother's heart is breaking. Surely you don't call that a fruit of the Spirit." But it did not seem as if I were singing at all: it just seemed to sing itself and came out without any effort.

"Blessed quietness, holy quietness,
What assurance in my soul;
On the stormy sea, Jesus speaks to me,
And the billows cease to roll."

Upon our arrival home we found my Father sitting by the dining-room fire, with his head in his hands, saying:

"Humph! Humph! Humph!" He always did that when he felt very badly over something. Leading me up to him, Mother said:

"Now I want you to tell your Father all about it. Tell the way you acted out before those people." Well, it certainly did sound dreadful to tell it, but Oh, that something kept whispering and echoing in my heart:

"E'en though the night
Be dark within the valley,
Just beyond is shining
An eternal day."

When at last they sent me to my room, I kneeled down quickly and began to pray. It happened that I was kneeling beside the stove-pipe hole and could not help overhearing a part of the conversation between my parents. It was something like this:

"Oh, what shall we do? Those people have got our girl under their influence, hypnotized her, mesmerized her or something."

"It is perfectly useless to argue with her, for no matter what we say, she only thinks she is being persecuted and will hold to it all the more tenaciously."

"Oh, what shall we do?" With this the door closed and I heard no more.

Oh, how can I describe the joy and the glory that had come within my soul? that deep-settled peace, that knowledge that He would lead and guide and would bring all things out right.

When next my Mother permitted me to go to school she told me of the decision which they had come to, namely, that if I went near those Pentecostal people once more they would take me away from school for good, education or no education. As she told me this the Holy Spirit gave me wisdom to make this reply:

"Mother, the Bible says that children are to obey their parents in the Lord, and if you can show me by the Word of God that what I have received is not in accordance with Bible teaching, or show me any place where we are told that the baptism of the Holy Spirit, with the Bible evidence, speaking in tongues, is not for today, I will never go to the Mission again." I staked my all on the Word.

"Why certainly I can prove it to you," she replied. "Those things were only for the Apostolic days. I will look up the scriptures and prove it to you when you get home tonight."

Dear Mother—she had been a student of the Bible and had taught Sunday School and Bible class for years. Oh, would she be able to prove that all these manifestations of the Holy Spirit's power and presence were only for by-gone days? I was not very well acquainted with the Bible on this subject, yet knew that what I had received was from God.

Assured that Mother would search the Bible honestly, I had pledged myself to stand by the consequences: Whatever the Bible said should stand. Thus it was that we both turned to the Word of God as the final court of appeal to settle the whole matter.

Mother got out her Bible, concordance, pencil and pad, and with heart and mind full of this one thing, immediately sat herself down at the breakfast table, spreading her books out before her, without pausing even long enough to gather up the breakfast dishes for washing—the lamps were not cleaned, and the beds were unmade.

(Oh, if any unbeliever will sit down with an open Bible and

an unprejudiced heart, there is no need for us to defend our position, so clear is the Word of God on this subject).

It was half past eight in the morning when I left home for school. At five-thirty, when I returned, Mother was still seated at the breakfast table, with her Bible and paper before her, and—would you believe it?—the breakfast dishes were still unwashed, the lamps uncleaned, the beds unmade, an unheard-of state of affairs for Mother, ever an excellent housekeeper.

I waited with bated breath for her decision. My heart softened within me as I saw by her reddened eyes that she had been weeping. Oh, what would her answer be? The smile upon her face encouraged me to ask—

"Oh, Mother, what is it?"

Now, dear reader, what do you suppose she said? With shining face she replied—

"Well, dear, I must admit that of a truth, *this is that which was spoken of by the prophet Joel, which should come to pass in the last days!*"

She had found that, away back in Isaiah 28:11, He had said —*"With stammering lips and another tongue will I speak to this people"*—that the prophet Joel had clearly prophesied that in these last days there should be a wonderful outpouring of the Holy Spirit, likened unto the latter rain, wherein the sons and daughters, the servants and the maids were alike to rejoice in this glorious downpour.

With one spring across the room, I threw my arms about my Mother's neck, squeezing her till she declared I had almost broken her neck. How happy we were as we danced around the table—laughing, crying and singing together—

" 'Tis the old time religion,
And it's good enough for me—"

If everyone who is skeptical of the reality of the baptism of the Holy Spirit would take the Word of God and search from cover to cover, he too, would be convinced without the shadow of a doubt that "This Is That."

CHAPTER VI.

CALLING INTO THE VINEYARD, AND MARRIAGE.

"Come, my beloved, and let us go forth into the field; let us lodge in the villages." S. of S. 7:11.

THE chain of events related in the foregoing chapters brings us right up to the place where God spoke to His poor little handmaiden, whose heart was rejoicing in the new-found Savior—the time when He called me to preach The Word, and ordained me in my room as related in the beginning of chapter one. (If you have forgotten, turn back and refresh your memory).

An intense, heaven-sent longing to be a soul winner for Jesus was born of the Spirit within my soul. He had done so much for me; He had plucked my feet out of the mire and the clay. Oh, to be able to win other souls, shining jewels to lay at His precious feet! Oh, to be able to tell of the Redeemer's love to perishing humanity! God spoke within the depths of my being and told me that "Before I called thee, I knew thee; before thou camest forth I sanctified thee; and I ordained thee."

"Why, you are but a child; no one would listen or have confidence in you," whispered the Enemy. "What do you know about preaching, anyway?" nodded Self and Common-sense. "Here are preachers, a country full of them, learned, college-bred, who have read books and digested theological studies for years. It is preposterous for you even to think of going out as a worker."

"But *not many wise men after the flesh, not many mighty, not many noble, are called: but God hath chosen the foolish things of the world to confound the wise; and God hath chosen the weak things of the world to confound the things that are mighty,*" argued the Word. "Has He not declared that with a worm He shall thrash a mountain—that when we are weak, then we are strong—and that a little child shall lead them? Has He not said that upon the servants and upon the handmaidens He would pour out His Spirit in the last days, and that they should prophesy? Did He not say that after the Spirit had come *'out of your innermost being'* (not out of your head, intellect or knowledge) *'should flow rivers of living water'?* You know the rivers are flowing. Just open your mouth wide and He will fill it."

"Yes, but remember in addition to your youth and lack of mental equipment," cried Human Affection, "there is your Mother to be considered. You are an only child, her only comfort and object of affection in this world. Surely you would not consider leaving her out here in the country all alone, after all that she has done for you?"

"Here you have love and home and comfort, all you can wish for. If you went forth as a worker you would have to leave all these," added Love of Comfort.

"If any man love Father or Mother more than Me, he is not worthy of Me," said the tender voice of Jesus. "No man hath given up houses or lands for My sake and the gospel's, but he shall receive a hundred-fold now in this time, and in the world to come eternal life. If you would come after Me you must take up your cross daily, denying yourself, and follow Me."

"But, Lord, these Pentecostal people have no earthly board behind them, no salary," cried Prudence and Forethought. "What about shoes and clothes, and necessary expenses?"

"Take no thought for what you shall eat or for what you shall drink or what you shall put on, for the Lord knoweth you have need of these things," calmly interrupted implicit Faith.

"Oh, yes, Lord, by Your grace I will take up my cross, 'twill be a joy," sang Consecration. "I will trust You and follow You, come what may. My all is on the altar, have Your dear way with me, whether 'tis 'go' or whether 'tis 'stay' let Your perfect will be wrought out in my life. I feel my own weakness and insufficiency—know not what the future holds—am but a child, but

'I can hear my Savior calling,
Take your cross and follow, follow Me.'

"Oh, here I am, Lord, send me. Such a burden for souls is mine that I would be willing to crawl upon my hands and knees from the Atlantic to the Pacific just to say to one poor, lost soul—

'Dear sinner, Jesus loves you.' "

"You must go with me, Jesus, you must help my infirmities and speak for me, for behold I can not speak, I am a child."

But the Lord said unto me, *"Say not, I am a child, for thou shalt go to all that I shall send thee, whatsoever I command thee thou shalt speak. Be not afraid of their faces, for I am with thee to deliver thee, saith the Lord. Then the Lord put forth His hand, and touched my mouth, and said unto me, Behold, I have put my words in thy mouth."*

The battle over, the conflict ended, the consecration made, come what might, no matter who should doubt the transaction that took place in that sacred hour, I had been ordained, not of man but of God.

Day by day the call grew louder, rang more clearly in my ears. Sitting at the piano I would sing, hour after hour, from the fullness of my heart,

"I'll go where you want me to go, dear Lord,
Over mountain or plain or sea;
I'll say what you want me to say, dear Lord,
I'll be what you want me to be."

Tears would roll down my face; my body was there, but my Spirit was far away out in the harvest fields working for Jesus.

So enwrapt was I in the call of the Master that I was often but dimly conscious of my Mother's leaving her work each time I began to play, no matter what part of the house she was in, and coming to the parlor door, leaning against it and wiping the big tears from her eyes on the corner of her apron. God was speaking to her Mother heart, taking her back to the day of her prayer for the little girl, reminding her of the dedication service when she had promised to let her go where He would send, even to the ends of the earth. She realized that the great divine call had come to her daughter, and that the time for her supreme sacrifice was near. She remembered the words of Hannah:

"Oh, my lord, I am the woman that stood by thee here, praying unto the Lord. For this child I prayed; and the Lord hath given me my petition which I asked of Him: therefore also have I lent him to the Lord; as long as he liveth he shall be lent to the Lord, and she worshipped the Lord there."

Just how it was all to come about, little did we know. The meetings were a feast to our souls. Workers came freely to our country home, and when the Evangelist, Robert Semple, that blessed man of God who, because of his Christ-like bearing, moved as a prince among men, passed on to another town, he continued to encourage and instruct me in the Lord by many long letters, all of which were filled with scriptures and food from God's storehouse.

Never has it been my privilege to read such letters as those that came from the inspired pen of this saintly man of prayer. He walked and lived and breathed in the atmosphere of heaven. To know him was to love and respect him.

Then came the time of his return visit to our town and the memorable night when I had volunteered to nurse the two little children of the sister in whose home I had received my baptism. The little ones had been stricken down with typhoid fever, and the mother was fatigued with long care and watching.

Late in the evening, as I was tending the little ones and setting things to rights in the room, the door opened and in walked Robert Semple, offering his services and prayers. After he had prayed, the children fell into a quiet sleep, and we sat down side by side to read the Bible by the light of the shaded lamp. Robert talked earnestly of the Savior and His love, of the work, of the great fields of golden grain, white already unto the harvest, of the need for laborers in these closing hours of the dispensation, of the soon coming of Jesus and the many souls yet to be saved, of what a life of faith meant—the sacrifice, the joy, the reward—then, reaching over he took my hand in his and, telling me of his love, asked me to become his wife and enter the work as a helpmate by his side.

This is the first time I have ever attempted to lift the veil even a little from that sacred, hallowed hour, when we kneeled side by side, hand in hand, and he reverently prayed God to look down and solemnize our engagement and send us forth as true laborers, in obedience to His call, to rescue poor perishing souls from eternal destruction.

While on my knees, with closed eyes and throbbing heart—(Why, this was the very room in which I had received my baptism!) the room seemed filled with angels who lined either side of the golden, sunlit path of life that stretched away into the vista of coming days of glorious love and joyful service to our Lord and King.

Here was the visible answer to the call.

Here was the loving human hand sent to unlatch the gate

of opportunity and guide my steps into that shining path and start me well upon the way—that way that has led through sunshine and shadow, tears and smiles, joys and sorrow, life and death, mountain-top and valley.

Little did I know that night, as I contemplated the shining way that led on and on to the Father's throne, how soon the strong, dear arm that was now about me as we prayed, and led me out into the work, would be removed; that after two years of married life I should be left alone, yet not alone.

The impenetrable mist with which God mercifully veils the future remained unrent, yet, had I known of the little mound of fresh-digged earth that should mark the grave of this dear heart in Happy Valley, Hong Kong, China, I should not have hesitated in that softly whispered "yes," with which I met his question; nor would I have shrunk one instant from the call to stand by his side. I deemed it one of the greatest privileges and honors I had ever known.

Oh, Jesus! Jesus! how wonderfully He had planned it all for poor, unworthy me! How he had sought and called and chosen me! Is it any wonder my heart sang with rapturous love and praise for such a Redeemer?

The straight-forward, manly way in which Robert went to my Mother for her consent, coupled with the dealings of the Lord in her heart on the subject, made her willing to part with her daughter, though she declared, mother-like, that it took the sunshine and the laughter and the music from the farm and from the home.

I am not going to try to describe the little wedding which took place under the flower-decked arch on the lawn the following August, nor the long tables spread beneath the apple trees for the wedding supper, nor the Mother-face that tried to keep brave and smiling as the little white wedding-dress was laid aside and the navy-clad bride entered the carriage that was soon hidden by a cloud of dust as it sped away to catch the train for Stratford—the mission field of which my husband was in charge.

"Were the whole realm of nature mine,
That were an offering far too small;
Love so amazing, so divine,
Demands my love, my life, my all."

CHAPTER VII.

EARLY MINISTRY.

"Let us get up early to the vineyards; let us see if the vine flourish, whether the tender grape appear, and the pomegranates bud forth: there will I give thee my loves." S. of S. 7:12.

THE happy days of service for Jesus which followed need not be described in detail. We had three little rooms in the heart of the city where swirling smoke clouds from nearby foundries swept over the roof and tiny back-yard where I struggled desperately with my first washing. I would wash and rub and rinse, and as fast as I washed the clothes the soot would black them. It was a battle between the smoke and me, and I was greatly troubled, having always heard that the housekeeping qualities of a good wife must be judged by her washing and her biscuits. Cinders would have won the day had it not been for the help and advice of one of the sisters.

Rooms were furnished in an unpretentious way, and even with my eyes filled with smoke from the broken door of the little kitchen range, my first pan of biscuits, hard and brown though they were, were considered a great and triumphant success by the husband who came in, from his toil in the boiler works, at noon. Never were biscuits praised so highly, and it is doubtful whether biscuits ever were quite so hard, but the spirit to learn and try to please was there just the same.

The little assembly was poor in this world's goods, and my dear husband, not willing to lay us as a burden upon them, had accepted this humble position of work, though in other cities he might have commanded a dignified position with a good salary. Like Paul he was not afraid to work with his hands.

The Lord blessed our labors in Stratford, Ontario, saving and baptizing precious souls, leading me on and out in a new way. From Stratford He definitely led us to the city of

LONDON, ONT., CAN.,

where the beautiful home of dear Sister Armstrong was opened to us. Meetings were held in her parlors until her rooms grew too small, and were then moved to the home of Brother Wortman.

Inside of a year over one hundred had received the baptism of the Holy Spirit with the Bible evidence, speaking in tongues, sinners had been saved, and there were several remarkable healings.

Then the Lord led us to Chicago, Ill., where in the North Avenue Mission with Brother W. H. Durham several happy months of teaching and service slipped by.

MIRACULOUS AND INSTANTANEOUS HEALING OF A BROKEN ANKLE.

WHILE at Findlay, Ohio, at Brother Leonard's Mission, attending the two weeks' special meetings conducted by Brother Durham, we prayed night and day for those seeking the baptism, and the Lord met every one. At times the whole floor in front of the altar was covered by the slain of the Lord. Amongst those seeking the baptism of the Spirit was a minister and a doctor of that city.

One evening, being tired in body, from the long hours at the altar, I went upstairs to lie down, during the tarrying meeting. I had hardly settled down to rest, when, hearing the big bass voice of the minister shouting, "Glory! Glory!! Glory!!!" I bounded off the couch to go and see if he was receiving the Holy Spirit, rejoicing that our prayers were being answered.

In running swiftly down the long flight of stairs I tripped, and, bending my ankle back under me, fell from the middle of the stairs all the rest of the way to the bottom. I could fairly hear the bones crunch under me as I fell. My toes turned towards where the heel ought to be, and my ankle swelled rapidly.

Up to this time, having always enjoyed the best of health, I had never had occasion to take the Lord as my personal healer, although I had witnessed many wonderful healings. Now, as the saints gathered about me and prayed, I must confess that my mind was more occupied with the pain and excruciating agony of my broken foot than with the Lord as my healer; consequently I was not healed that night.

The doctor examined my foot and said the bone was not only cracked, but that in wrenching my foot backwards in my fall, I had completely torn and severed four of the ligaments that move the toes, all being torn but that running to the big toe, thus pulling my toes around and backwards.

As soon as the swelling had been reduced sufficiently to permit a plaster of paris cast to be put on Dr. Harrison and his son, also a practicing physician of that city, set the bone, drew the bent foot back into place, and put on a heavy cast. He explained to me that the torn cords could not grow together; that my ankle would, therefore, always be stiff, but by keeping the plaster cast on for four weeks, till thoroughly healed, my foot would be straight. They both warned me not to touch it to the floor, or put any weight upon it. A pair of crutches was purchased, and by their aid I went hobbling to the train that was to take us back to Chicago.

The afternoon we arrived, I attended the service in the mission, and rested my aching and feverish foot on the platform in front of me. Every jar of the floor sent a stabbing pain through it, and, sick with the pain, I went to my room, a block away from the hall. While sitting there commiserating myself over the black and swollen toes, which were all I could see of my foot, a voice spoke to me and said:

"If you will wrap the shoe for your broken foot, and take it with you to wear home, and go over to North Avenue mission to Brother Durham and ask him to lay hands on your foot, I will heal it."

The idea of wrapping up a shoe, which was tight-fitting even with my foot in a normal condition, struck me so humorously that I laughed the thought away; but again and yet again came the voice:

"Wrap up your shoe to wear home, take it with you as you go to be prayed for, and I will heal you." The Word says, *"My sheep hear my voice,"* and, at last I reached for my crutches, hobbled over to my other shoe, wrapped it up, and with it tucked under my arm, started clumsily down the winding staircase to go to the mission for prayers.

On the way over the crutch slipped through a hole in the wooden sidewalk, and as my toes struck the hard boards, the perspiration stood in beads upon me, from the excruciating pain that shot up my limb. I felt dizzy and faint as I reached the foot of the steps (Brother Durham lived over the mission).

Trembling and white from pain, I felt unequal to climbing the stairs, so two of the brothers carried me up on a chair.

I told them just what the Lord had told me. There were twelve in the room besides myself, and all but one began to pray. The one who did not pray was an infidel, a brother of our Pastor.

As Brother Durham was walking up and down the room, calling on the Lord, he suddenly stopped, and laying his hands on my ankle, broke out praying in tongues, and then in English said:

"In the name of Jesus, receive your healing." I suddenly felt as if a shock of electricity had struck my foot. It flowed through my whole body, causing me to shake and tremble under the power of God. Instantaneously my foot was perfectly healed, the blackness was gone, the parted ligaments were knitted together, the bone was made whole. Glory to Jesus! I was healed!

Trembling with excitement and joy, it took me fully five minutes, with the help of the saints, to remove the plaster of paris cast. The infidel who was present said:

"Don't be foolish. Leave it on, you will only have to pay a doctor three dollars to replace the cast."

But, glory to Jesus, I was healed. At last the plaster was removed, the absorbent cotton off, my stocking on, also the shoe (which fitted perfectly now), and I leaped to my feet and began to dance and jump on the healed foot.

Everyone in the room was filled with the Spirit, and we all danced and sang and talked in tongues. Hallelujah! It is no wonder we shout His praises; when we have Jesus we have something worth shouting over.

Suddenly remembering my husband would be coming on the next elevated train, I ran down the stairs, my crutches left behind, and all the way to the station, and told him the wonderful news. My ankle was as strong as ever.

The mission was full to the doors that night, and when the Pastor asked me to step to the platform and tell of my wonderful healing, and the saints saw that the crutches and plaster cast were gone, and that I could leap and dance upon the foot, they shouted and praised the Lord. Many of the Chicago onlookers who knew not the healing power, doubted that the ankle had ever been broken. When the word went back and the healing was announced publicly in Findlay, Ohio, many of the public there who knew it was broken, would not believe it was healed. How like human nature. *"If they hear not Moses and the prophets, neither will they be persuaded though one rose from the dead."*

CHAPTER VIII.

CALL TO FOREIGN FIELDS.

"And He said unto me, Go ye into all the world, and preach the Gospel to every creature."—Mark 16:15.

IT WAS shortly after our return to Chicago and the miraculous, instantaneous healing of my broken ankle, just related, that my husband and myself were made to realize in a very definite way that the time had come for us to obey the call to China which the Spirit had been laying upon his heart more and more for some time.

We began praying for the fare and clothing which would be necessary. As I have explained, we had no earthly board behind us, no organization to lean upon. We, therefore, looked straight to Jesus, the One who had called us, and asked Him to supply our every need. In just a little over two weeks the necessary clothing and the fare had been donated by the dear saints of God, not by the rich, but by the poor.

We find, all over the country, in our meetings, that the rich and the near-rich will come to us and say:

"Oh, I am so sorry that I am not in a position just now to give something. My money is tied up and I am so situated that I am not able to do much now; how I wish I could." And while they are humming and hesitating over it, the poor step up, and with a glad light in their eyes, grip our hands with a hearty:

"God bless you! Here's a dollar, or here's five or ten," as the case may be; "Oh, I only wish it were more, but I will have more when next week's pay envelope comes in. How proud I am to have this privilege!"

Farewelling in Chicago, we went to Canada, accompanied by Brother Durham, holding revival meetings in different towns and cities in Ontario. In London we found the Lord still graciously pouring out His Spirit and had a glorious revival while there this time.

My home town being but twenty miles distant, I had the opportunity of saying farewell to my parents, but even when Mother waved me off at the depot, she smiled bravely as far away as I could see her waving her handkerchief from the platform. I held my hand out of the window and pointed up, bidding her look to Jesus.

After our last meeting was closed in Toronto, where many were baptized in the Spirit, we boarded the train for St. Johns, N. B., and as it was pulling out of the Union Depot, we heard the sweet voices of the saints singing: "God be with you 'til we meet again."

Leaving St. Johns, we set sail for Liverpool, England. From there we went to Belfast, Ireland. In Belfast the Lord sent a wonderful revival. In three weeks over two score were baptized in the Holy Spirit and all spoke in other tongues.

Mr. Semple's home, which was in Magherafelt, the North of Ireland, being but a few miles distant, we visited there. His dear father and mother, two brothers and two sisters, each vied with the other in packing the trunk of new clothing and good things for us. When at last the day of our departure had come they said "Good-bye" to their son, and Mrs. Semple (Robert's mother) declared that the Lord gave her the witness right then that she would never look upon his face again in this world. But Hallelujah! "Greater love hath no man than this, that he lay down his life for the brethren."

While waiting in London, England, for the boat on which we were to sail, we were entertained by dear saints who showed us the greatest hospitality and love. In attending Pentecostal services held in London we found that the Lord was pouring out His Spirit in the very same way as in America, and that hundreds of earnest Christians had been baptized with the same Holy Spirit, speaking with other tongues and praising the Lord. It was here that the Lord gave me that marvelous vision of the Dispensation of the Holy Spirit and the message in prophecy which has always seemed so glorious to me because He gave it.

Standing on the deck, as the boat slipped away from the wharf, we lifted our voices in song with the crowd of saints who stood on the pier. How sweet and encouraging their dear voices sounded as they rang over the ever-increasing distance between us. As far as we could hear they were singing:

"God will take care of you."

And when we could no longer hear them we could see the waving handkerchiefs and hats of these precious children of the Most High God.

Skirting the edge of the Bay of Biscay, we sailed on to Gibraltar, then in through the blue, sunlit waters of the Mediterranean, to the Suez Canal, and on into the Red Sea, through which the Children of Israel had been led dry-shod. We were surprised at the great width of the Sea, and learned that it was called the "Red Sea" because of the desert wind storms which blow the red sand across the water, giving it at times its red appearance.

Soon we were plowing through the waters of the Indian Ocean. After our visit at Ceylon it was not long until we were nearing our destination at Hong Kong.

En route we gathered good reports of the outpouring of the Latter Rain in Egypt, India, Ceylon, Malta, etc., too lengthy to relate at this time. Suffice it to say that they received the Holy Spirit as well as we, with the same Bible evidence, speaking in tongues. Sick were healed and signs and wonders were wrought in the name of the holy child, Jesus.

On the boat plentiful opportunity for witnessing for Jesus was given us. My husband spent hours and hours each day waiting upon God; the balance in reading the Word. It seemed as though we were being drawn nearer to the Master every day, and belonged less and less to this world.

After weathering a severe typhoon, came the day when we saw, in the early morning sunrise, the mountain of Hong Kong, and beheld the harbor with its numerous busy sampans.

We were met by saints and taken to the Missionary Home, of which Brother MacIntosh was at that time in charge. Brother and Sister Dixon and other missionaries were here, and we learned that the Latter Rain was falling in China, as well as in America, as God's little children faithfully proclaimed the truth. Yes, when the Chinese receive the baptism they speak in other tongues just as did the hundred and twenty on the day of Pentecost; the sick are healed and the lepers cleansed. Hallelujah!

In China we felt as never before the need of the Holy Spirit as a Comforter, and found it much more difficult to pray through. It seemed at times as though the air were filled with demons and the hosts of hell, in this wicked, benighted country, where for many centuries devil worship has been an open custom. We have seen Chinese bowing themselves down before their great gods, burning hundreds of dollars' worth of paper to feed their flames of devotion to their gods, and roasting their pigs and offering them with rice and other dainties to the great stone dragons in temple and cave.

Ancestral worship is observed by almost all. It is a peculiar sight to see them carrying food, rice, chicken, candied nuts and fruit, to lay upon the graves of their dead. A missionary once asked a young Chinaman who had recently been saved, when he was going to stop taking food to the grave of his dead. He replied:

"Why, I suppose when your people stop taking flowers as a tribute to the memory of their departed."

CHAPTER IX.

THE DEATH OF MY HUSBAND.

"When thou passest through the waters, I will be with thee; and through the rivers, they shall not overflow thee."—Isaiah 43:2.

WHILE in China my husband seemed to be drawn nearer and nearer to the Lord each day. He spent hours in prayer day and night. He really travailed in Spirit for the Chinese and often made the remark that he felt as though he would never return to America, but would rise to meet the Lord from China, carrying precious Chinese souls in his arms to Jesus. He used to sing over and over that little chorus—

"Bringing in the sheaves,"

only he worded it—

"Bringing in Chinese,
Bringing in Chinese;
We shall come rejoicing,
Bringing in Chinese."

After the heat of the day, we would often go out to sit on the beach in the evening, and while different workers would be talking together I would suddenly miss my husband. Diligent search would find him hidden away off somewhere behind a boulder or rock, praying earnestly for souls. At other times he would walk through the beautiful graveyard of Happy Valley, reading the inscriptions of missionaries who had laid down their lives for Jesus. How beautiful were flowers and fountains, and foliage—such rare beauty as we had never seen!

As we sat many hours studying and reading under these trees, little did we realize that soon dear Robert was to be laid at rest in this very spot in Happy Valley.

The intense heat and the filthy, insanitary condition of the country in which we dwelt began to tell upon our health. Malaria was raging, and to go out even for five minutes at noonday without a cork helmet and a heavy parasol meant almost certain death.

We were away down the coast at Macoe when my husband was taken seriously ill and was carried, in a very weak condition, to the steamer and back to Hong Kong and up the mountain to an English sanitarium, built especially for missionaries, where care was given free of charge.

Suffering with malaria in its worst form, I went with my husband to the hospital where we could be near (I in the ladies' ward, his ward some distance away), even though we could not see each other except on visiting days.

Robert was just in the hospital one week, and the anniversary of our second year of married life was celebrated during this time by a little exchange of notes sent by the nurse. During the few short visits I was permitted to make to his ward, I ever found his well-worn Bible (the one from which he had preached me under conviction and explained the way of salvation and the baptism of the Holy Spirit), my husband's constant companion. It was marked from cover to cover and his fingers seemed to be always between its pages.

Each day he grew weaker, and although I was confident the Lord would heal him, he felt as though his work were ended, that he had fought a good fight and finished his course, and henceforth there was laid up for him a crown of righteousness.

One evening, at the end of the week, the doctor gave me special permission to sit with my husband, and as my heart leaped with joy at the prospect, little did I dream the reason of this special kindness. I only felt grateful to the doctor, and the thought that my dear one was so soon to be taken from me never entered my mind. As I sat there by his bedside a great lump in my throat seemed to be choking me as I gazed at the thin, pale face, so changed in these few days, but feeling that I must be brave and encouraging I tried in a pitiful way to talk cheerfully of the soon-coming of the little one we had both planned and hoped for so long.

As we were talking thus I heard the click of the white-robed nurse's heels as she came down the long ward to tell me it was time for me to go back to my own ward now. And O, I shall never forget the sweet smile that lit up his countenance. Some way a terrible premonition of some sorrow befalling me, an idea vague and unformed, seized upon my heart, and as I clung to the white-enameled bar at the foot of his bed, I think he must have seen the look that swept across my face, for—still smiling encouragingly—he looked into my eyes and said:

"Good night, dear; I'll see you in the morning." These were the last words he ever spoke to me, but O, I know there is going to dawn a bright and cloudless morning some of these days, when there shall be—

"No more parting, no more tears,
No more crying, no more fears,"

for these things shall pass away when the Lord shall come. Why, it seems that I can almost see the early rays of dawn breaking in the sky just now, and the Spirit softly whispers:

"The morning is at hand; Jesus is coming soon; be faithful just a little longer."

"Good night, dear; I'll see you in the morning." Oh, dear reader, will you be there in the morning? Will you be ready to meet Jesus on that day?

I returned to the bed in the women's ward with an uneasy

feeling hard to describe, and lay for hours staring out into the darkness, listening to the irregular breathing of the other patients about me.

At midnight I sat up in bed with a frightened start. Out of the window at the foot of my bed I could see across the great square court, and in the window which I knew to be beside my husband's bed I saw a bright light burning. Some way a great terror seized upon my soul, as I heard the quick step of the night nurse coming along the corridor connecting the two wards. Straight to my bed she came, and with a tense catch in her voice that I will never forget, she told me to slip on my kimono and slippers and to hurry to the next ward, that my husband was very ill.

"He's not—he's not—not—d—dying?" I managed to gasp through my stiff lips.

"Come quick! He is sinking fast," were the words that sounded like a death knell, as we hurried down the long passage to—what?

"Death?—O, surely not; it couldn't be," I reasoned. I had never seen anyone die. I was not yet twenty years of age, and away out here on the opposite side of the globe from the Mother who had always shielded and protected me from every wind that blew.

"Dying? Impossible! Why, what of the little one that is to come? Surely he will live to see her clad in the glory of the tiny wardrobe so proudly tucked away?" All these thoughts raced like lightning through my mind. I was as one dazed. My lips were trembling; my knees shook till I could scarcely walk.

Then, as I stood by his bed, and saw that even unconscious as he was, the light of the glory world illuminated his face, I sank down in a heap by his side and clung to his cold hand. He did not open his eyes, did not see me. However, I think he must have been seeing Jesus, so rapt was the expression that lighted up his countenance.

Then, at that moment, when all the world seemed to be crumbling and slipping from beneath my feet, the Comforter, the blessed Holy Spirit, whom Jesus had sent, rose up within me and revealed Jesus in such a precious way, made the will of God so sweet, showed the prepared mansions so real that I shouted "Glory!" by the death bed of Robert Semple, from whom I had never dreamed of parting. Waves of joy rolled over my soul, and I was lifted from earth to heaven, and it seemed as though I accompanied him right to the pearly gates. *"The Lord gave and the Lord taketh away, blessed be the name of the Lord."*

When I felt the doctor shaking me by the shoulder, I at last raised my head from the bed, and loosened my clasp on the dear, cold hand. Stooping to kiss the cold forehead for the last time, I realized the great need of the Comforter. He did not fail me, but sweetly spoke in my ears:

"He is not here; he is risen."

O dear friend, never again say that you have no need of the Comforter whom Jesus sent. It is not only in the hour of rejoicing on the mountain-top that you need Him, but in sorrow's dark hour, down in the valley and the shadow of death, you too need the Comforter. Hallelujah! You must not think, when you see us dancing and shouting for very joy in the meeting, that it is all excitement and surface blessings, for this is not true. Ah no, the Holy Spirit still abides when the feet are led down into the dark waters and it seems as though the floods would overflow—then He is there to comfort and uphold; and when we pass through the fiery furnace He reveals the form of the Fourth, like unto the Son of God, as never before.

Oh, how we thank you, dear Jesus, that you ever said: "I will not leave you comfortless; I will send another, even the Holy Ghost."

I was never permitted to look upon the face of my dear one again, as the doctor was anxious to spare me all suffering possible, but Oh, how could I have borne it when I saw them pulling down the shades in hopes that I would not see, and heard the heavy tread of feet as they carried their burden past our windows and down the steps, if it had not been for this precious Holy Spirit?

Our slender funds were well-nigh exhausted and an immediate demand for money and funeral expenses was the next thing to be considered, so I lifted my heart to the Lord who had said:

"Take no thought . . . I will supply your needs." The

afternoon mail of that very day brought a letter from two dear sisters in Chicago, containing sixty dollars. The letter was dated one month previous and stated that the Lord had awakened them up in the middle of the night saying:

"Little Sister Semple is in trouble. Rise immediately and send her sixty dollars." They had gotten up and sent the money, and here it was at the spot just when needed. Oh, hallelujah! It had arrived long before the hasty cablegram to my dear Mother could have brought the necessary funds from her ever-ready heart.

Morning after morning, of the month that followed, I would wake up with a scream as my great loss swept over me, and I thought of the little one who would never see her father. Then the Comforter would instantly spring up within me till I was filled with joy unspeakable, and my hot, dry eyes would flow with tears of love and blessing.

Then came the little daughter, a tiny mite of a thing, but Oh such a comfort! Here again the Comforter was with me. Truly Jesus is a husband to the widow and a Father to the fatherless. I named the little one Roberta, after her father, Robert. It was in Hong Kong, on the top of the mountain, that my tiny little daughter was born, and when she was six weeks old I sailed to Shanghai.

On leaving Shanghai we went to Japan, Moji, Kobe, Nagasaki. Upon leaving Japan we set sail for Honolulu and the U. S. A., I carrying my precious little burden in a Japanese basket.

Mother had sent money, some of which I had not yet received, and on the boat I kept figuring up and found that there was not enough to take me clear across the continent. Without telling my needs to an earthly soul I kept looking up to Jesus and witnessing for Him every occasion I found on the boat. My feelings on this return trip I will not try to describe, but Oh, there seemed to be such a great big, vast emptiness yawning all about me, and I snuggled the dear little warm bundle, Roberta, closer to my heart.

As I was stepping off the steamer at San Francisco, the purser came running after me, and touching me on the arm, said:

"Oh, wait a minute! Here is something for you from the passengers." Opening the envelope which he slipped into my hand, I found sixty-five dollars which had been donated by them.

All through the trip it seemed as though there was not one thing which I needed but the Lord quickly sent. It was nearing Christmas time, and China being so warm, I had nothing but the lightest of bonnets for the baby. I was in my state room, turning the tiny bonnet on my fingers, thinking that I should have a warm one for her when I reached the snow of our own land, when a rap came at my door and a lady's voice said:

"Oh, we have just brought the baby a warm eiderdown bonnet and cape. You are sure to need it."

At another time I was wishing for a heavy shawl for her. The porter came to the state room, saying that Mr.——, who had gotten off at the last port in Japan, had left this warm woolen shawl, which he declared he would no longer need, with instructions that it was to be given to "that little missionary lady with the baby." It was a beautiful, expensive shawl. How I did praise Jesus!

At another time a thermos bottle was needed. Without a word to a soul it was brought to my door and quietly handed in. These are only a few of the many things that I might tell you of how He tempers the wind to the shorn lamb and tenderly watches over His little children.

On board the train, which was speeding across the Rocky Mountains and heading toward Chicago, I was afflicted for the first time in my life with train-sickness, and was obliged to remain in my berth for a couple of days. Different passengers had warned me that we had one of the crankiest old conductors on this car they had ever seen, and not to ask any favors of him under any consideration. But Oh, my Lord can make a lion as gentle as a lamb and turn the bitter into sweet.

That dear conductor walked the floor hour after hour and took care of the baby for me, even carrying her nursing bottle in his pocket to keep it warm. Praise the Lord!

After a few days' stop in Chicago, we journeyed on to New York City, where my Mother was engaged in Salvation Army work. As the train pulled into the depot she was there to meet me, and I held the baby in one arm, but with the other was still able to point up to the sky to Jesus, just as I had when the train had last pulled out for China. Praise the Lord. When you have the Holy Spirit in your heart He will help you to still keep your hand up and "Keep on praising God."

CHAPTER X.

NINEVEH TO TARSHISH—AND RETURN.

"Then Jonah prayed unto the Lord his God out of the fish's belly . . . And the Lord spake unto the fish, and it vomited out Jonah upon the dry land.

And the word of the Lord came unto Jonah the second time, saying,

Arise, go unto Nineveh, and preach unto it the preaching that I bid thee.

So Jonah arose, and went."—Jonah 2:1, 10; 3:1 to 3.

HAVE you ever had a secret tucked away in the closet of your Christian experience which you shrank from exposing to the sunlight of public gaze and criticism? —a spot somewhere on your spiritual anatomy, so sore that the very thought of its being touched by a curious, probing finger made you wince?—a certain period of your life which you would a little rather not have generally known or discussed, all of which has long ago been confessed, forgiven and buried beneath the cleansing blood?

Have you, in telling your experience, been tempted to take a hop, skip and a jump over your deviations from the straight and narrow path of God's best and perfect will for you? Have you felt like leaping over and omitting, when telling your Christian experience, the things which should have been omitted it real life?—Well, that has just been my case exactly.

If this were to be a fine-sounding story of a continued forward march, without ever such a thing as a waver, this chapter would never be written. The Lord has made me to long, however, that each step of my experience may be a blessing and an encouragement to someone. It is easy to tell of the times when we have lived in victory, run the heavenly race without a single tumble, and when God has blessed us and made us a blessing: the hours of defeat, when we stumbled in the darkness by the way, however, may be of more blessing to the poor backslider who is groping his way back to light, than any other experience could be.

The Lord had been wonderfully with me through the ordeal of my husband's death, subsequent events, and my return to the homeland. At times the awful waters of loneliness through which I waded, however, seemed as though they would roll over my head, but each time He was with me to comfort and bear me up.

The following year found me battling against the swift, contrariwise tide, struggling to keep my feet, and to take up the broken thread of my life where last left off. My work in the meetings necessitated taking with me, and often keeping out till midnight, and as late as two o'clock in the morning, my frail little daughter, who eventually became very ill. I was given expert advice upon her frail condition and was told that I would be responsible for her life if I did not "get her a quiet home and proper food, as the constant moving about and changing food would be the death of the child."

I had come home from China like a wounded little bird, and my bleeding heart was constantly pierced with curious questions from well-meaning people who could not see the will of God in our call to China, and who felt that there must be a mistake somewhere, either in Robert's sudden death or my return home. I could not answer them, not being able to see the will of God in all this yet myself. Wherever I went amongst the dear people who had helped to send us to China, I would seem to feel an atmosphere of questioning (whether spoken or unexpressed), which little by little wore upon me until soon I began to feel like some guilty thing who had no business to be there, but far away somewhere—I could not tell just where.

Oh! how I longed for some one who would understand or put their arms about me and help me at this critical moment of my life, and this was just the time that the Lord permitted those I loved best to seem to draw aside the arms that had been before so strong and dependable, causing a little curtain of reserve to drop between us, leaving me on the outside with my baby.

Looking at it in the natural, it is hardly to be wondered at that, like Hagar, with my child, I departed and wandered in the wilderness, and that I lifted up my voice and wept. Pentecost seemed as the mistress, dealing hardly with me and God as Abraham who apparently did not intervene in my behalf.

The loom of life seemed then to be but a tangled maze whose colorings had suddenly plunged from mountain-tops of sunlit glory to the depths of a seemingly endless valley of bewildering gloom. It is only now, after having watched through the succeeding years the steady flying to and fro of the shuttles of destiny, ever guided by the tender wisdom of the Hand Divine, that I begin to see the head and form of the Master being wrought out and woven upon the loom of my life.

It was just at the time of my greatest perplexity, when I had begun to lose out spiritually and wander away from the Lord, and was longing to make a home for the baby, that I married again. Before the marriage took place, however, I made one stipulation wherein I told my husband that all my heart and soul was really in the work of the Lord and that if, at any time in my life, He should call me to go to Africa or India, or to the Islands of the Sea, no matter where or when, I must obey God first of all. To this he agreed and we were married under these conditions, and settled down in a furnished apartment.

Disturbed and troubled in my heart, stepping out of the work of the Lord, I turned again to the world, endeavoring to stifle my longings to be reinstated at the banqueting table of my King.

I wonder if there is anyone on earth who is really as abjectly miserable as the backslider? It was such a relief to be able to stay away from the meetings, and yet such a pain to be away from them (if you can analyze that), that I was torn between the two conflicting forces. Some of the saints saw me backsliding and drifting into the world, and my position became still more intolerable.

When my husband received an invitation from his mother to come to her home in Rhode Island I was willing to consent to board the boat in my endeavor to "flee unto Tarshish from the presence of the Lord."

But Oh, dear reader, what a great wind the Lord sent out into the sea! Such a mighty tempest was there in the deep that our frail domestic craft was rocked to and fro, so that the ship was like to be broken.

Day by day matters grew worse instead of better; I grieved and mourned and wept for my Jesus and the old-time place in Him. I was a mystery and a constant source of discomfort to those round about me.

Earthly things—home—comfort—Oh, what did these matter? I was out of His dear will, and my soul refused to be comforted.

Shutting myself away in my room I would sit on the floor in the corner behind the bed, and cry over and over the one word that I could say when I tried to pray:

"Oh—Oh—Jesus! Jesus! Jesus!! JESUS!"

Seeing my unhappy, melancholy state, my mother-in-law advised us to rent and furnish a home of our own, saying that the work would occupy my mind and keep me from thinking so much about myself. This was done. With the help of our parents and our own earnings, a well-furnished home was made, containing all that heart could wish—*B-U-T J-E-S-U-S*, and Oh, without Him nothing matters!

"Why can't you be happy and act like other folks, and forget your troubles?" I was asked again and again. Time after time I tried to shake myself from my lethargy and depression and busy myself with household duties. Such a fever of restlessness came upon me that it seemed as though I must wear the polish off the furniture and the floors by dusting them so often. A dozen times a day I would take myself to task as I would catch sight of my tearful face in the looking-glass, saying:

"Now, see here, my lady, this will never do! What right have you to fret and pine like this? Just see those shining, polished floors, covered with soft Axminster and Wilton rugs. Just look at that mahogany parlor furniture and the big brass beds in yonder, the fine bathroom done in blue and white, the steam heat, the softly-shaded electric lights, the pretty baby's crib with its fluff and ribbons, the high-chair and the rocking-horse. Why aren't you glad to have a home like this for the babies, as any other mother would be?"

"Why, it's perfectly ridiculous for you to think of going out into the world again, and—remember—if you found it hard with one baby before, what do you suppose you would do now with two?"

Having had it thus out with myself, I would return to my work, half satisfied for a few minutes, saying:

"Well, yes, that's so. I had better give up all thoughts of such things, settle down and get used to my present life."

But, Oh, the *Call of God* was on my soul and I could not get away from it. For this cause I had been brought into the world. With each throb of my heart I could hear a voice saying:

"Preach the Word! Preach the Word! Will you go? Will you go?" and I would throw myself on my knees, tearfully sobbing:

"Oh, Lord, You know that I cannot go. Here are the two babies and here is the home, and here is husband, who has not the baptism and is not even seeking it. I will work here in the local mission, and that will do." But no, the answer still came back, clear from heaven:

"Go! DO THE WORK OF AN EVANGELIST; Preach the Word! The time is short; I am coming soon."

"Oh, Lord, I am in a pretty state to preach the Gospel, I am. Why, I feel so miserable and down and crushed. I need some one to help me instead of me helping others." At times, lifting my eyes quickly after prayer, I could almost see the devil rubbing his hands and leering at me, saying:

"There's no hope. You might just as well give up. Everyone knows you've backslidden, and would have no confidence in you." Then would ensue another spell of bitter weeping.

My husband and his mother would often say:

"Well, Aimee—I don't see what more you want. I don't believe anything could make you happy. It must be your disposition." (Why, bless the Lord, when in His will I am so happy and full of gladness, my feet and my heart are so light, that they cannot keep from dancing. It seems that no one on earth could possibly be so happy as I).

My nerves became so seriously affected that the singing of the teakettle upon the stove or the sound of voices was unbearable. I implored the little one to speak in whispers. I hated the sunshine and wanted to keep the shutters closed and the window-shades drawn tightly. The doctors said I would lose my reason if something was not done. I became very ill in body and inside of one year two serious operations were performed. Each time, before going under the surgeon's knife. and during many other times of critical illness, when it seemed as though I were going to die, I would call the saints to pray for me that I might be delivered, but each time they prayed I could plainly hear the voice of the Lord saying:

"Will you go? Will you preach the Word?" I knew that if I said "Yes", He would heal me. But how could I say "Yes?" Difficulties rose like mountains in my path. Oh, now I have learned, that no matter what the obstacles may be, if Jesus says "Go", and I start, by the time the obstacle is reached I will either be lifted over it or it will be gone. God does not ask us to do the impossible. If He tells you to do a thing, no matter how hard it seems, you just start to do it and you will find, like Christian of old, that the lions are fettered and unable to hinder your progress.

After the first operation I was worse instead of better. Complications set in, heart trouble, hemorrhages from my stomach, and intense nervousness among others. The doctors said that another operation would be necessary.

Oh, that home which I had thought to enjoy! Almost all my enjoyment was what I could see from my bed! I wonder if Jonah had nearly as rough a passage as I did when he ran away and disobeyed God. His trip was not as long as mine anyway. We read that Jonah paid his fare, and I certainly paid mine to the uttermost farthing.

The second operation was put off and put off, with some vague hope of trusting God, but how could I trust Him when out of His will, and when every time in prayer I got the answer which throbbed and pounded through my being with every pulse-beat—

"Will you go? Will you go? Preach the Word! Preach the Word!"

At last, doubling over with a scream with appendicitis, on top of all else, I was rushed again to the hospital. As I was being prepared for the operating table I prayed earnestly from my valley of despair—

"Oh, God, please take me home to be with You. It doesn't seem possible for me to go back and I certainly cannot bear it to go on. I am a misery to myself and to everybody round about me. Please, please take me home to be with You." But Oh, I am so glad that He spared me. Praise His precious name.

After I had come out from under the ether and the knife, wherein five operations in one had been performed, the poor, unconscious "what-there-was-left-of-me" was put back in the bed and I opened my eyes on the white walls of the hospital—quivering with pain from head to foot, which, instead of growing better grew worse and worse.

Twice my mother had been called by a telegram to see me die. Her heart was torn as the wheels of the train sped over the track, and she prayed that she might be there in time. From the depot she was rushed to the hospital, and chokes up yet, as she sits here beside me and tries to describe her feelings as she entered the room reeking with ether, and looked upon the little form lying on the pillow that had been the center of so many scenes of hope and life and happiness.

She thought of the day she had prayed for the little girl who should go out in the world to preach the Word, the day of the dedication under the banners of blood and fire, the golden future of joyful service, and—here—was the wreck!—Was this all?

Something within her refused to let go of God and His promises to her regarding me. Whilst the doctors and nurses in the outer room were gravely explaining to her the scientific reasons why I could not live, explaining that mine had been such an exceptional case, and endeavoring to reconcile her to my death, her heart was going out in an agony of prayer to God that her daughter's life would be spared.

Brokenly she wept and prayed, renewing and redoubling her vows to God to help in every way to get me back into the work and keep me there, to do all in her power to help me with my children and in every struggle, come what may.

The nurses, hardened as they were by long training, were frankly in tears, and the doctor "herumphed!" and cleared his throat as I came out of the ether, and declared that that hospital had never witnessed such a scene, for I was preaching, telling of Jesus, begging lost souls to come to Him, in that high strong voice which patients have when coming out from the anaesthetic. Broken though I was in body and spirit, the very moment that reason lost her sway, my soul began to sing and preach and pray to my beloved Jesus.

Later Mother came into my room, and kneeling down, looked into my eyes and said:

"Mother is here, darling. Mother will help. She understands and will stand by you, dear." In the look which was exchanged it seemed as though a spark of hope and understanding was instilled and glowed in both of our souls, which has never gone out, but has burst into a flame, ever mounting upward as days go by.

One evening, after a nurse and doctor had been in almost constant attendance all afternoon, three young internes came in and gathering me gently in their arms, carried me, mattress and all, into the separate room where people were taken to die.

About two in the morning the white-robed nurse, who had been stroking my hand, saying: "Poor little girl; poor little girl," seemed to be receding. The fluttering breaths which I could take were too painful to go deeper than my throat. Everything grew black—someone said:

"She's going." Just before losing consciousness, as I hovered between life and death, came the voice of my Lord, so loud that it startled me:

"NOW—WILL—YOU—GO?" And I knew it was "Go", one way or the other: that if I did not go into the work as a soul-winner and get back into the will of God, Jesus would take me to Himself before He would permit me to go on without Him and be lost.

Oh, don't you ever tell me that a woman cannot be called to preach the Gospel! If any man ever went through one-hundreadth part of the hell on earth that I lived in, those months when out of God's will and work, they would never say that again.

With my little remaining strength, I managed to gasp:

"Yes—Lord—I'll—go." And go I did!

I could not have been unconscious for more than a moment, but when I opened my eyes the pain was gone. I was able to take deep breaths without the agony which had accompanied the tiniest breath before. I was able to turn over without pain, and proceeded to do this, much to the alarm of the nurse. In two weeks, to the amazement of everyone, I was up and well, though weak in body. I have hardly known an ache or a pain from that day to this.

On several occasions before and after my return from the hospital, little attempts were made to break the news of my determination to go forth into the vineyard at once.

"Why, what a crazy notion for you to even think of such a thing! Why don't you be like other young women and be contented to stay at home and attend to the housework?" and other outbursts of like nature invariably met my timid, yet firm ventures to gain the consent of the household.

Too weak to argue, I was also too weak to dare even think of disobeying God. That great white whale, the operating table, had thrown me up on the shore. The Lord had spared my life under a definite promise that I would serve Him. Foolish and impossible as the idea might seem, I was going to strike out for Ninevah, without a moment's hesitation, live or die, sink or swim, praying for Divine guidance and filled with a determination to say "Yes" to that call—

"Will you Go? Will you Go?" I did not know just how or where I was to go, but intended to start anyway, and that at once, throwing myself at His feet and trusting Him implicitly. I was assured that He who parted the Red Sea and rolled back the waves of the Jordan would someway remove rivers and mountains for me and take me through the fires unburned.

Mother now being in Canada, I telegraphed there for money; and when alone in the house one night, 'phoned for a taxicab, and at eleven o'clock bundled my two babies inside while the chauffeur piled the two suitcases on top, and away we sped to catch the midnight train for home and Mother. To make a new start and begin all over again it seemed the most natural thing in the world to go back to the starting place from which I had set out before.

God was with me and I was conscious of His leading and support at every step. With my little baby clasped in one arm and Roberta sleeping in the other, I held them tightly to me as the immensity of what I was doing swept over me. The streets were dark and almost deserted as we rolled along toward the depot.

So here I was setting forth for the second time in my life to obey the great call to preach the Word, but how different it was from the first time—how changed the scene!

Scene One. The first time it was high noon and the warm, friendly sun smiled and beamed down upon us from the sky—life and hope spread their garments before the little rosy-cheeked bride as she was waved away by tearful but loving and sympathetic friends and relatives, one hundred or more of whom had gathered on the country lawn, some coming many miles to see her off, showering her with flowers, rice and "God bless you's." That time I had gone forth leaning in every way for strength, wisdom and guidance on the strong arm of my husband; blest and victorious in my soul. An open door of ministry lay before us; we were sure of our footing, knew just where we were going.

Scene Two. Setting forth alone—at midnight—almost running away—with my two babies—weak in body—empty and lean in my soul—no earthly arm to lean upon—no visible open door before me—no loving friends—no flowers or "God bless you's." But Oh, I praise Jesus for the experience! Nothing could tempt me to part with the lessons taught me in those hard places of going through alone with Jesus and thrusting my roots of faith and dependence, confidence and trust down deep into Himself.

My former life in the work had been like that of a vine which twined about the stalwart oak, but when that stronghold to which I clung had been taken away and transplanted into the heavenly gardens, when my clutch had been loosened and let go there was nothing left of the vine, that had reached so high, but a pitifully broken, crumpled little heap which lay in tumbled confusion on the earth. But now I had found One to cling to and fasten my hold upon who was as the cedars of Lebanon, who would endure forever, from whom I could not be removed—One who would never die nor leave me. Oh, it was Jesus! Jesus!!

Yes, thank God for the hard places, for the winds and the

icy blasts of winter's storm, for Oh, 'twas there I learned for the first time a little of what it meant to be rooted and grounded and settled—to die out and to go through a valley of crucifixion that led to resurrection power and glory.

Did you ever ride along through a tunnel or subway that was pitch dark and seemingly endless?—then all at once, away in the distance, you saw a tiny light which you knew must be the opening of the tunnel and sunlight? That's just the way I felt. I was still in the darkness of the tunnel, but I saw the door, the beacon light of God's dear sunlight—His smile of approval, and I was running toward it.

"Here we are, lady, just in time!" broke in the voice of the driver, as the car pulled up at the curb in front of the depot.

I cannot remember now how those two sleeping children and all the baggage were gotten on board, but I do know that a few minutes later, when the train steamed out into the night and sped through the fields and the sleepy towns, we were all on board and the babies sleeping as sweetly as they ever had in their lives in the snow-white Pullman bed.

I was obeying God, and although the enemy was still endeavoring to hound my tracks with accusations and forebodings of future disaster, he had someway lost his grip and his power to overthrow me. When he twitted me with the leanness and the barrenness of my soul, that hurt the most of anything because it was so true, my heart sang within me:

"Never mind, Rebecca's on her way to the well—to the fountain-head—to the sure source of supply—to the banqueting table of the King, and we'll soon be filled up now."

CHAPTER XI.

GETTING BACK.

"For ye were as sheep going astray; but are now returned unto the Shepherd and Bishop of your souls."—I Peter 2:25.

HEN the 11:55 pulled into the station of Ingersoll my Father and Mother were there to meet me—so was the pony I used to ride. She was only a colt then, but she knew me and whinnied affectionately.

"Suppose she knows you?" said Dad.

"Surely she does," I smiled. And as if to remove all doubts on the matter, Fritzie lifted her right front foot to shake hands and quivered all over as she nozzled my cheek with her velvet nose, smacking her lips and pretending to hunt for the old-time sugar lump—both tricks I had taught her long ago—my, how long it did seem! Was it centuries or was it just years?

Usually Fritzie was quite staid, but how she did pick up her heels and run that day! It seemed as though she couldn't get home and out of her harness quickly enough to play with me. I wondered if she remembered how we used to leap the fences, and the time she followed me right into the kitchen and stamped about, to the dismay of my Mother.

How familiar and restful and green the dear old fields looked on that drive homeward. Here was the old toll-gate. A mile beyond was the place where I had given my heart to Jesus and cried "Lord, be merciful to me, a sinner," as the sleigh jingled along, drawn by Fritzie's mother. A mile beyond that again was the little white school house on the corner. Every foot of the way was associated with girlhood memories.

No explanations were asked, but Mother informed me that it had all been settled that I was to leave for the Pentecostal camp meeting at Kitchener (then called Berlin) the next day. She herself had planned to attend, but immediately upon the receipt of my telegram had given up all thought of going and had written to engage accommodations for me.

"But, Mother!—the children—would I be able—"

"Never mind the children," she interrupted. "I have taken care of children before and cared for Roberta almost all the time anyway, and Rolf and I will get along fine, won't we, Sonny?" A delighted gurgle and a wide smile, that displayed the new baby teeth, was his response.

"Yes, and we've got the best Jeresy milk in the country to make him grow like a weed," boasted my Father, as if to conclude the subject.

"But—but—how can I get back to Kitchener, when I feel so leaked out spiritually? The last time I was there was with Brother Durham and Robert. I was so blest; prayed for the seekers. What would they think?

"But I'll go, Mother. Oh, I am so happy, so glad for the

opportunity. Are you sure that the extra work will not be too much for you?"

"Too much work?—I should say not! Oh, Aimee, nothing is too much or too hard to see you get back to God and back to the place where He wants you. Will you promise me that you will come back in this meeting? We will stand by you, and God will help you."

But I needed no coaxing or inducement—having set my face like a flint, and though all the world were pulling the other way I *MUST* go through—any other course meant death.

Before leaving the next morning for the camp, a telegram was sent to my husband, saying:

"I have tried to walk your way and have failed. Won't you come now and walk my way? I am sure we will be happy."

At Kitchener we were met with the wagon which carried the passengers and baggage to the camp grounds. I soon found myself alighting in the little city of tents, pitched in snow whiteness beneath the green foliage of the forest trees. Glad hands and familiar faces gathered round to welcome me back, but I felt conscience- and duty-bound to make an embarrassed, but hasty, explanation to one and all that I was not where I once was, and said to them—

"I prayed for others when they needed prayer. Now I need someone to pray for me and help me get back the blessing and fire of God upon the altar of my heart."

Perhaps some of you can imagine my feelings as I sat in the audience looking up at the platform whereon sat different ones whom but a few years before I had prayed with when they came through the baptism. There they were, shaking and quivering under the power, faces radiant—hallelujahs ringing—and here sat I, dabbing at my eyes with a wet handkerchief and saying:

"Oh, Jesus, You used to bless me like that. I used to shake under the power and praise you just like that.

"Oh, bless me now, my Savior;
I come to Thee."

(All through the months of my disobedience to God, the Holy Spirit had never left me, but had prayed through me in tongues many times, and was indeed an abiding Comforter. Oh, the mercy, and the long-suffering of God! How little I deserved it!)

When the call for the altar service came I stole forward amongst the others and bowed at the altar, feeling utterly unworthy to touch even one of the rough planks which formed its floor. All I could do was bow my head and weep. The brother in charge came along and said:

"Now, Sister, lift up your hands and praise the Lord, just as you used to tell others to do." But, Oh, no, I felt that I had much to make right with the Lord first—that I must beg Him to forgive me and apologize and humble myself in the dust before Him. How little we know after all of the great loving heart of God who runs to meet the penitent soul even as the father ran to meet the prodigal of old.

Brokenly I began to sob:

"Oh, Lord, forgive m—" before I could finish the words I felt as though the Lord had put His hand over my mouth and said to me:

"There, my child, it's all right. Don't say anything more about it." This was so sudden and unexpected I could not comprehend it, but thought surely I must be mistaken,—surely I would have to beg and plead for hours and it would be very hard to get back to God after having been so disobedient and wandering away. So I settled myself down and tried it again:

"Oh, Lord, dear Lord, can you ever forgive me—" again came the same peculiar sensation as of the Lord stopping my mouth and saying:

"It's all right; it's all forgiven. Don't say any more about it." It was just as though someone had injured me in some way, had come to me to ask forgiveness, and I had said:

"Oh, yes, that's all right. Never think of it again. Just forget it."

Well, the suddenness and the magnitude of this hearty reception completely bowled me over. It broke my heart and bound me to Him more than any whipping could ever have done. Such love was more than my heart could bear. Before I knew it I was on my back in the straw, under the power, saying:

"Dear Lord, just let me be as one of your hired servants. I

do not feel worthy to testify or work at the altar or preach, but just let me love you and dwell in your house, my Saviour."

The next thing I knew the Spirit was speaking in tongues through me, giving me the interpretation. A brother from London had a message in tongues—the Lord gave me the interpretation of that—and he fell back under the power. I was laughing and weeping and shaking. A little knot of people gathered round to rejoice with me. The Spirit lifted me to my feet and I walked up and down praising the Lamb for sinners slain. Falling on my knees I worshipped the Lord again.

A dear old Mennonite preacher who had been seeking his baptism for years was kneeling at the other end of the platform. It had been my privilege to pray for his brother as he came through to the baptism the night before we left for China. The Lord seemed to guide me to this brother now, and walking on my knees, with my hands outstretched before me, something within me spoke:

"In the name of Jesus Christ, receive ye the Holy Ghost." Immediately the brother fell to the ground and was speaking in tongues almost before he reached it. After all his years of waiting, the Comforter had come in like a flash of glory to abide forever.

The old-time power and the anointing for praying with seekers rested upon me. Many other instances, which I will not refer to here, took place. But Oh, the Lord did not let these wonderful answers to prayer, as I prayed for the seekers, come to puff me up, but to encourage me. It was balm to my wounded, troubled soul.

Never have I worked harder at the altar services in our own meetings than at that camp meeting. We stayed as late as twelve and sometimes two in the morning, praying for seekers and were up again to early morning meeting. He was restoring my soul, He was leading me out to green pastures. I had come to this camp meeting to see God, and Oh, how He did reveal himself to me!

Camp over, I returned to my Mother's to find her happily running the sewing machine on the piazza, making clothes for the children, who were laughing in the hammock that swung beneath the apple trees. Delightedly I repeated the story already written in my letters of the blessing of the Lord upon my soul, and added that I had but one week to wash and iron my things and get ready for the next camp meeting, which was to be held in London, twenty miles away, the very city where the Lord had taken my husband and myself to carry the message of Pentecost some years before.

Happy to do anything to advance my Saviour's cause, I had been given the task of painting a great twenty-five foot banner, roping and preparing it to go across the street, advertising the meetings.

Within the house was a little pile of letters, demanding my immediate return "to wash the dishes," "take care of the house" and "act like other women." But I had put my hand to the Gospel plow, and I could not turn back. I was going through, and I had the assurance that the Lord would bring my husband also. I certainly never could win him the other way and he would have had to have parted with me for good if I had died, which I surely would have done had I remained out of the work. I was going through; Jesus was with me and nothing in all the world mattered now. My heart was right with God.

Although in many ways the enemy endeavored to discourage, frighten and turn me back, as he did poor Christian in Pilgrim's Progress, and though the tests were hard and his tactics cunningly planned, Jesus held me firm and did not allow me to swerve from my path nor stumble in the way.

The blessed London camp meeting over, the Lord strongly impressed me to accept an invitation from Sister Sharp of Mount Forest, Ont., to conduct Bible meetings there in a little hall called "Victory Mission." The power and the glory of the Lord came down in a precious way. The mission soon became too small to hold the people; we were obliged to hold the services on the spacious lawn between the Sister's home and the mission. Such a spirit of revival came down upon the people that soon a tent was bought, hungry people filled it night after night and those who could not get in stood in rings round its border.

Then came the day when the power fell. It was half past ten in the morning, and in my room I was praying:

"Oh, Lord, send Thy mighty power today. Lord, send the power. Send the power, Lord."

Outside, in the tent, two brothers shook hands with each other and said:

"Praise the Lord." As they spoke the power of God struck them both; one fell one way, and one the other, and lay stretched out under the power shouting and glorifying God. Little children began to come in off the street to see what it meant. One look was sufficient and away they ran to bring others to see the strange sight.

Mrs. Sharp's mother, who had a very sore and badly poisoned foot, came hobbling out of the house, her knee on a chair which she used as a means of conveyance. No sooner did she reach the tent that the power struck her and she tipped over (chair and all), was healed, and later danced and praised the Lord.

Sister Sharp came running into the tent, and down she went. The town crier, who used to ring the bell advertising theaters, ball games, etc., came in, and over he went with his bell, and lying under the power added his voice with the others to the praises of the most high God.

It is not necessary for me to go on and relate the wonderful way in which Jesus worked in this meeting, to tell how the town was stirred, how our Sister was haled before the magistrate and liberated, how over a hundred were saved and scores received the baptism, as dear Sister Sharp has herself written an account of the meetings, which you will find related in Chapter One, Part II, of this book.

However, I must tell you the best news of all, for right in the midst of one of the meetings which was held in Mount Forest, my husband landed with his suitcase, to attend the meeting.

So changed was I, so radiantly happy, so filled with the power of God and the unction of the Holy Spirit, that he had to admit that this was indeed my calling and work in life. Before many hours had passed he himself had received the baptism of the Holy Spirit, spoke in tongues and glorified God.

How the Lord does vindicate and honor those who go through with Him! As my husband saw the workings of the Holy Spirit, sinners coming to the altar for salvation, believers receiving the Holy Spirit, and heard me delivering the messages under the power of the Spirit, for truly it was not I, but Christ that lived in me, he told me that he recognized that God had called me into this work and would not have me leave it for anything in the world. And through the succeeding years, though part of the time he is with me and part of the time elsewhere, the Lord has made him perfectly willing for me to go on, whether he is along or not.

The Lord has wonderfully blessed and supplied my every need and the needs of the two children, for food, clothing and traveling expenses. We have lacked no good thing. The way has been growing brighter and brighter day by day. The harvest of souls is increasing month by month. The work is spreading out and the nets are filled with abundance of fish. Glory! Glory!! GLORY!

CHAPTER XII.

REVIVAL FIRES FALL.

"And Elijah . . . repaired the altar of the Lord that was broken down.

Then the fire of the Lord fell, and consumed the burnt sacrifice . . . And when all the people saw it, they fell on their faces and said, The Lord, He is God."—I. Kings 18:30, 38 and 39.

FTER the meeting at Mount Forest the Lord called us back to the U. S. A. to dispose of our little store of earthly goods and to give me also an opportunity to work with my own hands and feet to help raise the money with which to purchase a new 40 x 80 Gospel tent which the Lord had shown me definitely it was His will for us to have. We had the assurance that the balance would be in by the time the tent was to be paid for, and true to His word, offerings began to be handed to us in the little meetings.

THE TENT MEETING IN PROVIDENCE, R. I.

The new tent was to have been ready for our camp meeting, which was to begin June first, but the Lord intervened and did not allow it to be completed on time. Knowing little of the winds and power of the elements which have to be taken into consideration when picking out a location for a tent meeting, we, in our ignorance, selected a fine, high hill, on the bluff of the bay where those who came to meeting could enjoy the breeze and the water. That there was a breeze no one who was there and saw the tents go down could deny. Whatever else the location may have lacked in, the breeze was ever there. If anything could have discouraged us with tent work, surely our experience in Providence would have done so, but praise the Lord, He did not permit our new tent to be completed, and therefore the tent company put up an old tent of their own which had almost seen its day, and cost us nothing for the damage done to it.

But in spite of wind and the hours of struggle to drive the stakes and tie the ropes and keep the tents up, the Lord sent thousands of people to the camp meetings and many precious souls wept their way to Jesus' feet and received the blessed Holy Spirit, the Comforter whom Jesus sent.

Neighbors who were utterly indifferent at first, when they saw our valiant struggles with the wind and storms, came to our help and toiled with us. Then, feeling they had some interest in the tent which they had worked so hard to keep up, came in to hear the message delivered in it, and were brought to the Lord—one whole family was saved in one night.

The series of meetings was almost over when one forenoon the last wind storm came, and in spite of all our efforts, down went the big tent with many tears in its rotten old seams which we had worked for hours to sew up, just a short time ago. My husband, who had worked faithfully each time, was discouraged, and declared that that tent could not be put up again. He had taken a position and returned to secular work, and would not be back that day, but I knew that hundreds would be there for the night meeting. I could not manage that big tent alone, so with the help of a little boy, in the heat of the noon hour, we set to work. We had ten small 10x12 tents scattered about in different places in the grounds; some had been erected; some were still in their bags. These we carried, one by one, raised them on their poles, stretched the canvas and drove the stakes, lashing them, pole to pole, all in one straight row. This had the appearance of one long tent, one hundred feet long and twelve feet wide (if you can imagine how that looked). Then we carried in the chairs. By this time people were arriving and they turned in and helped us.

How the Lord did bless our efforts; this tent was so low the wind could not take it down.

Two sisters from Onset Bay, Cape Cod, who attended the meeting, asked us to ship our tent there and, undismayed by the experiences in Providence, we shipped the tent. Although we have lowered our tent several times since, never once have we ever had our tent torn down by the wind from that day to this.

Before going to Onset a short meeting was held at Montwait Camp grounds, Massachusetts, and the Lord blessedly poured out of His Spirit, saving and baptizing hungry souls. The enemy was still testing my faith and endeavoring to draw me back from the work, but thank God, my feet were kept from slipping, even though many times I have had to go through alone. When the meeting was almost over in Montwait the Lord spoke to my husband, in Providence, R. I., in three dreams, calling him to leave his secular work in the plant where he was employed and come and assist me with the tents.

ONSET BAY

In Onset our new tent was pitched in the Holiness Camp ground, and though the battle was hard, Jesus gave victory. The war against spiritualism, Christian Science, and demon powers was hot and heavy, but we sang and preached the blood of Jesus until the break came and the Lord poured out His Spirit.

CORONA, L. I., N. Y.

While yet in Onset the Lord began to speak to me of Corona and different times when praying, would bring the word "Corona" before me. I had been asking the Lord for a typewriter and thought He was going to give me a Corona as the word kept ringing in my ears, when a letter came through the mail, however, from a dear colored sister, stating that the Lord had directly led her to send for us to come to Corona, L. I., (just outside of New York City) to hold a meeting. My spirit quickened within me as the Lord gave the witness that this was that which He had been speaking of.

The weather now being too cold for tent meetings in the East, we asked the Lord to supply the means whereby we might ship our tents to Florida, where it would be warm enough for a winter campaign, and still praying to this end, we went to Corona.

Upon first arrival this seemed a most discouraging field. No one but this precious colored sister was known to have received the baptism of the Holy Spirit according to Acts 2:4. Though we walked for blocks, not a hall could we find to rent, but I kept praying, and though everyone else doubted my call, I knew that God had sent me. Finally word came from the Swedish church that we would be welcome to open meetings there during the week.

The second night the church was filled to the door, though church members had been warned by their ministers to keep away from the Pentecostal people and have nothing to do with those folks who talked in tongues. Just one week from the day meetings were opened the break came. A Sunday School teacher from one of the large churches, a man whose sound Christian standing had been known for years, was the first to receive the baptism. The wife of a leading citizen was the second, and when the altar call was given scores from the audience, which was made up entirely of church members, gathered about the altar.

Never having seen a Pentecostal meeting, they were very stiff and did not know how really to get hold and seek the Lord. Knowing that their ministers had warned them that this was all hypnotism, however, I was very careful not to lay hands upon, or speak to the seekers, but prayed by my own chair earnestly:

"Oh, Lord, send the power. Lord, honor your Word just now."

Then it was that Mrs. John Lake, who had risen from the altar and taken her seat in the audience again, suddenly fell under the power, with her head upon her husband's shoulder. In alarm the people said:

"She has fainted. Run and get some water." But I knew she hadn't fainted, and I kept on praying:

"Lord, send the power. Baptize her just now."

Quite a crowd had gathered round her, but before they could get back with the water, praise the Lord, her lungs began to heave with the power, her chin began to quiver, and she broke out speaking with other tongues to the amazement and delight of all.

On and on she spoke, in such a clear, beautiful language, her face shining with the glory of the Lord. One would say to another:

"What do you think of it?" and others would say:

"Oh, isn't it wonderful, marvelous! How I wish I had the same experience!"

The news of this well-known sister's baptism quickly spread through the town. The next night three were slain under the power and came through speaking in tongues, and thus the meetings increased in power, numbers and results each night.

After preaching in the church one week, Pastor W. K. Bouton invited us to his church to preach on a Thursday night. (After warning his people not to come near our meetings he had come himself).

The Lord had convinced him of the truth that there was something deeper yet for himself and his church.

The night on which we spoke at his church I had to ask the Lord not to let me be afraid or overawed by the visiting ministers who sat behind me on the platform, and to give me liberty and power in preaching His Word and He never fails. He remembers our weakness, praise His name.

As I spoke, hearty "Amens" and "Hallelujahs" came trom all over the church. I felt that I must preach the truth without compromise or fear at least once in this church as they might never ask me again. When finished I took my seat, not presuming to give an altar call in someone else's church.

The Minister rose and said:

"How many of you people believe what Sister McPherson has said to be the truth, feel that you have not received the baptism of the Holy Spirit in the Bible way, and would like to receive this experience? Lift your hands."

They tell me that every hand in the church went up. (My eyes were so full of tears of joy I really could not say).

The people rose from their seats and flocked up the aisles,

gathered completely round the chancel rail, inside the chancel, right behind the pulpit, and prayed between the pews and all over the church for the baptism of the Holy Spirit. What a glorious sight it was! This church had been kept clean from concerts and suppers and worldly amusements. Through their consecrated pastor they had been brought up to the place where they were just ready to be swept into the fulness of the Spirit's power.

Three received the baptism that night. One lady fell by the organ, another at the other side of the church. Then two brothers who had not been on speaking terms with each other for over a year were seen talking to each other in the center of the church. One had asked the other, with tears in his eyes, to forgive him, and immediately fell back in his brother's arms under the power of the Holy Spirit. Alarmed, his brother lowered him to the floor.

I do not believe the scenes in that dear church could be described this side of heaven. Each time some one fell under the power the people would run to that side of the church. When some one would fall on the other side they would turn and go over there. It was all so new and strange.

The Pastor, however, did not run to look as the rest did, but kneeled by his pulpit with his hands over his face, looking through his fingers every once in a while to keep a watch on proceedings. (Laughing over it together later, when he had received his baptism, I told him it appeared as though he believed in the verse that told us to "watch and pray.") He was yearning for the power of God, and yet naturally fearful lest his people should be led into confusion and error.

Seeing the questions and excitement of the people as the power of God prostrated their dear ones, the enemy whispered:

"Well, you will never have an invitation back to this church now. There never was anyone stretched out under the power on that green carpet before. They will never ask you back here again."

Oh, ye of little faith, wherefore did ye doubt?

At midnight, when the meeting was beginning to break a little, the Pastor touched me on the arm and said:

"Sister, we have talked this over with the officials and the church is yours for as long as you want it, and when you want it. When shall we have the next meeting?"

"Tomorrow night," I replied.

Tomorrow night found the church not only filled to the doors, but the vestry and Sunday School rooms as well,—this night seven received the baptism. The Minister invited me to preach the Bible evidence of the baptism—speaking in other tongues as the Spirit gives utterance—and to take full liberty in every way.

During altar service he kneeled, looking through his fingers once in a while, at the strange proceedings taking place in his dignified congregation. Sinners broke down and wept their way to Jesus' feet—Protestants and Catholics alike. Such praying and calling upon the name of the Lord, the minister feared would result in the people's being arrested for disturbing the peace.

The third night nineteen received the baptism of the Holy Spirit. Down they went right and left, between the seats, in the aisles, in front of the chancel rail, up on the platform. Oh, Glory!

One night, while praying with a young lady who was receiving the baptism, I happened to catch the minister's eye as he was watching and beckoned him to come where he could really see and hear. He kneeled beside the young lady whom he knew well as a devoted Christian worker, and soon saw her face suffused with heavenly glory as she was filled with the Spirit and broke out speaking with other tongues and praising the Lord. As he watched and listened a wistful look came over the brother's face and without a word he went round to his pulpit again and kneeling down with closed eyes, lifted his hands and began to pray.

"Oh, Lord, fill me. Oh, Lord, fill me." Over and over he prayed this simple prayer in earnestness and humility before the Lord. The Spirit kept impressing me to go and pray for him. At first I hesitated, feeling my unworthiness, but at last I went and kneeled behind him and began to pray as simply as he:

"Lord, fill him."

"Lord, fill me," he would cry.

"Lord, fill him," was the prayer that filled my soul.

I do not know how long we kept on praying thus, but I do know that when I opened my eyes it seemed almost too good to be true. Then minister was swaying from side to side, and soon fell backwards under the power and rolled off the little step and lay under the glorious power of the Lord, just inside the chancel rail.

Someone spoke to his wife, who had been sitting in the audience, and said:

"Oh, there goes William!"

This was too much and with one bound she was in the aisle and ran to the front sobbing imploringly:

"Oh, Will, Will, speak to me. Speak to me."

Kneeling beside her I was praying with all my might that the Lord should baptize this dear Pastor as it would mean so much to the entire church and in fact the whole town. Fearful lest she should disturb him, I said:

"Oh, my dear, you wouldn't disturb him while he is under the power, for the world, would you?"

"Oh, but he's dying. He's dying!" she wailed. "I know he's going to die!"

"Oh, no, he is not dying," I hastily explained. "This is the power of the Holy Spirit, dear. He is safe in the arms of Jesus and if you watch a few minutes you will see him receive the Holy Spirit, I am sure."

"Oh, but I know he is dying! He had a vision once before and he almost died then! Will! Will! speak to me!" she implored.

I doubt if I could have restrained her much longer, but just at that tense moment, when the congregation were gathered round in breathless circles, leaning over the chancel rail, some even standing on the pews to see over the others' shoulders, Pastor W. K. Bouton was filled with the blessed Holy Spirit and gave such a Christ-exalting message as one seldom hears in this old world. The glory of God filled the place. The presence of the Lord penetrated the very air.

People fell to the floor here and there through the audience. Strong men sobbed like babies, and when at last the Pastor rose to his feet he walked up and down the platform, and said:

"Oh, friends, I have to preach!" And preach he did, under the inspiration of the Holy Spirit, telling the people that "This Is That," commanding them to be filled with the Spirit, to get oil in their lamps and prepare for the coming of the Lord.

In the two weeks that followed practically the entire congregation from pulpit to the door, besides members who came in from other churches, were baptized with the Holy Spirit and were afire with the Spirit of Evangelism.

All the trustees except one were swept through to the baptism. This one held aloof for some time, saying:

"Oh, I don't believe that all this noise and shouting and falling under the power is necessary. I believe in the Holy Spirit, but not in this enthusiastic manner."

"Well, brother, even if you don't understand it all now, do not sit back here in the seats. Come up to the altar. You feel it will be all right to seek more of Jesus, don't you?"

"Oh, yes, I will seek more of the Lord," he replied. "That's all right," and he took his place with the others at the altar.

It was only a few minutes later while praying—with the seekers, and they were going down one by one under the mighty rushing wind of the heavenly gales that were sweeping from heaven, that we heard a great shout, and something struck the floor with a thump.

Making my way as quickly as possible to the place where this great roaring was coming from, I found its source of origin was none other than the trustee who had but shortly before declared that all of this noise and shouting was unnecessary. I doubt if there was anyone in the church who made as much noise as he. He shook from head to foot; his face was aglow with heaven's light; he fairly shouted and roared forth as the Spirit gave him utterance, his heart was filled with joy and glory.

One brother who had thought it unnecessary to have a religion of real heart warmth and glory shouted God's praises for hours after he had been filled, and coming to me as I was on the sidewalk, just leaving for home, said, as he shook with the power:

"S-S-Sister M-M-McPherson, w-w-will I ever b-be able to t-t-talk in E-English again?" and away he went with other tongues again. Oh, hallelujah! Sometimes the greatest doubters get the biggest baptisms and the people who despise noise make the most noise of all when they receive this old-time power.

Many sick bodies were healed. A young woman, daughter of a Catholic family, was carried to the church in a taxicab, and came hobbling in upon crutches, crippled with rheumatism, unable to lift her hands and move the stiffened joints of her shoulders. Here is her written testimony:

TESTIMONY OF HEALING

"For the past six years I have suffered from one of the worst cases of rheumatism, known as 'Arthritis Rheumatism,' but praise God! He has healed me. For four years I was compelled to use crutches, and the stiffness was just taking a grip on each joint gradually. Until last December I could neither wash nor dress myself, and when one would even try to help me I would weep and moan with pain. My jaw became so stiff I could scarcely get a morsel of food into my mouth unless I broke it into very small pieces. But, praise God, since I have learned to say 'Glory to Jesus' every particle of stiffness has left my jaws. I have never again used the crutches since dear Sister McPherson's visit to the Free Gospel Church in Corona. Her prayers, together with the dear ones at that church, were answered, and Glory to Jesus, I have received my baptism with the Holy Ghost and fire.

"I am gaining in strength every day. Today I can wash, iron, sweep, run the sewing machine, and on days when mother is compelled to be away from home, I prepare two meals. I thank God today that we have a Pentecostal church in Corona, and also that God has placed in our midst our dear pastor, Brother Bouton, who is ever willing at all times to serve our Master, and lead his flock in the 'straight and narrow path'." (Signed) Louise Messnick.

I will not attempt to describe to you the wonderful way in which the work is going on day by day in this church. Brother Bouton has written a little of himself.

Now that the work was going on so beautifully here, the Lord told us the time had come to begin our journey to Florida. We announced our expected departure to the people. We did not tell anyone that we were asking the Lord for the means wherewith to ship our tent and pay our fares, but the last night of the meeting Brother Bouton set a table out and was getting ready to ask for an offering for us, but before the song which they were then singing was finished or he could get an opportunity to ask for an offering, the people started. Up the aisles they came, one after another, laying their offerings upon the open Bible.

The Lord sent us, through these dear saints, just the amount needed. As we explained to them that we were called to preach among the poor and go to those who had not yet heard the message of Pentecost, they promised to send us a box of clothing to give to the poor, and ship it to us as soon as possible.

Corona, its dear saints, and our own precious experiences while there will never be forgotten.

CHAPTER XIII.

CALLED TO DWELL IN TENTS.

FLORIDA TENT CAMPAIGN, 1917.

"For I have not dwelt in an house . . . but have gone from tent to tent, and from one tabernacle to another."—I Chron. 17:5.

OUR first Florida tent meeting was held in Jacksonville, the gateway to the lower south. A tract of land centrally located was loaned us free of charge, and we immediately set to work erecting tents, buying lumber, building seats, platform, installing lights and making the preparations necessary for each tent meeting. Some twenty-four hours before the meetings were to open all was in readiness, the last bill had been paid, and the piano installed, and we had five cents left over. How happy we were that the Lord had known just how much to give us!

While we were yet speaking of this wonderful way in which God had provided, a poor old colored lady came in, begging clothing, money or food for herself and children. We told her we were very sorry that we did not have any food to give her (we expected to fast ourselves until the meetings opened and offerings came in) nor any clothing at present, but we gave her the five cents which we had left.

Soon after she had gone, an automobile drove up to the tent, containing workers who had come from Atlanta, Ga. They were hungry and wanted supper right away, and not wishing to tell them that we had neither money nor food, I slipped away in my tent, and kneeling down, told the Lord about it, saying:

"Oh, Lord, if you want us to fast and pray until the meeting opens tomorrow—Amen. But if you want me to have something to set before these people, please supply the food."

Rising, I heard a man's big, gruff voice on the street in front of our tent, saying:

"Whoa thar'!"

Springing from the wagon, he came in with a cheery smile, carrying a box in his arms, marked "Prepaid," which he deposited upon the ground, with a—

"Right smart heavy box you got here. Sign on this line, please," and he departed.

"Why, here is the box of clothes which the Corona saints promised to send for the poor people! Now I will be able to give some clothes to that dear old colored lady and her children," flashed happily through my mind, causing the thought of supper to be forgotten for the moment.

Running for the hammer, we pried the top off the box. Sure enough, here was a coat and here were some dresses. The coat felt very heavy, and an experimental shake brought rolling out of its sleeves and pockets cans of corn, peas, salmon and a box of crackers. Still further search through the box revealed rolled oats, sugar, condensed milk and practically everything that was needed for supper. Oh, Glory to Jesus!

This is just one sample of the wonderful way in which the Lord provides for His children when they go forth without purse or scrip taking no thought of what they shall eat or what they shall drink or what they shall put on. He had sent us our supper all the way from Corona, L. I., to Jacksonville, Fla., and had it there right on the tick of the clock, for the bells were ringing six. The Lord is never late. Oh, aren't you glad He's on time? He's coming on time, too, dear ones. Very soon the floors of heaven will roll back and He will appear.

The tent meetings opened with a good attendance, and the crowds increased day after day. The altar was, time after time, filled with seekers for salvation, the baptism, and healing, and the Lord did not turn the hungry empty away.

Practically every state in the Union was represented by the tourists who gathered to this place, and many were amazed as they saw and felt the power of the Holy Spirit, heard the messages in tongues and interpretation, the heavenly music and singing, and saw the saints at the altar falling prostrate under the power, coming through to the baptism and speaking in languages they had never learned in their lives.

One brother spoke in Hebrew and a Hebrew scholar who was present, heard and understood. Hallelujah!

Two young men were healed, one of a broken arm, broken at three places, and dislocated at the wrist; the other of a broken hand. Both removed the plaster and the splints before the audience, convincing everyone that they were made every whit whole. One sister was healed instantly of cancer.

Note.—Of the many eventful meetings which took place, 1917 and 1918, we have selected paragraphs from reports.

CAMP MEETING AT TAMPA, 1917

Glory to Jesus! Glory! Glory! It seems you must almost hear us shouting and praising the Lord away up north. What a wonderful Saviour we have! He has taken the foolish to confound the wise, and the weak to put the strong to flight. He is laying bare His mighty arm. He is separating His people, yea, He is calling out a people *from* a people. Bless His name!

The Lord is blessing in Tampa. Meetings have increased in number and power steadily. Last night the tent was packed to the farthest corner, many standing and more turned away.

This has been a gathering under unique circumstances with this country standing under the dark clouds of trouble, on the brink of war. Tourists have heard for the first time the soon coming of Jesus and of the latter rain outpouring of the Spirit.

With joy many have received the message and been baptized, declaring that they will return to their towns and cities and proclaim the truth. An entire family from Minneapolis received the baptism the same night.

Great amazement fills the audience as the power of God falls. Many have been slain under the power and began to speak in tongues, prophesy and interpretation.

One lady did not have time to get to the altar. The power fell on her as she stood to her feet, and before she could get to the aisles the Lord had baptized her, as she went. The first sentence was interpreted—*"Jesus is coming soon, coming soon. Get ready."*

Sinners cried out for mercy, and came to the altar without urging. Young men and old have taken out pipes, cigarettes, tobacco and playing cards, left them behind and gone away with shining faces.

A brother—a professing Christian and church member for years—(without salvation) confessed his sins publicly as the power fell, and running to the altar gave up his beer, tobacco, and many things. He was so filled with joy, which, though he was an old man, he had never before experienced, that he danced and shouted and cried, much to the amazement of his neighbors, for he lives in a beautiful home right across from the tent. This is a wonderful opportunity to work. Just on the eve of Jesus' return to earth, this whole country is waiting with bated breath for—they know not what, and we hear His voice beseeching us—"Hasten! Preach the Word, for Jesus is coming soon."

The Lord has given us a Gospel automobile, with which we are able to hold eight or ten meetings a day, distributing thousands of tracts and hand bills, and carrying big display signs of the tent meetings.

PLEASANT GROVE CAMP, DURANT.

Durant is twenty miles from Tampa, and many of the people here are very poor. Some can not even read or write, but how hungry they are for God! Yesterday the ground was thick with teams, wagons and automobiles of those who had driven here from a radius of thirty miles around. The Lord is saving and baptizing souls and healing the sick. There are messages in tongues and interpretation. It is a wonderful sight to see people crowd to the front during altar service, standing on tiptoe on the benches to see the strange sight, men and women, slain under the mighty power of God, speaking in tongues as they are filled with the Spirit.

ST. PETERSBURG.

Just a shout of victory from St. Petersburg, Fla., this wicked city where Pentecost has never been preached.

A great celebration was on when our meetings opened. People play cards and gamble on tables by the sidewalk; the streets beside the park and city hall were roped off at night for dancing, and as the band played the people danced in masks and fancy costumes on the public streets.

Our snow-white tent, though comfortably situated, and decorated with palms and flowers to make it attractive, was but a poor inducement for such a worldly throng. Standing on the street, giving out hand bills and tracts, I looked at the long lines of automobiles and conveyances streaming by in the parades. This week was something in the nature of a Mardi-Gras and the cars were decorated to represent the state or business of the owner.

Suddenly the Lord spoke to me and said: "Decorate your car and join the parade!" At first this looked impossible. Surely the decorations must cost an enormous sum of money. But the Lord showed me how it could be done. We built a wooden frame just the shape of a tent; then taking a white sheet (which was one of the luxuries of our camp life) we made of it a miniature tent, stretching it over said frame, using cord for guy ropes, and large nails for stakes. On one side of the miniature tent we painted the words:

"Jesus is coming soon"; on the other side—

"Jesus saves"; on another side—

"I am going to the Pentecostal Camp meeting. Are you?"

Putting down the top of the Gospel auto, the miniature tent, some seven feet long, five feet wide, was lifted up and set over the car so as just to leave room for the driver. The car was also decorated with palms and wild flowers, which we gathered by the way, tied with tissue streamers.

Concealing a baby organ under the tent, I sat beneath it out of sight of the crowd, and the Lord shut the policeman's eyes so that we could slip into the grand parade of cars and get the full length of Main street with our advertisement. We *must* get an audience to our tent meeting, even if we had to sail forth with flying colors into the territory of the enemy to advertise our soul-saving business.

Early next morning we got in line with the other cars. The brass bands were going by; the liquor man advertised his business, the telephone, the wheat man and the florist; the butcher, the baker, the tourists representing their different states—all were there, having entered and listed their cars. When it came our turn to slip in, the policeman's back was turned, and he was motioning behind his back for us to come on, and holding back traffic from the other direction with his hand, so in we went. We were far enough behind the bands so that our little baby organ and chimes could be heard distinctly, playing—

"Just as I am, without one plea,
But that Thy blood, was shed for me."

and other familiar hymns such as—

"Oh, get ready, Oh, get ready, for the judgment day."

"For you I am praying,
I'm praying for you."

Thousands of people lined either side of the long street, leaning out of their windows, standing on the roofs—and after the first astonished stare the people began to laugh and clap their hands and cheer, and that night the tent was packed, and we had no more trouble getting crowds. Sinners were saved, believers baptized. The Salvation Army closed their doors and came in to work with us, bringing their drum and musical instruments.

**Note:* DOES THE WORK STAND?—Though two years have passed since this meeting, letters are still coming from Jacksonville, Tampa and St. Petersburg, from those who were saved and baptized during these meetings, stating that they are standing true to this day and going deeper with the Lord.

SAVANNAH, GEORGIA.

This great city, with its hundreds and thousands of living souls, that has never had a Pentecostal mission within its borders, nor heard the message of the latter rain, has been laid heavily upon our hearts.

After shipping our tabernacle, tents, and camping outfit on the railroad, laying hands upon it and asking the Lord to send it right straight through (though freight had been paralyzed by war shipments) we ourselves traveled in the Gospel auto, carrying workers and Gospel literature. The tent arrived almost as soon as ourselves. The Lord led us right to a spot of land which was loaned to us free of charge, and the first night several came forward for salvation. The second night one of those who had been saved the first night received the baptism. Never have we seen a more hungry, intensely earnest people than these, and although we are unable to stay, we are opening a mission, leaving our benches and fixtures here with Sister Swift of Durant, Fla., whom we brought with us in the car as a worker, and who, with her husband, will care for the work.

PREACHING IN THE COTTON FIELDS.

From Savannah, Ga., we traveled by Gospel auto through South and North Carolina, Kentucky, Maryland and New Jersey, preaching as we went, and giving out thousands of tracts. We find this a comparatively inexpensive way of reaching the people, getting to people who never could be reached any other way.

The poor people in the cotton and tobacco field districts, far from Pentecostal Missions, in this way receive the literature and testimony.

At night we run our car into some quiet field or forest, beside a stream of water, pitch our tent, build our camp fire, and put up our camping cots for the night; up and about our Father's business again with the rising of the sun.

We had but eighteen dollars on which to make the trip from Savannah to Long Branch, N. J., the scene of the next camp meeting, but the Lord made either the eighteen dollars or the gasoline to stretch, for we still had money when we arrived at our destination.

CHAPTER XV.

EASTERN SUMMER TENT CAMPAIGN, 1917.

CALL TO LONG BRANCH, N. J.

"The Spirit of the Lord God is upon me; because the Lord hath anointed me to preach good tidings unto the meek; He hath sent me to bind up the brokenhearted, to proclaim liberty to the captives, and the opening of the prison to them that are bound;

To proclaim the acceptable year of the Lord, and the day of vengeance of our Lord; to comfort all that mourn;

To give unto them beauty for ashes, the oil of joy for mourning, the garment of praise for the spirit of heaviness."—Isa. 61:1, 2, 3.

THE Lord witnessed to me concerning our going to Long Branch while in Savannah, Ga. I was waiting on the Lord for direct leadings. A number of letters, each containing a call to some particular city, were spread before me as I prayed.

"Oh, Lord, lead me just as You would have me. Do not let us get one step out of Your will in any way, or the place that You would have us to be. This call to Long Branch, N. J., seems to witness in my soul; speak to me, Lord, in some way, if this is of You. If not, take it away from me. How I wish that I could find out more about the place, its population, etc."

As I spoke, a New York paper was picked up by a little gust of wind and blown across the tent. Stooping over, still praying for the Lord to direct me and speak regarding Long Branch, N. J., I absent-mindedly picked up the paper and smoothed it out upon my lap, with amazement when, in large letters, printed half way across the paper, this sign met my gaze—"DON'T FAIL TO GO TO LONG BRANCH, N. J."

Beneath this sign was given a detailed description of the place, its accommodation, population, etc., and it wound up, with glaring letters—"WRITE AT ONCE TO LONG BRANCH, N. J., THAT YOU WILL BE THERE."

How wonderful that this New York paper should be away down here in Savannah, Ga., brought into the tent and right to my feet, open at this identical place! The Lord put the power upon me and witnessed that this was no mere accident, but truly another sign that He was leading.

(Condensed clippings and notes from reports.)

Showers of blessings are falling in Long Branch, where a tiny band, seven in number, have been praying for revival and an outpouring of the Spirit for years. Brother and Sister W. Martin had grounds ready, soon we had the tent erected and filled with the glory of the Lord.

Workers and seekers have gathered from other towns and cities, crowds increasing daily—Sundays people are turned away, unable to gain admission. Many have received the baptism of the Holy Spirit, and scores have come to the altar for salvation, and God is meeting one and all. A number have come out of the churches and received the baptism, and are going on in a precious way with the Lord. We go out daily with the Gospel car, upon which is painted in large letters on one side—"Jesus is coming soon"; on the other, "Where will you spend eternity?" Twenty and thirty miles of territory is covered daily with literature, street meetings and announcements.

During water baptism service by the ocean, the power of the Lord fell and those being baptized leaped, danced and shouted in the water, while spectators wept and praised the Lord on the shore.

Many of the young people have had marvelous and inspiring visions, some seeing our Saviour hanging on the Cross for our sins; others saw our Lord descending in the clouds to catch away His waiting people.

There have been many remarkable instances of healing, one of which we relate: A preacher came on crutches not believing that the Lord could heal as in days of old, and in answer to prayer God healed him instantly, in the middle of the meeting and he ran about the tent, dancing, without his crutches and shouting: "Why, the Lord still heals! He heals as in days of old!"

His wife was so overjoyed she ran up and down the aisles and right up on the platform, shaking my hand and making me dance over the platform with her in such a way that it was impossible to go on with the meeting for a time because of the shouting of the people.

CAMP MEETING, HYDE PARK, BOSTON, MASS.

It seemed impossible to ship our tents from New Jersey to Boston, Mass., as the embargo was on. The Lord opened the way for us to get a truck; and equipment was rushed through and put up on time. Praise God!

It was impossible to seat the throngs of people. The Pentecostal saints came filled with the glory and fire of God. Their testimonies and ringing songs of praises brought the entire neighborhood on the run to ask: "What meaneth this?" It was a hopeless task to seat the people, though seats were loaned us by the church and every available inch of space packed. Thousands nightly fringed the edge of the tent, standing clear out into the road as far and farther than it was possible for them to catch a word of the discourse.

At first the Catholic element did their best to disturb and break up the meeting, but praise the Lord, He gave us victory.

A policeman who roomed near the tent complained to his chief that he could not sleep for the noise of the people praying and shouting at all hours of the night, and the brethren were asked to appear at the station. They went in the Gospel car, leaving it in front of the door as they entered. The policeman who had made the complaint was not in, and the chief told them to sit down and wait for his return. Pacing up and down the floor, he at last went to the window, and looking out upon the car, with its lettered signs, drew back with a start, and said:

"Jesus is coming soon! Coming soon? Well, maybe so. I don't know."

"Are you prepared to meet Him if He should come?" they inquired.

"Have you been born again? Do you know that your sins are washed away, that you have passed from death unto life?"

"No, no, I can not say that I do." They further invited him to give his heart to Jesus, but this he refused to do, giving several reasons why he could not do so at this time. (This was the chief who refused us proper police protection at our tent meeting.)

Going over to the window several times, he read aloud, in a thoughtful voice: " 'Jesus is coming soon.' Well, well, maybe He is." And indeed He came very soon for this man. That night, the disturbing element, seeing no restraining hand laid upon them, were more disorderly than ever about the tent.

The next day the chief was stricken with heart failure at his desk and died in a few hours.

The news went round that entire section of the town that he had refused protection to the Gospel meetings then being conducted. Thereafter we had three men stationed by the tent at every meeting and perfect order.

Scores have come seeking salvation; the slain of the Lord are many, and deep conviction resting upon the people.

One young lady, a school teacher, came to mock, said she would never be one of those people, suddenly fell to her knees, crying for salvation, was wonderfully saved, and the next night baptized with the Holy Spirit.

Young men who ridiculed, were suddenly stricken with awful conviction while a message was being given in tongues and interpretation. The face of the young man who led the way to the altar turned white, his knees and hands trembled as he cried: "Lord, be merciful to me, a sinner." His friends followed him. They were all wonderfully saved and are now seeking the baptism.

A little girl with a paralyzed leg and a stiff knee was brought by her parents for healing. One leg was two inches shorter than the other. The Lord instantly healed her and she was able to bend her knee and the limb was lengthened and became as the other one.

Sunday morning the power fell so no one could preach; the Holy Spirit Himself spoke in prophecy through Sister McPherson. Then she played the piano in the Spirit, and all over the tabernacle pealed forth the heavenly anthem.

HUNTINGTON, L. I., CAMP MEETINGS

The camp grounds were a beautiful sight, with the many white tents nestled under the tall locust trees.

The meeting lasted ten days, souls were saved, backsliders reclaimed, sick healed, twenty-six received the baptism of the Holy Ghost. One girl who came to the altar to seek her baptism, wore a heavy steel truss around her waist, and running down both sides of her limb, it fastened at the bottom of a heavy shoe and strapped down her withered, helpless limb. The Lord baptized her in the Holy Ghost and healed her limb. She removed the truss, brace and shoe, stood up, and walked up and down, perfectly strong and without pain. Her mother wept and saints shouted. Surely we have a right to shout with such a wonderful Jesus.

Among the number who came to the camp meeting from out of town was a lady, educated, refined, a great believer in holiness. She brought with her her little son of about eleven years. She had come to study Pentecost, and analyze this baptism of the Holy Spirit with the Bible evidence, speaking in tongues, its effects, manifestations, etc. She was always asking questions and moving from one to the other as they lay under the power, coming through to the baptism. Sometimes her face would soften and then again the look of a doubting Thomas would come into her eyes and she would want to handle and see.

One afternoon her son, who, without a question, was seeking the baptism, fell under the power, his face, which was always bright, suddenly took on the radiance of heaven and his whole being seemed to be transformed, as he broke out singing in other languages, clear and beautiful, in poetry, the Lord giving me the interpretation of the song.

When the mother turned around from her investigating and seeking for information, and saw her son, who in his childlike faith had received that which she was questioning, it melted her heart and she herself fell under the power and came through speaking in tongues.

One night, during a severe storm, when the lights went out in the tent, we brought the Gospel automobile up to the edge of the tent, and lifting the side curtains, using the headlights of the car for illumination. This was one of the most wonderful meetings of this series. The Spirit took control in such a way that preaching was impossible.

Two ladies came from a Bible training school; one who had

been a Christian worker and missionary for years, was broken in health, and though she did not know much of the baptism of the Holy Spirit, asked to be prayed for for healing, during the breakfast hour in the dining tent.

We prayed for her and she fell off her seat and lay on the ground amongst the twigs and leaves, with the ducks, which were a constant source of annoyance to the cook, quacking about her. He does humble His people! No matter how great a worker one has been, everybody must get down. Hallelujah!

In a few minutes the dear sister had received the baptism of the Holy Spirit and was shaking from head to foot, laughing with joy and talking in tongues.

The last Sunday the floor was covered with those prostrated under the power. Many messages were given with interpretation.

MONTWAIT, MASS.

Here precious saints gathered from far and near and met in blessed liberty. The first night three received the baptism of the Spirit and sinners received salvation.

On Sunday nine received their baptism, some were saved and many healed. A dear Methodist minister and his wife and daughter received their baptism. Thirty or more received the Holy Ghost in the ten days' meeting.

WASHBURN, MAINE, CAMP.

Since writing the heading of this report, I have been sitting here before my typewriter wondering where and how to begin. It was all so wonderful, it would be impossible for me to describe, but longing to encourage the many poor, hungry saints who are shut away from the meetings, I will do my best.

The Lord was with us from the beginning. The first few days some fifty-four received the baptism, and the number increased daily until within two weeks and a half it was safe to say over a hundred received. Hardened sinners wept their way to the altar; many sat and trembled from head to foot under conviction, and sinners on their way to the altar, fell in the aisles. Often it was impossible to preach, the Holy Spirit conducted the meeting; messages in tongues and interpretation came forth from many empty vessels; waves of glory and marvelous singing swept over the audience.

A DRAMA ENACTED UNDER POWER OF HOLY SPIRIT

One night a drama was all worked out in the Spirit, showing forth the ten Virgins, going first with white robes to meet the Bridegroom. They said:

"He delayeth His coming; let us rest."

At first some argued that all should keep awake, for He that would come, would come quickly; but finally all were asleep.

Suddenly a loud cry—

"Behold! The Bridegroom cometh! Go ye out to meet Him!" Then all the virgins opened their eyes and examined their lamps in alarm. The five sisters enacting the part of the wise virgins, danced for joy because of the oil, but the foolish begged the wise to share their oil with them. The wise said it was impossible, and sent the foolish to buy oil of Him who had to sell

Then followed a scene where the foolish knocked at an imaginary door and haggled long over the price they would have to pay for the oil; they wanted to pay only a price which would not inconvenience them or cost a sacrifice, but the man who sold asked for all to give one hundred per cent sacrifice before they could obtain oil. At last the foolish went away, only to find that the wise had been taken up to meet the Lord; then they fell down and tore their hair and wept aloud.

This was followed by a ringing warning appeal to all to make full surrender, pay the price, buy oil now, for the Bridegroom is at the door.

This was only one of the many wonderful messages worked out in our midst which were beyond description. On Sundays hundreds of automobiles, horses and carriages filled the fields, and it was impossible to seat but a small part of the people. The altar was full of sinners seeking salvation, and Christians receiving the baptism. Several ministers and their wives received, also many church members and workers, several receiving right in their seats during service.

The fall of the year is coming and campaign in the north and east drawing to a close. The farmers' wagons are busily wending their way between the harvest fields and the barns, as they gather the results of their summer's labor. They mop their hot, perspiring faces, and heave tired but happy sighs.

Many a time, while working at the altar hour after hour, sometimes away into the morning hours, after a heavy day, we have sunk down upon a seat after it was all over and remembered that the Master of the harvest was weary for us. But oh, the joy of it! Row after row of hungry souls seeking salvation, the baptism of the Holy Ghost, divine healing, or a closer walk with God. The floors have been full of wheat—and the vats overflowed with oil and wine. The Ark has been in the midst and we delight our souls in the Lord as we live again the scenes of the past summer campaign.

CHAPTER XVI.

SECOND SOUTHERN CAMPAIGN AND GOSPEL AUTO WORK.

"Then shall the lame man leap as an hart, and the tongue of the dumb sing: for in the wilderness shall waters break out, and streams in the desert." Isa. 35:6.

FROM THE NORTHERNMOST TOWN IN MAINE TO THE SOUTHERNMOST CITY IN FLORIDA.

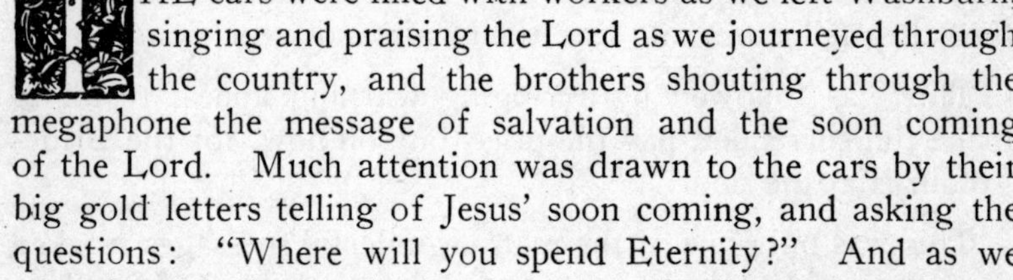

THE cars were filled with workers as we left Washburn, singing and praising the Lord as we journeyed through the country, and the brothers shouting through the megaphone the message of salvation and the soon coming of the Lord. Much attention was drawn to the cars by their big gold letters telling of Jesus' soon coming, and asking the questions: "Where will you spend Eternity?" And as we pass through the hundreds of towns and villages on our trips, we sing or testify, or give out literature, meeting many hungry souls.

We traveled all the day, slept by the wayside at night and the Lord always had a place prepared. We have our Gospel Autos so arranged that we can turn the front seat back and sleep in the car, and the big outdoors is our home. With joy we kneeled by the running board at night to pray and thank the Father for this glorious opportunity of preaching the Gospel far and wide in otherwise unattainable places.

Oh, that you could see the hungry faces that gather around and listen to the Word in the South. Frequently men step out from the crowd during street meeting, and kneel weeping, at the running board of the car, then rise to testify of a determination to go through with Jesus.

All through Virginia, North and South Carolina, and Georgia, we visited many poor homes, cotton and tobacco fields, etc., with the message of love. How eager the poor colored people were to hear the Word and receive the papers! In this way the poor have the gospel preached unto them, and those who could never hear in any other way, of Jesus' soon coming. Precious souls are at stake, no time to be lost—and we cry:—

"Here am I. Lord, send me." Pray that we may be faithful, unselfish, humble and quick—that we may never lose an opportunity of preaching, instant in season and out of season, the soon coming of Jesus, and what it means to be ready to meet Him. We want to lay down our lives for the Master as He laid down His life for us.

"He who saveth his life shall lose it, but he that loseth his life for My sake shall find it."

Sometimes, while sleeping by the wayside or under damp tents, the enemy whispers of rheumatism, etc., but that is the word we meet him with, and he disappears. He pictures others with comfortable homes and warm beds, and points in scorn to our hard canvas cots, with no home comforts, points to our smoky camp fire, and says the price is great. But, glory to Jesus, there is no desire in our hearts to go back, for we are happy with Jesus alone, and just one glimpse at the altar, filled with seekers after God, more than repays.

Pray for us, dear ones, as we go forth in the life of faith, with Him who said,

"Take no thought for what you shall eat or drink, or for what you shall put on, for the Lord your God knoweth you have need of these things."

JACKSONVILLE.

We rejoiced to find converts who had been saved and baptized during the first meeting, still walking with Jesus and growing in grace. The results at the second meeting surpassed that of the first. At times the entire altar was lined with sinners seeking salvation. Many were baptized in the Spirit, and many healed.

* * * *

The Lord then led us from the Atlantic Ocean to the Gulf of Mexico, preaching and distributing tracts, to Durant, Fla., there to conduct the

PLEASANT GROVE CAMP MEETING

God led us, with marching and singing, to encompass the camp and lay hands upon seats, altar, etc., and claim them for Jesus. The glory of the Lord was in our midst. The tabernacle was filled to overflowing and the groves strewn with autos and teams from forty miles around. A spirit of sweet unity and humility prevailed. There were wonderful messages in prophecy and prophetic song. Dramas were worked out, accompanied by tongues and interpretation. Heavenly music filled the place, and angel choirs were heard.

Deep conviction rested on many, and the altar filled with sinners seeking salvation. One dear little girl who received the baptism plead with all, in tongues and English, while under the power, to come to that beautiful city of God.

TAMPA, FLA.

With much faith and eager hands upon arriving we set to work getting up the big tent, and several smaller ones, making seats, installing electrical apparatus, painting signs, and advertising. The residence district and business section were visited with handbills, and God blessed our labor, and the tent was filled and a large number stood outside. There were many new faces each night, inquiring, "What meaneth this?" Coming closer and closer to the front, many soon plunged into the fountain.

An elderly lady, from a highly respected family of the city, after hearing Pentecost spoken against in persecuting tones, decided to come and judge for herself. Interested from the start, she attended regularly, later accompanied by her son and daughter-in-law. Soon she was gloriously baptized with the Holy Spirit; then the daughter, a dear, sweet Christian, began very earnestly seeking Him, and her husband said he could barely keep his seat, the power of God for salvation of his soul was so strongly upon him.

Street meetings were held from trucks and Gospel cars in many parts of Tampa and Ybor City, and from the band stand in front of the City Hall.

A CROSS COUNTRY TRIP—TAMPA TO MIAMI VIA OKEECHOBEE PRAIRIE WITH TRACTS AND GLAD NEWS.

When we left Tampa the car was well filled with tracts and from the west to the east coast of Florida, a distance of three hundred and fifty miles, we faithfully distributed literature until within a few miles of our destination, when all had been given out, and souls were crowding about the car asking for more.

In this trip we passed through the Okeechobee Prairie, and Prairie City, visiting each house with the first Pentecostal literature they had ever seen.

Our car being heavily loaded this trip, we did not carry a sleeping tent, and learned a little of what Jesus meant when he said, *"The birds have nests and the foxes have holes, but the Son of man has not where to lay His head."* The first night we spent in the car; the second night was spent wrapped in a blanket by the camp fire on the prairie near Okeechobee, a new prairie town. The third night was spent in a fisherman's shanty near Palm Beach, where also we witnessed for Jesus. The next night was spent in a little railway depot to keep out of the driving rain.

All the homes around us had their Christmas trees and fine dinners, but as our tents had not yet arrived, and we did not wish to spend the Lord's money on a room, we built a palm-leaf shanty on the beach, and hung our simple Christmas gifts on a little tree growing near. We kneeled down around it and read the story of Jesus' birth, and after prayer opened our little tokens. Praise the Lord! Though here we have no home and no abiding city, we seek one whose builder and maker is God.

TENT MEETINGS, MIAMI, FLA.

The first tent meeting conducted in Miami was held among the white people, the second among the colored saints. To the first meeting thronged the rich and fashionable in their automobiles and fine clothing. A tent meeting was a novelty. They came to be amused, but many remained to weep and pray. It was a beautiful sight to see the tears rolling down their faces, as they came humbly, and kneeled at the altar, giving their hearts and lives to Jesus in response to the simple message.

Because of the strong racial feeling, the dear colored people did not feel free to attend the white meeting. The Lord put such a love in my heart for the colored race that it was almost impossible for me to pass one of them on the street without such floods of love welling up in my heart that I had to step up to them and inquire:

"Have you ever heard of the latter rain outpouring of the Holy Spirit, the baptism of the Holy Ghost, and of the soon coming of Jesus?" I think they must have felt my love for them for they flocked about me whilst visiting and distributing tracts in their neighborhoods. Thus it was that after the white camp meeting we moved our equipment to the other side of town amongst these precious people.

MIAMI COLORED CAMP MEETING.

The tabernacle was filled, night after night, with precious black pearls to be gathered for Jesus. Picture a great platform thirty-two feet long and twelve feet wide, filled with baptized, colored saints, singing, clapping their hands, testifying with unction and a clear ring that carried conviction. Picture an audience where the power of God fell till often the evangelist could not minister, but the Spirit took full control; picture the colored saints, old and young, singing God's praises, sinners weeping their way to the altar, seekers receiving the Holy Spirit, and then you would see only a little corner of this meeting.

At times the power fell till every one raised faces shining with heaven's light, just shouted, and praised the Lamb for sinners slain, till the sound could be heard blocks away, and people came running to cry: "What meaneth this?"

At other times a holy hush, a spirit of weeping and great heart-searching and humbling swept the people from their seats and they fell on their knees in the aisles, between the seats, and at the altar and are now cleansed whiter than the driven snow, living pure, holy lives for the Jesus who said: "Go, and sin no more."

Drunkards testified to having been delivered from drink, gamblers to being set free from gambling; sinful girls and women of shame testified that the Lord had saved and cleansed them from sin.

Long marches were taken through the streets, and they sang as only colored folks can, played their musical instruments and shouted till people ran to know what had happened. Many leaped for joy on the march and demonstrated to all that "It is joy unspeakable and full of glory."

Some two hundred colored saints have the baptism of the Spirit in Miami, and many more are seeking and finding.

The people are very poor, and go to meeting in aprons and overalls. Collections very small, and were it not for the dear friends sending offerings in letters, we would have fallen further behind financially than we did. Several times, when we were wondering how to meet the heavy expenses of freight, gas, oil, lumber, lights, groceries, clothing, the needed amount came on the next mail from some child of God whom Father had been telephoning to. Thank God that even in these days when prices are soaring, it is possible to live a life of faith. It has meant self-sacrifice, and in our reports we endeavor to picture the sunny side, to encourage the many who live far from meetings, but fail, perhaps, to show the other side, where sometimes in driving rains, we find our sleeping tents ankle deep in water, our bedding wet, where we struggle to cook on smoky oil stoves and yet keep singing and smiling, fighting the good fight of faith.

KEY WEST FOR JESUS.

In the Island of Key West doors opened everywhere. Many begged us to ship our tent here and conduct an evangelistic campaign that would reach every corner of the Island, volunteering their help and prayers, declaring that few evangelists came so far out of the way, and that the whole city would turn out to the meeting.

The grounds of the Harris High School (beautifully

located) was chosen as a site for the tent meetings. Every seat was taken nightly and many were standing. New seats were obtained three times and arranged outside of the tent, but it was impossible to seat the large audiences. Ofttimes the tent was filled for two hours before meeting was to begin, so anxious were these hungry souls to obtain seats. Men and women came to the altar for salvation, and for the baptism of the Holy Spirit. Sick were healed and the Lord gave me blessed liberty in proclaiming the message of the hour.

My soul was so burdened for the dear colored people that I announced from the public platform that I had done my duty in the Lord toward the white population of the Island, and must risk their displeasure and disapproval now by going to the poor colored folk and telling them the same story. Some remonstrated, but as they saw the earnestness and longing in my heart, almost all agreed to help, and gave us no humbler spot for said meeting than the spacious grounds that surrounded the court house.

Then began earnest visiting among the colored people. At first it was impossible to make them believe that this was a

COLORED CAMP MEETING

or to persuade them that they were welcome to come inside and take seats, but when they really found it was true, how they flocked in!

One dear colored brother, whom everyone, black and white, admitted to be a saint of God, created considerable stir when he came up the aisle, and after looking at me, voiced aloud the amazement which was written upon his face—

"Why, Lawd a' massy! If dar ain't de berry woman what de Lawd showed me in ma' vision! She hab on de berry same dress—her hair am combed de berry same way! Yes, dat's de berry woman de Lawd showed me in ma' vision." He later explained to us that the Lord had given him a vision, some weeks previous, of a white sister coming, taking him by the hand, leading him through a river of water wherein a dove came down and rested upon him, and later leading him into the presence of the Lord.

It was impossible to keep the white people away. So for the

first time in the Island the white and colored attended the same place of worship and glorified the same Lord side by side. We arranged seats for the white people at the sides, reserving the center for the colored people, but so interested became the people in the meetings that reserve was a thing unknown.

The message of the Holy Ghost is new to the dear ones here. Some had not heard at all of the Holy Spirit and only one colored sister knew that He had come as a tangible Comforter.

Seven of the most spiritual of the colored workers and preachers have received the baptism of the Holy Spirit during the last four days.

We are not keeping count of the numbers of all that are being saved and getting through to God, but the names are recorded in the Lamb's book of life.

The poor and despised are having the gospel preached unto them, and God is honoring His own Word, preached in simplicity, but in demonstration and power with signs following.

Wonderful visions are seen by many receiving the Holy Spirit. A sister saw a vision of the coming of the Lord, just after she had received the baptism. Leaping to her feet she cried aloud:

"O, don't you see Him? Look! Jesus is coming! I see a beautiful star rising over the mountains and hills. Jesus is in the center of the star. O, see, he is bursting forth in glory and might! Jesus! Jesus!! JESUS!!!"

Another sister coming for salvation, prayed till she could be heard far away, and the people came running:

"Lord, be merciful to me, a sinner!"

Soon she sprang to her feet, dancing and clapping her hands, her face illuminated with the joy of salvation.

A colored preacher seeking the baptism with no one near him, fell prostrate and in a few moments was speaking with tongues and glorifying God. Suddenly his face convulsed as though in agony, and the Lord took him through the crucifixion scene. He described the death and love of Jesus, the blood trickling from His wounds.

A boy fourteen years old, was gloriously saved, and night

after night, pleads and exhorts in the most remarkable manner; many break down and weep all over the tabernacle.

My strength has been holding out in a remarkable way, through this strenuous winter, but at present I am very weak in body, and have to hang on to God for strength for each meeting. Please pray for me, saints, that I do not fail God. Souls are coming home to Jesus. All around are thousands of hungry souls. The harvest is great, the laborers few. I am alone, playing, leading, singing, preaching, and praying at the altar, besides having the Bridal Call to prepare; it is only the power of God that can sustain me. It is still a marvel in my eyes, the wonderful way the Lord helped me while left alone at Key West, to drive stakes, tie heavy guy ropes, and battle to keep the tent up, amidst wind and rain, sometimes preaching all day and sitting up the greater portion of the night to watch the tents and keep driving the stakes in with the big sledge hammer, as fast as the wind pulled them out, through the night watches, while a three-day nor'wester was on.

The wind died down and the meeting closed in triumphant success. The Lord sent a brother to help me take down the big tabernacle, and two colored sisters to assist me in taking apart some two hundred big long benches, pulling the nails and piling the lumber under the blazing sun, rolling the great strips of canvas, getting them into their bags and shipping them to the next place. Truly He gives His people supernatural strength when they are in the center of His will.

The farewell scene at the depot is a pleasant memory. The station platform was well-filled with both white and colored saints who had got up early to say a last good bye, bringing little offerings to help us with our fare, and wave us on our way. Dozens came up and gripped my hand as I stood on the steps of the train, telling how they had been blessed in the meeting.

It was just at the time of my departure from Key West that my dear Mother, with Roberta (whom she had been caring for), joined me. She had told me, when I entered the work, that if ever I needed her help, no matter what it was, she would give it, and now I did need her help as never before. Being left along so much, with the care of the tents, meetings, and an ever-growing correspondence which really needed the entire time of one person, the Bridal Call subscription lists, shipping of freight, arrangement of new meetings, my strength was giving way.

Sister N—— (who assisted in duties about the tent), and myself were alone at night in the big court yard, with drunken men and soldiers, reeling by the tents until all hours of the morning. God marvelously protected and cared for us insomuch that no one came near or molested us in any way. I was strongly impressed, however, to telegraph for my Mother to come to my assistance, not only because I needed the protection of a mother's presence, but to take hold of the business end of the work, and now, in answer to prayer and the appeal of the telegrams, here she was, sitting by my side as the train sped across the long bridges which spanned the ocean from island to island for the hundred miles back to the coast of Florida.

Mother has been with me from that day up to the time of the present writing. She has never shirked a duty nor one of the responsibilities laid upon her by the work, lifting from my shoulders the entire burden of the correspondence, caring for the long lists of Bridal Call subscriptions, overseeing the care of the children, packing, travelling, and a score of other duties, and I have been left free to give myself continually to prayer, the ministry of the Word, and writing. She has ever been a source of cheer and inspiration. How wonderful that she received the call first—that through her call I was brought into the work—and that the second time, through *my* call, *she* was brought into the work again.

After a short meeting amongst the colored people of West Palm Beach, and the colored camp meeting at Miami, we shipped our tents to Orlando, Fla., and journeyed thither ourselves in our Gospel Auto, distributing tracts and witnessing for Jesus all the way up the coast.

ORLANDO TENT MEETINGS.

Our freight was delayed by an embargo, and our time limited, having only a little over two weeks before we must journey northward to prepare for the Nation Wide Camp Meeting in Philadelphia, Pa.

Inquiring of the Lord, as we drove along Main Street in our car, I saw a large, brown tent which would seat at least five hundred people more than our own tabernacle would hold. Inside we found a fine floor, formerly used as a skating rink. The Lord touched the owner's heart to rent us the tent at a small cost for our series of meetings. This was the first time the holding up of our freight had delayed a camp meeting, and Father had a better tent all up, empty and waiting for us, floor and all.

People warned us that Orlando was aristocratic, we need not expect them to come to a tent meeting, but we were sure God had not made a mistake in sending us, so we went to work. Notices were put in the papers, seats engaged, handbills gotten out and meetings opened. So persistently did we advertise by handbills, by numerous street meetings, driving up and down the streets, inviting people to come to the tent and hear more about it, that it is to be doubted whether there was anyone within a radius of several miles but what knew that there was a tent meeting in progress in Orlando.

At first many merely lined up their cars in the streets around the tent and listened at a dignified distance, but soon the fire began to fall, and the ice began to melt, and leaving their cars they entered the tent and many, praise God, came to the altar

The crowds increased daily in numbers and interest. Six came to the altar for salvation the first meeting, and there was not a meeting but sinners were saved and believers baptized with the Spirit; night after night the long altar bench was filled and so were hungry hearts.

Never were we treated with more love and respect, each seemed to vie with the other to help and encourage us. First (our small living tents not having arrived) a cottage by the lake, with a garage, was put at our disposal free of charge during our stay. The best bakery in town sent their delivery wagon, with such great baskets of bread, pies, cakes and cookies, that we had enough to share with our people.

People who owned orange groves brought us fruit by the bushel. The grocer sent boxes packed to the brim with canned goods and vegetables, flour and surgar. People came to our door to tell us of the blessing they had received in the meetings

Oh, it means so much to be in the center of God's divine will. He will open doors and close doors, overthrow the mighty and make your enemies to be at peace with you. Bless the Lord.

The tent, with a seating capacity of nearly fifteen hundred, was filled to overflowing, rows of automobiles, and other vehicles lined the street. Ministers and workers from the various churches attended; some declared that this was the long-lost power their churches used to have. Others scoffed in derision.

Altogether the devil was afraid he was going to lose some of his people. So he had one lady who lived several blocks from the tent go to the police and protest that she could not sleep at night. The next evening a policeman brought a paper to the tent, stating that we must close our meeting at ten o'clock. Toward the end of my sermon I held a watch in my hand and kept looking at it as I spoke. I talked fast as I could, and at five minutes to ten told the people I knew they were hungry and would like to come to the altar, and that there were souls there that should be saved, but that a lady had complained of the noise, therefore we would all rise and be dismissed, and please not to stand or walk but to go out as quickly and quietly as possible.

Will I ever forget the look on those people's faces! Some of them almost owned the town, and for *them* to be told *they* had to close a meeting at ten o'clock—some of the men snorted at the very thought, and on the way out said:

"We'll see about this!"

"The idea! This place was open as a skating rink for months and was kept open until midnight. Now the Gospel's being preached they want to close it at ten o'clock, eh?"

"The Mayor's a friend of mine. I will see about that. Don't you be afraid, little woman. This thing will be all straightened out by tomorrow night."

Neighbors came up; people who had, up to this time, kept at arm's length and had not been quite sure whether they approved of us or not, hesitated no longer, but were our warm friends from that time on.

True to their word they got together in groups on the streets talking it over. Next day a lady who was the owner of a large boarding house, went about the neighborhood and had a petition signed that this order should be cancelled, declaring that the noise did not bother them. This clipping appeared on the front page of one of the Orlando papers next day:

MRS. ROONEY AIDS CHURCH.

"Mrs. Bettie Rooney deserves the thanks of all lovers of religious liberty for coming to the rescue and aid of Mrs. McPherson, who is conducting a series of meetings in the big tent.

"It seems that some one, whom Mrs. Rooney claimed lived at a distance, had the city officers close the meeting at an early hour on account of the noise of the speaking and singing interfering with their sleep, when Mrs. Rooney, good Christian woman that she is, immediately secured a petition with the names of twenty-five citizens living right near the gospel meetings, who protested to the Mayor against having the meetings broken up at so early an hour, which of course was acted on favorably, and the disgruntled ones will have to find something else to bring against the meeting.

"The only real charge against the meeting is that they preach the old fashioned GOSPEL, straight from the shoulder, and it makes some of the hifalutin frock-tails, who orate in the pulpit to swell congregations, who look through one eye-glass and wear silk tomfooleries, envious because of empty benches prevailing.

"It would do some preachers good to get religion and pass it on as these people are doing."

Immediately the order was cancelled and the meetings went on, ofttimes till midnight.

A young lady who came with a group of others from fashionable families, full of unbelief, was startled and throughly convinced when one night the Lord put His power down upon me and gave a message in tongues in the Spanish language, of which I knew not a word. Here is her testimony:

"I was very much impressed at one of the tent meetings, to hear Mrs. McPherson speak in Spanish, and directly afterwards to give exactly the same message in English. She was not conscious of speaking in Spanish. When told later of it she was quite surprised and said she did not know a word of Spanish. I also heard her talk in other languages with which I was not acquainted."

ANNIE L. TREADWELL.

When it came time to close the meetings and to move on toward Virginia and Pennsylvania, the town wherein we were told the people were proud and would pay no attention to us, turned out en masse to the closing meeting. One of the citizens made a speech in behalf of their townsmen, thanking us for our labors of love amonst them, inviting us to come back, saying that they would do all in their power to assist us. A sum of money was presented to help with the expenses of the northward journey.

CHAPTER XVII.

MEETINGS IN VIRGINIA AND GOSPEL AUTO NEWS.

"Let her glean even among the sheaves, and reproach her not. And let fall also some of the handfuls of purpose for her, that she may glean them, and rebuke her not.

"So she gleaned in the field until even, and beat out that she had gleaned." Ruth 2:15, 16, 17.

IT WAS late at night when we neared the state of Virginia, after reaching which we would still have a couple of hundred miles to journey. We all expressed the desire to press on and spend the night on good old Virginia soil. We had heard of the warm hearts of the Virginia people and wondered whether it was really true. Crossing the border we entered a sleeping little town and drew up under the trees by the side of the road to open out our automobile bed and erect our tent covering for the night.

Waking early and peeping out from under the protecting curtains to get our first daylight view of the place, we were surprised to find two houses near us, one just across the street, the other a little to our right. A man and his wife standing on the piazza of the former were looking toward us talking earnestly, no doubt wondering who we were.

Preparing to continue our journey, we had just finished our roadside toilet, when the man came hurrying across with a silver tray, with a large glass bowl brim full of ripe, crimsoned strawberries, a pitcher of thick cream and a bowl of powdered sugar. Then a little girl came running from the other house with a pan of hot steaming biscuits and a quart of fresh milk from the Jersey cow in the field. Neither knew what the other had done. This was our first experience of the far-famed Virginian hospitality.

PULASKI, VA.

PREACHING ON THE COURT HOUSE STEPS.

We were entertained in the beautiful home of Brother Z. Cecil during our ten days' meeting in the town. In order to reach as many people as possible with the message in the shortest time, it was decided to hold daily street meetings in addition to the regular meetings in the Pentecostal Holiness Church. When Brother Cecil went to ask the town officials for permission to preach on the street, they kindly invited us to come in and make use of the court house steps and spacious lawn.

The first night we went in a pouring rain and preached, feeling that time was too short to stop for a little rain. A large crowd gathered and the power fell. Nightly the crowd increased until it was a mass meeting and autos packed both sides of the street. It was a beautiful sight as we preached in God's big out-doors, and the people sat on the grassy lawn around this spacious building.

It was an unprecedented sight to see the power falling in such a place as the saints sang and danced upon the court house steps and down on the pavement. Hearts were touched and tears ran down the people's faces, and crowds followed to the meetings.

ROANOKE, VIRGINIA.

Before leaving Pulaski, the Pastor from the Pentecostal Holiness Church of Roanoke called upon us asking us to come to his church. The saints desired the meeting should be held in a tent, but the pastor insisted, and on our arrival in Roanoke, we drew up finally at the parsonage where our entertainment had been arranged. We saw a gentleman seated upon the piazza, and noticed that his face looked dark and forbidding, and that he did not welcome us in any way. Even when seated later with the pastor and his wife upon the piazza, and he had been introduced as "Brother So and So," he did not say a single "Hallelujah" or "God bless you."

The first meeting was held in the church. The Lord gave me the Wisdom not to go into the pulpit or even on the platform, so I stood quietly in the front and delivered my message upon the coming of the Lord, and the preparation of the Bride to meet Him. Fervent "Amens" came from the audience and tears filled many eyes.

This brother, who sat on the front seat, never looked up, but had the same dark, thunder-cloud look of sarcasm and displeasure upon his face. When I had taken my seat he rose and gave a discourse, which was fully as long as that of mine. Someone whispered:

"He is the state superintendent. He has heard about this meeting and come down to stop it."

I cannot repeat his discourse in words, but the substance of it was that if an angel came down from heaven and preached any other doctrine than that which was set forth in the rules and regulations of their church they were not to believe it; that the message of tonight was all very well, but he had heard that Sister McPherson taught actual transgressions and inbred sin were all taken out at one time, when we entered the fountain of blood. He said:

"We have the rules and regulations of our church to uphold. Take away our strong teaching of sanctification as a second definite work of grace and you will destroy the foundations and the pillars upon which our church is built."

The audience sat with their faces a mixture of misery and pity, but I was praising the Lord and saying:

"Oh, thank you, Jesus," as He poured the blessings into my soul.

When the dear man had finished speaking I rose and said that it would not be courtesy for me to make any reply in their church; that I had come under their urgent invitation and would be willing and happy to preach outside, from the Gospel car, or on a vacant lot, anywhere that the saints arranged for me.

I told them that I believed in the finished work of Calvary, believed that sin is sin whether it is actual transgressions, Adamic sin or inbred sin, whatever fancy name you give it, sin is sin; that while man looks on the outward appearance (so-called actual transgressions) God looks on the heart (inbred sin) and as for holiness, why, without holiness no man shall see the Lord. We must be saved, must be sanctified, but 'tis all through the precious atoning blood of Jesus Christ. "The blood of Jesus Christ, God's Son, cleanses us from *ALL* sin."

Several leaped to their feet and said they would get a place outside at once. (Both ministers said, "No, stay on for the time of the meetings in the church.") The Lord gave many the witness and the meetings being announced for Sunday, they started out to search for land.

Lots some distance from the church and on the main streets were traced up, but it was impossible to secure them. Every other place was blocked except the lot of land just opposite the Pentecostal Holiness Church. This was given free of charge. (How these precious saints worked all that Saturday!)

No tent being available, two great strips of canvas were secured and stretched over as large a space as possible. Three assemblies loaned their seats, lumber was hurried to the spot and a platform erected.

Each contributed something towards the erection of the hurried meeting place. One brother gave the electric light wires and fixtures; and though 'twas late Saturday noon the electric company sent out a special car and installed a meter.

A Sister loaned her lovely piano for these out-of-door meetings, and told us we were "welcome to the whole house" and paid the drayage on the piano for us. O, for more such consecrated people!

Thousands stood for hours packed all about the tent after every available seat was taken, altar filled, the saints sitting about the floor of the platform till it was almost impossible for me to move about without stepping on someone.

Men were saved, Hallelujah! Sick were healed. Two ministers who had been fighting the outpouring of the Spirit, said:

"We will fight you no longer," and came to the altar.

Street meetings were held every night on the busiest corner from our Gospel Car, and the city was stirred. People wept as they stood about the car. A dear man came with the tears rolling down his face and kneeled at the running board of the car as Brother Dougherty (who arranged all the meetings), prayed with him as he wept his way through to Calvary.

GOSPEL AUTO NEWS (JULY, 1918).

"Never did valiant warrior return with a more conquering tread, or more loyal heart throbbing within, nor more deserving of this public tribute than our faithful 'Pentecostal Gospel Car.' "

From the northernmost town in Maine, by the Canadian border to the southernmost city in the entire United States of America, undaunted by mountain or valley, it has steadily and safely carried not only the messengers but the message, and has been indeed and in truth a Flaming Evangel, declaring in letters of gold, that gleam ofttimes into the amazed eyes of the onlookers with as startling an effect as did the handwriting on the wall in Belshazzar's palace long ago.

Thousands of persons and vehicles have streamed by the side of the Gospel Car, but free from the man-fearing spirit, and impervious to criticism, instant in season and out of season, the Gospel Car has never hidden its light beneath the bushel, whether the gay bridal party dashed by with lilt of laughter and fragrant orange blossoms, or whether funeral procession, with sombre-plumed hearse, and black-garbed mourners, whether the dancing children rollicked by, or the aged man feebly leaning on his cane, it has solemnly inquired of one and all, *"Where will you spend eternity?"* declaring that "Judgment day is coming," and exhorting them to "Get Right With God."

Often, as we slow up amidst dense city traffic, it would seem to one uninitiated in Gospel Auto life as though many of the usually sedate pedestrians on the sidewalk, heretofore quietly pursuing their daily routine, had suddenly and involuntarily been transformed into fiery street preachers, who, startled out of themselves, demanded from one and all, in tones which electrify their fellow citizens, *"Where will you spend eternity?"* Those within hearing distance of the voice look up aghast into the speaker's gaze, they themselves see the car and take up the great question, *"Where?"*

Sometimes when we leave the car on some errand, we find on returning that a crowd has gathered about the faithful car which is holding its own street meeting and preaching all by itself; and who can say with what results for eternity?

No member of our party takes a more active part or renders more efficient and obedient service in every branch of the service than does the Gospel Car. Are there a thousand tracts to be distributed through the byways and hedges, or placed in the R. F. D. boxes? The Gospel Car is ready. Is there a street meeting to be held? There is one preacher that can always be depended upon—Gospel Car.

Is there a pulpit needed? Down goes the top and here is the car for a pulpit. Is there a stand needed? The windshield opens to hold Bible and song book. An altar needed where the penitent may weep his way to Calvary? The running-board does good service, ever ready to receive the copious tears of seeker and worker as they kneel together.

Is there an aged couple, or a mother who has stood long hours to listen with babe in arms, to be taken home? The Gospel Car is ready. A heavy burden to be carried? an errand to be run? street megaphone messages to be resounded? The Gospel Car is ready. Is there need of a table upon which to spread the modest evening meal prepared on the campfire by the way? dishes, or a can of food needed? The Gospel Car supplies the need.

Is there a need of bed and bedding for the weary traveler? The Gospel Car carries one folding bed upon its running-board, and another is formed by the front seat, which gently lays back upon its hinges, uniting front and back seats into a comparatively comfortable bed. When prayers (and good-nights) have been said by the flickerings of the campfire, the Gospel Car affords protection and rest under the whispering pines. When the editor, hard pressed on every hand, seeks quiet and rest with Bible or typewriter, it is the Gospel Car that bears her away to some quiet spot apart from the throng.

THE DYING BRIDE.

Meetings over, the last lights extinguished in the camp, are the duties of the Gospel Car ended? May she rest? No! Quick footsteps and an urgent message implores us to come at once to the dying bed of a young bride, who, but a few hours previous, had listened to our message and later had been suddenly stricken and was passing away. It is miles away, on a dark and perilous country road. How can we get there in time?

The Gospel Car is ready, and speeds a swift messenger of mercy, never pausing until she stands by the humble cottage door, where the midnight lights and shadowy forms bespeak the presence of the death angel, whose pinions are even now spread to bear away the slender form of the fair young bride.

Through the hours of waiting, wherein the dying and living alike clung to our hands and words for strength and consolation, until the last good-bye was spoken and the sweet voice trailed off into silence with the words: *"Meet me in Heaven!"* and the last breath fluttered gently away; and on through the hours of morning, while the sorrowing parents were comforted, and the hovering angels rejoiced as the young husband kneeled by the still form of his loved one and gave his heart to Jesus, the Gospel Car stood silently beneath the dews of the light, gleaming softly in the star light exhorting each neighbor as they reverently left the house with uncovered heads, to remember that for them too, the *"Judgment day is coming: get right with God."*

And when again the Gospel Car had brought me back to the home, this time to preach the funeral sermon, as I looked into the sweet face now reposing in the white, flower-wreathed casket, I could catch the echo of her words as she smiled into my face and said:

"Sister McPherson, I'm glad you are here, and I'll—meet—you—in—Heaven."

Then on behind the sure-footed horses that drew the hearse and carriages over stony mountain passes (considered too difficult for the other cars) and hills so steep that the nose of the car pointed heavenward, with a sheer cliff above and a precipice yawning beneath; then down into valleys where we found swollen mountain streams, where the water came over the running-board of the car till someone cried out:

"Surely we can go no further!" But NO, the Gospel Car, with a determined roar from her engine and a quick shift of her gears, emerged from her plunge dripping, panting, but *triumphant.*

When the little form had been laid at rest beneath the pines on the mountain top, in the sure and certain hope of a glorious resurrection in that land where tears are wiped away, the Gospel Car, having surmounted all difficulties (sometimes axle-deep in mud, again over jagged rocks which cruelly gashed its tires, tested and threatened on every hand), through it all kept up on the return trip till we reached our destination and her work was done, then with a long, expiring sigh, one tired tire sank slowly to the ground. Nevertheless (bathe and rub it as we will), like all other true warriors of steel, the Gospel Car bears its honorable scars of battle, without which no hero is truly decorated. Gazing upon each scar of battle, we recall with joyous hearts each scene these scars portray.

Through the many miles of travel the engine has never given us one moment's trouble, yet many a time tires have been patched and repatched, mended and reinforced until a cheery letter accompanied by a donation meets the pressing need, specifying that this offering was for Gospel Auto Work.

LIVES SAVED BY THE GOSPEL CAR.

"Dear Sister McPherson:

"Praise God for sending you and your Gospel Car to our town; if you had not come here, my brother, his wife and sister-in-law would probably have been blown into hell, as my brother had resolved to shoot both them and himself; but while he was on the piazza he saw *God's car* go by, and he read: *'Where will y-o-u spend eternity?'* It held and gripped him. He went in and told his wife (a very wicked woman—a saloon-keeper's daughter). She 'Poo-poohed!' and hardened her heart, although she knew him to be desperate. Only a very short time before they found him in the cellar basement, gas turned on at two o'clock in the morning unconscious; in five minutes more would have been past all earthly help, the doctor said.

"My brother was wonderfully convicted and has since been saved, and is now seeking the baptism of the Holy Spirit. It pays to pray. After fifty-five years of prayer by Mother, he has at last yielded to God. Bless His Name!" C. A. S.

VIOLA, DELAWARE

We were obliged to drive night and day to make our appointment in time. We found the saints full of faith and good works, and the meetings throughout were at a time of spiritual quickening and upbuilding. The building was crowded as never before with an earnest throng, listening eagerly to the unfolding of the divine plan of the ages for the salvation of mankind, and the conviction was great; one Catholic brother ran from the building, declaring he would have to go to the altar if he remained longer.

The meeting over, we started for Philadelphia and New York, driving all night, reaching Philadelphia before dawn. We did not pause, but pressed on to Atlantic Beach, where we rested on the sand for an hour, contemplating the greatness of the handiwork of God. Again pressing on to Long Branch to meet some of the dear saints and thence to New York, before we slept.

CHAPTER XVIII.

NATION WIDE CAMP, PHILADELPHIA.

"It came even to pass, as the trumpeters and singers as one, to make one sound to be heard in praising and thanking the Lord . . . that then the house was filled with a cloud, even the house of the Lord, so that the priests could not stand to minister by reason of the cloud for the glory of the Lord had filled the house." II Chron. 5:13, 14.

In the Fall of 1917, when we were passing through Philadelphia en route for Florida, it was our privilege to spend two days with the dear saints there and to attend meetings then being held in a large tent. The Lord graciously poured out His Spirit upon one and all, and when scores of saints begged us to come back for a series of meetings, the Lord witnessed in our hearts that this was of Him, and after much prayer and correspondence, a Nation Wide Camp Meeting was planned. Father told me to pray earnestly for money to buy a big Tabernacle tent which would be large enough to accommodate the people. A notice was inserted in the *Bridal Call.* Friends rallied and offerings came.

The problem was: Where was the tent? The government had commandeered the large tent-making concerns, and even though the Lord assured us that He had the right tent for us, and would deliver on time, I confess that we were anxious as the date for the Nation Wide Camp Meeting approached. Each time I went to the Lord He would say: "It is all right. You shall have your tent," but in the meantime my letters here and there to different people brought no hopes. The only tent that would at all fit my requirements was in New York City and was held at thirty-five hundred dollars, and this was out of the question. Sometimes the enemy would whisper:

"You have taken people's money for the tent, suppose you don't get that big tent, what are you going to say to them?" But Jesus said:

"Let not your heart be troubled."

After two years' experience, I had my own ideas of the kind of tent I wanted, its size, shape, seating capacity, texture, and make: One that would shed the rain, be mildew-proof, well roped and guyed, arranged with block-and-tackle system of lowering and raising. Where could such a tent be purchased?

When we arrived in the city of our summer's work, there was the very tent of my dreams and prayers, in an attic store-room of a downtown building, all tied up in bags, poles and stakes complete, ready for erection. Hallelujah! We went to look at it, climbed the stairs, and as we mounted towards the sky, our hearts mounted also as the tent was described to us, its size and material, ten ounce, U. S. Army duck, double fill and double twist, double stitched, splendid ropes, block and tackle, etc., which had never been erected, worth twenty-five hundred dollars today, and could be had at eighteen hundred cash, but I felt that fifteen hundred dollars was all the Lord wanted us to pay for that tent; and although at first they would not accept this, as the man stood in the door and read the sign, "Judgment day is coming, get right with God," his face became thoughtful and he said he would let us know later, and of course Father opened the way.

This tent had been ordered and built for an evangelist whom God was using blessedly in His service. When the baptism of the Holy Spirit was preached, this evangelist refused the light, took a stand against the outpouring of the Spirit, and he became very ill for months.

The tent, which God meant for our work remained brand new in its bags at the tent-maker's office, with the instructions that it was to be sold only for religious purposes. The news came that we could have it for fifteen hundred dollars, and it was soon up and packed, with throngs of people surrounding it drinking in the message of salvation through the precious blood, the baptism of the Holy Spirit, and the soon coming of Jesus.

Had this tent been purchased in any other city it is very improbable that we would have been able to have had it shipped because of the embargo which at that time paralyzed freight all over the country. And even if it could have been shipped it would have been necessary to have had it sent by express as the time was so short and the delivery charges would have been enormous, so our heavenly Father planned it all out and had the tent right in the very city where the meeting was to be held.

GLORY OF GOD IN CITY OF TENTS

The beautiful camp grounds were situated on a hill, near the river, and were sheltered by high shade trees. Rows and rows of small tents were erected in squares around the great new Gospel Tent with its snow white canvas.

The dining tents, dormitories, reading and rest tents were erected and soon the grounds assumed the appearance of a well-ordered camp. The leaders themselves rolled up their sleeves and helped with a good will for the future comfort of others. Heavy trucks were rolling up with great loads of cots, beds, seats, dishes, camp equipment, but 'midst all the bustle and the preparation brothers and sisters alike found time to shout and praise God. The trees echoed with the hallelujahs of the saints. As the newcomers arrived they in turn rolled up their sleeves and went to work. Even the night before the camp meeting opened the glory of God seemed to rest down upon the place as we gathered around the big bonfire to play and sing and worship the Lord for what He was about to do in our midst.

Note: (The following is a report which appeared in the September number of the *Bridal Call*, 1918.)

The picture of hundreds of saints standing upon their feet with hands lifted toward Heaven, eyes closed, and their upturned faces streaming with tears as they sing, as it were, a new song, and heavenly anthems voiced by the Holy Spirit through their lips in wondrous harmonic chords of love and thanksgiving, is a never-to-be-forgotten sight, and resembles much the conception that I have always had of what it must be to be in Heaven before the throne of the Most High God.

Oh, if you could but hear them pray, pray as never I have heard people pray before, each one forgetting their neighbor, forgetting all else but the Lord who answers prayer; praying out aloud with all their might, hundreds of them at one time, till no one voice can be distinguished in the midst, for they are all blended in one mighty heart throb of love and desire for God to have His way, which quickly turns into adoration, and flows forth as a river of praise straight to the throne of God. Needless to say, the answer usually comes before the prayer is finished.

The camp presents a very stirring and inspiring scene every night. After supper in the dining tent the people move out to prepare for the evening meeting. It is a common sight to see a little group of two or three people kneeling down in the paths, or under the trees, to present to God anything that might be upon their hearts. Then as the evening shadows lengthen, lights are turned on in the great Tabernacle Tent, and the saints soon fill the shining interior. Soon the night air resounds with the songs and the praise of hearts filled to overflowing with the love of God. After meeting it is not an uncommon thing to hear voices in supplication and praise continued on in the tents.

The night preceding this writing witnessed a scene that melted many a heart. One end of the large ladies' dormitory tent was given over to a children's meeting, and there the little tots were used in a wonderful way by the Spirit. Many a little one glorified God, speaking in other tongues. A number of parents were there and their hearts just welled with feeling as the Holy Spirit worked upon the children. It was a meeting never to be forgotten.

GOD LOCKS THE LIONS' MOUTHS.

When the city of tents was first erected on this beautiful hill, where earth and Heaven seem to meet, we found that we were in a neighborhood which was seventy-five per cent Roman Catholic, with institutions and colleges near-by. Gangs of boys patrolled the grounds day and night, keeping watch on everything and everybody, feeling great resentment at our invasion of the hill, which had been their special property since they could first remember. Then when the meetings opened and the power of God began to fall, and there was shouting, dancing and many prostrated, the whole community was stirred to its depths. They had never seen it after that fashion before.

The next night an enormous crowd filled the tent and stood all around the outside. Every time that there would be a manifestation of the Spirit, they would burst forth into peals of laughter, ridiculing and mocking. As an altar service was attempted, the hoodlums thronged into the tent in a body, standing over the seekers, mocking and jeering. The second Monday night arrived with the worst crowd that we had seen up to this time. It seemed as if the people were wild with anger, and many came with clubs and cudgels in their hands. There were organized gangs with leaders, carrying whistles, who gave signals to their men. Detectives afterwards told us that it had been a pre-arranged program to wipe every tent off the ground that night, and open threats had been made to this end.

The devil had carefully laid his plans. A riot took place down in the center of the city that night between the white and colored; there were no policemen available to keep order at the camp meeting grounds. Back and forth, to and fro, the mob surged about the tents. Speaking was impossible, and all we could do was to sing and hang on to God. "Rock of Ages, Cleft for Me," "Nearer, My God, to Thee," "It is Well for My Soul," "Jesus, O How Sweet the Name," were among the many hymns sung by the saints, as we all kept in the spirit of prayer.

The meeting was dismissed early, without any altar service. The crowd surged through the tent and over the grounds, like a hive of hornets. One policeman finally came on the grounds, but he was unable to cope with the situation.

The Lord seemed to lay it on me to call an all night of prayer, to settle this matter once and for all. The saints readily agreed and gathered about me. We began to pray one after another for the salvation of these boys and men. We prayed for a revival; prayed for God to have His way.

From this time on there has been no trouble of any kind with the outside pepole. The opposition has melted away like snow before the summer sunshine.

This outside trouble brought us the support of the different clergymen. One Baptist preacher stood on the platform and gave his word that he would stand by us until the end. Another clergyman of the Episcopal church said that he had told his boys to be in good behavior, and that if they felt a desire to go forward for salvation, to do so. Church members, class leaders, and ministers flock to us, and many have received the Holy Ghost since the beginning of these meetings.

We also find there is a large number who have no church home whatever, and many who have never been to church. These are a surprised and interested body of people upon whom God is also moving mightily. Our former enemies as well as our friends, are now asking for our literature, and great numbers of tracts and booklets are being given away.

The policemen who are used to handling large crowds, told us that there were between eight and ten thousand people on the grounds Sunday night, and I have never witnessed better order.

People of all denominations bring their sick to be prayed for. One father brought his little child emaciated and suffering from a weakness of the body that did not permit of its walking. The little one was prayed for, and when he was placed upon his feet, the proud joy and happiness just shone from the father's face, as the little one began to take steps for the first time in months.

One child, who was a pitiful sight to look upon, with a terrible skin disease, and was covered with sores, was instantly healed by the power of Jesus.

One young lady, in writing, says: "Saint Vitus dance and severe nervous trouble had tortured me for many months. My face and eyes twitched so that I was ashamed to sit in a meeting. I was prayed for and the demon rebuked, so that I am every whit whole—no twitching, no nervous trouble. Oh, what a rest! What a relief! What a Savior!"

CHAPTER XIX.

MEETINGS FROM MASS. TO NEW YORK.

"In the morning sow thy seed, and in the evening withhold not thine hand . . . for verily I say unto you, ye shall not have gone over the cities of Israel till the Son of man be come." Ecc. 11:6; Matt. 10:23.

For months the Lord had been burning the message on my heart:

"Go quickly into the highways and the hedges—go into the out-of-the-way places, and declare that Jesus is coming soon."

California rang in my ears, and the Lord had been speaking to us for some time about making a trans-continental, tract distributing-Gospel auto tour. The Lord had led us so definitely in the past that we were made to know that it was His voice. My husband, who had attended the latter part of the Nation Wide Camp Meeting had gone to Florida again, and it seemed a great undertaking for me to consider driving a car, which had been used as much as ours, myself on such a long trip.

Putting the Lord to the test, I asked Him, if it was His will for me to make this trip to help me to get a new and more powerful car. The committee who had handled all the financial end of the camp meeting said that though the offerings had been good, expenses were so high that there was very little left to divide amongst the numerous workers, so that by the time our own expenses were paid there would be nothing toward the car.

When I mentioned it to Mother she said: "Well, ask the Lord to help you sell the old car at a good figure, and I will pay the balance."

Needless to say, I lost no time in going down the street to see about it. Inside of half an hour I had sold the old car for almost as much as I had paid for it in the beginning, and in a few hours there was a new Gospel Car being lettered with six-inch golden letters saying: "Jesus is coming soon, get ready," and "Where will you spend eternity?"

Before setting out for California a chain of meetings was held from Massachusetts and Connecticut to New York.

LONG HILL, CONN.,

where a tent had been erected and adveritisements issued for a week-end meeting. Saints gathered in from the towns around about and the Lord bountifully poured out His Spirit upon us. Some were saved and several received the baptism.

Amongst the number was one young man who had been seeking for years.

MONTWAIT CAMP.

Here we were joined by our dear Sister, Elizabeth Sisson, who had worked so faithfully through the Nation Wide Camp Meeting at Philadelphia, and she traveled with us throughout this entire chain of meetings, blessedly used of the Lord.

The glory of the Lord came down, saints were there from Philadelphia, New York, Boston, Connecticut, New Hampshire, Rhode Island, and many were saved and baptized with the Holy Spirit, with the Bible evidence, speaking with other tongues.

WORCESTER, MASS.

A three-day convention was held and as the saints who flocked in from out of town lifted their voices in praise with the saints of Worcester the glory of the Lord came down and rested upon the people. The Lord saved sinners and baptized believers.

UNITY HALL, HARTFORD, CONN.

The saints, with their pastor, had engaged one of the most beautiful halls in the city. The Lord had given Brother Neilson the promise that He would pour out His Spirit in this meeting, and praise His name, He kept His word. God blessedly poured out His Spirit, and at some meetings four or five were baptized and a like number saved.

HARLEM CASINO, NEW YORK CITY. (REPORT)

Amongst the number receiving the baptism on Sunday afternoon was Mrs. Emma M. Whittemore of the "Door of Hope" work, well known the world over as a blessed child of God and earnest Christian worker of years' standing.

One of the crowning joys of the New York convention came when the wife of Pastor W. K. Bouton (who had been seeking earnestly for two years, ever since the power fell at Corona), was wonderfully filled on the platform and came through to her baptism. It seemed that our hearts would almost break with joy as we knelt beside both Brother and Sister Bouton when they received the blessed Holy Spirit. Brother Bouton just leaped and danced for joy. All glory to Jesus!

One woman who had been suffering from rheumatism was healed instantly and danced like a young girl. Two were healed of this awful epidemic which is going around. Many were healed from other troubles and afflictions, for which we give Jesus all the glory and praise. There were no numbers kept of those saved and baptized, but we know that they were many, praise the Lord.

NEW ROCHELLE, N. Y.

During the eight days we were there not one discordant note, or one unkind word or criticism, or tale-bearing did we meet, just Jesus and His praises seemed to occupy everyone. Before the first day was well opened every seat was full and saints were sitting on the floor of the platform and standing in the aisles, but no one minded in the least, and the power came down in streams.

As the meetings progressed many were saved and baptized, many bodies were healed and the last day found the church packed to the doors again and even the ante-room filled.

The influenza epidemic was raging in this city as elsewhere, but the Lord was marvelously good to us and did not permit us to be hindered for a moment in proclaiming the message.

Churches were closed up in cities just after we had left, opened in other towns just before we got there, but not a meeting was closed at a time when it would hinder the carrying out of the program which the Holy Spirit had mapped out for us.

In New Rochelle I was stricken with this disease Saturday night, but the Lord kept me up for the three services on Sunday. Sunday night I was taken with violent chills followed by high fever, but in answer to the prayers of the saints and a determined rising up in simple faith, the Lord enabled me to complete the week's meetings so that I lost only one whole meeting.

I went through a severe test, however, when my little daughter took the epidenmic which quickly turned to double pneumonia. For two days it seemed the dear little life which meant so much to me must pass on and be with Jesus.

Saints gathered to pray for her, and I was obliged to keep on preaching in spite of the lump in my throat and the weight on my heart. She had come to me in the Harlem Casino and whispered:

"Mamma, may I please give my testimony tonight?" I told her, "Yes," and she stood on the platform and testified, saying:

"I thank the Lord for ever saving me and washing me in the blood, putting upon me the white robes of righteousness. Two years ago He baptized me with the Holy Ghost and revealed to me His glory, and I am going all the way through with Jesus till I meet Him in the clouds."

Staying in the furnished rooms without heat or home comforts, I yearned for a little home where I could care for her properly, and I remembered how before becoming unconscious she had said:

"Oh, Mamma, I do wish we had a little home where I could go to school." I had said:

"Darling, would you want Mamma to leave work and try to get a little home together?" She said:

"Oh, no, Mamma, I don't want you to leave the work; I will try to teach myself." Dear little lamb!

One afternoon someone met me at the top of the stairs and whispered that Roberta was very low, I could not bear to stay and look upon her; I fell upon the floor and prayed God to spare her life and the Lord gave me assurance that He would not only raise her up but also poured balm upon my troubled heart by saying:

"I will give you a little home—a nest for your babies—out in Los Angeles, California, where they can play and be happy and go to school and have the home surroundings of other children. You fixed a home once before out of My will, and it was taken away; now I will give you a home in My will."

He showed me Abraham withholding not his only son, Isaac, laying him upon the altar of sacrifice and being spared the agony of seeing him die; then He showed me that I had yielded up not only one but my two children, had traveled these many months with them from city to city, and town to town, having no home or bed to tuck them into, and that, just as He spared Abraham his Isaac, He would spare me my two children and cause me to joy in His tender care.

It was all so real to me that I could almost see the little bungalow, floors, garden and all.

Brothers Brown and Thompson laid hands upon Roberta, prayed for her, and the Lord touched her body. She soon opened her eyes, and though very weak, knew us all and was able to smile again. I kneeled down and putting my lips close to her ear whispered:

"Oh, Roberta, God has told Mamma that He is going to give us a little home, where you can have flowers and roses and go to school."

Her face lighted and she answered back in a thin little voice: "Mamma, can I have a canary, too?" And little Rolf, who was listening, said: "Can I have some rose bushes and a garden?"

Through all the weeks that followed and the four thousand mile drive, the little children talked and planned what they would do when God gave them the little bungalow. Sometimes the enemy sought to test me, and said:

"Now, it is an awful thing for you to build these children's hopes up like this. What if you should be disappointed?" But Father does not disappoint nor break His Word. Praise His name!

CHAPTER XX.

THE TRANS-CONTINENTAL GOSPEL TOUR

"And the Lord said unto the servant, Go out into the highways and hedges, and compel them to come in, that my house may be filled." Lu. 14:23.

PASTOR of Tulsa, Okla., has been writing us regarding our going to Tulsa to conduct an evangelistic campaign and the Lord had given us a definite witness that we were to go.

Just as we were about to start out, however, in the Gospel Car, a telegram arrived, saying:

"Postpone coming. All churches closed and it is not safe for you to be abroad in the land."

Going to the Lord about the matter, He spoke plainly to me:

"Fear not, do not lose a single day. Go at once, and the day you arrive the ban will be lifted and the churches will be open."

(NOTES FROM THE LOG.)

At nine o'clock this morning the last snap was closed, the last strap fastened, the baggage, and the Gospel, testimonies and tracts in place, the last "Good-byes" and "God bless you's" said, and the motor purred softly, (every greasecup had been filled, the tires tested and the gasoline tank filled), and the car rolled away as quietly and efficiently as though it knew that we had been preparing for this trip for days, and that the hands of many saints had been laid upon it in solemn prayer and dedication. It seemed to realize what was expected of it on the long trip ahead, and importance of its mission, that of being a worthy herald of the great message of love. It seemed as though both our hearts were beating in unison with the thought of the great opportunity which had come into its life and mine.

From our starting point at 115th Street, we went along 7th Avenue to 10th Street, and from thence turned into Riverside Drive. A big policeman, who was leisurely directing the traffic, caught sight of the Gospel Car, and said in a loud voice:

" 'Where will you spend Eternity?' Well!! what do you know about that?" And as we smiled to ourselves we could not help thinking that if he were going to preach to fashionable Riverside Drive, he could not have selected a better text.

Crossing to Staten Island, thence to New Jersey, we gave out our tracts on the boats, at the ticket offices and to the passers-by.

Five hours' run brought us to Philadelphia, where we rejoiced at meeting the dear saints again. After attending to freight to be shipped to California, we crossed to Camden, N. J., where Sister Dr. Sharp, had her beautiful bungalow open and warmed to receive us.

After the illness of my little daughter, Roberta, and myself, and the hundred-mile drive of the day, the warmth and the light and love and hospitality extended to us in this home made it a vertiable haven of rest.

GETTYSBURG, PA., OCT. 26

Glory to Jesus. Gospel Car has left a trail of tracts one hundred and twenty miles long. How hungry the people are! The searching questions regarding salvation and our teaching, that they ask, reveal the longing in their hearts. At Lancaster, by congested traffic, the Lord held us ten minutes in the main street, during which time scores of men and women pressed about the car, reading the signs and asking for literature.

On through Mountville, York and New Oxford, passing the famous battlefields and reached Gettysburg in time to find the streets filled with soldiers who were off duty, and had a golden opporutnity for tract distribution. We are now camping by the roadside, near the Allegheny Mountains.

PITTSBURGH, PA., OCT. 27.

The tracts which we have been constantly distributing today reach back as a white thread for one hundred seventy-five miles. We have been climbing the Allegheny Mountains all day. At noon we reached Tuscarora Summit, at an altitude of 2240 feet, and are now outside of Pittsburgh. We have pitched our camp by the side of the main highway, on the property of Mr. Carnegie, the great steel magnate, and though doubtless he is unaware that he has guests tonight, the Lord directed us to this spot to camp. Today being Sunday we have had the most wonderful opportunity of distributing our literature to church members and thoughtful, energetic Christian people. No engine trouble, no tire trouble.

CLAYSVILLE, PA., OCT. 28.

Not nearly so much mileage today, but bless the Lord, we have been very busy for Him. You remember that the Lord led us to camp right by the main highway, instead of seeking a more secluded spot. Bless the Lord! As we were breaking camp this morning, we heard a rumbling that sounded like the coming of an army, and lifting our eyes we saw great long lines of camouflaged government auto trucks coming down the road, laden with soldiers and material. With "Gospels" and tracts I ran to the road. The Lord put it in their hearts, too, for without exception, every car paused and the soldiers reached for the Gospels and tracts, thanking us and promising to read them, and suiting the action to the word, began at once to read aloud to their companions.

In Pittsburgh we have been busy for the Master. Have had bad road, mud and detours today, and ahead of us tomorrow, but the Lord has taken wonderful care of us, and no accident has resulted.

Passing through Cecil and Claysville, through the great coal-mining section, just as the men were coming up out of the dark underground, their faces besmeared with coal and grime, the electric lights which they had used in their toil below still burning in their caps, we were privileged to speak and witness for Jesus, leaving them the tracts and literature.

COLUMBUS, OHIO, OCT. 29.

This morning we started out over the very bad roads which the residents of neighboring towns had warned us of, lost our way, and came on to a very dangerous mountain pass. One place there was just room for the wheels of the car to pass. A sheer cliff, hundreds of feet deep, yawned below us and

THE TABERNACLE TENT WHERE NATION WIDE CAMP WAS HELD FOR SIX WEEKS IN PHILADELPHIA, PA.

THE GOSPEL CAR IN WHICH AIMEE SEMPLE McPHERSON MADE HER FAMOUS TRANSCONTINENTAL TOUR—NEW YORK CITY TO LOS ANGELES

rocks hung out above us, but angels seemed to hold the car to the road even though it was wet and slippery. We stopped to inquire of a man the way. He set us right. The Lord gave us the witness that He had sent us this road to reach this man, for when we gave him our message and literature, he brightened and told us of their church on the hill and that the parson would be powerful glad "to know of the Latter Rain." The Lord took us through all the mire and the mud without trouble or skidding where dozens of cars had been stuck in the mud and had been hauled out with horses at great expense and labor. We feel perfectly conscious all the time of a guard of angels that are traveling beside the car, protecting it.

On to Wheeling, W. Va., and then to Zanesville, Ohio, and tonight we are camping by the roadside in a beautiful sheltered spot outside of Columbus, O. Usually the little brooks and streams serve as our wash-basins, but here we have two barrels of rain water, which stand beside a closed summer cottage. We are trusting to be refreshed and rested.

INDIANAPOLIS, IND., OCT. 30-31ST.

For years I have been longing to meet Sister Etter, and have been talking about it more in recent months. I have longed to hear her preach and be at her meetings. We have inquired of those who have read the newspapers, however, and they say that the ban is not lifted.

Blessed be the name of the Lord forever and forever. Oh, how good He is to give us the desires of our hearts. We have traveled some two hundred miles today, and still found time to distribute the literature to many people, also leaving it in the R. F. D. mail boxes.

Through Springfield, O., thence to Richmond, Ind., and we are now in a comfortable room in Indianapolis. Hallelujah! What a luxury it seems! How good God is! Let me tell you the marvelous thing He has done. Well, there was a special meeting of the officials of Indianapolis yesterday, and they decided to lift the ban at midnight tonight, this being just an hour and a half after we arrived. Tomorrow Mrs. Etter's tabernacle will be open and I will have the desire of my heart. Glory!

A day of rest and praise. Called upon Mrs. Etter, and attended the meeting in her tabernacle tonight. We rejoiced and praised the Lord together. The power of God fell; even though there were only a very few at the meeting, the Lord was there showering His blessings upon us. Tomorrow we proceed on our journey. The command of the Master to go into the highways and hedges is being literally fulfilled. From New York to Philadelphia we followed the "Lincoln Highway," from Philadelphia to Indianapolis the "National Highway;" tomorrow we turn into "Pike's Peak Ocean to Ocean Highway," thence into the "Big Four Highway" for Kansas City.

TUSCOLA, NOV. 1.

Have had a glorious day for Jesus, witnessed and gave out literature for one hundred and twenty miles. We are now passing through prairie farms and the great wheat section. We are now camping under the trees. It is very cold and frosty, but God is protecting each member of the party, that none shall suffer or take cold.

SPRINGFIELD, ILL., NOV. 2.

Only eighty-seven miles today, for shortly after noon we reached Springfield and the home of our dear Sister Osten, who in loving hospitality held us for the balance of the day; meetings in her parlor tonight, and will send us on our way in the morning refreshed, rested and fed, our lunch box packed with victuals for the journey. Hallelujah!

We are burdened for this beautiful city, the capital of the state, with no Pentecostal Assembly and only these dear ones holding up a little gleam of light in their parlor. They tell us they know of no assembly for a radius of one hundred miles. How we long to stop over to tell the people the burning message of the hour.

BARRY, ILL., NOV. 3.

Just eighty-three miles today, but O, the opportunity for distributing Gospels and tracts, and witnessing for the Lord has been glorious. Several young men, who received the Gospels eagerly, told us that they had never had a Bible in their lives.

Today a long funeral procession passed the Gospel Car, and almost all, from the driver of the hearse to the mourners, lifted heavy black veils and pressed close to the windows, read aloud, "Jesus is coming soon, get ready."

We are camping tonight by a wonderful spring of water that flows ceaselessly from a great high rock. Farmers come from miles around, bringing their tanks and vats to be filled from its flow. Questioning them as we gave out tracts, we learn that all of their cisterns are dry from the long drought and this water from the rock is their only supply. What a privilege to witness for Jesus, the rock from whose riven side flows the water of life that never runs dry.

MACON, MO., NOV. 4.

The Gospel Car has witnessed and given out literature today for one hundred miles. Oh! that you could see the expressions in the people's faces. Some look with horror, startled fear, some, with skepticism, spit on the sidewalk and say they "do not believe it." On others belief is written and eager longing to hear more about it. Some say, "Well, this is just exactly what I have been thinking, that this war, and all these plagues must be a sign of the coming of the Lord. Lady, give us some literature."

Crossing the Mississippi River into Hannibal, people from almost every walk of life gathered about the car, insomuch that as we stopped for dinner, one of the party stayed in the car to dispense literature and witness and answer questions. A saloon-keeper, a policeman, a traveling salesman, storekeepers, church members, a holiness lady, and many others, gathered about to ask questions and receive literature. The saloon-keeper was much in earnest and we are praying for his salvation. Eternity alone will reveal the fruitbearing of the seed sown on this trip. Hallelujah!

Traveled until late—and the night being raw and cold—we paused on a lonely square, wondering where to sleep. A gentleman seeing the car volunteered information, and we learned this was the Mayor of the town. So sorry we forgot to give him the literature.

BRAYMER, MO., NOV. 5.

At the restaurant this morning, watching at the window the

people who walked around the car, commenting upon its signs and wondering, "What meaneth this," one dear old colored brother was so interested that he couldn't leave the car until we returned, and was delighted with the *Bridal Call* and papers, saying:

"Ah's often he'ad of dese heah Pentecos' people, but Ah's nevah saw any befo'. Ah sho' am glad to get dez heah papahs."

As we were about to leave the Mayor came up again. Surely the Lord sent him to get his papers. He helped to tie a rope and spoke encouragingly of our work, and received the literature we gave him, gladly. Oh! Lord, work wonders in these dear hearts, we pray Thee.

Hoped to have made more mileage today, but are detained here in Braymer for some adjustments on the car.

OLATHE, KAN., NOV. 6.

We realized this morning that "all things work together for good to them that love the Lord and are the called according to His purpose." Our delay of yesterday caused us to pass through the little town of Polo, Mo., by daylight, whereas we would otherwise have passed through unobserved in the darkness. As we passed through this town, we turned and drew up at the filling station. The people trooped after us down the streets, came out of the stores and houses, and crowding around the car, almost made us gasp. They kept us busy giving out literature and answering their many questions about Jesus and our teaching.

One young man said that his mother saw the signs on the car out of the window and told him to run until he caught that car, and bring her some of those tracts that we were dropping by the wayside, and asked us to give him one of every kind we had.

Nowhere on our trip have we met with a more enthusiastic welcome. So eager were the people here that they seemed ready to search the whole car, and dissect all the pockets in the doors, and the boxes before they would be denied. Cries of "These are the Pentecostal people that speak in tongues. I have heard about them and I want to read about them," came from every side of the car.

One dear lady with quivering face, listened as we were praising the Lord, and then, catching hold of my hand, said:

"Oh, tell me how to get the baptism. I have read the Pentecostal literature before." She knew of Sister Sission, Sister Etter and others, but asked if Brother Simpson upheld this way of receiving the Holy Ghost. She went away laden with literature, exclaiming:

"Oh, what a feast I am going to have today! I am going to sit down and read every word."

One man came running up to the car, telling us he wanted some of these papers for a boy who was going to war the next day and was not saved.

On to Kansas City, Mo., thence on to Olathe, Kan., where we are spending the night.

OLATHE, KAN., NOV. 7.

Detained by rain today, but have had a quiet time of prayer and spiritual refreshing.

IOLA, KAN., NOV. 8.

Have made one hundred seven miles today through muddy roads. Great interest is manifested in the Gospel Car; the editor of the daily paper asked an interview that he might write it for his paper, and gladly received the tracts, *Bridal Call* and booklets, assuring us that he would be quite an authority on the subject by the time he had read them all, but promising to do so, nevertheless.

OOLOGAH, OKLA., NOV. 9.

One hundred and nineteen miles' traveling lands in Oologah, Okla. We are passing through great stretches of prairie country filled with oil wells, and nearing our destination, we are tarrying for the night instead of pressing on to Tulsa, because of the swollen condition of the river, which is flowing over the road we must take. The Lord has promised, however, that when we pass through the waters He will be with us, and through the rivers they shall not overflow us.

TULSA, OKLA., SUNDAY, NOV. 10.

Hallelujah! The Lord took us through the swollen river bottom without mishap. Surely He has given His angels charge over us to bear us up lest even our tires dash their feet against a stone. In all these fifteen hundred miles we have had but two slight punctures and no engine trouble. The Lord surely tempered the wind to the shorn lambs.

Although the water was flowing over the road and had filled the gullies either side and we could not see which was the road and which was the ditch, the Lord kept us right in the middle of the road for about one-eighth of a mile until the car emerged, dripping but triumphant, at the other side. (May he ever keep us thus in the middle of the King's Highway, through the waters of life.)

At noon, looking across the great stretches of prairie, the city of Tulsa came into view, and as we saw the skyline, the buildings and paved streets, after wading through the slough of despond, we shouted and praised the Lord, for it seemed that must be the way it will be when a soul is nearing Heaven, coming up the last lap of the journey—the beautiful city, with its walls of jasper looming just before, no more stones, mud, deep ruts or ditches to be avoided, but smooth streets that are paved with gold; no more camping by the way in darkness, for there will be an eternal day.

ARRIVE DAY CHURCHES RE-OPEN.

Sabbath morning, as we were driving into the streets of the city, the first service was being held. Hungry, tired and dusty, after having personally driven and cared for the large Gospel Car, we had but little time for refreshments when meeting hour arrived.

PRAYER PRECEDES REVIVAL.

For many weeks, the Tulsa saints were praying definitely for the coming revival. Days of fasting and prayer were observed. With such prayers it was no wonder the Lord brought us through in safety, no wonder the ban was lifted according to the promise God gave me, no wonder seventeen men and women who know not God lifted their hands for prayers and that sinners began coming to the altar from the first night, no wonder the Latter Rain came down in such showers, no wonder sick were healed and some were raised up from death's door, no wonder our tired bodies were rested and refreshed so that we could keep going day and night with scarcely a moment to ourselves.

SICK HEALED.

The epidemic still raging, and many having been weakened and afflicted, we stood hours at a time praying for the sick, and Jesus helped those who came to Him. Praise His name. One man, crippled with rheumatism, insomuch that he could not move without acute pain, walked, ran, danced, and finally danced and leaped, perfectly healed. A man with severe stomach trouble and a sister with running sores, internal troubles, were healed, also influenza, heart trouble, etc.

We were called into houses where poor people were lying so low their eyes seemed glassy, and the rattle in their throats, but the Lord marvelously raised them up. Bless His name!

GOSPEL CAR WHEELS FLY FOR JESUS.

The Gospel Car led a busy life in Tulsa. There were ceaseless calls for visiting among epidemic victims day and night. Wherever it went its signs attracted much attention on the streets. The Sunday newspaper printed the picture of the car with its golden sign, "Jesus Is Coming" showing plainly on the head of the paper. There were days of tract distribution, when the seven-passenger car, filled with workers, tracts and handbills, visited neighboring towns and villages, placarding every available window and post with the notices of the meetings and the soon coming of Jesus. Tracts were left in the mail boxes at the farm houses and at the big wells, etc.

The Gospel Car also attended noon-day meetings and preached its sermon faithfully at the Tulsa Iron Works while we preached within the foundry to the workingmen and iron moulders of Jesus and His love. Meeting some of these men at the revival meetings, we later had the joy of seeing them give their hearts to Jesus.

Perhaps the most important work of the Gospel Car in Tulsa was street meetings. Having secured one of the best corners of the city, the top of the auto was put down, and singers, with their musical instruments, filled the car; how those dear ones did sing and testify of Jesus. Illustrated charts were hung from a stand; these charts drew crowds from all about.

Such respect I never witnessed in a street meeting; men removed their hats and stood with bowed heads, and women with tears in their eyes. Then came a call for all who were tired of sin and wanted Jesus for their Saviour to lift their hands for prayer. The first night eighteen, the second night twenty-nine raised their hands, indicating that they wanted Jesus as their Saviour.

Then came a call to step out and kneel upon the sidewalk by "our penitent form," the runningboard, and publicly, before their fellow citizens, surrender to Jesus. Tears were on the faces of many. Two ladies stepped out of the crowd and knelt, their tears splashed on the running-board, as our tears of joy over repentant sinners mingled with theirs. At the close of the last meeting several hundred saints marched out of the tabernacle to the street and formed in circles about the car. The saints laid their hands upon the car, asking God to protect it and its occupants, and to send a guard of angels with it to keep it from all danger, and prayed that it might ever be a messenger of life and never of death. These dear ones also dropped their offerings toward gas, oil and tracts, inside the car.

TRANSCONTINENTAL TOUR CONTINUED.

Leaving Tulsa the Gospel Car turned south by southwest for Oklahoma City, where we expected to hold a meeting that night. Saints who had been at Tulsa had gone ahead of us on the train to arrange this meeting. While hastening along we found time to distribute tracts through the huge fields of oil wells and in each village and town.

HELD UP AND WAYLAID.

Hurrying along, trying to make every minute count, we were obliged to draw up at a filling station, in the little town of Stroud. As we stopped a man sprang from a doorway and leaped toward the car shouting: "Praise the Lord." Others came running. In another moment the car was encircled with earnest saints praising the Lord and telling us that they had driven from nine to fifteen miles, having learned that this town being on the highway, we must pass through it today. They had picketed themselves at various corners and doorways, and had waited all day since early morning to ask us to their ten-mile distant mission at Kendrick, for a meeting. We shook our heads and told them that this was impossible, as we had promised to be in Oklahoma City Mission that night, and offering them tracts and literature instead. But they held onto the car and one sister's eyes filled with tears, and she trembled with the intensity of her eagerness and hunger. Kendrick was a little place and off the beaten track, and no evanglist or Pentecostal workers ever came that way, and they were not going to let us go by without coming if they could possibly help it.

Our arguments that we must keep our promise gradually weakened under the steady fire of their pleadings, until we consented to telephone and call up Oklahoma City as a test, that if the saints there were willing, we should stay.

The Oklahoma City saints replied that Tuesday would be just as good, that they would have more time and could get a larger crowd together. While I was 'phoning, the saints were lined up praying. How their faces brightened as the Gospel Car was turned from the highway and out through the country ten miles away, where a hot supper was steaming on the table and preparations for our comfort had been made!

It was only a little village, but this seemed to be the largest building in it, and even before we got there we could see the lights shining inside and out and people standing outside looking in through the door. The seats were filled and some standing in the back as we sang and praised the Lord together. After a simple message an altar call was given, and one dear sister received the baptism of the Holy Ghost, speaking in a clear, beautiful language.

Next morning we pressed on to Oklahoma City, having left a goodly supply of tracts and *Bridal Calls*. As we traveled we were talking of and marveling at the great need of workers throughout the country and in the out-of-the-way places.

OKLAHOMA CITY.

The saints were ready and waiting for us. The Lord gave us a precious meeting, pouring out His spirit upon us without measure, and another dear sister received the baptism of the Holy Spirit that night. There were many calls for us to remain, holding meetings amongst the Indians; round-houses were offered us free of rent, but the season was late and the weather getting cold, great snow storms had been reported farther ahead in the mountains and we hastened on our way.

Our first point of compass was Amarillo, the last town in Oklahoma. From Amarillo to Tucumcari, New Mexico, and thence on to Santa Rosa. As we journeyed, Sister B—— and my dear mother gave out tracts through fields of cotton to the gangs of road workers, bridge builders, farmers, tent encampments by the way, and to the white-topped caravans as they lumbered slowly on their way.

Although there had been a heavy snow storm just a week before, and roads were heavy, we got along without any difficulty until after we had left Tucumcari. Here the roads leading to Santa Rosa became more and more dangerous, mud, snow, deep gulches, and steep mountain passes. Had we stopped to inquire about roads ahead (we afterwards learned), drivers would have told us this road was impassable in wet weather.

Miles and miles we traveled, where the only sign of life was an occasional prairie-dog or rolling tumble-weed. Deeper, ever deeper the wheels cut in the soft mud till it was flying clear over the top of the car. I got out and put the skid chains on, and on we went. Santa Rosa was only nine miles away, and our eyes were constantly on the speedometer, as we sighed with relief each new mile we covered.

Darkness had now overtaken us, but with the good lights of the car we crept on in low gear, the two sisters walking, Roberta and Rolf, my two children, asking how they could help me drive. The wind was sweeping over the prairie in icy blasts when the car at last settled down to the fenders.

Our first thought was to search for lumber to jack the car up on, but not a tree had we passed for a hundred miles. Sister B—— and myself at last set off over the plains to search for help, and the Lord directed us to the home of a Mexican, who came with team and labored till two a. m. without avail. It dawned upon us at last that the Lord did not want us to go on that night, and though we have always taught and believed that ALL THINGS work together for good to those who love the Lord and were called according to His purpose, we could hardly see that this was one of the "all things."

The two sisters spent the night in the two miles distant Mexican adobe house, I and the children (now asleep) in the car. I spent the night in prayer, and just at daybreak came the Mexicans in their wagon with more boards, and the first time trying we were out of the mud and on our way.

We had not gone more than a mile when we saw God's reason for holding us back; deep washouts and gulches had to be crossed, where only good light, and careful driving could have saved the car and its passengers. But the Lord was with us and the guard of angels was never more real to us, and though water came over the fenders at times, we never had to stop again.

SANTA ROSA.

Reaching the town, cold, hungry, wet and muddy, the Lord had a blessed surprise for us. As we reached the square a young couple rushed across the street crying:

"Praise the Lord! Won't you come right to our house? O, we are so glad to see some Pentecostal saints; haven't met any for over two years! Come and stay a week, can't you?"

How wonderful, here in the wilderness, where we never would have expected to meet a soul who had received the Holy Spirit. They welcomed, fed and warmed us, washed our muddy car, gave us dry clothes while ours were washed. Even the sister's shoes fitted our feet, and her children's clothes fitted the little ones. How we sang and prayed and the power fell; their hearts were starved, they needed us and we needed them, and we all needed the Lord, and He satisfied the need. Hallelujah!

From Santa Rosa we journeyed across the state of New Mexico, via Socorro. We had expected to go by the northern route, over the Datl mountains, but found the passes so full of snow that we turned down the southern trail to Deming, N. Mex., thence to Tucson, and on to Phoeniz, Ariz.

Many miles of desert with no signs of life; the giant cactus towered above the car and occasional coyotes skulked in the distance. Houses were sixty and eighty miles apart, and so our kind and thoughtful Father sent us through this long stretch of road with three other automobiles, making the party four in all, the other cars being seasoned travelers with kind-hearted men and women who offered assistance and encouragement all the way, one of them even driving the car for two days to rest my arms.

From Phoenix we were advised to go north to Needles, Cal., thus striking the old National trail again and avoiding the deep sand of Yuma and other southern points. This stretch of sand and stone took us over the last of our poor roads, for at Needles we struck a boulevard which ran through the desert to the top of the mountains, through the mountain passes leading on down the long grade, where we were able to coast many miles through winding grades and beautiful scenery, until we came to San Bernardino, Cal.

After the prairies, plains, deserts and mountains this was like a new world. For a week past we had been passing through great mining sections where the mountains were yielding gold, silver, amalgam, zinc, iron, copper and other minerals, but now all this was past and we were in the land where thousands of acres were filled with beautiful fruit trees, oranges, lemons, grapefruit, etc., hanging in abundance.

We hastened on to Rialto, Upland, Glendora, and Arcadia to Pasadena, and from Pasadena to Los Angeles, arriving Saturday noon, finding the saints prepared and waiting to welcome us. Every arrangement for our comfort and accommodation had been made by these precious children of the Lord, and Sunday the revival meeting opened.

"The toils of the road seem nothing since reaching the end of the way."

CHAPTER XXI.

LOS ANGELES, CALIFORNIA.

"Shout: for the Lord hath given you the city." Jos. 6:16.

With but two days to get the ache out of our arms, after the long trans-continental Gospel Auto trip with a car whose speedometer registered over four thousand miles, we opened our revival campaign in Los Angeles.

Our campaign opened in an upstairs hall, having a seating capacity of about one thousand. This hall, we were told, has been almost empty so that the dear Pastor had been preaching in his shirt sleeves to about a dozen people. But from the first meeting, crowds grew steadily. In a few days the people were not able to get into the hall. Prayer room, rostrum, stairway, and corridors overflowed, and many were turned away.

Here in this "city of angels," where the power had so wonderfully fallen years ago, we learned that divers doctrinal differences had gotten the eyes of many off the Lord, and that there was a dearth in the land. Hungry hearts were praying earnestly, however, and the Lord answered prayer in a wonderful way.

They who had lost their first love, caught the flame, and reconsecrated their lives to the service. One night the Lord gave me for a text "Shout, for the Lord hath given you the city." Little did we know at this time just how wonderfully God had given us the city, first as our home, and later in wonderful revivals and now as a base for evangelistic work at home and abroad.

The windows of heaven were open, hundreds were saved, scores were healed, and large numbers received the baptism of the Holy Spirit. People complained that they could not get into the building, so the

TEMPLE AUDITORIUM

with its rows of galleries, besides the boxes, auditorium and rostrum seating some 3500, was taken for the larger meetings; the rent being $100.00 for each three hours. This rental the Lord supplied through the plate offerings at each service without any special appeal.

This revival was not man-made or woman-made, but truly came down from the Father of lights. At times the whole audience would be melted into tears as the stillness and hush of the Holy Spirit descended upon the place. At other times, it seemed as though the gales from heaven swept the place and the heavenly singing would be indescribable. Wonderful messages in the Spirit poured forth and the glory of the Lord rested like a mantle upon the place.

It is impossible to describe the many wonderful cases wherein we have seen our God at work. A husband and wife who had not lived with each other for seven years, both got saved and ran and threw their arms around each other; she received the Baptism. Another couple who hadn't spoken for several years got back to the Lord, and the little girl came with such joy to tell how papa and mamma were going to have a happy home.

Another fine-looking man came, crying like a baby, asking us to pray for him, he wanted to be saved. We prayed for him, his face was bathed in tears, and in less than fifteen minutes the man was under the power, speaking in other tongues.

Two women who came in drunk, and were saved at one o'clock in the morning, praised God each meeting for having been saved from a life of sin and shame and filled with the Holy Spirit.

Oftentimes the messages were more than the sinners could bear, and as the sufferings of the Lord were described sobs would be heard, men and women from all parts of the building rose and came to the altar for salvation. Although no effort was made to keep track of the number saved or baptized in these meetings, we know the angels rejoiced one night at the spectacle of forty men and women coming to the altar for this glorious salvation. An entire Catholic family were saved the same night.

Many who were here say they have travelled the world over the last twelve years, since the latter rain began to fall, and that they have seen great revivals, but all declare that they never saw a revival like this, and all agree that it outshines even the wonderful days of old Azusa Street, of which they all speak with rapt faces; such a unity and melting together of workers, such a laying aside of quibbles and hair-splitting doctrines, such a going together for poor, lost sinners, God cannot help but bless.

The seats were filled long before meeting, then people stood tightly wedged for hours. Ushers struggled to keep the aisles open to conform to the fire laws; children and younger people sat on the floor in front of the altar, even on the platform itself, and every available foot of space was taken until the speaker found it hard to move to and fro without stepping upon someone. They raised the windows and stood on window sills; seats were put on the elevation that covers the baptistry, many stood in the halls and the corridors; overflow meetings were held in other parts of the building, one in the prayer-room where the singing and praising would be echoed in to us in the larger hall as believers received the baptism during the preaching. The pastor had thrown open his office suite of four rooms for an overflow meeting. Here many were filled with the Holy Spirit, others were in earnest prayer before God for conviction to rest upon the entire audience of the larger service.

CHAPTER XXII.

"THE HOUSE THAT GOD BUILT."

"Yea, the sparrow hath found an house, and the swallow a nest foı herself, where she may lay her young." Ps. 84:2.

All this time the Lord had continued to assure me that He would provide for me a little home for the children. He spoke to other people throughout the city on the same lines insomuch that they were calling me up on the telephone with the word that God had been showing them that the little children should have a home and place to go to school.

One Sunday night when the place was packed to the doors with people, a young lady sprang to her feet saying:

"The Lord shows me that I am to give a lot to Mrs. McPherson. I have four lots of land and do not need them all. I am not called to preach the Gospel, while she is, and by giving the land that the little ones may have a home and she may be free to come and go in the Lord's work, I will share in her reward." A brother sprang to his feet, saying:

"Yes, and I will help dig the cellar." Others chimed in with: "Yes, I will help lay the foundation," "I will do the lathing," "I will do the plastering," "I will furnish the dining room," and so it went until even the little canary bird was promised.

A lady promised rose bushes. Now the canary and the rose bushes touched my heart and caused me to shout more than all else, for small as the incidents may seem, I could see

God, for the canary and the rose bushes were the two things the children had asked for beyond all else. The Heavenly Father had not forgotten.

When all was arranged a day of dedication and earth-turning was set, and after singing and prayer the saints formed a long line and marched round the lot single file, asking the Lord for the needed means with which to erect the little home.

Away back yonder, when out of the will of God, how I had struggled to get a little rented flat furnished, and what misery I had gone through, but now God is Himself planning a home which would be our own, a home given and built by the saints, where every tap of the hammer drove nails of love into the building and into our hearts. Perhaps none of my readers who have always had a home for their little ones, a pillow of their own at night, could enter with me into this wonderful joy in their behalf.

Brother Blake was a builder by trade, and he undertook to oversee the erection of the little home. Soon the brothers were digging the cellar and doing the work either entirely free or at a very low figure. One brother who offered his services was tested by the enemy, who said to him:

"Now you know you should be working somewhere where you could earn a good day's pay to take home to the wife and family."

He knew God had spoken to him, however, and toiled away at the foundation. On his way home one night it began to rain, and right at his feet lay fifteen dollars. God had richly paid him for his two days' labor. Hallelujah!

This is just one instance out of many where God has blessed every undertaking about this little home. It was a wonderful thing, also, that the lot of land, just on the suburbs of Los Angeles, while away from the influence of the city, should be just across the street from a fine school. Let everybody that reads say "Glory." We ourselves are so full of thankfulness and praise we can cry with David,

"Oh, where, my soul, shall I begin to praise the name of Jesus?"

Just three months from the date the lot was donated, the "little gray home in the west" was finished and ourselves and babies in it. Each blow of the hammer, each smoothing oi the trowel, was done by Spirit-filled brethren who shouted and sang as they worked, whilst consecrated sisters cooked for them and sang in the garage which was erected first. What a little haven of rest it has been, that little home, a gift from the Father of Love.

TRANSCONTINENTAL JOURNEYS.

CHAPTER XXIII.

LOS ANGELES TO SAN FRANCISCO.

"The plowman shall overtake the reaper, and the treader of grapes him that soweth seed; and the mountains shall drop sweet wine, and all hills shall melt." Amos 9:13.

LEAVING Los Angeles at noon, via the San Fernando Valley, we passed through the citrus and olive ranches, through the Newhall Tunnel and on to Saugus with its great fields of oil wells nestling at the foot of the mountains, losing no opportunity with tracts and literature.

From Saugus we climbed the mountain grades of the San Francisquito Canyon, skirted the edge of the great lonely Mojave Desert spread like a vast, silent emptiness far away into the blue distance. Then up and up the mighty Tejon Pass with its rocky cliffs and precipices (Mt. Whitney in the distance). From the snowy summit we dropped to plains whereon a straight road stretched before us like a long, shining ribbon. Speeding over this highway, sunset found us in the town of Bakersfield.

We distributed tracts, and also held an open-air meeting at one of the principal corners, from the Gospel Car. Here we found special need for the little Gospels, which we gave freely.

On the journey toward Oakland and San Francisco, a blinding rain made driving not only difficult but dangerous. Hurrying along with side curtains buttoned securely and the windshield misty with the falling torrents, we failed to see an approaching freight train until within twenty feet of the track. The train was going too fast to stop, and had I slammed on the brakes the car would have skidded ahead into the train. Quick as a flash the Lord gave me presence of mind to whirl the car to the left and up the side of the track, thus avoiding the train and coming to a stop without injury. Hallelujah!

We prayed for dry weather; soon the sky cleared, and as we crossed the bay on the ferry from Oakland to San Francisco the sun smiled down upon us from a clear blue sky, as a promise that the Lord would send down upon us the showers of blessing and the sunshine of His love whilst in this city.

From the first meeting to the last the glory of God rested upon the people. The manifestations of the Spirit's power increased daily, hungry souls came from far and near and were filled with good things from Father's table. Crowds increased daily, and even though an extra gallery was built, the last meeting found the crowds standing clear out onto the sidewalk.

The way in which sinners rose to their feet in response to the altar call and came from the galleries and from various parts of the hall to the altar was a sight to warm the heart of any soul-winner. At the close of each preaching service the long prayer room would quickly fill from one end to the other with earnest seekers for the baptism of the Holy Spirit. The prayers of seekers and workers went up with such unison and in such accord that their voices sounded like the rushing of many waters. Many were prostrated on the floor under the power of God while they received their baptism, others were filled with the Spirit while kneeling or standing upright on their feet,with hands and face upturned to heaven.

These after meetings ofttimes continued until five and six in the morning. Among the many baptized with the Holy Spirit during these meetings were two ministers, church members and a number from a nearby Salvation Army corps.

Throughout our meetings everywhere we have put the ministry for the soul first, then the ministry for the body, nevertheless miracles of healing have been wrought in almost every meeting.

Among those who were healed in the San Francisco meeting was a child whose throat was to have been operated on the following day, instantly healed in answer to prayer. The doctor bade the mother take the child home, saying that she was perfectly whole.

A lady who had suffered with internal trouble and rupture for eighteen years was instantly made whole by the Great Physician, Jesus, in answer to the prayer of faith, insomuch that the truss has been removed and she leaps and dances and praises the Lord, absolutely free from pain.

A brother whose knee and ankle had been stiffened from a severe accident, was touched by the Hand Divine, and his joints loosened up so that he danced and leaped for joy, his limb made whole and sound as ever.

An elderly lady afflicted with neuritis in head and face, insomuch that for a number of years she had not had a sound night's sleep, came to ask for prayer. So tender was her head and face that she held her hands over it while we prayed, as though in terror lest the lightest finger touch should reach it. She was instantly healed, and through the entire balance of the meetings continued to praise God that all pain and tenderness was gone, and she slept soundly, free from suffering.

What a wonderful Saviour is He who has borne not only our sins but our sickness in His own body upon the tree, and by whose stripes we are made whole.

CONVENTION HALL, TULSA, OKLAHOMA.

(Condensed report of a marvelous campaign.)

Workers and ministers gathered in from seventeen states, while the local people surrounded the building (as described by reporters) with everything from a limousine to a buckboard, they came from thirty to sixty miles around, bringing their sick to be healed.

An artist, seeking new expressions of wonder, amazement, distress, yearning, earnest absorption, would certainly have found all that he sought portrayed upon the faces of spectators that gathered in and filled both sides of the galleries.

"Oh, what is it?—What does it mean?—What?"

"Have they fainted?—Are they dead?—What?—What?" cried others, as dozens were mown down under the power of the Holy Spirit.

Some anxious souls were so perturbed that they came to feel the pulse of those under the power. They went away with a peculiar, dazed expression, when the object of their anxious fears rose to his or her feet, their faces radiant with new-found joy, and ofttimes such spectators were soon at the altar themselves seeking the same touch from Almighty God.

Amongst the many wonderful manifestations of Jesus' healing power, was a woman with a broken arm, and a man twisted with rheumatism—both being healed instantaneously.

BETHEL TEMPLE, CHICAGO.

Upon conclusion of the Tulsa campaign, we were immediately plunged into the busy days of revival in Bethel Temple. For months letters of invitation had been coming, mourning over the dry condition of the ground, and declaring that for months very few had been receiving the baptism or being saved. All were praying and believing for a revival.

A special feature of this campaign was the tarrying meetings, wherein hundreds of earnest seekers for the Holy Spirit were filled and went back to their respective fields of labor, on fire for God and souls.

The large lecture room adjoining the main auditorium with a seating capacity of 500, was cleared in the same business-like way that a battleship clears her deck for action. Rows upon rows of hungry seekers took their places, while several scores of earnest and seemingly tireless saints and workers poured in to pray for them till the need of each hungry soul was met. The Spirit of God came down night after night till the floor was covered from the platform to the door with praying people, much to the amazed astonishment of spectators and reporters, who had never witnessed anything like it. Everyone prayed at the same time as all were too desperately in need, and too much in earnest to wait for another. Weeping their way through each found the blessing and the glory which he sought.

Such a wonderful effect did these scenes have upon the sinners that many of them ran to the altar, among the number being Jews and Roman Catholics. Church members of years' standing who had never known what it was to be born again, found the Saviour who filled their hearts with joy and flooded their faces with light and radiance. Conviction settled upon sinners like a mantle that they could not shake off. Two young men entered the church who had been robbing and stealing that day, and had come to the church with the intention of injuring the janitor and stealing whatever they could. Unable to stay in the room another moment, they fled to the door and down the steps. The convicting Spirit of God followed them, however, in such a wonderful way that one young man fell flat to the sidewalk under the rebuke of God, and came creeping on his hands and knees up the steps and made his way to the altar, where he was gloriously saved and later was followed by his companion.

A MOUNTAIN CAMP MEETING.

Among the foothills of the Blue Ridge Mountains, among tall trees that lift their heads in stately grandeur to the sky, there is a little farm and on the farm lived a little servant of the Lord whose name is Mary Walker. For over a year she had been bombarding heaven (and incidentally ourselves by way of letters and telegrams) for a revival.

Seeing her zeal and faith for a revival amongst the people shut away in the mountains, far from revivals and the preaching of the Word of power, we promised to go and shipped a tent to the spot. This sister trudged from home to home carrying the news and stimulating interest. Little did we dream the number that would be saved and baptized or the throngs that would follow us. Yet to this day 'tis a pleasant restful memory to dream about this little farm, with its winding brooks and streams murmuring and singing as they slip over smooth pebbles and glide beneath the down-reaching lacy arms of weeping willow.

Trees were removed from the apple orchard to make room for the big tent. The sleeping tents were pitched beneath fruit laden boughs. Sister Bent writes of this campaign as follows:

"Here is to be found the most ideal gathering of the Lord's children one could wish to find this side of Heaven. The platform is just filled with workers. It is quite beyond expectation, how the Lord has sent the leaders and workers from all parts to rally around His handmaiden, giving her their undivided love, sympathy and help. Many come twenty miles to attend the meeting, most of them having spent the day toiling hard under the blaze of hot sun, gathering in their hay and grain, for it is harvest time.

The Gettysburg Highway lanes as far as the eye could see, were lined with buggies and automobiles. They had come from the country-side for miles around, over the same road that Lee's retreating Army fled, when it took them an entire day and night to pass by.

A man was saved in his wheat field a short distance from the camp ground, where he could hear the singing of the hymns. They entered into his heart and were the means of bringing him to God there and then.

One sister walked five miles on purpose to get saved. Another woman walked twenty-two miles in one day to attend the meeting.

A baptismal service was held under the shade of the trees, beside the clear running waters of the creek. As the candidates went down into the water, one after another came up with lifted faces and hands, praising the Lord. Some had to be carried out of the water, so mightily was the power upon them."

NEW YORK CITY CAMP MEETING

Two days after closing the mountain camp, the New York campaign opened. A large field in the Bronx had been secured and a big tabernacle tent, dormitories and smaller tents erected. Electric signs bearing such inscriptions as "Do you want Salvation? Come!" "Do you want to be Baptized with the Holy Ghost and Fire? Come!" had been placed on elevated standards near.

Though God turned the tide and gave us many souls and blessed results, this meeting started under heavy odds. The brother who had been pressing us to come, informed us on arrival that he had incurred twenty-three hundred dollars expenses which he expected us to raise in the meetings for him. Money-raising in meeting being out of our line, our hearts were sorely burdened. Our friends, however, rallied to us and paid the money.

The tent was situated in the heart of a Catholic settlement, surrounded by various of its institutions. At the first meeting, we found an audience who had no idea of order in this as a religious service. Young men came galloping in with cigars in their mouths, and hats on the back of their heads; girls chewed gum, giggled, asking one another aloud what sort of show this was; boys rolled in and out under the canvas and the audience took its departure over the backless benches.

Next night was better. Whispering, hats and cigars were no more. The order and crowds improved until the finest people of the neighborhood were attending and God blessed graciously. Daily afternoon meetings were held for children, many of whom were ragged, barefoot street urchins. On Saturday afternoons we gave them a special treat of cake and ice cream, using 10 to 15 gallons.

Another special feature of the campaign was the rain. Down

it came—deluging, in torrents. Eight days it continued but the crowds packed the tent to overflowing. Hundreds stood outside under umbrellas, others stood with the rain pouring down their necks from the tent flaps or their neighbor's umbrella, and seemed totally unaware of it. Inside the tent the power fell and when the ground became a rushing river, the congregation stood on the seats, singing, testifying and shouting, holding their umbrellas over their heads to stop the rain that streamed through the old ramshackle tent. A plank bridge was built leading to the platform, and thus scores were soundly converted and filled with the Holy Ghost. Many still write thanking God for the Bronx Camp.

New York press representatives attended the meetings; also National Syndicates flashed the news of this (to them) wonderful revival to every state in the Union, making the bold assertion that we were "driving the devil from New York." Upon urgent request we wrote seven sermons to girls under the title "The Pitfalls of a Great City." These were illustrated by their artists, copyrighted and published throughout the world. Thus God widened our ministry and brought a victory to His name out of one of the hardest battles and most discouraging outlooks.

PACIFIC COAST CAMP—LOS ANGELES.

From New York and the Atlantic to Los Angeles and the Pacific, we hastened to arrange and open this campaign. Our great Tabernacle tent was situated in a nine-acre field and was adjoined by a large prayer-tent in the rear. "Tent town" was laid out as orderly as a little city, rows of camp tents were erected in streets, each bearing its own name upon a sign post, above which stood a little red cross. Here you would drive up "Hallelujah St.," then turn the corner to "Praise Ave.," and "This Is That Square," then on to "Victory Way," "Joy Blvd.," and "Amen Ave."

The tent grounds were filled with praise by day and by night until some of the less enthusiastic neighbors implored that they might be allowed to get a little sleep, at least between two and four a. m. The number of campers was amazing because of the street car strikes and national tie-ups in transportation, which occurred at that time. God had given us, several months previously, the "message of warning" prophesying these various conditions and the camp was fully prepared. Instead of hindering, this brought the people to the grounds permanently. Of this meeting, a visiting missionary wrote:

"Thousands upon thousands heard the Gospel and great mountains of prejudice, hard cold walls of doubt and unbelief had been literally swept away; hundreds wept their way to Jesus' feet, while between one and two hundred are known to have received the baptism of the Holy Spirit. The healings were very wonderful, the blind saw, the deaf heard and the lame walked.

"The great fifty-foot platform was packed with singers, workers, ministers, evangelists and missionaries, and not a murmuring word, critical remark, nor argumentative spirit intruded to mar the perfect harmony and love of this great campaign."

A liberal offering was given to visiting missionaries and after five weeks we reluctantly broke camp, giving the dear converts and precious baptized souls to the upbuilding and care of the church and missions here.

INTERSTATE CAMPAIGN—HOLDREGE, NEBRASKA.

Ministers and friends had been impressing upon us the great need of the Nebraskan territory, declaring that it was virgin soil and had never been touched by a real revival. When at last the way was open for us to give them a promise, the only available auditorium large enough was situated at Holdredge. How such a small town came to have such a large auditorium (with a seating capacity of 3500 and having every modern convenience) was a mystery, until the meeting was under way and we learned that the people who attended had driven from a radius up to fifty miles through mud and slush; sometimes on arrival these dear people would be mud bespattered from head to foot until their faces were scarcely recognizable; so earnest were they and so grateful for this full Gospel Revival privilege.

The townspeople (from the weekly newspaper, which devoted columns to the meetings, to the merchants who sent out our advertisements in their bundles and mailing lists) took an intense interest.

Behind the blessed results was a secret power house. Day and night without ceasing, throughout the three weeks' campaign, in relays, bands of seven consecrated saints continued in prayer and intercession.

Irresistible conviction settled down upon the audiences,

drawing scores to Christ. One convert was eighty-seven years, whilst amongst them were little children from four to six. At times the power of the Lord came down and dozens were prostrated at His feet. Happy converts still write us who were saved and baptized at this meeting.

STATE ARMORIES—AKRON, OHIO.

By C. A. McKinney, Pastor

Our hearts are overwhelmed with thanksgiving to God for his goodness in sending upon us this mighty outpouring of the Spirit and the wonderful revival.

The first Sunday night an audience of 1400 attended and it was wonderful to see how quickly and deeply the Spirit was convicting the people, and how definitely they reached the witness to their salvation. Men and women with tears streaming down their faces, some staggering under the power, made their way out of the seats, walked the length of the aisle, climbed the stairs to the stage, where the space a moment before by some fifty singers had been hastily transformed to a prayer room. Those tarrying for the baptism of the Holy Spirit poured up onto the platform from both stairways. Christians and altar workers followed and in a moment torrents of prayer rolled heavenward, sinners were being saved, believers baptized in the Holy Spirit and sick healed.

Tuesday night Sister McPherson told the story of her young life, and it is doubtful whether there was a dry eye in the building. When the altar call was given there was an instant response. The first was a soldier boy with broad shoulders and an erect figure and a determined look. Other men immediately followed him to the altar, weeping frankly and unashamed. Wives came with their husbands, mothers leading their sons and daughters. They marched down the aisles to the place where Sister McPherson stood on the steps to grasp their hands and to usher them into the prayer room. Here they wept out their hearts before the Lord and soon rose happy and triumphant. Many new converts received the baptism of the Holy Spirit the same night in which they were saved. A great many of these have declared they had never been in a Pentecostal meeting before.

The closing Sunday the Grand Opera House was secured. At an early hour the main floor and balcony were filled. People were held spellbound. Never had we heard anything so beautiful—how the Spirit revealed Jesus to us in His beauty and loveliness. Tears flowed down the cheeks of preachers, missionaries, saints and sinners alike. The management of the theatre stood outside looking in through the windows. Surely the Grand Opera House here had never witnessed such a scene! Words would fail to express our gratitude and praise to God for this great campaign.

NOTE—A large missionary offering was taken on the closing Sunday afternoon, which more than covered the fare and traveling expenses of Brother McKinney's daughter to Africa, in which field she works today.

FISHING FOR WHALES IN THE LYRIC.

WESTERN UNION TELEGRAM.

"Have secured Lyric -- seventeen days -- enormous cost -- reserve dates."

Such was the gist of the message which summoned us to Baltimore. Churches and assemblies had long been calling;

but were unable to complete arrangements. God had now provided the rental and expenses through a friend. This amounted, I believe, to three or four hundred dollars daily.

The Lord definitely spoke to us that this campaign was not so much for harvesting but a great plowing, seed-sowing and watering of the dry and barren fields. Our invitations had invariably been "Come empty and be filled." Here, however, the word went forth "Come filled, and pour out blessings for others."

This was an independent and undenominational meeting. In prayer the Lord spoke continually to my heart concerning it, "You are not fishing for minnows—you are fishing for whales." This seemed a strange message from the Lord, and for a time I could not understand it.

In this city were a number of Pentecostal saints, precious people, but some few of them were largely given to fleshly manifestations. A few impostors had brought bitter reproach upon the work. Our task, therefore, was to represent these glorious Bible truths in such a way as would win the respect and confidence of the churches and people. This, God enabled us to do in a wonderful way. Some of the mission folk, (accustomed only to reproach, and trained to believe that wherever there was power there must be a continuous noise and loud outcry) thought we held our fishing line and tackle in too firm a hand and were quenching the manifestations of the Spirit. Always having stood for the genuine power and demonstrations of the Holy Ghost, this accusation from those we loved, wounded our hearts deeply. We went to prayer and the Lord said over and over again: "Hold steady, my child, you are not fishing for minnows—you are fishing for WHALES."

Day after day the altars were filled with converts, and the prayer room with those seeking the baptism of the Holy Spirit; but on the whole our meetings were deep and quiet. We banked, not upon noisy manifestation, but upon the preaching of the Word.

Night after night, ministers, Doctors of Divinity, Jewish Rabbis, Medical doctors, and the best people of the city sat in the orchestra and boxes of this their finest theatre for which we were paying over three hundred dollars a day rental, in order to "Fish for Whales."

Soon the ministers were assisting us upon the platform, singing, leading in prayer and at the altar. Several times the persons for whom the ministers were thus praying fell under the power in their arms. Workers were anxious to rush to the front and assist in praying for them to receive the Spirit. But we said: "No—let the Holy Spirit run this affair. We are not fishing for minnows; we are fishing for whales." The result was that the ministers gently laid those under the power on the floor; and bade us not to worry as they had often seen such things in the earlier days of Methodism, in the United Brethren, and other churches. Soon, those upon whom God's power so sweetly rested were filled with the Holy Spirit and began to speak with other tongues, and the ministers, who were often the only ones near them at the time, (and therefore could not blame us) thought it was wonderful. Dear precious Pentecostal saints felt like leaping, dancing and shouting for joy and must have thought us hard for we shook our heads and softly said: "Sh-h-h—fishing for whales."

Urgent invitations to speak in several city churches were accepted and there God gloriously saved souls and healed the sick, as the congregations sang:

> "O, send the old-time power—the Pentecostal power,
> Thy flood gates of blessing upon us open wide.
> Let sinners be converted and Thy Name glorified."

Ministers were delighted to see their altars filled with penitents as never before. Interest was stirred throughout the entire city. Newspapers published columns with big head lines on their front pages, such as: "Blind Woman Has Sight Instantly Restored at Lyric Revival"—"Lame Man Skips"—"Modern Miracles Performed"—"Paralytic Woman Claims Limbs No Longer Useless"—"Deaf Ears Instantly Unstopped."

You can imagine the results; hundreds of sufferers and cripples flocked from far and near and I—well,—I was never so frightened in all my life. Taking one look at the throng of sick people, I ran down stairs, buried my face in a chair in the corner and began to weep: "Oh Lord, just see what's happened now! There are all those sick folks upstairs and Thine handmaiden never felt so helpless! Oh, I did want this meeting to be such a success and now just supposing these people should not . . . . ! Oh, Lord—Lord, what shall I do?"

"My child, who is going to heal these people, you or I?" was the question He brought to my heart.

"Why, Lord, it is You—You Who have all power in Heaven and on earth, I have no strength or power outside of Thee, dear Lord!"

"Then cease your weeping, rise, go up those stairs and pray in the name of the Lord Jesus Christ, with faith believing, and it shall be done even as you ask." And Oh, how God did work and lay bare His mighty arm in our midst. Great victory and honor were brought into the name of the Lord, Glory to Jesus!

So intense was the interest in ministerial circles that before the campaign had closed, several invitations had come to return and conduct campaigns in their churches, one being to hold a union revival in United Brethren Churches.

"But do you know just how the power of God may fall and that we preach the baptism of the Holy Spirit and believe that it is possible to receive Him in exactly the same way today as in the days of old?" we asked the ministers who called upon us.

"Why, that is just what we want, what the church is starving for," they replied. "We do not ask you to compromise but to preach the whole Word and only pray that it may bring some life into every valley of dry bones." After earnest prayer we were led to reply:

"Sunday afternoon we are to preach upon, 'The Baptism of the Holy Spirit.' Come and hear this message, then if you still want us we will come."

"Oh! we will still want you, never fear," they replied. "With all our hearts we want the real power of the real God."

Sunday afternoon dawned, bright and clear. Ministers, evangelists and the finest thinking people of the city were there. Dr. Shreve of McKendree M. E. Church of Washington, D. C., had caught the train immediately after the conclusion of his sermon and had brought with him several of his official men. Our hearts cried out to God to give liberty, wisdom and logic in the presentation of this great truth under favorable circumstances. Suddenly whilst sitting tense in earnest prayer, burdened for the cause of the Holy Spirit, I had a strange but overwhelming presentiment that the devil was going to lift up his head in this meeting and try to strike a blow somewhere at once, as the Lord was winning too mighty a victory, and would sweep many hearts with His power unless the devil put a stop to it. The strange and terrible feeling that a deadly serpent was right in the meeting, preparing to rise up, and strike, grew upon me.

Nervously I looked round over the platform, the wings, the boxes, the audience, but everything looked perfectly all right. All were singing and praising the Lord, and seemed serene and calm on the surface. Where, O where was the blow to be struck? Did I only imagine all this? No, the feeling was too strong, and for many months I could not doubt that God had given me the gift of discernment. Suddenly a woman rose to her feet. Sitting tense and rigid, I gave her one quick glace and the Lord said:

"There's the woman the devil has entered into, in order to try to frighten away the whales. This is the psychological moment for him to work. Day after day you have been piling up a mighty structure of teaching and impressions regarding the Holy Ghost and the results of the Spirit-filled life. This is the turning point, and the opinions of the people, their acceptance or rejection, their confidence won or lost, hangs by a thread, and will fall heavily one way or the other. If the devil can but make some misguided soul rise and do some foolish, fanatical, outlandish thing under the pretence of the Spirit's leadership and power, he can make the people think *this* is the result of the glorious message which you have been preaching. Hold fast in prayer; everything is at stake now; pray for wisdom and it shall be given you."

Keyed to the tension of the moment, these thoughts flashed through my mind like lightning. I prayed that the people would not notice the woman. With face flushed, she flung out her arms, made for the aisle and started for the front, beating her arms about like a flail, knocking off several ladies' hats on the way, crying, "Praise the Lord" in a strained unnatural voice all the while. There was not a second to lose. Grasping the arm of the brother who sat beside me, I whispered:

"Go! Go quickly, brother, get that woman in her seat; this is not of the Lord."

"Oh, Sister, I wouldn't dare!" he gasped, "that would be quenching the Spirit."

"Brother, go quickly, quickly!" I urged, "Tell the Lord to blame me if you like, but go quickly!" I gave him a little push and he was on his way. Asking God to help him, I started another chorus to cover the situation, for the hall was so large few had noticed the woman's performance. She was headed for the platform, but the brother, by walking before her, finally got her to her seat. He returned to the platform and in a moment the woman was in the aisle again; making her way to the boxes she began shaking her fists in the people's faces, knocking off hats with her flailing arms and screaming, "Praise God."

"Go, Sister, and get her out," I cried softly to a lady sitting behind me in the choir.

"Oh! But that's the Spirit of the Lord on her!" she exclaimed. (Oh why do not more people receive discernment of Spirits! How much reproach and misleadings would be avoided.) "Besides, she is bigger than I—How could I get her out?"

"That is the devil," I whispered desperately, "Go, dear, and God will help you. I dare not leave the platform. Every eye would follow me, and the meeting would be ruined." Away she went and in some miraculous way, God answered my prayer, and the woman was outside in another room. There the enemy showed his true colors and purpose. The woman proved to be a maniac who had been in an asylum. Her delusion seemed to cause her to believe herself a preacher. She paced the floor, crying disconnected sentences, raving and preaching to the chairs, and failing to recognize or be controlled by her own people. Yet, this was the kind of woman many of the saints would have allowed to promenade the platform and disgust the entire audience—fearing lest they quench the Spirit.

Attention soon reverted to the service, and I drew another easy breath. The strain had made me desperately ill at my stomach, and I left the meeting for a few moments, but returned in time to begin my message though still shaking from head to foot and in great weakness. In a moment, however, the power of God fell upon me and never had He given me such a clear mind, such an opening of the scriptures, and such a logical presentation of the truths of my message. The people laughed, shouted, and wept, and the day was won for God.

When the service was over, and hundreds of Christians had lifted their hands signifying that they desired this Baptism of power, I went to the boxes to shake hands with the ministers.

"Well, what is your opinion now?" I tremblingly asked, for I had preached Acts 2:4 in its entirety.

"Just that we want you in our churches more than ever," they replied. "We only wish we had the power you speak of and possess, and here, Sister, is $200.00 for your travelling expenses back to Baltimore."

Well, Glory to Jesus! Whales, Whales, Whales.

Looking backward, I can see that this meeting marked a turning point not only in my own ministry but in the history of the outpouring of Pentecostal power. Yet at the time (so far as I know) not one of the dear Pentecostal people understood the vision God had given me, and severely criticised what they called a "quenching of manifestations." Others of my friends said, "Well, we don't understand it yet, but we believe in you and if you say you have the vision we will follow." God bless them, they saw the vision a few weeks later when, upon our return trip to Baltimore, the power fell in the churches until the minister, Rev. E. W. Leech, with his beautiful wife, daughter, congregation and many of his official men and Sunday School teachers, received the baptism of the Holy Spirit in Pentecostal fullness. And the power began to fall in churches all about; then they came back and said, "We see it, Sister, thank God you had the vision and the courage to stand alone and be true to it."

CAMPAIGN IN UNITED BRETHREN CHURCHES.

After another hasty transcontinental trip to the "House That God Built" and the sweet babies at home, we returned to Baltimore, burdened with prayer for a great outpouring in the denominational churches. Gloriously the meetings opened with the Lord saving souls and bringing to His dear feet many members who declared that though they had belonged to church for years they had never known a real "born again" experience. What love, humility and hunger was displayed by these dear children of God.

After some days of blessed revival, in which many were saved and the altars constantly filled, a divine healing service was held upon the request of many and the power began to fall. For indeed, once we have opened the door to divine healing we have paved the way for the supernatural power of God to enter in. At the first healing service many were healed and, at the close of this service, the last young lady to be prayed for, swayed and seemed about to fall under the mighty power of God. "What shall I do with her?" I asked the pastor. "Why, why," said he, looking rather anxious, "I guess you'll have to let her go." We did; gently we lowered her to a reclining position and held her head in our arms. She seemed to be utterly lost in Jesus and her face shone as the face of an angel. Those who gazed upon her were melted to tears. A solemn hush came down upon the church, broken only by the sobs of the people and by her husband who wept his way through to salvation by her side. At six o'clock Mrs. Leech returned with us to the parsonage, leaving the young lady still lying just inside the chancel rail under the sweet power of God.

"Sister, I cannot go to church tonight," said Mrs. Leech on the way home. "I must tarry before the Lord and pray till I receive this wonderful power," she added with tears running down her cheecks.

That night we had a wonderful meeting; many were saved and three received the baptism of the Holy Spirit. Returning to the parsonage, we were met by the shining face of Sister Leech. We began to tell her enthusiastically of the wonderful meeting, but she said, "Oh you have not had a more wonderful meeting than I. When you left I began to wash the supper dishes, intending to get the work done quickly that I might spend more time in prayer; but as I walked about the

REVIVAL IN CHICAGO

Where Sister McPherson went to help win souls and God showed her many wonderful visions of His purpose for His Church

SISTER McPHERSON CONDUCTING A SI

AMEN CORNER—PRAISE AVE.-
Were visited daily by milkmen, bakers and icemen—for hundred

CK TENT MEETING IN LOS ANGELES

LELUJAH STREET AND GLORY DRIVE
e their home on camp ground, hungry to be fed with the Bread of Life

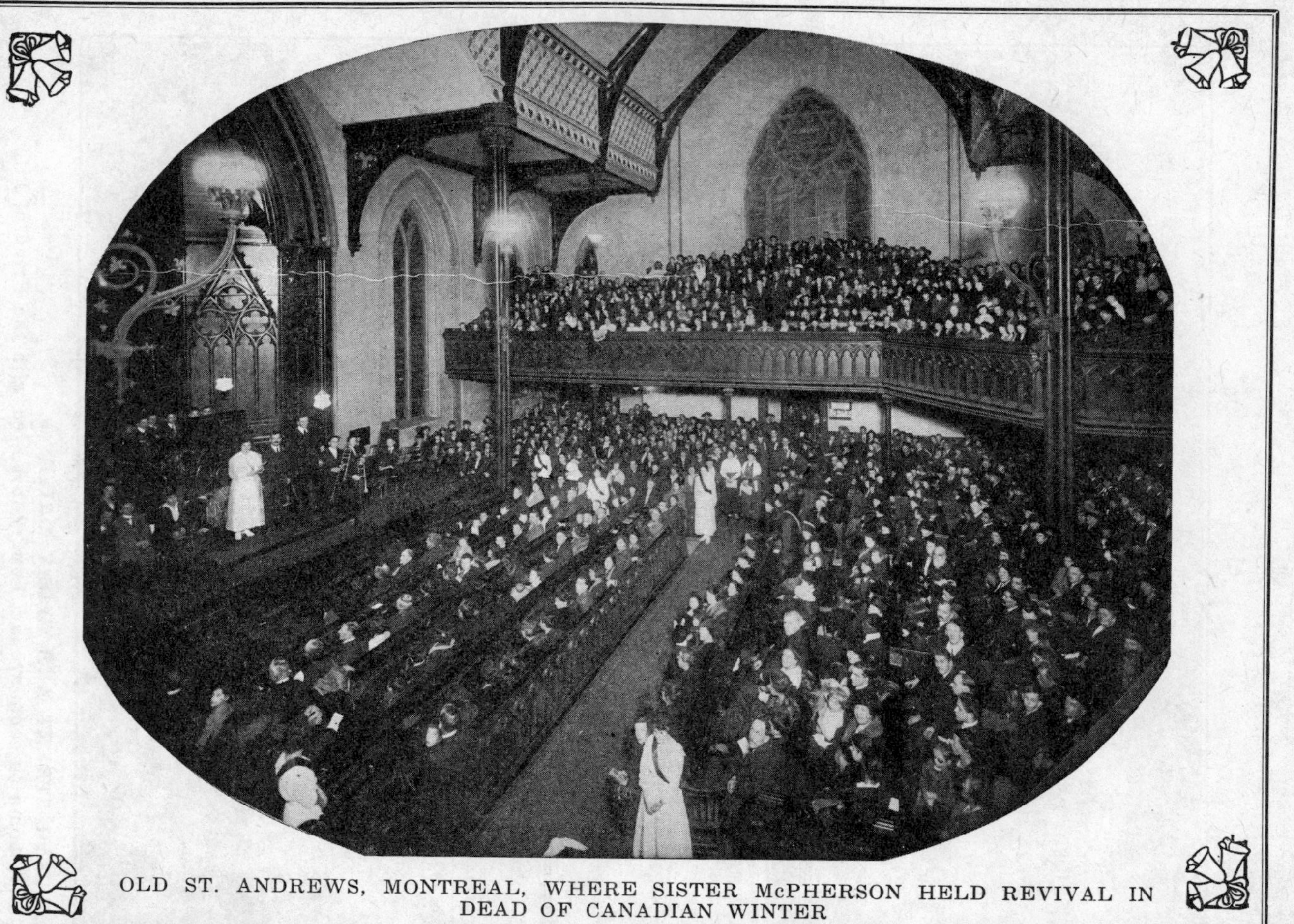

OLD ST. ANDREWS, MONTREAL, WHERE SISTER McPHERSON HELD REVIVAL IN DEAD OF CANADIAN WINTER

kitchen, the most peculiar sensation came over me, and I swayed as though I would fall. I caught the table for support two or three times and said to myself, 'Why, what's the matter? I'm not sick!' Then I realized that this was the power of God resting upon me and I made my way upstairs to pray. My little son was sleeping in my room so, not to disturb him, I went into your room and kneeled by your bed. Longing to be alone in the quiet with my Lord, I did not even stop to turn on the lights but dropped on my knees with my hands clasped and my arms across the bed. I had kneeled in this way but a moment, praying, when the power of God fell upon me and lifted my arms high above my head in praise. The whole room seemed to be flooded with a bright light and I fell over on the bed, then slipped off on your suitcase and then to the floor. I was just prostrated beneath His power, and quietly and gently my hands began to shake beneath His power. Oh, I have had a wonderful blessing and know that He will baptize me."

Next day when the power of the Lord fell upon her in the very same room, our dear sister was waiting upon the Lord. For many hours she lay under the power of God, and a most wonderful vision of the hill leading to heaven was given her. She saw the streets of gold, the gates of pearl and the throne of God. Even her little daughter Evelyn who, like a rosebud, had been transplanted in heaven's gardens, came before her in vision and prayer. So enraptured with heaven was she that she begged to remain, but the Lord said, "No, my child, go back and bring others with you."

"Then, if I must return, Lord," she cried, "fill me with the Holy Spirit that I may have power to lead them to your feet; baptize me now;" and was immediately filled with the Spirit and began to speak with other tongues as the Spirit gave her utterance. Hearing his wife's voice lifted in praise and prayer, Rev. Leech had mounted the stairs two steps at a time, and now kneeled by the bedside praying and praising the Lord.

That night, when he had retired to his own room, the power of the Holy Ghost fell upon this dear pastor—the most unemotional of men—and for twenty-four hours the Lord held him in the grip of His power and would not let him go. The next morning after Sister Leech had received her baptism, the writer was awakened from sleep, and with a start realized that some one had entered the room and was shaking her gently by the shoulder and calling her by name. Springing up, in the dim light, she recognized the form of Sister Leech. 'Twas not yet daylight,—what could be the matter?

"Please do come, Mr. Leech has been under the power of the Spirit all night, the bed is shaking with his tremblings; he is weeping and praying. I have not been able to sleep and wish you would come in and pray for him."

"Why, dearie, I do not think it will be necessary for me to go in, Jesus is the baptizer. I will stay here and pray." Praising the Lord for His goodness and praying that He might have His way with this dear man of God, the sleep of exhaustion soon claimed me again, however, for the days had been long and the night meetings had been very late, running usually to the "we sma' " hours. At 8:30 the Sister again called me to come. Hallelujah! our Brother was lost in wonder love and praise, and lay trembling from head to foot as waves of blessing swept over him as the billows over the sea. Cooking and housework and dinner were forgotten. Numbers of his congregation and chosen friends came tip-toeing up the stairs to peep in the door and bow weeping in the hallway in silent prayer. At nine o'clock the following morning, after wonderful revelations of Calvary and the burden for lost souls in Baltimore had been given him by God, Rev. Leech received the baptism of the Holy Ghost and began to praise the Lord in a new language as the spirit gave utterance.

Then, oh then, the power of the Lord fell. In spite of sleet and snow, the church was packed every day and night. In the back of the church, out in the lobbies, out on the stairs, in the aisles and clear to the street they stood. During the first week over one hundred men and women came to the altar seeking salvation, the number of converts increased steadily throughout the entire campaign, filling the chancel rail again and again, within and without.

Hundreds of church members seeing the power demonstrated in miracles of healing, became very hungry to be filled with the Holy Ghost. After a week of glorious revival in the church of Dr. H——, where many had been saved and several blessedly baptised with the Spirit, we returned to Franklin Memorial Church for the second week. After the Sunday morning service, a meeting for personal workers was called in the Sunday School room. A company of about fifty, being the choicest and most spiritual workers, gathered to organize a "Fishers" and "Altar-Workers" Band in order to have the very finest co-operation and draw the nets to shore.

When meeting was dismissed, no one seemed to want to go home, and all expressed their need of power. Suddenly a splendidly dressed, middle-aged lady fell beneath the mighty power of God, and in a moment was blessedly filled with the Spirit. No sooner had we turned to rejoice with her than another lady went down on the opposite side of the room, and lay under the power in one of the pews. Then God's power struck one of the official men and down he went, sobbing and pouring out his heart to God. In a few minutes he was blessedly baptised. Waves of glory rolled over him till he shouted aloud and began to speak as the Spirit gave him utterance.

What an afternoon we had! Sunday dinners were forgotten; people ran home to bring their loved ones to see the glorious power of God, and rejoice with them that the Holy Spirit had so honored their church, many were sweetly filled with the Holy Ghost. Hallelujah!

Hearing of the blessings received by the number who had tarried at the close of the morning service, the congregation became very hungry. Many requested an opportunity to wait before the Lord for His precious gift.

"Perhaps we can have a little prayer meeting after the service tonight," it was suggested.

"Shall we have it at the altar?" asked the Pastor, his own face aglow.

"No, experience of years has taught us that when a company of people wait before God for the baptism of the Holy Spirit, they should enter the 'Holy of Holies,' and with one accord in one place. This is too sacred and wonderful an experience for the gaze of the curious throng."

"Let us take them into the parsonage," suggested Mrs. Leech. "It adjoins the S. S. rooms, and we can walk from the church right into the house."

"Besides there will probably be no more than about seven or eight," added the Pastor.

After the night evangelistic meeting, in which many sinners and backsliders wept their way home to Jesus, the Pastor announced that any who desired to seek the deepening of the Spiritual life, and the baptism of the Holy Spirit might make their way to the parsonage immediately.

THE CONGREGATION STAMPEDES

Then Brother and Sister Leech, Mother and myself exchanged amazed glances and gasped with alarm, for it seemed as though almost the entire congregation of about fifteen hundred rose to their feet at the same time and filled the aisles leading to the parsonage door, many weeping and shouting, each trying to get there before the other.

The pretty little parsonage was like a doll's house, but every inch of space was put into service from parlor to kitchen. And still they came, until there was a blockade at the door, and the balance of the congregation moving in that direction. We dismissed the meeting as formally as was possible under the circumstances and stood on the outer edge of the crowd endeavoring to get into the parsonage. This was for some time an impossibility. But the people were in, at least scores and scores of them, and from the sounds of singing, prayer and rejoicing the Lord was certainly in.

At last, panting, but happy, I squeezed through the crowd yet outside, and oh! such a sight as met my eyes! There was scarcely a place to put one's foot; so tightly packed were the kneeling supplicants. I remember one lady was by the door which bumped her repeatedly as it was opened by people peering anxiously in to see if there was room for at least one more. The sister's eyes were closed, her hands upraised, and she seemed utterly indifferent and even unaware of any annoyance.

"Wh-wh-what shall we do?" gasped Mrs. Leech, as the people continued to press in. The people themselves solved the problem by moving the dining table to the wall and piling the other furniture upon it; and again crowding over, making room for more, till they were packed in like sardines.

And such praying! Mrs. Leech tells us that up to this time she had been obliged to write sentence prayers for her class, in order to have them pray audibly at all, and even this had been accomplished with great difficulty. Many had said they were perfectly willing to support the church, but begged not to be asked to take any active part in the service. But now they were started, and, like a dam that had broken from its boundary, allowing the great flood-tides of swollen, pent-up waters to sweep on and out, so did their prayers and adoration rise to God.

Seeing one lady kneeling almost tight against the gas radiator, trying to shield her burning face behind her hands, Sister Leech made her way to the woman and whispered: "Why, my dear! Aren't you very hot there?" Without stopping to look up the woman replied:

"Oh, I am roasting!" and went right on praying, "Lord, fill me with Thy Holy Spirit," and He did, praise His Name!

Was ever such a scene, in heaven or on earth? In the kitchen, hall, dining-room and parlor they were swept down beneath the mighty power of God. Outside, the crowds were standing, repeatedly sending in word that they were still waiting, and that as soon as those inside had received the baptism of the Holy Spirit, they did wish that they would come out so that they could enter and get their portion.

Was ever a house so filled to overflowing at prayer meeting as that parsonage! Even the stairs were filled with kneeling people, calling upon the Lord. One man fell under the power and came rolling down the steps. The others gave him but a brief glance and went right on with their own praying.

So great was the demand and hunger that it was decided to set apart certain days for waiting meetings where all could meet to "Tarry until." The church was divided at such services, brethren in one section and sisters in the others. Hundreds of supplicants would enter the hushed and sacred precincts of the church and quietly laying aside their wraps, would tiptoe to the altar rail, as though walking upon holy ground and slip down upon their knees, lifting up hungry, earnest hearts toward heaven. Their soft-voiced songs, mingled with the subdued tones of the great pipe organ, praying, "Fill me now, fill me now, fill me with the Holy Spirit, Jesus come and fill me now." Ministers, clergyman, trustees, laymen, Sunday School superintendents and members received the baptism side by side. It is estimated that between one hundred and one hundred and fifty were thus sweetly filled during the campaign. The number of conversions at the night meetings was simply marvelous, and the lasting work, on the same lines, goes on to this day.

JESUS HEALS THE SICK.

Each Tuesday and Thursday of the entire campaign was devoted to Divine Healing, and the sick folks flocked by the hundreds—blind, lame, deaf and dumb, paralytics, rheumatics, consumptives, and those having tumors, cancers, neuritis, palsy, and many other diseases found their way to the church and the altar.

A man wasted and weak with tuberculosis—scarcely able to speak above a whisper—a nervous wreck for many months, was instantly healed at the altar. Leaping to his feet, he shouted the praises of Jesus in a great strong voice, that boomed high above the voices of the people and the pipe organ. Drawing long breaths into the very bottom of his lungs, he clapped his hands and thumped his chest, declaring rapturously that the pain was all gone, and that as a healed man he would live to serve and glorify the Lord.

A deaf and dumb woman—born of deaf and dumb parents, was prayed for and declared she could hear our voices—the organ—singing—and finally, even a whisper! While with her lips she formed her first word in fifty-four years—G-L-O-R-Y !

A woman, whose eyes were blinded by cataracts so that she could not see her own teacup, who had been put on the street cars by a colored lady and guided into the church by the conductor, was touched in answer to prayer. She declared first that she saw a light—secondly, that she could see the electric lighted sign on the wall—*"Jesus saves."* She then read a small sign some forty feet away, next the title on the book, "This is That." After this she read portions from the "Bridal Call," praising the Lord loudly for His wonder-working power.

An elderly colored woman with a paralyzed arm, which had hung useless and dead by her side was instantly healed. In her delight, she swung the arm round and round and waved it high above her head, praising the Lord. So miraculous was her healing that she could pick up heavy articles and lift them the same as with the other hand.

A little boy, about nine years old, who was unable to stand or walk without the use of his brace was prayed for. The brace was removed and he not only walked, but ran and mounted the stairs that led from the chancel rail to the pulpit, and descended them again and again.

A lady was brought into the church leaning heavily upon a cane and an umbrella. She had had a fall some years previous which had injured the base of her brain, rendering her body, especially the limbs, almost useless. After prayer, the power of God struck her—surged through the weakened body—and throwing away her cane she walked alone for the first time in many long months; mounted the steps, descended them, turned her body, weeping and praising God, out of a full and faith-filled heart; and was seen last walking out of the church without the assistance of cane or supporting arm.

Many with crippled hands and limbs declared they could feel the warm blood and trickling life flowing through the disabled parts and soon could be seen moving them, to the delight of their friends and weeping relatives.

A TWENTIETH CENTURY MIRACLE.

Baltimore, Md., Feb. 9, 1920.

To Whom It May Concern: This is to certify that I, Mrs. W. W. Jackson, 906 W. 37th St., Baltimore City, was thrown from a street car on February 3rd, 1919, causing an injury to my back which resulted in a decayed spine.

I was treated by doctors and steadily grew worse. Finally I was given up by the doctor, who said he could not do me any good.

He then sent me to a hospital and had three X-ray pictures taken, which showed that my spine was decayed and holes eaten through it so badly that the doctors had no hopes of my ever getting any better.

They finally concluded to put me in a cast, reaching from my arm pits to my knees. This was done for a sham more than anything else, to keep from telling me how bad I was. I lay flat on my back about sixteen weeks, and no improved results. I thought I had to lie there and waste away till I died. But God sent Sister McPherson to preach to the sinners and heal the sick. I was prayed for and commenced to improve at once. They cut the cast from my limbs. In three days' time I was walking and doing light work about the house. Have been working ever since. Can walk a good long distance now, attend the revival meetings and give HIM all the glory.

MRS. H. W. JACKSON.

Mrs. H. W. J.'s Physician's Confirmations.

Baltimore, Md., Feb. 9, 1920.

I hereby endorse the above statement as correct. So far as medical skill can determine Mrs. Jackson's pelvic bones in the rear of the junction of the spinal column were diseased as proven by X-ray pictures and physical examinations.

S. R. WANTZ, M. D.

WINNIPEG, MANITOBA

Merry sleighbells and cutters were flying in every direction when we stepped off the train in the great metropolis of the Canadian Northwest. We were soon tucked behind warm robes, and snuggling our noses deeper into our collars, were on our way to the hotel. What a busy, worldly, pleasure-seeking city it was! How could the attention of this great throng be arrested and a real city-wide revival be brought about?

In the old Wesley Church we found a company of precious Spirit-filled saints. The church was but half-filled, however, and, questioning, we learned that the thousands of gay young people of the city were not in the habit of attending any church service at all.

"But we must reach them or 'twould not be a city-wide revival."

"But they are not in a habit of coming to church," they replied.

"Well, then, where are they, and we will go to them?" we queried.

"Oh—why—they're in the dance halls, thousands and thousands of them are whirling in the dance this very moment."

"Then, let us go and preach to them in the dance halls."

"But," they gasped, "do you think they will even let you?"

"God is able to open the doors; besides, the newspapers are so with us in Winnipeg that they would hesitate to refuse, lest the papers should say that they were afraid that a woman preacher would steal their crowds. Then, too, while visiting the jail, the other day, praying with the prisoners and leaving Bibles, flowers and literature with them, the Chief told me to call upon him for any service that he could render." Saturday night was set for the great enterprise and with fear and trembling, but much prayer, we started out.

Hearing of our intention, the Chief of Police had bidden us to come to his office. We told him of our decision to visit the notorious red light districts, enter the houses of sin and pray with women and girls and rescue them wherever opportunity afforded.

"Then you certainly do need our police-woman and plain clothes man to go with you.—Oh, I know that the Lord protects you—but our man knows all of these houses on Arabella Street and vicinity and will lead you to them."

This, of course, was too courteous an offer to be refused. We started out, making our calls from house to house, down the illy lighted street. The "plain dress" man giving a peculiar rap on the doors, gained admission for us in places where we could never have set our foot alone.

In our company, there was a lady whom the police-woman introduced as a personal friend. For hours we walked and visited together, first in the houses, then in five of the largest dance halls and, finally, in the cafes until after the midnight hour, before we realized this lady was a reporter from the

Winnipeg Tribune who had been sent to "cover" our expedition through the lines of the enemy. The following clipping was cut from the Tribune next morning:

EVANGELIST PREACHES IN DANCE HALLS.

(By Carolyn Cornell, Winnipeg Tribune)

"Persons who attended the dance halls Saturday night, went home humming a new refrain, one of the favorite campaign songs used in the revival services at the old Wesley Church.

"Through the courtesy of the managers, Mrs. Aimee Semple McPherson was introduced and accorded five minutes to give her message in several of the largest and most popular dance halls of the city last night.

"Two thousand dancers were at the Alhambra. The Evangelist and party arrived at intermission, and were the cause of interested comment as they entered. The balconies and refreshment booths were crowded. After the first dance at the conclusion of the intermission, the little woman in plain street costume went to the front of the stage and was introduced by Vic Joselyn, manager, who bespoke a kindly reception for her.

"Men and women swarmed to the front, forsaking balconies and 'sitting-out' corners. The orchestra was familiar with the campaign hymn, and after singing the chorus with her commandeered audience, the recruiting message was given.

"'Many of you men answered the call of your country for recruits to the King's army a few years ago when the call came for men,' she said. 'Conscription was not needed.'

"'You answered the call because you loved your King, your flag and your country.'

"'I am recruiting for an army—the army of the King of Kings, and the blood-stained banner of the Cross. Will you leave all and join our army?'

"At the close of her appeal Mrs. McPherson distributed tracts, scripture texts, and Bibles. On each occasion when she asked for a show of hands of those who would come to her meetings at the church, she was greeted with enthusiastic response. Without exception the attention given the speaker was respectful, and the managers voiced their respect for the religion of the Evangelist which brought her to the dance hall to tell her story.

"The party also visited certain houses of A-street, where entrance was gained, and the woman missionary spoke with the women in each and had prayer. Tears of penitence were shed by eyes from which no such tears had fallen for many years, when the petitioner besought divine love and forgiveness for the avowed sinner.

"'No one ever asked me to be a Christian before,' one woman said, 'and I know I am one of the sinners.' A testament was left wherever entrance was gained, and tracts and scripture texts and scripture mottoes for the wall at other closed doors.

"The party wound up about midnight at the Venice Cafe, which was crowded with after dance and theater guests, where she again delivered her message, standing between tables in the center of the great restaurant—later distributing literature. Each individual was personally addressed in the booths and at the tables."

THOUSANDS STORM CHURCH FOR ADMISSION.

The results were startling! Throngs immediately besieged the church, until the galleries creaked and groaned; aisles and passageways, doors, stairways and basement were jammed. Multitudes swarmed about the church and street, and were augmented momentarily by loaded street cars which emptied themselves at the door. Unable to cope with the throng of gospel-hungry people, the authorities were forced to turn the cars and crowds aside several blocks away.

If workers, bemoaning empty pews, deserted altars, absence of young people and failure to reach the unchurched people, could have looked into the faces of these people, could have seen the tear-filled eyes, and have rejoiced with us over the full altars containing many a mother's boy and girl who had been last night in dance and revelry, their questions as to how we get the crowds would have been answered. Our Lord's command, "Go ye into the highways and hedges,—compel them to come in that My house may be full," has never failed when one goes forth filled with the Spirit and love for souls.

As for the results of the meeting itself, let Brother A. H. Argue speak:

" . . . It was estimated that nearly 1700 were crowded into the main Auditorium of the church.

"The large basement was turned into a prayer room and seekers and workers would quickly fill it. The altar upstairs also, would fill up night after night with sinners, sometimes two and three rows all across the front, seeking God. It was wonderful to see the old-time conviction rest so mightily upon the people that they would rush to the altar and weep their way to Jesus. It was impossible to keep account of the numbers being saved and coming through to the baptism. One week we tried to get an estimate, and our count ran between forty and fifty who received the Holy Ghost according to Acts 2:4. Numbers saw visions. There were surely marvelous Bible signs in our midst. At the healing meetings one would be reminded of the time Jesus was upon earth, by the way the people thronged to the altar for prayer. Some very remarkable testimonies of healing were given; tumors, ruptures, rheumatism and gall stones being removed; in fact the many various cases of healing were too numerous to mention.

"Sister McPherson made her messages so simple that they were both easily understood and very impressive. Numbers of ministers of various denominations attended, and some received the baptism of the Spirit.

"The community has been stirred as never before by any other single spiritual effort in our city.

"Sister McPherson was untiring in her ministry, not sparing herself, holding meetings in railroad shops, visiting jails, poolrooms, and the largest dance halls in the city, where she was privileged to speak to thousands. Her earnest and sympathetic manner touched many hearts in these various places. The three daily papers took an active interest in her ministry, continually so that Winnipeg and the country surrounding were kept informed as to the progress of the Revival, and received the gist of her message."

IN MCKENDREE M. E. CHURCH, WASHINGTON, D. C.

Ever since the revivals in Baltimore,—Lyric Theatre and

United Brethren Churches—which Dr. Chas. A. Shreve had attended with his official men, he had been besieging Heaven for a spiritual outpouring upon himself and his congregation in the heart of the great city of Washington, and writing us.

Here again, we were entertained in the parsonage, and had the great joy of seeing the pastor, several of his officials and many of his membership and choir receive the baptism of the Holy Spirit, according to Acts 2:4.

Rev. Shreve was baptised with the Holy Ghost in the dining room of the parsonage one morning when, after returning from the meeting about two a. m. the power of the Lord came down upon him. From two till seven a. m. he lay beneath the mighty power of God and the Spirit announcing His incoming in his own inimitable way and language—just as the day was breaking. From the date of that great revival, McKendree M. E. Church has been on fire for God and has had a continuous revival. As to the conversions and healings in this meeting, we will let you see it through several clippings from various papers.

A REVIVAL WITH POWER

(From the "Methodist," April 29, 1920)

On Sunday came the closing special service of the most remarkable revival ever seen in McKendree, Charles A. Shreve, pastor, and, according to many old residents, the most powerful outpouring of God's Spirit ever known in the history of Washington. For three weeks the power of God swept the place. Christians were stirred as never before, and sinners came flocking home to God in penitence and tears.

Great crowds thronged the church at every service. During the last two weeks an overflow meeting was held downstairs every night. Both upstairs and down every corner was packed, and even then multitudes were turned away for lack of standing room. It was a common thing for the pastor and other workers to have to climb through a back window to reach the platform.

The altar was always crowded with earnest seekers after God. Many Christians were filled with the Holy Spirit, and about three hundred persons were converted. Great joy filled the hearts of the Christians as the big waves of God's glory rolled in. There was shouting and singing, and weeping. Many strong men and women were prostrated under the power of God (a number of these were persons who had been rather skeptical as to the present day working of the supernatural power of God), and some were swept by gales of holy laughter (and spake with other tongues).

Mrs. McPherson preached the Gospel in the power and demonstration of the Spirit, exhibiting a beautiful combination of faith and love and spiritual understanding of the Word of God. The driving method sometimes used by evangelists is entirely absent in her procedure, but the presence and charm of the Holy Spirit is manifest in her words and actions. The result is: God honors her simple trust in Him and sends His blessing upon her work.

Two services were held for the healing of the sick, and a large number of people were greatly helped. Many were definitely healed by Power Divine. Several cripples went away walking, and returned to bear witness of their deliverance.

On April 11, 60 persons were received into the church and 12 persons were converted in the evening service. On last Sunday, April 25th, 19 were received into the church and 13 were converted at the altar. Large crowds are attending all the services, and there is a keenness of spiritual interest which nothing can produce save a manifested presence and power of God.

The blessings attending this revival, we are glad to say, have not been confined to the local church, but the fire has spread to many sections of the city. People have been coming from all directions, and have in a large number of cases gone back with a new note of appreciation to God for the fact that He is still "Mighty to save and strong to deliver."

CHAS. A. SHREVE, Pastor.

A REMARKABLE REVIVAL

(From the "Gospel Mission Tidings" May 1920)

A most remarkable revival has just closed at McKendree Methodist Church, Rev. Charles A. Shreve, pastor. The services were for the conversion of sinners and a deeper work of grace among believers, and hundreds were converted and many believers received a real Pentecostal Baptism of the Holy Spirit. During the second week healing services were announced. From this time the church was not large enough to hold half the people; hundreds of crippled and sick besieged the doors many hours before the hour for services arrived.

The sick, deformed, blind, deaf, dumb, paralytic, and all manner of sufferers thronged the altar, in relays of thirty at a time. Some of these services were of five hours' duration, and on April 8 two were being held simultaneously, one in the church auditorium, another in the large Sunday School room. It is estimated 800 or more sick were ministered to on this date.

Then strange and wonderful things happened. Among the many healed that came under my personal observation was a case of a woman deaf for forty years, whose hearing was instantaneously restored; another, a paralytic, who had not walked for eight years, walked five times around the church, and when leaving, declared she intended to walk six blocks to get the street car to go to her home in a distant part of town. The last I saw of her she was going down the church stairs. This woman came in a taxi cab, was carried into the church like a bag of meal on the back of a husky man. A blind man rose to his feet and commenced to count and admire the beautiful church windows as vision gradually was being restored to his blind eyes.

A dozen or more of our mission clientele were healed and blessed, among whom was Nicholas Berezoski, twelve years old. For years he has been coming to the Mission, dragging his poor little body in a brace that seemed to barely hold him intact, a victim of the so dreaded infantile paralysis. Eight long years little Nick lived in this cage of steel. Laying her hands upon him, Mrs. McPherson exclaimed, "In the name of Jesus you shall be healed." "Gee, I can walk, and without holding my knee," and "I do feel so fine; let me see how far I can walk," and lo and behold, up and down the aisle walked our little Nick. "Ha'int you goin' to take my brace off," anxiously inquired our little friend. "Of course we will, if you feel that way," responded the evangelist, and a dressing room was formed by a human wall of women in the amen corner; little Nick was stripped and loosed from the steel bands, and, liberated, he walked again, to the joy of the multitude. "I never want that brace on me again," he fairly shouted, as he struck out for home, where his Russian mother fairly shrieked for joy as she rushed to the neighbors and told of the marvelous thing God had done for little Nick.

The effect upon his associates, the healing of this little boy, has been wonderful. He calls on us frequently to inform us he is growing stronger every day.

CRIPPLED AND DISABLED HEALED BY PRAYER

(The Washington Times, April 9, 1920)

Twelve hundred heads were bowed in prayer in the McKendree Methodist Episcopal Church yesterday afternoon. At the altar among scores of others, kneeled Miss Emily Kruger, an invalid since birth. The entire gathering united in praying to God to heal this woman. Suddenly a hush swept over the church. Praying stopped. Mrs. McPherson was looking upward. The invalid hopefully, with outstretched arms, was watching her. And then—

"In the name of the Lord Jesus Christ, you shall walk. Rise, and you shall be healed."

Walks Without Aid

The woman, hesitatingly, rose from her knees; she cast a swift glance about, as if bewildered and in a trance. She looked forward, then started out. One step,—two—three—four, then on and on to the end of the aisle. She turned and continued walking—up the aisle once, back up again, back again and on and on until she, unassisted, had paced the narrow aisle, six times. Then overcome she took a seat.

"It's wonderful," she murmured. "I have never done this before, I could only walk a few steps without help. God has cured me! Let me try again!" And the woman walked and walked. The crowd in the church, most of them sick, crippled and deformed, looked on bewildered. The woman for the first time in her life had strength to walk unaided. Friends had told her of Mrs. McPherson's belief that if one's faith in God were great enough he would be cured. Physicians had failed to heal her and she had decided to attend the service and pray earnestly to God for her recovery.

There was another woman who entered the church, deaf. She approached the altar and prayed to God. While Mrs. McPherson was kneeling and praying over her she suddenly heard. This woman told her story of being instantaneously cured of deafness.

It was the first time in twelve years she had been able to hear anything lower than a shout. Now she could even hear whispering.

It was these persons that "The Times" reporter saw and talked to. The reporter watched the entire services. There were many others who declared they were helped. One little girl, paralyzed in her left arm and unable to move it, was instantaneously cured.

The sight in that church yesterday, once seen will never be forgotten. There were the young and the old, the deformed children, the paralytic children, many persons with limbs bent and twisted, many deaf and blind, and several with St. Vitas' Dance.

There was some confusion at first; more than 500 persons wanted to go at once, but arrangement was made whereby some thirty persons gathered at the altar at one time. They were anointed with oil and told that with faith in God, their ills would be cured.

It was after the healing service was in progress for more than 15 minutes that a woman cried out:

"My God! Look at my son! He walks, his limp is almost gone. I thank God!" The woman began crying, and gathered her son in her arms and nearly smothered him with kisses. She put him down and the boy started out into the aisle. He hesitated at first, then walked a little faster and gradually began to run.

"Look, mother, look," he cried out, "see how I can run! Oh, mamma, see! Gee, you're crying, aren't you? but look, mamma, I can run and it doesn't hurt me, either."

Paralyzed many years, he so dragged himself, that at every step he took, one foot would hit the knee of the other. It was so much of a strain to walk that his body always surged backward. But he walked yesterday, his body erect, without exertion on his part.

Colored Woman Healed

Came another woman, colored, whose entire left side was paralyzed. She had little use of either her hand or leg. She was anointed and prayed for and, "In the name of Jesus," she was told to use her limb freely.

The colored woman, hesitatingly at first, began to walk. Then she hurried and then she danced.

"Praise the Lord, praise the Lord!" she cried out and for more than two minutes she danced and waved her hands in the air.

The colored woman—sixty-seven years old, had been paralyzed for more than fifteen years.

(Washington "Times," Monday Evening, April 12)

Long before 8 o'clock yesterday morning a crowd gathered in front of the church. Automobiles filled the streets nearby and it was necessary to call the policeman to direct the traffic in the neighborhood. Cripples came, carried in arms or in rolling chairs, the sick came leaning on the arms of friends and relatives.

By 9 o'clock there were close to 2,000 people in front of the church. Half an hour later the doors were thrown open and at 10 o'clock more than 1,200 had crowded into the upstairs. The downstairs service room was then opened, and by 10:30 it was crowded to capacity. Hundreds who reached the church after 10 o'clock were disappointed, it being impossible to accommodate them.

Blind Man Regains Sight

At 12:30 the regular services were concluded. Crowded with sick and crippled the church presented a pitiful picture. So touched was Mrs. McPherson with the requests of the afflicted that a "healing service" be held that she asked the sick and crippled to remain and be prayed for.

Many ill with internal troubles declared they were cured.

An interesting feature of the services occurred when a blind man, with one eye gone and the other covered with a cataract, his sight lost entirely, was prayed over, and in a few minutes declared he could distinguish the white garments of the leader. He then looked about the room, counted the windows on the wall, and took great delight in admiring the stained windows of the church.

"Thank God, I am well. I can see," he called out when sight was first restored.

Many aged and helpless cripples were carried to the altar in a pitiful condition. Mrs. McPherson prayed and offered sympathy to each one personally. There were several persons who had come hundreds of miles to be prayed for.

Mute Hears and Talks

Saturday a student of the Columbia Institution for the Deaf and Dumb in this city came to the McKendree parsonage. He asked for the Evangelist. But she was out. He then asked to be prayed over, and several members of the church gathered about him and prayed. Mrs. McPherson joined them a short time later.

For more than an hour they prayed to God that he might speak and hear. Gradually his voice came back to him. He mumbled unintelligible words. Then his utterance became clearer. He repeated, "In the Name of Jesus," several times and before leaving learned to say other words. His hearing, however, was not helped.

Yesterday he came to the church and attended the healing service. He kneeled at the altar to pray for the restoration of his hearing. Mrs. McPherson knelt with him and prayed. Several minutes later he was left alone, praying. Suddenly the boy looked up, glanced about. The evangelist saw a peculiar look upon his face.

"In the name of Jesus are you hearing?" she called to him. He looked at her for a second, then nodded.

"Has God healed you?" she asked.

"Yes," he answered. Other questions were asked. He answered.

When he left the church he was able to talk and hear, the first time since early childhood. The student returned that night to the services and continued praying, this time giving thanks to God for his wonderful recovery.

Church Crowded at Night

The afternoon services were ended at 3 o'clock. Shortly after 5 o'clock the crowd began gathering for the night services. There were more crippled and sick. The crowd was very patient and orderly and seemed content to wait many hours for the church to open. By 5 o'clock several thousand men and women had gathered in front of the church. There were more than twenty wheel chairs, carrying cripples.

The doors were opened at 6 o'clock and by 6:15 the church was crowded upstairs and down. More than 2,000 men, women and children were successful in gaining admittance. Men and women connected with the church then started singing and kept this up until the appearance of Mrs. McPherson. The crowd was so great that for her to preach both upstairs and down became necessary.

400 Seek Aid

At 8 o'clock services began upstairs, and continued until 10:30. So numerous were the crippled and sick in the church that Mrs. McPherson was asked to remain and pray for them. She consented and when the crowd cleared out of the room 400 crippled and sick remained to be healed.

For each one individually Mrs. McPherson prayed and spoke a word of cheer. There were many sick with internal trouble and numbers of them declared they had been instantly cured.

"As God healed when He was on earth, so will He heal now that He is gone," the leader told the afflicted. "God loves to do things now that He did when He was on earth. Have faith in Him. It is He alone who will cure you. God is with us tonight and we pray that He will help those gathered about here."

In the arms of several friends, Stella Blanchard, of the Stratford Hotel, was brought to the altar. For eight years she had not stood on her feet. Mrs. McPherson stood over her at the altar, prayed and anointed her with oil.

Crippled Woman Walks

"Oh God, heal this afflicted woman," she prayed. "You can make her whole and you will. We have faith that you will heal this woman." And for more than ten minutes they both prayed. Suddenly Mrs. McPherson stopped her praying. Her silence brought a stop to all other praying and singing in the church.

"In the name of Jesus Christ, I command you to walk. You are healed," she called out.

The woman rose to her feet. She steadied herself and began walking, slowly at first; then, step by step her strength was regained. It was the first time she had walked in eight years, in fact the first time she had stood on her feet alone. Mrs. McPherson offered to help her along.

"No, no, I can walk," she said. "Oh, please let me try." The woman continued and circled the church several times. Then she rested. A few minutes later she rose again, and this time, unassisted, walked about the church five times. When she left she walked to the street cars.

All Night Service

The services were not concluded until nearly 2 o'clock this morning. Mrs. McPherson, after praying for the last cripple and sick person, went into the parsonage and early this morning, before she arose there were many men and women gathered in front of the parsonage waiting for her to come.

ONE DAY AT MEMORIAL HALL, DAYTON, OHIO

Christ's healing of the sick today is so practical, tangible, undeniable, that it arrests the attention, sets whole cities talking of Jesus and draws multitudes as nothing else could do.

It is doubtful whether such scenes as we witnessed in Dayton could ever be forgotten. How I wish that everyone of my readers could have been there in person. Its memory would have ever been cherished as something sacred and inspiring. If you will come with me, walk along by my side, I will try to show it to you through my eyes and my memory as I write.

It is one of the closing Divine Healing Service days. Leaving our apartment at the hotel by auto, we are almost unprepared for the throngs that are to greet us. As we turn the corner, two blocks from the hall, the streets are filled with people. All are hurrying in one direction. A quiet excitement, an earnestness, and a something akin to awe can be felt in the very air.

Street cars, autos, ambulances, even hearses, pressed into service, are being unloaded. Sick are being brought in wheel chairs, on cots and stretchers, carried in the arms or on the backs of strong men. Cripples are carried bodily in rocking chairs. Men, women and children, leaning on crutches and canes, are crossing the streets, as policemen hold up the traffic. Many there are with arms, limbs or heads swathed in bandages.

"Oh God! Oh God," we moan. "Is the whole world sick? Are they all coming to Memorial Hall, to Thee for healing?"

Then we reach the hall itself. The doors are locked because of the press within. Kindly police and firemen are struggling to cope with the hopelessly jammed multitudes that surge 'round and 'round the building.

THRONGS UNABLE TO GAIN ADMISSION.

The stronger are pleading for the weak.

"Oh! We must get them in. We know they will be saved and healed if we can just get them inside."

Our car draws up at the side entrance. It is surrounded instantly. Clutching hands are stretched out everywhere.

"Oh, lady! Pray for me. Oh! Lay your hands on this man and pray just for a moment," or

"We have brought this child forty miles, surely you can let us in."

We are bewildered. What will we say? What will we do? 'Twould be impossible to do aught in this multitude. The weak ones and the children would be trampled under foot; besides, the great throng waits within.

There—a half-dozen policemen have cleared a space from the car to the side of the door. Tears stand in the eyes of these big, kindly men. Their voices are husky. Perspiration stands in beads upon their faces, as they hold back the pleading souls who reach above and under their arms in hopes of even touching us as we pass.

At a given signal an officer from within partially opens the door. We are hastily drawn within. The door closes. The lock snaps shut, but not in time to shut out the great sighing moan that has gone up from thousands of disappointed hearts, who realize at last that they are shut outside.

Within the lobby order and quiet prevail. The policeman is wiping his forehead.

"Oh, officer, isn't there room for a few more sufferers—just a few more?" we timidly ask.

"No, Sister, sorry, but we have far more in the building now than our fire regulations allow. Such a pitiful mass of humanity I never did see. 'Twould break the heart of a stone, it would!"

Entering thus by the side door, or carriage entrance, we catch a glimpse of the great basement. 'Tis filled with people, invalids, cripples, wheelchairs and comforting relatives standing by. Oh the dumb, pleading agony in their eyes, the outreaching hands! Will we ever forget that sight?

Police officers and ushers alike, touched with pity, are taking names on memorandum cards, and recording the worst cases, in hopes that if the hundreds upstairs are prayed for in time, those waiting patiently below can be carried above. Guards stand by the basement windows. Dozens of faces are pressed flat against the panes, looking in.

"We had to lock them, sister. They were passing the sick through the windows," some one exclaims.

Dazed, as though in a dream, we press on, and climb the stairs to the auditorium above. Through the open doors we catch a glimpse of the vast throng, as we make our way to the ladies' cloak room. It is situated to the right of the stage. Here some two score women are kneeling in earnest prayer, before entering the seats reserved for the choir on the stage. To the left in a corresponding room for men, we know that a similar company of brethren are bowed before the Lord.

Laying aside our wraps, we too, sink to our knees a moment in silent prayer; then tiptoe to the stage entrance, to see that all is in readiness.

Yes, quietly, efficiently, the nineteen special lady ushers with wide sashes of crimson ribbon, can be seen moving through the audience, under the direction of my mother, cheering and comforting the sufferers. Not a seat is vacant. Gallery and auditorium are packed to overflowing. Scores are standing at the rear. Seven hundred or more seats have been roped off across the front for the sick and afflicted. All are in their places. The entire altar space is filled with wheel chairs and rockers, cots and stretchers.

In spite of the press, there is little, if any confusion. Printed cards have been filled out, showing the name, church, disease and faith of each sufferer. These cards also state whether said sufferer is a Christian or is willing to become one this day; and whether healed or not, they will dedicate the balance of their lives to the service of Christ.

Each card is numbered, in the order in which distributed, so that the strong cannot press past the weak, the deformed, and the mothers with little children. All will have an equal opportunity and come in the order of their numbers, as shown upon the blackboard on the stage.

OPENING TIME.

A hasty glance at our watch—opening time has come. The grand piano in the center of the stage is opened. Brother Baur is already at his place. Under his light, reverent touch upon the ivory keyboard, a soft flood of melody flows out into the vast hall, like a burst of mellow sunlight. He is playing:

"Sweet hour of prayer, sweet hour of prayer
That calls me from a world of care;
And bids me at my Father's Throne,
Make all my wants and wishes known."

Both sections of the choir have now risen from their knees, and are standing in line, single file, each in his or her place, corresponding with their chair number. Each company has a captain; at a given signal from the musical director, Brother White, they file in softly, in perfect order and again sink to their knees in silent prayer.

"In seasons of distress and grief,
My soul has often found relief,"

Continues the welling notes of the piano:

"And oft escaped the tempter's snare,
By thy return, sweet hour of prayer."

Quietly, we slip into our places in the front row, reserved for ministers and workers. Pastors from the Methodist, Baptist, United Brethren and Christian Missionary Alliance, are there before us. We feel we are on holy ground. The very atmosphere is filled with a heart-cry of dire need, and an earnest faith, too deep to be clothed with mere words. Prayer is being breathed up. It wings its way to the very throne of God.

Looking up into the high, arched dome of the Memorial Hall, with the soft rays of light streaming through the upper windows, we feel as though a multitude of angels were silently filling the place. And the pitying face of the down-bending Christ is moved with compassion, as He looks again upon such a scene as He witnessed two thousand years ago upon the shores of Galilee.

We sink to our knees with the choir, and find ourselves praying softly, desperately as we have seldom prayed before:

"O Thou Christ of God—Thou compassionate Man of Calvary—Thou omnipotent Almighty King of Heaven and earth, Thou Sun, Who dispels all darkness, Thou Lion of Judah, Who breaks every chain, Thou Deliverer of the captive. Thou Hope of the hopeless, and Friend of the friendless, Thou Son of the Living God, if ever we loved Thee, needed Thee, trusted Thee it is now. Weak, helpless, desperate, we hide, hide away in Thee."

"O rise up! Rise up, dear Son of Righteousness, with healing in Thy wings. Lay bare Thy mighty arms, and glorify Thy name."

Wildly, our hearts throb up to Him in prayer. Sweetly the gentle calm of His Spirit falls o'er us like a mantle from the sky. The benediction of the Lord is resting upon our heads.

SONG AND PRAYER.

With a start we realize that the choir and ministers have risen. They are singing gently, thoughtfully. The whole of that vast audience catches up the refrain:

"What a friend we have in Jesus,
All our griefs and sins to bear.
What a privilege to carry,
Everything to God in prayer.
Oh, what peace we often forfeit,
Oh, what needless pain we bear,
All because we do not carry,
Everything to God—"

We rise to assist in the leading of the song. The spirit of God settles down more and more, like the cloud of His Presence. Hundreds are melted; strong men frankly weeping. Hard hearts have become a fountain of tears in the presence of Christ. How insignificant and puny the greatest affairs of the outside world seem in the light of His glory!

"Are you weary, are you heavy laden,
Tell it to Jesus, tell it to Jesus.
Are you grieving—"

continues the great choir. 'Tis caught up everywhere. Everyone is singing softly, from the pale face boy wrapped in blankets and propped up by pillows upon his cot, to the highest seat in the gallery. How sweet are their voices. Hark! 'Tis as though the angels of Heaven were joining in the chorus.

"You have no other
Such a friend and brother,
Tell it to Jesus alone."

And now, the thousands of heads are bowed in prayer. The Spirit prays through us as we lead them to the throne:

"O Thou Lamb of God, whose ear is ever open to our cry. Thou tender, loving Jesus, whose heart is ever yearning o'er thy little ones, fix every eye upon Thyself today. As the moon and the stars withdraw their shining before the sun at noonday, let earthly cares and hindrances pale and disappear before the glory of Thy power and presence. Stretch out Thine arms, our Father, and enfold this quivering, throbbing, suffering multitude unto Thy breast. Dry every tear, banish every pain, relieve the oppressed, heal Thou the sick and forgive the sinner every sin. Draw us up close, O close, Thou Son of God. As a Father pitieth his children, so Thou dost pity those that love and trust Thee. Give light in place of darkness. Give hope in place of fear. Give comfort, and sweet confidence to each heart gathered in Thy presence, for Thine own name's sake. Amen."

THE TESTIMONY MEETING

Song and prayer now over, a brief testimony meeting is opened. One by one eager witnesses rise in the gallery, stage and auditorium.

"O how I praise Jesus, for what He has done for me," rings a clear voice. "Last Thursday I came to this auditorium sick and sinful. For some years I had been suffering with spinal trouble and hip disease. Finally, tuberculosis of the bone set in, destroying the hip socket. O what pain and misery I suffered! But Jesus came and put his arms about me. I kneeled at that altar, and gave Him my heart. He washed my sins away. Then, in answer to prayer, and the laying on of hands, He healed me. My pain is gone, my crutches are gone, my sins and burdens are gone. I am happy, O so happy! And I grow stronger every hour."

A shower of hand clapping and "hallelujahs" fall upon our ears. Many of her friends are here. They know her and are so happy over the miracle wrought in her life.

"Let them see you walk. Stand up and walk," someone says. In a moment this dear woman with beaming face is up and walking swiftly toward us, hands lifted in praise, upturned face glowing, radiant. She reaches the steps, runs lightly up, grips our hands, is down again in her seat in a moment, amidst a roar of praise and joyful hand clapping.

But Hark! A clear voice is ringing out from the gallery.

"Saved and healed, bless the good Lord. Two weeks ago I came to this meeting. Jesus met me in saving and healing power. I had a complication of diseases and was tortured with pain from a cancer under this arm.

"I had been operated on once, but it grew again. I could not lift my hand to my head. Arm was growing fast to my side. But, in answer to prayer, Jesus instantly healed me! See me lift it now!"

Suiting the action to the word, she swings it 'round and 'round and lifts it high above her head.

"Glory to God! Glory to God! I know her, she lives right next to our house. It's all true," comes a chorus of voices, midst the ringing hallelujahs.

"I, too, must praise the Lord for salvation and healing. For four and a half years I had suffered with paralysis from the waist down." A heavy-set man in a quiet business suit is speaking now. "I walked with difficulty, leaning upon two canes. I heard of these meetings; and that Jesus was the same yesterday, today and forever. I came, sought Him as my Saviour and promised to give Him the balance of my days.

"He saved me, washed away my sins, and after three hours waiting in line I was prayed for. I felt the power of God go through my body. New blood and life seemed to circulate through my limbs. I threw aside my canes. Without them I walked, and walked, and, finally ran upon the stage and in the street after I had left the meeting. Jesus had healed even me!"

"Let them see you walk now, Brother."

In a moment the man had made his way to the aisle, ran lightly down it, mounted the steps leading to the stage, praised the Lord before the people, and taken his seat again.

"I, too, have been saved in this meeting, praise the Lord! I have received the blessed baptism of the Holy Spirit and have been healed of gall stones and other troubles. My little daughter, Maxine, has also been healed, and her crossed eyes straightened.

"After she had been prayed for, we went home, so happy. At the supper table my husband, who had come home from work, said, 'Why, Maxine's eyes are perfectly straight!' 'Why of course they are straight; what else could you expect?' The other night I was awakened by hearing my husband singing aloud:

"A little talk with Jesus,
Makes it right—all right."

No sooner has this dear sister taken her seat, than a clean shaven young man steps briskly to the front, mounts the platform and addresses the audience in a clear ringing voice:

"Many of you know me, Gibbons is my name. I am employed in the Ideal Cafeteria, in this city.

"For eleven years I have had a cataract on this eye, shutting out the sight. I came to these meetings, gave my heart to God, was prayed for and believed the Lord to remove the cataract. Look at me now! Both eyes are clear, and well as ever. I can read fine print and see perfectly with what was my poor eye. The cataract has completely disappeared, melted like snow before the sun."

On and on, one after another, they rise and give ringing testimonies concerning the power of God. 'Tis time now for

THE SHORT DIRECT MESSAGE

The people are leaning forward in their seats. Every face is turned expectantly toward the pulpit. Eagerly, they drink in the words we bring them from the sacred page.

"He was wounded for our transgressions. He was bruised for our iniquities; the chastisement of our peace was upon Him, and with His stripes we are healed."

Jesus came to destroy the works of the Devil. On Calvary's Cross He bore not only our sin, but that dire result of sin, sickness.

Whilst on this earth, the chief business in the ministry of our Lord was forgiving sin and healing the sick. The two were not divided; but went hand in hand. They should walk side by side, and know no division today.

Christ is the great physician for body, soul and spirit. It is He *"Who forgiveth our iniquities, and healeth all our diseases."*

When the multitude pressed upon the Lord in those years of long ago, He had compassion on them. His great heart of love yearned over them with tenderest pity. None were too weak, too sinful, too sick or deformed for Jesus to love, cheer, comfort and heal. None were in such darkness but He could bring them light. None so sorrowful and afflicted that He could not bring them happiness and health.

Now, Jesus is the same *yesterday, today and forever!* The things He loved to do when on this earth, He still loves to do today. His heart is still touched with compassion. His power is just the same. His ear is not heavy, nor His arm shortened.

Only one thing hindered the workings of His power, when He walked the shores of Galilee, that thing was unbelief.

God's power knows but one limitation, one boundary today, the boundary of unbelief.

Faith is the key that unlocks the storehouse of His power. Unbelief, the key that closes it, and bars it out. Fix your eyes and faith upon Jesus. Look to the Lamb of God. Draw near to Him just now. Come like the woman of old, saying, "If I may but touch His garment, I shall be whole."

Remember that though we pray for you, and lay our hands upon you, 'tis CHRIST Who heals, and He alone.

There are many here today who need the double cure, healing for the body, salvation for the soul. When Jesus healed the man sick with palsy, He said, "Son, thy sins be forgiven thee; arise and walk." When the people marveled He said unto them, "Why marvel ye? For *whether it is easier to say, 'Thy sins be forgiven thee;' or to say, 'Arise and walk?'"* 'Tis just as easy for the Saviour to say one as the other.

Put first things first. If you intend to take Him as your physician, accept him as your Saviour first. The fountain lies open, the precious blood is still efficacious to cleanse from sin.

Come to Him with your sins, your transgressions, and the burdens of years. Come in the old time way. Come with the simplicity of a litttle child, praying:

"Lord, be merciful to me a sinner. Make me Thy child—be Thou my Saviour. I give Thee this day my body, soul and spirit—my life—my strength—my love—my all." Then come with the golden flush of the new born day shining in your face, come to Him with a pure heart, and clean hands, saying:

"Dear Jesus, you have healed my sin-sick soul, please heal my body too. Not for my sake only, but that I may live and work, and testify for Thee; that I may serve Thee better and lead precious souls unto Thy feet."

And now, dear heart, remember that Jesus sees you. He is looking right down into your heart. He sees your thoughts, your motives and intents.

Be honest with God.
Be honest with me.
Be honest with yourself.

Hundreds of sick and suffering souls, are waiting to receive His healing touch. Let not a moment of this precious hour be wasted. If you are now unsaved, come quickly to Jesus. Rise from your seats—make your way down these aisles, kneel at His feet in heart contrition. Surrender your life. Forsake your sins, then, on believing ground, you can press in to claim His promise

THE ALTAR CALL.

"That's it, Brother! Don't wait a moment."

"Come, Sister, come, Brother, that's right, don't be ashamed of the tears. Come as you are.

"'Here bring your wounded heart—
Here tell your anguish.
Earth has no sorrow,
That Heaven cans't not heal—'

"Ah! Here they come, Jesus—they are coming to you now. O, who could stay away from such a Saviour as Thee! Who could resist such unfathomable love!"

Only thirty seconds have passed since the first sobbing man left his seat, and hurried to the altar. But already the long row, containing some three score seats is full from end to end. The choir is singing softly, almost in a whisper:

"Just as I am without one plea,
But that Thy blood was shed for me—"

The aisles are filling up with men and women sobbing aloud. A second and third row of benches are quickly placed in order by silent, skillful ushers. Devoted Christians, wearing golden ribbon badges, bearing the words, "Personal Worker," are passing in and out among the penitents. Tears—sacred tears, are flowing down and splashing on the chairs. Men and women are doing business with God, for time and eternity. There are few dry eyes in the building. The choir sings on and on, softly, "Take me as I am"—"I believe Jesus Saves"—"Where He Leads Me, I Will Follow."

DIVINE HEALING SERVICE.

Meanwhile, one-half of the stage has been cleared. The choir are all at the right now. Seven chairs are placed on the left side of the platform —the backs partially turned to the audience. A small table, upon which rests a little silver urn of anointing oil, is placed before them. Seven of the lowest numbers are written upon the blackboard. Seven sick folks bearing cards with corresponding numbers, are brought from the audience. They fill these chairs; lifting hearts and hands toward Heaven, they pray as we anoint their heads with oil and place our hands upon them.

"Sister, do you believe that Jesus heals you now?" we ask.

"Brother, do you believe and step out upon His promise now?"

"I do—thank God I know He heals me now! His power flows through me."

"Then in the name of Jesus Christ, rise up and walk!—In Jesus' name, be thou made whole." And now as these are walking and praising the Lord we turn to the next, a lady.

STONE DEAF FOR THIRTY-FIVE YEARS.

"Sister, do you believe that Christ can open these deaf ears, right now?" we write upon her pad.

"I do. I do!"

"Then in the name of Jesus Christ, thou deaf spirit, I command you to come out of her! O, ear be opened, and hear the word of the Lord!

"Sister, rise. In Jesus name, can you hear me now?"

"Yes! O, yes—thank God!"

"Can you hear me *now*—and now—and n-o-w?" We lower our voice to a whisper, but she declares she can hear every word. "What is your name?" we whisper. She answers every question. Her ears have been restored—her joy almost too full to be contained.

"Glory to God! Glory, glory to God! 'Tis the first I've heard in forty years," she sobs.

"Sister dear, we are going to sing for you, how sweet it will sound after all this time."

"Safe in the arms of Jesus,
Safe on His gentle breast—"

With rapt, radiant face she listens, lost in a wonder, love and praise, that is beyond all description.

But we must not waste a moment! See the lines and lines of waiting people. No sooner is one of the seven chairs vacated than it is filled again. On and on they come. The following is a partial list of the diseases prayed for during the afternoon service.

Weakness, spinal trouble, neuritis, kidney trouble, deaf and dumb, hip diseases, varicose veins, disease of the throat, ulceration and paralysis after effects of the flu, meningitis, St. Vitus dance, crippled, loss of voice, cataract of eyes, palsy, afflictions of ear, diabetes, crossed eyes, curvature of the spine, paralysis, rheumatism, nervous diseases, locomotor-ataxia, loss of finger nails, hand and foot disease, broken hand, bronchitis, asthma, heart disease, tumor on arm, deafness, blindness, goiter, tuberculosis, growths on different parts of the body, valvular heart trouble, gall stones, epilepsy, dislocated hip, shell shock, stiff knee, chronic disease, dropsy, cancer and inflammation of the stomach, liver trouble, broken ankle, etc.

Prayer is made for afflictions extending from that of tiny infants, to the most aged soldiers from the military home. Deaf, blind, lame, halt, they walk, hobble or are carried bodily, up the steps of the platform. How many cases of paralysis there are! See here is a woman with no use of one side of her body. She takes her place in one of the chairs. She is praying even before we get to her. Instead of watching us, her eyes are upon the Christ—a good and encouraging sign! Let us go to her quickly—

"Sister, I was once a Christian but have been a backslider for many years. I have consecrated my life to Christ today," she tells us with quivering, but shining face, "and I just know He is going to heal me."

THE LAME WALK.

"Then according to thy faith be it done unto thee. In the name of Jesus Christ, the resurrected Lord, rise up and walk."

Her first act is to lay crutches aside. The next, to struggle to her feet by aid of the chairs—

"Rise and walk, Sister—just forget that limb has ever been paralyzed and dead, your faith has made you whole! Step right out and walk—in—His—name." In a moment she is walking, she leans heavily upon our arm at first; then as life and circulation course through the dead half of her body, she withdraws her hand and starts to walk alone. The choir is singing now, softly, prayerfully,

"My faith looks up to Thee,
Thou Lamb of Calvary, Saviour Divine."

Everyone is praying—the woman is walking better now, more and more rapidly and with greater ease.

"Just step right out, like a little girl again," we encourage—

"Jesus has made you whole."

In a moment the dear soul, taking us literally, is running across the stage, light as a child; descending the steps—mounting them again—waving her once useless arm and lifting heavy articles with it, as she alternately laughs, shouts and weeps. The whole of that vast audience is shouting, clapping and wiping away happy tears.

CURVATURE OF SPINE INSTANTLY HEALED.

A young woman suffering with curvature of the spine is brought to the platform, accompanied by her mother. We anoint her with oil, and pray for her in the name of Jesus Christ. Like a flash from heaven we have a witness that the work is done, and confidently lift her to her feet.

"Where is this curvature in your spine, dear?" we ask gently.

"Right there," she answers, pointing to the spot. We lay our hands upon the spot, but can locate no curvature. It seems to be perfectly straight.

"Where is it now, dear? Put your own hand back and see if you can locate it." Both mother and daughter search in vain for a moment, endeavoring to locate the curvature. They cannot find it. It is gone. They look blankly into one another's faces for a moment—then with a wild cry of delight, the arms of the mother are about the daughter, the daughter's arms about the mother. Their tears are mingling together. Now they are both standing at the front of the stage. The music has stopped. They are testifying, laughing, rejoicing over the work that has been done. How that throng rejoices with them, as they praise the Lord together.

DEAF MUTES SPEAK AND HEAR.

Two young men are prayed for. Attendants give us a brief history of their cases. They have just been saved, and have mighty faith for their healing.

How eagerly they look upon us! Faith fairly radiates from their countenances. Hastily we point up to Jesus, smilingly encouraging them to look up to Him, the one to whom belongs all power in heaven and on earth. They are looking up now too, praying. Suddenly a mighty wave of the Spirit's power sweeps over us. Putting our lips to their ears, we cry—

"In the name of Jesus Christ, thou deaf spirit we command thee to come out of him! Thou dumb spirit—we rebuke thee in Jesus' name, release him and let him go! O ears, we command you to hear the Word of the Lord! O lips and tongue, speak forth His praise!"

'Twas the voice of the Holy Spirit speaking through us. The brief wave of power passes—we open our eyes and question the young men.

"Can you hear me now?"—pointing to our ears.

"Yes, yes!" They are nodding their heads with delight—pointing to their own ears. They look at each other, and rise to their feet, listening a moment—then nodding violently and smiling again.

"Now speak! s-p-e-a-k!" We point to their lips, for having been born deaf and dumb they cannot understand us, even though they hear.

"Try to speak, say, 'Praise the Lord!'"

The singing has stopped entirely now. Even the soft notes of the violin are still. Their lips are moving as they watch us, and listen like a child learning a lesson.

"Praise the Lord!" we repeat, pointing up and smiling. Then the mouth of the first young man opens, his lips are moving—"PRAISE—THE—LORD!" comes in a high, hoarse voice that can be heard clear to the gallery. 'Twas only a squeaky, wavering attempt, but a wave of clapping and amens sweep the place. The choir have lifted up their hands and are praising Jesus, too.

Thus encouraged by hearing his own voice, he tries again.

"PRAISE—THE—LORD!" This time he is more sure of himself, and the voice is better controlled.

"PRAISE—THE—LORD!" he cries again and again.

'Tis too much for the throng to bear and keep their seats! As one man, they rise to their feet, and give vent to the praises of their Saviour in a loud burst of shouting, clapping, weeping, laughing that sweeps out and up like a mighty river, then turns into the channel of song:

"All hail the power of Jesus' name,
Let angels prostrate fall.
Bring forth the royal diadem,
And crown Him Lord of all."

They are waving their handkerchiefs as they sing. What a scene it is! Thousands of white handkerchiefs flutter and wave like heavenly doves on wide-spread pinions, and just to think that the audience is made up of people from almost every creed and faith, Protestants, Catholics and even Jews, exalting the power of the mighty Christ. Those two deaf and dumb young men were made to speak and hear before our eyes by Jesus' wondrous power.

SAMPLE OF THOSE NOT HEALED.

And is everybody healed, at such a meeting? someone may ask. Indeed, no; 'tis only they who come with faith, believing. Here is a man, for instance, with an afflicted limb stretched out before him. Two canes clutched within his hands. Instead of praying, he is watching us, and seeking to protect the painful limb from injury through passersby.

Some way we wonder whether he has faith: that glow is missing from his face. His eyes seem to say, "Well, I will let them pray for me, it might do me some good, and certainly can do me no harm."

"Brother, have you faith that Jesus Christ will heal you; and make you walk whole again, right NOW?"

"Well, I wish He would—I hope He can," is the evasive answer.

"But have you not a living faith, that He WILL make you whole? When we pray, can you not put your faith into the present tense and say 'I believe, He does it now—I take my healing now?' "

"Well, I *hope* He will heal me now, I've certainly suffered enough, God knows."

"Just why are you seeking healing, Brother," we seek to probe his heart's intent.

"Want to be rid of this pain, and to be about again, of course!"

"But is it not for His dear glory?—that you may work and witness for Jesus Christ?"

"Oh y-e-s, of course I'd work for Him"—but ah! the ring of sincerity is missing from his voice and face.

But there, we mustn't hold up the streaming lines of sick folk who wait for prayer. And though we feel his faith is not where we can get results we cannot becomingly refuse prayer for those who come. No mighty stirring of the Spirit now,—the gifts of healing lie dormant.

We pray—ask God to give him faith and healing; but through the prayer he sits there passively with open eyes not troubling to pray or call upon the Lord himself, Oh, if he just had faith the size of a grain of mustard seed—perhaps it will come to him now.

"Now, Brother, we have fulfilled God's Word. If you but believe, you may rise up and walk away, well and strong, and leave those canes behind—rise up in faith right now."

"Oh, lady—I couldn't put my weight on that foot!—It's years since I have walked upon it."

"But, man, we've prayed for you. Do you not believe Christ heals you now? All He requires is faith and a miracle will be wrought"—but no flicker of faith crosses his face or heart. He goes away the same as when he came.

DYING CONSUMPTIVE RAISED UP.

As a contrast to this case, a dying woman was carried to the auditorium. Doctors had predicted that she would not live through the day. "Take me to that meeting," the wasted consumptive had implored in a thin, weak voice. "And I am sure that Christ will heal me." When my attention was drawn to her she was wrapped in blankets and laid out upon the long table in the cloak room at the rear end of the stage. I was shocked at her appearance —face grey as ashes, lips almost black, cheeks fallen in, eyes sunken, scarcely able to draw a breath—sick unto death. What an awful thing for these people to bring her here to die, is our first thought.

"Darling, are you ready to go, if Christ should call you just now? How beautiful it would be to see Jesus; and dwell in the land where sickness and pain never come."

"But I am not going to die! Jesus is going to heal me right now," the young woman whispers weakly. Ashamed of our unbelief and waverings, before this pure, white light of glorious faith, we anoint her with oil, lay hands upon her and lift our hearts in prayer.

In a moment her friends are loosening the blankets. She is sitting up, for the first time in four months.

"I want to walk," she declares. "You don't mind if I get up and walk into the meeting, do you?"

"Why no," we gasp weakly. "Obey the Lord, of course!" Up to her feet she gets, and in her house slippers, pink silk kimono, and loose-sleeve cloak she walks in onto the stage, healed by the Saviour Divine. This same young lady walked to the platform, stood for half an hour, testified, sang and invited sinners to come to the altar, then made her way to the prayer room below; after which she climbed the steps, and drove home in the auto. She attended the closing Sunday afternoon meeting again, testifying to the power of God. Hallelujah!

INFANTILE PARALYSIS HEALED.

Next is a little child—a pretty, winsome little girl, four years of age. She is sitting upon her mother's knee.

"What is the trouble, dear?" we gently ask. The mother's face is bathed in tears—an agony of prayer shakes her frame. "O, it's this arm and leg!—infantile paralysis left this limb so weak that she drags it and has not proper use of it. But Jesus will heal her! I know He will—right now!"

The child is anointed, we kneel in prayer, and lay our hands upon those weakened limbs. Supposing this was our little girl! "O Jesus, come and heal!"—the spirit gives the witness—springing up we bid the mother set the child upon the floor.

No hesitancy here!—the child is walking to and fro across the stage, clinging to her mother's hand. *Walking*, did I say? No, dancing, skipping. Mother is too slow. She looses her hand, and unassisted, runs ahead, bounding, skipping like a playful little lamb; stopping ever and anon to gaze with wide-eyed childish wonder and delight upon the limb now made whole, like unto the other one.

The mother stands like a statue for a moment; then lifts both hands and eyes to Heaven, too full for words. Someone steadies her as she stands swaying, as though about to faint, completely overcome. But joy never kills; and in a moment she is watching again as the little tot dances to the music, then stops and looks at her foot; runs and stops again to lift up the foot and inspect it all over again. Running to the music director, clinging to his fingers, she is dancing up and down to the ringing chorus of "A little talk with Jesus makes it right, all right."

The audience is clapping, and weeping, and laughing all in one again—God bless them!

But we must not stay to watch! Pray on and on, for hundreds are yet feverishly watching the clock—"Will there be time! O will they reach my number?" is the feverish question burning upon their hearts.

"Ah, dear ones," we cry, "do not fix your eyes upon us; but look away to Jesus. 'Tis not we who have the power to heal, it is the Lord. If you but *believe,* He will heal you where you stand,"—and so He did. One woman with a dislocated shoulder, causing intense suffering and sleepless nights, was healed right in her seat. Removing the sling she walked away completely whole.

On and on, on and on, we pray and work. God is working with us; the signs are following. Every now and then someone comes who has no faith and is not healed, but many there are with faith who walk away, new creatures, bless the Lord. The blind receive their sight, the deaf are made to hear, the lame walk, praise the Lord. Among the number might be mentioned—

Mrs. J. J. Fraga, 125 Park Street, crippled for life, healed instantly, ran back and forth on the stage and attended succeeding meetings, praising the Lord.

Mrs. Lurch, confined to her bed for two and a half years, brought in a wheel chair, raised up almost instantly and walked home.

Mrs. Della Hartnum, suffering from gall stones for sixteen years, on her way to the operating table the evening she was healed, brought on a stretcher but raised up to live and glorify the King.

On and on we pray—How hot it seems! How our backs and feet do ache from the long standing! Are we nearly through?

No, there are hundreds more waiting! Whatever will we do? And then what of all those poor cripples waiting so patiently in the basement?

DISAPPOINTED HUNDREDS TURNED AWAY

It is after six o'clock. Evening service is due to begin in one hour and thirty minutes. Our heads are almost swimming, from the hours of constant tension, prayer, sympathy and emotions of joy and victory. We understand what the Master felt, when the Word declares, *"He was weary."*

"You really must stop now, dear. The car is waiting to take you to your room. Throngs are gathered outside for the evening meeting already. The officers are waiting to clear and air the building, before letting in the new crowd." It is the voice of my mother, who with Bro. Gortner and others, are urging us towards the stage exit.

"O don't go until you have prayed for me, and me and me." A chorus of protesting voices cried, "I have waited for hours and hours. Three different days I came and got so near! O, pray—please pray for me." Scores of sufferers who have waited patiently, unmurmuringly, through the long hours, even though many had gotten up from the sick beds to come, break down now. Their faces quiver! They choke with tears. "Oh! Oh! Won't there be time to pray for me?" We reach as many as we can. 'Tis almost seven now. The crowds who have waited so long outside the closed doors are anxious to get in. Workers almost pick us up bodily to get us out of the crowd, and away from the clutching hands.

Oh, dear reader, can you see it with my eyes? Do you see those reaching, clutching hands, and hear the longing cry?

'Twas after just such a mighty healing service that Jesus, gazing upon the multitude, was moved with compassion and cried, *"The harvest truly is plentious; but the laborers are few. Pray ye therefore the Lord of Harvest will send forth laborers."* Matt. 9:35-38. We had never realized that these words were used in connection with the sick before. Perhaps in His human body, even Jesus could not begin to reach them all Himself.

At last, we find ourselves descending the steps to the carriage door again. Officers have cleared a passage way and tucked us in the car. The motor is running, and we are soon under way.

How good the air feels; 'tis like stepping into another world. M-m-m-m-h! How good it feels to be off our feet! But O, just look at the crowds gathered in thousands on the steps, the sidewalks, the streets, waiting for admission. (See picture.)

Some one is waving their hand. Our car is held up! Two men are running, carrying an old lady in a rocker. What is the matter? We open the door—"O Sister, you simply must pray for my mother! We have come so far and waited so long; she has such faith." We stop a moment in the street and pray, other workers gather round. We drive away; but news is brought to us later, that the dear old lady rose from her chair and walked.

We are at the hotel now, and have only a moment to change our saturated, perspiring garments for cool, clean, fresh ones. We wash, eat a hurried bite—

"The phone is ringing!—the car is at the door," calls mother's cheerful voice.

"I tell you we have one crowd tonight, Sister!" exclaims the driver who has called for us. "Doors locked three-quarters of an hour ago, and brethren preaching to an overflow audience on the steps."—I have tried to take you to one meeting; and will not attempt to describe another in detail. Were time and space not at such a premium, there are many other scenes I would long to have you witness, dear, precious reader, far away in homes, on farms, or in the foreign fields. shut out from meetings, such as these.

THE NIGHT'S EVANGELISTIC SERVICE.

The Evangelistic services at night, for instance, where hundreds rose without a moment's hesitance, and wept their way to the altars. They came, not to sign cards, or shake our hands, but to fall upon their knees before Almighty God, and plead the cleansing blood of Jesus as we gave the invitation:

"Jesus is standing here tonight."

"His arms are open—He is calling you by name. He sees, and knows, and understands you. He loves, and wants you. Come with your burdens, your sorrows, your heart-aches, your sins. Come as you are—you've kept Him waiting too long now!

"Come on! Come quick—quick!"—and come they did, from all parts of the building.

Glory! Glory! Glory! 'Tis a sight to make the angels in heaven weep and shout for joy.

Then, saved and radiant, I would have you see them, stand upon their feet and testify, one after another:

"One week ago, I was filled with the world and the devil—running from one dance-hall and theatre to another, smoking, swearing, looking for earthly amusement. Then I came to this meeting, to see whether these things I had been hearing were true. For three days I have been under conviction. Tonight I came out and gave my heart to God. Jesus saves me now. By His grace I'll live for Him. Pray that I may receive the baptism of the Holy Ghost." These are but samples of the ringing testimonies.

"For years I have been a professing Christian, a church member—but as Sister McPherson says, I had a name that I lived but was dead. Since these meetings I have seen Christ—seen myself—and tonight I have been born again. I know *now* that I am saved! I know that He is mine and I am His."

THE PRAYER ROOM.

Then too, I would have you come with us to the prayer room below. A door-keeper questions all who enter—

"Are you a Christian? Are you seeking the Baptism?—only seekers and workers admitted, as space is limited."

We enter the door—what a picture meets our eyes. Hundreds kneel in prayer, hands uplifted, singing, praying. Several are lying under the power, speaking in tongues as the Spirit gives utterance. Some appear to be fairly lost in God. Here too, is the faithful pianist, softly playing as the people sing:

"Fill me now. Fill me now.
Jesus come and fill me now.
Fill me with Thy Holy Spirit,
Jesus come—"

Oh, the indescribable sweetness, the holy, reverent seeking after God—no excitement or loud outcry, but everywhere that earnest, seeking, longing after God's Holy Spirit.

Members from practically all the different churches are seeking together. Roman Catholics saved upstairs, now seek the Baptism in the prayer room below. A Methodist Episcopal minister seeks and receives with the others.

I would have you see the spacious kitchen, the quiet, efficient workers, the meals served cafeteria plan, the long tables in the banquet hall, which seat several hundred at one time.

How near to heaven it all seems! The hearty handshakes—the God Bless You's—the sound of distant voices raised in prayer—the voice of the male quartet from another room as they practice for the next service.

I *must* close. My pencil has been running on and on for hours. But I did want you all to see it so; and asked the Lord to help me as I wrote, and bless you as you read.

Could you see it? Were you blessed and encouraged as you read? Write and let me know.

DAYTON REVIVAL.

By L. S. Shires, Pastor of M. E. Church, Covington, Va.

One day at Sister McPherson's great meeting in Washington, D. C., filled me with a hunger to know more and to experience more of the deeper things of God. After the meeting at Dayton, Ohio, began, I grew more and more restless every day, until I found relief by boarding a train for Dayton, on May 13.

No tongue can express nor pen describe the overwhelming power and the wonderful spirit of the great Dayton meeting as I saw it and experienced it for four days.

As I approached Memorial Hall early Thursday afternoon and saw the long flight of steps thronged with people, the mass extending far back into the street, I was encouraged by the thought that possibly I might get close enough to get in when the doors were opened. I hurried on only to find that the healing service had begun over an hour before, that the immense hall was packed with people and that the doors were locked. The great throng on the outside were unwilling to leave. About four o'clock I gained admittance to the hall. There a most wonderful sight met my eyes. On the large stage were seated the sick or crippled people for whom, one at a time, Sister McPherson was praying to be healed in the name of Christ, the Great Healer and Physician. Oh, that I had the power to describe the miraculous cures I saw there.

One young girl sixteen years old, who had never walked, was healed and walked back and forth on the stage completely cured. That night when I came for the evening service, I was pressing my way up the aisle of the rapidly filling hall trying to get as near the front as possible. When I had gotten about as far as it was possible for me to go I heard the remarkably sweet voice of a girl say, "Here's a seat." I occupied it promptly and in a few moments I noticed that the little stranger who spoke to me was the sixteen-year-old girl who had never walked until that day. She walked to the service and I saw her walk away just like the other girls. This thought came to me, that when Jesus comes in as our Healer and our Saviour He puts a thoughtfulness in our heart and a sweetness in our voice that impresses even strangers.

I saw on the stage a little Catholic boy who was deaf and dumb. He was healed; he could hear people in the audience who would speak to him and he could answer back to them.

A man who was paralyzed was taken to the stage in his wheel-chair. After anointing and prayer by Sister McPherson he said he was greatly helped. In this case the cure was not instantaneous. His family reported the next day that as they were wheeling him home he said he felt so much better he believed he could walk. He got to his feet and in a few moments he was walking along with his family, pushing his own chair. As some one said the next day, during Christ's time it was, "Take up your bed and walk," but the twentieth century version seems to be, "Get out of your chair and push."

Another man was taken to the stage suffering intensely with a severe rupture. He was instantaneously cured and took off his truss. He was so overcome that he leaped and shouted on the stage for fifteen or twenty minutes before he could control himself, so overcome was he with joy.

It is simply impossible to mention the miraculous cures among people affected with cancer, blindness, deafness, heart trouble, paralysis, broken bones, tuberculosis, gall stones, appendicitis, rheumatism—so many cases which absolutely could not be benefitted by treatment from physicians. During that afternoon and evening between six hundred and seven hundred afflicted people were annointed and prayed for by Sister McPherson. The healing service continued to within thirty minutes of the evening preaching service. The helpers kept urging the sick people not to try to make their way to Mrs. Pherson; that she would simply have to have a few minutes' rest and get her supper before facing the great throng at the evening service. They kept pressing on, anxious to have the tender touch of this patient, compassionate, self-sacrificing woman, and hear her earnest voice in prayer, pleading with Jesus to heal them and set them free. Finally her helpers tried to pull her away from the crowd that was thronging her and her own mother pleaded with her to rest a few minutes and get supper before she had to go into the preaching service. But she said, "Oh, Mother, supper or no supper, I can not leave these dear suffering people." She then came down to the foot of the steps leading to the platform and shook hands with the sick ones with a "God bless you and heal you." Quite a number of miraculous cures were effected in this hurried handshaking before she was finally literally taken away by compusion for a few minutes rest before she began preaching. It made me think of the accounts that are given us of how the people thronged the Master and how they resorted to every conceivable plan to get the sick ones to Him, even letting them down through the roof. And then I wondered if Jesus Himself could have been any more patient and tender and compassionate and self sacrificing and any more anxious to minister to those who were afflicted than this dear woman of God.

But as miraculous and soul-stirring as this all is, yet it is not given first place in the great Dayton meeting. It comes first in this article only because I happened to reach Dayton on the afternoon for this service. The emphasis is on soul-saving, and tarrying for the Baptism of the Holy Spirit.

I have attended some wonderful revivals, but I am frank to state that I have never witnessed such overwhelming power as was manifest in every service at the Dayton meeting. Even at the afternoon services at which the sermons were addressed to Christians, there was the same conviction among the unsaved and that eagerness to come to the alter. They would begin coming before the choir could begin singing, and sometimes before the speaker had finished giving the invitation. At the afternoon meetings there were always fifty penitents at the altar; at the evening services there were from one hundred to two hundred seeking Christ.

The testimony meetings were wonderful. Only a small per cent of those who wanted to tell what the Lord had done for them in the revival could be given a chance to speak. All over the house people were telling how the Lord saved them; hundreds were waiting to tell how Jesus had healed them, scores were eager to tell how they had received the Baptism of the Holy Spirit,—just one constant stream of testimony out of grateful hearts filled with love and praise to God.

Another impressive feature of the meeting were the services in which requests were made for prayer. There were scores of people on their feet at the same time waiting for a chance to request prayers for their unsaved loved ones, children asking prayers that their parents might become Christians, others asking prayers that their sick, crippled, or blind loved ones might be healed. One request after another was made until finally they had to be made simply by the lifted hand. There wasn't time to hear the oral requests. Oh, the burdens that were on the hearts of the people for the unsaved.

The mighty hunger of God's people to know more of Him and to have His power for service was shown in the large number that were found in the prayer room tarrying for the Baptism of the Holy Spirit. The atmosphere of that room was simply charged with divine power. You could feel the very presence of God the moment you entered the room. A number of people each day I was present received the Baptism. One young business man from Chicago happened in at the meetings one day. He was so impressed that he wired his wife to come at once, not stating in the telegram any reason why she should come. After she arrived they were both seen regularly in the prayer room tarrying for the Baptism. His wife received the Baptism and at the first opportunity testified to the joy that filled her soul.

The influence of this revival was not simply local, but hungry hearts were there from all over the Middle West. From a section of country stretching from New York to Texas the people kept pouring in on every train and by automobile until it was becoming a perplexing problem for the committee to find rooms to accommodate them. It became necessary to make public appeals from the platform for people to open their homes and rent rooms to those who were coming to the revival. At some of the meetings fully three thousand people were turned away unable to gain admission to the large hall.

This letter about my four days at the big revival would be incomplete without a brief statement, at least, in regard to my own Baptism. I had been tarrying for the Baptism of the Holy Spirit since April 11, the day

I first heard Sister McPherson at Washington, D. C., the closing day of her campaign in the capital city. At the first service that day I was filled with a hunger to know more of God. At the evening service I asked some of the personal workers if I might not seek the Baptism at that service. They all said there would be no tarrying service. Finally a little personal worker came along who saw how hungry I was for a deeper experience, so it was suggested that I go to the prayer room. The next morning I sent a note to Dr. Shreve, pastor of McKendree Church, in which the revival had been conducted, requesting the opportunity of talking with him awhile about the things that had so deeply impressed me. I did not get to see him until after ten o'clock that night. That consecrated servant of God, though almost exhausted from his strenuous work of the day, and having had but very little rest, even at night, for over three weeks, sat there for over an hour telling me his own experience in tarrying for and on receiving the Baptism, and explained the Scriptural teaching on the subject. Then he called in Joe and they prayed with me until after one o'clock that night. I remained in Washington two days longer that I might keep in touch with the three people who had given me such encouragement and instruction. After leaving I continued to tarry for the Baptism. When the Dayton meeting began I simply could not stay away. On Sunday, May 16, in the prayer room in Memorial Hall, I received the Baptism. The Holy Spirit came in like a torrent, as though He would tear my body to pieces. One of my besetting sins has been my unwillingness to speak out boldly for Christ, but when the Holy Spirit came in He made me shout the praises of Jesus until He verily split my throat. However, as one brother said to me, the Lord is able to repair any damage He does to the old temple. After being tossed about violently for quite awhile until I was panting for breath and wet with perspiration, I then lay for quite awhile in blessed quietness and poured forth praise to God in tongues for over half an hour. Oh, the joy that filled my soul was unspeakable and full of glory.

IN THE ALBERTAN PRAIRIES, CANADA.

The trip, with its changing of cars at the peep of day, was particularly hard, and our bodies were particularly weary and exhausted when we stepped from the train at four a. m. in the bleak, gray dawn.

"Wh-o-o-o!" said the biting wind that whistled across the level stretches of prairie and drove the stinging sleet into our faces as we waded through the mud to a waiting car.

With difficulty we secured one small bedroom in a third-rate hotel. Shivering with cold and hunger, it was only our utter exhaustion that caused us to seek a little warmth and repose upon a bed which had not been changed since its last occupant. In the morning other guests departed and we secured better accommodations, then set out to find the building in which the meetings were to be held; upon inquiry we learned that it had recently been burned, and were informed that, in their extremity, the large curling rink which, during the winters was covered with ice for fancy skating, and during the summers flooded with water, had been hastily secured.

What a change from the splendidly heated and ventilated beautiful Memorial Hall! Friends were now working desperately to build a platform, seats and prayer-room, and to lay down planks to carry the people over the mud as far as the benches, where is was hoped they would bring enough newspapers to protect their feet from the raw dampness of the sodden ground that had never been dried in years. They decorated the old beams overhead with flags and bunting so that during the services, if one could just forget the chill and clap their hands fast enough to keep them warm, and fancy that the soft mud was a nice thick carpet, it helped some.

While this campaign seemed difficult to us, it was heaven on earth to the dear starving saints of the great Northwest and so great was the financial struggle that we were happy to donate our time as a missionary work to this great and needy field. The following is from a report by W. E. McAllister.

"The great meeting has come and gone, but thank God the results still remain; for although three hundred were saved, and three score or more sealed by the blessed Holy Spirit, many are still being saved and filled in almost every meeting.

"As we look back over the past two weeks, our hearts are moved with praise and thanksgiving to God for the many dear ones who found Salvation for their souls, healing for their bodies, and the blessed Holy Spirit to be their abiding Comforter, during these meetings. It is the unanimous opinion expressed everywhere, that this has been the greatest spiritual awakening that the City of Lethbridge has ever known.

"When our dear Sister McPherson arrived from Dayton, with a little tired, pinched look in her face, our hearts went out in sympathy to her; for the prospects here did look discouraging. The weather was cold and damp, which made the Curling Rink very uncomfortable, putting our Sister under a very heavy handicap. However, this brave little woman cheerfully started in. She was at every meeting, with enough fire prayed down from heaven to warm things up.

"Even as I write, I can see her as she catches up her tambourine and comes to the front of the platform, calling for volunteers to follow her in a march around the building, singing, "We're Marching to Zion." To me, one of the most impressive parts of her meeting, was the prayer-room. We had only a small one, with room for one hundred and fifty, but from the beginning God began to pour out His Spirit.

"The first Sunday, a young Holiness worker received the Baptism. Quite a number of the choir from one of the most prominent churches of the city were filled with the Holy Spirit, and at last, the Sunday School Superintendent of the same church.

"God sent the sunshine and warmed up the atmosphere, and also sent

His blessed Holy Spirit and warmed up the hearts of the people, and today there are scores of clear, definite testimonies of what God has done in two short weeks.

"People came to attend these meetings from as far east as Winnipeg, Man., as far west as Prince Rupert, B. C., from the states of Montana, Washington and California, and from all over Alberta, for 400 miles north of Lethbridge. Sick ones came and were healed by the mighty Power of God, and many dear ones were filled with the Holy Spirit. The total result of the fire that is thus spread throughout the country will never be known, till that great day when the books are opened and the names are read. These meetings have inspired more zeal and enthusiasm, and have been of more encouragement to the work as a whole than any meetings in its history; and we feel that this revival will be the mother of many other revivals all over these Western Provinces.

The Divine Healing Services

"Scores of sick folks were prayed for, and many testified to the mighty healing power of God. One man who had been crippled with rheumatism for over two years, who was assisted into the building by friends and ushers, after the prayer of faith was offered on his behalf, skipped and ran up and down in front of the platform, and left the building, running like a boy, to tell his wife that the Great Physician is just the same today. Another young man was brought in from the country in a bed, so crippled with rheumatism that he was unable to work. He heard of the meetings, came and found Salvation, and after being prayed for, he testified to God's saving and healing power. A doctor's wife knew this young man intimately, and was so deeply interested in the case as to go and visit him in his home. He said his pains were all gone and that he was perfectly healed. She called again the next day to see if the healing still lasted, and found that he had gone back to work on the farm. It would take too long to tell of everyone who was healed. Suffice it to say that there were a cloud of witnesses with clear, definite testimonies to God's healing power."

BEAUTIFUL ALTON ON THE MISSISSIPPI.

Only a little handful of praying saints they were, but full of faith, zeal and desire for a revival. Their church was tiny, but their faith and hearts reached out for the city. So burdened were they for a revival, that after writing us their petition, the saints continued in fasting and prayer whilst waiting for "a cloud the size of a man's hand" in the form of a favorable reply. At length God mightily answered their prayers and sent a gracious revival which stirred the city and community, stretching forth His hand in blessing, salvation and healing. One result of this revival was the enlargement of the church, in which the revival work has never ceased and glowing reports continue to cheer and bless us.

The following clippings from the "Bridal Call" and newspapers will best tell you the story of this meeting:

BENEATH THE BIG TOP AT ALTON, ILL.

Through our car windows to the left, the great, shimmering expanse of the "Father of Waters" swept gleaming by; bearing big steamers and pleasure boats on its placid bosom.

What a large crowd were gathered at the depot! Fellow passengers put down their newspapers and looked curiously out, as the "White Hussar" City Band filled the air with "Revive Us Again." Loving, earnest saints and Christian workers had formed a reception and march. Stepping from the train we were instantly surrounded, presented with beautiful bouquets of roses, welcomed and hurried to a waiting automobile, and were soon falling into line in the parade, dazed and excited by these unusual demonstrations.

The large tent erected on the high school campus, in the heart of the city, and under the big shade trees, was estimated to seat 2000. No detail had been overlooked by the Pastor and his consecrated flock. For many months they had worked, planned, and prayed for this meeting. The very air seemed clear as heaven from the beginning. From the very beginning the crowds were good; after the first few days it was impossible to accommodate them. Hundreds came to the altar of penitence sobbing out their sins, and receiving pardon through the precious blood of Calvary's Lamb. Hundreds came for healing and many touched the hem of the Saviour's garment

THE TARRYING MEETINGS.

Many afternoon meetings were set apart for Christians seeking the baptism of the Holy Ghost, the gifts of the Spirit, and enduement of power for service.

With uplifted hands and faces, seeking and praising Jesus for His unspeakable promise, one after another were filled with the Holy Ghost—filled till they overflowed, and spoke in other tongues as the Spirit gave utterance. Some were baptized while sitting quietly; some while kneeling at the altar; some were slain under the mighty power of God, and laying prostrate at His feet, had marvelous visions of Christ on the cross, with streaming wounds in side and hands and feet. Some saw Him coming in the clouds of Heaven. Others caught glimpses of that celestial city, through opening gates, and heard the glad hosannas of angelic hosts. Still others had glimpses of the harvest fields, panting for laborers, and were consumed with soul-winning zeal.

A blessed baptismal service was held on the shores of the Mississippi, and scores of converts were baptized in the "Father of Waters," whilst throngs of spectators sang on the banks, and stood upon every available roof or elevation that commanded a better view. During the baptising of men, women and children many of whom had been converted during the meetings, many citizens would interrupt by begging to be allowed to testify to the great change that Christ had wrought in their lives, then go down beneath the waves.

Oh that I had power and space to describe the scene—the blue heavens, laced with fleecy clouds of purest white; the blue waters of the broad and noble river; the multitudes assembled on the river's edge as in the days of Christ; the flotilla of little boats, drawn near by those determined to see, as fortunate enough to possess them; the white robed children singing; the radiant joy and shouting of those baptized as they came up from their watery grave; eyes and hands uplifted to the open heavens.

Some stood in this posture for minutes at a time, looking raptly upward without moving a muscle, and afterwards told us they had seen the face of Jesus smiling down upon them, surrounded by an innumerable company of angels. Strong men wiped tears continually from their eyes, and declared that they had never witnessed such a scene before.

Several gave their hearts to Christ on the shore, and went into the water. One dear lady, who had battled with conviction at home, suddenly gave her heart to Christ in her kitchen, and ran all the way to the river, arriving just in time to be immersed.

As for the Divine Healing services, the reporters of the Alton daily newspapers have written such splendid word pictures, and given so much information about cases they themselves witnessed and interviewed, that from their columns we have selected clippings. We have endeavored to eliminate all personal references to the evangelist, that Christ alone might be exalted; and trust our readers will pardon any slight mention which may still remain. It is her greatest desire to give unto the Lamb all praise and honor and glory. Amen. For it is He who has done all the miracles, and who has all power in heaven and on earth.

CHURCH THRONGED BY AFFLICTED PERSONS—WORK IS CAUSE OF WONDER.

Cured!

That was the breathed as well as the spoken prayer of hundreds of people who witnessed the healing services at the First Methodist Church yesterday afternoon. Such a jumble of human sufferings relieved, of blind, lame and halt, to all appearances cured; and such wonder and fervor not unmixed with a certain tragedy on the part of the sick as well as the whole, has never been witnessed in Alton.

The statement was made by enthusiasts and skeptics alike, yet it hardly tells the entire story. It does not relate of the indefatigable, tireless work of the evangelist lasting through hours of praying. It hardly tells the story of an audience wrapped in wonder, men mute with marvel; women shedding tears, and paying little attention to the breathless heat that grew as 2,000 people remained to the very end. The actors in the drama were the evangelist and the same hundred crippled and sick in the front pews who were either brought up to the altar in wheel chairs or cots, or who painfully sidled up, each in his own fantastic and pitiful way.

Mrs. McPherson prayed over and anointed with oil at least a hundred sick and crippled and 50 per cent of these found relief, either complete or partial.

CROWD THRONGS CHURCH.

Long before the hour of the service, people were swarmed in front of the church, including the sick who could walk and stand. The sick holding admission cards were first to be allowed into the church. It was soon filled to capacity.

They came, the halt, the blind, the paralytics. Came also the victims of cancer, tuberculosis and arterial hardening. Carried in were the young and the old, male and female, those with horribly distorted limbs, misshapen heads, twisted muscles.

Such a mass of twisted, suffering, misshapen humanity as was assembled in the First Methodist church yesterday afternoon had never been seen by any of those present.

Kneeling at the chancel rail were relays of the sick, presented in the order of their ticket numbers. Bending over them was the devoted woman whose prayers are sought for healing. Her bearing is that of true sincerity. One is impressed with her absolute confidence that if there is sufficient faith on the part of those who would be healed the healing can be accomplished.

Mrs. McPherson is filled with an energy that seems to be almost tireless, almost inexhaustible.

Never in the history of the city has a revival attracted so much attention. The wonderful work is the talk of the town and the physicians, ministers and business men are made to marvel.

Another service held at the First Methodist church and the people flocked there by the hundreds. The church was filled and overflowing long before the services began and hundreds were turnd away unable to get even near the doors.

AUDIENCE IS HELD IN SPELL.

Before a tremendous crowd Mrs. McPherson prayed over hundreds of sick and crippled. A lame man who had been on crutches walked away, little paralytic children discarded braces, jumped up and down and ran, while reports continued to reach the rectory that many people who had been prayed over in previous divine healing services were improved and even entirely cured.

The crowd that packed the church was probably the biggest that was ever within its portals. Many people stood during the three hours of the service. The galleries of the church were crowded and all aisles were blocked. Outside the church were automobiles lined up for a block. The heat within the church was terrific, yet the people all undismayed fanned themselves listlessly, wrapt in attention. There was a continual hubub of voices and an undercurrent of profound excitement as cripples brought in on cots and beds and wheel chairs suddenly rose and shouted while the soft peals of the organ rose to a thunderous noise in expressison of applause.

At the beginning of the healing services everyone was alert and it seemed as though the soul of everyone was stirred to the highest pitch of enthusiasm. The light from the beaming face of the evangelist could be seen reflecting out into the audience as she moved about the platform continually praising Jesus and asking for His presence.

So the healing went on, the cripples were brought to the platform and made to walk, the blind to see, the deaf to hear, and the dumb to speak.

THREE THOUSAND IN BIG TENT PRAYED ALOUD.

Did you ever hear three or four thousand people pray at once? Not in unison, reciting the Lord's prayer, but every individual praying, using each suppliant his or her own words? Well, the reporter never did before last night and it made a wonderful impression. It was something new in Alton. The fervor could be understood though the words were not. Somehow it caused one to think of Niagara. The mind shifting about for an analogy contemplated the deep roll of thunder. The Spirit mounted upward as if to the top of the mountain.

During the experience meeting the lights went out. The experience meeting went right on in the dark. The lights were out perhaps five minutes and when they came on once more, it was observed how little attention had been paid to the fact.

CROWD ESTIMATED EIGHT OR TEN THOUSAND.

The gathering at the tent last night was probably the largest that ever attended a religious service in this vicinity.

The converts at the meeting last evening swarmed the aisles like bees around a bee hive. When the evangelist asked for those who wanted to be saved to come forward there was a rush for the front and the number was so large that it was impossible to accommodate all of them in the space reserved in front. The number of converts last evening were surpassed in only one meeting so far.

MOVIE MAN SIGNS PETITION—SAYS REVIVAL IS CRIPPLING HIS BUSINESS.

Rev. A. W. Kortkamp announced that four or five different petitions were sent to him bearing the names of the most prominent business men of the city requesting the lady evangelist to stay another week.

Even the name of a picture show manager was on the list, who stated when he signed the petition, that although the meetings were crippling his business, the woman was doing so much good in the city that he felt like he wanted to sign the petition also.

REVIVAL IS HELPING TO COLLECT BILLS.

Beside the spiritual content derived from the McPherson meetings, there is a practical side which has come to light. In the great service which had as its text to "come to the altar and give your hearts to Christ," Mrs. McPherson told many who came to pray, to "Go home and pay their debts." This was also taken literally, and it has been reported that it has had its effect on business. Bills which have been of long standing have been paid voluntarily.

"Thousands upon thousands heard the Gospel and great mountains of prejudice, hard cold walls of doubt and unbelief had been literally swept away; hundreds wept their way to Jesus' feet, while between one and two hundred are known to have received the baptism of the Holy Spirit. The healings were very wonderful, the blind saw, the deaf heard and the lame walked.

"The great fifty-foot platform was packed with singers, workers, ministers, evangelists and missionaries, and not a murmuring word, critical remark, nor argumentative spirit intruded to mar the perfect harmony and love of this great campaign."

IN THE MINES AND MOUNTAINS OF WEST VIRGINIA.

"Where in the world is the town anyway?" we asked ourselves in bewilderment as we stepped, grip in hand, from the train in Piedmont, W. Va. Grim mountains 'round about, railroad tracks, shunting engines puffing and blowing smoke a-plenty; but where is the city, and where is the great tabernacle we have heard so much about from the brethren who for so long have been urging upon us their burden for a revival? We gaze forlornly through the smoke-filled air, at the towering hills, in which straggling streets and houses seemed to hide from view. Also on either side of the tracks can be seen a few little narrow streets of smoke-begrimed buildings, looking as dejected as though thoroughly discouraged and disappointed with life in general. A peculiar vapor of strong acids was filling the air and biting our throats (already sensitive from recent meeting) till we coughed, strangled and choked. A large paper mill nearby was belching forth these poisonous fumes and, gazing fascinated at the hills immediately behind it, we saw that all the noble trees which had once clad them with beauteous verdure were now but like gray ghosts, dead where they stood.

We had arrived a little sooner than expected, so it was with difficulty we located a brother who, with beaming face and many "God bless you's" piloted us across the street to the hotel. Here we were met by the proprietor who graciously moved the cuspidor and offered us a seat on the piazza (draped with a newspaper as a protection from the cinders) and in a few moments, climbing two long flights of stairs, were in our rooms on the third floor. Here for three long weeks our windows afforded us a perfectly good, unobstructed view of the railroad tracks, where, day and night, (particularly night) miles of trains of open coal cars puffed, panted and smoked as they passed to and from the mines with which the entire country was intersected.

The tabernacle in which the meetings were held had been recently used as a storeroom for lumber and was situated within a few feet of the tracks and switches, where (if I remember rightly) seventeen engines congregated each night at the hour of our evening service. This was their hour and place to fire up and prepare to draw the great trains of coal up the famous seventeen-mile grade. At another side of the tabernacle was an ice cream factory that had just then installed heavy engines and noisy machinery, which seemed to be in almost continuous operation. The tabernacle was only accessible through a muddy back alley; boards were soon laid down to bridge the mud, however, and the tabernacle, the outside of which resembled an old barn, had been made really beautiful within. Volunteer workers and brethren had whitewashed, by machinery, and the firemen turned out to decorate with flags throughout. The seats were comfortable and a great platform and elevation for the choir had been erected.

The meetings opened with a good attendance, although where the people came from was a mystery to us. Within a few days not only was the large tabernacle filled to overflowing but throngs were in the street and lanes. Special revival trains were run from Cumberland, Md., and outside points. The meetings increased in power and glory; the orchestra and workers were the greatest comfort and assistance. I preached, however, under great handicap, having to cough and choke from the coal dust, acid fumes and warm smoke which at times poured through the building from the great engines standing so near that one could almost reach out a hand and touch them.

Fancy trying to preach to two thousand or more people nightly for three weeks under those circumstances. It was necessary to yell at the top of one's voice to be heard. Almost every sentence we would utter, the trains would say: "Sh-h-h-h-h-h!" but we refused to be silenced and arranged a signal that whenever I was not screaming my sermon loud enough an usher at the rear was to lift his hand so that I could raise my voice still more to be heard above the railway engines.

For a half hour we had had almost perfect quiet one night, and only two trains had rumbled past when suddenly, just before the message which was to comprise one of the greatest subjects of the campaign, the engines pulled up and started the blowers to fan their fires. The noise was (to put it mildly) excruciating to overwrought nerves, and I turned, in desperation, to a dignified preacher who sat by my side, and whispered:

"Brother, do go and stop that terrible noise!"

"Why, how can I stop it?" he asked, with a face so miserable and worried that it was almost ludicrous. "How can I stop the blower letting off steam?"

"Oh, I don't care how you stop it! Put your hat over it, or sit on it, only do, do something." Glancing nervously at his hat (it was a very nice one), he picked it up and went hastily through the door and, in a few moments, I heard the engine pulling noisily up the track to a more distant point.

About the altar were enacted scenes never to be forgotten; those dear, warm-hearted miners and factory people had been untouched by revival fires for many a year and hundreds had never heard the Gospel preached with power and demonstration of the Holy Ghost. The altars were filled to overflowing, scores were saved and baptized with the Holy Spirit and many healed of their infirmities, to which precious letters and messages testify to this day. The divine healing services created such interest that, in spite of the one policeman the town afforded, those who had journeyed for many miles were determined to get in or, at least, to see whether or not Christ really healed the sick. We were reminded of the days when those who would not be denied took off the roof to admit their sick. Here they took the siding off the building in several places, weeping and pleading to see at least the miracles of healing. Scores of people scaled the lower roofs of the tabernacle, lying flat on their stomachs at the open windows. When we lifted our eyes in prayer, we gave a start for our astonished gaze beheld long rows of eager faces peering in in triumph from above. Then would come mysterious scratching noises as someone was being pulled unceremoniously back down the roof and such undignified snatches of conversation as:

"Hey, there, you let go my foot, I tell ya, le-go, I say!"

"Well, come down, then and hurry up about it. Do you want that roof falling in and killing everyone?"

"Well, there's lots of others up here, and I want to see and hear after coming thirty miles, don't I?"

"Don't argue with me, young fellow, you come ———" etc., would punctuate pauses between the songs, as the one lone little policeman battled with the crowds ere he finally gave it up and he, too, looked through a crack.

One night the throngs were so desperately determined to hear the message that at five-thirty the building was packed and the throngs outside so insistent that a hasty message brought us from the hotel to the scene. An open air meeting was held; I preached to the people from the back of an automobile and several dozen hands were held up, expressing the desire to become Christian followers of the Lamb.

This had been a hard field in almost every respect, largely because former workers had been unfaithful. God gave us the confidence of the people, however, and enabled us, by His Spirit, to cleanse the standards in His dear blood and the water of the Word, and plant them again on the pinnacles of respect. Hard, also, because of the terrific strain of preaching against the engines for the cause of Pentecost, which has been so dear to my heart, almost finished me there. At the last meeting, while shouting my loudest (preaching over the noise of the blowers, as engineers stoked their fires), my throat felt as though filled with splinters, and a sudden pain pierced my right lung as though I had been shot with a bullet. Many months have passed since that day and though much prayer has been offered, an inflamed and painful spot in my chest still reminds me, not only of the meeting in the mines and mountains but of the "Greater Love" which causes us day by day to lay down our lives for the brethren.

Out of it all there are a few scenes that stand out very clearly before me yet; I would like you to see them too. Shut your eyes now and picture it. See—here is the church, a great stone structure, builded solidly, as though to last for centuries. And yonder, high above is the big steeple, where pigeons and doves are busy preening their feathers, and cooing together as they look down upon the throngs below. The street cars come clanging up one after another, unloading at the doors. Automobiles draw up from every side, and seek a place to park. The steps are crowded, though it is hours before the doors will be unlocked. Every fifteen minutes sees the crowds augmented, like waves that are rolling in and have forgotten to recede. Old and young, rich and poor, are standing there, pressed tight against each other. There stand a poor Russian, and an Italian woman, with their black shawls pinned over their heads, nervously clasping and unclasping their hands, or clutching a poor twisted little sickly babe to their hearts, struggling to protect them in the jam. Beside them stand women of refinement and wealth from the finest circles in the city, dressed in silks, satins, and duvetines, aristocrats to the tips of their jeweled fingers. The rich and poor stand on one level here in these hours of waiting; social rank and difference forgotten, they are accentuated by the same motives; they are driven by the same desperate need; they are all seeking help from the same Source. They are sinful, they are sick; they have come to seek the Saviour, and to touch the hem of His garment. They have come to see Jesus—poor, old, hungry, heart-breaking world, you have not changed one bit from what you were in the days of Christ, have you? The same sick bodies—the same sin-laden hearts—the same bitter anguish—the same scalding tears—Oh, yes, you are just the same old world. You still need Jesus, the wonder-working

Jesus, as they needed him 1900 years ago. And here He is, poor, weeping world, here your loving Saviour stands, a smile of welcome's on his face, and blessings in His hands.

Oh, what a jam! How tight and breathless it is becoming in the middle and close up to the door! Many have come from scores of miles, and say that they have eaten nothing since morning, except a little lunch which they have carried with them lest they should lose their place by the doors and be shut out. It is after supper time now, and many are growing faint. But there is no possible way of going back, even if one wanted to! You are almost lifted off your feet in the press. Policemen are coming now. Sixteen to eighteen of them are detailed to care for the doors and see that none are injured in the press.

Christian workers, choir, ushers, church officials, ministers and their wives, etc., are being taken in through the Seventeenth street doors now.

Then the main doors are opened, gradually, and a dozen strong men, aided by the police are needed to keep that sea of humanity from sweeping in like an irresistible sea. Not because they want to come tumbling in like this; but because of the pressure behind them. I stood in the door myself on two occasions when the doors were first opened and saw ladies fall in headforemost in a fainting and dazed condition from being pressed against the doors and having stood so very long. Why if the hour was set ahead to five o'clock in the morning I verily believe it would be packed at two.

This old world is hungry for God, dear people. Men and women are desperately hungry—not for oyster suppers, concerts and social gatherings, but for the power of God to be manifested and their poor hearts strengthened and fed. If you were once caught in a crowd like this, if you once looked into their hungry faces, if you once heard their cries of distress when they found they could not get in or be prayed for, and if you saw them pressing and thronging in and in, till the church was filled, the great balcony overflowing down the steps, the aisles roped, and all standing place packed, chairs brought and the chancel filled, men sitting on the altar cushions on the floor, and standing in the vestibules, and twelve hundred or more packed into a space that should hold but one thousand and the chapel (seating five hundred, at the rear of the church proper) filled and then saw the ushers filling the basement Sunday-school rooms, and getting folks to preach to them. If you then went to the doors and saw the crowd outside was still larger than the crowd inside, and they pressed you, and coaxed you, wouldn't you just realize why Jesus had to get into a boat and push away from land, in order to preach to the people? And wouldn't you realize what He meant when He said the harvest truly is great, but the laborers are few?

Well of course, the only thing that could be done was to do the best you could, and then steel your heart and lock the doors, and send some one out to speak from the steps. And the strange thing was that even if there was no one to preach they would not go away, but would stand patiently hour after hour outside the locked doors, just content to be near, and catch what words they could through the opened windows.

And although we had exceptionally good weather all through the campaign, there were two nights when it poured rain. I saw the crowds and felt so sorry when the place was filled, and many still shut out. As we entered the edifice we said—

"O you poor, poor things, we are so very sorry you can't get in! You will be soaking wet, won't you?" And they replied:

"Now don't you worry one bit, little Sister! Don't worry about us. We don't care if we get soaked to the skin, if you just leave the windows open so we can hear your voice as you speak and sing; that's all we ask. And when service is over and some go out, we can get in to the last altar service." I tell you I just have to wipe my eyes as I write, and every time I think of the beautiful spirit of those wonderful and hungry people. Oh, how Jesus loved and yearned over them in the days when He was upon this earth, and how He yearns over and loves them still today. Jesus give us a heart like Thine!

And now the scene within the church—Every available inch of space is packed, and the song service is under way. Rev. Crowell is himself directing the singing, and the chorus loft is filled with singers. The two front rows are filled with ladies, dressed in white; while the male voices are at the rear.

How sweet the singing is! And how they all take up the refrain! Many are weeping frankly and forget to wipe the tears away as they sing. The ceiling is remarkably high, and studded with lights, the gallery runs—horse-shoe like—round the church, and is outlined with a circle of electric lights set close together. How beautiful it looks! Then those stained glass windows—the one that attracted me the most was the one directly in front of us as we sat in the pulpit. It depicted the Lord Jesus returning in the clouds of heaven. How that Form lit up during the service, and there were many times, when I looked up through my tears during prayer at that window, when it seemed as though that dear Form moved in that gorgeous stained glass window and stretched out His hands in blessing o'er the bowed and prayerful heads of that assembled throng. Of course it must have been just the tears that made it so appear, but I know my Lord was there, and all felt His sacred presence.

The preaching service, the writer would rather not describe, as she was but an instrument within the hand of God. Suffice it to say, that Jesus blessed and filled her full to overflowing and poured the message forth to eager ears and hungry hearts. And it brought forth fruit. Ah yes! What gracious, glorious and abundant fruit! And altars filled again, again and yet again, and then they kneeled—those weeping penitents far down the aisles, and in the pews and gave their hearts to Christ.

Nor was the meeting all for sinners; there were glorious tarrying meetings for the saints. The first was held just for the officials' wives. In that first sweet tarrying meeting, the first to receive the baptism of the Spirit, and to speak in other tongues, was the wife of the Sunday-school superintendent. She slipped to the floor like a leaf in a summer's breeze, and was sweetly filled with His presence. Others cried to God for a like experience. The next was a mid-week meeting. We had preached that night on the power of the Holy Ghost, the altars had again been filled and filled with sinners; but O, we yearned to call the Christians next to the prayer rooms for the Holy Ghost. The altar place was filled with ministers; Dr. Shreve stood beside me (from McKendree M. E., Washington, D. C.), and Dr. Wilson, the District Superintendent, who writes in this issue.

I spoke to them of what was on my heart, and they said, "Yes, that's what we all need—the baptism of the Holy Ghost." Turning to Rev. Crowell we asked what he thought of turning the entire channel of the after meeting into a regular Pentecostal seekers' meeting. "You go right ahead, and obey the Lord," said this dear soul, "You are the engineer on this train, I'm only the fireman!"

And so the call was given. How those dear hearts did respond. They came from all over the church, and from the galleries and poured into the prayer rooms till the ushers had to close the doors. Brethren tarried before the Lord in one room, with Dr. Shreve (who, you remember, received the Pentecostal baptism of the Holy Spirit according to Acts 2:4 in the M. E. Church revival in Washington, where he is still pastor) in charge. Dr. Wilson assisted also, and God did the rest. Bless His name. The sisters were in another room, packed in till the writer, who took charge of this meeting, could scarcely find a place to put her foot down in the press. And then

THE POWER FALLS!

We began to sing softly, "Fill me now, fill me now. Jesus come and fill me now," and as the people lifted up their hands and prayed and praised, the glory came down. In the centre the power struck first and five were slain under the power of God at the same time. O it was so sweet to see their faces light up as the Spirit came in, and to hear the Spirit speaking through them, just as He spoke through the 120 on the day of Pentecost, even though in all their lives they had never seen or heard any one receive the baptism. Those nearest to them would stop to listen raptly for a moment, and then shut their eyes and pray all the harder. Some said to me as they contemplated those under the mighty power of God, "O sister, tell me, is it sinful for me to be envious? I never envied anyone anything so much in my life, as I envy those dear people the power that is on them now." And we would reply, "O don't ask their blessing, but look up to Jesus, dears; He is standing just by your side, waiting to fill your cup to overflowing."

And there goes someone down at the farther end of the room—she is one of our oldest church members, they tell us.

"Well, I don't believe in that!" said a sweet-faced Holiness woman who stood by in her uniform and bonnet. "Stood by," did I say? Well, you could hardly call it standing, for she scarcely had the words out of her mouth, when the power of God struck her and over she went, and soon received the baptism of the Holy Spirit just like the rest; and made more noise than all the comparatively quiet ones put together. She was the only one throughout the entire revival that I ever heard question the power, and she did not question it long.

"Who is that beautiful lady over there?" I would ask as one after another were swept with the gales from heaven.

"O that's one of our Sunday school teachers," or "that sister is in the choir," or "well, that's one of our best members, who has been wandering from God and has just come home in the meeting." And in the men's meeting the power would be falling, too. I think the first to receive was a doctor, one of the official men. Many declared that they saw visions of Jesus on the cross, coming in glory, etc., and would rise with faces that shone as though transfigured and exclaim:

"O, if you had only seen the vision! O, I have just seen Jesus!" And indeed you could see heaven as you gazed into their eyes. In our undenominational city revivals, so very many have received their baptism on their knees, or sitting in the pews. But here they all seemed to go down in good old-fashioned John Wesley Methodist fashion, and were so very proud of it. God bless them! Not for one instant did pastor or people draw back, but when I would question them a little fearfully as to how they thought things were going, they would say: "O Sister McPherson, isn't it grand, the old Wesleyan days have come back again. This is what my father used to tell about, and to think that I have lived to see it!" And the pastor said, "I know why God has deigned to honor us so with His power—it is because we cleaned this church up two years ago, and it has been clean and straight for God (no concerts or tickets sold). And it has paid—O look at it now, Hallelujah!"

On each Saturday night there was a "men's only" meeting,

where officials and church members and ministers met to seek and to receive the Baptism. The power fell in the church, too—but there I must stop or I'd write on and on till there would be no room for the report of the pastor, superintendent, and reporters. I only meant to say a few words of introduction when I started—

And must close by again thanking God for the souls saved, healed and baptized. Dear Mrs. Crowell, wife of the pastor, sweetly received her baptism, whilst the godly pastor is earnestly seeking. One thing that greatly impressed me in the meeting was the way in which sinners would eagerly await the altar call and then come running to the Christ. No matter what the messages were on—ofttimes on the deepest things concerning the baptism of the Holy Spirit—they came just the same. In fact, after such sermons, sinners would exclaim, "Well! If that's religion! If there is a power like that I want it! I'm going to get saved, so that I, too, may receive the Gift of the Holy Spirit."

Another thing which must have impressed all who came in contact with their influence, were "The Official Men." Never in my experience have we been privileged to meet more godly, consecrated, efficient men. No wonder God picked out this church in which to kindle the fire, which we hope and pray may spread to all the churches in the city.

GREAT DAYS IN PHILADELPHIA

By John J. Wilson, D. D., (District Supt.)

Rev. A. E. Crowell and his Official Board invited Mrs. Aimee Semple McPherson to conduct a series of meetings in the C. C. Hancock Memorial Church, Philadelphia, Pa.

This woman of God opened the campaign Sunday, October 24th, and for more than two weeks preached to congregations crowding every part of the church.

People came from all parts of the city, and many came from other cities. The people fairly stormed the church, anxious to see and hear. Thousands were unable to gain admission, yet so earnest were the hungry hearts, that hundreds waited for hours in the street, hoping to catch, at least, a part of the message. These crowding thousands represented all classes, Jews and Gentiles, Catholics and Protestants. Many nations were also represented. Many came for healing; many out of curiosity, but hundreds came for the touch of God, that their hearts might be healed and their sins forgiven.

What days these have been. Who, fortunate enough to be present, can forget them? Days of marvelous and awakening blessing to thousands in Philadelphia Church Centres, giving promise of greater things in the life of many churches during the coming days. Oh, how our hearts pray, that this may be gloriously fulfilled. And our prayer ascends, in the name of the dear Lord and Saviour, Jesus Christ.

What wonderful scenes we have witnessed. Who can describe them? Words are inadequate. From the very start, one thing was evident: God was present, Christ was seen and the Holy Spirit was in His temple. Men and women recognized the Spirit's presence, and quickly responded to His nearness and gladly honored the Christ. What scenes followed, thrilling, uplifting, and soul-inspiring in their effect.

Oh, they carried you back to the dear old days of Pentecost. Once more the windows of heaven were opened and the Power fell upon hundreds every night. So marvelous the Power of God, that frequently the people tarried until the early hours of morning, that they might see the Glory of God manifested and sing the praises of the Risen Christ.

How the Spirit did manifest His Power. What a response to unquestioning faith. The lame walked, Hallelujah, the sick were healed. The deaf declared God had unstopped their ears. Men, women and even little children, gave such evidence of blessings, physical and spiritual, that ministers and laymen, who came doubting and questioning remained to shout the praises of God.

The more thrilling results were seen in the transformation of sinful lives. How hungry the people were. It was not necessary to beg, pull or drag people to the Cross. The Spirit's power was so real and persuasive, that as soon as the door of opportunity was opened, they rushed to the Cross.

Sinners were converted, believers were baptized, as in the olden days, and why not? God is the same, Christ is the same, and the Holy Spirit is the same. O, Church of God, Awake! Put aside every hindrance. Put on your beautiful garments. Open your heart's door to the Holy Spirit; and give Him right of way. This is the day of opporunity. God is calling, calling, calling to His Church.

Will you hear His voice? We heard it in Philadelphia. Will you not say to the blessed Holy Spirit—"Come in. Come in. Fill Thy Church with Thine own Power, that they may go forth, in Thy Power, to get the world ready for the coming of the King."

"A PICTURE THAT CHANGED A CHURCH, OR A MODERN PENTECOST"

Rev. A. E. Crowell, Pastor Hancock M. E. Church

It is impossible to tell the story of spiritual fervor and power, and to describe the manifested presence of the Lord of Hosts in the language of mortals.

First, let me tell you of the Church. It is a beautiful, commodious stone structure, located in the midst of a residential district of the busy city. The seating capacity of the main audience room about 900. We have as fine a type of people as any pastor could wish to serve. The Church has always been more or less of a popular church, has a membership of about 600, and the audience about as large or a little larger than most of the churches about us.

Now, as to the story—: A little less than a year ago, a card came to my desk; it had on it a representation of a woman preaching, holding the Bible in one hand, the other outstretched toward heaven. The background was black with representations of stars, also the words "Soon the starry floors of Heaven will burst and Jesus will appear." I took a fancy to the "cut" and the card remained on my desk for weeks. There was an announcement on the card of a meeting held somewhere, I cannot now recall, nor was there anything on the card to indicate from whence it came.

Some time after the foregoing a copy of the *Bridal Call* was placed in my hands by a friend; this I read, and was specially interested in the account of the meeting, and of the good done.

The third link in this chain was a little tract that I read and compared with the New Testament, and was somewhat impressed with its little message.

The next link was the appearing of an article in our New York Christian Advocate, of a wonderful revival in the McKendree Methodist Episcopal Church of Washington, D. C. I wrote to the pastor, Dr. Shreve, and asked him for a few of the details, also for the name of the Evangelist. He replied, giving the name of Mrs. Aimee Semple McPherson, of Los Angeles.

I then began putting my scattered links together and I found that this name corresponded with the name of the writer of the tract, the editor of the magazine, and was the name of the woman represented on the card. You may call it what you please, but we folks call it the leading of the Holy Spirit.

Then began a correspondence with Sister McPherson. Our first reply was not very encouraging, except as to her possible coming next spring. My reply was that it must be now, that is, in the fall. I met Dr. Shreve at Ocean Grove, and had a talk with him, and felt very much encouraged as to the possibilities of a fall campaign. A meeting of the Official Board of the Church was called, and we discussed the plans and possibilities of securing Mrs. McPherson. We made it a matter of prayer. Every official present prayed audibly, some of them for the first time, hearts were melted, tears flowed, but we arose from our knees confident of the Lord's leading.

The pastor was authorized by a unanimous vote to invite Mrs. McPherson to hold a series of meetings in our church, at the earliest possible date. Thus the correspondence was continued and one day we were pleased to receive this reply from our good sister:

'Dear Brother:

Truly "the Spirit beareth witness." We had risen early under a strong impression that you should have the offer of a meeting following Piedmont, and wrote you to that effect. Your letter requesting same time has made us realize that our

God is gathering the stored-up blessings and they are ready to break and fall in a deluge of heavenly latter rain."

Thus, I think you will agree with me, the links put together made a strong chain.

THE MEETINGS

First: the crowds. Never in the church history of the city of Philadelphia were such crowds seen waiting to get in, and waiting outside after the church was filled. On one occasion, after the church and chapel were filled, thousands were still outside. The pastor stood on the corner step for over a half-hour and preached to the crowd. About seventy-five feet away, on another step, stood another minister and preached to the crowd gathered about that door. The crowd opening up for the trolleys to pass through. On Sunday afternoon they started to gather as early as four o'clock for the evening service; the doors opening at 6:30, and in just four minutes every available inch of space was occupied. This condition was manifest every night of the second week.

The Spirit of the Meetings. So often in similar meetings, it has been more like a religious circus, but not so here. It seemed like holy ground, and it was, thank God! The presence and power of God was such as could be felt. People everywhere speak of the religious atmosphere of the meetings. The hymns breathed the prayers and confessions of the people in holy rhythm. Hearts as well as lips were tuned to sing His praise. What music we had! To Him be all the glory.

The Altar. The whole church was like an altar, and on one occasion, when everything was crowded with penitents, and they were penitents, weeping their way through to conscious salvation, people were asked to kneel right where they were, and all over the house folks were weeping their way to God's mercy seat. Again and again, one night I suppose it happened six or seven times, the altar would be cleared, and another "altar call" made, when the crowd would come filling the altar, inside and out, all about the front, and at the end of the seats in the aisles down almost to the doors. They came without coaxing or arguing, I believe most of them came without a worker having a chance to get to them, elbowing their way through the crowd, from every quarter of the house. A glorious sight.

A Midnight Altar Call. Dr. John G. Wilson, the District Superintendent, cancelled all his official engagements that he might be with us in the meetings. What soul-stirring prayers! What inspiring, pleading exhortations he made! His own soul had caught fire, and he had just laid himself on God's altar to be used of Him. On one occasion, so manifest was the presence and power of God, that we could not get the people to go home. It was midnight, the church was still filled with people. Dr. Wilson gave an altar-call, when they came from every quarter of the house filling the altar, and kneeling anywhere to weep their way through to God. Mrs. Wilson was present in nearly every meeting, helping by prayer and tender sympathy, and wise direction, those who were seeking Christ. She was especially helpful in the "Tarrying Room," where she and the pastor's wife, with other of our consecrated women waited in prayer and song and helpful suggestion. I do not believe any minister has ever been privileged to witness deeper conviction than was seen in the faces and tears of those who came to Christ. It was more than mere surface emotion. The great deeps of their hearts were stirred, and God spoke to them in unmistakable language for their faces showed it when sorrow and sighing fled away, and the joy of the Lord just flooded their souls. You don't blame us for saying "Glory to Jesus" and even "Hallelujah" right out loud, do you?

All classes, all religions, and quite a few nations were represented in the list of seeking ones.

Two afternoons of the first week were given to meeting with the wives of theological men of the church. The first was to get a little better acquainted, the second was a "Tarrying meeting," where the first of our folks received the baptism (Acts 2:4). Two Saturday evenings were given up to the men of our Church, who were so busy with the crowds, etc., that they did not have time for prayer. What a time we did have. Now don't tell anybody, but they made as much noise as any pentecostal crowd you ever heard. Excuse me, it was not noise; it was the anguished cry of hungry hearts, desperately in earnest, seeking the baptism of power. Thank God, we were not disappointed. Several of our men went up by going down.

The "Tarrying Meeting." Four afternoons were given up to the prayer meetings. Each one having a larger attendance than the one preceding. What hours of fellowshipping with God! Heaven came down, the soul to greet and glory crowned the mercy seat. I do not know how many received the Baptism. But of this I am sure, that each one who did receive it knows it, and Jesus knows. The Sunday school superintendent of a neighboring Methodist Church was stricken under the power, near the close of one of the meetings, about midnight, and at 2:30 a. m. he came through. When I heard of the meetings lasting up into the morning hours, in the McKendree Church, I said, there will be none of that in my church, but here it was 2:30, and I just say "Glory to God" and

> "Have thine own way, Lord; have thine own way;
> Thou art the potter—I am the clay."

One evening, or night, rather, at the close of the meeting, we went to one of the neighboring homes, for a little fellowship and prayer with an afflicted one. Dr. Shreve was with us. What a time we had. My own wife, lost in prayer for the afflicted one, until swept by the gentle breezes of the pentecostal breath of God up into loving fellowship with her Lord, talking with Him in languages that they two alone understood. (See Acts 2:4.) Again it was 2:30 a. m. when we went home. We just say "Glory to Jesus."

The Healing Meetings. What demonstrations of the power of God to work wonders, and even miracles in the morning of the 20th century. When I was at the Piedmont meetings, my own heart was touched, as I looked upon the scene there presented, of the sick, the afflicted, the lame, the halt, the blind, and emaciated and wasted. I could not but think of the days, long ago, when Jesus was here on earth. I fancied I saw just such a sight as must have greeted him again and again. Such was the sight here in my own church. At Piedmont, it was in a wooden tabernacle; here, it was more like the lame man at the gate beautiful. And, thank God! a disciple was here who could say, "In the name of Jesus Christ, rise up and walk." Some were made whole, some began to mend from that hour; a number of our own people have been wonderfully helped and healed.

A physician friend of mine was present. His pastor told me the other day that this doctor admitted to him that he went there skeptical, but came away convinced of the power of God to heal, and with a great spiritual blessing to his own soul.

We kept no records of seekers for the baptism, nor of those who came for healing, but have the names of just about 500 who accepted Christ as their Saviour. When Sister McPherson asked me "For how many shall I pray, as I go to God for the meetings in your church," I said "500." He has answered the prayer. About 100 have expressed a preference for our church.

A new day has dawned for our church. It can never be what it was before. As God said to Israel, "Go forward," so He has spoken to us, and we must go, "Strong in the strength that God supplies through His eternal Son."

CANADA'S LARGEST CITY IS VISITED WITH FLOODS OF THE LATTER RAIN

By C. C. Baker, Pastor

How shall we begin to lay before you the wonderful things that took place during the ministry of our dear Sister McPherson here; words seem almost to fail, but can truly say, "God poured His Spirit on us as He did on them in the beginning."

Truly the "Latter Rain" is falling and the floods have reached Montreal, the city of spiritual darkness and one that lies in the grip of Catholicism.

The date was set and preparations were being made for the greatest spiritual awakening that this city had ever seen, the saints of God were with one accord; night after night they met together for no other purpose than to reach through to God on behalf of this city. Afternoon prayer meetings were held in the different homes in the city, until it came to the night before the opening day of the campaign—Saturday evening. Down in the basement of the church could be heard the volume of prayer going up, for lost souls and an enduement of power on Mrs. McPherson, a real message for the people now sitting in darkness.

Altars Filled with Penitents First Day

Sunday came. Every heart was opened before God, and the searching time began. Altar call was given at the close of the address. What a scene—those who had been living at a distance from God and in a cold and miserable condition were the first to lead the way, then falling in rank, as it were, were others weeping and crying for mercy, asking that their sins might be forgiven. The Spirit fell and souls came through to the Baptism, in the first service. The first evening meeting revealed an altar filled with sinners seeking salvation, with a prayer-room below filled with hungry children of God seeking the Baptism of the Holy Spirit.

Miracles of Healing

Thursday was set apart for healing, and prayer for the sick; it came and the throng with it. What a sight, the lame, halt, and blind, seeking deliverance, their very faces spoke of the terrible suffering they were undergoing, but wait—these faces were to be changed and indeed many were. After a glowing talk from our sister, preparations were made for prayer. The sight we will never forget, those who had been bound for so long were now being set free through faith in Jesus' Name. Quietly and sweetly the music floated over the air, suddenly all eyes were turned on a young girl with crutches, who ascended the platform in great difficulty. Mrs. McPherson relieved her of them, laying them down on a nearby chair, asking her in the meantime of her faith in the ONE who was to heal her. Prayer was offered, she arose to her feet and to the amazement of the crowded house she walked across the platform with Mrs. McPherson's aid but no crutches, suddenly she started out alone, and there was no longer silence but great exclamations of joy and praises to God arose all over the congregation. Shortly she ran like a child of ten, throwing herself into the outstretched arms of Mrs. McPherson. The people could no longer keep their seats but stood to their feet and in one volume there arose the sound of many hands clapping together for joy at what God had wrought among them. Many other cases in this service that I wish I could here tell but space is limited.

The tide was continually rising being very marked on the attendance, shortly the building, seating some 2000, was too small and many standing eager to hear and see the works of God. Many from outside points were attending, namely: Toronto, Ottawa, Chicago, Winnipeg, Kingston, New York, Newfoundland, New Hampshire and others.

Oh what a week, filled with events Montreal will never forget. By this time the press were bringing before the public the things that God was doing in our midst. Reporters coming in our meetings were amazed at what they saw and heard and at times were so lost would almost forget their task and find themselves one among the many who were looking on in wonder and amazement. The last Thursday came for prayer for the sick, people thronged the place with hundreds on the outside unable to enter, policemen were jostled about in the crowd and jam, at times nearly taken off their feet by those seeking to just get in. This was the scene from without, but look inside the building—and there were those in chairs and on beds, many blind, halt and lame, suffering from many diseases seeking the great Physician. At times one would feel moved with compassion for those who were suffering severely and then would come the sight of those who were completely delivered walking back and forth over the platform, praising God for what He had done. I cannot do justice to these services nor am I able to touch on the emotion and high spiritual tide that was felt so keenly in the meetings. Ministers of the city confessed that this was nothing else than the real "old time Religion;" this resulted in churches and ministers feeling their need of more power and opened the doors for our dear sister to tell to them again the simple story of Jesus and His power to save and heal. All we can seem to say is that it was truly wonderful. Blind were made to see, lame to walk straight, sick rising up and leaping and praising God. Oh that men would praise God for the mighty works that are being done in these last days.

Hundreds Throng the Altars for Salvation

Saturday afternoon was indescribable. The crowds were intense, policemen were unable to cope with them at times as they pressed their way to gain an entrance. What a scene as our dear Sister moved among the suffering throng in her spotless white apparel, laying hands on many suffering and aching heads, offering the prayer of faith that moved the heart of God and brought relief to many. This service never closed except for a short time of recess, but went right on into the evening meeting, and hundreds thronged to the altar. As they would come in such numbers our dear sister would put her hands to her face and exclaim, "What shall we do with them? Where shall we put them? Already *every available space around the altar and six rows from the front are filled.*" Strong men throw themselves on the platform as they responded to the call, weeping and calling on God to save them from their sins, tears flowing freely from those who were now returning to God and giving themselves up to Him.

Our closing day had come when our dear sister was to deliver her last message to this people, and the morning service was a feast to those hungry for more of God. Many more seeking salvation, and the prayer-room was one not to be forgotten; men and women—rich and poor alike, with great tears rolling down their cheeks, some kneeling, others lying prostrate under the power of God, tarrying to be endowed with power from on high. God's presence was real the moment you entered the place, the air being charged as it were with His Spirit. This service went on into the evening meeting. At 6:45 p. m. the house was filled, with many standing, unable to get in.

Scores of young men and women again flocked and crowded the altar, praying to God for salvation. As the burdens rolled away young men would be seen emptying out of their pockets cigarette cases and tobacco, getting cleaned up ready to join the mighty army of redeemed soldiers.

Although they are leaving for other fields, where precious jewels must be won for the Master, still they leave behind them memories that will never fade, and hearts inspired for the battle and winning souls more than ever. With fresh zeal we press in, taking up the work where they left off, not only strengthened in faith, but determined to keep the banner floating high in this city for Jesus Christ our Lord.

PENTECOSTAL POWER IN MT. AIRY M. E. CHURCH, PHILADELPHIA.

SO wonderfully was the work in Philadelphia impressed upon our hearts, this being the beginning of one of the greatest church revivals we have ever known in America, that we made special arrangements to accept the invitation of Dr. Tindell, of Mt. Airy M. E. Church, whose heart and people were burdened for a revival of the old time power, in the most aristocratic residental section of this beautiful city of churches.

THE TARRYING MEETING

Yearning for a revival, and realizing like the disciples of old, and our beloved Bishop Berry, that "every real revival must begin with a genuine Pentecost," they started in right with a "men's only" tarrying meeting, on the Saturday night that heralded the revival. Dr. Trindell specially invited my Mother to be present. The large Sunday School room was well filled with men, pastors and officials, all seeking alike this precious gift of the Spirit. The first sound to greet our ears as we neared the church, was that of hundreds of men singing with great volume and fervor:

"O send the old time power,
The Pentecostal power,
Thy flood-gates of blessing
On us now open wide.
Let sinners be converted,
And Thy name Glorified."

What a glorious meeting it was! Such humility and hunger are seldom witnessed. The power of the Lord fell, hundreds of hands and hearts lifted to heaven, brought the answer. The first to receive His baptism was a Sunday School Superintendent. He was gloriously filled, and spake with other tongues as the Spirit gave him utterance. Several others "received like precious gift as we did at the beginning." Every one was drawn closer to Christ and filled with a zeal for souls.

During the Campaign four "special tarrying meetings" were held, afternoons and Saturday nights, not in any way interfering with the nightly evangelistic services. This was the dynamo which supplied power for the whole campaign. Afternoons were for those who felt their need of the Holy Spirit. We were delighted to find a filled church.

After a flowing testimony meeting where the cream of Spiritual church members and workers poured out their heart-hunger for the enduement of power for service, and concise message from the Word, upon the subject, the entire company broke up and made their way to the prayer rooms, separate rooms being occupied by brothers and sisters.

The glorious results of the experience received in those hours will tell for time and eternity. Such singing! Such praying! Such demonstration of power and the Holy Ghost! These meetings are beyond description; more than a score were swept down by the mighty power of God at one time, and many would be receiving their Pentecostal baptism, whilst others were sweetly filled as they knelt by their chairs. Not one would waste a precious moment watching those to the left, or right, and none were content with anything short of the Bible standard. Among those to be gloriously filled, as were the hundred and twenty of old, were ministers, laity, and Christian workers.

The closing Saturday night saw the greatest of this series of waiting meetings. The large Sunday School room was filled to the doors for the "men's only" meeting. Many from Rev. Crowell's church wore small cards on their lapels, identifying them as *"This Is That Band"* and *"Tarry Until Association."* Glory! Hallelujah! When these Methodists do a thing they do it up right.

Upon learning of the large company of prominent clergymen and church officials from far and wide who would unite with the men of Dr. Tindell's and Rev. Crowell's church to seek the old time power, we were impressed to commandeer our beloved friend, the Pastor of McKendree Church, Washington, D. C., Rev. C. A. Shreve, who with his church so graciously received this blessed baptism of the Holy Spirit almost a year ago, during our campaign in his church. He came, and at the conclusion of our message gave a graphic description of his own wonderful Pentecostal Baptism, and the after results since that time in his own church and city. This account was a blessed inspiration to all. Men laughed, wept and shouted together as he talked. Then came the hours of prayer, hundreds of voices storming Heaven, uplifted hands, tear-drenched faces—and THE OLD TIME POWER. Hallelujah!

How many received the baptism? you ask. So vast was the work of the Holy Spirit, upon that large company of men, so tightly packed together were they that it was at times impossible to get through or keep count, but almost everywhere we turned some radiant faced man would wipe the tears from his eyes and say:

"O Glory to God, Sister, here's another man, just receiving, and three or four over there who have just swept clear through. O listen to the Spirit speaking through them! Can you tell what language that is, Sister?" And we would say, "Brother, it is a river of praise flowing right to the throne, and must be the tongues of men or angels." "O look at that shining face over there," another would cry; "it just lit up as with an electric light from within." The oldest Christian workers present, some of them doctors of divinity, renowned authors, and world travelers, declared that in all their lives they had never witnessed such a scene nor attended such a meeting. All rejoiced to know that the Ark is being brought back, and believe that dear John Wesley would be the most rejoiced of all. All of our own forefathers having been of the staunchest early day Methodism, some of them preachers and teachers, this meant perhaps as much to us as to any. None realized the flight of the hours. It was already Sunday, 2 p. m. ere we tip-toed from this room, made doubly sacred through the Spirit's presence in those hours.

Small wonder then, that jubilant messages were brought to us ere the Sabbath sun was set, that the revival fires had spread to many other churches.

At the close of the first Sunday morning service, the altar was filled with penitents seeking pardon and salvation. O could you have witnessed these same scenes, when at night, the long chancel was filled three times across, with yielded hearts, who with tears of penitents who publicly confessed their sins and accepted Christ. Whilst this wonderful altar call was at its height, Dr. Wilson (the District Superintendent), who had cancelled every engagement to stand with us that time, came in with Rev. and Mrs. Crowell. All had hastened hither upon the conclusion of their respective services, whilst real old Methodist shouts of victory and rejoicing filled the place.

When all was over, with flushed face and happy hearts, we all shook hands, thanking God for this wonderful day. A young lady greeted us and exclaimed:

"Oh! If my father could have lived to see this day, how happy he would have been. My father built this church and always prayed that it might be filled. Thank God, though he did not live to see it, it was filled tonight, and O that altar call!" This was the daughter of the devoted former Pastor, of whose work and prayer meetings we heard repeatedly while in that city.

Each evening the power continued to fall. The chancel rail was filled with sinners within and without, and at times the front pews must needs be vacated to make place for the penitents to kneel. At times the platform and pulpit was cleared and used for another row of converts.

One splendid feature of the campaign was the large attendance of ministers, from various churches of city and state, who at times filled the entire chancel space between altar and pulpit. There were at times from fifteen to twenty-five in this company, including such God-used preachers and evangelists as Dr. L. W. Munhall, editor of "The Eastern Methodist," Dr. Garett and others.

Splendid men they were, and hungry for a revival of Pentecostal power. Great was their joy as they beheld throughout the week the hundreds weep their way to Jesus' feet. Nothing could be more like Jesus than the way in which these dear ministers of the gospel threw themselves on their knees beside the penitents and prayed, as tears of preacher and penitent mingled and melted together upon the altar.

SERVICE OF PRAYER FOR THE SICK.

Friday night a divine healing service was held, upon the urgent request of many. The audience overflowed every door and stood in the street. Again the meeting was marked by the large attendance of ministers. After the divine healing sermon, Rev. Beiri, pastor of the Siloam M. E. Church, ascended the platform, and calling a young lady from the audience to stand by his side, gave a thrilling account of her marvelous healing in answer to prayer during the meeting a few weeks previous at the C. C. Hancock Church. She and her family were Roman Catholics, and have been converted and joined his church as a result of her healing from curvature of the spine and other troubles. Her spine, which had resembled a letter "S," has been straightened, and her brace laid aside from that night.

Sixty or more came to the platform, who were prayed for by the writer personally, and probably as many more went to the altar and were prayed for and anointed by the various ministers. There were a number of remarkable healings, many of them instantaneous.

THE FINAL SUNDAY.

When we entered the church that morning after just a few hours absence since the great tarrying meeting, referred to in the beginning of this report, we knew that the place was filled with the presence of the Lord. As through the great stained-glass window at our right, the morning sun came tumbling in waves of multi-colored glory, the praiseful notes of the great pipe-organ caused the oak-beamed roof to vibrate,

"Have Thine own way, Lord,
Have Thine own way,
Thou art the Potter,
I am the clay."

sang the congregation through their tears. What a time of melting! It seemed to many as though the very place was filled with angels, and that Christ was walking in the midst.

Then the entire congregation fell on their knees between the pews, and prayed. All had forgotten Sunday dinner, and had no desire to go. Falling on his knees on the platform, tears running down his dear face, Dr. Tindell prayed—prayed till the power came down in such an irresistible manner that several were prostrated in the choir, at the altar, and between the pews, as in the days of early Methodism. Thank God that we have lived to see the power which our mothers and grandparents used to talk about in this dear church.

Loath to sever our Spirit-born union, these dear ones came to the train from both churches in hundreds. A prayer, song and praise service was conducted by Drs. Wilson and Crowell, till the train pulled out at eleven o'clock and their "God be with you till we meet again" was swallowed up on the rapidly widening distance 'twixt our train and them.

GLIMPSES OF THE SAN DIEGO REVIVAL

HUNDREDS of our readers in the snow-bound North and East have besought us to take them with us through the written story to Southern California and the San Diego revival. So, though volumes might be written concerning the wonderful workings of God in thousands of lives, who, body and soul, entered the troubled waters during the five weeks' meetings, if you will come with us on the wings of prayer and thought, we will ask the Lord to help us give you at least a few glimpses of the great revival.

There—we are nearing the city, after a hundred and forty-mile drive from "The House that God built." All the way we have been praying and planning for this meeting, as we clung to the steering wheel of the car which sped lightly up hill and down through the ever-changing panorama of mountain and sea.

We are thinking of the building, the singers, the workers—we seem to be so handicapped. First, that boxing arena—Who ever heard tell of a woman evangelist attempting a revival in just such a place! In memory we picture it. There's the elevated boxing ring in the center; fenced in by ropes through which we must climb several times each night. Then there is the audience on all four sides, in the seats and on the bleachers. Will we ever be able to make them all hear? If the evangelist were only a man with a pugnacious, fight-till-you-conquer, biff, bang, bing! message, it might be all right, and meet the expectations of those whose curiosity brings them to the arena to witness the novel sight of the Gospel being preached from the boxing ring, and the Devil's taking the count, in many a hardened life.

But a woman! Would it be possible that the soft, appealing message of one who has a woman's and a mother's heart could accomplish nearly the same results?

We feel our weakness and shake our heads in doubt, but just with that the Spirit whispers—"Not by might, nor by power, but my Spirit, saith the Lord."

"Why yes, Jesus; that's so; please forgive us," we cry. "Neither man nor woman, with all their power has been able to move this sinful city. It is only you, dear Lord, by Thy power that can do it now. Make us clean and empty channels through which Thy power may flow."

Then, too, there's the singing. There is no one here whom we know who would be able to swing the singing for such an audience and building—

"I will help you, and send you help," says Jesus.

"But the 'fishers' and the altar workers—three score will be needed; and the precious little band of Spirit-filled, consecrated saints who are planning and praying for the meeting are so few in number—"

"I who am able to raise up seed to Abraham from the stones, will raise up more than you need. Be of good courage. Fear not, but believe."

Yes, yes! Dear Lord, we know You've never lost a battle! We do—we do trust Thee. Only keep us very yielded in Your hands, and give us strength and wisdom for such an hour."

THE CITY.

We have been driving automatically, our minds upon the Lord. And suddenly, here we are, right in the midst of the city. Slowly we make our way through the traffic of Broadway and then turn over to "Fourth" and climb the hill, on our way to Sister Branch's home, where we are to be entertained.

What a dear little city it is—this San Diego nestling close to the blue Pacific. Not so very little, either, with its thousands of inhabitants; but just big enough for every one to get acquainted and be aroused to interest by a great revival. Beautiful little city. The longer one stays the more they are charmed with itself, its people and its surroundings. "Beautiful for situation—the joy of the whole earth," might well be written on its portals.

ITS SURROUNDINGS.

Let us stop the car a moment on this hill and look about us! Yonder to the north we see the boulevards and railways leading over valley and hill toward sunset cliffs, La Jolla and Los Angeles, and hugging the coast as though they must not lose sight of even one of the countless breakers that roll in snowy beauty o'er a sea as blue as indigo, and break upon the shore.

To the east, in silent grandeur, like straight sentinels standing erect to guard this sun-kissed land from snow and cold, lie the snow-capped summits of the Coast range; and the Gateway to Imperial Valley, whose wide and fertile acres slumber 'neath the golden sun and drench the land with perfume of the orange blossom, while busy bees sing all day long their droning song and speed from flower to flower.

And on the south, just eighteen miles away, lies Mexico; its distant mountains lift their heads and look from out the hazy veil which drapes them each from head to foot as with a blue chiffon and fills each crag and canyon with a hundred mysteries.

On the west the ocean, deep and blue and sparkling like some rare jewel. Yonder strip of land is Coronado—and over there Point Loma, with its Naval Base. Above the bay the alert sea gulls circle over vessels ranging from the busy man-o'-war and ocean liner to the submarine, pleasure yacht and fishing craft. And above it all, the air is vibrant with the roar of wide-winged aeroplanes that circle, dip and glide. And yonder calmly sails the great dirigible, like a silver fish, too lazy to move a fin or tail. Still looking to the west we see the business section of the city, which runs clear to the water, and then with busy piers and wharves which appear to stretch out their feet and dip them into the sea.

ITS PEOPLE.

To this beautiful city come the tourist and traveler from every clime; escaping the cold of winter and the heat of summer, for this is an ideal and almost unchanging climate.

What a place for a revival! How far-reaching would be its effects—like tying messages to homing pigeons and sending them abroad unto their different homes in every quarter of the globe.

San Diego needed a revival if ever a city did. For just as the Devil invaded Eden in the form of a serpent, bringing deception, sorrow and sin, so he had entered this harbor and port, wrecking the bodies and souls of hundreds of young men and women upon the rocks of immorality, gaiety, dancing, smoking, gambling, drinking; for Mexico is but eighteen miles away, and Tia Juana, with its "Monte Carlo," its cock and bull fights, its streets of saloons, gambling houses and haunts of sin and debauchery, eats like a festering sore into the purity and morals of them whom the Devil tempts. Ah! the tales which mothers have sobbed into our ears, mothers whose hearts were breaking over children gone astray —the stories which girls and young women whispered at the altar, and when we prayed for the healing of the sick—the broken lives—the bodies devoured by ravages of sin—ah! yes, we saw, we heard, we know it needed a revival.

And others knew it too—praise God; and so for weeks and months and years God's people had prayed—"Lord, send us a revival. Arrest the attention of this giddy throng. Give us a revival of the Gospel of Jesus Christ that will awaken the churches, and bring sinners in hundreds to the cross."

But there! We must not spend another moment talking and looking—Now is the time for work! So away we speed to the home of Sister Branch. She has given us the downstairs rooms of her house. A hurried dinner, a hasty toilet, and dressed as for a meeting, we are on our way downtown again, for this is Wednesday evening and we are to speak to the boxers and fight fans at the arena.

No, the revival does not begin till tomorrow, but Manager Keran of the arena has invited us to speak to the house packed with the howling multitude of fight fans, who clamor for the sight of blood and knock-out blows or any kind of thrill that will satisfy the craving of their souls, which nothing else can really satisfy, except the love of Jesus. O! If we could only tell them of the Saviour's blood so freely spilled on Calvary; and of the victory He has won o'er death and hell; and of the shouts of joy that fill His children's mouths.

"But aren't you nervous, Sister—entering the ring before that multitude, like a lamb among wolves?"

"Why certainly I'm nervous—scared is a better word! See, my hands and limbs are shaking; but I am going, and Christ is going to help me arrest their attention and snatch some brand from the burning."

Now we are approaching the building. Automobiles are

parked for blocks around. The hoots and cheers and screams and—O how can words be found to describe those hideous "yowls" that rent the night, and could be heard for blocks. Men were fighting—fighting with bleeding nostrils—fighting till one went down and took the count, and was carried limply from the ring, uttering weird animal cries of pain and distress.

We do not go in to see this sight but nervously pace the sidewalk, trembling more violently every moment.—"O God help us!"—"Jesus, You were not 'too good' to eat with publicans and sinners: and You came to call 'not the righteous but sinners to repentance.'" "God help m—"

But there! Quiet reigns at last. Intermission has come and the Manager is coming to get us. Hundreds of curious eyes are turned upon us as we make our way through the blinding, smoke-laden air to the ring. Queer, how one's mind will stop to take in smaller incidents at a time like this, but as we climb from the floor to the chair, and from the chair to the platform, we notice hard-faced women smoking cigarettes, chewing gum, and laughing intimately into the faces of their escorts; we notice that the tight-drawn canvas which covers the floor of the boxing ring is besmirched with blood. Now we are beneath the ropes, then standing beneath the blinding glare of the great shaded light overhead, trying to see the faces of the men and women whose curious eyes are lifted to us on every side. Trying to see, I say, for though the great light above covers us with a merciless glare, they are all in semi-darkness.

"Scared?" Yes, worse than ever; but as Manager Keran introduces us, we have one consolation, and that is that though he has introduced the famous fighters from all over the world, he was more nervous than we when it came to introducing a woman. And although he is of the politest of men, in his excitement he not only is shaking from head to foot but has even forgotten to remove his hat. While he is speaking we wonder desperately how we are going to keep from strangling with the smoke, and then suddenly find ourselves talking—talking of Jesus and His love, of His precious blood, of the coming revival and inviting them all to come and see our Jesus win the victory over the Devil.

The very audacity and courage of the thing which we had done in meeting the Devil on his own ground commands the admiration of the people. They clap and cheer at every interval. Wonderfully God helps us keep them in control, though after we have told them of God's love for every one, and requested them to bring to meeting with them "the worst sinner to be found in San Diego," there was one disconcerting moment when several hands pointed and voices cried out:

"That's him over there, Sister!"

"No!—That's him over yonder!"

as they picked out certain citizens in the audience whose notorious lives and reputation were well known. It looked as though competition would be lively tomorrow night, but with a laugh, and a last invitation to "be there tomorrow night" we find ourselves on the way to the door whilst the audience continues to cheer and clap.

Once back in the car, we take a long breath of pure air and say—"Well, thank God, that's over!" and in our relief scarcely know whether to laugh or cry.

THE NEXT DAY.

Now, the scene at the arena is changed—even the building seems different—happy songs and hallelujahs make it echo as busy hands are mopping, dusting and decorating.

Whilst driving in the car this morning, we passed a house where a beautiful palm and pepper tree had been felled to make room for the enlargement of a building; and upon securing permission we have had a truck load of these beautiful boughs and branches hauled to the arena. Now, transforming pillar, post and wall it looks as though we had entered a cool forest, fragrant, restful and inviting. The canvas covering has been cleaned as white as snow. Palms, calla lilies, carnations, orange blossoms and ferns are being carried in by the loving hands. A grand piano is lifted to the square. The shade lamp advertising restaurants and diamonds is taken down, and a new one advertising Jesus is lifted to its place; and almost before we know it, the clock hands have crept around, the meeting is begun—the campaign opened.

The power of God is with us from the very first. Saints stand firm together heart and soul, with one accord, praying to one end. The revival is undenominational, they tell us again and again, and no one is to have a corner on it, no one to seek selfish ends from its results. A city's wide revival of the Gospel of Jesus Christ, is their cry.

Hallelujah! How it grows—from the first afternoon's meeting, where the little company met to encourage our hearts, and to express their longing to be hidden away in the meeting to give us a clear field, and to see God work. They told us also of their longing to see every church, minister and worker made to feel the undenominational spirit of the revival, and to realize that the responsibility and blessed privilege was equally divided amongst them all. Through the entire campaign a blessed spirit of love and unity is on us all. We feel that every heart is made to throb as one—that is—nine hundred and ninety-nine out of a thousand. Once in a while some earnest soul whom Paul would have classified as having zeal without knowledge, would arrive from outside points, and not being in the spirit of the revival would express the opinion that more fish could be caught with a club than with the bait of love, held in a steady, patient hand. But, as in the days of Moses, God permitted Aaron's rod to bud before their eyes, and all were made to remember, "By their fruits . . ."

For the first night's text God gave to us the words, "And when Christ was come near, he beheld the city, and wept over it." There and then the altars began to fill with penitents. Soon the arena, accommodating from 2500 to 3000, is filled to capacity twice daily and the hundred-foot altar is filled to overflowing also, twice each day.

One must really be in this blessed atmosphere to realize the joy and exultation that floods the soul and dims the eyes with tears when the lifted-up and honored Christ draws men and women, first by dozens, then by scores, and then by hundreds to Himself.

But there—you asked us to take you right along with us to some of the meetings, and give you some real glimpses of the revival, didn't you? Well, come along—let's hurry up, or we'll be late for the afternoon service.

TWO WEEKS LATER.

The morning has been spent in writing, reading and prayer. But now there is not a moment to lose. A hasty telephone call has bidden us, "Come at once, as the arena is filled to overflowing with the most hungry and expectant crowd assembled since the Bible days."

Sure enough, as we approach the building the neighboring streets are filled with automobiles. We can scarcely find a place to park the car. The men ushers, wearing red badges, part the crowds at the door, and pull us through—but not till a score of hands have reached out and plucked at our garments while an anxious voice cries:

"O Sister! I don't know what to do; I brought my husband here last night to be saved and healed, but we could not get near the doors for the throng. He works till 6:30, and though he comes straight here without supper, this is the fourth time he has been shut out. Whatever will I do?"

"Why, dearie," we reply, "here is a reserved seat ticket for tonight. There is always room for those who want salvation. Tell him we will expect him to lead the way to the altar tonight."

"O Sister, just take one look at Dorothy, won't you?" cries a mother, tugging at our coats. "See her little paralyzed arm that was prayed for the other night has been healed—

"Move it, Dorothy—pick up that book. Look! Look!" continues the delighted mother as the child obeys her bidding with ease. Then throwing her arms about our neck, this good woman hugs us tight and cries, "Praise God! Husband and I have both been saved during this meeting, and our home is O so happy now. I—" but we had time to hear no more.

Hurrying on, we make a desperate effort to straighten the wrinkles from our crumpled-up collar before reaching the platform. We trip over a crutch, and the foot-rest of a wheel-chair which protrudes into the aisle; and while we stop to apologize, the arms of several invalids, cripples and mothers with babies have had time to reach us. A babel of voices is beating upon us from every side.

"O won't you please wait a minute—Sister—when—Sister, what about—Cancer—tumor—Benny's rheumatism—mother's cataract—varicose veins—husband's paralysis—Oh! Oh!" A dozen people are all pulling us in different directions and trying to talk at once, asking prayers for salvation and healing; each in their trembling eagerness interrupting the other till our heads are whirling with confusion as we break away and climb through the ropes of the boxing ring. O those welcome ropes! The very things that we had once dreaded now enclose our only haven of refuge.

Unquestionably, as you can see, the revival is on—the entire city is shaken. In every store, shop and street car, the one subject is the power of Christ and the meetings. So now we realize, as never before, why Christ got into a row boat and pushed away from land in order to talk uninterruptedly to the clamoring and needy throng. Poor dear, helpless little sheep—how our hearts go out to them! How they need Jesus as their Saviour, and healer, and His precious Holy Spirit as their Comforter!

True to his promise, God has sent helpers. Brother and Sister Pierce are here now, also Brother and Sister Black, Brother and Sister Waldron and many others. Brothers Pierce and Black are in charge of the singing, with solos, duets and male quartettes, while a mixed sextette from the leading churches of the city freely volunteer their splendid services. And how the songs do soar from the full hearts of the congregation!

"I am coming to Jesus for rest,
Rest such as the purified know—"

Every one, young and old, sick and well, sinner and saint catches up the song till the building shakes with its volume.

"And my soul is athirst to be blessed,
To be washed and made whiter than snow."

Two rows of chairs on the platform are filled with ministers from Methodist, Baptist, Episcopal, Evangelical, Presbyterian, Christian, Salvation Army, Pentecostal and Nazarene churches, sitting side by side; doctrinal differences forgotten in the great welling love and pity for lost souls and the eager willingness to help draw the full nets to land. God bless these dear men! What a beautiful spirit they manifest. How earnest and spiritual are their faces:

"Revive us again,
Fill each heart with Thy love."

The audience is standing now with uplifted faces and hands as they sing:

"Let each soul be rekindled
With fire from above.
Hallelujah! Thine the glory."

How they praise the Lord together! Is it possible that only two short weeks ago, the majority of these people were strangers to each other, and strangers to these ringing Hallelujahs? I declare in this campaign it has almost been an impossibility to tell the Catholics from the Protestants, and the convicted sinner from the saint, for they all weep and shout and praise the Lord together. Many a time God wrought a notable miracle before our eyes and sinners stood up and shouted the praise of the Lord, lifted completely out of themselves at the sight.

And now they are praying. Dr. Belding of the First Baptist Church is leading, humbly, earnestly, his head crowned with hair as white as snow and his face is lifted to Heaven. Sobs and amens come from many parts of the building. When the congregation have united in the Lord's Prayer, and the last amen has been spoken, the tension is broken by the ringing chorus—

"It's the old time religion,
And it's good enough for me,
It was good for our fathers,
It was good for our mothers,
It is good for San Diego,
And it's good enough for me."

and then still standing, they all joyously obey the command to "turn around and shake hands with at least three people, smiling and saying, 'God bless you!'" and singing all the while:

"It makes you love everybody,
And it's good enough for me."

Hallelujah! What a happy, loving family we are! No one goes away without a touch of love, a smile, a handshake, and a "God bless you." Who can say how many are won into the Kingdom by this very act?

Brother and Sister Black are singing that song which they have made so popular during the revival that it is being whistled in the stores and streets throughout the city:

"Speak, my Lord, speak to me,
Speak, and I'll be quick to answer thee.
Speak, my Lord, speak to me.
Speak and I will answer, Lord, send me."

Alert, happy and expectant, the people are now ready for the testimony meeting. A dozen or more are on their feet at once, ready to tell of blessings received, and blessings needed to prepare them for the service of the Lord.

TESTIMONY MEETING.

"I want to praise the Lord that this has been the happiest day of my life!" cries the ringing voice of a U. S. Marine in uniform—"I gave my heart to Jesus Christ last night, right down at the altar. I've cleaned up my life, and made things right today, and now I'm going to live for Him. And O! I believe that He has called me to preach the Gospel.

"I have a Godly mother," and here his voice grows husky and wavers for a moment—"She's been praying for me a good many years. I wrote her a letter last night that will make her dear old heart glad. I—I—" but too full for utterance he can go no further and sits down with his face buried in his hands.

"And I want to praise God too, for what He has done for my baby and me." 'Tis a little mother, speaking now. Her face is all aglow as she steps to the front, and mounts the platform, holding her baby in her arms.

"Three months ago, my baby accidentally drank a mixture of gasoline and kerosene, which burned its way down her little mouth, throat and tubes, so severely that when the passage leading to the stomach began to heal, it grew together. Consequently, no food or water could be gotten to her stomach, and doctors put the poor little thing under ether and operated on her six times. With each operation they would put instruments down her throat to force the passage open, but it only grew together again, and a large pouch was forming on her chest. Doctors gave her up to die — but O! she was all we had, and 'twas hard to see her go.

"Two weeks ago we brought her to this meeting to be anointed with oil and prayed for, according to James V. She hadn't swallowed a drop of water for days and was starving; but praise the Lord, Jesus healed her—

"Look at her now! She drinks bottle after bottle of milk and is gaining in flesh and strength every day—and my testimony," she happily adds, "is that Jesus has just baptized me with the blessed Holy Spirit, according to Acts 2:4, in that blessed Prayer Room. Now I want to live for Jesus and serve Him every moment while I live."

A shower of hand clapping, like hail on a tin roof, comes from every part of the building. Mothers with sick babies are wiping their eyes, and others are shouting "Hallelujah!"

What a character study are the faces of this audience! What emotions they depict, leaning forward in their seats, oblivious to all else—but S-h-h!—a broad-shouldered Italian, in neat business dress, is speaking now. He is a Roman Catholic who was healed during the first week:

"Glory to God! Glory to Jesus!"

"I'm afraid he's spoilt for a good Catholic now—What would his priest say if he heard him shouting the praises of the Lord like that?" we whisper.

"Never—never can I praise God enough, for that which He has done for me. For the last five years cataracts have been growing on my eyes, till I was losing my sight. I am an engraver by trade, but though I wore heavy glasses I could not see to do my work. One week ago yesterday I was prayed for; and I prayed to God also. When I had been anointed, the Sister touched my eyes, and said softly:—'Brother, open your eyes and see whether you can see now?"

"I opened them slowly, then stared about me, for I could see clearly! Springing to my feet I flung the glasses clear across the room, and I could see still more clearly—perfectly in fact—

for the cataracts were entirely gone. The words, 'O my God! I can see! I can see!' kept bursting from my lips. All the way home on the street car I kept walking up and down looking at the signs and crying 'I can see that; I can read that, and that,' till the conductor thought I was crazy—so I was, with joy, from Jesus. In this book," tapping a black note book, "are the names of the specialists who pronounced my eyes incurable except by operation, but Doctor Jesus healed them—Hallelujah!"

This same brother has been preaching to the Italians, and interpreting for the workers since that day. "But shouldn't you go to work?" we protest. "How can you be here every afternoon and evening?"

"Oh, work?" said he, as though he had forgotten that such a thing existed, "I go to work when the revival meeting is over. I no got time now—I'm too busy."

"Glory to Jesus, I gave my heart to Christ night before last, and received the baptism of the Holy Spirit yesterday afternoon; I'm so happy."

One after another the testimonies roll on and on; there are people on their feet, in the benches and on the bleachers on all four sides.

"Words cannot express the happiness in my heart or my gratitude to God for sending this wonderful revival to our city." An elderly man is speaking now.

"My seven children, grown men and women, have all been saved in this meeting, and the prayers of years have been answered in a moment."

"I am sick—I have come for healing." A lady in a wheel chair is speaking. "This is the first time I have attended a religious service in thirty years because of my affliction. Oh, it is so good to be here, and God is going to bless me body and soul."

"I am a sinner, I want to be a Christian" is the startling testimony of one who sits in the fourth row, and who has the appearance of a prosperous business man. "The miracles which I have seen in this meeting convince me of the reality of a living God." Tears are in his eyes, and he is visibly trembling as he repeats, "I want to be a Christian, I must be saved today." (Such precious testimonies were not uncommon during the revival, for conviction is resting like a mantle on them all.)

"Wait a moment! Wait—you who are standing on your feet. Let us all bow our heads. How many here this afternoon will take the same noble, courageous stand, and say with our brother—'Sister, I'm not a Christian, but I would like to be before the sun sets this day. Pray for me.'

"Every one who will say that, lift your hands, and let me see where you are, even before the message—

"God bless you, brother! That's right, sister! There they go—one, two, three, four, five, six, seven—Oh, look at those hands going up all over the building. Look, dear ministers on the platform, open your eyes and look! Did you ever see such a precious sight?" Hands are lifted in every quarter of the building; many are weeping; others trembling with conviction.

So, though these afternoon meetings are really intended for deeper teachings and helping the spiritual Christians through to the mighty baptism of the Holy Spirit, we must bring a message from the Word which will reach both classes before we call the sinners to the altar and the Christians make their way to the prayer room.

"Oh, Jesus, help us now," we pray. "Help us make straight paths for their feet. Help us make the message simple and plain. Oh, Jesus, you are right here now; you are walking up and down in the aisles, and between the seats. We feel Thy presence brooding o'er the place. Open our spiritual eyes that we may see Thy face. Lay your hand in tenderest blessing on each head.

"Bless these dear people, Jesus; save the sinner, heal the sick, comfort the sorrowful, baptize believers with the Holy Ghost and with fire, then send us all out in Thy harvest field to win other precious souls for Thee, dear Lord."

In our message, we do not talk about Hebrew, Latin or Greek; we could not if we would—but stick to the simple story of Jesus' love, and the outpoured Holy Spirit who has come to convict us of sin and draw us to the cross of Calvary, where, as we confess our sins, Jesus, the faithful and just, cleanseth us from all unrighteousness; we tell of the 'born-again-life' where old things are passed away and all things have become new, of our new love and duties as a child of God and a winner of souls; of our dire need for the enduement of power from on high, and of God's provision whereby this need is met, even the mighty baptism of the Holy Spirit. Teachings along the line of consecration and life after receiving the Holy Spirit are also set forth and then, having yielded body and soul to Jesus, they who are sick are invited to seek the Lord as their healer, not with a selfish motive; but that with strong, whole bodies they may serve Him better with all their strength and life.

The audience is made to feel that Jesus is right here, penetrating their heart of hearts, reading their thoughts, realizing their needs better than they know them themselves, waiting with outstretched arms to pardon, to comfort, to heal, to fill with the Spirit; calling every one in the building by name with His tender, loving voice, saying, "Come, my child, I am waiting to bless you. I know all about your defeats, your sickness and your burdens. See, my arms are open to you. Come, let me take you beneath the shadow of my wings; I will give you rest, I will bless, strengthen and heal you—"

In other words, the secret of power—the reason that scores and hundreds are lifted to their feet and drawn to the altars is that "Christ, lifted from the earth," draws all men unto His own dear self. Who is there that could resist such a Saviour, Friend and Lover? Well, we couldn't in San Diego, anyway.

THE ALTAR CALL.

And now, with bowed heads, we ask God's help and blessing on every seeking soul; then dividing the audience into two classes, give two altar calls. The first is to the sinners, who rise in scores, and weep their way to the altar without a moment's hesitation.

Here they are met by altar workers, wearing white badges bearing the word "altar" which distinguishes them from those seeking help. There is no confusion, except when the 100-

foot altar becames too small and the front benches must be cleared to make room for the overflow. There is no hurry at the altar; every one is bidden to tarry till they know the work is done; then names and addresses are taken on cards by the workers; for the city is later to be divided into sections, and visiting committees formed whose duty it is to visit these homes, offer prayer, and if possible establish a family altar and encourage the new convert in the Lord. Expert "fishers of men" are combing the audience. These wear green badges, bearing the word "Fisher." These three score workers (God sent as He promised) are from Methodist, Baptist, Presbyterian, Salvation Army, Pentecostal, Nazarene, Y. M. C. A., Epworth League and many other groups of Christian workers throughout the city. Each has been carefully selected after they themselves have received a blessing, and an outpouring of the love of the Master.

The whole center of the building is filled with penitents and workers now. See, there are three young married couples coming to Jesus together in this one meeting.

And here is a dear old man with silver hair, how he is weeping! A little boy, surely not over fourteen or fifteen (himself saved only the other night, and now an earnest and tireless worker) is kneeling by the old man with his young arm thrown lovingly across the trembling shoulders.

During a momentary lull between the songs we hear the childish voice of the lad interwoven with that of the older quavering one in earnest prayer, then both voices melt away in the next song:

> "Just as I am without one plea
> But that Thou bidst me come to Thee."

Ah! the old man has a witness now that his sins are all forgiven. A bright smile lights up his face, he is wiping the tears from his cheeks, but we see several drops still shining like diamonds in his beard, where they have dropped unheeded.

"How old are you, brother dear?" The little lad is speaking again, pencil poised over his altar card, ready for action.

"Eighty-three, come next March," is the answer.

"Have you been a Christian before, brother?" The earnest little wide-eyed face is lifted to the older one in sympathetic inquiry.

"N-n-n-ever before."

The poor old man begins to sob afresh and his head goes down again. No wonder he wept so hard. "All my l-life has been wasted, wasted, wasted!"

"Oh, that is too bad, brother; you've missed so much, and others have missed so much help too, that you might have given."

"That lad will make a preacher some day, if Jesus tarries," we whisper joyously to ourselves.

"But the past is all under the blood now, sir. Oh, just begin to serve and work for Him with every bit of your strength, from this minute, and maybe you can win souls for Him yet. I was saved last Sunday night. I've got all life ahead of me and I mean to work hard and win lots of souls for Jesus, I do."

God bless the child with his chubby little cheeks and his sparkling eyes, with all of life and hope lying just ahead. We feel as though we would like to hug him and tell him ever to be true to Jesus.

"Here, sister—" he cries enthusiastically, shoving the altar card in the pocket of my white dress, "Here's your card for this brother," and he is off to find another needing help.

Will he ever, we wonder to ourselves, if he lives to be a hundred years old, forget this revival? Never, for these are the scenes which our fathers and mothers describe to us with bated breath as happening in their own early days.

But while we have been engrossed with this scene enacted before us, the meeting has taken a new turn. Brother Pierce who has been leading the singing, has swung the channel of song into the chorus:

> "I believe Jesus saves.
> And His blood makes me whiter than snow."

And all around the square enclosure men and women are on their feet praising God for salvation through His Son, Jesus Christ.

As soon as possible now the second altar call is given. This appeals to Christians who long to go deeper in God, and to be filled with the Holy Spirit even as the 120 were filled on that memorable day of Pentecost. They are made to realize that the revival must not stop; and that they, in order to carry it on and care for the new converts after this meeting is over, must be filled with the Spirit and endued with new power.

Again a show of hands is asked for. This time the question is as to the number of Christians who feel their need of, and are candidates for, the baptism of the Holy Ghost. Hundreds of hands are lifted in answer to the call. God bless these dear, humble, earnest hearts! "Oh, to be filled with His Spirit, that I may the better lead men and women to the Lord!" is their cry. "Not for my own pleasure, not for the sake of any evidence that will accompany the baptism, but for the glory of God, and the advancement of His kingdom, I ask."

THE LUTHERAN CHURCH OUR PRAYER ROOM.

Long ago, the little prayer room across the street had proved too small, and though the overflow had filled our dressing room, and even the great refrigerator which belongs to the building and accommodates some twenty people, there was not half enough room. Speaking of the ice box refrigerator, it is laughable, but many received their Pentecostal baptism in this very place, and are on fire for God today. Not quickly will we forget the shock it gave us when word was brought that Rev. So-and-So was under the power of God in the ice box, receiving the baptism. We had heard of people being blessed under strange circumstances, but were horrified at this and ran quickly to the door to investigate. Needless to say there was no ice in the refrigerator which proved to be a goodly sized room, and it would not have lasted long had there been any, for that men's prayer meeting would have melted anything that could be melted, with its fire and fervor.

Just when we were desperate over the need of a prayer room, the Lutheran Church, one short block from the arena, was kindly offered. So, after dismissal, and a last word of invitation was given, we find ourselves pressing our way through the crowded aisles and leading the way up the street to the church.

"Pit-a-pat, pit-a-pat," say the scores of feet that hurry after us. Looking back at them, as we turn the corner, makes us feel like a mother hen with all her hungry little brood following after. No wonder dear Jesus thought of the same thing, and longed to gather them under His wings.

But we have reached the church now. A keeper is stationed at the door to direct the men into the Sunday school rooms, and the ladies into the main auditorium. Here they come in a steady stream, the chancel is filled inside and out, the front pews; then all pews clear to the rear are filled. Some are kneeling in the corners, in the aisles, by the door. How holy and reverend it all is! What a blessed quietness prevails. It is as though we were in the presence of a king. Some one begins singing softly:

"I need Thee, O I need Thee.
Every hour I need Thee."

and other voices catch up the refrain:

"O bless me now, my Saviour,
I come to Thee."

There is no excitement, no working up of emotions, no suggestions that the Spirit will come this way, or that—only an earnest, full-hearted seeking after God; and e'er many moments the power begins to fall and the slain of the Lord are many. Some are sweetly filled with the Spirit while kneeling upright; some are prostrated beneath His power like Daniel, or Peter, or John, in the days of old. Others are clasped in the arms of their dear ones; yonder, a mother sees her only daughter (a young woman in her twenties for whom she has been praying for years, and who gave her heart to God the other night) under the power of God. Running to her she snatches her up in her arms and kisses her with delight, as filled with the Spirit she begins to speak with other tongues as the Spirit gives her utterance.

"But, does it not hinder the Spirit for any one to disturb or touch those whom the Lord is so blessing?" you ask.

No, indeed! This is not some passing fancy, or imagination, but the mighty power of the Third Person of the Trinity, and usually, we have noticed that the harder the conditions under which the Spirit has to work, the more wondrous is His manifested power.

Glory to Jesus. One after another is being filled with the Spirit. How wonderfully illuminated are their faces! Praise the Lord! Praise the Lord! And each infilling is in accordance with the Bible pattern of Acts 2:4. But Sisters Pierce, Black, Waldron and Steele will look after the ladies' department of the prayer room now, whilst the brothers take charge of the men's room. The ever faithful little mother, Sister Kennedy, has sent in word, saying, "Come, dearie, you must hurry now. You know that you are hot, and tired, and hungry. It is six o'clock and a large crowd is standing outside of the doors of the arena right this minute."

So away we go—but we must take one peep at the men's prayer meeting before we go.

There they are, praying away as though nothing mattered in all the world but seeking the face of the Lord and the fulness of His Spirit. Our sailor boy whose lung was so miraculously restored in answer to prayer, has been seeking earnestly. We pause and pray for him, bidding him look up and receive his portion, and in a moment of time he is sweetly filled with the Holy Ghost, and begins praising Jesus in a new language which flows like a river to the throne of God.

Just a word of help and prayer and two more splendid Christian men have received the baptism. Oh, how the power is falling! How dear Jesus is! But we must hurry, hurry.

We grab our coats, have a desperate hunt for our Bible bag, find it, whisper to the workers that we are leaving them in charge, and run a block to our car. Sure enough, there is the crowd, congregated not only on the sidewalk in front of the door, but clear into the streets, for tonight we are to pray for the healing of the sick. Cripples, invalids, wheel chairs, people on crutches, the blind, the halt, the deaf and dumb, and those having all manner of diseases, are being admitted at a special door by ticket. Our little mother has never stopped even a moment for supper, but is interviewing, registering and helping to a place of believing faith the sick and afflicted. The audience in the streets, which is increasing every moment, have twenty minutes more to wait till the doors are open, and they sing as they wait, "Rock of ages, cleft for me, let me hide myself in Thee." It can be heard for streets around, as we speed away to our rooms.

It is now the middle of the campaign. The people have found out the place of our abode, at Sister Branch's home, and there is not a quiet moment left, day or night, between door and telephone bells and mothers pressing their way right into our very bed rooms, with little children to be prayed for. So it has become necessary for us to move to a quiet hotel, and bind the clerk and bell-boys to silence; and yet even here there is no real privacy. The entire city is really stirred, and we find that the guests and owners of the hotel are attending the meetings and begging reserved seat tickets for the special nights and registration cards for the sick.

We run to the cafeteria and hurry to our table with some steak and potatoes to keep up our strength. "You say you are tired, reader? Why, this is no time to get tired; the real day's work has but just begun; brace up now; we have just five minutes to eat. We shouldn't really have stayed in that prayer room so long."

"Lord, bless this food to the nourishment of our—"

"Excuse me, but isn't this Sister McPherson?"

"Ye-e-s, dear," we falter.

"Oh, I am so glad! I have been trying to get hold of you for so long," the owner of the voice complains.

"Papa, papa! Come over here and sit down; we can talk to Sister as she eats."

"Now, Sister—Papa here" (a hasty glance at Papa reveals an elderly man of perhaps 65 or 70). "Papa has a cancer on his neck beneath that soft hankerchief; it is so painful—and raw, just like that steak."

"O-o-h!" we shudder, and push the plate from us; it would be impossible to touch another bite. Seeing our pallid, tired face blanch at the description she continues to give of "Papa's" suffering, the woman at last excuses herself and goes. We go too—without supper, determining to lay in a supply of sandwiches in the room tomorrow (we are staying at a reasonable hotel which has no dining room).

There is barely time to don a fresh, clean dress, and run now. We phone and learn that the singing was started promptly at seven, as the house was full, and many standing in the streets. Again we rush to the building. Again the streets are full of cars—again the police and ushers part the crowd and seizing our hands pull us through. Again the singing, praying, preaching and overflowing altars, each service dearer, sweeter, deeper and of more absorbing interest than the last; but you know, dear reader, that the Bridal Call is small and that we could not take you to all of the meetings, so, after a brief glimpse into this healing service at the arena we will pass on to the mammoth outdoor divine healing service in Balboa Park.

ARENA—DIVINE HEALING SERVICE

It is now about 8:30 p. m. The message from the text, "Jesus of Nazareth passeth by," has brought scores to the altar for salvation, for we ever seek to put the ministry for the soul ahead of the ministry for the body.

Not only are the ministers from the leading city churches with us tonight, but from other churches for miles around. As the aisles and altars fill with "sinner-folk" coming home to God, the ministering brethren leap from their seats, and through the ropes to welcome and pray for them. Down on their broadcloth knees they go, toiling with the workers, helping harvest in the grain. God bless and reward them for their sweet, sweet spirit! With hearty handshakes—pats—and "God bless you's" they are sent back to their seats singing "Happy Day, Happy Day, for Christ has washed my sins away."

And now, the ropes are lowered at one corner, so that the sick may be brought to the platform. (Whenever it is possible we prefer to pray at the chancel rail, or the altar; but they don't seem to build them in boxing arenas, so we had to do the next best thing and use the platform.)

In a steady procession they come, there to be prayed over and anointed with oil in the name of the Lord. Brothers Black and Pierce are leading the congregation in:

"My faith looks up to Thee,
Thou Lamb of Calvary,
Saviour Divine."

and other songs. Dr. Ferris, of the First M. E. Church, Dr. Belding, of the First Baptist and Rev. Wilt are assisting us in prayer, whilst Rev. Wood and Rev. Weyant are assisting the people to and from the platform, and Jesus is doing the work and bringing glory to His precious Name.

The building is packed and breathless with interest from floor to ceiling. People are sitting and standing on windows, ledges, on top of the dressing room and in most unexpected places. The doors are jammed as far as the policemen's ropes will permit; and in the street crowds stand perfectly still for hours hoping for a fleeting glimpse of the plâtform through the opened doors.

Because of the great demand (multitudes have come to Southern California seeking health, as in perhaps no other place) two or three divine healing services have been held each week during the revival. Faith is rising higher and higher like a great flood tide that sweeps all before it. For indeed, if "Seeing is beliving" one could not be a doubter long. Blind eyes were opened, deaf ears unstopped and the lame in several instances left their crutches behind, leaping and jumping with joy as they went away.

The effects of such miraculous and instantaneous cures in answer to the believing prayer are curious to witness.

A young woman who had given her heart to Christ in the meetings persuaded her fiance, a wordly minded young man, and who seldom gave a thought to God or his soul, to attend the meeting. Upon seeing a paralytic man fling his crutches from him and walk, jump and even run up and down the steps and aisles in his joy at again finding the use of his limbs, the face of the worldly young man, who in his eagerness had unconsciously risen and pressed his way to the front, turned perfectly white. He pressed the back of his hand against his forehead, and his eyes were wide and staring, as though he had seen a spirit rise from the grave. He swayed as though about to faint; and a few moments later was kneeling at the corner of the altar sobbing as though his heart would break—such is the convicting effect of these scenes. Surely they preach a louder and more convincing sermon than the most eloquent words ever could do.

At another notable miracle, where stiff and doubled joints were visibly straightened before our very eyes, so that a crippled sufferer from arthritis rheumatism ran like a child, waving his arms above his head and finally holding up his crutches in his joy, and offering them to any one who wanted them for firewood, I saw a man—the finest, sanest type of level headed American, leap to his feet, absolutely oblivious to his surroundings, his face working, his eyes burning with excitement, and throwing his hands straight up above his head, he gave utterance to a loud

"WH-E-E-E! ! ! !"

whilst his mortified and fashionably dressed wife pulled desperately at his coat tails and said: "Sit down, Charles; you're forgetting yourself; sit down." He did so after a moment, looking rather shamefacedly about him to see whether any one had noticed, but no, they were too busy wiping away the tears, clapping their hands and praising the Lord, to divide their attention with him for an instant. Poor man, the only difference was that he had never learned to say "Hallelujah," and as he had to give some vent to his feelings or burst, he said "Wh-e-e-e."

PARALYSIS AND BLIND EYE HEALED

A little girl of twenty, but looking more like fourteen because of her long illness, is prayed for. She has never walked alone in her life; her relatives and grandmother have been praying and fasting all day, and "know" she will be healed.

Sure enough, in a moment, she is up and walking to and fro across the platform, hands uplifted, face transformed. Now she is descending the steps and walking again in the aisles; till suddenly, after she has taken her seat, a new thought strikes her and a little shadow falls over her countenance. Going quickly to her side, our little mother, who is overseeing them all, asks the trouble.

"O-o-h, I became so interested in Jesus making me walk that I entirely forgot to ask Him to heal my blind eye,—this one eye" pointing, "has been blind since infancy, and I do want it healed so much, but now my opportunity is passed."

"Why, dearie," mother makes reply, "who was it that healed your spine and limbs."

"Why, it was Jesus," the girl replies emphatically through her tears.

"Then lift up your head and ask Him to heal your eye also, right now whilst the waters are troubled."

Mother passes on her work of preparing and forming the steady line which is flowing over the platform.

The little girl is praying earnestly the while. Then suddenly, a wild glad little cry is heard from her corner. We look around, and there she is, on her feet again; one hand tight over the good eye whilst she gazes happily about her with the other. She picks out her relatives and grandmother in the distance—sees the hundreds of handkerchiefs which the delighted audience are waving to her, describes the objects in front of her, counts the fingers lifted before her eyes and can see clearly "Praise the Lord!"

This is just the opportune time to impress upon the audience the realization that it is not "me" but "JESUS" who heals the sick and answers prayer. Bringing the meeting to quiet we give the little girl an opportunity to testify, and have her relatives rise to confirm the story, then, after drawing the attention of the people to the fact of her eye being healed in answer to her own prayers, after she had taken her seat, we ask the multitude:

"Every one who has seen the notable miracle of this girlie walking and seeing, say 'Amen'!"

A thunderous "A-A-A-A-M-E-N!" shakes the place.

"And now, let me ask you—WHO HEALED HER? How many think we did it? Say 'Aye'—"

Not a sound.

"Every one that knows that Jesus Christ did it say 'Hallelujah'!"

A near splitting roar of "HAL-LE-LU-JAH!" rocks the building.

These are the moments when sinners and former unbelievers praise the Lord and cry "Hallelujah" in unison with the whole audience. Why, how could one help it? "Who could resist such a Saviour as this?" we ask them. "What man or woman among you would not want such a Saviour, healer, companion and friend? Why, He is a friend worth having! You cannot afford to live another day without HIM. Every one here tonight who has not yet given his heart to Jesus, but would like to be a real Christian from this hour—lift your hands."

And then we stand, ministers and laymen together, gasping with amazement and delight—scores of hands are shooting up on every side, thus saying, "I am coming to the altar at the very next opportunity and will give my heart to such a Christ."

But, without another word, we must hasten on, if I am to take you to the open air mass meeting in Balboa Park.

THE ENTIRE CITY STIRRED AND SHAKEN

For five big unbroken weeks the revival has swept on and out, higher and wider and greater, until to say that the whole city is shaken to its depths by interest in the power of Jesus Christ, is to put it mildly.

Such crowds are being turned away from the doors that there is a continuous clamor for reserved seats. This system of reserving at least half of the building and admitting by ticket those who have not been able to get in before, seems the only solution. The employees of the large department stores appeal through the store manager for tickets, and come in a body one night; the employees of another, the next; the marines, sailors, service men and young people, the next. Another is Church Members' night, the Methodists in one section, the Baptists in another, then the Presbyterians, etc. Wonderful love and unity prevail. And when "The Old Time Religion" was sung, and the words added:

"It makes the Methodists love the Baptists,
It makes the Baptists love the Methodists,
It is good for San Diego,
And it's good enough for me,"

all the church members who could do so reached across the

aisles and shook hands with all members of other denominations they could reach, still singing: "It makes you love everybody, and it's good enough for me."

It has now become impossible to enter a hotel, restaurant, store, or even to walk a block on the street without several people recognizing and stopping us, either with a shining testimony of salvation and healing, or a fretful grievance that they have to work late and have been shut out for a week.

"And Sunday afternoon, I did so want to hear that sermon on 'The Second Coming of the Lord,' but I was too late. Oh, if only I hadn't stopped for dinner; I was there more than an hour and a half before the doors were opened as it was; but I couldn't get near the building. Sister, I believe that fully 2,000 people were turned away; what are you going to do about it?"

"Why, brother, we have good news for you," we reply. "By request of hundreds this message is to be repeated in the First Presbyterian church tomorrow night, and admission by reserve seat ticket will ensure our reaching those who have not heard the message and keeping out those who have. Here's your ticket, and one for the wife, right now."

"Oh, thank you so much; but couldn't you give me four or five more? My boss in the shop and his wife were shut out too, and there's so and so, and so and so, etc.—"

This is a sample of the gauntlet one must run now to get anywhere. We run into a store for a clean blouse—no time for laundry now—we select it quickly, but not before a clerk in the distance recognizes us, or thinks she does, and calls a little whispering group together to confirm her suspicions. They are coming toward us now:

"Pardon me, but aren't you Sister Mc—?" You know the rest—

"Mrs. McPherson, we'd like to know why it is that reserved seat tickets have been sent to the —— and to —— and we have had none. My little niece was healed of infantile paralysis at the meetings. We think they are wonderful, why haven't you thought of us? etc."

Apologetically we gently explain that we did not know that they wanted to come.

"Wanted to come!!! Who wouldn't? etc., etc."

These few samples are enough to convince you of the scope of wonderful interest aroused in the city. The meeting has been extended twice, and has not had a single break. One night each week when the arena had been otherwise engaged, the revival services were held in the largest churches of the city. First in the Normal Heights M. E. Church, where Rev. Weyant is pastor, we had a precious meeting and many souls were born into the Kingdom. The second week, in the First M. E. Church, with Dr. Lincoln A. Ferris (who is a well known national figure) we had a still more glorious outpouring of the Spirit of the Lord, the long chancel rail being filled, within and without, with sinners weeping their way to Jesus' feet. A Divine Healing service was also held at the conclusion of the service this night. The third week's church service was held in the First Baptist Church, of which Dr. Belding is pastor, and to this church we returned later for another service which was exclusively for the Young People's United Christian Endeavorers of the city, and their friends. At both services the long chancel rail of this beautiful cathedral-like church which is called "The White Temple" was filled again and again. The fourth week's meeting was held in the First Presbyterian Church, and the repetition of the message on "The Second Coming" saw the entire front of the church, pews and platform, filled with earnest seekers after Jesus, the Light of the World.

On one Saturday afternoon a large water baptismal service was held in the First Christian Church, where scores of new converts were given the opportunity of being buried with Christ in baptism. Every moment is busier than the last; every day more precious, and laden with precious fruitage, gleaned from the fields of harvest.

MULTITUDES OF SICK CANNOT BE REACHED

Sinners were being saved by the hundred; believers receiving the baptism of the Holy Spirit in numbers—but the sick, pray as hard as we could and see as many healed as laid upon the promise in real faith, nothing doubting, yet though we stayed and prayed until exhausted, we had only touched the fringe or the outskirts of that great multitude clamoring for prayer. They declared that they had been fasting and praying, and KNEW they had faith to be healed. Patiently yet with dauntless persistence, cripples, paralytics, people in wheel chairs, mothers with little children upon whom the sin of the parents had been visited would stay on and on till the whole audience had gone, and then waylay us asking when they could be prayed for.

So again, we would pray, and again God would answer, but even so the great bulk could not be reached except by general prayer. It seemed that as soon as one was healed she ran and told nine others, and brought them too, even telegraphing and rushing the sick in on trains; we begged them not to do so lest it would be impossible to reach them in the throng. But no, they said they would fast and pray and stand their chance with the others to get up; and that if they did not, they believed that the power of God was so strong in the place that they would be healed where they sat. Then they would go to bring others. No wonder that in certain instances where Jesus healed the sick He commanded them to tell no man of it.

Of! if Jesus were only here in person and could show us how to manage it all. How could it be done—was it impossible? Was there *no* way in which it could be managed? These questions brought to our mind other questions. How did Jesus manage to pray for so many when He was on earth? How did the Apostles manage with their crowds? Then, from the sky, a brand new thought rent its way like an illuminating flash through our tired minds, exclaiming—Why, Jesus didn't attempt to pray for the 5,000 in a building like this: He went out into the fields and deserts, and they brought their sick and laid them down at Jesus' feet and He healed them. Then, too, there was Peter, in Acts 5:15, where they brought the sick forth into the streets and laid them on beds and couches; and where there came also a multitude out of the cities round about Jerusalem bringing sick folks that were healed, every one.

Why—why hadn't we thought of it before. 'Twas because there was no building large enough that they took them into the streets and fields and held out-door services under the canopy of Gods blue sky. That's exactly the solution they found to the problem.

Then came a startling suggestion which almost took our breath. 'Twas the little mother who put it into words:

"Why couldn't we let the sick fill the streets, or a field—or —perhaps the Park, and pray for them there as they did in the Bible days. Never having heard of such a thing being done in modern days, we hesitated a little—"What would the people think?" (eternal question), came to us. Could we do it? Where? When?

Putting it to the audience inside and outside of the building, we asked all that were in favor to lift their hands and say "Aye." The result was deafening, and so Chaplain Spotts, Chaplain of the U. S. Marines, and a man of wide influence and respect, took the matter up with the Park Commissioner. A hasty Board meeting was called; and not only was beautiful Balboa Park ours, but the magnificent Organ Pavilion was placed at our disposal, with seats for many thousands, standing room for a thousand more, a platform before the only outdoor pipe organ in the world. Besides this all the U. S. marines and soldiers that should be needed to assist the Chief of Police and his men with the automobiles, ambulances, pedestrians and the sick, were offered.

And so the days were set for two such mammoth meetings to be conducted in the Park. We do not suppose that such a gathering has ever been assembled for an out-door religious service, and Divine Healing meetings since the days of Christ upon the earth. The writer believes that had she known such a meeting was to have been held by any one in any part of the globe she would willingly have crossed the waters to behold it. Having witnessed it ourselves therefore we long to make you see it too. Now both of these meetings were so wonderful, so identical in power and results, that they merge and mingle together in our minds as we write, so that it would be almost impossible for us to give a separate account of each. We will therefore consider them collectively as we go.

MAMMOTH OUTDOOR DIVINE HEALING SERVICE, ORGAN PAVILION, BALBOA PARK

At 9:45, dressed and breakfasted, we get the car from the garage across the street and are on our way to the Park. The meeting is scheduled to begin at 10:30. Mother has been gone since before we were up, and with her staff of twenty ushers, who were dressed in white from head to foot, wearing crimson sashes, and the trained nurses, men ushers and Marines who had volunterred their services, is caring for the comfort of the sick, and placing them in the most advantageous position.

The entire city has been called to fasting and prayer through the meetings and the columns of the newspapers.

As we approach the Park we are forced to stop many times and drive slowly because of the traffic which is almost all moving in the same direction. It would appear that every one who can possibly get to Balboa Park today is either there already or on the way.

Passing over the bridge which spans the canyon and through the great arch that adorns the entrance to "The World's Fair Grounds," we find throngs of pedestrians, wending their way to the Organ Pavilion. Special street cars are unloading hundreds more, while every street, court and square is filled with automobiles. The uniformed Marines and Service men, are handling the traffic admirably and without confusion.

But now we have reached the court with its entrance and exit road to the Organ. All other cars are stopped today before they reach this entrance except ambulances and those bringing invalids who must be carried. A guard holds up his hand for us to stop—then with a word from his superior officer, smiles and beckons us to come on. Another guard who has been detailed to pilot us in, jumps on the running board, and the car proceeds more slowly than ever. We are just creeping along now, for pedestrians, wheel chairs, stretchers and those carrying cripples on easy chairs, fill the road ahead. We sound the horn continuously and at last have gotten the car as close to the front as possible, and drawn it close to the circular curbing.

We stop the motor and look out over the sea of humanity gathered in the great Organ Pavilion. Whilst driving through the throng we had to attend strictly to our business and keep our eyes upon the road lest we injure some of the blind and lame and now we get our first real glimpse of the gathering.

Photographers, newspaper men with panoramic cameras and men with moving picture cameras are scattered around the outskirts of the crowd, and scaling the high buildings and walls to get a better view of the throng. But no picture that we have yet seen has been really able to depict the enormity of that multitude, which Police and Park Commissioners estimated through the day to range between ten and thirty thousand. Certainly it is a scene of humanity. There is no jesting, very little talking and at first seldom a smile; perfect reverence and awe is upon them all, for this is the most solemn and momentous occasion that the city has ever known. One bond of sympathy and Christian love has bound them all together and has made their hearts to throb as one.

Poor souls, they have sat here so long. The morning sun is shining but the long shadow of the great organ still falls across the people. 'Twill be gone when the sun gets an hour higher.

We leap from the car with a guilty feeling as though we have kept them waiting, though we are really half an hour early, and make our way to the platform. Tears are in our eyes, and we can hardly see.

Mounting the platform we look down upon those pale and emaciated faces; some are almost skeletons; upon beds, upon chairs, sick babies carried on pillows; the sufferer who has been unable to lie down for years and has to sit bolt upright on air cushions in her chair because of rheumatism; the blind, the the halt, the lame, the children whose little bodies are devoured with the results of Tia Juana's sins; the sufferers from cancer, tumor, and all manner of diseases; the young woman whose limb is decayed and poisoned and must be amputated unless Jesus heals it; the human bodies in cages of steel and plaster; the deaf and dumb who have never spoken nor heard, the epileptic, the insane, the demon possessed and those incredibly bloated with dropsy; the rich, the poor, the old and young, the sick and well, the sinner and the saint; the Catholic and the Protestant—we realize that if ever anywhere a people needed Jesus in this wide world it is here and now.

"No—no, dear reader; if you stay right by us and see it through our eyes, you must not break down or give way now! We are going to need every ounce of energy, faith, sympathy and endurance before this day is o'er. Besides there is not a second to lose and we might as well start the meeting right this minute as keep them waiting longer."

All the ministers and clergymen are seated on the platform. Thank God, there is dear Dr. Ferris, with his strong encouraging face and smile. He stood by us from the very first, anointing and praying for the sick by our side, hour after hour, in each healing service.

And yes, the choir, selected from the various churches and admitted to the rostrum by platform passes is ready to begin. There is our little orchestra with cornets, trombone, saxaphone, etc., and yonder are the Salvationists in uniform with their music and band.

Another look at the sufferers in the audience and we drop down beside our chairs for a word of prayer. Poor darlings, how we have learned to love them; the compassion of the Lord Himself has filled our hearts. How much more then does Jesus love them! Wildly our hearts throb up in an agony of prayer:

"O Jesus, look down from the open heavens of blue this morning upon us all.

"Dear Lord, here we are, just the same, poor, old, heart-broken, sin-striken world that we were when You walked upon the earth. We are still the same needy people, Lord—shedding the same tears, feeling the same woes, subjected to the same ills, feeling the same pains. We have the same blind eyes, the same deaf ears, the same burdens that oppress—and O! thank God, we have the same, same Jesus.

"You have never changed—dear, faithful, covenant-keeping Jesus—always ever just the same. Thine ear is not heavy that Thou canst not hear; nor Thine arm shortened that Thou canst not save.

"O blessed Jesus— we dare to trust Thee. We dare to believe Thy word. We're walking to meet Thee on the waters, like Peter, today; and whilst we keep our eyes on Thee Thou wilt not let us fall.

"Put faith in our heart, Lord, meet the expectations of thy people, that all may know our God still lives and answers prayers, in Jesus' name—Amen."

And now the entire congregation is standing singing, with faces lifted to the open Heaven:

"All hail the power of Jesus' Name,
Let angels prostrate fall."

Yes! Yes! The Power of Jesus' name. Why, it is because of that very power we are here this morning.

And now there is silence. Even the waving date palms, planted in a wide circle about the pavilion are still for a moment. Dr. Belding, that splendid man of God, is praying—praying such a prayer as one seldom hears in this day and age. Every heart is lifted with him, as his voice rings out, clear and strong over the heads of the assembled multitude and mounts to God above.

Look! See those soft, fleecy clouds floating overhead. Does it not seem as though the sky were filled with angels? and yonder are the feathers of a mighty angel's wings.

"Rock of Ages, cleft for me,
Let me hide myself in Thee.
While the nearer waters roll,
While the tempest still is high."

Was ever such singing on earth, as well from those thousands and thousands of full hearts?

"Hide me O, my Saviour hide—
Safe into the haven guide."

Now they are seated again, the sweet song of the male quartette (arranged by one of the Park Commissioners, who himself sings in the number) is winging its way into the hearts of the people.

Suddenly it is time for the message; but before we speak, several requests are sent up, asking that James R. Flood, of the U. S. Navy, who was so miraculously healed two weeks ago, should relate the wonderful story. Summoned from his position in the audience, where he is assisting and encouraging the sick, he vaults lightly to the platform, and, taking his place beside us, gives the following testimony in a strong, clear voice:

MIRACULOUS RESTORATION AND HEALING OF DISEASED WITHERED LUNG

On June 7, 1918, while serving with the United States Army Engineers, in France, I was gassed with Chlorine gas. A piece of shrapnel from a bursting shell went through my gas mask, breaking the mouthpiece and rendering the mask useless. I stumbled around the shell-torn wood for the few moments that consciousness remained with me, strangling from the fumes. When I fell, unconscious, I lay for seventeen hours before stretcher bearers reached me and carried me to a First Aid Station. My mouth, throat and lungs were so babdly burned by the gas that I was bleeding from my mouth when picked up. Army Medical Officers sent me back to the States, and until September 24, 1919, I remained in Army Hospitals under treatment. Some strength came back into my body slowly, but *BLEEDING FROM MY LUNGS* was a daily occurrence. If I coughed or even laughed heartily, or tried to lift anything a hemorrhage started.

X-Ray pictures of my chest showed my right lung slowly shriveling, and drying up. In September, 1919, I was discharged from the Army Hospital as being *BEYOND ANY FURTHER MEDICAL AID.* The last X-Ray picture taken showed only a small mass of shriveled matter about the size of a goose egg in my right chest, all that remained of that lung, and I was given the compensation and insurance allowed to a disabled soldier and *SENT HOME TO DIE.*

But I didn't believe God intended me to die just yet, so I refused to give up. My father and mother had been Christians and had brought me up to believe in Christ as the source of all Goodness and of all Power. Dad was a doctor, a chest specialist, treating diseases of the heart and lungs; and I have heard him over and over again tell his patients that it was not necessary for them to die from lung trouble; if they lived the right life and believed in their healing, praying God to give them strength, He would answer their prayers. I have seen my dad pray with his patients about as often as I have seen him give them medicine, and I have seen a lot of those he gave pills to, die. Don't think from that, that dad was a better preacher than physician, but he was a better doctor because he was a good Christian.

And so, although father and mother were no longer with me in this world to help me, when the Army physicians told me nothing more could be done for me, I refused to believe it, and I kept on practising what dad and mother had taught me—to live right and to call on Jesus for help. The hemorrhages kept coming, however, but I felt sure they would stop.

A few months after I was discharged from the Army an opportunity was given to me to enlist in the Navy as an Instructor in the Training School at Great Lakes, Illinois. I went there in December, 1919, to deliver lectures in the theory of operation and repair of aviation and navigation instruments. But the climate there on the shore of Lake Michigan was very unfavorable for my condition. During the ten months I was there most of my time was spent in hospitals, and as the next winter drew on the Navy physicians ordered my discharge fearing that I could not live through another Illinois winter. But I asked to remain in the service, and my request was granted on condition that I be transferred to the West Coast.

Praise the Lord for the order which sent me to San Diego. The hemorrhages from my lungs still continued out here, however, and the right side of my chest was as flat and immovable as a board when I breathed.

I went to the Navy Hospital at Balboa Park for treatment and the Navy physicians there wanted to discharge me from the service, saying that I could not continue in the service and live.

One night a lady came to the house where I stay, and told of the wonderful things the Lord was doing in Dreamland Arena, praising Him for the souls He has saved, and the sick bodies He has touched and made whole.

I went to the meetings and the devil tried to drive me away. Every time I tried to sing or shout the praise of Jesus my lung started to bleed and I would cough up blood until my handkerchief was saturated with it, but I kept going to the meetings.

On Saturday night, January 29th, 1921, as I sat coughing blood into my handkerchief, Sister Kennedy sent an usher for me, who with herself led me up on to the platform. The Rev. Dr. Ferris, pastor of the M. E. Church, came and took my hand and Sister McPherson asked me to stand up and pray to Jesus to come into my body and cleanse it. I don't know if Sister McPherson put her hands on me or prayed for me (friends have told me these things were done), but I only know that when I asked Him to come near me, that He came. Oh! Praise the Lord, He touched me! I felt the withered tissue in my chest begin to tingle like your hands or feet do when they have been asleep and wake up. I felt the cool air rushing into my right side as I had not felt it before. I looked down and saw the right side of my chest rising and falling when I breathed, as it had not moved before. Oh! Praise the Lord, a drop of His precious power had fallen on me, and I was made whole again.

I went back to my seat a new man, and though I sang and shouted His Blessed Name for the rest of the evening, I did not cough up any more blood. It has now been some weeks since He sent His mercy into my body and I have not had a hemorrhage. I have worked and lifted heavy weights during this time as I had not done for two years and a half, and it has not tired me nor caused bleeding. Oh, precious blood of Jesus; it can do all things for those who will only believe. My lung which was gone is restored, and I am given new strength and new life to work for Him and shout His praise.

Mrs. M. E. H., in whose home I stayed since coming to San Diego, has seen me having hemorrhages, and has carried the bowls of blood from my room, and has added her testimony to mine. I hope to get the old X-ray of my chest, and also a new one, and when I get them I shall send them to Sister McPherson so that she may make cuts from them to show the readers of the Bridal Call the miracle of the withered lung restored.

(Note—This testimony has been spoken, written and signed by Mr. Flood.)

Upon the conclusion of this remarkable testimony, a great handclapping and cheering rises from the audience. They who look upon this young man in his sailor uniform, surely gaze upon a great and notable miracle. Praise, oh, praise the Lord!

And now, after a short sermon, which embraces the "Double Cure" salvation for the soul and healing for the body, (which message is listened to with breathless interest by the silent reverent throng, who lean forward in their seats, eyes riveted lest one word of the message of hope be lost) the long and seemingly endless stream of cripples and sufferers has begun to flow over the platform, and we are praying for the sick.

Dr. Ferris, Dr. Belding and Dr. D. U. Wilt stand with us in prayer, hour after hour; as we are anointing, praying, encouraging, lifting the sufferer from his or her bed after prayer is made, steadying them as they begin to try their limbs made weak from long disuse, rejoicing as strength flows back and they lift up their hands in praise to God and walk away shouting, "I knew He'd do it! I just knew He would!"

"The great Physician now is near,
The sympathizing Jesus.
He stoops with drooping heart to cheer,
Oh, hear the voice of Jesus."

The choir is singing in soft, encouraging, almost caressing tones, as though by their very song of faith they would carry the sick to the arms of the Christ who waits to bless and heal.

Here is a man, carried up lying face downwards, on a stretcher, prone upon his cot. He is suffering from tuberculosis of the spine.

"Oh, Lord," we pray, "for Thy name's sake touch and heal this suffering and afflicted body." As we pray he also lifts his voice in earnest supplication.

"Let Thy Power, Thy resurrected life, stream down through this body, heal this tubercular spine, and make him whole from this very hour."

"Brother, have you faith that Jesus Christ will heal you now?"

"Sister, I have—I have been praying and fasting, and I know that He is able and willing!"

"Then, in the name of Jesus Christ of Nazareth, take your healing in His Mighty Name; rise up and walk!"

In a moment be scrambles off the cot, is on his feet, walking to and fro, descending the steps and walking in the midst of the crowd below, clapping his hands like a prisoner just liberated from confinement, glorifying and praising the Lord in a loud voice. His minister, who has assisted him in getting to the meeting and the platform, adds his testimony to that which our eyes have seen; declaring that he knows this man's suffering and faith, and praises God for answered prayer.

JESUS SAVES LIMB FROM AMPUTATION

And this young woman, is a "run-away." For many weeks she has been a "shut-in" at the hospital with her limb strapped to the ceiling. About three months ago she had been struck, and dragged by an automobile. Her limb was fractured in four places and the bone refused to knit. After she had suffered untold agony, it was found that infection had set in and abscesses formed on the bone. Four operations had been performed, but the pus would not flow, (this was Tuesday) and the limb was doomed to amputation on the coming Friday. Her heart was heavy and sad.

Then came a ray of hope: she heard that right in this very city, in answer to believing prayer, the Lord was healing the people from their diseases, as He did in the Bible days. If He could heal others, why could He not heal her; and save this limb from amputation?

There and then, she decided to give her heart to God, and become a Christian at the first opportunity, giving her strength, her love, her all to Him in service, when He had made her whole.

But how could she—with her tortured limb in a cast (which opened in front to permit dressing of the wound, which ran through the limb from front to back) ever get to the meeting? Asking the doctor's permission she was met with the reply:

"Why, child, you are crazy to think of such a thing! Positively not! There is no hope for your limb now that it has refused to drain and has become so infected, except in amputation."

Oh, what would she do! She just could not give up when there was this chance to go to the Great Physician and have it healed. She sat in the hospital and thought and prayed. A lady friend came to visit her, helped her dress, and with help, carried her to an automobile and away they went to the Park.

Speaking of her as the "run-away" and telling of her pitiful case, the workers now carry her to the platform. But, before thinking of her body, the suffering young woman thinks first of her soul. Burying her tear drenched face in her handkerchief, she sobs out:

"Oh, I am such a sinner! I'm such a sinner! Jesus save me, forgive me, and I'll give my heart and life to You."

Receiving the heavenly witness that the work is done, she begins to praise the Lord, and we anoint her head with oil and pray that she may be made whole.

She removes the blankets from the limb, which is held straight out before her on another chair, and we gasp at the terrible sight; a gaping, angry hole runs through the limb which is discolored and perfectly black. Yet, even as we pray, the Great Physician Jesus touches her and honors her faith. The blackness disappears almost at once and the natural color returns.

"Oh! the pain is all gone!" she cries in a voice that carries far to the people. Delighted she begins pressing and tapping the limb with her fingers, joyously declaring that the Lord has made her whole.

Upon her returning to the hospital, she found the hospital staff were very much annoyed at her "daring escapade." But, the following morning when the examination was made, they were amazed and delighted at the marvelous improvement and gave her permission to go back to the meeting again that night; and said that there would be no need for amputation. It was the writer's privilege to see this young woman at the meetings two weeks later, and to hear her say that the only anxiety the doctors now feel is that the limb is healing too rapidly and that they could not understand it. The abscesses drained immediately and the bone is knitting together. Hallelujah!

Oh, see the streams of people coming for prayer—would you ever have believed that there was so much sickness and suffering in the world! See, the sufferers range from the tiniest little babes, some of whom have never grown since birth and are thin and haggard from sickness, to the oldest man that leans upon his staff and is assisted up the steps.

CANCER, DROPSY AND RHEUMATISM HEALED

Here is a dear old lady, suffering from cancer, dropsy and rheumatism. How she is praying as she stands in line and waits her turn. No looking curiously about, her mind is fixed on God.

"In the name of Jesus Christ, we rebuke this cancer and command it to melt away like snow before the sun! Dropsy, and rheumatism, we rebuke you in the name of Jesus and command you to loose this body! Sister, in the name of Jesus, be thou made whole—go in peace and serve the Lord in a well, sound body from this hour."

As we pray, she declares that she can feel the power of the Lord streaming through her entire being and instantly she is healed.

NOTE—This, too, is a wonderful testimony; for two weeks have passed since that day. Last night we heard this sister testify in Liberty Hall before a thousand people that not only is the cancer gone, but the dropsy and rheumatism, too, have disappeared. She declares that she is the happiest woman in the world.

Not all are healed who come. A few there are who have not the least idea of what it means to exercise active believing faith in the Lord Jesus; but come to see if *we* can heal, or do them any good. Of course, *we* have no power within ourselves and try to get their eyes on Jesus. There are some who stand or sit coldly, like a piece of wood, while we pray for them. They are not healed, for coming to Jesus for healing is like coming to Him for salvation. If one kneels at the altar to be converted, but never prays or makes any effort to confess their sins, or call upon the Lord, they go away in exactly the same condition as that in which they came. No matter who shall pray, or how earnest the petition is, it is a personal matter 'twixt them and the Lord. *They* must seek if they would find, and believe if they would receive. Such cases of unbelieving are few and far between, however, for the vast majority have wonderful implicit faith—faith which rises higher every moment because of the mighty miracles which are being performed before their very eyes.

THREE GIRLS FROM TUBERCULAR HOSPITAL HEALED

Mr. Mutters (keeper of the San Diego Zoo, with its wonderful lions and other wild animals) is a devoted worker in the meeting and brought with him three very sick young ladies from the Tubercular Hospital. They were prayed for and instantly healed at the first meeting in the Park, and are here again at the second service testifying to the wonderful power of Jesus that has made them whole. Coughing is gone, lungs are dried up and soreness healed. They have been permitted to leave the hospital after two years' confinement.

"Oh," cries one of the young ladies, "the nurse told me the other day, as I was leaving the hospital after my wonderful healing, that the doctor had said that he did not expect me to live through the spring. Praise the Lord, just look at me now —hear my voice—see me breathe, my lungs are perfectly sound. We three are all out of the hospital to stay and, oh, it seems so, so good, like being set free from a prison where we were destined to serve a life sentence. Now, we will work for Jesus, and testify to His power as long as we live."

All day long, the procession never stops. From 10:30 in the morning, till the sun is far in the west, we pray and pray and pray, and yet seem to have made no great inroads upon the multitude who have come for healing. The seats vacated by those who have been prayed for are instantly filled by others who press to the front.

At one o'clock, loving hands pull us away from our task for the moment, and draw us through one of the doors at the side of the great organ and into a room where we are made to eat a couple of sandwiches "to keep up our strength" they say. But oh, we are not hungry—we are receiving strength from above. Thousands of eyes watch us jealously as we leave, and brighten with appreciation when we hastily return.

In fifteen minutes we are back on the platform and the long procession begins to move again. The sick, the lame, the blind, the halt, those on beds and those who come in wheel chairs, they who hobble on crutches or lean upon a cane—what a procession! One man is bowed over with an infirmity such as we read of in the Bible, and cannot lift his head above his waist. On and on, on and on they come—those with cancers, tumors, goitres and every disease known to mortal man.

One man is healed of a goitre so quickly that his collar is left loose and hanging. Others declare their tumors are gone.

We were supposed to end the meeting at 2:30, for the organ recital begins at three each day; but Dr. Stewart and the Park Commissioner send up word that we are not to stop as long as our strength holds out, as they would not interfere with the meeting, or hinder one poor sick body being healed for the world. So, we take another long breath—wipe the perspiration from our burning faces and begin again.

DEAF EARS UNSTOPPED

The number of deaf ears that are opened is truly wonderful. Many who have not heard a sound, or even their own voices before in years leave the platform declaring that they can hear a whisper.

During the revival, one dear old soldier who fought in the Civil War, and whose ear-drums were punctured by the bursting of a shell, was healed. Jesus, by His mighty power, restored the broken ear-drum instantly and gave the man his hearing once again.

"You say you think it's wonderful?" So did he. He leaped and danced and shouted like a boy. His delight was wonderful to behold. For two weeks after his healing he attended the meetings, testifying again and again to the fact that he could hear every song and sermon from beginning to end.

Three hundred and eighty sufferers, each having numbered registration cards, have already been prayed for on the platform today. Not merely touched, but really dealt with and personally prayed for.

But hundreds and hundreds who have sat patiently all day, are beginning to get uneasy and ask each other with anxious, quivering faces, "Will they get to me? Will I ever be able to get up?"

You say that you are "so tired, you can't stand up another

minute," dear reader? Oh, you must not give up yet! Why, I would rather face a battery of guns than face the disappointment of those people who have sat here all night and day without food or drink, waiting to be prayed for, if we leave.

"But," you say, "my feet are aching and burning like fire from standing so long on this cement floor, my eyes are aching from the sun, my back——"

But there! You know that Jesus was weary, many's the time, for us. Think what He suffered on Calvary to bring deliverance to US! Shall we not then be willing to forget our own exhaustion, in bringing His deliverance to others?

"But, will we not be sick in bed ourselves tomorrow?" you ask.

No, indeed—as our days so shall our strength be. "He that loseth his life for My sake," says Jesus, "the same shall find it." Tomorrow we will be as refreshed and rested as ever; for the Master will lay His healing hand upon us.

But—come to think of it, we cannot wait till tomorrow, to regain our drooping strength, for announcements have been made by Dr. Belding and by the press that we are to speak to the young people of the city tonight, under the auspices of the United Christian Endeavorers. Our subject is to be "The Four Steps in Christian Life as Taught in the Book of Ruth," and we MUST be fresh and at our best for this.

"Impossible!" you say. "How could the fatigue and nervous exhaustion from lifting and praying for this mass of suffering humanity, all day, be taken away so quickly? Why, you have poured out your strength and sympathy like water upon the ground!"

But the same spirit that raised up Jesus from the dead, my dears, will quicken this mortal body, praise the Lord. But come, we must not stand here talking a second longer. Each moment we lose, means another disappointed one that will be sent away without a touch of prayer. Of course, when all else fails and the time is gone, we will pray for them all collectively and many will be healed as by faith they touch the hem of the Master's garment; but they all long to receive the "anointing," and be prayed for personally.

On and on we pray; wonderful instances of healing which would take a volume if written are wrought out before our eyes. But now the day is going. Another hour and the long shadows will be filling the pavilion. Hour after hour the stream of sick, who come in orderly rows, attended by nurses, ushers and marines, has never stopped. But now thinking to reach more in a shorter time, it is thought best for us to come right down among the multitude and pray from seat to seat. This is done for a short time but soon we are beaten back to the steps by the press; who, forgetting themselves in their anxiety to get to the front, are crowding the cripples and the mothers with babes.

Here we pray again, leaning over the banister for protection and incidentally for support, for though I cannot speak for the dear ministers, Doctors Ferris, Beldin, Wilt, Weyant, Wood, Morgan, and others, I, personally, am swaying and dizzy through the long strain and anxiety of knowing that so many cannot possibly be reached in the remaining time.

Wonderful things take place at this closing moment and the last to be prayed for are

TWO DEAF MUTE YOUNG LADIES

They are sisters and have never heard a sound or spoken a word in their lives.

"Oh! Thou deaf and dumb spirit, in the name of the Lord Jesus Christ, we command you to come out of her!"

"Oh! Ears be opened! Tongue be loosed and speak the praise of Jesus," we cry as the power of God falls on us.

Instantly a light breaks over the face of the girl for whom we pray and she points to her ears, in the most delighted gestures, indicating that she can hear. Then we bid her speak the name of "Jesus."

"She-sus"—is her first attempt, and her joy is wonderful to behold when she hears her own voice.

"Jesus! Jesus!" she is saying now and the voice is becoming stronger, so that the crowd can hear it. They clap their hands in unspeakable delight and shout until the pavilion echoes. How wonderful that her first spoken word should be the Name above every name—"Jesus!"

"Now, say, 'Praise - the - Lord,' " we direct.

"—aise - the - 'ord" is her first attempt here. For never having spoken in her life or having heard a spoken word, she must learn to talk, like a baby. Soon, however, she is saying clearly, "Praise the Lord" and "Hallelujah!" to the delight of the crowd that surge about the steps.

During the time that we have been praying for this young lady, her deaf mute sister has been standing by, wide-eyed with joy and wonder; for though she could not hear, she could read in the expression of her sister's face and the moving of the lips, the wonderful story that Christ had set her free.

Trembling from head to foot, she is now passed through the gateway, which has been formed by human hands at the foot of the stairs to hold back the crowd. And praise the Lord, Jesus heals her in exactly the same manner as that in which He has healed her sister. Now they both stand praising the Lord and making new sounds, as they begin to talk, delightedly, to each other, and point to their ears, signifying that they can hear. GLORY! GLORY! GLORY! Do you wonder we all sang:

"What a wonderful change
In my life has been wrought,
Since Jesus came into my heart;
Floods of joy o'er my soul,
Like the sea billows roll,
Since Jesus came into my heart."

All are standing now, and a sea of waving handkerchiefs are floating above the heads of the people. Bless them—they are giving a wave offering unto the Lord, and now Dr. Ferris is closing in prayer, thanking the Lord for the miracles which our eyes have beheld, and praying His richest blessing upon each head.

At last the meeting is over. The crowd is breaking past all barriers to get to us. A cordon of workers and a couple of men in uniform rush in to rescue us, for our white faces show that strength is at an end, and we are piloted to our car. In walking we feel as though we are on the deck of a heaving vessel, or that the ground is swelling beneath our feet, but praise the Lord, He is whispering, "Well done!" and we have the satisfaction of knowing that we have done our best and that thousands of lives are cheered and strengthened by a touch from our loving Lord.

Away to the hotel, to wash, comb, and don a fresh, clean dress, out to the restaurant for dinner—and then off to the White Temple Baptist Church and the Young People's meeting.

Automobiles are parked far and near. Hundreds of bright young faces greet us as we mount the platform. The finest young men and women of the city must be here tonight, and at the close of the service, in the neighborhood of one hundred rise and make their way to the altar, there to renounce the world and accept Christ as their personal Saviour.

Many splendid service men, marines and soldiers are amongst the number. A little pile of pipes, tobacco, cigarettes, dice, etc., is emptied from pockets and left inside the altar railing as they come. Tears are in their eyes, and joy in their faces as they rise to take their seats, saying, "Henceforth for me to live in Christ."

And now, dear reader, though we have written and written of San Diego we have only taken you through a portion of two days' meetings—but we pray that they may contain a blessing to your soul. Poor "shut-ins," some of you far away in other cities and states on farm lands, far from revival fires —others across the sea in Australia, India, Africa, China, Japan, Great Britain and Europe, we have been thinking of you as our busy pencil flew across the pages. We long to bring to you new blessing, inspiration and encouragement. If this has been accomplished and we have carried you to the meetings and made you see them through our eyes (we have tried so hard), would it be too much trouble for you to drop a line and tell us so, that we may know just what is needed most another time.

And just to think, we've never said a word about the wonderful *"Workers' Meeting,"* where ministers, Sunday-school teachers and superintendents, elders, deacons, church officials, Y. M. C. A., Y. W. C. A., W. C. T. U., leaders and workers, Mission workers, Christian Endeavorers, Epworth Leaguers, etc., met together to express their heart-felt need of the baptism of the Holy Spirit, and to receive an enduement of power for service. The results of the "tarrying service" that followed this meeting, only eternity can tell. Many were filled with the Holy Spirit and spake with other tongues as in the days of old. Neither have we told of the water baptismal service.

Then there was the aeroplane flight, wherein the evangelist preached from the aeroplane to a large crowd in the Aviation Field and then made a flight over the city, which she showered with fifteen thousand hand-bills and announcements of the revival meeting, bringing a message from above. This aeroplane flight was donated freely by Mr. Hennessey, of the Hennessey Flying Squad, at the foot of Broadway, at the Municipal Pier.

SUFFER THE LITTLE CHILDREN TO COME

Neither have we told you of the blessed afternoon service, which was held for little babies and children at the arena.

Because of the press, it was necessary to request that the infant orchestra be left at home during the night service, but this one afternoon, the coming generation held full sway. Over one hundred babies were held in our arms and dedicated to the Lord by the mothers and fathers. Parents who were not yet Christians came and gave their hearts to the Lord before presenting the little children, and asked wisdom that they might bring them up to live for Him. Many parents had been converted in the meetings and all solemnly promised to establish a family altar in the home and to make it a house of prayer from this day; also, to bring up their children in the fear and admonition of the Lord and to yield them to His service gladly, and render whatever help they can give, if the Lord should call them to His service at home or abroad.

Mothers who did not possess a Bible were each presented with a beautiful leather-bound volume, and prayer was made that each parent might have wisdom and strength to meet each problem as it should arise and hold their little ones for Jesus. Sick babies were also anointed and prayed for and the sweet little cherubs had a wonderful time as an orchestra with special inimitable selections all of their own.

Upon our first return visit we were privileged to open a campaign fund for the saints with which to build themselves a San Diego Tabernacle for the continuation of the work. Upon our second return visit, we were privileged to preach the Gospel under the canopy of a tent to a large audience upon the lot of land which they had secured. Thirty-six hundred dollars was raised for their building there and then, this sum being contributed almost entirely by new people who had been converted touched or interested during the late campaign. This has been one of the effects and great after-results, spiritual, numerical and financial, reaped by pastors and workers in various other cities wherein our campaigns have been held. Oh, how happy we are to be able, under the guidance of the Lord, to so build up, establish and leave upon such a firm foundation, the work of the Lord, from place to place; leaving it well known, respected, and looked up to by thousands of people who have, perhaps, never before been interested in just such a work!

JESUS HEALS THE SICK

TUBERCULOSIS HEALED.—I was in the hospital a little over two months. I had tuberculosis and the doctor said I would have to stay in the hospital for a year at least. I praise the Lord I found a new Physician, who promised to heal all my diseases. On a Wednesday I left the hospital against the doctor's wishes and went to the Organ pavilion at Balboa Park to be prayed for. I was healed and have felt better since then, than in all my life. "Glory to Jesus."—Dorothy L., San Diego.

TUBERCULOSIS HEALED.—I had been in a hospital two years with tuberculosis. After prayer, the blessed Jesus healed me. I was not expected to live the year out, but praise the Lord I have left the hospital and hope to live many years in the glad service. Jesus, the Great Physician, is my Doctor forever more.—E. W., San Diego.

KILLED 40 RATTLESNAKES.—I deem it the greatest privilege of my life to testify in these columns what the blessed Christ, the Saviour of mankind, has done for me. I have been quite deaf for 20 years. When attending church and sitting on the front seat, I could hardly ever hear the number of the hymns given out and had to ask some one next to me. I have lived in Colorado ten years and in that time I have killed not less than 40 rattlesnakes and never heard one rattle. I have attended the McPherson revival meetings in the Dreamland Arena, San Diego, California, and the evening of January 15th, the dear sister had a healing service and I went up on the platform and was anointed in the name of the Lord, and I had my hearing restored instantaneously. Praise the dear Lord forever and forever. I also had the joy of salvation restored to me. I witnessed to the above on two occasions on the platform. Yours in the Lord.—William T. Ewing, Civil War Veteran, San Diego.

NEURITIS, ETC., HEALED.—In January, 1911, I had a sudden attack of multiple neuritis, developing into complete general neuritis, causing a condition of intense pain throughout every portion of my body. Soon my hands and feet became crippled and powerless and I was unable to turn or move. Doctors declared the case hopeless and this terrible condition lasted eight months without relief. I fully believed that God's power alone could help me and prayed with an earnest faith in the full *ability* of God's power, but without any conviction as to whether or not it might be His *will* that I should be cured. During 1912 there were several months of marked improvement and I struggled to be able to cope with the conditions of my life, which were exceedingly hard.

Suddenly I was again gripped by the full force of the old neuritis, and soon became critically ill. I was treated by some of the most noted physicians and nerve specialists in Santa Barbara and San Francisco, but in January, 1913, I was again pronounced in a hopeless condition and was carried back on a stretcher to my home in Philadelphia. There I was taken from hospital to hospital during the many long months in bed, until at the close of 1914, I was able to begin the painful struggle to get about on crutches. Electrical treatment and massage were kept up constantly, but there was little further gain in the next year. By the fall of 1915, however, I was beginning to use the crutches quite freely and considered myself blessed with a wonderful recovery. When the revival services opened in San Diego, I was at the very first meeting and was tremendously impressed by the power of the message.

I learned of the barrier which I had set up by not coming with simple, loving, positive faith, sure of the dear Saviour's loving eagerness to heal and to bless with the same and immediate and complete power as of old in His earthly ministry. At this time I was depending on crutches for getting about except that I could get around in the house on the smooth level. I could not go up steps or walk as much as a block on the street without cramping pains and the danger of a troublesome attack. Both feet were partially paralyzed and I was not able to raise them from their down-hanging position. The toes were entirely numb and senseless. I was never without pain of more or less degree, very, very easily fatigued and sensitive to the least chill and dampness. Sleep was constantly disturbed by cramping muscles and sharp pain and after the general aching weariness kept me from resting at all. On the night of January 22, 1921, I was amongst those who were to be prayed for and after the careful instructions was able to come with full faith that "By His stripes we are healed"—and that I was then to receive the merciful blessing. I was hardly conscious of anything but *thankful praise* until after I had stepped down from the high platform and was walking about amongst the people, filled with entirely new power and soundness. I walked home that night, a distance of fully a mile without the least bit of pain or even fatigue. On taking off the shoes, I found the feet entirely straight, alive and active, as normally. I slept that night and ever since in perfect peace and comfort. My crutches were the first of many to follow, left as trophies in the arena, a silent testimony of the power and loving mercy of God. It is now nearly a month since then and I have walked two miles or more almost every day. Also, my sight, which was quite seriously impaired, I had not thought to pray for at the time of my other healing, was restored to me later through prayer, so that I can now read without glasses. This is the record of my principal cure, but the spiritual blessing is far more wonderful and more prized. This no one else may quite know, though I pray my life may yet show what my lips cannot utter. May all glory and praise be to God.—Marian W., San Diego.

RUNNING TO HEAR THE WORD.—The following came to me Sunday evening at 5:15, January 6, the last night of your meetings in the Dreamland Arena, in San Diego. I had given up going that evening as I thought I would give up my seat for the unsaved, but, ah, how my heart longed to be there and I had a battle with myself to give up going to a feast like that, so after I had conquered and was thinking, "Well, I won't hear Mrs. McPherson's last message, but I hope my sacrifice will prove a blessing to someone else," a voice said to me, "If you want to meet the Saviour once more in the arena, you'd better run." As the voice struck my ear, then in my heart there was a wonderful power come into my body. I looked at the clock and it was then 5:15 and I had only one meal that day, so felt the need of something to eat, but when the voice spoke to me, the feeling of the need of food left me, so I picked up an apple and ate it as I was getting ready to get off as quickly as possible. I had four and a half miles to go on the street car. The power remained with me and I just felt as if the car did not go half fast enough, and if I was off, I could outrun it. I never in all my life was able to walk as I walked after leaving the car. When I was within a half a block of the arena, I saw the doors were open, and it looked as if every seat was taken. The voice said again, "You'd better run," so I did run, and as I looked around wondering what people would think of me running, I saw several others from different directions running also, and I tell you my heart just went in leaps and bounds in praise and thanksgiving to God, thanking Him, to think I lived to see the day, when I saw people running to hear the word of God. Glory to His name for hearing and answering prayer. This is what my heart has yearned and prayed for, for many years and my heart's prayer is now, Burn on, burn on, oh, Holy Fire! till all the dross is consumed and the gold is refined and we shall see the dear Master coming for His own. After I found a seat it was just 6:15, so I rested a few minutes, then closed my eyes and as I lifted my heart in prayer, asking God's blessing on the speaker and on the hearts of the hearers, the dear Lord gave me a vision of the affairs as they were at the arena. It seemed as though the dance floor overhead was removed and just a little above our heads was the Saviour in His beautiful robe of white. I say "white" as I don't know any other word to use, but, oh, it is so weak in describing anything like that, that had the sheen of glory in it as that had, and the beautiful halo around His glorious face, with hands outstretched to us all. The response to the altar call was wonderful at that service, as at all other services. My heart's prayer is that not one soul who has been sealed with His precious blood by the power of the Holy Spirit, will go back to the world, but be kept and used for His honor and glory. Lovingly your sister in Christ.—A. B., San Diego.

VOICE RESTORED.—Among those healed was Mrs. E. C. She lost her voice one year ago and could not swallow food. Now she can eat without choking, sleeps well and is beginning to talk. She is amazed at the wonderful things Jesus will do for those who believe and trust in Him. Praise God from whom all blessings flow. San Diego.

SPINAL TROUBLE HEALED.—This is to certify that I, the undersigned, was healed by our Lord, Jesus Christ, through the intercession of Mrs. McPherson, from spinal trouble and sciatic rheumatism, I myself suffered for fifteen long years, and know what it means.—Mrs. Anna C., Lemon Grove.

PRAISE GOD.—I have been healed by attending those grand meetings through my faith in God; I give Him all the praise. Praise God I am free from bondage and I'm determined to trust and serve Him to the end. I had inflammation of the bladder and catarrh of the stomach for years, and I praise God for such a grand revival as San Diego has never known and my daily prayer is that God may sustain and protect and keep our sister that she may go forth and go on with this grand good work.—Mrs. Jennie M. McL., San Diego.

HEALED OF TUMOR.—I was healed of a tumor, heart trouble, high blood pressure and neuritis, about two weeks ago, January 22, 1921. The tumor was internal but I am sure it is gone, or is going. My heart beat very rapidly sometimes, 101 or 102 times in a minute. It is normal now. I had high blood pressure, testing 184 for about six years; now my head is relieved and feeling fine. I have not felt the neuritis for two weeks and am sure I will not again. I am truly thankful to God for the healing.—Mrs. Cora L., Huntley, Minn.

HEART AND STOMACH HEALED.—I was instantly healed of heart and stomach trouble about two weeks ago, January 22, 1921. My heart was beating much too slow. The doctor told me I was losing about twelve beats in a minute and there was a continual ache and pressure around my heart. I would bloat up and could not sleep well at night. While they were praying for me, the ache and pressure left. It was a great relief and it has not returned and neither do I bloat any more and I sleep fine, for which I earnestly thank God. I was here in San Diego for the winter.—S. A. L., Huntley, Minn.

TERRIBLE GOITRE HEALED.—I am happy to say that Jesus has healed me, through prayer. Four years ago I went to Rochester, Minnesota, to consult Mayo's regarding my health. After thirteen of the specialists had examined me, they pronounced my disease an ingrown butterfly goitre, which I knew had been of twenty years' standing, and was crowding my heart, and affecting my nerves badly. I had a fluttering as of a butterfly through my entire body, which I could not control. The doctors there advised an operation as soon as my heart could be quieted, but I could not consent to this and came home. But thanks be to God, He has healed me and I thank Him many, many times for sending this blessed hand-maiden to San Diego.—C. N. B., San Diego.

SAVED AND HEALED.—I have been wonderfully revived spiritually on the afternoon of January 21, 1921, while kneeling at the altar, praying, by faith. I saw my dear Saviour standing in front of me, His pure white robe was lying in folds around His feet and, by faith, I took both hands full of the snow white garment and kissed it. I felt blessed and happy and believed it a token that I had received not only pardon, but would be fully healed, for was not Mary Magdalene healed and forgiven when she merely touched the hem of His garment? I said nothing of this vision, but my faith was strong, so strong that on Saturday night when I went up for healing, while I didn't do anything different from many others, yet they spoke of my great faith. This spiritual healing I value above the healing of the body, yet my eyes are greatly improved, and I'm feeling better, looking better and eat because I'm hungry. And the deep hollows in my cheeks are filling. My troubles were many—end of spine curved in from a fall, stomach, bowel and kidney trouble, poor circulation and rheumatism of the joints and sciatic trouble. These troubles may take time to heal, but praise God I feel a hundred per cent better in mind, soul and body.—Ada W. A., San Diego.

I THANK JESUS, over and over again for touching my body with His healing power. I suffered many years with nervous indigestion and bowel trouble, also tuberculosis of the left lung for the last eight years and invisible goitre and eye trouble. I was prayed for at your first healing service, but could not say I was healed; on the following morning after seeing so many healed and myself not healed, I took God's Word and asked Him to show me why I was not healed. He plainly showed me that my heart was hardened so I would not be healed. Praise His holy name, He took that away right there. The next message I heard, one of the workers said, "with His stripes we are healed." I said to the Father, "that is for me, hallelujah," and I have rested on that promise ever since. My stomach is healed, my lung is healed, and I am stronger and trusting Him to take the goitre away. The evidence I have had that my lung is healed—the devil passed some of his cold germs around promiscuously at the arena and some lodged in my throat and head, but, praise the Lord, Jesus used them to bring praises to His holy name, instead of me becoming weak as usual. They did not affect me that way and my lung is healed, so they could not lodge there. God has been good to me ever since I was stricken, just waiting I now know, to heal me. I was an orphan girl without a home when stricken. There was a young man loved me and I him. When I was told to seek another climate, he said, "I won't let you go alone; I'm going to take care of you." God bless my husband, he has taken care of me for eight years, demonstrating to me every day of his life the blessed love of Jesus. Pray for us. From one who intends to serve Jesus in His way with the body He has healed.—Mrs. B. Lulu McL.

WISHING TO TESTFY to what the Lord has done for me, will say that I was healed at the meetings held in San Diego. Glory to God for it. I had ulcer of the stomach for about eight years, also rheumatism which caused a lump on my left knee, but thanks to God, I am well now. Blessed be His name, since Jesus came into my heart, there is sunshine in my soul. —J. E. D.

I HAVE RECEIVED wonderful healing during the revival meetings. I had a rush of blood to my head, night and day, at frequent intervals for years. It was almost unbearable. Doctors and chiropractors did me no good. I am a Christian and have been praying for healing for many months, but I did not receive it. The Lord so filled me during these meetings, and by almost constant prayer myself, I received the healing. Praise the Lord. Hallelujah! Glory to His name. I can truly say that the Lord doth with me dwell and I will always be ready and willing to do what He would have me do.—Mrs. B. J. B.

HEALED OF BOWEL TROUBLE.—I have been healed of the after effects of the "flu" that were so bad that I would have to move to drier location and sunny rooms if I expected to live. And also healed me of chronic bowel trouble that baffled all methods of treatment, that I had before the "flu" came on. —R. H. B., San Diego.

DRUM OF LEFT EAR PUNCTURED—HEALED.—While I was in the U. S. Army service at the Presidio, during target practice, the concussion was so great that the drum of my left ear was punctured. Was discharged from the service February 6, 1906, then landed a job as gripman on the Haight street cable line in San Francisco, but my hearing kept getting so bad (such a roaring in my ear) that I had to give it up. Then went east to Findlay, Ohio, to visit my people, returned to the coast that fall, where I remained until the fall of 1913, then to Australia with a party of land seekers. While in Sydney they were begging for men to go to work in the train service for the Government railroad of New South Wales; I knew that I could not pass the strict Government physical examination on account of my hearing. I then came to Honolulu, where I thought I would try once more; landed a job on the Honolulu Rapid Transit as motorman, but after riding the cars for several days, could not hear well enough to tell one bell from the other, on account of the roaring in my ear, so had to give up the job; then sailed for San Francisco. Had my ears examined by two specialists, one at Honolulu and the other in Los Angeles, both of whom pronounced the drum punctured. I have been gloriously blessed and healed at the arena meetings. The Lord has both saved me and restord my hearing. Praise Him forever.—Azotus H., San Diego.

BECAUSE GOD HAS BLESSED us so wonderfully in healing our grand-daughter, Margaret Morse, we want to tell everybody about it, and to thank Him for bringing this precious hand-maiden of His to San Diego, where she has done so many wonderful things in the name of Jesus.

Margaret Morse is twenty years of age. When she was barely two years old she was stricken with spinal meningitis or infantile paralysis. Doctors did not understand her case. After she recovered she walked a few months, but her head grew too large, her spine was curved, her left hip higher by two inches than the right. She has walked with great difficulty.

On the afternoon of the last healing service at the arena, we succeeded in getting a card and that night Margaret was healed. She was wonderfully helped immediately, walking with ease and going up and down the steps of the platform confidently. Since that evening she continues to improve. Her spine is almost straight, her hip is normal, the great masses of flesh which had accumulated around her body from sitting so much, have disappeared.

But more wonderful than all, the left eye, in which, according to doctors, the optic nerve was dead, is seeing again. She is reading with it, and that too, with the good eye covered. Praise the Lord! She will, by the grace of God, soon be perfectly well. May the Lord bless His dear hand-maiden and spare her many years as she goes from coast to coast doing many wonderful works in the name of Jesus.

REVIVAL FIRES AT SAN JOSE, CAL.

EIGHT WONDERFUL DAYS IN THE FIRST BAPTIST CHURCH

WHAT wonderful days of cyclonic power and glory they were!

The Lord has just given us the most wonderful eight-day revival in the First Baptist Church of San Jose (pronounced San HoZay). In addition to saving hundreds who wept their way to the altar, and healing scores of sick folk, the Lord gloriously baptized the pastor, Dr. W. K. Towner, with the Holy Spirit. Several of the deacons, and church officials, including the treasurer, Sunday-school teachers, and even the church sexton and his wife received the baptism according to the pattern shown us in the New Testament Mount, Acts 2:4, 10:46, 19:6. Many members of the church and choir were also filled with the Spirit. The Shekina Glory of the Lord came down upon the place until there was not room to contain it all. Hallelujah! Glory!—and this is the way it all began:

Upon our return from San Diego, the usual stacks of mail were piled up and waiting attention. Scattered amongst them were several calls to conduct revival campaigns in denominational churches in various parts of the country. Each expressed precious humility, hunger and a burden for a revival of the old-time religion. But after reading and praising God for their contents, we had to shake our heads, sigh, and say: "Oh, how we wish it were possible to go—but everything is booked so full for months in advance, and these cities are so far away. Besides, the few remaining days before leaving for St. Louis and Dallas, must be spent in writing and prayer and getting the third edition of "This Is That" on the press.

Then we came to Dr. Towner's letter, telling of their need, their hunger, the unanimity of their official board, resulting from an intensive scriptural study of the Holy Spirit, His personality and office work, in the Acts of the Apostles; and God spoke to me:—"That's my call—go at once."

Hasty telegrams flew to and fro, work that a moment before seemed imperative and all-important was postponed for a week and dropped where it was (Dear ones, waiting for "This Is That," please take note and extend your patience further), and almost before we knew it the Evangelist-Editor found herself bundled bag and baggage into a sleeper of the "Sunset Limited," which tore its shrieking way through the night towards Santa Barbara and on to San Jose.

"We are a hungry and a ready people," said Dr. Towner, on our arrival. "We have been reading The Bridal Call to our people, and the fires of revival are ready to burst into flame at a moment's notice. . . . When someone told me that if you came the church would be full to overflowing, I told them that I was not much interested in the coming of someone who would fill the church to overflowing as in the coming of someone who would *fill the pastor and his people to overflowing with the power of the Holy Ghost.*

But would God be able to accomplish such a mighty revival as they expected, in one short week? Yes—the clouds of blessing were ready to burst upon us the very first Sunday morning. Although there had been little time to advertise, the news was flashed by telephone and telegraph till visitors were arriving from almost every city of Western and Northern California. At the close of the first service, in which the fact was emphasized that all great revivals must begin in the hearts of the people themselves, the altar was thrown open to those coming for conversion or consecration. The hungry people arose like a wave at full tide and swept to the front together till the whole altar space was full and then overflowed into the aisles from front to the back of the church.

What a time of weeping and heart-searching. Many were saved, many reclaimed, and scores reconsecrated themselves to the Lord Jesus. Sunday night the power of God fell till again the altar overflowed, this time with unconverted only. "Praise the Lord!" cried the pastor; "never has this church witnessed such a scene in all its history!"

In looking to the Lord for a promise concerning this people and my message to them, the Lord spoke from His Word, and said: "Speak, and hold not thy peace, for I have much people in this city," and Peter's experience in the household of Cornelius was brought forcefully to our minds. Monday night, not only did the Lord meet in saving power the two score penitents at the altar, but gloriously baptised five young ladies, Sunday School teachers and choir singers, with the Holy Spirit in an after-meeting of God's own appointment.

The main service was over, and being rather weary from the two services of the day, Mrs. Dr. Steele, of Los Angeles, and ourselves were about to leave the church when word came that "a group of our finest young ladies are seeking the baptism of the Holy Spirit in the Sunday School room and would like you to come in for a moment to pray for them."

But, thought I, tomorrow afternoon we are to speak upon the baptism of the Holy Spirit; as yet they have not heard just what or how to receive or even expect this pentecostal infilling. —But there, neither did Cornelius' household, and God took care of that; perhaps He would do the same here, and be His own instructor.

Hallelujah! In a few moments five of these beautiful young women, including the pastor's secretary, were swept down beneath the mighty power of God. And although they had never seen any of us receive the baptism of the Holy Spirit, or heard the Spirit speak to them, they were every one filled in exactly the same way as the 120 on the memorable day of Pentecost. One young lady, a Sunday School teacher, spoke and sang in other tongues, which sounded like the language of Heaven, for over two hours. Such interpretation and singing one would scarcely hope to hear this side of Heaven. As loving, weeping friends and church members stood 'round this group till almost 1 a. m., numbers of unconverted gave their hearts to Christ; and the music director, with tears in his eyes, said: "She has been singing for me for a year and a half and I know she cannot sing like that of herself. Her voice is low contralto, and she is taking notes as high as a prima donna,—it is the Holy Spirit Himself."

This was but the beginning; all week, two meetings a day, the revival swept on, gaining impetus at every service. Word was brought again and again, of people being saved and baptised with the Spirit in their homes. One man stayed away from service to resist conviction, but God so gripped his conscience that during the altar service at the church, he fell to the floor in his own home, sobbing: "Lord, be merciful to me a sinner!" and was gloriously saved. His wife came to the morning service next day and gave her heart to God.

Day after day, afternoon and evening, the altars were continuously filled with sinners and backsliders, weeping their way to the foot of the cross.

Three services were held for the sick and some wonderful healings resulted, insomuch that the people marveled and wept and shouted and glorified Jesus of Nazareth. From eight o'clock in the morning until two the next morning, I am told, there was almost always some one in the church seeking God, praying through to victory and the Promised Land.

What a revival! On the closing Sunday, after the morning service with its great altar call, we had returned to the hotel to rest a few moments before going to luncheon—(there had been no time for breakfast)—but a sudden call on the phone from the church, said:

"Will you please come over to the church right away—at once? Several of our deacons are under the power—so are the members of our choir, our church treasurer, etc! Will you come?"

Would we go? I should say we would! Down the elevator, through the long lobby, out the door and down the street we flew, till several guests of the hotel came to the door with a most surprised look on their faces and gazed after us inquiringly.

"Where is the fire?" they wonder.

"In the First Baptist Church," our hearts sang. Glory!

When we opened the door—oh, the sacred sight that met our eyes. We will not attempt to describe it here. Suffice it to say the slain of the Lord were many and the vats o'erflowed with oil and wine. In the choir loft lay the deasons; in the aisles, on the pews, were the lady ushers and singers—while between the front pews and the altar was the preacher, prostrate at the Saviour's feet—all being sweetly baptised with the precious Holy Spirit, who now spake through them in a language of praise and worship that was all His own. Out of their innermost beings was made to flow the rivers of living water described by Jesus when He spake of the Spirit.

'That man struck a gusher," said one brother, in the language of the oil fields, in describing the mighty infilling of one prominent church official, whose unspeakable joy and praises to God in the Spirit were incessant and indescribable.

All afternoon the power of the Lord continued to fall. At six o'clock, great crowds gathered at every entrance and overflowing the sidewalks, waiting for the doors to open, those still under the power of God were carried into the choir room and we made our way through the throngs at the doors and away to the hotel for a combination breakfast, luncheon and dinner all in one.

The night meeting opened at seven o'clock. The mighty response to the message and altar call was the crowning joy of the campaign. Scores and scores of men and women, young and old, filled the choir loft, the pulpit platform, the altar space and the aisles, seeking Jesus the Christ as their personal Saviour.

Repeated implorings to stay at least another week tore our hearts. How we longed to remain with this precious people. But work and piled-up letters clamored for immediate attention and we must away. But God is with them, and the Comforter has come "to abide forever."

DR. TOWNER'S REPORT

Right in the midst of the spring glory of blossom season in Santa Clara Valley, God graciously visited San Jose, its metropolis, with a mighty baptism of the Holy Spirit sent from heaven. Out of the open windows came the poured-out blessing until there was no room to contain it. Seekers were at the altar by the scores from the opening meeting, Sunday morning, March 20th, until the close. Every one of the seventeen services was fruitful in a harvest of precious souls, who were weeping out their hearts in contrition at the altar before the mercy seat, and rising with songs and everlasting joy upon their heads in the consciousness of sins forgiven and an inborn experience of the new life in Christ Jesus.

It became at once the outstanding religious event in the history of the city. Great crowds surged through the doors of the church, filling every chink and cranny of the large auditorium and overflowing through the vestibules into the street. Thousands were turned away.

Sister Aimee Semple McPherson came to us in direct answer to prayer and in demonstration of the Holy Spirit and power. The story of how God prepared us for her coming by intensive study of the Person and Ministry of the Holy Spirit, and how He directed her to us "to declare all the words of this life," is too long to recite. It is sufficient to say that from the beginning the very auditorium was charged with supernatural power, Hallelujah! Into one short week was crowded the experiences of a generation.

On Tuesday evening, at the tarrying meeting, the power fell. Wednesday night witnessed the miraculous touch of Jesus in Divine Healing, the eyes of the blind were opened, deaf ears unstopped, cripples arose from wheel chairs and walked. Jesus won all hearts through the gracious and potent ministry of His hand-maiden. Before and after the healing services the altar was thronged and the church aisles were choked with inquirers.

The interest greatened in its intensity and power until men and women over all the city fell under the spell of the Holy Spirit and sinners were saved in their own homes during the time of the altar call at the church.

At the Men's meeting on Saturday afternoon, hundreds of the city's best men were brought under the blessed spell of the Saviour's power and grace. Strong men were filling the pulpit and choir loft on their knees with cries and tears seeking the precious blood for cleansing and the enduement of the Holy Ghost from heaven. It was a sight to make the angels rejoice, a sight never before witnessed by men who have attended revivals in all parts of the country.

Sister McPherson's sermon on the "Two Photographs," at the Sunday morning service, melted all hearts in contrition. It was a memorable service. At its close the Holy Spirit fell in precious fulness on a tarrying meeting which the Lord appointed and not man. Many were prostrated under the mighty power of God and arose rejoicing, sweeping through the gates of praise.

The crowning service was on Sunday evening. Crowds gathered an hour and a half before the service and hundreds were turned away. Every available space that could be used for kneeling penitents was requisitioned and the aisles of the auditorium, even the pews, were centers of little prayer services where Christian workers were experiencing the joy of leading souls to Jesus.

One man, over ninety-three years old, was saved and baptized during the meetings. Another veteran of eighty-four kneeled at the altar by the side of a seeking flaxen-haired cherub of four. Hundreds have said we never saw it so before. "God hath done great things for us whereof we are glad." So, smiling, praying, rejoicing, singing, weeping, we sang the old hymns of Christian fellowship and joy and said good-bye and God-speed to our Sister, whose remarkable messages and indefatigable labors had led us into the experience of a religious revival that comes down out of heaven from God.

Already a movement is well under way to prepare a great tabernacle campaign for her return and the work goes sweeping on.

SOUL STIRRING REVIVAL IN ST. LOUIS, MO.

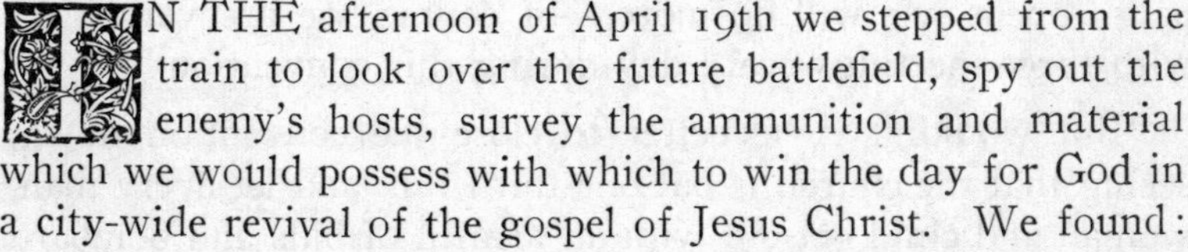

IN THE afternoon of April 19th we stepped from the train to look over the future battlefield, spy out the enemy's hosts, survey the ammunition and material which we would possess with which to win the day for God in a city-wide revival of the gospel of Jesus Christ. We found:

A busy bustling city of 773,000, rating sixth in the United States, clanging street cars, roaring automobiles, streets congested with the great city's usual hurrying throng on business and pleasure bent. Theatres ablaze, cabarets and dance halls aglow, a beautiful city with churches aplenty, but a reputation of being immune (?) to revivals.

A beautiful Masonic auditorium—the Moolah Temple, accommodating (at most) some three thousand, which was to be ours for three weeks and four Sundays.

Our earthly backing—the smallest church in the city, with only 67 members.

Our choir—anxious questioning revealed the fact that some 15 members (out of the little 67, many of whom were well along in life) were all that could be mustered for choir duties—the platform seated 500. These few were inexperienced singers, but were willing to do their best and hoped others would come to their aid.

The ushers—a small company composed of a few consecrated, hard-working brothers from humble walks of life, who, though totally inexperienced in handling crowds or executive ability, offered their faithful services and were ready to be shown.

(When it came to trusting God for numbers, Gideon was left far behind. St. Louis was much greater than the camp of the Midians and he had 300 against our 67.)

Dropping in unexpectedly at the little "convention" being held in the tiny church, our hearts asked the tremulous question: If this is their state convention and the church is but one-third filled, will that great auditorium down town ever be filled?

"What advertising has been done?" we asked.

"We began to put some cards in the windows yesterday," replied the Pastor, "and as we have five days before the campaign opens, we will do more,—of course, we are very busy with three meetings every day during this convention."

"But wouldn't it be better to close the convention down, seeing that the church is but one-third full, and let every man, woman and child get out with an armful of bills and bombard the town? If this is to be a city-wide revival, every one must be made to know it—any paid ads in the papers yet?"

"No—there was a small news item in the other day on an inside page in one of them, however."

"Um-hum!—permitted to put banners on the trolleys here?"

"No—against the rules."

"Allowed to put banners across the streets?"

"Don't think so—but have a nice sign outside Moolah Temple."

"I see—well—the time is short. Better get more cards, posters and bills and cover the city as far as you can in these few days. Must let people know the revival is on or they cannot come! What's going on at the Temple tonight?"

"A Masonic dance, I think."

"Well, if you will get a Brother to drive us over, we would like to have a look at it." Soon we are in the building walking through the auditorium, platform, corridors, prospective "prayer rooms," groaning within ourselves: "Oh-h! that dear little 67 will be but a drop in the bucket! Lord, send the crowds. Help us to awaken this city, said to be immune to revivals, dear Lord." That night we lay for a long time wide eyed and thoughtful, looking desperately to the Lord.

MOOLAH TEMPLE, ST. LOUIS, WHERE THE REVIVAL STARTED

FLYING OVER SAN DIEGO, CAL.

SCENE AT ST. LOUIS, MO.

Where thousands witnessed the converts being baptized in the Mississippi River by [illegible]

SISTER McPHERSON BATTLING FOR JESUS IN DALLAS, TEXAS

MISSIONARY WORK AND EVANGELISTIC CAMPAIGN IN EXHIBITION BUILDING IN DALLAS, TEXAS

"Oh, I expect this place to be full next Sunday," said the enthusiastic driver next morning.

Not wishing to dampen his ardor, but feeling duty bound to prepare him, I replied: "Why, brother, it couldn't be full next Sunday, for only comparatively few even know there is to be a meeting. The main floor will be about half full in the afternoon, three-quarters at night and by the end of the first week the meeting will advertise itself and the place be full to overflowing."

THE OPENING

Just half full it was the first afternoon. But the glory of the Lord was upon us and the crowd was larger at night. Our little choir spread their chairs very far apart and sang bravely. They were augmented by a splendid delegation from Alton, and all did their best. After the message and altar call, the altars filled and many gave their hearts to Christ that first service.

The crowd swelled night by night as one told the other, and by the middle of the week the place was filled with those who declared they had "just heard about it." Preaching service twice every day, sometimes a third service being held, soon the building became too little. Hundreds were being saved and healed, many receiving the baptism of the Holy Spirit. Ministers, laymen and workers began to pour in from every denomination and take their stand beside us on the platform, thanking God for the revival which He had sent totally unannounced and from the most unexpected quarter. Nobly they sang and prayed and toiled, helping us bring to land the nets that were now full to the bursting. Pastors brought their best singers and choirs to our assistance. Official men, presbyters, elders, deacons, trustees, Sunday-school teachers, Y. M. C. A. workers, members of the Gideon band, led by its St. Louis president, came to our assistance, and still we were short of workers, for conviction and fear fell upon the people and hundreds rushed to the altar crying: "God, be merciful to me, a sinner."

THE MULTITUDES COME RUNNING TOGETHER

By the beginning of the second week regular details of policemen, headed by the Sergeant, were needed and changed twice daily, to help protect the people and guard against any being trampled beneath foot or crushed against the building, for multitudes were unable to gain admission.

Sick and sinful who were shut out the day before would begin to congregate about the Temple doors as early as seven and at times five o'clock in the morning, there to wait patiently hour after hour in the blazing hot sun or the pouring rain (and we had plenty of each) for the doors to open. By 9 and 10 a. m. the streets would begin to fill. By 12:15 the doors would open and the house pack in a few moments, leaving disappointed throngs in the streets.

Police and ministers declared that four and five thousand were turned away from several services. Some would stand outside through the entire night meeting, holding to a corner or ledge of the building, believing (poor souls) that by touching even the outside of the building in which God was working so mightily that they would receive a blessing. Police could scarce keep the people back. They wept, plead, coaxed to get in "just one minute," but all to no avail, for they assured them that far more than the law allowed were in already.

On one occasion a basement window was removed, while an officer had his back turned, and a score or more gained entrance before they were discovered. At another time some ingenious souls borrowed or made a ladder just long enough to reach the narrow fire escape and scores of men and women, risking their lives, scrambled up the steep steps and entered the balcony "emergency exit" doors before the officers came rushing around and seized the ladder.

"Did you ever see people so hungry to hear the gospel?" exclaimed Dr. Bitler, of the Chateau Place M. E. Church, and Rev. Markley of Scruggs Memorial.

"Never," replied dear Dr. Claggett, a saintly Presbyterian minister and President of the Board of the Texas Presbyterian University. "I have just celebrated my 50th anniversary and have been through the great revivals from Moody and Sankey down, but never did I see multitudes rushing and struggling to hear the Word like this in all my experience. It breaks my heart till I go home and weep at seeing them shut out," continued this noble man with tears in his eyes and a quiver in the rugged lines of his dear face,—"something must be done about it!"

"Yes," we replied. "But what can we do? 'Tis the same in every city. The world is hungry to hear the Gospel. Not hungering for suppers and concerts and social gatherings, but heart-hungry for a *real* Jesus who saves and heals and baptizes with the Holy Spirit."

THOUSANDS SEEK SALVATION

How the sinners and blacksliders did respond to the altar calls! The entire platform, now hurriedly emptied of singers, would fill almost instantly. Then the entire altar space, running the full width of the building, would fill until at times there was no more room and we would be obliged to halt the singing and stop the people where they were in the aisles until we could clear whole rows of seats, and even then they would ofttimes break the fire-laws by kneeling right where they were and weeping their way to Calvary in the middle of the aisles, which they completely blocked.

Methodist, Baptist, Presbyterian, Congregational, Lutheran, Pentecostal, Salvation Army, Nazarene, Evangelical, workers and deaconesses from various churches all toiled side by side, denominational walls happily forgotten in the great overwhelming glory of seeing sinners born into the Kingdom, and the sick being healed of their infirmities.

The number of acceptance cards handed in by those professing conversion with tearful faces at the altar of repentance mounted into thousands now and careful records were kept with names, addresses and notations as to whether they had ever been saved before and with whom they wished to worship, etc. This latter method we find of great assistance in conserving results, guiding visiting committees who call at the homes after campaign is closed, pray with the converts, leave Bibles where needed and seeking to establish the family altar.

MAN DEAF, DUMB AND LAME SINCE THE AGE OF TWO YEARS HEALED

At the Divine Healing Services God worked in mighty power, insomuch that we can truly say the blind saw, the deaf heard, the dumb spake, the lame walked and the poor had the Gospel preached unto them.

A young man had been deaf and dumb and lame as a result of infantile paralysis since two years of age. He was instantly healed in answer to prayer. The crooked and paralyzed leg was crooked and paralyzed no longer. The deaf ears were completely unstopped in an instant insomuch th. t he heard the slightest whisper and his face was illuminated at the music. His tongue, lips and voice were unsealed at the command of the Lord till this young man, who had learned the deaf and dumb language and talked on his hands for years, began to speak with a loud voice the praises of Jesus till every one, even in the top gallery, heard his voice.

First, we taught him to speak the sweetest word in all the world—Jesus. Then he learned to say: "Praise the Lord." His first attempt sounded like: "

"Aise—de—'ord." His second:: "Prai—thee—'ord," and at last: "PRAISE THE LORD" in a clear, distinct voice as he learned to move his tongue correctly and enunciate. For several minutes he talked and listened as the audience clapped and cheered and shouted until the building rocked. His father, a practicing physician, came to the platform, threw his arms around his boy, then gave his own corroborative testimony and repeated it a few nights later, declaring that now his son could hear his own voice, his father's voice and footsteps, in fact, could hear everything, and like a child was learning to talk rapidly and was soon going home to his little baby to hear his voice for the first time.

He declared that he felt himself called for the work of the Lord and hands were laid upon him for service. He reads verses of Scripture to the audience and on his last night before departure read a whole chapter in Revelation, beginning with the words: "And I beheld a new heaven and a new earth." His mother stood by his side (she had caught the train and joyously hastened to the meetings at the good news). Tears stood in her eyes as she said:

"Oh, I've been praying for this for years and years. And during this meeting I have been at home upon my knees praying and now the answer has come. Before my son (now 25 years old) was born, I gave him to God and prayed that he would preach the Gospel, but when he was two years old, came this cruel stroke of paralysis, crippling his limb and sweeping away his speech and hearing. Oh, how I thank God for what He has done and pray that the prayers of years may be fulfilled in this miraculous way and my son be led to enter the ministry as a winner of souls." When she had finished the son smiled brightly and said aloud:

"A-a-a-m-e-n!"

THE EFFECT

The effect of all this on an audience is hard to describe. They may sit stiff and unyielding through songs and prayer and preaching; they may even hold back during altar call when they see hundreds going to the cross and rising with the glad smile of heaven transfiguring their faces; but when they see and hear such miracles as that just described, they are jolted from their indifference and complacency as though a stick of dynamite had exploded beneath them. There is nothing left to do but believe.

Involuntarily they clap their hands and weep and cry, Hallelujah! just like other folks — wouldn't be human if they didn't. And soon this living, loving Christ of Galilee has won their hearts and they rise to follow and worship Him. Who could help loving such a Saviour? They might resist a cold, marble God—trillions of miles away, who *once* forgave sin and healed the sick some nineteen hundred years ago, in a far off land called Palestine—a country they have never seen—a God whose ear is heavy that He cannot hear or who is too busy to bother with their small infirmities—but, when it comes to resisting and treating with indifference a living, loving, tender Saviour Physician, who is the same yesterday, today and forever, a Jesus whose ear is not heavy that He cannot hear and whose arm is not shortened that He cannot save; a Lord who really cares, whose heart is touched with our woes;

a Redeemer who can meet every need of His people, whether that need arise in body, soul or spirit; who still forgives sin, heals the sick, comforts the broken-hearted, dries the tears of the sorrowful, cradles the aching head upon His bosom, sets the prisoner free from his every chain, drives back the clouds of night with the dawning sunrise of His own dear love, as He comes "with healing in His wings"—Ah! that is a different matter! "Who could afford to slight and wound such a Saviour as this—who could afford to live without such a Friend, Lover, Physician and King?

"Why, He is not afar off—He is real!" we cry. "He is standing right in our midst today. Though our eyes are holden that we do not see His face, we feel and see His power and hear His tender voice crying: Come unto Me all ye that are weary and heavy laden, and I will give thee rest."

And praise God they do come in hundreds, and falling down at His feet acclaim Him Lord and Master of their lives.

TUMEROUS CANCER AND RHEUMATISM HEALED

A dear sisiter, Mrs. E. Gregg, Vandeventer and Evans Avenue, a member of Scruggs Memorial Church of which Rev. Markley is pastor, came to the meeting suffering with rheumatism and a cancerous tumor. After prayer she was instantaneously and miraculously healed. The arm, which could be lifted no higher than the shoulder—and that with great pain and difficulty—was immediately released from the fetters and shot above her head perfectly healed. Her stiffened knees were loosed in a moment so that she ran up and down the steps clapping her hands and crying:

"I am healed—Oh, I am healed!—Thank God! Thank God!"

A few minutes later she left the auditorum hurridely, only to return in about thirty minutes with a face almost transfigured. She walked straight to the platform, climbed the steps, and in the expectant hush (she was personally known by many people) announced to the startled audience that the entire cancerous tumor which had been of internal growth had passed away and that she was completely healed.

This sister had suffered tortures before, but, hallelujah! she attended every meeting now and came to the depot two weeks and a half later to see us off. There, standing on the station steps, she witnessed before the assembled throng of her perfect healing from that hour. Relatives and physicians have corroborated many of these testimonies.

CANADIAN SOLDIER RELEASED FROM STEEL CAST

A Canadian soldier, wounded in France in such a way that his body must be contained in a great case of steel that looked like a small half barrel, declared himself instantly healed in answer to prayer. Leaving the auditorium for the dressing room, he removed the entire contraption, and to the surprise and bewilderment of us all, came in bowing his aforetime stiff knees and back clear to the floor with every step and holding the great steel case and trusses triumphantly aloft as he came. They went to adorn the walls and hang beside the ear trumpets, braces, crutches, canes, etc., others had discarded.

Not all were healed, for many did not meet the conditions or have real faith; a large percentage, however, possibly 80 per cent, were gloriously healed, some instantly, some gradually from that hour began to mend.

I remember praying earnestly for one man, paralyzed, I think he was, but saw no change. Dozens had been healed this night one after another and I had learned to look for some cause now when no healing resulted in answer to our prayers. Instinctively my eyes fell upon his vest pocket—'twas full of great black cigars. My instant diagnosis was: Temple unclean—life unsurrendered—body not healed.

HEART-BROKEN MULTITUDES TURNED AWAY

And so the meetings went on, day after day, till two weeks and two days had elapsed. The throngs who stood without were heart-broken. Audiences of eight thousand would congregate and wait for the doors to open and only three thousand be able to gain admission.

"But please—we want to be saved—we want to be healed!" they would plead.

"Sorry—can't admit another one," the officers would reply. "Crammed to capacity now—better go home and come again."

But they refused to go home. Great fear was upon all the people. One dear, sensible looking woman declared that as she stood in that crowd in her fashionable apparel, the realization of her unsaved condition swept over her till she thought Judgment Day had come and she was shut outside the doors with the multitudes of lost waiting for the verdict. She cried out to God for mercy and was saved where she stood.

We give but a few instances here and there in the meeting that you may form an idea of the flood tide of conviction resting upon the meeting within and without.

FORCED TO MOVE TO COLISEUM SEATING 12,000

It was by this time impossible to cope with the crowds which I am told were at times twice as large outside as within. My mother, burdened for the people, would rise at break of day and go to the Temple to comfort and pray for them until the doors opened and they were admitted, then conducting blessed morning prayer meetings specially for the sick and afflicted. Many truly found Christ in these early morning services.

"I simply cannot bear it!" cried dear Dr. Clagett. "I went home and wept last night to think of the multitudes that were shut out, even though they struggled to hear the Gospel." This dear man of God rose one night and addressed the audience saying:

"Mrs. McPherson and mother do not know what I am about to say, but my heart is breaking to think of the throngs being turned away. I believe and several of our other ministers —Dr. Bitler of Chateau Place M. E. Church, Rev. Markley of Scruggs Memorial and many others (hearty amens from the long rows of ministers on the platform—believe that we should make an effort to secure the Coliseum seating 12,000 (and said to accommodate, including standing room, some 16,000) for the balance of the meetings." Here such a storm of applause, shouting and clapping of hands rocked the building that the doctor could not proceed for sometime. "I have been in personal touch with the owner, Mr. Bates, today and though the Coliseum usually rents for $500.00 a night, we can secure it for $1500.00 for the balance of the campaign and it will be ready for occupancy tomorrow morning. Now I will give the first $100.00 Will fourteen other men and women rise and give the balance?"

In almost less time than it takes to tell it, the sum was given or pledged, the audience in the street cheering as the news was sent out. The next morning Mr. Bates, with tears in his eyes and a lump in his throat which he declared was as big as his fist, made still another reduction through his personal check, so some balance was left for advertising in order to help us make this great change in twenty-four hours.

But oh what a tremendous building it was! One city block square. It reminded us of New York Madison Square Garden outside, but within it was a palace by comparison, beautifully arranged, comfortably seated with opera chairs, the great circle of balconies and galleries ran the entire oval of the building. Why, in the dim light I could barely see the top seats way up by the roof yonder—"surely we will never see this building filled on such short notice," I gasped.

"See it filled! I should say we will see it filled," cried others who had been brought in through the meeting and now wished to encourage us. "This building will be packed and hundreds will be standing in the street." And unbelievable as it sounds, that's exactly what happened. Oh, dear Jesus, 'tis really true that when *Thou* are lifted up *from the earth,* all men are still drawn to Thine own dear side!

Just as quickly as the news could be scattered the people came running together from every quarter and the place was filled. From break of day till midnight my darling mother never left the building. Day after day she went without meals or ate a sandwich standing in the corner, meeting and registering the sick, caring for the delegations constantly arriving from distant towns, directing the ushers who did noble service unmurmuringly, losing the messages night after night. I have seen mother retire at three in the morning and be up at five preparing to leave for the building. At this early hour she would find cripples and invalids clinging with trembling fingers to the doors that they might "not be shut out today." (Some heart-touching incidents came to our notice in this way where a sufferer had prayed the entire night and risen before dawn to meet my mother and receive the precious registration card and some wonderful healings were graciously given by Jesus.) It was this tireless, faithful service on her part that left me free to snatch a few minutes rest between the long strenuous services, now three a day, and enabled me to keep up till the end of the campaign.

The balance of the meeting was so wonderful and of such magnitude in numbers and results that it would need a clearer head and a better writer than myself to describe it all. Thousands and thousands and thousands of people, row after row in auditorium, boxes, balcony and galleries, encircling the entire building—the hundred and fifty foot platform filled with ministers and clergymen of all denominations—just back of them an elevated choir, ladies in spotless white, men in business suits—the grand piano, the lights—the songs—the ringing testimonies—the prayers of earnest clergymen who rallied to every service, even closing their own doors in order to help our weary arms bring the nets to land—the sermons shouted in a voice that seemed almost to burst my lungs as I attempted to make myself heard to the uttermost parts of that great building—the consciousness of having to stand immediately under the great sounding board—the immense altar calls wherein hundreds rose from all parts of the building and fell in contrition at the Master's feet filling the platform, the altar space and the aisles—the soft invitation songs—the busy, earnest workers flying to and fro praying with the penitents, securing names and addresses of same, supplying with Bibles those who were in need—the infinite sigh of relief when the Pastor of the Calvary Baptist Church, in splendid assured efficiency took charge of the singing for the balance of the campaign—the getting the converts back to their seats, the platform re-arranged and ministers seated—the swinging of the channel of song and prayer into the divine healing service which followed—the bowed heads and silent prayer as the piano and violin led into the soft whispered "My Faith Looks Up to Thee"—the long endless rows of sick and crippled which flowed over the platform—the anointing with oil, the prayers, the healings wherein numbers rose from their beds, others cast aside crutches, wheel chairs, braces, trusses, casts, supports, ear trumpets, glasses, bandages, etc., declaring to the great throng that they were healed—all these things blend and mingle and whirl round and round in my mind with the clapping and shouting of the throng till I cannot seem to sort them all out and write them in order someway. But the Lord was with us in great power. The Holy Spirit filled the place with a cloud of glory and the whole city was made to talk of the power of Jesus Christ.

GIRL BLIND EIGHT YEARS INSTANTLY RECOVERS SIGHT

A girl 13 years of age, who stated that she had been stone blind for eight long years, instantly regained her sight, describing and pointing with delight to all that she saw. A white veil melted visibly from her eyes and she saw clearly.

A young man, who had not walked for some years, threw aside his crutches, which he had used with great difficulty, shouting: "I am healed!" ran from the platform, descending the steps, wringing the hands of all he met, embracing his mother and wife joyously and exclaiming: "Now I will live for Christ and I will be able to go back to work and support my wife and family."

Tears fell from the eyes of thousands when the deaf ears of a mother of perhaps 68 years of age were instantly opened. Her face was radiant as the deaf ears were unstopped after the silence of years so that she heard our voices, the singing and even a whisper. Because of the throngs only occasionally were relatives permitted to ascend the platform with those prayed for, and that only when the crippled were in need of their assistance. But the beautiful daughter of this mother could keep her seat no longer. Breaking through the line of special ushers in their white dresses and crimson sashes, she ran up the steps, threw her arms about the mother and pressed her wet cheek to hers crying:

"Oh, mother, can you hear me?"

"Yes, dear—I can hear every word now. Praise the Lord!"

"Oh, sister, I am a singer," the daughter began, turning toward us.

"Yes, and an accomplished singer, too," cried other voices.

"And in all these years," she continued, "mother has never heard me sing."

"Then let her hear you sing right now, dearie. Never mind this great audience, sister, they're with you heart and soul. Look, darling, they're all crying harder than you are. Just forget that they are there and sing to Jesus and mother."

And there and then, with an indescribable light on her face, this beautiful young lady threw back her head and before the great multitude sang with a voice clear as a bell:

"I can hear my Saviour calling
Take your cross and follow me,
Where He leads me I will follow
I'll go with Him all the way."

During the song the mother's face was a study. (Oh, for some really great journalist who could write these scenes as they are.) She stood with clasped hands and radiant face assuring her daughter with tears of joy as they left the platform with their arms still about each other, that she had "heard every word."

Several goitres went down instantly before the gaze of the whole multitude. A tumor on the spine of a certain lady melted like a snow ball before a hot flame, when she was prayed for. She put her hand to her spine, so did one of the leading physicians who stood by. Both declared it gone and glorified the Lord.

A man with a cancer on his face—another with a cancer on his hand—were healed; not instantly, but the next morning both found that a thin skin had grown over the place, by noon a scab had formed, and in a couple of days it fell off leaving the place healed. Praise God!

A man whose varicose veins had been removed by surgical operation had suffered for years with an open leg, which was like a seething fire of pain. He found the place healed and filled in with perfect flesh the next morning and returned to give the Lord the glory.

WHEEL CHAIR AND STRETCHER MEETING

Through all the rush and thronging multitudes we struggled to protect the helpless invalids, but the press became so great that we were at last, for the sake of their own safety, obliged to ask them to remain away till we could have a special service for them alone.

Saturday morning therefore was set apart exclusively for those on beds and in wheel chairs. From the break of day, the management, the ushers and my dear mother worked desperately to accommodate them all. First the long lines of opera chairs must be unbolted from the floor in front of the platform, wheel trucks must be brought in for their removal from the auditorium. The floor space thus cleared was roped and reserved for the rows of stretchers that were carried in from waiting ambulances in a stream. Beds and cots began to come in from every direction, as excited voices cried, "Where shall I lay this one?" or "Where should this stretcher be placed?"

There were those with broken backs, broken necks in great casts, those with total paralysis drawn in queer contortions, those dying with tuberculosis, those eaten with cancer, young and old, rich and poor lay side by side till one could easily believe they were in a large hospital. Courteous, thoughtful ushers were moving softly about under Mrs. Kennedy's directions, encouraging and attending the need of each sufferer till meeting began.

Then came the rows and rows of wheel chairs. 'Twas almost impossible to look over that great company and realize that they were all tied to those chairs, unable to rise. But, praise God, Jesus came to set the prisoner free, and nothing is too hard for our God, we assured our pitying hearts as we went from one to another before opening the service.

The streets were lined in every direction with invalid cars and ambulances hours before opening time. The rich came bringing the poor. All seemed to be thinking of the other first. The poor old newspaper woman and the street urchin sat in their chairs side by side with the rich and the influential. Those wrapped in tattered, greasy quilts beside those on their air pillows and eiderdown wrappings. Denominational and social barriers were all down, tears and songs mingled together as all lifted their eyes to the tender Saviour who had come to save and heal and comfort. Great armfuls of hundreds of fragrant roses were brought and given to the sick, as a token of the dear Rose of Sharon, and then the meeting began.

We wonder whether such a scene has ever been witnessed since the Bible days. O praise the Lord for Jesus, the ray of hope in the darkened soul, the hope of the hopeless, the strength of the faint.

From nine in the morning till two in the afternoon we prayed, prayed till the afternoon crowds were filling the streets before the door. When we dismissed the morning crowds we directed them to leave by the left hand side of the building, and asked that the other doors be kept closed till we had them safely out. But by some means the orders were confused, some one opened the street doors and in poured the afternoon crowd in thousands. Once the big doors were swung open and jammed with people it was impossible to get them closed and the afternoon crowd telescoped the morning crowd. You can imagine the work and thinking needed on the part of the already worn ushers. But oh, it was the glorious meeting.

THE CLOSING SUNDAY

The morning service of the closing Sunday was devoted to a service of prayer and praise. One after another, men and women, young and old, eagerly mounted the platform, and standing beneath the sounding board endeavored to make the multitiude hear as they testified to having been saved, healed and baptized with the Holy Spirit. Ringing testimonies they were, almost too miraculous to be believed were we not able to turn around and gaze at the casts, braces and crutches adorning the gallery rail behind the platform.

The closing night was the greatest of all. Many had fasted all day, never leaving the building lest they lose their seat and opportunity to be prayed for. Long before dark the great structure was crowded to capacity and the doors locked. Whole street cars of people and a special train had to be turned away in addition to the disappointed crowds without.

That last night the people streamed to the altars and kneeled in the aisles as though they never would stop coming. After that we prayed for the sick. The healings were amongst the most marvelous we had yet seen and the testimonies of those previously healed were glorious and convincing.

The whole multitude wept and laughed and praised God as one soul till we rose to sing: "Blessed Be the Tie That Binds" and "God Be with You Till We Meet Again."

Next morning a ministers' meeting was held in Scruggs Memorial Church to make arrangements regarding the conservation of the work. The Secretary of the Federation of Churches met with them. And after a glorious season of prayer, where ministers of all denominations kneeled at the altar, praying for a mighty baptism of the Holy Spirit upon them all, giving power and wisdom to continue the work, the meeting was turned over to an appointed committee of ministers from the various churches who will assist in appointing visiting committees to call upon every home to help establish the work begun in the revival, that when Christ shall come we shall be able to say: "I have not lost them which Thou gavest me."

At 1:30 Monday afternoon, in "The Father of Waters"—the Mississippi, a baptismal service was held. A Methodist, a Baptist, a Presbyterian, a Congregationalist and a Pentecostal minister all assisting in the baptismal ceremonies, while thousands stood on the banks and sang.

'Twas a great, great meeting. From the loaves and fishes and a little yielded basket, the Master's hand fed the hungry thousands. Jesus did all the mighty works. He alone shall have all the glory.

A PRESBYTERIAN MINISTER'S COMMENTS ON MRS. McPHERSON'S MEETINGS IN ST. LOUIS, MO.

By Rev. Wm. H. Clagett, D. D., President of Board of Trustees Texas Presbyterian University

For three weeks this great city of St. Louis has been in the grip of probably the most remarkable series of religious meetings in the history of the city, the meetings conducted by Mrs. Aimee Semple McPherson.

These meetings were remarkable in their beginning, in their development from day to day, and most remarkable of all in their close.

For the first time in my life, with mine own eyes, I have seen enacted before me scenes such as we read of in the Bible as occurring in the days of Jesus Christ and the Apostles.

I have seen the lame made to walk, the dumb to speak, the deaf to hear, the blind to see, and devils cast out.

I cannot blame any one for not believing things that can and will be told of these meetings, for I probably would not believe them myself had I not *seen them*, but *I have seen them*, and "we are *witnesses* of these things."

There were thousands of persons who confessed conversion, hundreds and hundreds who were prayed for for healing, and thousands of others who begged and pleaded with tears in their eyes for cards for prayer for healing, to whom cards could not be given because it was physically impossible for Mrs. McPherson to reach them.

In a movement which in three short weeks developed into the proportions that this movement did, of course, there will be chaff, probably a good deal of chaff among the wheat; chaff among the professed conversions; chaff among the professed healings; and chaff among the professed consecration of lives to Jesus Christ.

In regard to the genuineness of the work in these meetings, I will say that I myself have preached the Gospel and listened to others preach it for fifty years. I have heard all the great evangelists from Moody to those of the present day, and I have never heard the simple Gospel of Jesus Christ and Him crucified more simply, more faithfully, more lovingly preached, nor the unconverted more lovingly and more tenderly pleaded with than I heard this from the lips of Mrs. McPherson, nor have I ever heard a stronger condemnation of the fanaticisms, extravagances and shams that are so common and that are parading as a higher type of holiness. I never heard more scathing sarcasm than that with which she cuts these shams to pieces and insists upon the *sane,* the *true,* the *real* acceptance of the *real,* the *living,* the *ever-present* Jesus as the *only* Saviour and Sanctifier. I have never heard a preacher who seeks more sincerely to exalt Jesus Christ and who hides herself more completely behind Christ and His cross.

I have never seen in any one a *greater passion* for souls.

The *salvation* of souls—everything in her services is *secondary* to this. The only purpose for the healing of the body is that the body may be a consecrated dwelling place of the Holy Spirit in order that the healed one may bring others to Christ; and Mrs. McPherson will not pray for the healing of adults until they have first accepted Christ and definitely consecrated themselves in writing to live for Him.

It is not my purpose to write of the meeting in detail, of the individual cases of conversion, of healing, and the miracles that Jesus, through His hand-maiden, wrought in these meetings. This I will leave to others.

The feature of these services of which I wish to write especially is the miracle of the meeting itself.

Thirty years ago, on a farm in Canada, a devoted woman with a passion for souls and a heart breaking over the worldliness in the church, prayed for "a baby girl," and that God would use this baby in reviving the great Bible Truth that the *Church of Jesus Christ is His Body*—a people *"called out* of the world"—in whom He now dwells, through whom He reveals Himself to the world, and to whom He has given His Holy Spirit—the Third Person of the Trinity—to be *in them* "the power of God" to do *through them* what Jesus did when He was in His physical body here on earth.

God answered her prayer, and laid a little baby girl in her arms.

If there are those who would criticize these meetings, let them explain these simple, but significant facts, facts to which there are thousands upon thousands of witnesses to testify, facts to which the whole city of St. Louis must testify if the truth is spoken.

Three weeks ago, this mother and this "little baby girl," now grown to be a young woman twenty-nine years of age, came to St. Louis. They came very quietly, unheralded and unknown to the great city. There was no advance agent in human form, coming weeks before them to prepare the way, to organize a campaign for them, to herald their coming by announcement of it in the churches and through the papers, to organize prayer meetings throughout the city for weeks of prayer in preparation of their coming, the methods now used in preparation for the great union Religious Campaigns, and of which methods of preparations I have only the most hearty commendations. Their only advance agent was the Holy Spirit. He was unseen by man, and His mission in reference to these two women was unknown even to the Christian people of the city.

A small band of Christians—less than seventy souls—knowing how wonderfully God had used Mrs. McPherson in other places—in their faith that God would bless the coming of His hand-maiden to St. Louis—had succeeded in renting the Moolah Temple, an auditorium that seats 3,000. An advertisement, telling when the services would begin, was put in each of the city papers. The ministers of the city, each one filled with his own work, knew nothing of the meeting.

In this quiet way the meeting began. Only about 300, I understand, were present at the first meeting. But God began to work. From the very first service, lost men and women came to the altar crying, "What must I do to be saved?" At the first service for prayer for the healing of the sick, sick were healed. These went out and told what Jesus, through His hand-maiden had done for them. The people came running together, many ministers among them, myself among these, and by the end of the week, the great building was filled to its capacity, and hundreds, and then thousands were turned away, unable to get into Moolah Temple. At the close of the second week, the police stated that there were 5,000 people outside the building, many of whom remained through all the service although they could neither see nor hear anything that was transpiring inside the building.

On Monday evening, without Mrs. McPherson knowing anything of his purpose, a gentleman rose on the platform and proposed that the meeting be transferred to the Coliseum, the largest auditorium in the city, a building that seats 12,000 people. In ten minutes the money was raised to rent the Coliseum, this too although the rent of Moolah had been paid to the close of the three weeks' meeting.

On Wednesday, the transfer of the services to the Coliseum was made. There were 5,000 people present at the first service in the afternoon, and 8,000 at the evening service.

Then the city awakened. The Coliseum was crowded. Many ministers came to offer their help. People, well and sick, came from cities round about. Hundreds and hundreds of men and women came weeping and asking "to see Jesus," and thousands of requests came for prayer for the sick.

These two godly women, assisted by many pastors, worked to and beyond the limit of their physical strength, and yet, there were thousands of calls to which they could not respond.

At the closing service on Sunday evening, Mrs. McPherson prayed for the sick as long as she could stand. Then she sat in a chair and prayed until eleven o'clock, when, seeing she was about to faint, we took her away although hundreds and hundreds were still pleading for prayer.

This is the story of the meetings conducted in St. Louis by these two godly women. How can it be explained? It can be explained only in one of two ways. It is the work of the Lord or it is the work of the Devil. It is one or the other. Does the Devil make the blind to see, the deaf to hear, the dumb to speak, the lame to walk? Does the Devil lead people to call Jesus Lord and to set up family altars in their homes to offer prayer to God in the name of Jesus? "IT IS THE LORD'S DOINGS AND IT IS MARVELOUS IN OUR EYES!"

CANCER PASSED AWAY.—While attending the meetings in Moolah Temple, St. Louis, I was wonderfully healed, saved and filled with the Holy Spirit. Through the prayers of Mrs. McPherson, I was completely healed of cancer of the stomach. Almost instantly, as she placed her hand upon my stomach, I could feel the cancer breaking loose, and I had barely time to get into privacy before the cancer passed from my body, though it was so large I had to assist in its removal. It weighed about a pound and one-quarter, and had roots ranging from one inch to six inches in length. I showed it to four persons, but did not make an effort to preserve it.

I was also healed of rheumatism of years' standing in my arm—could not raise it high. Praise the Lord! I expect to serve Him the rest of my life in whatever He bids me do.

My little daughter 12 years old was healed of deafness and blindness.—Mrs. R. T. Gregg, St. Louis, 312 Evans Ave., May 17.

MIGHTY REVIVAL IN DENVER, COLO.

THE CROWDS AND THE ALTAR CALLS

THE opening service was held in the Second Congregational Church, of which Rev. Wright is pastor, on Sunday morning of June 19th. Though the meeting was not scheduled to begin until 10:45 A. M., people began to gather as early as 7 and 8 o'clock. Long ere we arrived the little church was overflowing, and people standing in the streets, in hopes of hearing at least a few words.

During the prayer and the message, the power of the Spirit so enveloped the people that almost all were melted to tears, and hundreds of hands were lifted by those signifying their desire to become a Christian, or to reconsecrate their hearts and recover their first love.

The second service was held in the People's Congregational Tabernacle at 2:30, the largest Protestant auditorium in the city. This was also overflowing. Clear around the seldom-used galleries the people stood, and down the stairs into the street.

The altar call, found hundreds struggling to get to the mourners' bench. Looking desperately about us, we remembered there was no altar in this church, as the front pews reached close to the special platform.

ALTARS FULL ON FIRST DAY

What should we do? There was not a moment to lose. The aisles were filling and many coming from the galleries and from all directions. Ministers and pastors attending looked wild! Was the harvest to be gathered on the first day, instead of pleading, coaxing and "working up" to a little altar call at the end of the first week?

Seizing the outstretched hands of those penitents nearest the platform, we did the only thing possible, helped them to step on a chair and climb to the platform whilst we hastily emptied the choir lofts and lower gallery wings in an effort to make room for them. On and on they came, till the platform and choir were filled; the front pews emptied and refilled; and even then we were obliged to ask the balance of those desiring to accept Jesus as their Saviour to kneel in the aisles and pray where they were, as there was no more room to contain them. And this the first day! Ministers and workers rubbed their eyes and began to deal with weeping sinners. But the converts were packed so solidly and the workers were so amazed and unprepared in numbers or expectations that for the greater part we must needs kneel and pray on the fringe of the crowd, that God would plead His own cause and have His own dear way.

At the close of the service, Dean A. C. Peck (pastor of the People's Tabernacle, under whose auspices we were) declared to the assembled throng that the cloudburst of God's glory in convicting and saving power had been so sudden, almost unexpected, that it found their congregation totally unprepared.

"I am ashamed," said this dear man of God, "but we are going to be ready tonight, or at least do our best, and Oh, let us all pray for a genuine baptism of power of the Holy Ghost and fire upon the ministers and the workers, that we may not be found wanting in this great hour for which we have prayed so many years."

"Can you suggest any way to make more room at the altar?" he asked us after the meeting.

"Only by taking up the front row of pews," we replied. "But they are all fastened securely to the floor and this is Sunday."

"Never mind that! Souls are at stake, and—out they come!" They did, too. And that evening found a larger altar space but not nearly large enough, for again many scores wept their way to the dear Savior's pierced feet.

Monday afternoon we expected to find the lower floor partly filled; but caught our breath at the hunger of the world for Jesus, when we found (if that were possible) a still larger crowd packed into the church than that of yesterday. And thus it continued two and three times a day for the balance of the first week.

After the first Divine Healing Service and the miracles of Wednesday night, when the lame walked and ran, throwing their crutches and canes away, when the Lord worked miracles and the newspapers came out with startling headlines: "The Deaf Hear—The Blind See! The Lame Walk!" police had to be called, but there was no holding the crowds!

Greater throngs stood in the streets, we are told, than were able to enter the building. So great became the pressure, so piteous the pleadings of the throng to hear the Gospel, that special arrangements were made by Mayor Bailey, and the Auditorium, which had been engaged by a Labor Convention, was opened to us ahead of time.

THE MUNICIPAL AUDITORIUM

The great Auditorium is built in two parts, the theatre end, the convention hall and dance floor end. The two are separated by a great stage and asbestos curtain which can be removed and the building made into one when occasion demands, thus seating 12,000 people and admitting an additional 3,000 to standing room.

For Sunday morning service the theatre end was opened to us—the management being fully assured that this great Auditorium with its two rows of galleries and boxes would be sufficient.

The place was packed and more thousands were turned away. By evening the curtain was lifted and the convention hall was filling with eager throngs, who begged to hear, even though they might not see. The altars overflowed with hundreds who sought salvation.

Monday morning a corps of men were put to work and the change made, swinging both buildings into one. Then the *real* crowds began to come! The entire building became too small for the larger services, and again thousands upon thousands were turned away.

THRONGS REMAIN AND PRAY IN STREETS

The doors might be locked, but kindly police and firemen could not persuade the people to go home. At times hundreds kneeled outside on the steps and sidewalks, or stood with uncovered heads. Though they could see nothing but the blank walls and closed doors, they knew that Jesus of Nazareth was passing by in that building, saving, healing and filling with His Holy Spirit. They were determined to hold their ground and be admitted to the next meeting.

The eagerness and the hunger of these people to hear the preaching of the Gospel and to receive His blessed touch for body and soul cannot be put into words. Though thousands and thousands (surely more than 10,000) came to the altars for salvation during the meetings, thousands of others could not get through for the throng. And though a multitude of sick folk were reached and prayed for, other multitudes came more quickly than we could pray. Hundreds fasted and prayed for days, asking God to give them an opportunity to get in and be prayed for.

Some were so desperately afraid that they could not get in on the next day, that it was found necessary by the custodian of the building to organize a searching party to scour the building each night. Numbers of people would climb to the attic and scramble over a net work of electric wires to seek a hiding place; or creep beneath the gallery seats taking a litttle bag of lunch with them, with the intent of hiding there till the morning meeting when they would be sure to be admitted. On several occasions, after we had gone home, women and mothers were found who had locked themselves in the ladies' rest rooms where they had dragged heavy boxes and barricaded the doors, determined to spend the night in the basement so as to be in the building in the morning.

"But—but—but! why, Sister McPherson, why did you not pray for these people?" some horrified readers may ask. "How could you be so heartless as to go home for a moment and leave the people so?"

My dears—we did pray. We prayed and prayed and prayed and sang and preached and prayed again, hour after hour, day after day. Prayed till the audience swam in a mist before our weary eyes, and the floor heaved like the deck of a vessel, and our limbs seemed as though they would crumble under us. Prayed with smiling face, to encourage others; and yet ever with an aching heart, knowing thousands would be unreached. Prayed, standing on the brink of exhaustion, when sleep held out inviting arms—brushed back the weariness from our eyes and smiled again. We prayed on and on each day and night till at last workers picked us up bodily and carried us out to another long room, lined with sick and crippled, where we prayed oftentimes for at least an hour after the balance of our audience were in their beds. When at last we would wearily drag our foot-steps to our waiting car in the alley, we would find there many who had stood clinging to our car for hours for just a brief word of prayer—and still they clamored to be saved and healed and be filled with the spirit, for indeed the harvest is plenteous and the laborers few.

GENUINE PENTECOST REPEATED

The enormous altar calls of this campaign were the most mighty visitations of God's convicting and saving power the writer has ever known or dreamed.

Without exaggeration, at times when the altar call was given for sinners and backsliders, it seemed as though one-half of the congregation arose to their feet. The aisles, stairs and passage-ways would become so blocked and congested that it would take minutes for even the most skilled band of police and workers to get them untangled and placed in the seats cleared to accommodate them and act as an altar.

It became necessary to give two separate altar calls—one for men, another for women. One would need to be an eye witness in order to realize the thrilling inspiration and noble spectacle of seeing one thousand five hundred men rising to their feet simultaneously and rushing to the altar from every side of the building. They swarmed up the aisles and over the steps. They filled the large platform and choir space. They filled the altars and then overflowed into row after row of front seats. And still they came from the galleries and balconies till the great staff of workers were at their wit's end to know where to put them.

Oh, hallelujah! If there is joy in Heaven over one sinner that repented, what a jubilee there must have been over these thousands of splendid men, rich and poor, old and young, from every walk and station of life, coming home to God.

Next the call would be made for the women, and into the space (now cleared by the men) they in turn would pour like a river till again every inch was taken and hundreds were obliged to kneel in the aisles. Converts of tonight would be altar workers tomorrow. It seemed as though business was at a standstill; bankers, lawyers, reporters, policemen, firemen, storekeepers, laundrymen, real estate agents, automobile salesmen, men from all walks of life, from General Hale of the U. S. Army to those of the humblest stations, gave their hearts to God and immediately turned around to help their neighbor find Him too. They were taught that way and immediately went to work at it.

The moment the altar call would be given, the solemn stillness which had been brooding o'er the place would be broken by the most peculiar clicking noise, which would resound from the lower auditorium to the topmost balcony. 'Twas the click of hundreds and hundreds of the seats of opera chairs being closed as the people rose to their feet and made their way to the altar. 'Twas as though the fluttering of angels' wings could be heard throughout the entire building, helping sweep these men and women to the Master's feet.

The press table filled with reporters, editors and journalists would be enveloped in a moment with supplicants seeking salvation. The press staff would be obliged to stand on their own table, or sit perched on the altar rail. Some of them wept frankly themselves, and later confided that they, too, had been converted in that hour. Rich and poor came together, the high and the low, in this revival. Never was American democracy more strikingly exemplified or manifested in a better cause.

So strong became the current of God's spirit, that the people like straws, were swept upon its bosom into the sea of His love. Mayor Bailey and his wife, the Governor and his wife, the Judge of the Superior Court, attorneys, lawyers, officers of high standing in the U. S. Army, business men, Congressmen and society women rubbed shoulders and mingled tears with their poorer brothers and sisters of the factory, shop, farm and gambling halls of Hop Alley and Chinatown.

Oh, how we lift our hearts to God in praise and thanksgiving for these many thousands who have sought the shelter of His love and found Him precious to their hearts. The writer in preaching the Gospel, has always had a firm conviction that if she could but succeed in lifting Christ above the earth—succeed in making Him real to the people, in sweeping back the curtains of doubt and unbelief by the hands of faith and the preached Word, insomuch that the people should glimpse the face of Him who is altogether lovely, they would be unable to resist His call and would come trooping in multitudes to fall in loving contrition and surrender at His beautiful feet. And, Oh, now we have seen it proven. "And I, if I be lifted up from the earth . . ." The trouble is with so many of us, that we are forever *lifting up the "earth,"* telling how good "I" am, how important "I" am, and what great things "I" have accomplished, what certain theories "I" hold, that the poor people never see *the Christ.* But Oh, if the capital "I" can only decrease and our blessed Lord increase until it is no more "I" but Christ that lives in me, then will the human indeed be hidden away behind the Cross and the glorious Christ will be all and in all, speaking anew from Calvary, stretching forth again His beckoning hands and drawing all men unto Himself.

MAMMOTH DIVINE HEALING SERVICES

Not only was this a mighty revival in the healing of the sin-sick soul, but also in the healing of the body.

Special sections were arranged for the sick and invalids who were able to walk and sit up. Other sections for the bed-ridden and those in wheel-chairs. At stretcher service there were as many as 150 beds, I am told. One door, called "the wagon door," was kept specially for the blind, the crippled and the bed-ridden. Special railings were erected to protect them from the pressing throng.

Was ever such an assemblage of sick, blind and lame gathered together in one place since the days of the Master we wonder?

See these sufferers from arthritis deformans lying in wheel chairs and on beds and on cots. Did you ever realize that bodies could be so gnarled, twisted and tortured? One poor woman is so twisted with rheumatism that her feet are drawn completely over her shoulders.

There are tiny children drawn double with the same disease and their little twisted hands look like bird's claws and are stiff and brittle.

Yonder a woman is clutching the coverlet of her bed to keep back the moans, caused by a great cruel cancer which gnaws and eats its way to her heart.

And yonder lies a man swathed in bandages, whose whole body from head to foot is covered with a fearsome disease, till his skin resembles the scales of a fish. His patient faced wife sits fanning him and wiping the tears from her tired stricken eyes. Don't cry, lady dear, we will pray to Jesus. He who cleansed the leper's spots can cause these scales to fall off and this flesh to become as the flesh of a little child.

Over there sits a young husband, clasping his little white faced wife in his arms, as she pants for breath. Death has laid its icy hand upon her, and unless Jesus sets her free that little babe nestling in dewy slumber close by her side, with little pink fingers which curl contentedly about her own, will be left to face the world without a mother.

Yonder a row of dope victims (whose arms are purple and raw from oft plied needle) sit twitching and trembling of body, but with eyes now brightened by hope. All else has failed, but they have heard that Jesus—the Lion of the tribe of Judah—can break every chain, and that He can set at liberty those that are bound. Dumbly their eyes plead for prayer and a sister's practical love and help.

Yonder are the deaf, the dumb, the blind, and rows of crutches like corn stalks in a field. And yonder—

But we must not stop a moment more to look—dare not cry nor let our face quiver—but must keep right on smiling and believing for "they" are searching our faces, reading our every expression, big, dumb eyes of pleading, look out from pallid, drawn faces and seem to burn into our very souls, and read the message hidden there, to see if there be hope and faith.

"Am I too sick for Christ to heal? Is my load too heavy for Him to bear?" their eyes question.

"Is my poor quivering frame too bowed and broken for Him to raise me up?" "Are my sores too loathsome, my disease too great?" "Is there hope for me, or must I be shut out in the dark?" ask those eyes, that are focused unwaveringly upon us wherever we go—watching—watching our every move.

MUSTN'T CRY BEFORE THOSE SEARCHING EYES

Policemen, used to all sorts of conditions, weep like children. Newspaper men, "hard-boiled," as they term themselves, tremble with emotion. Ministers on the platform (two long rows of them from practically every denomination) and ushers weep from sympathy. Everyone (whose heart is not a stone) is moved—but *"we"* dare not weep before these sick folk who are watching with those fever bright eyes.

We blink back the threatening tears, swallow hard that gulping lump in our throats and smile bravely, flashing to their waiting eyes the message:

"No darlings, there are none too sinful for Jesus to save—none too broken in body or soul for Him to heal. All things are possible to him that believeth! Have faith in God, dear hearts, the sun will shine. Jesus loves you, He will help you, He will bear your load. Be of good courage—doubt not—only believe."

Row after row, to the right and the left, the great building is filled to capacity. See the top galleries are full, thousands standing all over the building. All doors are open on the right side of the house. Open gates have been so placed that the thousands waiting in the street without can see, at least, part of the service. And by some miracle, hundreds declared that even though they stood far across the street they heard every word of the evangelist's message.

PARALYSIS HEALED

One of the first to come to the platform for healing was a man by the name of Mr. O. A. Priest, 3205 Adams Street, a member of Dean Peck's church. He had suffered three strokes of paralysis on one side of the body and had been unable to clothe himself for months.

While sitting in the audience, the helpless limb had protruded into the aisle and the ushers and people moving in had constantly tripped over it, but he was unable to draw it in till he took the crook of his cane in one hand and lifted the limb by degrees to a place of safety. When this brother was helped to the platform he looked to the Lord and prayed earnestly.

"Oh, Lord Jesus," we cried, "In Thy Name, we command this paralysis to be gone! Let it fall from our brother like a mantle that is worn and old. Pour in Thine own, warm, life-giving virtue and strength in Jesus name. Amen!

"Brother, have you faith to believe that Jesus heals you now?"

"I have."

"Then in the name of Jesus, this side is restored to life and strength—lift up your arm!" Up went the arm. "Now lift the limb!" He lifted that, moving it freely backward and forward.

Stepping high, and swinging his arm like a flail, the delighted man walked to and fro across the platform, seemingly oblivious to the audience, who were clapping and shouting till the building resounded. Opening and closing his fingers and testing the strength of his hand and arm, he walked across the platform to a spot where stood a solidly built Sunday School chair. Picking it up with the once paralyzed hand, he lifted the chair high above his head with perfect ease.

Leaving his cane and his helpers he ran down the steps of the platform and up again for sheer delight in being once more able to climb the stairs, then away down the aisles, shaking hands with old friends, and answering the questions of reporters who were looking on with amazement.

BABY SISSON HEALED OF TWO HUNDRED SORES

A little sick baby was brought in the arms of its mother at the close of the service. She had braved the crowds for hours, with this tiny, pale, and wasted mite of humanity clasped to her breast. Her own face, white and haggard, plainly bespoke her anxiety and suffering for the little one. At last she had almost reached the steps—but there a large tightly packed crowd were even yet between herself and the platform.

"Oh, God," she whispered, "if I can only get my baby through! If the sister can only take my baby in her arms and breathe one prayer, I KNOW he would be healed of this terrible affliction!—Oh, God—Oh, God!"

As we turned to leave the platform after hours and hours of steady prayer (expecting to go into another room, where the crippled and bed-ridden were waiting us), our eyes were irresistibly drawn to those of that dear mother. Dark and troubled, framed in a brave white face, they flashed their message. But how could we stop now!—there were thousands of others who were also waiting!

Then it was that with the instinctive appeal of one mother heart to another, she unfolded the baby from her breast, lifted it high above the heads of the people and held it out to us. Involuntarily, our mother arms shot out to take it. The crowd parted to let her through, and the child was in our arms.

"Just what is this disease, mother dear?—and don't cry so hard!—Jesus will heal the little lambie," we encouraged.

"Sister, it is virulent eczema,—had it ever since he was four weeks old—as many as two hundred sores have eaten their way into that little form at one time. Every time I dress baby, the blood runs from the little body. And, Oh sister, he is so brave—he tries so hard not to cry," she choked,—"just holds his breath and shudders."

"There, there, mother dear. Forget that frightful nightmare of seeing baby suffer what you would have borne for him a thousand times if you could. Jesus bore that pain for you and baby, too, dear. He will help you."

"Oh, I know it! I know it! I know He will—just now."

Anointing the baby with oil, we pressed it close and prayed earnestly, returning it to the young mother as she dried her tears and the sunshine of her smile suddenly revealed the beauty of her face before these months of sleeplessness and suffering had blanched her cheeks.

She took her baby and departed, but returned a few days later to testify at a mammoth children's service. She declared that her baby was well and, indeed, its flesh looked perfectly whole.

Pressed on every hand that morning with some 5,000 children sick and well, we could not stop to question her. But the next morning, waking early, the writer jumped up and into her automobile (a beautiful Oldsmobile Sedan which the Denver Olds Company had loaned her during the revival) and went in search of the little mother to hear the rest of the story.

Out and out we went, beyond the suburbs of the city, and then over some very bumpy roads to Downing in search of our number.

"Why, that must be it over there," we puzzled, "and yet it's so tiny—is it a house at all?" The weest, little doll-house of a place, it was about as big as one ordinary room. But it wore a fresh green coat of paint, and a humble little window box made from four boards, in which struggled some tiny plants. "Why, I believe it's the smallest, humblest and yet the neatest, little house in Denver!" we exclaimed.

Suddenly, having heard the motor and auto horn, Mrs. Sisson is at the door, the baby in her arms. How she loves that frail, little life! In a moment she is at the car.

"Oh, sister! I am so happy! I'm singing all the day long. My baby is all well. Instead of some 200 sores ranging from the size of a pin head to large open holes, my baby's flesh is sound and whole.

"When I came home from meeting, he slept like a top. No itching or burning at all! When I gave him his bath the next morning, I found that every sore—except four of the deepest ones—had disappeared, and this morning, in the baby's bath-tub, the last scab of the last four sores fell off—and Oh! My baby is well! Thank God! thank God! Christ has visited our little home."

"Little home, indeed! It was little more than a sweet bird's nest. These dear people must be very poor, and struggling hard. What this must mean to them—why this is the very home of all others Christ would have visited in Denver, we mused. And surely He had visited it, this blessed man of Galilee, surely His own dear feet had crossed the threshold of that door, bringing Balm of Gilead to a fevered, tossing babe and a mother's bleeding heart, and lighted the lamp of salvation and blessing on the altar of that home.

"Yes," she replied to our question, "I took him to Dr.——— and he did the best he could for baby, but finally told me that he had grown so bad I would have to take him to a specialist in the city and have each sore treated every day. But (here a brave, twisted little smile told the struggle) but—husband is only a substitute in the post-office, you know. Some weeks he brings home ten dollars; sometimes ten dollars in two weeks. It takes some planning to keep soul and body together and clothes and doctor bills. So even though the baby bled and suffered so cruelly each time I changed or bathed him, I couldn't afford the specialist, but walked the floor and wept.

"Then one day came the ray of light! We had heard of a revival meeting being held in town, but did not give it much thought, until word came that Jesus was healing the sick today just as He did in olden days.

"Here was my door of hope, for if it was true that Jesus still healed the sick, I had found a '*Specialist*' to whom I could take my baby free of charge, had He not said: 'Suffer the little children to come.' Was not this salvation and healing without money and without price?

"That day I just dressed and wrapped up my poor baby and went,—The rest you know. Only look, sister, see how his little arms are filling out! He is eating everything, and putting on weight—Oh, I'm so happy!"

And so were we, as we backed the car to turn and drive away. We wiped the tears from our eyes, to see those ruts better, for the road was full of them, and wiped them again, several times on the way to town.

"Oh, Lord, I'd rather have you visit that tiny box of a house, with its coat of fresh green paint, its brave little window box, and poor young family than the richest mansion in the land," I whispered, and drove back into a day brim full of duty and demands.

It would be an impossibility to attempt giving you more than a few samples of those healed by Christ. But the words of the Master: *The blind see, the deaf hear, the lame walk, the sick are raised up, the poor have the Gospel preached unto them, and blessed is he that shall not be offended in me,* described the whole scene in a sentence.

MEMORIAL HALL, DAYTON, OHIO

Where for three weeks the throngs were so great that is was necessary to use firemen and police to empty the auditorium from rear exits in order to admit other multitudes waiting to hear Sister McPherson preach "The Four-Square Gospel"

MEMORIAL HALL
During a service where thousands were saved and healed during revival by Sister McPherson

Not only from the homes of the poor did they come to Jesus, however, but from every walk of life. From the wife of the Mayor, Mrs. Dewey C. Bailey, who was healed of lameness from which she had suffered for many years—the elite of the city left their limousines by the pavement, attended the services and were prayed for as humbly as the rest after giving up their theatres, parties and cards and turning to the Lord Jesus.

FOUR BLIND PEOPLE RECEIVE SIGHT IN SAME MEETING

Four blind people, three men and a woman, instantly received their sight in one afternoon meeting.

The first man was not prayed for on the platform at all. But kneeling at the altar, giving his sin-sick heart to God, the Lord opened his physical, as well as his spiritual eyes. He bounded to the platform with cries and shouts of joy:

"I can see—I can see! God,—I can see! Oh, I've been in total darkness so long. Lady, excuse me for making a noise, but I can't help it! Oh, I can see! God—God!" and the big man, clad in immaculate palm beach suit, evidently of good family, buried his face in his arms and sobbed like a child.

"William, William! Is it true—can you see? Oh, brother, can you see?" rang out the clear voice of a beautiful young lady, who came running down a long aisle from the gallery door, her cheeks wet with tears.

Jerking up his head, he looked over the audience. Straight to the aisle up which she was running he turned and fixing his delighted eyes upon her, brushed away the tears with the back of his hand, and with husky voice, shaking with emotion, replied:

"Yes, sister, I can see you—I see you as well as ever." Holding out his arms to her, he lifted her to the platform. Right over the reporters' press table she came, steps forgotten in the excitement of the moment. "Why, I can see everything and everybody! Look—'way up in the top-most row in the top gallery, they are waving their handkerchiefs at me, and I am waving back.

"I see you—I see you all. Why, I see as good as I *ever* did." Then brother and sister are locked in each other's embrace.

THE CLAPS AND CHEERS OF THE AUDIENCE

Their delight and their tears you must picture for yourself—'tis too much for me to attempt.

Did you ever see 12,000 people wiping tears from their eyes at the same time, with everything from the farmer's red bandana to the elegant lady's silken handkerchief with the real lace edge?

Did you ever see 12,000 people clap and cheer and laugh and cry and shout and sing and pray and weep all together, till every heart beats as one and the difference of social standing is forgotten? Well, anyway, that's what happens in meetings of this kind in Denver.

THE WELL APPLIED LESSON

"But wait a moment, audience. Here is just the opportunity I have been looking for!" They are still in a moment now. "I want to ask you some questions.

"Did I pray for this man?"

"No."

"Or anoint him with oil?"

"No."

"No, I have never seen him in my life, I am very sure—then, did I heal him?"

"No! No-o-o-o!"

"Well, then, who *did* heal him?"

"J-E-S-U-S!" they all shout back in unison.

In praying for the sick, no matter how busy you may be, never fail to take advantage of every opportunity to draw the attention of the multitudes to the fact that it is Jesus, not the preacher, who heals the broken body. Say to them in the words of the apostles of old: "Why look ye upon us, as though by our own power we have done some great things"—this is the work of Jesus, whom God has raised up and of whom we are all witnesses.

O, LAWD, AH DONE SEE AGAIN

A man blind for twenty years was prayed for and healed in this same meeting. His delight beggared description. Only a poor colored man was he, but:

"Oh, Lawd! Ah done see again—Ah jes knowed ma Savior could do it!" he affirmed. "Fo' twenty years Ah've lived in de da'k; but now—bless de Lawd—Ah kin see!"

"What am I holding up in front of you?" we asked, expecting him to say, "Your hand." We are startled and the audience convulsed with relieved and happy laughter when he replied with ceremonious exactitude:

"Fo'r fingers—and—one—thumb."

"How many now?" we asked.

"Two."

"How many?"

"Three."

"How many now?"

"You've put yo' hand behind yo' back."

"Correct—can you follow me, brother?"

"Sho' Ah can—" and in and out, through the line that waits for prayer he follows us, then down the steps where a colored "mammy," evidently his wife, is wiping the tears from her eyes, and the open armed reporters with pads and pencils pounce upon him. Again the audience is swept with billows of rejoicing. Mothers clasp their blind babies tighter with new hope. Tears of joy steal through the closed lids of many a sightless eye in the audience where they await their plunge into the troubled waters of Bethesda's pool.

Many who were carried in on beds, rose and walked out. Scores left their crutches and canes to be added to the steadily growing line behind the platform.

Once in awhile, some one without faith or any real intention of living a surrendered life, would get through the line and go away in the same condition as that in which they came; but for the greater part, the supplicants were well taught and prepared by my dear mother before coming to the platform, and were healed there and then. Sometimes even those seeming to possess great faith showed no apparent results—we know not why.

OFFICER WHITE'S MOTHER

A sweet, little lady was healed instantly one afternoon meeting from paralysis of a pronounced form. She ran down the steps with the lightness of a young girl, and away happy as a bird to her own home. Her son, we were informed, was one of the officers on duty at the Auditorium, but did not happen to be there at the moment of his mother's healing.

He was very skeptical when he heard of the same, and had thought there must be something "phony in it somewhere." Hastening to his home he was astonished beyond measure to find his little mother walking all over the house, singing about her work, as well as she had ever been in her life.

"Mother!" he exclaimed. "Are you walking, are you all right?"

"I certainly am, son. Christ has made me whole."

"And can you lift your limb? Can you stand on that chair?"

"I certainly can." And suiting the action to the word, Mrs. White leaped like a girl, first to the chair and then to the table, and jumped again to the floor, before being swept into the arms of her great manly son, who crushed her tight against the brass buttons of his policeman's coat.

They both returned to the meeting almost every day after that; both became active workers in the meetings; both stood side by side on the platform to testify, and the last we saw of "Officer White" he was advising and helping the sick people as earnestly as any preacher of the Gospel.

THREE ENORMOUS CHILDREN'S MEETINGS

Each Thursday morning between ten and one mass meetings were held for the children. Fully 5,000 children were congregated on those occasions in the Municipal Auditorium. Here the well children met to sing to the sick children.

Before the heart talk to children, prayers for the sick, crippled and bed-ridden little ones, a mountain of flowers were brought and banked high upon the great platform. Wagon loads of toys and candy were also sent with the compliments of several department stores, the commissioner of supplies and private individuals attending the meetings. Mr. Goodman, the owner of the Flarorine Candy Co., sent 500 bags—250 pounds of pure candy. So that not a sick or crippled child went away without a flower, or a toy or a bag of candy.

Hundreds of little orphans and poor children, whose parents were able to afford little more than the bare necessities of life were made glad.

But the thing they wanted most was prayer for their sick. So after the song service and music by the Olinger Highlanders' Band, a stirring song, "Stand Up, Stand Up for Jesus," rendered by several hundred uniformed Boy Scouts, who marched in, in a body, a short message and a call for acceptances of Christ, to which some 3,000 little ones responded by praying aloud together for forgiveness of sin and consecration to Christ's service, the meeting was turned over to prayer for the sick and crippled children. What a heart-rending scene it was!

It was an Auditorium filled with one black mass of people that watched this procession of sorrow.

Outside an equally large throng clamored for admittance.

At 8 o'clock, two hours before the time set for the opening of the "children's healing service," thousands surged in the streets outside the building.

Pushing and edging, crying and begging, it was finally necessary to rope the streets in order to keep them in order.

Within the building, though, all was quiet. Even the youngsters seemed to realize the solemnity of the occasion.

Mothers carrying babies in their arms, orphans brought by their friends, children on crutches, in wheel chairs and stretchers, babies shrunken to skin and bones carried tenderly on pillows, little tots twisted and drawn with rheumatism, too pain-racked to bear handling were carried in trundle beds. Young mothers brought children whose sightless eyes were white as milk, many with unspeakable diseases where the sins of the parents were visited upon the children, paralytics, those with spinal curvature, St. Vitus' Dance, demon possessed, imbeciles, epileptic victims, tubercular babies and those having tubercular bones, tiny babies, apparently no more than six months old, having heads as large as an eight-quart bucket, carried on pillows and beds—this condition caused by water on the brain.

Oh, how the compassionate father heart of the Savior, who said: "Suffer the little children to come unto me and forbid them not," must have wept o'er the sight!

Row after row, seat after seat, the long lines flowed across the platform. Many men who had gone through the awful scenes of the great World War without flinching were utterly overcome and made to weep aloud before this scene of the little children in their sickness and suffering.

Blind children danced for joy, and declared that they could see their mother's face, and described the flowers, the toys, the flags. Deaf and dumb children spake and heard, calling their parents by name and hearing their own voices for the first time in their lives.

The first word the dumb were taught to speak, after their lips were opened, was always the precious name of Jesus. Three deaf and dumb boys in one family were healed by the same Jesus of Nazareth, who cast out the Spirits by His word in the days of old. They stood, as though in a trance for a few moments after their ears were opened, looking first at the great pipes of the Municipal organ, listening as the welling notes of a hymn of praise rolled forth, and then at their mother who stood with hands lifted high above her head, shouting praises to the Lord for their deliverance.

Several lame children left braces and crutches behind, and walked off, straight as reeds. Spines were made to straighten even as we beheld.

One little girl, of about twelve years of age, whose parents had been too poor to bring her, was sent for by a kind friend, who paid all expenses. The child was deaf and dumb through scarlet fever, contracted in infancy. The Lord instantly healed her, opening her ears and lips so that she spake and heard clearly. She returned that night to testify before the marvelling multitude.

Oh, the simplicity of the faith of these children! They wept and prayed and praised the Lord just like older folks and hundreds of parents, giving their hearts to God, wept at the sight. They determined to go home, to live a Christian life, establish a family altar and bring up these darling little ones in the fear and admonition of the Lord. Bibles were given to those in need and all went away with hearts and arms full to overflowing.

"And there was great joy in the city."

SPECIAL STRETCHER DAY.

This service was held in the forenoon of the closing Sunday.

Even though we had been expecting and planning for it, it was a shock to the writer when she entered the building to see the great number of beds, scores and scores of them, placed row on row in front of the platform. Many of those invalids lying upon their death beds were still unsaved. How they needed Christ! Many of them had not been to church, nor had they heard a sermon for years. Many knew little or nothing of real salvation. Scores of invalids had come to hear the Gospel.

Scores of invalids raised their hands for prayer at the end of the message, signifying that they were sinners or backsliders and wanted someone to pray with them that they might be converted. As they were unable to arise from their beds and come to the altar, ministers and gentle workers went to their beds—death beds in several instances, where the feet of elderly people were already at the brink of the chilly waters, and pointed the sufferers to the Lamb of God who taketh away the sins of the world.

A great scene indeed, a scene never to be forgotten! Of this you will read more in an interesting newspaper comment appearing at the bottom of a page brimful of pictures, in *The Denver Post.*

AUDITORIUM HOSPITAL SCENE

Twelve Thousand Persons Are Moved to Tears by Impressive Service That Is Likened to "Revival of Bodies"

(By Albert W. Stone)

Reporters, as a class, are reputed to be "hard-boiled."

They see life in so many of its phases, and from so many angles, they become calloused to its heart throbs and thrills.

It took Mrs. McPherson to demonstrate that even reporters' emotions can be touched, when she stood on the Auditorium platform Sunday morning and directed the singing of twenty or more old hymns, for the benefit of the special guests of the meeting, bed-ridden invalids of all ages and classes.

It is safe to say that a stranger assembly of guests never were gathered together—at least, not since the time of the Man of Galilee.

They were spread out before the great organ in fan-shaped formation. Cots, stretchers, adjustable invalid chairs, beds—every conceivable kind of furniture designed to hold and add a mite of comfort to the hard lot of a cripple or an invalid—were lined up in solid windrows, each one with an occupant whose gaze never for an instant left the face of the woman in white up there on the platform.

Twelve Thousand Attend Service

On every side was the audience—12,000 strong—filling to capacity the main floor, balconies and galleries. Palmer Christian sat at the immense console, down in the orchestra pit, his fingers on the keys. Back of the chair loomed the great organ, ready to peal forth harmony.

"We are going to sing for these poor people in these cots this morning," Mrs. McPherson announced. "We are going to sing the songs they ask for."

She consulted a card in her hand.

"Here is a little woman, an invalid for thirty years, who hasn't been to church in all that time," she said. "She used to go when she was young, and had her health. She remembers, dimly, how they used to sing in the little church she attended back home, and she has asked us to sing for her 'Pass Me Not, Oh Gentle Savior.'"

Mr. Christian's fingers touched the keys, and the old song leaped forth under the magic of his genius. The audience, as one person, joined in. Twelve thousand voices rose. The tremendous volume of melody, gathering strength from every quarter, rolled down upon the men, women and children in the cots. Frank Farmer, tenor, kept time with his baton. It seemed that everybody knew the song, and knew it well.

Tears Dampened Eyes of Invalids

Even the quavering, cracked voices of the guests joined in. Some of them sang with closed eyes, hands clasped on their breast. Others couldn't sing, and tears seeping forth from under their white eyelids told why.

The song ended. Mrs. McPherson's eyes were wet. She leaned over and spoke to a worker at her side.

"See that girl reporter down there," she said in a low voice. "She is crying like a baby."

She was. So were her companions at the press table, fourteen of them. One man, a journalistic political war horse who had covered every Democratic and Republican convention in Colorado in the last twenty years—many of them in the same Auditorium—touched another reporter on the shoulder. His hand was trembling and his eyes were suffused.

"Never saw anything like it," he said. "Never."

Song after song was sung—each one familiar to most of the audience from childhood. "Jesus, Lover of My Soul" was one. "Lead Kindly Light" was sung at the request of a paralytic. "Where the Lord Leads I Will Follow" rose in plaintive melody. And "Nearer My God to Thee" was rendered with such spontaneity that the thousands waiting out on the sidewalk joined in.

Service Seemed a "Revival of Bodies"

The healing session was one of the most impressive of the revival services. It was literally a "revival of bodies" for many of the victims. Person after person rose from their cots and declared themselves healed as their hands and faces were lifted heavenward.

City firemen, their blue uniforms making a picturesque blotch of color against the white dresses of the feminine workers and their brass buttons gleaming, carried the cots to the stage. Members of the Salvation Army entered the hall, the American flag carried at their head, and set to work. Stretcher bearers labored with the perspiration streaming from their faces. Mrs. Kennedy, mother of the evangelist, flitted about among the cots, stroking fevered foreheads and saying soothing things. Outside the barricaded doors the waiting thousands craned their necks and tried to see.

For two hours and forty minutes Mrs. McPherson labored. When she declared a recess every cot patient had been reached.

WHOLE CITY CALLED TO FASTING AND PRAYER

When at the close of the third week it was found impossible to pray for more than one out of every hundred coming for healing, because of the thronging multitudes, a special day of fasting and prayer was called.

Twenty thousand requests for prayer cards were distributed for as many people in two services. The hour was set for "twelve to one" Saturday noon. Friday night the city began its fast, eating nothing till the next evening. At noon hour in stores, shops, churches and streets the people prayed. Before the closed doors of the Auditorium crowds gathered and kneeled with uncovered heads during the hour of prayer. On the sidewalks of the downtown section, people also kneeled in several instances, and as the church bells rang and the noon whistles blew, a torrent of prayer arose up to heaven in behalf of the suffering and the afflicted. The results were glorious indeed, the afternoon meeting being filled with testimonies of those who had been instantly delivered in that hour. Hearty thanks and appreciation are due to Mayor Dewey C. Bailey, to the newspapers, the ministers and employers of the city, who assisted us in calling the city to prayer.

THE CLOSING HOURS OF THE CAMPAIGN

saw thousands turned away, filling the streets in all directions; but also saw thousands coming to Jesus for salvation.

MONDAY SPENT IN VISITING JAIL AND HOSPITALS

On Sunday night, July 10th, the campaign ended. Monday, from early morning till late at night, eleven hours and thirty minutes were spent in active service, visiting hospitals, the jail, the Old Ladies' Home, and private residences of poor and rich.

Tuesday forenoon was spent in a trip to Lookout Mountain, whither we were accompanied by a procession of some 150 automobiles. There seemed to be a little feeling as to which of the cars we were to ride in, several claiming they had asked first—God bless these dear people for their love and kindness to us! The problem was soon solved by riding a part of the way in each car.

On top of the mountain a glorious testimony meeting was held by those who had been saved, healed and filled with the Spirit. Gen. Irving Hale, who led our armies in the Phillipine War, again witnessed as to his healing. Dope addicts testified that the chains were broken and the desire for the needle gone. Husbands and wives testified that homes which were once filled with wrangling, quarreling and unkind words, had now become a heaven on earth, and asked us to sing:

"What a wonderful change in my life has been wrought
Since Jesus came into my heart."

After song service and testimony meeting, the party moved on to a still further mountain peak, where basket-luncheon was served and all broke bread and praised the Lord in sweetest fellowship; then, after a short sermon delivered from a picnic table, which answered for a pulpit, and the final exhortations to the converts to keep close to Jesus, we returned to the city by way of Bear Creek Canyon and were soon on our way to the depot where a large crowd had awaited. There were reporters, ministers, business men, converts of the revival, those who had been healed, and even here the sick came to the very steps of the train, and were prayed for just as the train was pulling out and the notes of "God be with you till we meet again" rose from the waving crowd.

Not a kind word could they have spoken that they left unsaid; not a loving deed that they could have rendered that was left undone from the beginning to the close of the campaign; suggestions for the betterment or help of the meeting were no sooner made than the suggestion was instantly carried out.

Oh, angels, hover over Denver; dear Son of Righteousness, spread forth the feathered pinions of Thy loving, healing wings o'er their heads in protection and blessing we pray. Keep the new converts, strengthen the weak, baptize with Thy

Spirit those who seek Thy face and grant that we may all meet again in glory when the morning breaks and the shadows flee away. Amen.

WIFE OF MAYOR HEALED

When at the close of the meeting Saturday night, Mrs. Dewey C. Bailey, wife of Denver's mayor, walked up the stairs to the platform at the Auditorium, seeking healing for a foot that had caused her much anguish for three years, she had faith that what she asked would be granted unto her. Wednesday morning Mrs. Bailey reports the foot is fine.

"Saturday night was the first night in three years that I have had any rest with my foot," she said. "For months and months I have had to get up and rub my foot before I could go to sleep. Now that is past. The trouble grew out of a broken arch, and an X-ray taken a short time ago showed inflammation had set in. I have always believed in the potency of prayer, backed by faith, and I am sure Mrs. McPherson's prayers, added to my faith, have resulted in a cure."

Mrs. Bailey asserts that in her opinion "Mrs. McPherson's meeting is the finest influence that has blessed Denver in many years."

Ascending the rostrum with tears of gratitude streaming down her face, Mrs. Mollie E. Kane of Aurora, testified that her daughter, who suffered a double curvature of the spine, had been cured.

SAW SPINE STRAIGHTENED

"As my daughter stood beside me," said Mrs. Kane, "I could see, because of the miraculous straightening of her back, that she was fully two inches taller."

WORKS WONDERS IN DENVER CHINATOWN

Women Derelicts Fall at Feet of Evangelist and Declare They'll Spurn "Poppy;" Blind and Deaf Orientals "Healed"
(By Eileen O'Connor, Denver Express)

It was 10 o'clock in Hop Alley, Denver's Chinatown, Friday night. The air was warm and still, but an occasional breeze wafted the perfume from an opium pipe or carried the little clinking sound of fan tan chips.

Here and there could be heard the cry of a baby or the shuffling tread of some Chinaman as he poked his way through the narrow little street, silently nodding to his friends who sat on the steps of houses bordering the alley.

To all outward appearances, Chinatown was no different Friday night than it is any other night. But to those who know the secrets of its little world, excitement was rampant. For the word had gone the rounds that Mrs. Aimee Semple McPherson, evangelist and faith healer, was to visit its precincts after the closing of her mammoth evening's services at the Auditorium.

And such an unusual crowd it was that ran to meet the white-robed woman, as she alighted from an automobile, and with her mother, Mrs. Minnie Kennedy, was escorted through Hop Alley by Chief Narcotic Agent Harry V. Williamson, Henry A. Larson, supervising agent of the United States federal prohibition service, Prohibition Agents Carpenter and Westover and Sergeant Reed of the Denver police force.*

Down through the dark recesses of the alley she went, smiling to the silent, wondering figures that squatted on the dark steps and patting the heads of the little Chinese children that danced and swarmed about her feet.

As a salute to her entry, one Chinese woman lighted a small rocket that went whizzing in the air and alighting square on the roof of the Lee Wing-Kook Long lottery house, started it afire.

The House of the Lily

The Chinese Lily gambling house had been lighted in anticipation of Mrs. McPherson's visit and it was there that the revival was to be held. In and out of the door ducked dark clad figures, some in their native dress, others in Americanized garb.

Within the white-washed den everything had been removed but an electric fan, a few rough chairs and a deal table. And such a crowd it was that packed the little room to its utmost capacity. Like so many blackbirds on a fence, little Chinese children sat on a shelf bordering the room. Chinese youths, who had assimilated American dress and customs; Chinese who still clung to their native customs, young Chinese with their little ones, old Chinese grandfathers and grandmothers—all were there.

The White Outcasts

And in the midst of these were gathered a few negroes and the unfortunate American men and girls who had fallen victims to the drug habit. Then there were the onlookers, the Americans who had gone with Mrs. McPherson to help her sing and pray.

And it was into the midst of such a scene as this that the evangelist smilingly and cheerfully went. Unmindful of the skeptics, she preached and ministered.

There were those who, perhaps, feeling the stings of conscience. abruptly edged themselves out of the throng and fled from the world of God, but there were those, too, the Chinese, who had lingered outside, sitting behind the barred doors and windows of their homes, that ventured timidly out and finally sought the door of the former most famous gambling den in Hop Alley.

Obeying the admonition of 1900 years ago, "Go ye into all the world and preach the gospel to all nations," Mrs. McPherson stretched out her arms and gathered the unfortunates into them. Although her ministry and preaching was for everyone gathered in the little room, it was most especially directed to the men and girls who had become addicted to dope.

Mounting a chair, she sat on the back of it and drank a glass of water proffered her by Mrs. Lily Look.

Seemingly fresh and unexhausted after her long evening service at the Auditorium, she took up her Bible and called the little service to order.

Addressing the little throng as "brothers and sisters," she told them of the love of Jesus for humanity.

"We've all wandered away," she said, "but Jesus loves you and He's here, right in the midst of us tonight. Oh, I do love Jesus, and I want you to do the same. The Lord was tempted on the mountain, He knows what it is to fight against evil, and He knows how hard we have to struggle. But he's coming here tonight to bring you a ray of sunshine and salvation. Oh, I love you, too, and I'd love to put my arms about you all."

Hymn book in hand, she led the singing and joined with the little Chinese children in singing "Oh, We're Little Sunbeams." And with each smile, with each word and with every movement of her outstretched hands, some of the unfortunates drew nearer her and tears began to flow more freely.

And by the time the evangelist asked, "How many would like to come give their hearts to Jesus?" sobs were audible in every corner of the room. Down from the chair Mrs. McPherson sprung and right down on the dirty floor on her knees, she went. Her arms encircled the poor unfortunate dope addicts, she hugged their poor, emaciated, trembling bodies and loved and kissed them.

Prayed With Them

And then both she and her mother prayed. Such prayers as would melt a heart of stone. From their very hearts the words came. "O Jesus, they can't set themselves free from this horrible morphine habit. O Jesus, Lion of Judah, come and break the chains that bind them."

And even as the words were uttered it was accomplished. Heads of the unfortunate victims dropped onto the shoulders of Mrs. McPherson and Mrs. Kennedy, tearful eyes entreated theirs, and then one of the addicts, a young girl who had been using drugs for ten years, was heard, "I'm going home to mother."

Arms that were blue and disfigured from morphine were thrown about her neck and she soothed and rubbed them and obtained the promise that never again would they feel the prick of the needle.

And the promises of reform that came from these poor, unfortunate girls were sincere and genuine. Some have been users of drugs for 40 years, yet they have promised to break away from the habit.

And they have declared their intention of attending every meeting during the remainder of the revival here.

Give Up Needle

As a first step in their reformation, some of the girls, knowing they were going to attend the meeting last night, refused to take any drug yesterday.

One gave her needle to one of the federal officers, while others came from houses where companions were "rolling pills," and stood shaking and trembling throughout the meeting, refusing to stimulate themselves with any dope.

At the end of the prayers the reserve of the Chinese was broken. They crowded around, embracing and loving her. And she went amongst them praying for them and putting her arms about them. The little Chinese children virtually smothered her with kisses.

News of the wonders of the healing powers had spread to Chinatown and again Mrs. McPherson was called upon to lay hands upon the sick and afflicted. Little Robert Look was brought with a broken arm, while Joseph Schwartz declared he had been cured of neuritis, from which he had suffered for the last three years.

Veritable miracles, though, were worked in the cases of Luke Jung and Charley Fong. No sooner had the healing hands been laid upon Jung, deaf for 30 years, than he instantly regained his hearing.

There was a veritable skirmish in Hop Alley when Mrs. McPherson left.

Crowds trailed her to the automobile, tugging at her and begging her to come again. And amid tears of joy and good wishes, she left behind her a night in Chinatown that will long be a memory to its inhabitants.

And what was going on behind those boarded up windows and doors lining Hop Alley, only the imaginations of the whites passing up and down the alley could picture.

Those boarded entranceways gave one a creepy impression of Oriental eyes peeping out at passersby. There were none of the evidences of prosperity in the alley, or in the lottery rooms, in which the meeting was held, such as is described by the imaginative writers of the old five cent thrillers.

All in all it was a sordid picture that held no lure for the visitors.

Jack London never painted a starker picture in his "People of Abyss."

For here is the Abyss—the very mud sill upon which society crushes her failures.

AGED CHINAMAN, BLIND TWENTY YEARS, CAN SEE

By Charles W. Clogston,

Managing Editor, Denver Express

Charley Fong can see! He was made to see after 20 years of darkness.

He told me so himself.

I know he can see, for he described to me in his quaint "pidgin" English a roof fire that occurred in Hop Alley just before midnight Friday night.

I was introduced to Charley Fong by Mrs. McPherson just after she had concluded a remarkable revival meeting in the Chinese lottery rooms of Jimmy Look in Hop Alley.

"Can you see this man? If so, shake hands with him," she said. Charley took my hand and looked up at me with a broad grin that indicated his happiness in his rediscovered vision.

I walked down Hop Alley with Charley. He stepped gingerly over obstacles in his path, despite his years, and looked joyfully at the faces and forms of his countrymen and countrywomen who sat along the alley in the dim light of the incandescent lights dotting the narrow, ugly thoroughfare through Denver's Chinatown. They looked like gnomes in the semi-darkness against the background of brick and mortar and boarded-up doorways and windows.

At the corner of Hop Alley and 20th street is the Lee Wing-Fook lottery house, which was selling fireworks. The room was on fire.

Charley Fong stood by me, fascinated with the spectacle of the fire.

At his other side stood W. H. Robinson, a negro, who has lived neighbor to Fong for 18 years and who led him to the McPherson meeting.

"Can you see it, Charley?" asked his colored neighbor.

"Yeh," said Charley, "I see him," and he pointed to the fire on the roof.

The fire wagons came dashing up. Charley missed none of the scene.

"Laddah," he said, as the firemen put a ladder against the building.

"Wlattah!" was his next exclamation as a stream from one of the hose lines went splashing into the air and came down on the flames.

"Allee out!" was his next exclamation, and he turned to look at me.

And then Charley ambled off with his black companion, who seemed almost as happy as his Chinese neighbor that the weazened yellow man could see.

"He ain't been able to see even sunlight in the 18 years I have knew him," said the negro neighbor of the Chinaman, as the two strange companions departed. "It shore am wonderful—Ah say it is."

SOME MARVELS OF THE LAST DAYS

By Dean A. C. Peck

Among the many "Signs of the Times" foretold in the Scriptures, which indicate that the last days of the age are upon us, none are more apparent and convincing than those of the new evangel which have summoned us to review the days, methods and works of Jesus during the time of His residence upon the earth. The recent substitution by the Church of ways, designed by the wisdom of men and financed to attract and hold men to ecclesiastical communions by other means than the preaching of the full Gospel which Christ unfolded, has met open rebuke from heaven. To our amazement we are seeing with our eyes and hearing with our ears that the Holy Ghost is still the commander of the Lord's hosts, and that the baptism, gifts and fruit of the Spirit are to be had for asking to credential and empower believers to become effective witnesses for their crucified and risen Redeemer.

Denver has been swept by the fire of machine guns from Heaven. The slain of the Lord are many. The entire city is talking about the greatest revival in the history of Colorado, and, many believe, in the history of the world since the early days of the Church. We have been unable to take care of the crowds of people who have thronged our streets seeking admittance to behold the wonders wrought by divine power and hear the emancipating truth of which Jesus Christ is the embodiment. In three short weeks a thousand homes have been blessed by the healing touch of the Christ and ten thousand penitents have openly sought Jesus as their Saviour. Many people have journeyed for a thousand miles from every point of the compass to behold these amazing manifestations of divine grace.

The attention of the writer was attracted during the early months of the present year to the work of Mrs. Aimee Semple McPherson in San Diego, and, a little later, in San Jose. Inquiry and correspondence by both wire and letter established the facts of the genuineness of the work and the worker. An invitation to come to Denver at the earliest possible day was extended and accepted. Engagements to hold meetings at St. Louis and Dallas were, however, first on the program.

The writer attended both of these meetings and was thoroughly convinced by the evidence of his own senses that God was working mightily through His hand-maiden.

The preparations for the coming of Mrs. McPherson were those usually carried out. The daily and weekly papers were friendly and printed authenticated stories of what had been wrought in other cities. The state was thoroughly advised of what had occurred and of the coming and expected results through the work of the evangelist. Denver itself was sown with attractive invitations to attend the projected services. Banners were hung across the streets at various strategic points. The street cars carried advertisements on their fronts. Much difficulty was experienced in securing co-operation from either churches or pastors. The People's Tabernacle, the Second Congregational Church and the Pentecostal Mission were the only organizations united in the work. Before the meetings closed, however, with very few exceptions, nearly every church and pastor in the city were thoroughly convinced that the work was from God and gave their influence and labor to enlarge its scope.

The revival began on the morning of June 19 with a meeting at the Second Congregational Church, of which Dr. E. F. Wright is pastor. In the afternoon the services were removed to the People's Tabernacle, where they continued until June 26. The building has the largest seating capacity of any church in the city—1640. About 400 chairs from the vestry were added to the regular accomodations and, beginning with the initial service, every seat was filled and every inch of standing room occupied. The police estimated that fully as many were turned away as were assembled together, twice and thrice each day, during the first week of the meetings. At the first meeting, and indeed during all the services of the first three or four days, the work was purely evangelical. At no service were there fewer than 200 seekers at the altar, which was of the old-fashioned Methodist mourners' bench variety. The intelligence of this great turning to God immediately attracted the attention of the whole city and state. When the service for healing began, the overflow crowds increased and would remain for hours, filling the streets adjacent to the church.

On Sunday, June 26, the meetings were removed to the City Auditorium. This building has an advertised seating capacity of 12,000. One-third of it can be separated into what is known as the theatre. This seats about 4,000. Our faith, at first, only accepted the theatre end of the building. We were amazed, when, on Sunday morning, we gathered for the first service to find it packed and thousands seeking admittance who could not be accommodated. The number of seekers was doubled. On Monday the whole building was thrown together and for two weeks, at every service, always held twice a day, (at least three times a week, three times a day), the great building was packed to capacity. Not only were the seats occupied, but the standing room on the main floor and in the balconies and galleries gave footing to the multitudes.

In the meantime the good news, carried by the papers and the telegraph wires, had traveled all over our western country. People began to come in by hundreds and thousands. Most of these were seeking healing for their bodies. All of them were interested beyond expression. For the first time we realized how Jesus advertised and got His crowds. The head of our street car system told me that his corporation carried at least 20,000 people per day, each day, on their cars to attend the services. In every store or wherever men gathered for work, lunch or to transact business the meetings were discussed and the wonders seen talked over. The mayor attended several services and, with his wife, twice occupied a seat on the platform. The city government attended in a body. Many prominent citizens occupied boxes and not a few were healed. Interest grew more intense as the days passed. The very atmosphere was charged with deep realization of God's presence in the city of Denver. People believed that He was working among them as Jesus worked when upon the earth. The crowds which attended were similar to those which followed Him. The preaching was the same Gospel which He preached and the miracles performed in opening the eyes of the blind, unstopping the ears of the deaf, healing the paralytics and all manners of disease made the deepest impression imaginable on our population.

Twice during the series Mrs. McPherson held special services for children when they were told the truth of the Bible, where thousands of well children, who had been trained, sang to the thousands of sick and crippled children who were there for healing. Once she went down into Chinatown and held a midnight service among those who reek with filth and disease and who are surrounded by the vilest exhibitions which Satan can devise. She also held meetings with workers, and indeed, met with as many as possible at all times. The reporters attended her everywhere. The day after the meetings closed about fifty visits were made to institutions and the sick unable to see her otherwise. Lawyers, ministers, doctors and prominent men in all professions, the wife of the Mayor of the city and the Chief Justice of the Supreme Court of Colorado were among those to whom she ministered.

But few doctrines were presented to her audience by Mrs. McPherson. They were:

1. The deity of Jesus Christ.
2. The blood of atonement.
3. The new birth.
4. Baptism of the Holy Ghost.
5. The right of the present day Church to all the gifts and privileges of the Church when first organized.
6. Jesus Christ the same yesterday, today and forever.
7. The imminent return of Christ for His Church and to rule the world.

Much stress was constantly placed on the fact that the weakness of the Church today, manifested in her spiritual experience and scant fruit, has been brought about by the relinquishment of the doctrines and practices which brought conquering power during the first 300 years of her existence. Jesus Christ was so presented as to make the people feel that He was one of their number—present in the midst of the congregation. The effect of her preaching sometimes was bewildering along these lines. One could almost see the Lord. Nothing could exceed the simplicity of the preaching. The language was such that the simplest and most ignorant hearer could compass her thoughts. Some of her illustrative figures were tremendous. She preached with great directness and straight from the shoulder. There was no hesitation nor appearance of fear as she openly and squarely battled with the social fads and commercialization which have enervated the Church. The theatre, the dance, the bridge parties and all useless and time-absorbing devices of Satan were unsparingly denounced. Likewise, was the dress of woman, abbreviated at both top and bottom, held up as the pest of decency and the enemy of right doing. Her invective against sin, at times, was vehement.

She also insists, when the crowds come to the altar, and especially whenever some particularly great effect is produced in the healing services, that the work is not performed by herself, that God only uses her as an instrument and that all the glory must go to Jesus Christ by whose power the work is wrought. Time after time, when the audience would break forth in great cheers over some great miracle of healing performed, she would stop, lift her hand and demand that the glory be given to Jesus Christ.

Not all who appeared before her were healed. Some went away as they came. At this writing, which is but two or three days after the termination of the meetings, we are glad to say that, so far as our knowledge extends, the results of the healing services are substantial and that many bless the name of the Lord for what He has wrought in them through His servant.

Mrs. McPherson, while among us, was particularly strong in her preaching concerning the baptism of the Holy Ghost. The narrative she gave of her own filling with the Spirit was very graphic and convincing. She placed such emphasis on the fact that a blood-washed soul and a clean body were necessary to prepare the individual to become the temple of the Holy Ghost. In other words, she believes that the doctrines of perfect love and entire sanctification must precede the baptism of the Spirit which bestows power through the gifts of the Spirit and bears the fruit of the Spirit. She was inducted after much prayer and long waiting. She believes that there must be some special evidence, as on the day of

Pentecost and other subsequent similar occasions, given to every individual who has thus been baptized.

While the revival meetings remained at the Tabernacle we had plenty of rooms in the vestry for what Mrs. McPherson called "tarrying meetings." These were prepared as places of retirement where people might wait before the Lord and pray for the baptism of the Holy Ghost. Many took advantage of the opportunities thus afforded and some received this great blessing. When we removed to the City Auditorinm, however, there were no such rooms and the waiting before God had to be transferred to the homes of the people after the public meeting adjourned. We cannot tell to what extent this necessity affected this part of the work. Many professors of religion appeared who were dissatisfied with their Christian experiences. At one of the meetings held at the Tabernacle this week, after Mrs. McPherson had left the city, more than fifty seekers came to the altar with the definite purpose of seeking the baptism of the Holy Ghost. Last night, at a similar meeting, there were about one hundred such seekers who expressed their purpose of continuing the quest until the bestowal satisfied their souls.

Five churches in the city are continuing the meetings. As intimated before, the People's Tabernacle has taken up the work where Mrs. McPherson left it. During the week there have been many seekers for spiritual blessing. The attendance has been large and 43 have been anointed and prayed with for the healing of the body. A goodly proportion of these gave instant and direct evidence that God had touched them. We are greatly encouraged. It is a fact that, when God's commandments are obeyed, and we put ourselves in the line laid down for the application of either divine grace and forgiveness through Christ's blood, or divine healing through the appropriating faith of God, We shall see results. At this time we have no exact data from the work of the other churches, but have no doubt that wherever these great fundamental New Testament teachings are presented as Jesus and His Apostles taught them. that results must of necessity follow. These things are based on the direct promises of God.

Our people have been reconciled to the departure of the evangelist only through her promise to return to us next June. Knowing her as we do, and having become familiar with what is necessary to produce the best and largest results, and being familiar with the methods of her work, we expect when she returns to us, to have such preparations made as will result in harvests commensurate with her faith and our faith, with her efforts and our efforts, so that the very best results may be harvested, gleaned and brought into the garner of our common Master. We bid her God speed in all the labor which she has planned to perform in the days to come.

JUDGE OF JUVENILE COURT WRITES

July 12, 1921.

My dear Mrs. McPherson:

My friend, Senator Dunklee, told me that after I left the meeting at the Brown, you were good enough to do me a very great honor to ask if I would send a short statement for your paper, *The Bridal Call.* This I am more than glad and privileged to do and will enclose it herewith. I should be more than pleased if it should be acceptable for your purposes.

May I express to you again the same appreciation which of course has been voiced by thousands and thousands for what your coming into our midst has meant to our entire city. No such spiritual uplift has ever come to Denver in my time, and we shall always praise and thank the Lord for sending you to us.

With all good wishes to you and your dear mother from both myself and my wife, I am

Sincerely and gratefully yours,

BEN B. LINDSEY.

May we be included in your prayers and some day we hope to hear you from *our* seat in your great Echo Park Temple.

Twenty-one years as Judge of the Juvenile Court that, after all, is a family court, gives one a great experience and insight into the trials, tribulations, sins and sufferings of the people. No institution perhaps comes more intimately in contact with human failings and difficulties. It is not generally known that a work of this kind also attracts thousands of people who are seeking help. I am satisfied that we know far more about the extent of sinfulness than the public could possibly know or even the average school or church. I think even these institutions would be surprised if not indeed startled if they knew how much sinfulness there is in the world at this time, and, therefore how much need for the healing power of Jesus Christ. Laws, for example, are important; but my experience teaches me that these laws seldom accomplish the purpose they are intended to accomplish. I am coming more and more to the belief that too many man-made laws and a dependence upon them to save the world from sin is really doing much to get us away from the real remedies that were promised by the great divine Healer. With all due respect however for the power of "Caesar" but much more for the power of Christ, I do not hesitate to say that the bringing of the spirit of Christ into a community after the fashion of one of His real disciples like Mrs. McPherson, is doing more to destroy the powers of Satan, sin and lawlessness in that community than all the police departments, sheriffs, and courts combined. That is why public officials especially have abundant cause to welcome the glorious work for Christ that Mrs. McPherson is doing and that is why I am proud of Denver officials because from the Mayor down to the humblest man in the police department she has been given a glad welcome and support.

It is a great privilege for me to bear testimony to what has been a thousand times demonstrated in Denver that the bringing of the real spirit of Christ to a community through the true Gospel in revival services conducted by Mrs. McPherson and Mrs. Kennedy, is positively the most precious, the most priceless, the most wonderful thing that could happen to that community.

BEN B. LINDSEY.

Juvenile Court of Denver.
July 12, 1921.

WHAT MAKES A REVIVAL

CANTON—OHIO

Is it Advertising? Is it Organization? Is it the raising of Advance Subscriptions to guarantee Expenses? Is it the training of big Choirs, expert direction of music, and instruction of workers? Is it the wisdom and diplomacy of Advance Representatives to solicit and secure co-operation of the denominations?

NOT necessarily so—although all of these are to be desired and are blessedly used of God when directed by the Holy Spirit, as was the case in the recent glorious campaign in Denver, Colorado, with Dean Peck and the Congregational churches, the Dean himself being of national reputation in religious and benevolent circles, and with Dr. Towner of the First Baptist Church of San Jose being loyally supported and planned by his splendid board of official men six months in advance. In both of these meetings brains, money and experienced, capable men were thrown into service in unstinted measure by the churches backing the meetings and a glorious revival crowned their efforts.

But the fact that these splendid and much to be desired aids are not absolutely indispensable to the magnifying of the name of the Lord Jehovah, and that it is not these alone that constitute a heaven-born, heaven-sent revival was strangely evidenced in the recent campaign at Canton, Ohio.

It was not the Reception Committee that brought the Revival to Canton.

Stepping from the warm shelter of the sleeping car at 7 A.M. Saturday morning we stood for a moment shivering on the platform, found ourselves unmet because of a delayed telegram and picking up our suit cases made our way to the depot, called a sleepy taxi man and packed in behind our baggage, sped away to locate the one brother with whom we had corresponded regarding the business of the meeting.

He had secured the building from the Councilmen, rent free, (we paying the actual running expenses) but there his responsibility ended. Here was the city—here was the City Auditorium—and here were we on this frosty October morning. Now, dear Lord Jesus, for the Revival you promised when you bade us come to Canton!

Making our way to the Cortland Hotel, rooms were secured and we hurried to the Auditorium for our first acquaintance with the building, which was to constitute the battlefield of the Lord for the coming three weeks.

It was not the careful advance arrangement and creation of Revival atmosphere that brought the Revival, for when we groped our way through the darkened Auditorium we found a moving picture show for the children in progress. No arrangement of platform, altars, prayer rooms, etc., had yet begun—these were arranged after the dance that night.

It was not the advertising campaign that brought the Revival to Canton. Outside of a few scattered window cards and a sign above the door of the Auditorium itself there had been little advance advertising done, with the exception of a two-column sermon which one minister was stirred up to preach against the Revival before we arrived. His declaration that the day of miracles, healings and supernatural power of God was gone, and his announcement that some people were coming to Canton to preach, who believed that they were *not* past and that Christ had the same power and willingness to do today that which He did yesterday and warnings against us were our chief advance newspaper advertisements. They did waken more interest than any paid Ad. of our own could do, we admit, but were not of the nature which most Evangelists (ourselves included) would most choose.

It was not the securing of advance Denominational co-operation—not in Canton at least: For a chill struck us to the heart when, missing the presence of the one minister we had expected to work with us through the campaign, we drove to his parsonage the next day to inquire just what co-operation and help he could give. We were informed that his superiors had warned him to beware of the meetings as we claimed to have received the Pentecostal Baptism of the Holy Spirit and that he felt it the part of wisdom to go slow.

By the end of the first week, however, more than a thousand men and women had kneeled at the altars seeking salvation.

Clergymen from practically all the leading churches were on the platform speaking, singing, praying, planning, organizing workers' squads, and the dear Brother mentioned came and helped us too, bringing his choir, orchestra and workers.

It was not a large, well trained choir that brought the Revival to Canton. On the first Sunday afternoon we had about twenty-six members in the choir which we recruited from the audience; many of them were our visiting friends, some were members of local choirs; the majority of them had never met before, consequently having never sung together till that hour.

The platform accommodated some five hundred singers and when, (after praying together in the little dressing room and taking many peeps through the stage entrance at our slowly growing audience in the center of the auditorium.) we finally sent in our little choir of singers, they huddled close together in the center of the rostrum and looked lost in its vastness. Hasty word was sent in, bidding them spread their chairs further apart and make themselves look as much as possible.

Long before the campaign was over the platform was jammed to capacity and extra supports were needed to keep it from sagging—but 'tis of the opening days and the bringing about of the Revival we are now speaking. Having no other pianist at hand, Dr. Price (a Congregational minister of Lodi, Cal., who, with his wife, is assisting us on this transcontinental series) took the piano. A brother volunteered to help lead the singing as I sat behind him and anxiously whispered instructions, vainly endeavoring to help him keep the choir and audience together in the vast spaces of the echoing galleries, for indeed, it was bewildering to tell which was the choir, which was the audience, and which the echo.

N-no, we don't think that anyone who was present on that first Sunday would say that it was the big, well-trained choir that brought about the Revival! And yet—that first afternoon the altar was filled from end to end with penitent sinners and back-sliders seeking the Christ. And they were filled and refilled meeting after meeting, day after day, for three weeks and four Sundays.

It was not the advance training of workers—these were volunteer helpers from the audience until the altar calls grew so tremendously that resident clergymen, Salvation Army and Y. M. C. A. workers who were with us heart and soul, formed committees and brought ten and twenty workers from each of the churches and instructed them on the moment as to the expert handling of the thronging penitents, and appointed secretaries over these again.

It was not the sending of advance representatives to boost us or our work, or to secure co-operation, for there was no mortal to do this in Canton. Yet the Holy Spirit led the way, softening and warming many's the heart through the Bridal Call. It must not be thought that we were friendless in Canton, even that first Sunday, however, for this was our third campaign in Ohio and the State was well sprinkled with Bridal Call readers and warm-hearted children of God, many of whom had been converted, healed or baptized in our Dayton or Akron campaigns. These flocked from far and near and at times practically every state in the Union—Mexico, Canada and Panama were represented.

Was it paid newspaper publicity as some have suggested?

Positively not! There were wonderful articles in the best positions on the front pages of the city papers every day from the opening until the closing of the campaign for which special Press representatives were detailed, but this service was rendered gratuitously, as the Revival presented from their standpoint, was the news of the day and concerned countless thousands.

The Revival was *the* subject of conversation in the streets, banks, restaurants, pool rooms, barber shops—everywhere. At the close of the campaign the Canton Daily News presented us, not with a bill for services rendered, but with a check for $50.00 for two chairs in the Echo Park Revival Tabernacle, one for the editor and one for the reporter.

Was it the eloquent preaching of the Evangelist? Well, not the first Sunday anyway, for we found to our consternation the sparsely filled building abounding with echoes rendered it most confusing for the hearer to distinguish between the speaker and the echoes which seemed to be thrown back from every empty seat in the gallery. These echos disappeared immediately when the building was filled on the fourth day of the campaign.

Yet, notwithstanding the above mentioned adverse conditions, from the very first hour the city seemed to be in the grip of the Revival and so marvelously did God undertake that from the first service to the last the altars were filled to overflowing with men and women seeking and finding Jesus as their personal Savior. Many of these were business men who had never before taken any interest in religion or confessed Christ as Lord.

No, it was not the preaching of the Evangelist alone, for this was proven daily when, even before the sermon or altar call, those desiring to be saved were asked to hold up their hands and request prayer. At such times scores, often hundreds of hands were raised in every section of the building and almost as many professed themselves ready to then and there come to Christ as filled the altars after the sermon.

Was it the so-called "Knock-them-down-and-drag-them-out" tactics employed by so many wherein expert "fishers" are trained to watch the hands or indications of even mild conviction, then go, plead, coax, argue and finally drag the sinner to the altar against his will?

No, these tactics were not adopted, for every worker was needed on the platform to assist the long lines of penitents coming to the front and few were left for audience work. Besides this, the aisles were so congested and choked with people who were rising to their feet and with streaming eyes making their way to the front that all the traffic must needs flow in one direction and every worker be on hand to bring out new chairs and find places for those who *were* coming. Scores at each service were under a gripping conviction for sin that was unmistakable and seemingly unescapable. No, it was not the power or persuasion of man but of God.

Was it then that the Devil was asleep and failed to oppose bitterly the inroads into his kingdom, the overthrowal of the citadels of doubt, and the liberating of his captives?

Decidedly NOT—for from start to finish his Satanic Majesty not only trembled for his hold on hearts and lives, but wove diabolic plans in a vain endeavor to overthrow the work, cunningly chose and instructed emissaries to do his bidding, through whom he raged and roared like an angry lion.

I. A MESSENGER WITH A MESSAGE AND THE POWER TO DELIVER IT

Through all the ages God has been seeking and using yielded and believing messengers through whom He could pour His message from Heaven to earth. The messenger must be in direct contact with the Lord and with the people, through a heart filled with love. God wants a Revival everywhere and is looking for empty vessels through whom His message can flow. Such a messenger must not only take, believe and have confidence in the message, but must lose himself in it and be absorbed by it. The message must be in direct accord with the word of God, not as theologians would explain it, but as it reads in its simplicity, power, fullness and blessing. The messenger must be inspired of God by the Holy Spirit to deliver it, changing printer's ink, paper and mere words into the living voice and power of the living Christ.

II. THE LIFTING UP OF CHRIST, THE GREAT "I AM"

And if I (Jesus the same, yesterday, today and forever) be lifted up from the earth, I will draw all men unto me. The messenger must hide away behind the Cross in order that the people may see less earthiness and more Christ. Christ must be lifted up until He is made real to the people. The preaching of the great "I Am" instead of the great "I Was" accomplishes this by making real and bringing near to the people the ever living, loving, unchangeable Christ of Galilee ready, waiting, longing to do today for the simple, the sick and the heavy laden that which He did of yore. The lifting of Jesus high above the earth, Jesus with the loving heart, the tender voice, the nail pierced hands; Jesus whose ear is not heavy that He cannot hear and whose arm is not shortened that He cannot save, is one of the great secrets of bringing about a Revival.

In order to do this the one who lifts Him up must have lived and walked with this Christ, sharing in His love, sharing in His sorrow and suffering, sharing in His glory, and be really a reflection of the Christ. Thus He is made no longer a marble God in the far off yesterday who neither loves nor cares, but becomes a vital, pulsing, living reality so near that the hungry heart may reach out and touch His robe.

III. THE ANOINTING FROM ABOVE AND THE UTTERANCE FROM WITHIN

In pouring out His Revival spirit, God used human instruments. The Evangel should be imbued with power from above—the power of the Holy Ghost and fire; should be under the anointing and have the holy oil that makes the face to shine, even as Aaron o'er whose head ran the oil that reached to the end of his beard and the skirts of his gown. Even a sinner can tell in a moment whether the preacher has the oil and the holy anointing.

Jesus intends that rivers of living waters should flow out of the innermost being of His messengers, and this spake He of the Spirit. 'Tis not so much that which flows from the head as that which flows from the heart that makes a Revival. Keep the joy, the lilt and the glory of your first love. Make salvation attractive, and the Christian life a heaven to go to heaven in and example of that which you preach in body and soul.

IV. THE PREACHING OF THE FULL GOSPEL

The clipping shears should be put away and the wonderful story from the old book should be preached with faith and simplicity just as it reads—Salvation by faith, healing for the body, the baptism of the Holy Spirit and the glorious imminent coming of the Lord Jesus. There must be no hedging or letting down the bars but a fearless presentation of Bible truth in the good old Bible way. A straight, dividing line must be drawn between the Church and the world, the sinner and the saint, and Jesus must be proclaimed as the only way by which a sin-burdened soul can find salvation and deliverance.

V. A PASSION FOR SOULS, COUPLED WITH THE DRAWING POWER OF LOVE

In order to have a real Revival God's messenger must needs have a vision and God-given realization of the value of a human soul, then every song, sermon, testimony, word and action should be but sure, firm, stepping stones that lead directly to the throne, the goal, the one great important thing towering above them all—*the altar call.* Souls, Souls, Souls—should be the battle cry; all other things being subservient until the battlements of Heaven are made to echo with the joy bells welcoming the wandering ones back home. If one preaches the Gospel 'tis to win souls. If one prays for the healing of the sick and afflicted, 'tis so that they may have more strength with which to go out in turn and win other souls. If one climbs to the mountain top experience and receives the baptism of the Holy Spirit, 'tis so that one may go forth with the power of God and be a more efficient, practical, level-headed winner of souls.

We, as Messengers, must have been drawn so close to the heart of Jesus that the o'er flowing love welling from His own great heart has come trickling down into our hearts, making them to overflow with divine love that looks out in three directions: (1), toward God, the Father in consecrated abandoned yielding, obedience, service and zeal; (2), toward the brethren, for hereby men know that ye are My disciples; (3), toward a world of lost, sin-benighted, briar-torn, wandering sheep for whom the good Shepherd is seeking and calling through His under Shepherds that preach the word.

VI. SPARE NOT YOURSELF

Put your all, personal ambitions, health, life, strength, means —everything, on the altar and count not your life dear unto death. Keep humble and lowly at the Master's feet, ever being careful to ascribe all the honor and glory to Jesus.

VII. FAITH

To bring about a real Revival God's Messenger must have faith. Faith in God—Faith in His word—Faith in the Call and in the Message He has given you and burned in your very soul—Faith to believe that the world is hungry and waiting to be brought to Christ—Faith in the outpouring of the Holy Spirit and the copious showers of blessings that are falling in these last days wherein God is pouring out His Spirit upon all flesh—Faith that if we preach the word the Lord is faithful to confirm it with signs following—Faith to believe that Christ is at the Helm—Faith to believe that God can bring a Revival out of the hardest, most impossible circumstances, make the wrath of man to praise Him and turn every missile of the enemy back into his own ranks to work his own undoing—Faith to believe that God is greater and more mighty than the devil and keeping our eyes upon the author and finisher of our faith, never doubt for a moment that He will win the day—Faith to laugh at defeat and obstacles and to see nothing but God's power, promises and sweeping victory.

ADDRESS BY REV. MANCHESTER, D. D.

President Canton Ministerial Association

I AM going to be perfectly honest this afternoon in what I say. When I came into these meetings first it was on Thursday afternoon of the first week. I am going to say another thing. I came from Missouri when I came here. (Applause.) Not that I really doubted but I simply did not know, and wanted to be shown.

I do not think I had been sitting here more than about ten minutes (for I was late and Sister was preaching) before I said to myself, "God has sent that message to me." Then I kept on coming. I want to say to you in order to make it very short this afternoon that this has been to me the greatest meeting that I ever attended. (Applause.) And I have been fifty years a Methodist preacher and it has been the greatest one to me that I have ever attended. I have seen some great ones, too, but I will tell you why it has been great to me. It is because I have seen more of God's plan than ever before.

The first thing that came to me with great power was that Jesus Christ is exalted. People began talking about healing. "Well," I said, "I do not know about the healing just yet but I know that Jesus Christ is being lifted up and that is the biggest thing that can come into any meeting. (Applause.) If souls can be saved for all eternity that is a bigger thing than healing a body for fifteen or twenty years, perhaps, at the utmost.

I have come to this conclusion that the healing of the body is a part of the plan, (applause) just as much as any other part of the plan and God forgive me that I have prayed so many times by the bedside of the sick and I have asked God simply to make them more comfortable and get them home to Heaven when they died. I am going to pray for more than that now. (Applause.) I am going to realize too the mighty power of Christ to do these things.

I wish you could have seen what a half dozen of us saw yesterday morning in that little room. Mr. C——— was the crookedest man physically in this city, bent over this way. I was quite interested in the man and I did not know his heart was hungry. I knew him to be a good Christian man, a sterling member of the First Baptist Church of this city. I went down and spoke to him two or three times. He thanked me for my kindness in going to him, he not knowing his words were a benediction to me.

Yesterday Mrs. McPherson went into this room and anointed him and we began to pray for him. That man could not have been on his feet for three years. He arose and began to walk up and down that room shouting the praises of God. (Applause.) And he kept it up. After he had been in there a couple hours he started to go home and he walked through that crowd at the door, out to the automobile, and climbed in alone. His dear wife had been handling him, lifting him into the automobile all this time. She said God gave her strength to do it because she loved him so. Those who live in Canton understand me when I say he got out on Cleveland Avenue and walked down to his home without a crutch or cane, walked up the stairs, went into his room, spent the hour from twelve to one in prayer for others of us.

He called us up last night and said he was happy and at twelve o'clock this morning said, "I am the happiest man that ever lived. Oh, I do not know what to do, I am so happy." Then he went down to the Baptist Church, taught his old Bible class down there, told them the wonderful things God had done for him. I never was so conscious of any other Presence in my life as I was on Sunday afternoon when Jesus Christ came to him with His mighty healing power.

THE PEOPLE'S TABERNACLE DENVER, COLO.—DEAN A. C. PECK

THE MUNICIPAL AUDITORIUM, DENVER, COLO.

THE COLISEUM, ST. LOUIS, DURING S

THE GREAT MUNI

Scene of the two world-moving campaigns, where scenes like thi
by 1000 men and 1000 women. Mayor Baily,

:RSON'S GREAT REVIVAL CAMPAIGN

ORIUM, DENVER, COLO.
ıous for many weeks. The Altar calls often were answered
y and Dean Peck were supporters and helpers

MANY WERE HEALED AND WENT WALKING OUT REJOICING DURING THIS WONDERFUL DAY AT DENVER, COLO.

THE FRESNO REVIVAL VIEWED

(NOTE: Mr. Frisbie is a well-known real estate man, formerly President of Theosophical Society, but recently converted through Bridal Call.)

HE McPherson party arrived from Los Angeles via the Southern Pacific, at 11 A. M., Saturday, January 7th.

They were greeted by numerous friends and interested people from far and near, who cheered, waved handkerchiefs and sang Gospel songs, while struggling to obtain a closer view of the Evangelist.

The committee on arrangements, assisted by railroad officials and police, hurried Mrs. McPherson through the crowds to a waiting automobile. She was then driven to the City Hall, where Mayor Hart and his official family were waiting to greet her. After this cordial welcome by the city fathers, who have been her staunch supporters from the first, Sister thanked the Mayor for his hearty co-operation in opening the way for the coming revival campaign.

The campaign opened at 2:30 P. M. As very little advertising had been done, we were not looking for a large audience, it being Sister's intention merely to organize the work at the first gathering. To our astonishment, an audience of 3,500 or more thronged the Civic Auditorium, long before the hour announced for the first meeting; and I may here remark that, during the entire campaign, the Auditorium, which seats over 6,000 people, was crowded to the limit, with crowds outside clamoring for admission, often standing for hours in the rain, so as to be ready for the next meeting.

The Mayor, Truman G. Hart, introduced the Evangelist in a most kindly and enthusiastic speech, and closed his remarks by saying:

"It is with real delight that I have accepted the invitation to introduce this splendid woman, and true friend of humanity;" then, leading her to the front of the platform, he said, "All of you who are really glad to see her, please stand and extend to her a hearty welcome."

It is needless to say that the entire audience were on their feet immediately, waving handkerchiefs and applauding enthusiastically.

Sister McPherson now took charge of the meeting, and the campaign was on. Singers and workers from several churches in this city, and out-of-town, were present to take part in the great campaign.

Although somewhat fatigued from her recent campaign in the East, and long railroad journey, Sister McPherson preached a powerful sermon; at the close of which she invited the sinful and backsliders to come to the altar and give their hearts to Jesus. As nearly as I can estimate, some 200 people responded to this first call of the Evangelist; a thing never before heard of in Fresno, as all previous evangelists have preached many sermons before giving an altar call.

The Fresno campaign, from start to finish, was essentially a revival meeting, particular stress being laid on that part of the Gospel which deals with the salvation of the sinner and the reclaiming of the backslider.

These meetings were held daily at 2:30 and 7:30, extra meetings devoted to prayer for the sick and afflicted being held regularly on Monday, Wednesday, Friday and Sunday mornings at 10:30. There were also other extra meetings, from time to time, held in the early morning or late at night, at which Sister McPherson prayed for the afflicted whom she was unable to reach at the regular meetings. It seemed to me that these prayer meetings were given to the sick and afflicted from the goodness of her heart, and as something outside of the regular evangelistic work. We all observed with wonder and amazement, the seemingly superhuman strength given to our dear Sister, which made it possible for her to accomplish the otherwise impossible.

Too much can not be said in praise of her wonderful mother, Mrs. Minnie Kennedy, who took time from her strenuous duties in connection with the campaign, to pray with and for the sick and prepare them for the touch of faith which was later to make them every whit whole.

Surely it is woman's day, and God is pouring out His spirit on His handmaidens. Ten, or even five years ago, no one would have dreamed that two little women could have conducted, unaided, except for a few volunteer workers, such a wonderful campaign; in fact, no one ever dreamed of such a campaign. If my memory serves me correctly, all previous evangelists coming to Fresno, have required that their expenses be guaranteed in full before accepting a call to preach, but Mrs. McPherson had no human support, either financially or otherwise. She simply trusted Jesus to open the way and to supply her every need. That this prayer was abundantly answered, one need only to have been present or to ask some one who attended the revival.

From my viewpoint, this was the first Full Gospel message that has ever been preached in Fresno by any of the big evangelists; consequently we need not be surprised at the mighty works which were accomplished in the salvation of sinners, the healing of the sick, and the baptizing of believers with the Holy Spirit.

Mrs. McPherson seeks, with all her heart, to eliminate the personality and to lift up Jesus, and "I if I be lifted up from the earth, will draw all men unto me."

As near as is possible to estimate, more than 6000 people came weeping to the altar during this revival. They did not have to be urged to come forward; in many cases they actually ran. There were no fishers in the audience to help the more timid ones; they came of their own free will, with no incentive other than the plain, simple presentation of the Gospel of Jesus Christ. The sense of excitement or over-persuasion was entirely absent in these meetings. The only real difficulty incurred was in finding room for the penitents to kneel.

On two occasions Sister did not preach a sermon, but simply prayed for the sinful, then gave the altar call. They came as usual and filled the platform and aisles.

A gray-haired minister, with tear-dimmed eyes, said to the writer: "I have been preaching for forty years. I am a very old man, yet I have never seen such a wonderful revival, such a mighty outpouring of the Spirit, such a throng of people seeking salvation." Looking over the vast audience, he said, "See that sea of earnest, prayerful faces, that multitude with uplifted hands, imploring Sister McPherson to pray for them. Fresno never witnessed such a sight. I have attended the meetings of all other evangelists of my time, and nothing approaching this has ever been witnessed before."

Surely no other evangelist has loved and honored Jesus Christ more than Sister McPherson. When the sick are healed or the sinful saved, she asks the audience, "Who did this?" and they soon learn to answer, with one accord, "Jesus!"

Day after day, the multitudes who came to hear and to witness the mighty works, increased. Blind eyes were opened, deaf ears unstopped, the lame walked, and the poor had the Gospel preached to them, as in the days when Jesus walked the earth. The results obtained through prayer for the afflicted have been simply wonderful. I can only take time in this letter to recite a few cases.

One brother was brought to the platform in a wheel chair. His form was greatly emaciated, his face pale and distorted from long suffering. He was afflicted with tuberculosis of the knee joints. The writer must admit that his faith failed as this poor man was lifted upon the platform and brought forward in his chair. The great audience gasped in astonishment as Sister took hold of his hands and commanded him, in the name of Jesus, to arise and walk. As the power of God began pouring through his emaciated form, some one standing nearby, said, "Now I shall not be surprised to see the dead raised." He not only stood upon his feet, but actually walked back and forth upon the platform, amidst the tears and cheers of the vast audience. He then walked unaided off the platform, down seven steps, and out in front of the audience. With every step, new strength seemed to permeate his body; new life flowed through his veins; color began to come into his face, and he was healed. Glory to Jesus! This case was one of the earliest manifestations, during the meetings, of the power of Jesus to heal the sick.

We have had the opportunity of seeing this brother, almost daily, in the meetings, after prayer was offered. His testimony is that he is now completely healed and growing stronger daily. Surely "He hath borne our griefs and carried our sorrows," and "by His stripes we are healed."

Another interesting case which occurs to me at this moment, is that of an Armenian boy. The writer saw this boy come onto the platform with his mother. His eyes were covered with cataracts. He had never seen any object, and could only distinguish between light and darkness. After Sister McPherson had anointed him and prayed the prayer of faith, saying: "Jesus, open these blind eyes," a look of intelligence and surprise became noticeable, immediately he looked with delight and astonishment at the waving handkerchiefs in the audience. A moment later, Sister McPherson pointed to his mother standing a few feet away, and said to him, "Who is that sweet faced lady standing there?" Looking up in wonderment, he replied, "I don't know." Then the mother said, "Why, darling, don't you know your mother?" Flying to her arms, he said, "Oh, mamma, I can see." This remarkable healing was witnessed by more than 5000 people, many of whom took the little boy in their arms, just to satisfy themselves as to whether or not he could really see.

It is needless to say there was scarcely a dry eye in the audience, and the applause was deafening. Jesus of Narazeth had passed by, and it was again proven had lost none of His ancient power to open the blind eyes. Glory to His Name, forever! Sister McPherson speaks truly, when she says, "He is the Great I Am and not the *Great I Was.*"

We witnessed the case of another brother, who ascended the platform with great difficulty, being so bent with rheumatism that his hands almost touched the floor. After being anointed according to the command given in James 5:14, Sister took hold of his hands and said, "In the Name of Jesus, arise, stand upon thy feet and walk!" He not only stood erect, but raised both hands high above his head, shouting "Glory to God! Praise Jesus!" After walking back and forth upon the platform, he actually ran down the seven steps leading to the main audience room, and up one aisle and down another, amid the shouts, the applause and the tears of the vast audience.

One lady approached the evangelist, who had been suffering from a repulsive goiter on her neck. After being prayed for, she raised her eyes toward heaven and gasped, "Praise Jesus, it is gone," and sure enough there was no further sign of a goiter. Fifty people standing nearby witnessed this remarkable healing.

Space will not permit me to write of the many cases wherein those suffering from cancer, rheumatism, goiter, paralysis, tumors, ulcers, deformities, etc., were instantly healed or began to amend from that hour.

The only unfortunate aspect of this great Revival seemed to be the utter inability of the ushers to find seats for the people. Day after day, as long as the revival continued, the police struggled with the multitude who were seeking admission into the already crowded auditorium. One night, the throng outside was so great and so insistent to hear the message on the second coming of Christ, that they actually broke through the strong guard of police, and before they could be stopped, more than a thousand people had crowded into the aisles and anterooms of the already full auditorium. Although Sergeant of Police Fornes, and Fire Chief Berkholtz loudly protested against this over-crowding of the building, the people refused to move, and as Sister McPherson began to speak, she looked over a vast unbroken sea of humanity, which had flowed into the aisles, into the ante rooms and even onto the platform.

"They shall mount up with wings as eagles, they shall run and not be weary; they shall walk and not faint." We cannot help applying this precious promise to Sister McPherson personally, for ordinarily, no human being could stand the great strain which is put upon the little Evangelist. After three sermons, two or three altar calls, besides praying for the sick and attending to the multitude of other duties, including dictating replies to letters, writing articles for the Bridal Call, to say nothing about family duties, she often seems as fresh and vigorous at the end of the long strenuous day as at the beginning.

Glory to Jesus for the wonderful works which our eyes have beheld during this campaign. Sister McPherson seems to have no regard for her bodily comforts. Some days she scarcely takes time to eat. Her mind is so intent upon ministering to the needy, and answering every cry for help, that oftentimes her attendants must actually carry her through the crowds of pleading people who bar her way.

Let us sum up the results of this splendid revival, or some of them which appear on the surface, for Eternity alone can tell the whole story.

Looking at it from a Spiritual viewpoint, thousands have been saved from a life of sin and shame, and converted to the religion of Jesus Christ, washed in His Precious Blood and started on the road to Glory. Hundreds of family altars have been established, and people who never knew how to pray before are now kneeling reverently at the feet of Christ Jesus. We have learned to love our Bibles, to love the Church of Jesus Christ, and to reverence the ministers of the Gospel, and best of all we have learned to love one another as never before. From a purely commercial city, given over almost entirely to money making and worldly pleasures, Fresno has been transformed overnight, as it were, into a God fearing, church-going and praying city. Hallelujah to Jesus!

Even from a commercial viewpoint we are gainers, for our city has been filled with visitors from nearly every state in the Union. The hotels and rooming houses have been filled; the restaurants have flourished, and other lines of business greatly stimulated. I believe our population has increased a thousand or more by reason of the people who will locate here, having learned to love the city and its people during the Revival.

Again I thank God, with a full heart, for sending Sister McPherson and her faithful mother and co-worker, Mrs. Minnie Kennedy, to Fresno. "Praise God from whom all blessings flow!" Thousands of my fellow townsmen who read this will say "AMEN."

THE MAYOR OF FRESNO

Jan. 30, 1922

It is my distinct impression, after attending several of the meetings of Mrs. McPherson, and having since the meetings begun, talked to some scores of people who have diligently attended them from the beginning, that Mrs. McPherson's ministry here has been peculiarly beneficial to the people of this city and county. I have viewed almost with amazement the calm religious fervor that Mrs. McPherson has seemed to spread throughout the thousands of persons daily thronging the auditorium, and the conversion of thousands of people, young and old, during her work here, has, I think, filled our people with astonishment.

How a demonstration of this sort can fail to be of inestimable benefit to the rank and file of our citizenry, is more than I can comprehend. It seems to me that if Mrs. McPherson can hold her force and strength and persist in the tremendous work she is now carrying on, she must in the end, become a distinct moral benefit and uplift to our nation and to the English speaking world.

Yours sincerely,

(Signed) T. G. HART, Mayor.

Fresno, Cal., Jan. 30, 1922

COMMISSIONER OF PUBLIC WORKS

I want to express to you, Mrs. McPherson, in this simple manner my deep appreciation of the wonderful good you have done for our community since you have been with us this month.

I can truthfully and honestly say that there has been nothing in your meetings at any time, nor in any way, which could offend the most sensitive person. There has been nothing, in any meeting, at which any minister could take the slightest exception.

You have told thousands upon thousands of people, in a gentle, simple way, your version of the Scriptures. Personally, I feel that if our ministers would have attended every one of your meetings they would have been greatly benefited and would have been better able to have preached the Gospel of Jesus Christ as He intended it to be preached.

You have done me good, amongst the thousands of others, and you have done the City of Fresno good, and I thank you from the bottom of my heart. I hope and trust that you will be able to be with us many times in the future, and I am sure I am expressing the sentiments of thousands of our citizens.

May God bless you and keep you strong to carry on your wonderful work.

Very sincerely yours,

WM. STRANAHAN,

Commissioner of Public Works.

Jan. 31, 1922.

FRESNO CAMPAIGN

By Rev. H. E. Wilkinson, Moderator
San Joaquin Valley Baptist Association

AS Mrs. McPherson's campaign draws to a close we begin to realize how much we will miss her, and what a blessing she has been to Fresno and the San Joaquin Valley.

We think of thousands who stood for hours in cold and stormy weather at the auditorium and we regret that the building did not seat 15,000 instead of about 6,000. Even with the larger seating capacity the house would have been filled at every service. Many refrained from coming to hear Sister McPherson because of the uncertainty of finding a place to sit. They too were as eager for the Gospel message as those more fortunate.

The newspapers have been generous in their reports of the meetings, and through the Herald thousands will read those matchless sermons that they could not get otherwise. Praise the Lord!

Much that was opposition to commence with soon turned to marked support. Many ministers skeptical at first, have yielded to the Gospel message as preached in its simplicity and power by this messenger of God. Business men, including bankers, lawyers and manufacturers, have heard her tell the thrilling story. Thousands have confessed the Lord Jesus as their personal Saviour and a new citizenship will mark the personnel of Fresno's people from this time on. We have heard the name of Jesus spoken in our stores, our clubs, our business conversations in such a reverent way as to convince the most callous man that He has been walking with us during these three weeks. People who never lisped the name of Jesus have learned to talk of him without restraint and often with the silvery tear of repentance dropping from moistened eyes.

Many have reason to praise the Lord for renewed bodies, as well as for renewed souls. I want to bear testimony to Sister McPherson's service as a soul winner. Some would place emphasis on the healing meetings. Good as these have been, those meetings when the altar call brought response of thousands who for the first time confessed Christ as Saviour and Lord have been characterized by her greatest effort, and she has been faithful in telling her hearers that healing was incidental, not her main purpose.

Fresno has been filled with people from every section of this great state and from other states. Such earnest people too. Some came that their barren lives might be quickened. We have seen the gambler changed to a Christian gentleman, the burglar halted in his quest and converted, the cigarette smoker cleaned of his filthy habit, and every form of sinful habit changed to be in keeping with these renewed lives, Praise the Lord!

Our hotels have been filled to overflowing. The spare room in many homes has been the "room of blessing" to many, and how glad we have been to entertain these seekers. Throughout the valley for miles in every direction the meetings have been a topic of conversation so general has been the influence. People have abandoned home on the farm for weeks at a time to be present to hear the message. Such meetings have never been known in California before.

And the message. I have listened to great preachers at their best yet I want to testify that never have I heard such wonderful preaching. Nothing spectacular, no funny stories, no abuse of the churches and ministers—on the other hand Sister McPherson has urged churches and ministers to be supported in every manner, just the plain Gospel story of Jesus and His Love for sinners. It convinces one that God's Word has not lost power and that even today we can witness scenes such as marked the ministry of the apostolic age. That splendid face portrays a life filled with the Spirit.

I wish I could close without a word of regret, but as I think of those thousands of men, women and children who have confessed Jesus being without adequate care by consecrated Christian workers I confess a sorrow that may be overcome by prayer to the Lord that He will care for them, every one to His glory.

As a member of a great denomination I shall watch with keen interest the influence of this campaign which has already manifested itself in some of our churches. Such a message as Sister McPherson has preached cannot but strengthen our faith in God.

IN THE SUNFLOWER STATE OF KANSAS

"By His counsel guide, uphold you;
In His arms securely fold you:
God be with you 'till we meet again."

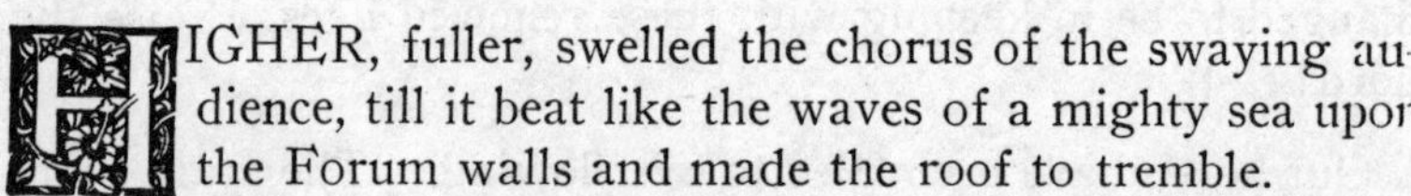

HIGHER, fuller, swelled the chorus of the swaying audience, till it beat like the waves of a mighty sea upon the Forum walls and made the roof to tremble.

And as they sang, o'er their heads there floated—was it a sea of many thousand hankerchiefs?—or was it the fluttering wings of innumerable doves that filled the building, hovering above the tight packed throng that filled the parquet floor, the circling balconies, gallery and the stage? Through a mist of tears 'twas hard to tell unless one rubbed one's eyes and looked a second time. But unquestionably the Heavenly Dove was there and thousands had come to trust beneath His feathers.

The last convert risen from the Altar, the last benediction asked, the last handshake and God bless you from the human river that flowed by, and the electric lights in the great chandelier and arched dome began to blink out one by one upon the closing scene of our first Revival Campaign in the famous Sunflower State of Kansas.

What a mighty and blessed campaign it had been! Our weary hearts sang joyously as we were surrounded and supported through the stage door and through the crowd on limbs that had grown suddenly a little tremulous and uncertain now that the great strain was over.

What a campaign it had been from start to finish—a sweeping cyclone of God's power of soul winning and blessing come down upon the hungry hearted who came from practically every state in the Union, Canada, Alaska, and Mexico who dipped their cups of blessing into the flowing stream of His abounding love.

Day by day the recording angels had been busily employed writing the new names of the steady throngs of newly blood-washed souls who had sought and found the Saviour at the long altars which filled the floor in the front of the building, now on row.

A LAYMEN'S COMMITTEE

Back of the campaign, staunch as the rock of Gibraltar, capable as a fleet of dreadnaughts, stood the most wonderful Interdenominational Laymen's Committee with whom it has ever been our privilege to work.

From the moment we stepped off the train on arrival, till the last farewell was waved at the depot, they stood by in quiet efficiency, encouragement and service. One earnest prayer filled every loyal heart—Lord send a Revival and give us souls, Souls, SOULS. And Praise the Lord, the answer came!

The great Wichita Forum, ideal for such a meeting, was leased. The Lord and the City Officials threw wide its doors at a nominal rent to us for the entire campaign.

And surely for their acts of courtesy and kindliness toward the Revival they were not unrewarded as the following clippings from The Wichita Eagle would show:

REVIVAL AID TO BUSINESS

WICHITA RETAILERS GRATEFUL TO EVANGELIST FOR TRADE STIMULANT

Wichita business men have received more than $100,000 directly through the revivals conducted for the last three weeks by Mrs. Aimee McPherson according to estimates based upon averages used by the Board of Commerce. Both the board and business men have stated that the out-of-town persons, drawn by the revival, have had a marked and beneficial influence on business.

According to Joseph Noble, secretary of the Retail division of the Board of Commerce, visitors will spend, on an average, $5 to $8 a day. At least 1,000 visitors have attended the revival daily, and many estimate 2,000. Each spending $5 to $8 according to the average, makes the total range from $100,000 to $320,000.

The revival has drawn a large number of country people, states A. W. Hinkel of the Boston Store, and country people always buy when in the city, he adds. Shortly after the close of each meeting, it has been noticed stores fill and a rush of business follows, he says.

CITIZENS REPENT AND INSIST THEY PAY UP OLD DEBTS

MONEY HANDLERS OF WICHITA CORPORATIONS SEE RESULTS OF MCPHERSON REVIVAL—OFFICERS ASTONISHED

"If Wichita never before had an acute conscience, it has one now," observed L. O. Ripley, vice-president and general manager of the Kansas Gas and Electric company, in discussing results of the Aimee Semple McPherson revival.

"It is noticeable in our office that some magic power has descended upon the city and people who once were inclined to procrastination are becoming scrupulously prompt in meeting their obligations. If Mrs. McPherson possesses the power to impel people to pay their debts, she has solved a problem touching upon finances, over which hairs have grown gray and great minds have flickered out."

"Come here, Gow, and tell this reporter some of our late experiences," commanded Mr. Ripley.

TREASURER SPEAKS

Mr. Gow, who is treasurer of the company related how he has been astounded during the past few days at receipt of letters breathing the spirit of penitence, telling of the writers moving away leaving their last month's gas and electric bills, and offering restitution in the way of pecuniary redress. In each instance, the writer had been attending the McPherson meetings and had become converted, he said. Furthermore, Mr. Gow said there is a strange absence during the past few days of trouble with patrons tapping wires, or gas service pipes, in their desire to steal these products.

FELT OTHER PLACES

Several days ago, T. J. Williamson, superintendent of the Wichita Water company, placed a special collector in the field, in the effort to clean up some old scores.

"I have been astonished at the amount of cash that has been collected, much of which we never expected to get," Mr. Williamson said. "We have received partial, or payment in full of accounts of two, three and four years' standing. In several instances, we have learned that bills were paid by new converts at the McPherson meetings."

J. S. Martin, commercial superintendent of the Southwestern Bell Telephone company relates that collections of back accounts never have been more satisfactory than during the recent past, which he attributes to the religious awakening in the city.

Mr. Martin relates one instance of where a woman sought to pay for a long distance phone call which she had put in at a pay booth and had departed without depositing the coins requested by the operator. This was three years ago. "I forgave her the amount whatever it was and told her I was glad she feels better over her confession," said Mr. Martin.

In a story published in The Eagle a few days ago, the experience of Howard W. Patton, general manager of the street railway company, was related; how he had encountered several persons who desire to make restitutions for wrongs they admitted to have perpetrated against the company in times gone by. They still are coming, he says.

It is reported that several local merchants have had experiences with customers of past years who had forgotten to liquidate their indebtedness and that as a result, several mercantile coffers have been replenished.

Mrs. McPherson, night after night, has preached the doctrine that requires a sinner to make amends for past misdeeds before he shall become the chosen of God.

What an awe inspiring sight to see these thousands of hungry hearts pouring into the Auditorium day after day for three weeks and the doors often roped and barred to hold back other thousands who would gain admittance just to hear the Old Time Gospel of Calvary's rugged Cross!

What a revelation of the hunger that fills human hearts from coast to coast, to gaze upon the hundreds upon hundreds of visitors to whom thousands of miles and the expense of entertainment in the city hotels was no barrier. Surely the harvest is great, the time of a mighty revival, a tremendous outpouring of the Holy Spirit is upon us and the Lord is near, even at the door.

THE GYPSIES

Among those who came to visit us from afar were the Gypsies. They came in throngs from practically every tribe. Dewy Mark, Chief of the Mark tribe, was in command of scores of camps and was to a large degree responsible for the revival among them.

In gay colors of the rainbow they came showering us with smiles, love and gifts; kissing our hands, our dresses, and if we were not ever watchful, dropping to the floor and kissing our shoes (much to our embarrassment). Looking up with dark, adoring Gypsy eyes they would cry: "O, lady, you told us about Jesus! Now—I saved—I healed and oh, so happy. Praise the Lord! Praise the Lord!"

Such devotion, such love as they heaped upon us we had never imagined. They donated chairs for the Temple at Echo Park; they loaded our arms with flowers and baskets of roses; they took us to Riverside Park and ministered to our temporal needs at the most unique and sumptuous banquet we have ever witnessed.

Here under the trees they spread their table cloths upon the grass and arranged a low table for us. Then they heaped upon the cloths, dozens of delicately baked chickens, roasts of meat, potatoes, vegetables, salads, fruits of every description and ice cream. Then, strewed the whole with flowers; planted gay American flags in the loaves of twisted bread and dropped to their knees, bidding us ask the blessing of the Lord upon the food. Surely never was a more picturesque scene since the days of long ago. The Mitchell tribe presented the Evangelist with an entire Gypsy costume which they insisted that she wear at all Gypsy services; and in order to become all things to all men that by any means we might win some, it incidentally became necessary to wear this costly gift home to the hotel (whither we returned in a Gypsy car decked with soft silks within and without) or to run the risk of offending these new converts who have the heart of a child.

After a moment's hesitation the Evangelist decided that it would be unworthy of the spirit of Christ to do other than as requested or conceal their gift, and wore the whole costume home.

Needless to say, all business and conversation hung suspended for a moment of wondering silence as we passed through the lobby of the great hotel and entered the elevator.

But it was renewed with a buzz that could be heard through the closed doors as we shot upward to our rooms.

Surely it is a heart of love, and entering into the spirit of understanding and sympathy with these precious people that is winning them for the first time to this full gospel and this born again experience. Methinks were such a thing to happen in a foreign land, 'twould cause joy throughout the earth and be recorded everywhere, but happening in our own America we scarce realize the import of a Nation turning to the Lord. Communion service was later administered and a testimony meeting held for them. It brought tears to the eyes of all to hear them tell how smoking, drinking, gambling, theatres, wild parties and dancing had all disappeared beneath the precious cleansing of the blood of Jesus. And how when the soft night mantle falls and the merry sparks leap upward from the camp fire, like flaming rubies through the night, they gather close to sing the songs that we have taught them, to pray and to commune with God beneath the twinkling stars of the open Heaven, which is the canopy of this wandering race. Surely God, who looketh down from beyond the shining moon, which swings ceaselessly through the cloudy space—the God, who made Heaven and earth and the Gypsies with their loving hearts, looks down and smiles his peace and blessing upon their upturned eager faces through the night. In his testimony, the Chief is ever quick to declare that the beginning of this Revival came about through the Denver meeting where one year ago, he himself was healed of a disease of the lungs and where his mother was healed of a fibroid tumor which, they declare, melted and was gone within fifteen minutes after prayer. These things stirred their nation and resulted in their turning to the Lord.

THE OSAGE INDIANS

From the Osage tribe of red-skinned Indians came numbers to attend the Revival and to give their hearts to the Lord. Three Chiefs were among the number and for the first time in our lives we saw the stoic calm of the race melt as they wept aloud and later cried for joy at the Master's feet. This tribe presented two magnificent wreaths, floral pieces, an Indian blanket and an invitation to their Reservation which we hope to accept at our earliest convenience.

Aside from the Gypsies and the Indians, who occupied one section at one side, the balance of our congregation was composed of the finest type of American citizens, thoughtful, earnest people who came to Christ in hundreds as the calls went forth.

A large chorus led by Brother Nichols, Wichita's singing Evangelist, entirely filled a large elevated platform on the stage. Singers and musicians came from the various churches and in every sense of the word this was a Laymen's Revival. It would seem as though laymen all over the world are rising up and demanding a return to the old time religion and an old time revival and as though they are oftimes outstripping the clergy in their efforts and success. Special services for aged and children were conducted with blessed results. Free distribution of Bibles was made wherein the word of God was put into the hands of hundreds of little children under the age of fifteen, who declared that never in their lives had they remembered seeing their mothers read a Bible, or of seeing the good book in their homes. Hundreds of tiny tots came to the altar and gave their hearts to Christ. A meeting for young business men and women was also held and out of the fifty evangelistic services conducted in the city, four special morning and one afternoon service was dedicated to prayer for the sick and afflicted. And by many definite answers to believing prayer were hearts and lives rejoiced.

SUNSET HOUR IN RIVERSIDE PARK

A glorious sunset hour testimony and prayer service was held one evening under the spreading trees of the city park at the band stand. The sermon, "Zacheus in the Sycamore Tree," brought many to the Lord and quite appropriately one man who had climbed unwittingly into a tree, the better to see and hear over the heads of the people, was one of the first to whose heart conviction was struck by the direct application and who came down to the feet of the Lord. Later a service of prayer was held for the afflicted and the glory of the Lord fell upon all the people, as the sick were raised up, the deaf heard, and the lame walked.

THE NEWSPAPERS

wrote most glowing and kindly reports of the meetings daily, placing the same upon the front page often with the leading headlines. Two of the highest salaried staff of reporters were put to cover the meetings and we regret that space will not permit a reproduction of many of these reports in this book. The splendid article which follows by Mr. Waggoner, who is a most thoughtful and earnest writer, should prove a blessing to all.

REMEMBERING THE POOR

Having heard of a poor section by the River bottom where the poverty stricken live in frail shacks made out of canvas and tin cans which they had opened and nailed flat, and where people dwelt under wagon tops, which had been placed upon the ground, we went to investigate one morning.

The reports which had reached our ears had not been exaggerated. We found sick and dying people living without the bare necessities of life, empty cupboards, filth, squalor, and half naked people living among the city dumps covered with flies and dirt. Going from home to home to pray, we soon realized that something more than prayer was needed. Groceries and clothes were the crying need of the hour. We were unable to visit all of these poor hovels ere the writer turned desperately ill between sympathy and the sickening conditions.

Returning to the afternoon meeting, the needs of this section known as "Squatter Town" were laid before the audience and a splendid offering received for the poor. Food, clothing, great baskets full of groceries, mosquito netting, toys, etc., were taken thither in trucks and automobiles and distributed by the Committee instead of being handled by The Associated Charities.

MAMMOTH COMMUNION SERVICE

On the closing Sunday of the Revival, a mammoth communion service wherein some five thousand saints were privileged to participate in the sacrament which was held, and a Communion sermon preached by the Evangelist from Exodus 12:3 "A lamb for a house," showing forth the blood of the slain lamb applied to the door posts of the heart for salvation, and the body of the lamb as our food for strength and might. His blood for our salvation, His body for our body, His strength for our weakness. And there was a shout in the camp as thousands caught a fresh vision of the great Redeemer even the Lamb slain from the foundation of the world. So expertly was this mammoth communion service conducted by the Committee of Arrangements that it was possible to serve bread and wine throughout the entire building in less than twenty minutes.

How the power of the Lord came down as Saints wept and consecrated their lives anew to His service! After the Sacrament was served, the call was given at the request of many for hundreds of young men and women who would there and then pledge their lives to the service of the Master at home or abroad to come forward, and by the laying on of hands the power of God and the baptism of the Holy Ghost was invoked for special anointing for service. The platform and the steps leading to it and the aisles were crowded with hundreds who surged forward, thus pledging their lives. 'Twas a never to be forgotten sight.

ARKANSAS CITY

Closing the campaign in Wichita, Sunday, May the 23rd, with three enormous services and altar calls, we journeyed the next day to Arkansas City for a mass meeting in Wilson Park.

'Twas by the following telegram our invitation was tendered:

WESTERN UNION

Arkansas City, May 12, 1922.

DEAR MRS. MC PHERSON:

FROM THE HEARTS OF THE ARKANSAS CITY PEOPLE WE EXTEND TO YOU AN INVITATION TO BE WITH US THE DAY YOU CLOSE IN WICHITA. EVERYTHING WILL BE MADE READY. COME.

MINISTERIAL ASSOCIATION, CHAMBER OF COMMERCE, MAYOR OF ARKANSAS CITY, Y. M. C. A., Y. W. C. A., DAILY NEWS, DAILY TRAVELER AND VARIOUS CLUBS AND ASSOCIATIONS.

Arriving in the city at four p. m., we saw hundreds assembled in the park. Many we were told had sat there since morning to have their seats for the seven o'clock meeting. By six o'clock the rotunda was overflowing and a throng standing all round. Oh! the hunger of this world wherever one may turn for the old time Gospel, but alas, just as the meeting was to open, down came a perfect torrent of rain. The following quotation from the Daily Press tells a little of the story:

ARKANSAS CITY, May 29.—With a crash of thunder that startled thousands of persons, many of them drenched to the skin, a deluge of rain lapsed into a drizzle and in ten minutes stars were shining after Aimee Semple McPherson called upon the Lord to roll the clouds away and stay the rain, at the beginning of religious services in Wilson Park here tonight.

All the ministers of Arkansas City excepting one were seated on the stage of the park tabernacle. They were endeavoring to make addresses preliminary to the services, but their voices were inaudible to those beyond the pale of a narrow circle. Suddenly Mrs. McPherson sprang forward.

"STAY THIS RAIN"

"Oh Lord, stay this rain and this storm," she prayed. "You can just hold it in the hollow of your hand. Lord, don't ycu see these people have come these many miles and don't you see we have come these many miles to preach this word to them. We don't mind going home in the rain, dear Lord, but if it is Thy will stay it and if the land hath need of it, let it fall after the message has been delivered to these hungry souls."

Expectant persons marveled when there was an instantaneous cessation of the downpour and soon the sky was entirely clear. With persons wading through slush, the circle of faces widened until a sea of faces stood back of the seats and the evangelist continued with the services. The stage was banked with some of the most beautiful floral pieces that could be assembled, local workers said. Singling out one of roses, sent by Senator and Mrs. R. C. Howard, Mrs. McPherson carried it back to Wichita. Others were contributed by business firms, civic organizations and women's clubs.

ALL SEATS FILLED

All available seats in the tabernacle were filled before 5 o'clock and many were there at noon. Max Coulter of the Traveler and James Weeds of the News estimated that five thousand or more heard the discourse, while hundreds more sat in automobiles lining blocks of streets, unable to get within range of the evangelist's voice. Newspaper men and other occupants of the stage estimated that 500 held up hands requesting prayers for salvation.

NOTED WICHITA JOURNALIST REVIEWS REVIVAL

By W. R. Waggoner
(Wichita Eagle Staff Reporter)

(Note—The subjoined article was written for the Bridal Call on condition that references to Mrs. McPherson should not be penciled or eliminated. She protests against particular reference to herself on the grounds that the Bridal Call is her personal organ, but I submit that an imposition of this character would rob the subject of much of the inspiration.—The Writer.)

LOOKING back over a three weeks' revival campaign just closed, as one who in the capacity of a newspaper reporter covered the majority of the services, I seem to be navigating as a rudderless ship at sea. Few times in my life, if indeed ever before, have I felt almost wholly helpless in an endeavor to do simple justice to a subject.

Summed up in brief, the inconceivable has happened. Wichita has been shakened and churned until thousands appear to be in a haze of wonderment, while hundreds of Godless homes have swung wide open their portals and invited the Savior in. Professed Christians, admittedly outside the pale of Christ's love, have emerged from the folds of the clock of inconstancy and buckled on the whole armor of God, with open confessions; the indifferent have flocked to the altar in droves, while the scoffer has knelt in agonized prayer for complete redemption.

That miracles have been performed for both the spiritually and physically sick, now goes undisputed. I have seen the power of God work upon the afflicted in body, with a startling strangeness calculated to inspire terror in the hearts of the lost. I have heard the blind praise the Lord for restoration of sight. I have heard suddenly inspired hallelujahs ring through the great auditorium when human ears were unstopped. I have seen paralytics and rheumatics, those afflicted with tuberculosis, cancer, tumor and other diseases, manifest their unspeakable joy as the bonds were loosed—the fetters severed that held them captives. And, all under the character of supplication taught by this little woman in white, who will bear the love of Wichita to her home in the Golden West and to Eternity.

Taking her at her word—that she is an evangelist and not a healer, I submit that the revival is without a parallel here in the measure of good accomplished for the whole city; to the countryside about and to the distant municipalities and commonwealths that have sent their quotas to this Mecca of religious awakening.

She—this little woman in white—has come into the midst of a sinful population, spreading the doctrine of the Great I Am, with an awfulness beyond the breaking of the seven vials of wrath—with a power that has gladdened human hearts and transfigured souls.

I can see her yet, as I believe thousands can see her, standing in the pulpit, or beside a suffering form, face uplifted and arms stretched outward to the father in Heaven, praying through tears—those pure crystal diamonds of the human soul—with an agony such as must have been the Savior's as he knelt in historic Gethsemane. I—we, it would well be said—can see her bending over an invalid's chair, or a penitent sinner, gently imploring Our Lord to touch them with the magic of his love. We can see her with a halo about her and with a tenseness over seas of silent weepers, uttering in plaintive tones:

"Jesus is here; O, I know Jesus is here."

While I do not believe Mrs. McPherson is conscious of the effort, I am certain that she has brought many a man and woman out of the "Slough of Despond," by invoking the power of satire. Through this medium, she has revealed to himself, or herself, persons who otherwise would sit as stone, unscathed by the firebrands of truth which she levels at them.

However, the light that radiates from Mrs. McPherson's altar—the power that emanates from her shafts of Divinely-directed oratory—obviously are inspired by her faith in God's word. The Old Time Religion she preaches revivifies slumbering consciences into scintillating stars of hope. She prays for the Old Time Religion and decries the higher criticism and psychology that apparently have fastened their fungused tentacles about the modern church. She preaches non-sectarianism and reveals herself in the attitude of believing the Bible in its entirety.

Mrs. McPherson's narration of the fall from the Apostolic church and its rise, beginning with Martin Luther; her pictures of the re-incarnation of sin-blighted souls and her inspired story of the second coming of Christ are impellingly convincing to the skeptic—unassailable, based on the Gibraltar of truth, incontrovertible.

She speaks of the Hills and Valleys encountered since her evangelistic career began and in her descensions, has met her Gethsemanes and Golgothas. But the masses that have heard her in Wichita cannot picture her in the lonely stretch between the peaks. Rather she appears as one on the mountain top, walking and talking with her Savior, as Moses communed with God from the rugged heights of Sinai. Her one approach to the "valley," to those who drink in her words of wisdom, is when she is bending toward the chasm of lost hope, lifting sorrowing souls to God.

She goes apart with the Savior, casts conventionalism to the winds and takes a broad view of humanity as she meets its various units. She knows not one creed, one color, one nationality, one condition from another. In the depth and breadth of her vision, she contemplates but one end for them all, and that is where at the termination of a vista set with the jewels of hope, the gates of the New Jerusalem stand ajar for the redeemed.

Never, constant attendants at the meeting attest, has the word of God been expounded as this humble servant of the multitude presents it. Hers is a brand of religion that melts adamant hearts with its acetylene fire as the all-pervading sun scatters a "wreath of mist at eve." It is gripping, impelling, matchless, irresistible. From its depths springs the illumination that lights many a weary way and quickens slow tread into a Marathon race for Glory.

There has entered into my being, and I believe the same consciousness prevails with thousands, a conviction that if all the ministers of the gospel in the nations of the earth embracing Christianity, would sow the same seeds Mrs. McPherson is sowing—if they would preach the same plan of redemption in unison for a period of three weeks, as she has done in Wichita, the world would be turned upside down, the Angels of Heaven would sing for joy and the face of Jesus would appear to a regenerated world.

No one knows as yet, how many souls in this city have been brought to Christ since Mrs. McPherson began preaching The Word, first to comparatively small congregations and latterly to packed houses with thousands turned away on single nights. She had no time to count them and her faithful workers have not yet undertaken the task. Certain it is that they run into hundreds upon hundreds.

Nothing like it has been experienced in this city and nothing may ever again happen that even will approach its magnitude from the religious point of view. From the cold standpoint of the average reporter, it is without doubt, the biggest succession of big news events ever registered in Wichita. From the standpoint of soul-saving it stands forth as an oasis in the desert of sin and will go down through the days and weeks and months and years as a fadeless, immortal monument to the cause of Jesus Christ.

I verily believe that the Angels are rejoicing with the Godly men and women of Wichita, over the miraculous delivery the city has had. I believe that the mighty work of this Godly woman whom we might eulogize if we dared, is receiving special recognition upon High. Somehow I feel that when the rewards for merit are distributed on the other Shore, there will be a few more jewels in her crown—a diadem set with rarer gems will be placed upon our sister's brow. I feel that from across the broad expanse, seraphic music will float back to earth to warn those she has left behind of her arrival, and that the winged hosts will welcome her home.

And now, as the form of our little woman in white is receding into the east, we of Wichita are breathing in unison "God Speed" and wishing her and the crucified Jesus she holds up to the multitudes, a measure of success even more phenomenal than was attained here. Mrs. McPherson has gone, but her gentle spirit is everywhere present, counseling the followers of the Lord and praying that Divine touch may fall upon those yet groping about in darkness; while it breathes a benediction over scores of souls, saved by the Heavenly power she invoked while in our midst.

WITHIN THE GOLDEN GATE OF SAN FRANCISCO

SAN FRANCISCO—what thoughts the name suggests! San Francisco—the beautiful, the incomparable, through whose Golden Gate the sun feels duty bound to cast its last watchful gaze ere being folded behind the blue waves of the Pacific in the flaming Western sky.

San Francisco—the city of earthquakes, tragedy, revelry night life, underground city, gambling and opium dens.

San Francisco—the city of big hearts, wealth, fashion, gaiety; noted for its hospitality and art of entertaining; with its blazing lights, its hills and valleys, theatres, dance-halls, great hotels and clubs; the eddy, surge and roar of its rolling automobiles, its mixed multitudes and distinguished guests where author, artist, statesman, politician, opera-star, business magnate and tourist rub shoulders with the boot-legger, gambler, the thug and the painted women of the underworld.

Into this city alone we came to preach Jesus Christ; to

kindle the flame with His love and fan into an exultant glow the fires of a city-wide revival.

For a long time we have prayed and others have prayed that God would move this city. We made several visits to look over the situation and walk around its walls, looking for a loop-hole in which, by the hand of the Lord, we might place the dynamite of God's Word that should blast its way through the unbelief, gaiety and business rush into the hearts of its inmates. We had considered the Civic Auditorium, but though we had cast longing eyes in that direction, we found the rent too steep. Surely there must be some place—but where?

Then it was that we were led to the great Coliseum—old, battle-scarred, enormous, scene of the prize-fights' howling mob, just now the home of the roller skating rink, but still boasting as ever the greatest seating capacity on the Pacific Coast or west of the Rockies; estimates ranging from 12,000 to 15,000—none being just sure what it did seat because of the enormous bleachers which entirely circled the building and rose to the roof, row on row.

Coming in one night to look at the building—I climbed to the topmost seat of the topmost bleacher and sat thoughtfully with my chin in my hand, looking out over the immense area, over the fancy-dress skating carnival which was then in progress, over the blaring instruments of the brass band which played frantically to be heard above the roar of the skates over the polished hardwood floor and peering out through the haze of smoke that hung above it all, considered the building pro and con with regard to its possibilities of housing the revival that was to be or not to be.

It is a peculiar feeling to sit alone like that, high up in a big building and decide so momentous a question; one which is to affect the lives of tens of thousands of people through time and eternity—to be or not to be—and as I sat soliloquizing, gazing through the smoke and listening to the roar, I mentally addressed the Coliseum.

"Good evening, Mr. Coliseum."

"Good evening, lady! I am glad you spoke. Perched up there on my topmost bleacher you look a little different from the rest of the folks here tonight—rather out of place, in it but not of it, so to speak. Several others as well as myself have been curiously speculating as to who you are and what you are doing way up there."

"Why, I am just a little Evangelist lady, thinking of coming to San Francisco to conduct a revival campaign to preach Jesus, who when lifted up from the earth, draws all men unto Him. But since you have asked the first question—you are quite a battle-scarred, curiosity-arousing old building yourself—never remember seeing one just like you before. How old are you, Mr. Coliseum?"

"Well now—I don't usually discuss my exact age, but from my weatherbeaten sides, you can see at a glance that I have stood here many a weary year. I have seen the young children grow up and their grandchildren married. I shuddered and shook through the earthquake and gazed upon the great fire but have stood through it all."

"You certainly look like an ancient and grizzly warrior. You must have a startling and interesting history."

"Yes, if the history of the thousands of lives that have flowed in and out of my doors like the waves of a sea could be written and the story of my prizefights and carnivals codified, the city would not be great enough to contain them all."

"Prize fights, did you say? What is your business, may I ask, Mr. Coliseum? Also as to how you prosper and are in health?"

"I am an old and nationally known prize ring. Right in my heart yonder where the band stand is tonight, some of the greatest battles of the ring have been fought. Tens of thousands of men have stood on my floor and bleachers, howling, booing, hissing, cheering, shrieking—till it seemed my wooden sides and great arched roof would be rent as bleeding, unconscious fighters were borne to the dressing rooms and the Victor bowed in triumph.

"I have also housed many a political meeting. Gov. Johnson spoke in me just a little while since. Just at present I am far from prosperous, however, for now in my old age, the young people are rolling all over me on their roller skates and my reputation is as scarred as my sides.

"As for being in health, I fear my days are numbered, for even now the neighbors are signing a petition asking the city for my death warrant. They declare I am leaving my mark on the lives of the youth of the community, scarring their minds and souls with the influence of my hectic career and desecration of the Sabbath."

"So I am told, but I figure that if I am going to use you in my work as an Evangelist—if you will pardon my saying so, I think it high time you were converted, had a complete change of heart and begin to undo some of the guilty past of which you speak. Perhaps you have never had much opportunity along this line—but if your lease of life is extended as we expect, I am to have you first of all for a revival meeting, if you could adapt yourself to such a thing. Have you ever seen a revival meeting, Mr. Coliseum?"

"No, my only experience with church work was when visited by the International Sunday School Convention who once used about half of me for a short time. This was to transact business, however, and was not a revival. But aren't you in the wrong city, lady? You know San Francisco is one place where they say it is impossible to have a revival. Considerably more than half of our population are absolutely Pagan and attend no church, either Protestant or Catholic. Why, there hasn't been a revival here—a real one, which would shake the city—that I can remember."

"So I am told, but I figure that if I am going fishing, Mr. Coliseum, it is always best to find water that has not been all fished out. If there hasn't been a revival here recently, so much the better. The waters must be literally teeming with fish, I should think."

"H'um—maybe so——"

"Well, what would you say to the thought of having a revival right here in this building?"

"Why, my dear lady! You cause a blush to mount my brow—though I never thought I could blush again. Surely, I am too wicked and disreputable an old sinner to be considered worthy to shelter a city-wide revival. Besides, I am old and have not the conveniences you might need for such an enterprise. Why don't you go down-town and get the Civic Auditorium? That seats from 8,000 to 10,000 people, is magnificent in its appointments, has opera chairs, pipe organ, ante rooms and all ready to step into. While by comparison, I am a great barn of a place, draughty and seatless lest you bring your own chairs, and would take an awful lot of sprucing up before I could make myself passably presentable. I appreciate your thought for an old sinner like me, lady, but I reckon you had best get the Auditorium."

"But—my dear Coliseum—I did inquire about the Auditorium, and the lowest possible rate was $12,000.00 a month, and for two little women who are coming in to finance their own meeting, that would be an unthinkable sum—yet, oh, you are right, if we only *could* afford it. There in the center of the city, in that beautiful building, God could command the attention of all and turn the city upside down."

"But others get it for the world—why not you for the church?"

"Well now, Mr. Coliseum, I will tell you, it's like this, since you really press me for an answer. Two women want that Civic Auditorium:

"Mary Garden, the opera singer, and

"Aimee Semple McPherson, the Evangelist.

"Mary is to sing to the rich; Aimee is to preach to the poor; Mary's seats will be paid for weeks in advance—money no object, for the world lavishes its dollars on its favorites, loves its own and the average seat will sell for between two and three dollars.

"Aimee's seats are free; our average revival meeting offering runs under two cents per head and no matter how often she counts her pennies, they will not reach around that rental, so, while I preach here, if you can manage to hold us, Mary will warble down there."

While I tried to make these mental observations with a cheery smile and a brave air, the grizzly and weather-beaten old Coliseum did not seem at all deceived by my levity. Was that just a breath of air? or another of those draughts that came constantly through the open ribs of the bleachers—or did the old Coliseum sigh and swallow a lump in his throat? Seemed like one could sense a friendly sympathy running all through his giant frame.

"Hem! If that's the way the land lies, I guess we'll have to see what we can do about it. Come to think of it, I've heard how Christ was not born in a palace, but cradled in a barn, and I guess His revival can find shelter here if it wants to. And though it is pretty late in life to begin, I guess I'll try to slick myself up a bit and make myself respectable. I've heard by reputation of the crowds that come to hear you lift up the Christ, and while I've not much else to boast about, I certainly have plenty of room, if that's any consolation, and I'll do my best to be converted and help."

"Oh, Mr. Coliseum! the room is a conclusive argument. We'll take you. The roller skating people move out at 11 o'clock one night and we move in at 2:30 the next day, and I am sure you will do your best. We'll put the platform at the other end—use that one great bleacher for a chorus of 800 voices and make our altar down below. What could you offer in the line of prayer rooms, Mr. Coliseum?"

"P-p-prayer rooms?—ahem—prayer rooms! Why, er—such things are a little out of my line. Contractors often forget to build one on when erecting prize rings, but—wait a minute, lady—how about the dressing rooms where we used to rub the prize-fighters down? You will see the pictures of the battlers hanging on the walls right now. Then there is the room where the skates and bottles are stored. The bottles have been congregating since long before the days of prohibition—but I'll turn them all out and slick it up 'fore you get here and do at least one good, respectable thing by this revival effort before I die."

"Thanks. Now I had better be going, I guess; mother will think I am lost. And it is closing time for you, I see. Your skaters are thinning out, and your electric eyes are blinking shut one by one. Good night, Mr. Coliseum."

"Good night, Evangelist lady. I'll do my best for you!"

And so it was that at 11 P. M. one night, a few weeks later, when the last note of the band was silent, the Coliseum, instead of going to sleep behind closed doors, put on its working togs and labored all night. Clouds of dust and snatches of song—revival songs from the band of Christian workers who made the dust with busy brooms, emanated from the doors, while truck after truck brought in thousands of rented chairs which were quickly unloaded, nailed together and slid into place; flags, bunting, plants, palms and flowers rose into position on the hastily constructed platform. Altar benches were piled near at hand ready for use. But, though the Coliseum heaved and resounded all through the night and until meeting time the next day, he was just caught in the very act of smuggling out his truck-loads of bottles, skates, prize-fight paraphernalia and well nigh had a collision at the doors with the trucks bringing in Bibles, gospel literature and revival paraphernalia.

"Here—where do these tracts and Bibles go? Where do I put this pulpit?" one driver would call from an incoming truck.

"Why—right in here, I guess, but wait until I get out with these bottles, skates and things," would come the panting answer from the outgoing driver, as he mopped his head.

But at last it was completed. The platform finished, busy carpenters having completed the steps and railing, tacked the last flag and strip of bunting into place; deft fingers of the women had arranged the floral pieces contributed from all sides, thousands of rented chairs had been placed on the floor and the aisles formed, under the supervision of the fireman's vigilant eye.

"It's such a rat trap of a wooden building, if there ever came a fire, how would we get the people out?" he fretted.

"The Lord will not permit any fire in this building during the revival," we prophesied. "Except the fire of the Holy Ghost!" And praise the Lord, His fire did fall.

The campaign opened on a Saturday afternoon with a message on Evangelism, a talk intended for the inspiration and arousing of Christians, but when the altar call was given, scores of men and women came to the front declaring themselves to be sinners in need of salvation. In such multitudes did they pour to the front, even on that first day, that we were bewildered as to how to find workers enough to pray for them.

That night after a message from the subject, "If Jesus Christ came to San Francisco and viewed the city from Twin Peaks," another altar call twice as large as that of the afternoon occurred as men and women streamed down every aisle and deluged the altar as they wept at Jesus' feet.

Dr. Gordon of the First Congregational Church was there

to introduce us with the well chosen and enthusiastically fitting words of which only he is capable (Dr. Gordon, by the way, is editor of that column in The San Francisco Chronicle entitled "Sense" and is the brother of the Mr. Gordon who is the author of the "Quiet Talks" series we have all so much enjoyed).

From this point on the meetings grew daily in attendance and interest in spite the cold and fog, until hundreds daily sought Christ as their Savior at the altars.

CITY CLERGYMEN TO RESCUE

The city clergymen came to our rescue as the crowds and altar calls grew to gigantic proportions. Letters were issued by the Ministerial Federation of churches and an appeal for help made and received. The President and the Secretary of the Federation took charge of the altar cards, for the name, address, church preference, age, business and spiritual history of our converts are kept as carefully as possible to aid in follow-up work. These altar cards were distributed by the Federation to the various churches and missions of the city, the same following up the converts by personal contact by house-to-house visitation.

A chorus of 800 voices came from various churches and rendered noble service; a splendid orchestra of some score or more pieces filled the air with music; a male quartet from the Bible School sang many into the kingdom and indeed, to the splendid, sane, well-taught Bible students from Brother Craig's mission and school, the campaign owes a debt of gratitude, for they sang in the chorus, played in the orchestra, acted as ushers, worked at the altars and were ready at a moment's notice to render any service, and have greatly added to their number and strength many converts and friends.

The San Francisco Choral Union visited us in a body and lifted all by their songs of Christ. The male chorus from Turlock came 100 miles by auto to assist in the services and were enthusiastically received—such singing one scarce expects to hear this side of Heaven.

In ever widening circles the revival influence swept out, until the result showing in the altar calls saw literally hundreds responding to each appeal. At first, the space between the platform and the front seats seemed so wide as to be disconcerting and almost to make one feel out of touch with the audience. Once the altar call was given, however, that space would fill so quickly as to take one's breath away.

THOSE ALTAR CALLS

How I wish you could have seen the inspiring sight! As soon as the call was given for sinners to come to Christ, the aisles would be black with scores coming from every direction to the altar; coming as though they were trying to see who could get there first! Never have we seen people so literally rush to the Savior's feet!

And, rushing to meet them would come the altar workers, pouring down from the front bleachers and chorus, determined to be there as soon as the penitents.

Rushing in between the two tidal waves ere they met, would come the ushers, running like trained athletes, with the long altar benches which had been piled up in readiness.

All of this would happen while an uninitiated one could but blink his eyes a few times, and indeed, the writer never grew quite accustomed to the scene. Then, without confusion, those two tides would meet with the benches slid in between them and the scene would suddenly change—the penitents going down on their knees on the one side, heads down, handkerchiefs pressed to streaming eyes, while the workers dropped simultaneously to their knees on the other side—arms thrown about the penitents' shoulders; women workers praying with women, men with men.

The soft strains of music:

> "Just as I am, without one plea,
> But that thy blood was shed for me,
> And that thou bid'st me come to Thee.
> Oh, Lamb of God, I come,"

would be wafted up from the moist-eyed, soft-voiced audience as they rejoiced over sinners' turning to the Christ. Jumbled up snatches of prayers and conversations would reach our ears, "Lord, be merciful to me, a sinner—O, Jesus, save him just now—Thank God, there is my big son at the altar—There goes my husband, that's five in the family now saved in this meeting—Pray, sister, pray, brother—Just ask Jesus to save—But I can't pray. I don't know what to say, never prayed in my life—Teach me, sister—Teach me, Jesus—Teach me to pray."

Oh, those scrambled up sentences that floated up from the altar benches to us who hovered above on the platform, directing workers and music! Seemed as though the heart of a stone would melt at the revelation of those opened hearts!

Hundreds turned to Christ who declared that never in their lives had they been saved before, and that never had they prayed nor read a Bible. Several declared that they had not been inside of a church for 50 years; infidels were calling on God and oh, we had a happy time of it. Wiping my eyes I looked up through the mist at the old Coliseum whose arched roof seemed to span the whole scene like two friendly arms:

"Well, Mr. Coliseum, what do you think of this for a busy scene? You may have had lots of crowds and thought you had seen the human race run the entire gamut of emotions, but did you ever see such a sight as this? Did you ever see emotions so profoundly, so sincerely, and yet with all quietly and without trace of excitement stirred to the depths? Just look at that mother over there with her arms around a son most twice her size. See him hold her tight and wipe the tears from her eyes as he chokes out: 'It's all right now, muzzy—I have taken the step—life is going to be different for you now, dear! Your prayers are answered.' "

"Oh, I think it's wonderful, lady—wonderful—the power of God Himself, and I believe I am getting converted or well on the way—glorious is the Lord and greatly to be praised!"

PRAYER SERVICES FOR THE SICK

Toward the middle of the campaign, hundreds, having heard of the power of Christ to heal as well as to save, came to the special prayer services for the sick to be borne to the throne of grace and miracles were wrought by the living Lord. The pressure at last became so great that the city ministers and clergymen who sat on the platform with us, helping, encouraging, praying, volunteered to take this part of the work off our shoulders.

"Sister," they said, "this work is too much for you, with all your revival duties—you just leave it to us and we will

THE "FORUM", WICHITA, KANS.
Scenes like this were the order of every day during the campaign held by Sister McPherson

form the lines and pray for the sick in several groups. This work is too heavy for a woman, and we men preachers should do it, anyway."

And so they did. Dr. Lundy of the Howard Presbyterian church, Dr. Gilchrist of the Ministerial Federation, Dr. Phillips, Dr. Reid taking command. Then to still more fully meet the demand without taking the time from the revival, they organized morning Divine healing services in the Howard Presbyterian Church, where the ministers of the various denominations of the city, Presbyterian, Congregational, Methodist, Episcopal, Baptist, United Brethren, etc., met to pray for the sick. The writer was not present, but the Lord was, and according to the accounts of the ministers, who returned with shining faces after having prayed for and annointed over 700 in two days, and according to the people who declared they had been healed, they must have had one glorious time in that church.

SUFFER THE CHILDREN TO COME

The great daily newspapers of San Francisco wrote wonderful accounts and ran pictures that sometimes occupied almost a whole page. Their busy flashlights grew to be a familiar sight, so interested were they. Not one unkind or critical word was spoken during our visit to the city. The following is clipped from the account of children's services in "The Call":

"The kiddies had their day Saturday afternoon. The word 'remarkable' can be applied to any of the services Mrs. McPherson has held since opening her San Francisco campaign two weeks ago. But it goes double for the children's services. Never was there such a spectacle seen in San Francisco before.

"Nine thousand men, women and children were there, and of these fully 4000 were little ones. There were 500 little boys and girls in the children's choir. Five hundred little white and black boys and girls, Japanese and Chinese, Orientals and Occidentals, children of the Near East, the Philippines, Europe, Africa, the Americas. It was a crowd of children thoroughly representative of San Francisco for it was cosmopolitan in its types and its manifestations.

500 ATTEND

"Five hundred children, in robust health and sickly, sound of limb and crippled and deformed, children bright and normal and children whose brows were oppressed with the stamp of near imbecility, children in gay Easter dresses, their faces shining, and children in rags, their faces innocent of the manifestations of soap and water, answered the altar call. They came along, with big brothers and sisters, with fathers and mothers, with grandfathers and grandmothers.

"It was this that formed the most remarkable spectacle of its kind San Francisco has seen. Five hundred tots and little boys and girls in a great semicircle about the altar, on their knees, heads bowed reverently, dedicating themselves to the service of God, pledging themselves to lead clean, pure lives. Ministers and women church workers went among them, knelt with them, put their arms about them and whispered in their ears.

"And then, following the altar calls, scores of little sufferers made their way up to the platform, or were led or carried, and received the prayer-for-healing ministrations of Mrs. McPherson. The lame, the halt, the blind; little ones afflicted, with withered arms and legs; children incapable of thought; babies in arms.

TRIES THE SOUL

"It was a spectacle to try one's soul, these little afflicted ones raising their eyes to heaven and praying, with Mrs. McPherson, to God to make them well.

"The altar—never was such an altar seen in San Francisco before! It was banked with flowers—roses, lilies, tulips, the blooms of spring—and with books, toys, candy. There were little brown and gray bunnies, baskets of eggs, dolls, express wagons, cookies, chickens, horses, teddy bears, story books. Every little one who sought a healing received some toy or a book and some candy, and then the remainder was distributed among the other children."

BROADCASTING BY RADIO

A unique and interesting diversion came one Sunday morning, when, by special invitation of the Rockridge Radio Station of Oakland, the writer was accorded the gracious honor of being the first woman in the world to preach a sermon over the wireless telephone. Tens of thousands on the Pacific Coast are talking radio just now, and thousands of receiving sets are in private homes, hospitals, hotels, clubs, halls and public buildings. But in addition to being heard for a radius of 2,000 miles across the continent and by the ships at sea, this was the day of the enormous blossom festival, where some 50,000 people were assembled at Saratoga. Saturday night they had danced in the open air to radio music, but this Sunday morning they were to hear the voice of a preacher coming out of the open heavens and falling through the air—the voice I mean, not the preacher.

All the way across the ferry, our hearts beat nervously as mother and I talked of the great possibilities and prayed for the words to speak. When facing the machinery and electrical apparatus of the sending station, our nervousness was increased, especially when we found a newspaper camera man there for a picture and story, also neighbors assembled to hear the sermon. But, after putting them all out except the operator, I felt more at ease—that is, as much at ease as it is possible for one to feel facing that great horn and having only its dark, mysterious looking depths for a visible audience.

But closing my eyes, I looked to the Lord for help and began to speak—taking my text from Luke 4:18, "The Spirit of the Lord is upon me, for He hath anointed me to preach the gospel to the poor; He hath sent me to heal the broken-hearted; to preach deliverance to the captives, and the recovering of sight to the blind; to set at liberty them that are bound and to preach the acceptable year of the Lord."

In a moment I found myself talking into that great receiver—talking somehow as I had seldom talked before. The room with its electrical apparatus was forgotten, and all I could think of was the thousands at the Blossom Festival, the sailor boys, mothers' boys on the ships at sea, the sick in the homes where receivers had been installed, and I prayed and preached and prayed again and did most everything but take up the collection.

When the doxology was pronounced and the beaming operator turned some little adjustment, shutting off the apparatus and we dared speak again, the room filled with those who had been listening through receivers in the other room and the long-distance 'phone began to ring as people, one after another, enthusiastically declared that they had heard every word and had been thrilled and blessed by a message from the Lord coming through the air that Sunday morning. In a few moments we were again crossing the bay, ready for the afternoon throngs.

MIDNIGHT IN RESCUE MISSION

Another interesting diversion came when we visited the Sunshine Mission, though how it got the name of Sunshine, I do not know, lest 'tis from the Sun of Righteousness—for it is away down cellar under a poor section of the city. Some call it Cut-Throat Mission, because of the poor down and outs of the underworld, jailbirds, counterfeiters, drug addicts, drunkards, etc., who attend it to hear the gospel and to be fed beef stew and served hot coffee and bread. The hearing of the former being incidental and essential to the receiving of the latter.

The hall was packed with an expectant throng that night and in waiting for us, we verily believe they almost forgot the supper, for it had been announced by the wireless that runs through the underworld of San Francisco that we were to preach to the sinner and pray for the afflicted. How those men clapped and cheered and wept and wiped their eyes at the simple story of the Savior's love! How they flocked to the altar!

Workers of this mission, Brother and Sister Steele, had long prayed for a break when many would come to Christ, and it came this night. Men fallen to the depths, but in whose faces one could read the story of a splendid mother and home; boys who had been caught in the toils of Satan and broken in body and soul came to the altar; drug addicts asked prayer to be healed of the habit; a bottle of denatured alcohol was thrown from the pocket of a man with trembling hand; tobacco cans followed from others and were added to the pile.

But oh, their eyes as they looked up expectantly into ours! "Lady, you say this Jesus can forgive me and heal me and break these fetters? Then I hope He will, right now."

Of course he will, brother dear; pray now:

> Ask the Savior to help you,
> Comfort, strengthen and keep you.
> He is willing to aid you,
> He will carry you through.

At last all were prayed for, for salvation and healing. Baskets of Testaments which we had brought were then given out freely to them all, and supper served. Those men ate ravenously—they were really hungry. Oh, the histories, the stories back of some of those lives! Surely, fiction could never be as interesting as real life.

MIDNIGHT IN CHINATOWN

One night after the close of the evening service in the Auditorium, it was our privilege to hold a service in Chinatown in the Congregational church. It was packed to the doors for almost two hours ere we arrived with the various ministers and the orchestra who came to assist. A Chinese choir sang and the message went forth—that same old story of a Savior whose hands and feet were nailed to the cross on Calvary's brow. The old, old story that is ever new of a Savior who lives again, who loves and cares, lifts the burden, dries the tear and brings joy in place of sorrow as in the days of yore.

An interpreter helped me and when the altar call was given, Chinese men and women rose all over the church and in the balcony and wept their way to the front, just as did you and I. They seem to feel the same conviction, shed the same tears and breathe the same broken prayer as did we, and are saved by the same gracious Savior.

How good it was to see them come, whole families in certain instances, who had never confessed Christ before! Then we prayed for the sick and saw our Lord do glorious things before our eyes as the lame walked and the deaf rapturously declared they could hear. The Chinese audience clapped and shouted the praises of the Lord. It would seem as though such a religion of power would win all heathendom, had we but the faith.

THE CLOSING HOURS

The closing hours of the San Francisco campaign were filled to the brim with new victories and the meetings closed Sunday night with a building packed to capacity and the doors closed. But best of all, three times that day the altars were full to overflowing with new converts, and our two hundred altar workers were utterly unable to cope with the crowds seeking salvation. So calls were given for workers to volunteer from the audience. It was a glorious sight!

The closing moments, when between 12,000 and 15,000 stood upon their feet, singing and waving a sea of white handkerchiefs—there appeared a surging sea of linen, the memory lives with me yet, and those voices sing on in my mind:

"Yes, we'll gather at the river,
The beautiful, the beautiful river,
Gather with the saints at the river
That flows by the throne of God."

It was over. The lights were out. The streetcar inspectors shouting directions to the multitudes on the sidewalk that their cars were waiting in line, could be heard in the distance. Mounted police busily directed traffic at the corners. Officers shook our hands, calling Godspeed and declaring that never in the history of San Francisco had such a multitude assembled in the name of religion or such a crowd been in the Coliseum. A moment more and we were in our car and away.

But the next day, when the crowds were gone and the workers were removing the seats and packing up, I slipped away quietly—almost reverently—into the Coliseum for one last look at the building which had grown so dear and friendly through the past weeks.

"I have come to say good-bye, Mr. Coliseum."

"I knew you would, Sister. I was waiting for you—good-bye and God bless you! I am glad the revival came and though I may be used for other purposes a little while before I am taken down and laid to rest, I want you to know that I'll never be the same again. I am a changed Coliseum."

"Of course you are. No one could go through the experience of the last three weeks without being changed for the better; and I thank you for your shelter and light and friendliness and oh! I do hope you will be converted and used no more to lead the young astray.

"Good-bye, Mr. Coliseum."

"Good-bye, Sister—may the blessings of God go with you."

"Good-bye—good-bye."

THE SAN FRANCISCO REVIVAL

By Dr. Reid

Presbyterian Minister. Secy. Ministerial Association, San Francisco

HE spake as one having authority and not as their scribes. These words concerning Jesus come to my mind unbidden as I attempt to tell the story of the coming of Mrs. Aimee Semple McPherson to San Francisco. No more striking act of audacity is to be found in the history of the spread of the gospel than that of Sister McPherson's coming to the city by the Golden Gate.

It required firm faith, calm confidence and contagious courage for her to come into this great city, half of whose population is not connected with any religious organization, and, without backing from any source, to hire a prize-ring and proceed at her own charges to convert it into a pulpit from which to preach the gospel of salvation for sinners and healing for those who are sick. But that she "endured as seeing the invisible" is perfectly patent to all of us as we look back on those three wonderful weeks which have just closed.

Like many of his brethren in the ministry, the writer was exceedingly slow to accept any responsibility in connection with her coming. When approached by her fore-runner to prepare the way for her coming by handling the advertising and publicity, he said very frankly that he would undertake it only with the definite understanding that he was doing so in a purely professional capacity, as a newspaper and publicity man, being religious editor of the San Francisco Journal and publicity representative of the Federation of Churches, the San Francisco Presbytery and the Synod of California.

No sooner had she arrived and begun to preach, than we began to discover for ourselves that she was not only possessed of an apostolic passion for the salvation of men, but that she preached the gospel of Jesus Christ with a power and persuasiveness such as few, even of America's greatest evangelists possessed, and that, blended with this simple, appealing gospel, was a pleasingness of personality which captured the hearts of all who heard her, both saints and sinners. She had not finished her first week before many of the leading pastors of the city who had attended some of the services began to assure her of their sympathy and prayers and, before the revival closed, a large number of them had become enthusiastic supporters, contributing all they could to the success of the work.

The first service was held on Saturday night, April 1, the most unpropitious night possible for any kind of religious gathering, and yet there were fully three thousand five hundred people in attendance—a perfectly wonderful thing to those of us who know San Francisco. More than ten thousand heard her in the two services held Sunday, April 2, and, in spite of the unprecedented number of cold nights, aggravated by the fact that there was absolutely no way to heat the old wooden barn of a building in which the meetings were held, the audiences increased steadily until the last Sunday, when more than 25,000 people attended the three services of the day, the Coliseum being packed to its fullest capacity—12,500—at the evening hour, while many were unable to gain admittance. The writer asked a man who has lived in San Francisco for fifty years if he had ever seen such an audience in attendance upon a religious service; he replied that it far surpassed anything he had ever witnessed.

It would be impossible to give an adequate idea of what these meetings have accomplished—time, possibly eternity alone, can tell how far-reaching they have been. Hundreds crowded the altar at the close of every service, seeking salvation from their sins and the infilling of the Holy Spirit. Most of these surrendered their lives to Christ and signed confession cards before rising from their knees. The number of penitents in the last few services was so great that they literally choked the altar space and all but swamped the altarworkers, thus necessitating the handling of them in groups from the platform. How many have already united with local churches or missions—of which we have an unusual number in San Francisco—the writer has no way of knowing, at this time.

Suffice it to say that literally thousands were led either to confess Christ for the first time or to reconsecrate themselves to the service of God.

Wonderful as were the results of her purely evangelistic work, more wonderful still were the healing services. Let it be said right here, however, that "Sister McPherson," as she is affectionately called by all, never held a healing service without first urging in an earnest appeal that those present who knew not Christ should "Seek first the kingdom of God and His righteousness and all these things"—including healing—"shall be added unto you." It would not be within the province of this article to attempt to tell of the many cases of seemingly immediate healing. Two of the most remarkable instances were of women afflicted with goitre, each larger than a hen egg; to the amazement of those of us who stood near, including a number of local pastors and representatives of the press, in both instances the goitre seemed to "melt away" as prayer was being offered—before our very eyes! Many who were either totally or partially blind received sight; a large number who were either stone deaf or partially deaf were restored to hearing, the most remarkable instance being that of a little girl who was mute, whose ears were opened and whom the evangelist taught to say "bless the Lord" and to call the name of Jesus.

But, to my mind, the most permanently benefiical result of this revival has come already, more or less as a by-product; not only Christian people in general but ministers of the gospel in particular, have been given a new conception of God as one who is near at hand, not far removed from human affairs; as one who is just as eager and just as able to save sinners and heal the sick today as He was in Jesus' "days of the flesh"; that, with apologies to the evangelist for slightly modifying her telling aphorism, He is *"the Great I Am,"* not "the great I was" nor yet "the great I will be"! For four or five days before the meetings closed, groups of pastors spent hours in praying for the sick every morning in Howard Presbyterian Church (directly across the street from the Coliseum), whose pastor, the Rev. J. Wilson Lundy, was changed from an active opponent to an enthusiastic supporter of and worker in the meetings, and many healings were recorded there. So confirmed are these pastors in their new degree of faith, that they announced that these spiritual clinics would be continued every day so long as there were those desiring the ministry of healing.

One pastor frankly stated to his congregation, after assisting in one of the platform healing services, "I am frank to tell you that I have gotten religion—the good, old-fashioned kind," and the tears were streaming down his unabashed face as he spoke! Just as the fogs and cold winds of this most delightful of climates, taken the year around, are wont to chill the body to the marrow, betimes, so the spiritual atmosphere has been such as to all but freeze the most ardent of preachers. The San Francisco Bay region has been the burial-place of many a ministerial ambition. Mrs. McPherson's unbounded faith and unquenchable fervor aroused in all of us a determination to preach 'the full gospel" with greater confidence than ever before, relying upon the Holy Spirit to give efficacy both to prayer for the sick and to our exhortations to sinners. This, I am persuaded, is her greatest contribution to the metropolis of the Pacific Coast! While the meetings have closed, the revival is going on, bless the Lord!

On Sunday afternoon, more than 10,000 people stood and, with waving handkerchiefs, expressed to Mrs. McPherson their grateful appreciation of the great work which she had accomplished and, by the same token, extended an eager, pressing invitation to her to come again; and a more representative and cosmopolitan group could not be found in any American city. She carried the key of the city away with her and can re-enter at her pleasure, finding a grateful group awaiting her arrival.

THE SPIRITUAL EARTHQUAKE

By Dr. J. Wilson Lundy

Pastor Howard Ave. Presbyterian Church, San Francisco

SAN FRANCISCO has had many and varied experiences, but the one it can never forget, the one that has thrilled it to its heart's core has grown out of, and is identified with, the great revival campaign of three weeks, conducted by Aimee Semple McPherson.

Some years ago our city was rocked by a mighty earthquake, and as a result of the shaking much damage was wrought, but the spiritual upheaval of the last few weeks has brought to the people of our city the greatest awakening they have ever experienced and the richest outpouring of blessings they have ever received. This city by the Sunset Sea has been visited by many distinguished people—kings, famous generals with their laurels fresh upon them, distinguished scholars, world renowned statesmen, scientists, poets and artists, but no visit we have ever received can compare in point of thrilling interest, heartfelt enthusiasm, and far-reaching results with the visit of our beloved little sister. No one that has ever entered our gates has ever won such a large and warm place in our hearts.

The truth is, we have all fallen hopelessly in love with our little sister. By her sweet womanliness, her unaffected goodness, her winsomeness of personality, and her altogether marvelous gifts as a herald of the cross, she has won our heartfelt admiration and love.

I feel that I have been very fortunate, in that my church is located in the immediate neighborhood by the Coliseum, the scene of the revival. This brought me into close and vital touch with the great meeting. Our building was used as a place of rest during the interval between the afternoon and evening meetings, by people coming from points across the Bay and up and down the Peninsula, and also for conferences of the workers and for prayer services; we felt, as perhaps no other church did, the pulse and throb of the mighty awakening.

This was made evident in our last two Sunday morning services. I looked over my audience and I felt that I had a new congregation—the same people, yes, and yet not the same, for it was easy to see that they had become transformed in spirit—eyes radiant and faces aglow with a new-found joy and happiness. And to see to the wonder of it all, our church for the first time in all its long history, was not large enough to accommodate the people who came to worship, and many were turned away.

But what shall we say of the scenes witnessed in the great Coliseum, as thousands upon thousands responded to the overture of the Christ love and at every altar call pressed with eagerness to the front to make the great surrender, and to find forgiveness and salvation through the precious blood of Christ?

Time and again we were embarrassed by the difficulty of finding room in the front for the penitents who flocked from all parts of the great building.

Who could look out upon such a scene as was presented at every altar call and not be thrilled to the very bottom of his soul? If there were tears of penitence on the faces of the men and women who flocked by the hundreds and thousands to the improvised altars, there were also tears of joy and gladness on the faces of ministers and other workers as they witnessed the soul stirring and never-to-be-forgotten sight. We thank God for what this means to us who have been laboring here in a city given over to pleasure seeking and the worship of Mammon, for the encouragement it gives us, for the hope it inspires, for the joy with which it fills our souls. How often we have been disheartened as our appeals and labors have yielded no apparent results, how time and again we have been depressed by the carelessness, lukewarmness and wordliness of many in our churches when we have earnestly desired to reach and win for the kingdom. But now that the tide is turning, now that indifference is giving way to earnestness, and coldness to warmth and easy-going unconcern, to deep searchings of heart, we feel a new thrill of joy, we feel that we are receiving a new baptism of courage and hope.

The ministry of healing was so wonderfully owned by God to the relief of hundreds of afflicted ones that it contributed much to the success of the meetings. To many of us this was something altogether new, but in the presence and the manifest and unmistakable evidences of the Great Physician's healing power, we gave to it our unqualified approval.

I am glad it was my privilege day after day, to be in close touch with Sister McPherson while she was in the act of ministering to the afflicted. Her tenderness, earnestness and spirit of compassion, coupled with an unconquerable and unwavering faith were channels through which the blessing of health and strength flowed into the bodies of the afflicted ones. I have seen in these meetings many wonderful cures—sight restored, deaf ears opened, goiters melted away, the crippled and helpless walk off the platform carrying their crutches, and many other ills of the flesh either mitigated or entirely removed. The wonderful success achieved along this line has led a number of the pastors of our city to plan for a ministry of healing in connection with their respective churches.

While I am writing this message there are two companies of ministers in the adjoining auditorium of my church earnestly seeking through prayer and the anointing of oil to give relief to a large gathering of afflicted people, and already God has signally honored their ministry, and many are rejoicing because of their restoration to health and strength.

Taking it all in all, this campaign has been an unqualified success and will go down in the history of San Francisco as the greatest religious revival the city has ever known. It is also exceedingly gratifying that in all the meetings there has been a wonderful spirit of hearty co-operation and delightful fellowship on the part of the ministers representing all the evangelical denominations. We, the clergy of the city, unite in the verdict that it was the greatest, the sanest, the sweetest and the most fruitful in blessed results of all the revivals with which we have ever been identified.

In view of this tremendous religious upheaval in our city, we have good reason to thank God and take courage. Revivals outgrown? Never, as long as men sin and God loves them and the cross makes its transcendent appeal. As well talk of spring showers and summer suns being outgrown. Revivals are biblical; they are historical; they are reasonable; they are a part of the economy of God in nature and in human progress, and they are on the stage at this hour, arousing churches, turning communities upside down, attesting to critics and gainsayers and unbelievers the power of the gospel to save and to heal. In bringing this message to a close I can say for myself and for my brethren in the ministry, that San Francisco cannot have too many of the Aimee Semple McPherson type of revivals, and it is hoped that next year our beloved sister will return to us for another blessed season of spiritual awakening.

THE EVOLUTION OF A WHEAT WAREHOUSE

WILLING hands, devoted hearts, a small town, a wheat warehouse, an urgent petition signed by the merchants, four meetings and a hungry community—these were the constituents that went to make up the whirlwind two-day revival campaign in Turlock, California.

A royal welcome, the hospitality of Turlock's most beautiful Christian home, the electric thrill of excitement running through the streets and homes and we were on our way to the meeting. Within three blocks of the warehouse, we saw cars parked in every direction in streets and fields. Coming closer, we saw that the door-yard on all sides of the building was packed with people. Three strenuous but ineffectual attempts to enter the doors were made wherein the people laughingly but good-naturedly tried to part the crowd to get us in, but all to no avail.

When at last, howover, we succeeded in gaining admission by the rear door, the interior of the steel warehouse presented a wondrous picture. The great structure had been emptied by willing hands of its thousands of sacks of wheat and decorated with boughs, palm branches and blossoms from one end to the other. An elevated choir loft, a platform, an altar that would have done credit to any meeting, had been put in place. A chorus of 250 voices were singing behind a platform lined with ministers and containing a piano, a tuneful orchestra and a profusion of flowers.

Before us, as we mounted the platform, we saw a sea of upturned, eager faces, waiting to hear the message for which we are all athirst—more, more about Jesus. Two balconies constructed out of sacks of wheat seated many people.

What a transformation these precious people had made in this building during the few days they had to prepare! No trouble had been too great, no thoughtful deed left undone. Surely had the Master Himself come to Turlock as he went to Bethany in the days of yore, they could not have done more. Surely, they deserved a blessing and a vision of the Master. "Oh, Lord, help us sweep back the curtains. Rift Thou the clouds that these dear hearts may glimpse Thy blessed face and hear Thy voice sweeter than the rushing water, then shall they be repaid an hundred fold," we prayed.

Space is too limited to herein describe the meetings in Turlock. Suffice it to say that the floors were filled with wheat of another nature now, as golden grain of never dying souls was harvested from the fields of life and laid at the Savior's feet. Sinners were saved, sick were healed and the name of the Master glorified.

RETURN VISIT TO FRESNO

Three times Sunday, April 30th, we preached to packed houses in the Municipal Auditorium, Fresno, reviewing the recent revival and calling for testimonies as to how the conversions and healings had stood through the three months that had elapsed since we were last there.

The results surpassed our fondest dreams, as scores of splendid men and women fell into line and streamed over the platform to give testimony as to their conversion and healing during the recent revival. Mrs. Hart of the Sunnyside Grocery described the melting and total disappearance of her fibroid tumor, and told of X-ray proofs of its former existence. Others testified as to their healing from paralysis, deafness, growths, and diseases of almost every description. A man 82 years of age, always an infidel till the January meetings, told of his conversion, and the ringing declaration of young men and women converts, that they had been saved and were going into the missionary work, was a delight to the soul. The stage of the Auditorium was one mass of roses and lilac, the gift of loving hands. Scores accepted Christ. 'Twas a wonderful day of encouragement to convert and evangelist alike.

THE ROCHESTER REVIVAL

ON Wednesday the campaign proper opened in Convention Hall with a seating capacity of three thousand five hundred. The seats were placed in order, a piano lifted to the stage which had served as a support for the great boxing bout ring but a few hours before. Flags, palms, mottoes were arranged, a pulpit procured and the meeting was on. From the very first visitors and delegates began to pour in from surrounding states, as many as twenty-two states being represented at one time. People came from as far west as California and Oregon, from northern Canada and Nova Scotia, from the south of Florida, Alabama and Georgia. Many of our beloved Bridal Call readers, staunch friends who had stood by us through the years, came streaming in from Connecticut, Pennsylvania, New Jersey, New York, Rhode Island and other states. A saner, more loyal, loving band of soul winners it has never been our privilege to meet. All set to work with a will serving in any capacity that they could. A choir was quickly formed from the various churches of the city, pianists volunteered, numbers of musicians volunteered for the orchestra, flowers were donated for the rostrum, an elevated platform was installed for the choir.

The meeting opened with victory and the close of the first afternoon service found the great altar filled from end to end. The first night service found twice as many seeking salvation as this altar could hold and it soon became necessary to invite them to the platform and to kneel in the aisles after the altar space was filled.

"But what do you mean by 'the altar'?" some one may ask. "I did not know altars were built in theaters and in municipal auditoriums and boxing arenas!" Then turn back to the life of Abraham and you will see just what the writer means. We read of Abraham that when he ascended the mountain he builded an altar there; when he went down into the shadows of the valley he builded an altar there; when he crossed the plains or the desert he builded an altar there. Surely this is a pattern for the evangelist. We have learned to build an altar wherever we go from coast to coast for the Lord Jesus Christ. Sometimes it has been the running board of our automobile; sometimes it has been a kitchen chair; sometimes we have converted the platform of the prize fight ring into an altar of the Lord; sometimes it is the stage of a theater; at times it has been the piazza of a cottage from which we have preached the Gospel. Anywhere, everywhere we have learned to "build an altar there."

What a glorious time soul winning it was. The thing that must impress visiting ministers and workers from every section of the country is the great soul hunger to know Jesus Christ as the Savior, the unhesitating rush to the altar of hundreds of men and women in every city to seek salvation at the very first altar calls without any coaxing, without any personal work or fishing whatsoever being done in the audience. Surely this old world is hungry, hungry, hungry for the Gospel power of the Lord Jesus Christ. They are not hungry for oyster suppers, they can buy oysters at the restaurant. They are not hungry for a social church, they can enjoy social life at the club. They are not hungry to hear in church about politics or the disarmament of the nations, they are longing to hear the old, old story of Jesus and His love. Wherever this story is preached with simplicity and power, wherever Christ is lifted up above the earth He draws men and women to Himself and hundreds come daily running to His precious feet, leaving their burden of sin beneath the crimson blood.

Soon the splendid band of workers were selected and the altar work systematized. Dr. Thompson of the Asbury M. E. Church took charge of this branch of the work and though pressed with many other church duties attended almost without an exception the three services daily, registering the converts, instructing the workers and conserving that beautiful harvest which is indeed more precious than all the silver, gold and jewels of the world rolled into one. Other city ministers came in one by one, assuring us of their prayers, co-operation and assistance in every possible way.

TWO GYPSY BANDS ARRIVE

The meeting in Convention Hall was no sooner opened than a wonderful thing happened. A band of Gypsies, headed by their chief, came to attend the revival services. The chief had been in communication with others by letter and telegram for some time as the whole of the tribes of Gypsydom from Atlantic to Pacific were stirred to the depths through the healing of one of their number from a terrible tumor during the revival in Denver, Colo. They state that the great tumor had melted away within two or three days after prayer had been offered for her and the news had spread like wildfire. It resulted in the gathering together of these Gypsies and their quaint heart-touching pleading that we tell them the story of Jesus and "all 'bout how get saved, how get healed, go back tell other Gypsies everywhere 'bout Jesus who maketh happy and healthy." Of their seeking and finding the Lord as their Savior and Physician, of their showering us with kisses, flowers, gold and love we will let Dr. Price speak elsewhere.

Just before the campaign closed a second band of Gypsies arrived under the leadership of Dewey Mark, head of the Mark tribe of Gypsies. This time they came from five states, an entirely new band to be saved and healed. The first meeting that the second band entered they almost snowed the writer under with chrysanthemums, carnations, roses, daisies, ferns and baskets of multi-colored flowers, reiterating the plaintive cry, 'Oh, lady, tell us 'bout Jesus, all 'bout how to get saved, healed and happy." God bless them with their dear, simple, childlike hearts, with their love, unselfishness, generosity and yieldedness to do the will of the Christ. Truly it put one in mind of the customs of ancient days when the wise men came bringing gold, frankincense and myrrh to place at the feet of Jesus.

My mother and myself could scarcely keep the tears back. We felt as though we almost wanted to go through the floor when we would be standing on the platform and the Gypsies would be kneeling at the altar seeking salvation and we would realize with a start that they were kissing our shoes and the hem of our dress, saying brokenly through their tears, "Oh, thank you, thank you, lady, you brought me to Jesus, you told me of His love! Now Jesus made me happy! Jesus made me well! I love you, lady, dear!" And yet one could no more think of scolding them than one would think of slapping a little child who offered you a piece of candy out of the goodness of a loving heart.

'Twas wonderful to see their simple faith. Were they saved? Yes, Hallelujah! Were they healed? Glory to God, they were! A chief who had not been able to bend his knees because of the stiffness with which rheumatism had locked his joints, fairly danced a jig on the platform after his healing saying, "Oh, golly, I can bend by knees, golly, I can! Thank God, I can bend my knees!"

It took the writer a moment to realize what the man had said, and I looked at him with dumb horror for a moment but his face was shining and he was sublimely unconscious that he had said anything wrong. I went to him quickly and said, "Oh, brother, you are saved now! You have given your heart to Jesus! 'Golly' is not a good word, you must say 'Glory!' now." But he was so full that he could not stop and he continued, "Oh, golly — I mean glory! I can bend my knees. All right, Sister, I say glory! Now I know!" God bless him!

One of the ladies among the second company, who was healed from broken limbs and arm had never been able to lift her hand but could only swing the arm from the shoulder, was instantly delivered and joyfully lifted the arm first a quarter of the way, then half way, then three-quarters, then all the way up above her head, freely swinging it to and fro—completely healed.

The whole company found Christ and were healed of their diseases. They remained till the end of the meeting, then went happily to their various states—for they had journeyed many hundreds of miles—to tell the story to all the other Gypsies, declaring that they were coming to California to see them saved and healed and to bring gifts for the tabernacle.

Practically everyone of these Gypsies bought a chair in Echo Park Revival Tabernacle and even secured a chair for their little children! If the people of our own race had done this the Temple would have been up over night. What a lesson they taught us in unselfishness, in giving, and in receiving!

ALTARS OVERFLOWED AT EVERY SERVICE

On and on swept the revival meetings opening in Convention Hall on Wednesday night and seeing the building packed by the first Saturday night with hundreds standing and swarming at the fire-escapes trying to gain admission.

The divine healing services were of necessity held for the most part at an early morning hour, and even so found the building overcrowded. But the great soul cry of the people was for salvation and to know the Lord Jesus Christ as their Redeemer. Therefore, with the exception of the three Saturday nights, the other afternoon and evening services were devoted entirely to evangelism. The morning prayer meetings being devoted to services for the sick, the afternoons and evenings being kept clear and free for the ever widening sweep of the revival, hundreds sought and found salvation every day. Attendance grew by leaps and bounds till at times as many were turned away as gained admission to the building. They came not to see anything spectacular but to hear the old story of the cross of Jesus Christ and to await the first opportunity of rising to their feet, rushing up the aisles and giving their hearts and lives to Him.

"And it shall come to pass in the last days saith the Lord, that I will pour out my Spirit upon all flesh." Surely the first droppings of this great prophetical spiritual outpouring are upon us. Multitudes are just waiting for the opportunity and the troubling of the waters that they may plunge into the revival fountain and be saved.

The large number of men seeking salvation was considered a remarkable feature of the campaign. Meeting after meeting the large platform would be literally packed, row after row with men only, seeking, weeping and finding forgiveness of sin and the full salvation of the Lord Jesus Christ while the women knelt at the altar below. Some of the finest citizens and business men of the city, I am told, were among those thus finding the Christ and consecrating their lives to His service. Twice the greater part of the main floor was reserved for and filled by men only whose work prevented early attendance and admission.

On the closing night of the revival campaign Judge Gillette of the County Court came to the platform and gave a beautiful talk on the power of the Gospel and expressed his approval of the soul winning work of the campaign.

In the opening of the Saturday evening meeting the people broke into applause and rose to their feet singing "My Country 'Tis of Thee" as the women of the Grand Army of the Republic entered the door bearing in their hands, upon a long standard, an enormous flag whose stars and stripes were waving as they made their way to the front and presented it to us to adorn the Echo Park Revival Tabernacle in Los Angeles, Calif., declaring that such revivals were making this land of the free and the brave a better, happier and more wholesome place in which to live and praying that the work might ever go on in increasing power and glory.

Yes, it was a glorious revival for soul winning. Enthusiasm ran high in this dear old conservative city, and as Dr. Thompson of the Asbury M. E. Church was wont to say, in their conservatism it might take a little while to start the fire but once it had caught ablaze nothing could put it out; it would burn ever higher and higher. God grant that the revival flames may never die till Jesus comes. Amen.

Not only did singers come in from the various churches but the Salvation Army silver band, under the leadership of Adjutant Wiseman, came to the services at two different times, making the building resound with the sound of victory. We could almost close our eyes and picture that last great triumphal day when with waving banners and playing bands the redeemed of the Lord shall go marching into the beautiful city of gold. (This band have also contributed a seat in the Echo Park Revival Tabernacle. God bless them.)

On Monday nights the Convention Hall was engaged for theatrical performances or boxing bouts, but not an hour's time was lost, thanks to the co-operàtion of the city churches, the Asbury M. E. Church being specially gracious in the opening of their doors at all times.

The last Monday service before the close of the campaign was held in the largest church in the city, the Central Presbyterian, and it was packed to the topmost seat of the gallery and many stood. The platform and all spaces also were jammed and overflowed till men and women knelt in the aisles seeking salvation when the altar call was given. Oh, what a wonderful Savior is Jesus, our glorious Lord!

THE FAREWELL

At the depot at 10 P. M. when we came to take our train, we found in the neighborhood of five hundred brave faced, laughing, singing young men and women to see us off. Standing on the steps we conducted a farewell service of song, testimony and prayer. Even the policemen and the station officials uncovered their heads and bowed reverently as we lifted our hearts in prayer and thanksgiving to our glorious Father above who had given us these hundreds of converts, sheaves from the harvest field of life now being gathered into the heavenly garner. Oh, how they testified as to their being saved, healed and filled with the Spirit! The angels above must have rejoiced with us as we wiped our eyes and rejoiced on earth below, over lambs that were lost and found again as the Lord brought back His own.

At the time the train was due we all made our way to the upstairs station platform. The train, however, proved to be over an hour late. Nothing daunted they insisted upon staying with us to the last moment, and another outdoor service was held. A large rubbish can was turned upside down, we were lifted to it by the encircling throng and "we builded an altar there," singing, praying, testifying, advising and counseling, seeking to establish one another in the most holy faith till at last the train pulled in and the last good-byes were waved from the distance.

We are soon seated in the speeding coach of a Santa Fe railroad train looking out upon the mountains and plains of New Mexico, but our hearts, prayers, and tender love are with the newly made converts of the Canton and Rochester revivals and our lips are breathing a prayer that they will be kept close to the heart of the Master till we meet at Jesus' feet.

WINNING THE GYPSIES FOR JESUS

DR. CHARLES S. PRICE

THE telephone bell in the apartment of an evangelist must grow almost as tired as the evangelist for it keeps up a constant jingle at all hours of the day and night; this is especially true when the evangelist happens to be Aimee Semple McPherson. Sometimes I have thought that the evangelistic party ought to be enlarged by our acquiring an additional helper to be known as the telephone secretary, but on second thought I am convinced that no one would want the job because they would have to eat and sleep with the receiver fastened to their ears. The wires themselves must laugh and cry as the requests come over the telephone; all kinds of strange and peculiar questions from "What must I do to be healed?" to "What time does the eight o'clock meeting start?" Anybody having the permanent job of "telephone secretary" would very soon, I am convinced, be asking dear Mother Kennedy for a healing card on which they would describe their malady as "Telephonitis." But then, sometimes we receive messages that gladden our hearts. On the second day of the great campaign, that will be known in religious history as the Rochester Revival, the telephone bell rang. Now there was nothing unusual in that. It would have been unusual had it kept still; but there was something unusual in the message that came over the wire.

Sister McPherson is answering, "Hello," "Hello, who is speaking?"

"This is Mrs. McPherson."

"Oh, lady, lady—we come here—we here—please tell us 'bout Jesus—we come a long way—we want know 'bout Jesus —lady—we sick too—lady, please help—lady—we got gold ——"

"Yes, just wait a minute, tell me who you are—I can't see you over the telephone, you know."

"Yes, lady—we come—we here— we got gold in our pockets —we bring it to Jesus—tell us 'bout Jesus—some baby very sick—Jesus help us—tell us 'bout——"

"Yes, God bless you. I will tell you all about Jesus—but first tell me who you are."

"Oh—we gypsies—we come long, long way—lady, you remember Denver gypsy woman healed—her tumor go—she know all 'bout Jesus, we want you tell us too—we get telegram from our king—he say come to Rochester—lady, we got gold in our pockets—we want give it Jesus—we want you tell us 'bout Jesus——"

"All right, God bless you—go to Convention Hall—wait till I come. There is a meeting there this afternoon and I will tell you all about Jesus. Jesus loves you all. He wants all the gypsies. Tell all your people to be there. God bless you!"

"Yes, lady, we be there, good-bye."

"Good-bye, God bless you."

"Good-bye, lady."

An hour or two has sped by and it is time for the meeting in the Hall. Because it is my custom to go a little early and see that everything is orderly and ready for Sister McPherson when she arrives, I make my way to the Hall, and am greeted by a riot of color and glory in the front seats. If it were not for the more soberly dressed American people in the other seats you could almost imagine yourself translated to some Oriental country, and standing in the throne room of an Oriental potentate.

Imagine these gorgeously dressed, dark skinned Romany wanderers, doing obeisance to their monarch. I am informed that yards and yards of almost priceless silks made up their dresses. White shawls from the looms of Persia were wrapped around heads and draped around shoulders. No pauper gypsies are these, for around the necks of all women are hanging string after string of gold coins gathered from all countries of the globe, in such quantities that it seems they must be too heavy to wear.

Their hair, as black as a raven's wing, is hanging in closely braided plaits over each shoulder, their fingers are heavy with rings, their wrists glisten with the shining gold of bracelets, and diamond ear-rings flash in the light, glistening almost as bright as the pearl-like tear drops of expectancy that are seen in their coal black eyes.

I go up to them, and introduce myself, and immediately there is a torrent of questions, "Where is she? When is lady coming? Tell her touch me, please, mister, I very, very sick. Tell her gypsy king send us, we got gold."

"Oh, please now, don't everybody talk at once. I know Sister McPherson will tell you all about Jesus. I know she will pray for you; just be patient, and perhaps she will have a meeting for you gypsies all by yourselves."

It is impossible to quiet them. It seems they can hardly wait; their hearts are bursting with expectancy, and tear drops are glistening in their eyes.

"Please, mister, please, you tell lady she heal my baby, my poor little baby——"

"Oh, but, sister, the lady can't heal your baby, it is Jesus—she can——"

But the choir room door is opening and slowly the choir files in. The seats on the platform are being filled. The gypsies are silent, they are watching the procession, watching, watching, watching with a tenseness that is almost painful, watching for the lady, waiting, waiting. Oh, they just can't wait any more. One young gypsy mother clasps a baby in her arms and starts toward the door. Dr. Thompson, of the Asbury Methodist Church, is climbing the steps to the platform now and then a subdued murmur from the gypsies — their "lady" is climbing the stairs at last.

Sister McPherson walks toward the edge of the platform and her eyes are immediately riveted on the gorgeous array of color in the front seats. They are moving around in the seats awkwardly. I feel in my heart they will tear themselves away in a moment or two, they can't sit quiet there. But Sister is talking. Now she is looking right at them.

"You poor darlings," she says. "I am so glad you are here. I am going to tell you all about Jesus. I will tell you ——"

That is as far as she got. Some of the women start to courtesy, dropping on the floor in such a graceful manner that their skirts spread around them until they looked like little poppies in a garden of flowers of resplendent hue. Others throw kisses, and still others clasp their hands and bow their heads again and again.

As I look into Sister McPherson's face I see she is crying and laughing at the same time. Then unable to stand it any longer she holds out her hands and says, "Oh, I just love you, and Jesus loves you too."

That is all they need. Out of their seats they come. They kneel and make the sign of the cross, they kiss her hand, and, although Sister herself did not know it at the time, they kissed her feet and the hem of her dress, and cried out their petition: "Tell us 'bout Jesus, lady," they cry. "Heal my baby, he is so sick, lady. Please, lady, we come long, long way."

Back of me the choir is sobbing, front of me the gypsies are praying, holding out their hands appealingly to a little woman in the garb of a servant. Truly she is a servant now, a woman who loves the common people so much that, laughing and crying at the same time, she can look into the coal black eyes of a gypsy band and say, "I love you, I love you, and Jesus loves you too."

I look at the audience. Is there a dry eye anywhere? Did Convention Hall ever see such a scene before? Oh, it must be that angels looked over the battlements of glory, and smiled when they saw the outstretched hand of a gypsy chief and heard the cry for Jesus that came from the heart of a gypsy maid.

It is very reluctantly that they take their seats, and the audience joins in singing, "Oh, How I Love Jesus." None of the gypsies are singing, they do not know the hymn. They simply sit and watch, most of them with a hand raised in the air and an appealing look on their faces as their gaze is turned upward.

The sermon is over now, and Sister McPherson is praying. She is praying that God will touch the hearts of the people, and bring them to the altar to find peace and pardon and salvation at the feet of Jesus Christ.

The gypsy band needs no second invitation. The big broad shouldered chief rises to his feet and starts toward the altar. In an instant every gypsy is headed for the altar chairs and every last one of them, thirty-two in number, are praying for salvation and the coming of the Friend of the Gypsies, Jesus Christ, into their hearts.

By their sides kneel their white brothers and sisters, crying to the same Christ, blending their voices in a melody of prayer and weeping their way through to the same old rugged cross in the same old-fashioned way.

It is a sight that one can never forget. Some things in life stand out above all others; some incidents stamp themselves indelibly on the brain, and the sight of those dark-skinned Orientals, in all the gorgeous finery of their race, and with all the warm blooded impulses of their southern natures, crying for salvation, can never be eradicated.

That afternoon they vowed allegiance to another Monarch, they became citizens of a new country, they subscribed to the constitution of a spiritual empire and Jesus of Nazareth became a Gypsy King.

The meeting is over now and tears of joy on faces dark-skinned have been wiped away. I am surrounded by a group of men, foremost among whom is the gypsy chief.

"We don't know much," he says. "We want to be saved, we want to go to heaven, yes, we believe Jesus can heal the sick. Mister, won't you teach us how to pray? Won't you teach us how to have faith? Mister, tell us what to do when the Holy Lady——"

"Oh, but you must not call her that," I remonstrated. I knew how Sister McPherson recoiled from any such titles and how she would feel if they called her that. But he came back at me quick as a flash. "Why not, she is Holy Lady."

"No, brother, she is——"

"Well," he interrupted, "is she bad lady?"

"No," I said.

"Then if she not bad, she holy lady. Everybody bad or holy—me all the time bad—now try to be holy. No more shoot craps, no more swear, no more gamble."

"That's right," I told him. "You try to be a real Christian."

It was this conversation that led me to call a special meeting for those gypsies at ten o'clock on the following morning, the purpose of the meeting being to teach them how to pray, how to look up in faith when they were anointed for healing, and how to walk with Jesus when they went back to Salt Lake City, to Baltimore, and New York, the towns from which they came.

What a prayer meeting that was! They filled the room where they were kneeling, they filled it with dark-skinned forms, with prayer of supplication and shouts of joy. What simple childlike faith they had, what assurance they had that they would be healed.

I moved along the kneeling rows praying with each one individually and at last we rose to our feet. The chief made a brief address in a tongue that was foreign to me, but I knew from the expression in their eyes that he was telling them of Jesus. I knew from the fingers that pointed upward that his story was of a land that is fairer than day, a land that sometime will be Home to a wandering gypsy band.

The hours soon sped by and the time arrived for the gypsy service in Convention Hall. Only the gypsies were to be prayed for that night, only the gypsies were to move across the stage with uplifted hands in supplicating prayer, only the gypsies I say, yet who can see the potential possibilities wrapped up in those black-eyed gypsy boys who came into Rochester with diseased bodies and sin-stricken hearts but went back to their tribes with healing for the body and Jesus in their souls. Can I describe that scene? Can I tell it just as it occurred? It seems to me that no human pen could tell it right, only the keeper of heaven's books could really write the scenes that that night were recorded by him in the ledgers of the Eternal City.

First in the line comes the brother of the chief. He is a

big fellow, broad shouldered and swarthy, but his heart is heaving and his eyes are filled with tears. I hand his card to Sister McPherson and in a moment she is praying, "Jesus, bless this gypsy. Oh, Jesus, You saved his soul, touch his body now. Jesus, just one touch of Your finger and it is done. Oh, Jesus, help him to pray. Take away this rheumatism, Lord, and oh, Jesus, restore this deaf ear." "Brother, in the name of Jesus of Nazareth receive your healing."

I am watching his face. Faith is there, not the passive hope that it might be done but the active faith that takes the promise and says, "It is done." Slowly he bends his once stiff joints, and a smile of radiant happiness comes over his face. He bends his back, his knees, his arms, and then he says something in gypsy language that I cannot understand but I know it must be the gypsy equivalent to "Praise the Lord!"

His pain is gone, the joints bend freely for the first time in years, he hears a watch tick with his deaf ear, and with a smile of satisfaction he takes a seat on the platform.

Healing after healing follows, shouts of joy come from the audience, tears are flowing freely and the whole building is stirred as the power falls. Sister is happy, so very happy that Jesus is working in such a wonderful way. She is standing now holding in her arms a gypsy baby. She cuddles it close to her heart, and kisses it, and then kisses its mother, a beautiful young gypsy queen. That mother's head is thrown back, arms are outstretched in prayer, tears flow from those coal black eyes and fall in large drops upon the stage.

"For of such is the kingdom of heaven," the evangelist is saying. "Mother, your baby is well. Jesus has touched your baby."

"Thank you, thank you," sobbed out the gypsy mother, as she clasped her baby in her arms. Slowly the gypsy mother is led from the stage and the great audience looks on with eyes of amazement at the scene that Jesus of Nazareth invisible on the platform has enacted before them.

But the line is moving along faster now and in the row is standing a dark-eyed, black-haired gypsy boy. Because his ears are deaf his eyes are wide open looking with a gaze of amazement at the scene that is transpiring before him. His dark face is radiant with the light of expectancy and hope as he stands before Sister McPherson and he strains his deaf ears to catch the words that leave the lips of the evangelist.

His deaf ears are anointed and then in a moment the smile broadens into a grin and the grin develops into a laugh as he turns around to the gypsies behind him and says, "I can hear now, I can hear, I am healed."

Slowly Sister McPherson backs away from him and says in a whisper, "Can you hear me now?" But his eyes are riveted on the grand piano and he is listening to the strains of "My Faith Looks Up to Thee," that is coming from the piano and the crying, singer choir. Test after test is given him and the audience, becoming thoroughly satisfied that his ears are really opened, breaks into a cheer while Sister clasps her hands and lifts her eyes in gratitude to the Christ who is working such miracles.

At this juncture of the proceedings the gypsy who was suffering from rheumatism before he was anointed is unable to contain his emotions any longer. There he is sitting with his great big frame in one of the choir chairs, his hands clasped in front of him and his eyes turned upward toward heaven. Great big tears are coursing down his furrowed cheeks and fall in large glittering drops on the floor.

"Pain all gone," he keeps saying. "No more hurt, praise the Lord, pain all gone."

A gypsy brother by his side evidently interrogates him and asks him how he knows that his pain is all gone? And the chief immediately starts a little meeting of his own by jumping up on the stage and promptly dances a gypsy jig. The audience saw and wondered and applauded. Never before have I seen such radiant, happy faces as those of that gypsy band who with the faith of a little child in the power of Jesus Christ came with their infirm bodies to Him on that glorious night.

Now Sister is standing in front of a gypsy women that is resplendent with dresses that are of all the colors of the rainbow. Magnificent shawls are draped around her shoulders and her head dress is dazzling in its brilliancy. Row upon row of gold coins jingle around her neck as she approaches the praying woman in white. There she is with her large black eyes glistening because of the tears, gulping something back in her throat and standing with her hands outstretched toward heaven calling upon Jesus Christ with all the emotion and passion of her race.

Sister is anointing her now, and then a cry of gladness escapes from her lips as putting her hands to her body she shouts, "It is gone, it is gone, all gone."

A moment or two later that gypsy woman is standing before that vast audience telling the story of how her own sister was healed in Denver, Colo., of a tumor and how the king of the gypsies wired to the gypsy bands telling them of the wonderful story of the power of Christ to heal.

"It was my own sister," she cried. "Tumor all gone. Sister McPherson anointed her—pretty soon tumor go away—now she very, very well." And so the story went.

It seemed that the power of God so flooded the building that every gypsy in the line was healed.

The doxology has now been sung and the crowd is slowly wending its way through the doors engaging in just one general topic of conversation, the things that their eyes have seen and the things their ears have heard, for this was the first divine healing service in the city of Rochester.

The gypsies stayed on the platform, reluctant to leave the great building, crowding around Sister McPherson eager to get an opportunity to kiss her hand or reaching for her hand, place it themselves upon their own heads in benediction.

Sister was radiantly happy, so happy that these romantic people had received the touch of Jesus in their physical bodies but happier by far that they knew the meaning of the old rugged cross, some of them for the first time in their lives.

There is an old gypsy custom that gypsies always follow when traveling over transcontinental highways. Sometimes as the gypsy caravans come to a cross road they will take one road toward their destination and strew flowers along the highway that gypsies coming after them might see the road they have gone. Is it not significant that the following morning the gypsies should come with their offerings of gold for the Tabernacle and flowers of love for their dear white Sister before they said their fond good-bye? The trails of the rainbow hued women of Romany origin and the little woman in white of Caucasian blood must needs go in different ways. One will go on carrying the blessed message of Jesus in tabernacles from coast to coast while the other will lead to country byways, to verdant meadows or rippling brooks and gypsy camps, but who knows that in the end the roads will meet again before the gate of that city whose builder and maker is God.

A GREAT REVIVAL CAMPAIGN

REV. FRANK C. THOMPSON, D. D.

HREE weeks ago a spiritual aeroplane flew over Rochester and dropped Sister McPherson, as it were, from the clouds.

There was no great excitement or blare of trumpets when she landed. No organization or committee from the Federation of Churches with elaborate plans to advertise her meetings beforehand.

She came in as quietly as Paul entered Rome in the olden time.

A few friends with audacious faith had secured the largest auditorium in the city, trusting in God to fill it with hungry souls.

Looked at from a purely human standpoint, such an enterprise was bound to fail. The average evangelist that had come to our city in late years, even when backed by several churches, had counted himself happy if he had three or four hundred people out to hear him on week nights.

But here comes a woman with absolutely no local organization behind her, who within a few days after she has stepped on the platform, has filled our largest hall to overflowing and soon thousands are being turned away.

My father's home was in Rochester and I have kept in close touch with the city during a ministry of forty-one years and I can testify that nothing like this series of meetings has ever occurred here before.

The services were phenomenal in several respects:

(1) In demonstrating the attractiveness of the old-time Gospel.

The messages of Sister McPherson were beautiful in their

simplicity, yet mighty in their convicting power. They rang true on all of the great fundamental doctrines and threw a flood of new light on many passages of Scripture which heretofore had seemed comparatively unimportant.

The speaker drew a very sharp line between the church and the world, but unlike many modern evangelists, there was no bitterness in her messages nor underhanded flings at the church nor criticisms of ministers.

(2) Again, the meetings were pre-eminently above others in the thoroughness and depth of the work done. Sin was portrayed as an awful reality and not merely as "an error of the mortal mind."

The necessity for repentance and the new birth was driven home in almost every sermon. The "straight gate" and the "narrow way" were held up as the only entrance into the kingdom of God.

This was no hand-shaking, card-signing campaign. Our Sister insisted that those who were seeking salvation should show their sincerity by coming forward to the "penitent form" and seeking for mercy.

The warning bell which has so long hung silent in many church steeples, was rung at every service. Yet the beauty of it all was, that the dominant note of all the entire series of meetings was *the love of Christ* and the sufficiency of His blood to cleanse from all sin.

(3) The power of the Altar Calls I have never seen surpassed.

As our Sister closed her sermons and came to the exhortation, she was upon her tiptoes, and made such a telling and ardent appeal that the audience was swayed as the waves of the sea and with tears in their eyes moved to the altar in crowds.

At this point in the service she seemed doubly inspired, as her voice reached the farthest corners of the vast auditorium, and like her Master of old, she cried, "Lazarus, come forth," and scores and hundreds at every service came out the graves of sin into the new life in Christ.

God grant that the churches in this city where these resurrected souls are standing, may hear and obey the second call of Christ at the tomb, "Loose him and let him go," thus helping them to put off their grave clothes and get into spiritual activity.

(4) Another feature which was phenomenal in these meetings was the wonderful exaltation of Jesus Christ. Whatever the topic selected by our Sister the keynote of every service was Jesus Christ, the same yesterday, today and forever, not the great "I was" but the great "I am."

"Jesus all the day long was her joy and her song." I have never listened to an evangelist who so continually enthroned the "Man of Galilee" in every message. To this fact I attribute Sister McPherson's great success: for it is written in John 12:26, "If any man serve me, him will my father honor."

This continual glorifying of Christ is a strong proof that the messenger is baptized with the Holy Spirit, for in John 16:13, 14 it reads, "When he, the Spirit of Truth, is come (in you) he shall glorify me."

(5) The emphasis laid upon the baptism of the Holy Spirit was very unusual in these meetings. There was a sane and powerful presentation of this great truth throughout most of the sermons.

This vital doctrine is greatly obscured in the church today. Ministers and people are struggling to move the gospel train up the grade by pushing behind with their puny methods and organizations, when all they need is the *fire in the engine* to drive the wheels forward.

The great watchword of our Sister's messages was the Master's last recorded words, "Ye shall receive power after that the Holy Spirit has come upon you."

The most startling and pathetic feature in the campaign was the faith healing services.

Never before had I fully realized what the passages in the Gospels meant when they said the multitudes pressed upon Christ and thronged Him, seeking healing.

In many services large portions of the hall were filled with those seeking physical relief.

When the moment came for prayers for the sick there was a dramatic scene beggaring description. Scores of the afflicted came to the platform with uplifted hands where Sister McPherson anointed them and prayed for their recovery.

A large number testified to their complete healing from tumors, deafness, blindness, goiter, lameness, and many other diseases.

These scenes confirmed the opinion which I have long held, that there are special spiritual gifts bestowed upon Christians. One is the gift of healing.

All men are commanded to pray for the sick (James 5:14) and if the conditions are met and it is the will of God the healing will take place; but some Spirit-filled believers have a *special gift* of faith and of healing (1 Cor. 12:9) which enables them continually to accomplish results in this sphere of service which the ordinary believer can only attain in special cases.

Although Sister McPherson makes no such claims for herself, the work accomplished by her seems to point clearly to the fact that she has a special gift and calling along the line of healing.

The meetings closed with vast numbers beating at the doors trying to get in to hear the message.

The night Sister McPherson left on the train a great crowd of hundreds thronged the railroad station anxious for a last glimpse of the face of the faithful evangelist.

The crush was so great that only a few succeeded in shaking her hand, but she spoke to the crowds in two different places —once in the large waiting room, where songs were sung and testimonies given, and again on the long train platform which was filled with friends. Good-byes were shouted, handkerchiefs waved, and the train rolled away near midnight, carrying with it the one who had brought salvation and healing to hundreds of homes and captured the hearts of all who heard her.

TWO SPEECHES BY COUNTY JUDGE GILLETTE

Stenographically Recorded

LADIES and Gentlemen: I want to congratulate you on the opportunity you have had these past few days of seeing this marvelous exhibition of the power of Jesus Christ to save men. I am a layman, but I believe that we laymen should do more in the way of testifying to our faith in Jesus Christ than we have in the past. (Applause.)

I did not come here to speak. I came here to listen, but inasmuch as I am on my feet I want to give testimony to my abiding faith in the power of Jesus Christ to save men even to the uttermost. (Applause.)

Many of you know that my daily avocation is largely in dealing with those who are apprehended for crime. I want to say to you that over seventy per cent of the boys who come before me come from broken-up and non-Christian homes. Seldom, if ever, do we have a boy come before the county court accused of crime who comes from a Christian home.

I want to testify to the power of religion and of Christ to save criminals. We judges in the children's court, in the county court, and probation officers find the only way to save some of these people leading this sordid life is to get their feet upon the solid rock of faith. Probation officers and judges are not miracle workers, but Jesus Christ is and we can only surround these people with religious influences that their lives may be made whole.

In conclusion I want to commend to you the life of that lowly, humble Nazarene Carpenter born in Bethlehem of Judea, reared in ancient Galilee, who travelled up and down, healing the sick, making the lame and halt to walk and the blind to see, who said, "Suffer the little children to come unto me and forbid them not"; who brought a shield into this world and not a sword; who came to minister rather than to be ministered unto; who taught His disciples, he who would be the greatest among you should be the servant of all.

I want to commend the ministry of this noble woman who has been ministering to you for the past few weeks, one who is following closer in the footsteps of that Holiest One than anyone I know of. (Applause.)

And in conclusion I want to commend to you that life, that greatest life that ever lived upon earth, perfect because of its honest simplicity, perfect because of its love and divine humanity—the life of Jesus Christ. (Applause.)

JUDGE GILLETTE'S SPEECH AT THE BANQUET OF CHAIR HOLDER MEMBERS OF ECHO PARK EVANGELISTIC ASSOCIATION, GIVEN AT THE SENECA HOTEL, NOV. 21, 1921

Ladies and Gentlemen: I want to congratulate you on this wonderful revival evangelistic campaign which has been going on, which has resulted in the redemption of so many souls for Christ. The redemption of souls to Christ is far more important than any physical healing. Mrs. McPherson, this servant of the Most High, believes also that healing is merely an incident in the great service of redemption of souls.

Since the great war many of us have turned more than ever before to the full realization that a man or woman is great or small in the proportion that he or she renders real service to mankind and to humanity. Some of us have chosen the public walks of life because we feel that in the public service the avenues of opportunity for service are more abundant than they are in some other walks of life. In our position we have had to do with social welfare, broken-up homes, homes headed by drunken and dissolute parents. We have been highly gratified at the service probation officers and other social welfare workers have been enalbed to do along those lines. *But, my friends, all our combined efforts pale into insignificance compared to the supreme service* this sister, most faithful minister of God, has been rendering not only in this community but in other communities she has visited.

In conclusion I want to congratulate her again upon the good she has done to this beautiful city of Rochester and other cities she has visited because, I repeat, there is no work that is so beneficial to mankind and humanity as this work of saving souls. And I hope that some co-operative movement shall be made after her departure that will see these souls garnered in the churches, placed amid religious surroundings where the temptation to backslide will not be great.

In conclusion I again want to acknowledge our obligation to Mrs. McPherson and bid her God-speed in this noble work. This whole community extends our most sincere good wishes to you, Mrs. McPherson, I am sure. (Applause.)

DENVER'S GREAT REVIVAL

By Dean A. C. Peck, Pastor Ogden Avenue Methodist Episcopal Church and Manager of Revival Campaign

IN response to a very cordial and unanimous invitation to 12,000 people, given at one of the closing meetings of the revival held in Denver in 1921, Mrs. McPherson returned to our city and began her second series of meetings on Friday, June 9, 1922. The evangelist was in fine form and health, and her preaching, if possible, was more effective than even that of the year since. One of the most frequently expressed sentiments heard from many of her audiences was over the fact of her ability to preach so constantly with such power and persuasion. It seemed like a miracle to all who weighed the facts.

Our meetings this year were shorter in duration than those of last year. Because of previous plans they continued but two weeks and three Sundays. A year ago they were held three weeks and four Sundays. Also they were begun earlier in the season and closed two weeks before the time of adjournment taken last year, thus escaping the tourist season, which filled the city and meetings with strangers a year ago. Our crowds, then, were prodigious. The municipal auditorium was packed at every service, and usually there would be thousands who could not secure entrance. It was estimated that Mrs. McPherson preached to close to half a million people. Such crowds, of course, seriously interfered with the best work for evangelism. This year we had plenty of people, but were not swept from our feet by the crowds. The estimate of the newspapers this year is that she preached to about 100,000 people per week.

Our organization this year was much more complete than that of a year ago. Not having had experience, we then had to feel our way along as the interest in the meetings developed. This year we had six splendid committees who were in constant operation, directing the music, work at the altar, ushers, examinations of applicants for healing, printing and providing accommodations for visitors. They did their work well and greatly facilitated the conduct and efficiency of the meetings.

One of the most pronounced features of the entire series was seen in the faithful and constant adherence to the old-time methods of getting "pure and undefiled religion." The truth was declared with no uncertain sound from beginning to the end. The modern swirl of amusements, social occupations, ecclesiastical compromises and the substitutes of service for salvation was denounced in unequivocal terms. At the same time, the possibility of old-time faith and power to accomplish the new birth, bringing new creatures into the eternal life, was held before the people. The cards signed indicated that about 100 per day responded to the call for repentance and faith in the Lord Jesus Christ. There were, also, many seekers after the baptism with the Holy Ghost. Frequent testimony meetings were held where converts were given opportunity to witness to their conversion, and many responded at every such meeting.

Many attended from Colorado and other states, some coming more than a thousand miles. There were some very happy and pronounced healings. The emphasis, however, is ever placed on conversion rather than physical cures. Usually, before healing services, the evangelist would make a call for a dozen or twenty of those who had been healed last year to come to the platform and give their testimony concerning the work God had wrought in them. There were always more of such witnesses than could be heard. A deep impression was made on the audiences by those who testified to the benefits previously received.

One of the happy features of the services found expression in a great children's meeting. Well children who could sing came beautifully dressed and occupied the platform, and, under the leadership of the precentor, and following the music of the great organ, sang to the sick and afflicted children. Much clothing, candy, toys, and great quantities of flowers were distributed. Also those who suffered from troubles and diseases which attack children presented themselves for healing, and many went away whole. There was probably no meeting held which attracted larger attention and accomplished greater results for good. We were deprived of our great place of meeting one day during the series because of the commencement exercises of the Denver public schools, the building having been secured for this purpose a year ago. The weather on that day was cool and some rain fell and no evangelistic service was held until evening. As the day waned, the clouds disappeared and the sun came out to make dry the grass and seats of our great Civic Center. This place of meeting has seats for 4,000. It is flanked on the south by the great Greek theatre. As previously planned, this splendid camp meeting ground was used for the evening service. Every seat was filled, every inch of standing room in both theatre and amphitheatre occupied and thousands of people stood outside, eagerly watching and listening to the exercises of song and sermon. A great response was made when the altar call was given. Fully a hundred people knelt on the steps of the theatre to seek the Savior.

Another of the most noticeable and unique characteristics of the meeting throughout was the attendance of a band of sixty gypsies. They were present at nearly every service. In Denver, a year ago, Mrs. McPherson had been used of God as the agent to pray for the healing of one of their number from a deadly disease. Since that time they have followed her everywhere, bringing flowers and unique offerings of many kinds and making a contribution for the revival tabernacle at Los Angeles. I talked with several of them and concluded that they were genuinely converted and anxious to do whatever they could to bring others to Christ. They told me that the heads of the gypsy tribes, who travel to and fro over America, were doing everything possible to help Mrs. McPherson in her work. They also said that some of their number throughout the country have been converted. Their enthusiasm and love for Sister McPherson are unbounded.

The choir numbered about 200 and special features were introduced at nearly all meetings.

During the last week the number of sick, many of whom had come from great distances, was so great that it was found to be impossible for Mrs. McPherson to meet and pray with all of them. In this exigency twelve ministers banded themselves together to help meet the pressure. Morning meetings at 10 o'clock were held five days at Christ Methodist Episcopal Church. There the Bible doctrines of divine healing and faith were briefly presented, testimonies of those who had been healed were given and the afflicted ones came and bowed at the chancel, while three or four groups of ministers, with oil and prayer, directed their faith to the Maker, who is also the great Physician. It is a great pleasure to record that these meetings were successful almost beyond precedent. They were largely attended and hundreds were prayed for. Many testified later at the greater meetings in the auditorium to the grace and power of God in healing their bodies, as well as in converting their souls.

It has been determined by the ministers who thus took part in these meetings to continue them in different parts of the city. Five churches have been secured—one central, one in North Denver, one in South Denver, one in West Denver and one in East Denver. Every week at 2:30 on Thursday afternoons at one of the places named, in rotation, the people in the different sections of the city will be invited to come for instruction, conversation, healing and the Baptism with the Holy Ghost. The interest in these meetings is great, and we anticipate large results. We invite the prayers of those who believe in these doctrines, all over the country, for God's presence in these meetings, and that we may have tangible results along both spiritual and material lines.

Our organization for the conservation of the results of the Denver meetings is, also, to be extended. We have been most fortunate in securing the services of Miss Mae Adams, who understands the Bible and the doctrines we believe and teach. She will organize, this week, in the Colfax Avenue Methodist Episcopal Church, a class which will meet each week for the study of the Scriptures and for seeking the deeper spiritual life. We hope, also, that at least three other weekly classes will soon be organized. Our ministers and laymen, who are interested in this work, will aid in every possible way to secure the largest results.

We expect, also, as soon as possible, to systematically organize a propaganda in as many churches of the city as will open their doors for our efforts. We are in receipt of a considerable number of invitations from outside cities and towns of Colorado, and from adjacent states to carry the glad tidings into the regions beyond. All this is most encouraging. The writer is of the opinion that no meetings have ever been held in Denver, the widespread results of which are so patent, as this recent series. While the meetings last year were great, those of this year have been intense and have succeeded in stirring not only the interest of a multitude of Christian professors, but have moved them to a surrender to God for Christian service which they never felt before.

Our meetings this year presented another testimony of large interest to the throngs which attended. We built a baptistry about 12 feet long, 6 feet wide and 4 feet deep. The water it contained was provided from the city waterworks and the necessary warmth provided from the great hot-water tanks of the auditorium. This baptistry was beautifully adorned on every side with plants and flowers. An arched canopy top was wound with beautiful red roses. A white dove hovered over the spot where the candidates were baptized.

Into this place, dressed in baptismal garments, the ladies being clad in white, the candidates descended and were buried with Christ into His death and raised into the blessed fulness of His resurrection life. It was all most beautiful and significant. Several hundred converts were thus inducted into Christian fellowship. This method of baptism was, on each occasion, fully explained by the evangelist. She, herself, with an assisting clergyman, performed the rite. A deep impression was made upon the people by this public confession of faith and surrender, in which Christ was obeyed and His name accepted before men.

The last Sunday of the meetings, June 25th, was a day in which the power of God was manifested in many and wondrous ways. At 10:30 o'clock several thousand people gathered to receive the Holy Communion. This was administered by sixty church stewards and deacons gathered from Denver churches. The elements were consecrated by the evangelist. The great organ played softly the dear old music of familiar sacramental hymns. Sometimes the choir would chant in low tones the story of Christ's sufferings and death and His coming again. We never saw so many people commune together before. The atmosphere was sweet with the fragrance of Heaven. One could feel the presence of God's guardian angels hovering about the heirs of salvation to whom God has made them ministering spirits. It was an occasion we shall talk about in Heaven some time in the future.

The afternoon sermon was given wholly over to evangelism. The preacher probably never declared the Gospel with greater power. The sermon occupied nearly two hours in its delivery, and the "slain of the Lord were many." The whole of the front central section of the building was used as a "Mourners' Bench." People knelt at the chairs and several hundred workers directed them to the "Lamb of God which taketh away the sins of the world." Never was there more convincing demonstration that the old Gospel has not lost its power than in that Sunday afternoon meeting. Many were converted and their future lives in Christ will be dated from that service. We thank God and take courage.

The Sunday evening and last service of the series witnessed the gathering of a great throng—too many for anybody to count during one meeting. Every part of the great building was alive with the expectant multitude. The mayor was present, and publicly expressed his belief, not only in the evangelist, but with thankfulness for the great good she had wrought among our people. Mrs. McPherson, in most happy rejoinder, returned her thanks and voiced her appreciation of the co-operative efforts of the city, the churches, the workers and press, which had resulted in the great success of her efforts in Denver. As she came on the platform, the whole front of the auditorium being decorated with summer flowers, from an opening above there fell upon her such a shower of beautiful, fragrant and many-colored petals as to inundate the floor ankle-deep all about her. It was impossible to still the applause of the people. Time after time the demonstrations over the forethought of the workers who had arranged this beautiful display broke forth, expressing their joy and happiness. The invitation of Mayor Bailey for the evangelist to return to Denver again next summer, given in words of hearty esteem for both herself and her works, was enthusiastically approved by the audience with many demonstrations of gladness. The people stood on their feet, waved their handkerchiefs and sang songs of hosannas and hallelujahs to the mighty Christ.

On the whole, to sum up briefly the results of the work accomplished during the last two weeks in this series of revival meetings: We believe that no work of any sort, ecclesiastical, political, commercial or social, has ever been effected in this city which has reached more people, accomplished greater or larger results, blessed more souls and given greater hope, both for this life and that which is to come, than the series just closed. Ten thousand people bade our evangelist farewell with a quiver in their hearts and the glisten of tears in their eyes, but in the hope that some day she will return again with messages to inspire and direct the souls of men beyond this vale of tears to the home eternal which is without sin, sickness or death.

THE DENVER REVIVAL AS SEEN BY EDWARD CHARLES FINTEL

Pastor First M. E. Church, Scottsbluff, Nebraska

EARLY on Monday morning, June 12th, we started overland with our little family toward the great auditorium at Denver, Colorado, which was to be the scene of another great revival campaign.

We motored for two days, and the nearer we came to Denver the deeper stirred the memories of the wonderful campaign of a year ago, when thousands were converted, the blind were made to see, the deaf to hear, the lame to walk and all manner of diseases were healed. We remembered the great throngs that pressed for entrance at each door for hours before the services began and our hearts were all aflutter with anticipation, hungry for the great hours of uplift and privilege of service.

When we arrived we found crowds of from five to fourteen thousand at each great afternoon and evening service. A great heavy burden for souls was upon the heart of the evangelist and all the workers. There was a consciousness of wonderful power and depth. We soon found ourselves under the burden and doing what we could to help carry the mighty load.

Never was the evangelist's message more deep and pungent with power. Every sermon seemed greater and stronger than the one before. The trials as by fire of the year had drawn her closer to the Christ and had seemed to enrich and deepen every fibre of her being. Mighty power was manifest in the great altar service of Tuesday evening, which was followed by prayer for the sick, when again the deaf were made to hear, the lame to walk and all manner of diseases were healed.

GREAT DEPTH AND SPIRITUALITY

Each successive meeting seemed greater than the one preceding. The throngs increased, the spirit deepened and the power was more manifest. Early Saturday morning the writer started homeward to take care of the Sunday services. Just as he was leaving the city, starting out on the 245-mile journey, he passed a Swiss gentleman who threw up his hand asking for a ride. His face was beaming with joy. Upon asking him what made him so happy, he said, "They prayed for me at the Civic Center last night; I was so deaf that I could not hear at all out of one ear, and they had to holler (holding up his hand to his ear), and they had to holler very loudly into my other ear, like this (keeping his hand to his ear), but now (taking his hand from his ear), I can hear perfectly." And all the way in our drive to Brighton, where he alighted to walk eastward to his farm, we conversed without difficulty amid the hum of the motor and wonderfully enjoyed the visit over the wonderful things he had seen and heard.

It was a wonderful joy to tell the people at home. In the great morning service the people voted unanimously the Pastor should tell them of the meetings instead of preaching the regular sermon in the morning. My heart was full and *The Spirit came upon me with mighty power* as I began to declare the wonderful works of God in the conversion of hundreds of souls and the healing of the sick. Seldom have I seen my congregation so moved and swayed by the mighty power, not by my own, but the Lord working through me until it seemed every one believed.

Early Thursday morning we started back to Denver with a mother whose daughter was already here, a blind man and a sister whose spine had been injured. In spite of the heat we drove the 245 miles, arriving in Denver at five o'clock, in time to get into the great service and hear the sermon on the Second Coming of Christ. How it thrilled us and lifted us! It seemed so much bigger and stronger than the one on the same great subject last year.

We could easily discern that the meetings in our absence had very perceptibly deepened. Instantly the power seemed to take hold of those whom we had brought with us.

CITY CLERGYMEN PRAY FOR SICK

The ministers of Denver held special services for the sick in Christ's Methodist Episcopal Church each morning. They thus relieved Sister McPherson of much of this burden of anointing and prayer for the afflicted, leaving her free for her great ministry of the Word. Upon going into this great service we were overjoyed to find that the Lord was answering the prayers of the ministers in behalf of the sick, as well as those of Sister McPherson.

It seemed to us that there was the sanction of the Spirit in the lifting of this load for the thousands of sick and lame and blind and deaf from the evangelist's heavily burdened shoulders.

In James 5:14-15, salvation and healing are still united. And in the apostle's instructions to the Church, and the tribes scattered abroad, we read: *"Is any sick among you? Let him call for the elders of the Church; and let them pray over him, anointing him with oil in the name of the Lord; and the prayer of faith shall save the sick, and the Lord shall raise him up; and* (note the connection) *if we have committed sins, they shall be forgiven him."*

Some of us felt exceedingly unworthy and very weak when called upon for this mighty service, but the Lord helped us and we were thrilled as our faith grew and we saw the manifestations of God's power. I was so thankful that after the revival of last year I had purchased all the books and had read the "Bridal Call" through and through as each number came from month to month, and that many of the Scriptures were fresh in the mind.

On Friday afternoon we hastened to the auditorium; we soon realized that the closing days of the great campaign were at hand. The announcement of another baptismal service and the service for the anointing of workers greatly interested us. In the meantime, the sister with the injured spine, who was not even a Christian before we started on our journey, had given her heart to the Lord, was wonderfully converted; had trusted the Lord for healing and had given her whole life to the service of the Lord. We had witnessed the first great baptismal service, but without any suggestion from us that this was her opportunity, she made the decision and desired to be buried with Christ in baptism. She was one of the 112 baptized in the great service, so beautiful and so sacred, on Saturday evening.

TREMENDOUS ALTAR CALLS

Almost every service was closed with the wonderful altar call. Unlike any other great evangelist I had ever seen, Sister McPherson depended absolutely upon the power of the Holy Spirit and prayer of believers to move upon the hearts of unbelievers as they came by hundreds and hundreds from all over the great auditorium. She did not depend upon any type of emotionalism, warnings of wrath or death-bed stories, nor does she permit personal workers to go out to implore folks to make a decision for Christ, but at the close of each of her wonderful messages she would simply say, "Let us pray."

ENTIRE ABSENCE OF EXCITEMENT

After prayer she would ask those who wanted to become Christians to raise their hands, first in one section then in the other. While she made this appeal in the simplest, tenderest possible way, standing in the place of Christ, pleading "Come," she would ask all the Christians to continue in the spirit of prayer. Then she would ask all who had raised their hands to stand to their feet and then come to the altar. Scores and hundreds would come, come almost running, tears streaming down their faces. As a pastor I have had them turn to me, after kneeling and praying with their face buried in their hands for a moment, and in a choking voice say, "Come and pray for me."

The genuineness and depth of these converts is proven in a story told me by Dr. Wright, pastor of the Second Congregational Church, Denver. Pointing to a sister sitting in the fourth row back in the workers' section, he said: "There is a sister who was converted in last June's meeting. She joined my church immediately after, and since then has brought in at least a dozen fine folks." He continued: "That lady sitting right by her side is one of the folks brought in through her personal work; she was an infidel, and now is a splendid worker."

THE WONDERFUL TESTIMONY MEETINGS

One of the things that thrilled us all was the wonderful testimonies given by the people who were converted or healed in the June meetings of a year ago. To hear these testimonies of wonderful conversion and marvelous healing and see in the closing part of the same meeting other wonderful conversions and healings convinced the most doubtful. We had the privilege of talking with those who had been healed, afterwards, and we simply could not doubt.

It seemed to us that one of the wonderful missions of this series of meetings was to establish the work already begun and to obliterate any possible doubt as to the work being absolutely of the Lord. There will need to be an invention of a new type of "fire extinguisher" if the fire of this revival is ever put out. We were so glad that our sister asked each one testifying to healing, in answer to prayer, to give his name and address, before they told the story of the work the Lord had done. Hundreds of the folks who gave their testimony were eager to tell of their experience and answer any question, and pledged to write letters in response to any inquiry. Truly the work was genuine.

THE WONDERFUL CONSECRATION SERVICE

Some were a bit afraid that there might be a tinge of fanatacism in this consecration service, but not so. All through the services we were conscious of the sweetest, sanest and deepest teachings of the Word of God in the full gospel. I have had charge of the life work services in great institutes of our own church, where hundreds have surrendered their lives in full life's service for the Master, but never was in a meeting which seemed to me so deep, so sane and so far reaching as this one. Scores and hundreds came forward with radiant faces, with tears of joy streaming down their cheeks; quietly, with thoughtfulness and with evidence of having won a great battle against selfishness to give themselves in whole life's service for the Master. Scores of young men came forward, many of whom will enter the ministry of the Gospel. Glory be to God for that wonderful service, for Pentecostal Power came down as of old, but was manifest in the deepest quiet and radiant faces, not the slightest tinge of fanatacism or excitement. It was as though He had said, "Be still and know that I am God." Each great body of young people, and then older and still older, until those who would give themselves as Sunday school teachers and personal workers had knelt at the altar, were blessed as they prayed, and the pastors and evangelist laid hands gently on their heads.

MAYOR INVITES RETURN

At the closing service a mighty crowd filled the great auditorium, and many were standing. Mr. Reynolds was as usual at his place at the great municipal organ. He played "Onward Christian Soldiers," and many other stirring hymns. The people were singing lifting songs of praises from thousands of voices. A great cheer arose when the evangelist came into this closing service, and she had no more reached her place than a great rose shower fell from the heights of the great municipal building, covering the floor ankle-deep with rose petals and flowers all around the pulpit. Then Mayor Bailey gave splendid words of appreciation. In response to his suggestion that we would like her to return next June, the crowd arose and applauded and cheered and waved handkerchiefs and uttered fervent Amens. There are many we would mention in connection with this service besides the ministers and pastors, who so faithfully did their full part in co-operation, but for Dean Peck and Mrs. Kennedy, the sweet little mother of the evangelist, we feel like giving thanks to the Lord from our hearts for their tireless, unassuming helpfulness. Soon the preliminary services were over and the closing message was being given. Thousands listened eagerly and hung on the words. In response to the invitation literally hundreds crowded to the altar. Estimating space and chairs, there must have been close to one thousand people kneeling in that last great altar service. Then, after the Benediction, many thousands pressed forward to shake Sister's hand, say a parting word and receive freely a copy of The Bridal Call. One would think the Evangelist tired enough now to drop in her tracks, but she was not too tired to pray for the sick and even after that, when she might have rushed to her apartment for rest, she came back with arms full of her flowers and divided them with the crowd that lingered. Shower upon shower of beautiful roses had been given her, and she wanted to share them.

Many prayers will follow her to her next great campaign in Oakland, California, and then across the seas to the five great campaigns to be held in Australia. Many of us have been lifted until we say within our hearts:

Higher than the highest heavens,
  Deeper than the deepest sea,
Lord, Thy love at last hath conquered
  Let me know my soul's desire
None for self and all to me.

A PRESBYTERIAN MINISTER WRITES

I DESIRE to state in reference to Aimee Semple McPherson, and her meetings in Denver, that, last year while she was here I attended all of her services for more than two weeks, and this year I have been present at every service for just two weeks. I have had the pleasure of being present during a whole campaign—or nearly so—with all of the leading evangelists of our day and time, commencing with Dwight L. Moody, Dr. Chapman, Dr. Campbell Morgan, Billy Sunday, Dr. Torrey, Gipsy Smith, Paul Rader, and many others of lesser note, sometimes traveling hundreds of miles for the purpose of getting into their meetings, hearing them preach, seeing how they caught their fish and how they strung them.

I only had to hear Mrs. McPherson preach a few times and to note the result of her ministrations—a year ago—in order to determine for myself that she is undoubtedly the greatest preacher-evangelist in the world of today—and I so stated at that time. And now, after listening to her again for two weeks and noting the great work that God Almighty enables this little woman to accomplish in the salvation of lost souls and in the healing of the sick in answer to prayer, I am most assuredly not in a position to retract. In her preaching she makes the first and the most important thing—the saving of the human soul; but I have witnessed many cases of healing in her meetings in answer to prayer and the laying on of her hands. I have seen goiters the size of my fist instantly disappear, the lame to walk, the deaf to hear, the blind to see, and the deaf and dumb both to hear and to speak, and many other remarkable cases of healing too numerous to mention in this brief letter.

She preaches the gospel of salvation by repentance, and faith in the Lord Jesus Christ to be followed by the baptism with the Holy Spirit, and she does it with power and in demonstration of the Spirit, with the simplicity of a child and without any flourishes or objectionable features, making the plan of salvation so plain that "a wayfaring man though a fool need not err therein," and yet she does it with an unction and a divine anointing and with a sweetness of spirit that enables her to bring to the altar in true repentance more men and women than any other soul winner of our day and time can do.

Is the hand of the Lord shortened in the days in which we are living, or, is He "the same yesterday, today and forever?" Is He "the great I Was," or is He "the great I Am," now and forever? These were questions among others propounded on the streets, in stores, in the homes and parks of Denver during the McPherson meetings, held in the Municipal Auditorium with its 14,000 seating capacity.

Those of us who were there were convinced that the *Lord's* hand is not shortened, that he cannot redeem, and that "Jesus Christ is the same yesterday, today and forever."

I attended the McPherson meeting in this city last year and again this year, and the marvelous things my eyes beheld in the wonder-working power of God is more than tongue can tell or pen describe; the inconceivable happened. Denver has been shaken until thousands appear to be in a haze of wonderment. I have seen hundreds come to the altar for prayer and salvation and leave bearing testimony that they were saved; I have seen hundreds anointed for healing, and my eyes have seen goiter melt away as the snow before the sun. I have seen the deaf ears unstopped so they could hear, the dumb anointed and thep did speak, eyesight restored, and they bore testimony to their being saved, healed and blessed.

Hundreds of godless homes have been made happy and invited the Savior in. Hundreds of professed Christians admitted their backsliding, returned to their Lord and Savior and buckled on the whole armor of God, with open confession; hundreds of indifferent flocked to the altar for prayer, while the scoffer was seen to kneel in agonizing prayer pleading for complete redemption.

So great was the power of God upon the meetings and so numerous the requests for salvation and healing of soul and body, that twelve ministers banded themselves together to assist that little woman, Mrs. McPherson, by holding forenoon meetings in Christ's Church, where large numbers were saved and healed. I assisted in the services by prayer and anointing, and I bear testimony that never before in my twenty-four years of ministry as pastor have I seen the like, tears flowing from the penitent and the suffering ones in such a flow that it bathed the hands of the minister praying with them.

Is she a second Billy Sunday, as some have asked? No; no; there can be no comparison; it is an entirely different message that this little woman in white preaches. She is an evangelist called with a message for this particular time; she is a voice crying in the cities everywhere she goes, "Repent for the Kingdom of God is at hand."

She is one of God's specially anointed in the midst of a sinful population, spreading the doctrine of the Great I AM, and a fourfold gospel, with a power that gladdens human hearts and transfigures souls.

E. L. KRUMREIG.

DR. ADDISON BLANCHARD, DENVER'S OLDEST, MOST HONORED MINISTER WRITES

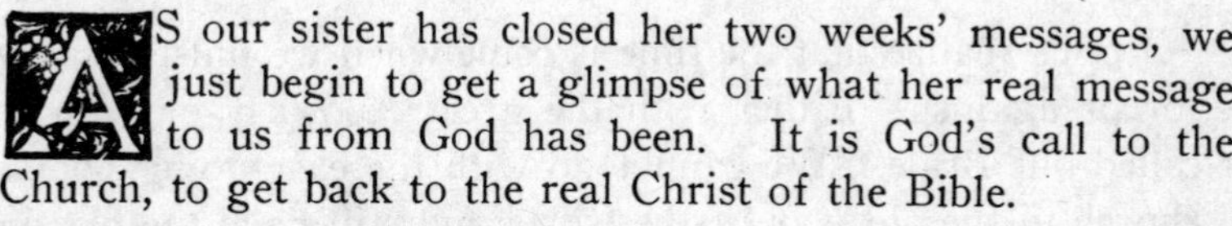

AS our sister has closed her two weeks' messages, we just begin to get a glimpse of what her real message to us from God has been. It is God's call to the Church, to get back to the real Christ of the Bible.

God is summoning His followers to the ministry, and the power He conferred on them as He left them for the Father's right hand, is falling today. That one great message of hers, "LOST AND RESTORED," contains the substance of her entire teaching. It is not for a little reviving, that a few souls may be gathered into our Church fellowship, as it is and has been. It is not only for the joyous singing of a few hymns, with a little more fervor than formerly, and a new consecration along old lines. . . . Oh this and far more!

It is a call to get back to the promises that have always been ours—always for the Church, but not understood or entered into. Jesus Christ the same, yesterday, today, forever. He is coming soon! But before he comes, he shall have a bride that shall know, and be ready to die for Him, as the early Church did—a Church with all the gifts and graces—ready to follow Him to the cross—to be taken out of the world, because not of the world.

Are we coming to the great Apostacy? Yes! But also to a great restoration of the devotion of the early church, ready for service unto death; ready for persecution and martyrdom if need be. We see it already in the world. The Clarion Call is on us. She comes to the SLEEPING BRIDE of our day with an unmistakable message. Why has it taken us so long to appreciate what she was driving at? Why? but that it was so tremendous we could not begin to comprehend it. The events that are soon to unroll in our world and perhaps in our own land will be the best commentary on her words. We are still asleep. When you wake up children they are sometimes cross. Let it seem strange to us that the sleeping Church wakes up at first very, very cross—with all sorts of objections and criticisms and oppositions—unwilling to recognize the facts in the case and to accept the message as God would have us.

Let us realize that the time is come when we must be either for or against. Either with the great Apostasy or with the called out Bride. We cannot go with the easy-going popular church in the old way of the world and still have the blessing of the Spirit of God. God is calling for heroes who will take up the "Faith of our Fathers" and their cross of sacrifice and service. "If we suffer with Him we shall reign with Him." "If we deny Him, He also will deny us."

Let us not think that by refusing Mrs. McPherson's message we have ended the matter. The clarion call is to be sounded out by many voices as the time goes on. Shall we be apostate with the rest of the sleeping Church?

We stand where we must give answer to God.

DR. ADDISON BLANCHARD,
Pastor Emeritus 2nd Cong. Church, Denver.

FAREWELL SPEECH BY MAYOR BAILEY, DENVER, COLO.

I HAVE stood on many platforms before tonight, but never in rose leaves up to my ankles before. (Applause.) Of course, these were not showered for me, but for Mrs. McPherson, who has put in two weeks of such successful meetings in this city. We hate to see her go, you will all agree with me on that. She has done a world of good in this city. I know from the way people talk to me that the city is better, and I am sure would continue to be better if she stayed among us. (Applause.)

But Mrs. McPherson has to move on doing good wherever she goes. Many places she has to visit to carry on the great work that she has started. I am sure that all of you people that have heard her, not only this year, but a year ago, are her steadfast friends. You believe in her, and *so do I.* (Applause.)

I was here with my dear wife a year ago, when she was closing her campaign, and I was here the night that she opened these meetings. People tell me who come to my office and meet me on the street that they heard Mrs. McPherson preach when she was here before and this time; and, speaking of the first meeting, they say they have felt better this whole year because they came and heard her and believe in her. (Applause.)

Now, ladies and gentlemen, I know you all agree with me on this, and that I may be the spokesman of the people here in Denver, and thousands who are not here tonight, in requesting Mrs. McPherson to return a year from now. (Applause.)

Mrs. McPherson, with this wonderful demonstration that you see before you and hear, a great majority of the citizens of Denver wish you Godspeed to your home, and a pleasant trip, and we ask you, for the good work that you are carrying on and the good work you are doing in this great city, that you return hêre the first of next June and carry on another meeting as you have done this year. (Prolonged applause.)

This seems to be unanimous, and thousands and thousands of people that are not able to be here tonight would show as much enthusiasm in Mrs. McPherson's coming back again to carry on her good work as you have done. I thank you.

ADDRESS OF JUDGE BEN LINDSEY OF THE JUVENILE COURT, DENVER

MRS. McPHERSON, and My Friends: I feel greatly honored at this opportunity of just a minute or two to add my testimony to that of the Mayor in the way of appreciation for what Mrs. McPherson's meetings have meant to this city. I have to deal with sinners, mostly young sinners, but I also deal with all kinds of sinners. I want to tell you of a sample of her work.

I came to the meeting the other night and met some of my old friends among the crooks, one of the most notorious burglars in the country, and I was particularly astounded to meet this particular gentleman, because I thought he was about the meanest crook I had ever met. I helped him out of some trouble one time, and he robbed $5.00 from me. But he got religion down here and told me he was doing fine, was back on his job, and from the evidences that he gave me I was satisfied that he was thoroughly redeemed. . . .

Mrs. McPherson has found her way to the hospitals of this town, the jails, the sick and afflicted, the homes of the poor. She has also found her way into the heart of every man, woman and child in Denver. She has found a way into our hearts and leaves behind more converts, and in my judgment, has done more good than any other person in the country.

UNDER THE BIG TOP IN THE HEART OF THE BAY CITIES

(From The Bridal Call, July, 1922)

COME reader-o'-mine—put on your traveling cloak of faith; don your happiest revival spirit; close the door of immediate cares and surroundings softly behind you; settle yourself firmly upon this printed page; hold tightly with both hands and sail away through this midsummer day, on the widespread pinions of "The Bridal Call" to the last, great Evangelistic Campaign the Editor will be privileged to hold on the American Continent this year.

On the wings of the July-August, double issue you were carried from Rochester, N. Y., to Denver, Colorado. We now, however, in a straight course, sail due West to the sun-kist shores of the Pacific Coast.

The snow-capped peaks of Colorado ranges fade, and far below us lies the desert's arid waste. The cactus and the sage-brush spin dizzily past as we journey. The Salt Lake glimmers like an amethyst, in a setting of gold and silver sands. A buzzard soars o'er our heads and a prairie dog scampers for his underground home as we glide. The Coast Range appears, is crossed; suddenly a salt breeze blowing fresh from the sea kisses the memory of burning desert heat from our faces. A sea gull sweeps very close, calling to his mate in a voice echoing the wildness of the sea itself. And there, rolling in with a thousand foam-crest billows, sweeps the Sunset Sea to kiss the foot-hills and the beaches of the great Pacific Coast.

Yonder lies the city of San Francisco, with its clang and roar and multi-lighted Market Street. Just this side, its waters flowing through the Golden Gate, lies the bay some six miles of whose deep waters, constantly churned and plowed by noisy steamers, ferries and freight boats, lies between San Francisco and the bay cities. And now, just beneath us, spread out in a great panorama lies Oakland, called the bed-room of San Francisco; Berkeley with its colleges and universities and wealth, and Alameda with its beautiful homes and brilliant populace. And here—just in the throbbing heart of it all—rising, falling, the billowing expanse of canvas of "The Big Top" in the arms of a gentle breeze. The last preparations are being made for the long prayed for Revival. Deft fingers of the decoration committee have placed the last flower and flag in place; but, sailing on past the tent pass over a busy scene at a railway depot, we find ourselves among the spectators of a great enthusiastic throng that are waiting at the station platform.

THE RECEPTION

What a peculiar gathering! How bright and expectant their faces. All are looking in one direction, searching the distant bend of the railway tracks. An orchestra of silver and stringed instruments are pressing to the front. Newspaper photographers and movie-men are setting up their cameras at various points of vantage above the heads of the singing, happy crowd.

In bewilderment one might well ask: What meaneth this? What manner of reception is this, and whom are they to welcome? Can it be that they are here to welcome some victorious baseball team, a theatrical troupe, the Shriners? Any of these might be frequently welcomed by throngs at the depot without rousing comment. But there is surely something different here, for as they wait the whole multitude take up as with one voice the refrain, scattering it on the winds abroad:

"Revive us again,
Fill each heart with Thy love,
May each soul be rekindled,
With fire from above."

Dr. Knox springs to a baggage truck to lead the chorus. The orchestra catch it up, and carry it on and out till it collides mid-air with the shriek of the engine which now flashes into view, puffs noisily down the track and comes to a halt, with a grind of air brakes on its burnished ribbons of steel.

Every face is lighted now. Swift feet are running down the platform. Silver instruments of the musicians are glinting in the sunlight. But if these are here to meet some worldy amusement bringers, why are they singing:

"Give me the old time religion,
Give me the old time religion,
Give me the OLD TIME religion
For it's good enough for me!"

One expects the world to grow enthusiastic over their own but it is possible that Christians can grow as enthusiastic over Christ and a revival as does the world over a ball-team? Alighting from the incoming train is a surprised and delighted Evangelist and her little Mother. One moment they stand alone, looking rather dazedly at the throng, and the next are swallowed up in the midst of it. Music, singing, large bouquets presented by the laymen's committees, a speech by the local clergyman who has come to tender the official welcome to Oakland, exuberant cheering of the children of the Lord, a return speech of appreciation and thanks from ourselves after we have been boosted to a handy baggage truck, the click of cameras, and an amused wonder as to what the movie man would do with the picture of Evangelists who preach against their business, gets all tangled up together here, and in a moment more we are running the gauntlet through hundreds of outstretched hands that line our way to the car.

"God bless them. God bless them!" We find ourselves weeping, "Oh, Jesus, look down upon the warm, enthusiasm of these dear hearts. They have waited so long for this revival. They have worked and labored and given for months—oh, God grant that they may see the travail of their souls answered in the salvation of thousands of men and women, and be satisfied."

In a moment, without any confusion, a long parade is formed. Our car and that containing the chairman of committee Dr. Sherman, M. D., of Oakland, have been beautifully draped in green and white by the campaign decoration committee, symbolic of fragrant green pastures and of purity. A large truck, containing the band and chorus carrying banners, is in the lead, and streams of automobiles, reaching several blocks and carrying banners announcing the Tent Meeting, bring up the rear, and escort us through the business section to our quarters in the Oakland Hotel.

THE OPENING NIGHT

And now it is Saturday night. Instead of having to work

up an interest and pray down a revival spirit, the praying has been done in advance. A committee meeting, begun many months previous to the opening of the campaign, had six persons in attendance, the last committee meeting found six hundred ready to serve in any capacity great or small. Usually we have had to raise all the moneys for expenses out of campaign, but here about three thousand dollars had been pledged and given and expended to cover one-half of the expenses. The tent was well filled on the first night and the power of God streaming down. O, reader, does it not thrill your very soul and make the heart of you sing for joy to see in every city from coast to coast the same wonderful manifestation—altars filled to overflowing the very first meeting?

How they troop to the altar this opening night, scores and scores of them seeking Salvation and restoration, after the preaching of the sermon from the text: "They have taken away my Lord," (a portion of which is given in this issue). Young and old, rich and poor kneel together, seeking the Christ who saves and keeps.

The Sunday meetings find the tent-tabernacle filled to capacity and multitudes standing. The great Chorus are in place, hundreds of trained voices carried by a grand piano, and a large orchestra can be heard for two blocks, we are told. An enthusiastic, responsive, sympathetic audience catches up the refrain, till the canvas seems to lift with the power and glory of it. Many are wiping their eyes, many hands are raised, all are singing and entering into the spirit of the meeting. One realizes in a moment that one is among staunch, loyal, proven friends. No need to beat down prejudice, win respect, then confidence, then hearts here. Confidence is already won and full sympathy assured, for this is our sixth campaign in Northern California alone in less than one year—intensive work that cannot help but make this the most wonderful meeting to crown them all.

And thus indeed it proves to be. Not one heart-ache or moment's anxiety. All has been arranged and carried out by hundreds of warm friends from all over California and many from other states. Meeting after meeting the saints weep and sing and shout and rejoice as the message of the "Four-Square" Gospel goes forth and hundreds daily troop to the altars, seeking and finding Jesus as their only Savior. The inspiration of that mighty tent-tabernacle with its vast sea of upturned faces can hardly be described. Thousands stand at times about the tent unable to gain admission. Special police were requested to come, but after standing idle for several hours, went away again, reporting that though some ten thousand people at times were on the ground not one officer was needed as this was the quietest and most perfectly behaved throng they had ever handled.

Throughout the press of the entire two weeks and three Sundays no officer is required, except to handle the auto traffic, which at times lines the streets from shortly after daybreak till after midnight in every direction.

From three to five meetings are held daily. Three altar calls each day in the tabernacle the first week saw, without exception, the seven long altar benches crowded with sinners seeking Salvation. Scores who have passed the ages of seventy and eighty find the Lord, declaring that this is the first time in all their lives they have opened the door to let the Master in. Hundreds of splendid young men and women, talented business folk, also kneel at the nail-pierced feet of Jesus, accepting the Lord and pledging their lives to His service at home or abroad.

At times the glory and power of God so sweeps the tent, during the preaching of the Word, that men and women sit on the very edge of the benches, clinging to the seats with their hands, trying to sit still till altar call comes, then, finding it impossible to resist the appeal a moment longer, start for the front. One afternoon, startled at seeing men and women rising in various parts of the tent and pressing past all others to get to the aisle, we pause in amazement, and say to this heretofore well-behaved audience: "Please let no one leave while we are speaking." But see the lines turn, not toward the rear, but toward the front of the tabernacle as they speak out and say:

"We are not going out, Sister, we are coming to the altar. We can't stand it another minute. O, Jesus, save me, save me now." Hallelujah! Multitudes in the valley of decision. Multitudes coming to the Lord in genuine and sincere repentance every service. Oh it is a glorious sight to make the angels of Heaven shout for joy.

OLD FOLKS AND CHILDREN'S MEETINGS

Special meetings are held both for the old and young. Each Friday afternoon we enter the tent and mount the platform to look out over the vast sea of silver heads. The oldest dozen, over eighty and ninety, one being ninety-nine years of age, are called to the platform.

Only favorite hymns, sung sixty and seventy years ago, are selected by the old folk. Many a time the requested selection is totally unknown to the young. Then it is that the old folk enter most into the spirit of the song, and their sweet, quivery voices swell the chorus "way over Jordan," in such sweet words and music that we of the younger generation wonder why such songs were ever allowed to die. The testimonies and songs of these old folk are most marvelous and bring tears to all. One old lady over eighty years of age, straight and slim as a girl, sings a solo of the olden days in a sweet voice many a younger sister soloist might envy.

Then comes the altar call for the aged folk, immediately following the sermon and the number of men and women seeking Christ for the first time who have passed their sixtieth year is amazing beyond words. Testaments are brought out of the offerings and given freely to the thousands one meets in the course of a two and three-week campaign who have never heretofore owned or read a Bible.

And then great baskets of roses, carnations, sweet peas, etc., which have been made up into beautiful corsages by loving fingers that have stripped many a garden, are presented to the aged as a little tribute from the younger generation. The tent is cleared and another throng is pouring in for the nightly Evangelistic meeting.

Again—it is Children's service. The streets for blocks in every direction are dotted with little children and their parents dressed in spotless white, coming to sing and testify to the sick and needy children. Children from the orphanages, and charitable institutions, children from homes of wealth and refinement, all pouring into the tent till the audience in front of the platform is packed, and the choir loft just back of the platform is overflowing with children in white, who are to sing. The orchestra is composed of child musicians, the solos and quartets are rendered by children. The Chinese and the Japanese Sunday School children mount the platform and sing, eclipsing the music of the older folk, if that were possible.

Then comes the sermon direct to children, little faces are lifted to us as we speak, sweet as dewy rosebuds, drinking in our every word. How they love and trust us! "O, Lord Jesus," we breathe, "Thou who lovest the little children and bidst them come unto Thee, help us to gather these little lambs into the fold, direct their little feet into Thy paths in the days of their youth. O how glorious it would be, if instead of waiting till these little ones are hardened sinners, and then making great, heroic efforts to bring them to Thee, we could mould by Thy power these little lives just now, that they never go astray, far down the darkened paths of sin and sorrow."

And now the message, which has held the breathless attention of the children every moment, is concluded and the altar call is given for those little boys and girls who have not been attending Sunday School, and for those who have never yet learned to pray and give their hearts to Christ. Suddenly the aisles are filled with children, hundreds and hundreds of them. Some of them have tear drops like sparkling diamonds on their cheeks; kneeling at the altars, boys on one side of the platform, girls on the other, they clasp their precious little hands, close their eyes and begin to pray.

O those blessed little fragments of broken prayer! How they clutch at our heartstrings and cause us to yearn as a mother over them all!

"O, Jesus, please forgive me my sins. Let me be naughty and cross to Mamma no longer. Jesus me don't want to be bad, me wants to be dood, like you. Make my heart clean in the precious blood." Hallelujah! Scores of the little folk from six to fourteen and fifteen years of age seemed to get a most wonderful witness that they were children of the Lord and that Jesus had come into their hearts to abide.

"Now will every little boy and girl who has never seen a Bible in his or her home to your recollection, and who never remembers having seen his or her mamma read a Bible, and would like to take one home to their parents and ask them to read it to each other and to you, please stand up." Scores of children from eight to sixteen rise and are all supplied with the Word of God freely to take to their several homes. As we cast the Bread of Life upon the water we pray that it may return after many days.

Great baskets, that it requires a strong man to carry are lifted one by one to the platform, filled to the brim (by stores, and individuals interested in children) with dolls, wagons, drums, horns, Bible story books, clothing for poor children, gifts for orphanage and charity sections, etc.

INTERDENOMINATIONAL CONFERENCE

During the last week of the campaign a ministerial conference was held wherein the "Four-Square Gospel Association" was organized for the purpose of banding together ministers and laymen of various Evangelical churches in fellowship and co-operation to further the cause of Evangelism throughout the land.

How we wish you could visualize these scenes! The conference sessions are held in the Trinity Episcopal Church. Seventy-five denominational ministers and evangelists present at roll call the first day, grow each session. Songs, prayer, and addresses upon the following subjects are brought before the session by Congregational, Baptist and other speakers filled with the Holy Ghost: "The Ministry of the Word"; "The Ministry of the Spirit"; "The Ministry of Healing." Special emphasis being laid upon the incoming gifts, fruits, and objective of the Holy Spirit. Then questions, and problems are discussed, and the whole assemblage fall upon their knees—an Episcopal Rector is weeping and praying with soul stirring earnestness—a Presbyterian Pastor catches up the petition where the other leaves it, and prays like an old-time Methodist that unbelief, higher criticism, wordliness and pride may be swept from all of the churches of the land, and the old-time power of the Holy Spirit falls as it did on the day of Pentecost. First one and then another call upon the Lord, and wind up by announcing a Preacher's prayer meeting call in the Christian and Missionary Alliance Church for the purpose of praying for the baptism of the Holy Spirit at eight o'clock in the morning.

The final session of the conference finds the evangelist in the question box, ready to answer to the best of her ability with the help of the Holy Spirit, the questions upon healing and the Baptism of the Spirit asked in the open forum. The Glory of the Lord seemed to settle down in such a vivid and realistic manner, as the sun came streaming through the stained glass windows, that all were conscious of the Master's presence. Question after question came in the most kindly spirit from hungry and seeking men of God, and the Lord graciously assisted in the answers of the same, till scriptures opened up and were expounded as to the necessity for and the manner of the coming of the Spirit, till not a question remains in the minds or upon the lips of any present. Tears are in the eyes of clergy and laymen, as all expressed their desire for an outpouring of the Holy Spirit, even as received in Apostolic days.

Over one thousand names were signed to the statement of doctrine and purpose contained in the Four-Square Gospel the first day by those pledging themselves to its cause in their various churches.

ENTHUSIASM AND KINDLINESS UNBOUNDED

Never during our fourteen years of ministry from Coast to Coast have we ever met a more kindly, enthusiastic people. Never have we been treated with more consideration, confidence and tender solicitation. Just as a sample of the splendid things done by the Oakland people, the Stephens Agency loaned to us for the entire campaign a new "chummy" roadster, finished in black and tan. The Excelsior Laundry insisted upon doing our laundry freely. The churches opened their doors for special prayer meetings, many ministers closed all evening services during the campaign that they and their people might attend the meeting and pray with seekers at the altars, ready to jump in at a moment's notice to sing or pray or speak. The newspapers, specially the Oakland Tribune, contained daily columns and photographs from beginning to end of the meeting, every word being constructive, loyal to the cause of Christ, and written by a staff reporter. The Tribune Radio called us to speak by wireless to listening thousands. The Ku Klux Klan carried us away by auto to their secret meeting, marching the Evangelist, Dr. Towner, and Tribune reporter through long double formations of white-robed men to a platform, there bidding us preach a sermon of salvation to the Klansmen, following which they presented us with a hundred dollar bill for four chairs in the Angelus Temple at Echo Park. The women of Alameda County started a window fund, and pledged to raise $1500.00 for a beautiful stained glass window. The California Bridal Call readers present opened a fund in which all were invited to take part, to place a window, depicting the scene in the Garden of Gethsemane, donating same in memory of Robert Semple, who gave his life for the sake of the gospel in China. Only a little marker has been placed on his grave. What a blessed memorial this window is, for if ever there was a man of intercession and prayer, who knew Gethsemanes, 'twas he.

THE CLOSING SUNDAY

What a triumphant, victorious closing day is this last Sunday! From early morning till almost midnight the streets are blocked with automobiles in every direction. Thousands of men and women are pouring in from parts all over the country. Songs, prayer, praise, preaching, the weeping of sinners at the altar, the joy of born again souls, the strains of the Salvation Army Brass Band, and the sweet song of the uniformed "hallelujah lassies," who have come to render their music and love, the volume of a mighty choir, the testimonies of scores of witnesses, and the cheering of responsive audiences, can be heard throughout the day. Communion is served to 3000 saints in the morning hour of worship, and then at the two great services afternoon and evening, wherein in the neighborhood of 10,000 are on the grounds, the altars are constantly filling and emptying with those seeking and finding Christ Jesus as their Saviour.

THE HEAVY TRUNK

Before the close of the night service, there came to the platform two stalwart men who seemed to be having great difficulty to lift a new steamer trunk which they carried. Lifting, tugging, puffing, what can make it so heavy, we wonder. At last with a thump it is laid upon the platform and a very pretty speech made by the representative of the chorus who are presenting the trunk as a love gift for our voyage.

"It is not the weight of the trunk that burdens us down, Sister," he declares; "the trunk itself is light, but into it has been squeezed and crammed so much love and prayer that two strong men can scarcely carry it all."

WATER BAPTISMAL SERVICE

Though the campaign closed on Sunday night, a mighty water baptismal service is held on Monday at 1 P. M. in beautiful Idora Park, where the large outdoor swimming pool has been specially prepared and loaned by the management. Idora Park is filled with many amusements, but these and the music attending the same are stilled during the service. Many thousands of people assembled about the edge of the great pool greet our eye as we enter. Special music has been secured by the management of the park and sacred hymns are rendered through the world's greatest magnavox, easily leading the singing of thousands.

Climbing a ladder, thus mounting to a high platform, easily seen by all, we bring a simple, direct message, descriptive of the symbol, water baptism, and bid those who have not yet made Jesus Christ their Saviour make this the day of decision, and now they are singing again. Scores of men and women are stepping into the waters of baptism. Five clergymen, Baptist, Methodist, United Brethren, Christian and Missionary Alliance and Congregational, are immersing the candidates.

Dressed in spotless white, many young women kneel upon the edge of the pool, lifting their hands to the open heavens, dedicating their lives for service at home or abroad, as hands are laid upon them, imploring God's blessing upon their lives ere they rise, and with clasped hands and lifted faces, step down into the sparkling waters. Baptizing five candidates at one time, as rapidly as they can be handled, the entire service lasts two hours. The glory in the faces of the people is a never-to-be-forgotten scene.

And now the meeting is being brought to a close, thousands of handkerchiefs are waving in the sunlight, and mirrored in the placid waters beneath, as the throng takes up and makes the heavens echo with the song:

"Yes, we'll gather at the river,
The beautiful, the beautiful river,
Gather with the saints at the river,
That flows from the throne of God."

And now it is over; that great heart-trobbing, filled to the brim, two weeks of whirlwind evangel has come and gone, but the revival is going on. Churches and missions everywhere are putting on special prayer services, that their people may be filled with the Spirit, pastors announcing hours of prayer for the sick, converts uniting with the churches and missions of their choice. We have come to the closing hours, and can truthfully say, as we look back over one of the most successful campaigns of our ministry,—one which has not caused us a moment's anxiety, a tear or a sleepless hour,—that our friends have been more loyal, the presence and power of God more manifest, the depth and spirituality of the meeting more profound than ever before, and are memories of the most happy and blessed one great experience this side of heaven.

SALVATION ARMY OFFICER'S REPORT

By Mrs. Staff Captain C. E. Baynton, Oakland, Calif.

HOW can such a meeting be described with cold type? What can I say to convey to you, dear reader, something of the victories won? The more I think of it the more impossible the task. I can only think of one word which in any way describes what we who were present experienced. Wonderful! O it was wonderful! What a glorious manifestation of the presence of God among men. How the Holy Spirit filled the great tent, moving the vast audiences and causing hundreds to seek Christ as their personal Saviour in every service. Hallelujah! How our hearts were filled with praise and our eyes were dimmed by tears as we found ourselves present at and witnessing one of the most wonderfully successful revivals of old-time religion that has swept the Pacific Coast for many years. There was no excitement, no death-bed stories to excite emotion or play on the imagination. Just the old, old story of Jesus and His love—Jesus Christ the same yesterday, today and forever—told by dear Sister McPherson in a sweet. humble, forceful manner. As we listen we are sure she lives in close vital conscious contact with the Master each day and therefore is able to present the scriptures with true interpretation and as a result thousands are being saved.

In addition to the great number who were saved there were many who received the baptism of the Holy Ghost and others again who were healed. The lame discarded their crutches and walked. Praise God for the old-time Gospel and for Sister McPherson's meeting in Oakland.

As I write my mind travels. It journeys away to Eastern Canada. To a little farm near Ingersoll, Ontario. I see it all so clear now. In fancy I am again in the little home, so clean and sweet and pure, pervaded with such a beautiful atmosphere. I remember listening to the story of an earnest little woman; she is on her knees before an open Bible making a request of her God, and at the same time entering into a contract with him. "If thou wilt O God," she is saying. "If thou wilt . . . she shall be dedicated to you." God heard and answered that prayer; dear Mrs. Kennedy has kept her part of the contract. Aimee was given to God and trained for His work, and out of that little woman's consecration over thirty years ago on a Canadian farm has come all these glorious McPherson revival campaigns throughout the United States and which are now to reach out to other countries. To God be all the glory.

REPORT BY DR. WILLIAM KEENEY TOWNER

FIRST BAPTIST CHURCH, SAN JOSE

SO many wonderful events featured the sixteen days of "wonder love and praise" in Oakland that it is difficult to select a starting point for our narration. The most significant feature was the throngs of hungry church members that hung with breathless attention on the delivery of the "glorious gospel of the blessed God."

How intent and earnest the sea of expectant faces that met the Evangelist day after day, to drink in the "rivers of living waters" that flowed straight from the "Fountain of grace rich full and free." They came in thousands, overflowing the great "tent of meeting" and standing in silent awe and wonder outside the tent for hours. So hungry and thirsty were the little sheep that they seemed fairly to crowd the sinners and prodigals away from the feeding troughs. And what a feast they had! What fat things from the Father's lees and what rich new wine! Hallelujah! East Bay saints certainly recognized the verdant pastures of tender grass and the sweet still waters of peace. No such crowds were ever assembled before in these regions. The Tribune estimated the closing audience at twenty-five thousand, and at least eighty per cent of them were spiritual starvelings out for a wholesome supper at the King's table. Never again will the sour ensilage from the silo of liberalism, or the chaff from the orthodox separator satisfy them. They have learned that springs of joy are gushing and rivers of peace are flowing bank full; that father's house is not a land of famine, but a house of bread where the hungry soul may "eat that which is good and delight itself in fatness."

The orderliness of the vast crowds was remarkable. Not a policeman was necessary, not a ripple disturbed the serene and reverent atmosphere of real spiritual worship. The corps of ushers handled the congregations with great skill and tact. It was an easy task. They were there to hear the four square gospel, to understand and receive it and they sat or stood in quiet expectance as the spirit filled messenger "preached the word."

The gypsy tribes, with their picturesque garments, their olive complexion, raven hair and sparkling eyes lent a tinge of oriental charm to the picture. Who will ever forget the eager, generous response of their warm and unspoiled hearts to the call of Christ. From Boston, Mass., Rochester, N. Y., from Honolulu and from almost everywhere under the sun these children of the open sky and the King's highway motored to the meetings prepared to hear with their ears, to understand with their hearts and to be saved and healed.

The children's meeting was a marvel of beauty, grace and power. Fully twenty-five hundred children were in the attendance. The children's choir, the soloist from among the little folks, the rapt attention and ready response was a revelation of what can be done with a simple gospel message presented with naive directness and spiritual power to the child mind and heart. What a rebuke to the modern theory that gymnastics, basketry, fancy-work, folk-dances and other fol-de-rol are necessary to win an audience for the word of God.

When the altar call was given they flowed out of the choir gallery and the auditorium into the aisles and up to the altar where they yielded their lives to Jesus. Who can compute the immeasurable results of such an experience on these hundreds of lives surrendered and sealed in a real experience of grace during these morning glory hours of life's sunrise.

Perhaps the most marvelous experience was the altar call in Chinatown, given at midnight on Saturday preceding the close of the meeting. Nearly, if not quite fifty of these "children of the sun" came out from their associates and knelt with humble courage at the altar. More than half of them were staunch young men, men of superior intelligence from high school, college and business life. Splendid young women were there too giving their lives to the service of Christ.

Sunday, July thirtieth is a memorable day. The great communion message on "A Lamb for a House" prepared our hearts to receive the elements of the Holy Supper with a depth of truth and reality, hitherto lacking in many of us. Sister McPherson presided in person and was assisted by ministers and deacons from all denominations. It was a rich and wonderful experience for all. Scarcely an eye was dry, but the tears were expressed from souls too deeply moved by adoration for our blessed Lord Jesus, and by a communion of heart as brothers bound with ties of blood for any other utterance than the silent tribute of tears. The communion was served to fully three thousand people with a divine orderliness in just fifteen minutes.

The concluding services on Sunday afternoon and evening are beyond description. As the great audience stood in silence while the cadence from the chorus—"Sweep over my spirit forever I pray, In fathomless billows of love" swelled and echoed and vanished out over the sleeping city enveloping its spacious avenues and rolling hills in a wraith of melody and worship, it seemed to us that the one momentary heart throb of that great audience was worth all the faith, sacrifice and effort put into the Campaign. These cities of the East shore of San Francisco Bay—destined, if Jesus tarries, to be the metropolis of the world some day, will never be the same again.

A Presence has been felt walking in majesty and power, in understanding and in love among them and the radiance of that Presence will dispel the mists of unbelief and banish the chill of doubt until the glory of the Lord shall shine round them and the "knowledge of the glory of God shall cover them as the waters cover the sea."

The Conference of pastors and workers that assembled on Tuesday, Wednesday and Thursday morning of July 25, 26 and 27 was marked by a spirit of unity and power.

The addresses of various spirit-filled ministers, on Wednesday morning and Mrs. McPherson's masterful and convincing exposition of the fourteenth chapter of First Corinthians on Thursday morning contributed largely to the delightful season of fellowship in the deeper truths of the gospel. Out of the Conference grew a new banding together of the laity and clergy in America who hold and practice the four-square gospel. The new fellowship is to be known as "The Four-Square Gospel Association." Already many hundreds of pastors, evangelists, teachers and prominent members of the recognized evangelical churches have enrolled and many thousands in all the churches stand ready to enroll as fast as the new project is presented to them by returning delegates and visitors.

Altogether the short campaign in Oakland will compass the most far reaching results in quickening the faith of the churches, arousing them to their task and to the power present and available for its achievement. The great congregations have dispersed, the radiant messenger has departd for the Antipodes, the ringing "hallelujahs," "glory to Jesus," and the mighty swelling chorus of praise from ten thousand throats are silent, the great "Tent of Meeting" has disappeared but the spirit of power newly generated in souls that were born again, and revived in hearts that had grown chilled and seared will spread and greaten—carrying salvation and healing everywhere until He shall come whose right it is to reign.

EPISCOPAL RECTOR'S COMMENT

Rev. Augustas Martyr, St. Clements Episcopal Church, Berkeley.

THE reflections of one who went to the McPherson Revival in Oakland with an open mind, determined, at least, to be sympathetic, may well be revealed in what I experienced in the participation of the meetings.

Having heard that God was using His Servant, Mrs. Aimee Semple McPherson, in a wonderful manner as a winner of souls and as a channel by which He might bring the healing touch of Jesus to those who were afflicted in body and mind, I determined to go and see for myself.

As a result, I am convinced what I saw was this: a humble servant of God presenting the simple Gospel of Christ to a multitude of men, women and children, assembled as we might picture the hungering crowds seeking truth in the days of the Master and His disciples.

I beheld the power of the Lord holding sway. I saw and felt the conviction of truth and belief in the Divine power to save and to heal. In the presence of so great a demonstration of thousands of souls seeking salvation, and hundreds besides seeking the healing touch of Jesus, who could doubt the wondrous power of the presence of God in His servant?

Personally I am persuaded that my life and ministry have been stimulated and blessed in the service of the Master. I pray that God's Spirit may use me to accomplish far greater results than heretofore under the spiritual stimulus which I derived from participation in this remarkable revival.

Convinced as I am of the good that has been done and is being done, I shall continue to pray that God may use our dear Sister to bring thousands of souls to the feet of her dear Lord.

CHRISTIAN AND MISSIONARY ALLIANCE PASTOR

Rev. R. H. Moon, Oakland

HE long prayed and hoped for McPherson revival meetings have come and gone in Oakland. But even though the tent is down and the meetings have been closed the revival has by no means stopped—on the contrary it is just beginning. Since the meetings we have not had an opportunity to meet our congregation in a Sunday service but last Tuesday evening we met them at the mid-week prayer meeting. This meeting convinced us that the revival is still on. Our prayer meeting was doubled and a number were there who testified to being saved and reclaimed. One unsaved man was there with his wife and daughter. But the sweet part to us as pastor was to listen to the testimony of our own congregation of how they were revived and taken deeper into the things of God as a result of the meetings. Some told of how they entered into the meeting with prejudice in their hearts, but it was not long before they were convinced that these meetings were of God.

As a pastor who sat on the platform and listened to almost every one of the messages, I am glad to say that nothing but a Scriptural, sane, old-fashioned gospel was preached. There was not even a tinge of fanaticism or wild fire present in any of the meetings. The crowds were exceedingly large, reverent and orderly. The spirit of God held them, meeting after meeting, as if in a vice, and when the altar call was given, it seemed the perfectly natural thing for people to flock to the altar for salvation. How could they do aught else since the presence of God was so powerfully manifested?

While the blessed ministry of Christ for the body was preached, yet never once was it emphasized out of its place. Always salvation for the sinner was put first and not as is commonly reported did the seekers come to the altar thinking thereby to be prayed with for healing. I dealt personally with a number of seekers and not once did I find one who was coming for healing. A deep seated, Holy Ghost conviction for sin and a desire to be forgiven and cleansed was everywhere present.

Personally I was glad for the message of the necessity of the baptism with the Holy Ghost for the believer subsequent to conversion. It is this message that has precipitated a revival in my own church and has rekindled the old passion for souls. Our church is now going out into the highways as never before to compel them to come in.

The messages on the second coming of our Lord were the finest I have ever heard, and I believe that the largest crowd that crowded onto the lot (the tent was altogether too small to hold them) was that which came to hear about the return of our Bridegroom from the skies. I praise God for having had the opportunity of participating in these meetings and may God give us another opportunity soon.

OLIVET CONGREGATIONAL CHURCH

HAROLD GOVETTE, Pastor
Oakland, California, August 3, 1922.

HAVING been anxious, for several years, that Sister McPherson should come to Oakland to conduct a revival campaign, it is not surprising that when it was definitely understood that she was coming, I entered with enthusiasm into the movement to help prepare for her great work.

I had no misgivings as to the final outcome of the meetings, for after having visited Fresno, and seeing something of the results of her meetings there, and having visited the meeting in San Francisco, I was fully convinced that the Holy Spirit was with her and would use her mightily, in stirring up the Christian people of Oakland, and in bringing hundreds to a knowledge of the truth as it is in Christ Jesus the Lord.

Well, the revival has been held. And I readily say that it was certainly the most successful revival that has ever been held in Oakland, at least during my stay of eight years.

All Oakland has felt the power of her life and preaching. Every church in our city will be helped. I am confident our own church, Olivet Congregational has received a wonderful uplift from the effects of the meeting.

The way she reached the masses, and led them in her simple, gentle, earnest manner to our Lord was refreshing to the heart and faith of any Christian worker.

Sister McPherson is one of the sanest, most conscientious, most earnest and most thoroughly consecrated evangelists it has ever been my pleasure to meet. I like the way she endeavored all the time to turn the tide of her labors into the various organized churches of our city.

She believes the Bible as the inspired word of God and so presents it to mankind. She believes in the Deity of Jesus Christ, the power of the Holy Ghost, the healing of the body through prayer and in the personal and visible return of our Lord. It is my candid belief that if the great leaders of our church in America would give her earnest and sincere backing it would bring the drifting church back to God and lift our whole nation into the safety of the righteousness of true christianity.

A thousand thanks to God, for the wonderful work she, through the Lord, has accomplished in our city. She has taught me more about the spirit of gentleness than I ever learned from any other source.

THE VOYAGE

A FINAL shriek of the whistle, the scampering of a multitude of feet across the decks and down the gang-plank. Laughter, songs, good wishes, smiles, flowers, and "God bless you's" of the friends who had come to see us off. Hundreds of happy upturned faces of converts, ministers in clerical garb, laymen, newspaper friends, Salvation Army uniforms, business men, and homey housewives passing up boxes of cakes and love offerings from home and fireside, composing the singing, testifying group on the wharf below.

The final rumble of the great crane lifting the last pile of freight and baggage aboard. The cry "Cast off!"—quick dexterous hands at the pilings—the creak of slackening ropes—the scream of the sea gull—the soft plash of the waves against the vessel—the slowly widening distance 'twixt wharf and ship—six inches—a foot—two feet—three—four—five—ten—twenty. The wild impulse for a moment to leap ashore or to cry "Stop! Stop the ship!" "Take us back to shore—this is our country—there are our friends—there lies our work—our Temple—our earthly all. We cannot leave it to go to the other side of the world on this boat!"

A second steadying thought—and we realize that we are going on the Master's business to hungry hearts in Australasia—"They have waited many months, and we must go *now,* as we could not get away for a long time after the Temple is opened."

Thirty feet, thirty yards, thirty rods—through the blur of tears—hundreds of handkerchiefs waving on the pier, flying feet running to keep pace with us round the end of the dock. Three or four songs, in as many keys and from as many groups, mingling one with the other.

"God will take care of you
Through all the day over all the way"

is sounded out by a Salvation Army cornet, yonder many voices are lifting:

"God be with you till we meet again," while from the end of the pier comes the clear voice of the young folk:

> "When we asunder part,
> It gives us inward pain;
> But we shall still be joined in heart
> And hope to meet again."

Fifty rods—a hundred—two hundred—the bend is rounded. A chill sea breeze makes us clutch our wraps more closely. We have passed the Golden Gate. The S. S. "Manganui" is nosing her way to open sea. The land of the Stars and Stripes is an outline of sky-scrapers and mountains—a fading but well-defined ridge—a melting line—an indistinct shade—GONE!

Our little horizon is bounded by the constantly changing circle of sunlit waves and never-ending sea. The seagulls that have been following, waver uncertainly, seem instinctively to realize the length of the voyage, turn back one by one—and we are on our way. On our way to work for the Master in Australia, but almost a month's time to get there in. What shall we do with the days—relax, sit still with folded hands? We have lived at too high a speed and tension to do that at first. Other passengers are able to spend whole days in aimless wanderings, or cards, or idle conversation, but our minds must still be busy with the many things concerning the Kingdom. The interior of the Temple is planned first, then the windows, with full instructions for placing. The story for the "Bridal Call," the final editing of September and October numbers, made ready for mailing at the first port of call—the leading articles for November, December and January are written, the Word of God read—designs for the dedicatory stone for the Temple drawn—a multitude of letters written on our busy typewriter, while a constant wondering fills our minds as to how other passengers, having nothing to do but eat and dress (which they did some five times a day, ladies seldom wearing the same garment twice on the entire voyage), could possibly be happy in so aimless a life.

Slowly the days and nights pass, till the Big and Little Dipper begin to slip beneath the eastern sky and the Southern Cross to appear in the east. And then, after some thirteen days without sight of land or ship of any description, great excitement prevails—we are nearing our first port of call—the small town of Papeete, on the island of Tahati, owned and ruled by the French. Rugged, sheer mountains reach skyward.

Unbelievably high walls of granite pierce the clouds like bristling spears. A softer sea-line of harbor lies below, many smaller craft, the dark form and swift flash of a great shark by the side of the boat, a frightened school of flying fish skimming the water. Sails, buildings, forms, faces, becoming more distinct. Brilliant sunlight and foamy billows breaking over the coral reefs. The soft plump of the steamer against the wharf and we are ashore on a South Sea Island.

Our eyes fell upon an island that might have come out of a tale of the Arabian Nights or a fairy story book—an island that flows with milk and honey as must Eden of old—cocoanuts, bananas, oranges, pineapples, mandarins and every kind of fruit and flower one could name growing in their native state yielding abundant harvest without the aid of man. Natives, French and Chinese living together 'neath the azure blue of a wonderful sky that never knows snow or frost.

Then away to the island of Raratonga, owned and ruled by the French, some forty hours' journey. Here, again, a veritable garden of Eden but much more advanced and prosperous because of the splendid work of the British Foreign Missionary Society, is unveiled before us. An island almost entirely surrounded by a coral reef—water blue as the sky and clear as crystal—enormous sea-shells, all one can carry—sands like snow—palms—flowers—t r a i l i n g vines—huge banana groves—oranges—all manner of fruit lying on the ground—fish for the taking—milk for the breaking of a cocoanut—shells—birds of wondrous plumage—shaded streets—laughing natives, singing happy islanders—the original plan of God for this world before the fall of man is borne in upon us as never before.

THE PRAYERS THAT HELD A SHIP

And now we are sailing again, bound this time for the rock-bound coast of New Zealand, almost a week's steady sailing, after we have been notified that we are expected to arrive in Wellington Friday morning and to sail for Australia Saturday evening. Yes, the sailing schedules were all fixed up splendidly to get away for Australia Saturday, but the praying saints of Wellington had determined otherwise.

Great preparations were being made, unknown to us; the Town Hall taken, advertisements posted, and from towns and cities all about hungry souls were gathered for meetings which they had planned for Friday night, Saturday and Sunday.

Then came word to their ears that the boat was to sail Saturday evening! What could they do? They questioned one another in consternation.

"We must have the meeting. Go ask the ship office to hold the boat in the harbor," suggested one.

"Might try," said another. "Perhaps they do not know it is God's will for the boat to wait till Monday, I will tell them."

"Hold the boat! The idea! Why £1,000 could not hold it! Hold the boat over Sunday, indeed! Well, I never! Humph!!" snorted the official. "The idea of such an impossible thing."

"Well, if you cannot, God can," they averred and believed it, too, but how? Their faces were downcast and troubled.

"Let us pray," suggested a dear child of the King and soon a prayer meeting was in progress.

"Dear Lord, hold the boat," they prayed, "hold it till Monday. You might let the firemen go on strike, Lord, or send a storm if all else fails. Yes, Lord, send a wind, not enough to hurt the boat but enough to delay their arrival a few hours, to cause delay in unloading so they must stay till Monday."

And so it came to pass that the elements began to threaten, the barometer dropped, and though the sky looked clear, a wireless from New Zealand reached our ship bidding us prepare for storm as heavy weather was riding off New Zealand. Canvas was lashed over the open decks, wind breaks put up and all set—yet no storm.

Then it came, rain and wind and high billows—a glorious sea depicting the power of God—the first real sea we had had, because saints in America had prayed for calm weather, till almost everyone on board had remarked that they never could remember so calm a passage. We knew nothing about praying people in Wellington and wondered what we were going to tell the people in America when they asked us whether we had had any storm.

At last we made the harbor, but not in the morning as had been expected. Night had fallen, the lights along the shore were lighted and notices were posted stating that we could not sail till Monday afternoon. No work is done on Sunday in New Zealand and the cargo could not all be removed and loaded in so short a time.

Joy reigned among the children of the Lord in Wellington, for God had held the boat and it had not cost £1,000 either.

Entertained in the home of Captain Gifford of the School of Navigation, we were whisked away to the week-end services in the Methodist Church and to the Town Hall meetings. Here we were given the joyous privilege of seeing some scores of penitents kneeling at the mercy seat crowning Our Savior as theirs. The songs, the testimonies, the conversions, the hunger, the hallelujahs, the amens, the rejoicings, the tears, seemed just the same as those of the children of God in America and Canada.

The congregation were deeply spiritual, earnest thinking people, with a mighty hunger for more of God, closing our series of meetings on Sunday night with the Town Hall packed to capacity. We could not suppress the longing to be able to stay longer or to come again to minister to these precious people. The land slide of converts pouring to the altars to give themselves to Christ overjoyed them beyond measure.

Were they stiff, conservative, or cold, you ask? No, indeed! Had you been able to see the scene at the pier as the boat sailed, had you seen the throng of people who came to see us off, had you heard their songs, and God bless you's, I doubt whether you could have told the difference from the farewells said in San Francisco some three weeks previous. There were the same upturned faces, the same interdenominational spirit, ministers of the same denominations, mission workers, and Salvation Army uniforms.

Once more aboard and we were on our way to Sydney, Australia, but not alone this time, for a party of New Zealand delegates sailed with us. Once more the sea was like a placid lake day by day, until one morning we woke to find our ship noiselessly rounding "the Heads" and turning into that magnificent "Queen of waterways," Sydney Harbor. The most common phrase in Sydney seems to be "What do you think of our Harbor?" They ask the question of all as commonly as we would say "Fine day, is it not?" and indeed it is one to be proud of and deservedly heralded.

We hasten below to close the last handbag—but what is that sound as of singing?

It is not the phonograph or the passengers in worldly song! Hark! It is coming across the waters and flowing in through the porthole:

"Revive us again,
Fill each heart with Thy love;
May each soul be rekindled,
With fire from above."

Can it be someone to meet us? Quickly we come to the deck trembling with emotion and joy of reaching our ocean journey's end. There they are, a crowd of bright-faced Choristers on the pier to meet us, handkerchiefs waving, and over their heads is held aloft, by stalwart hands, a large and brightly printed banner

WELCOME
MRS. MCPHERSON AND PARTY TO
AUSTRALIA
AND GOD BLESS YOU

And then we are suddenly in their midst. They are shaking our hands, kissing us, wiping the tears from their eyes, shouting the victory. Cold? Conservative? you ask. Maybe so—they have the name of it, it is true, but we have not found it yet. They seem just as full, or, at least, almost as full of the feeling of love of God and souls, as American audiences.

A busy day in Sydney looking at buildings, talking of plans, then away by the evening express to Melbourne with a goodly crowd on the station platform to bid us Godspeed. Newspaper reporters were aboard the ship to interview us before we landed and were again at the depot to see us off, till had it not been for the strange tramcars and the trains with separate compartments, we might have believed ourselves in our own land.

The shrill voice of the whistle, the jerk of the engine, and we are on our way again, the Melbourne "flyer" making 40, 50, and, the guard told us at times 60 miles an hour over a smooth roadbed. The next morning we awoke in Melbourne, the scene of our first Australian mission.

TRIAL AND TRIUMPH IN MELBOURNE, AUSTRALIA

IF YOU were going to a far-away city to conduct an evangelistic campaign, and if traveling far, you were eagerly anxious for success to crown your mission, and if, upon arrival, you found that the company under whose auspices you were to be introduced were, while small in number and humble in quarters, loved, honored, respected and trusted by the earnest thinking Christian people of various churches because the fruitage of their labors for the past years had proven them to be sound in doctrine, clean and wholesome in ministry and methods, blessed and loved by the best Christian characters of their neighborhood because of their charity, good works and general constructiveness to the church of Christ in general, and now, ere you began, the result of this ground work was that—.

The bands were playing, the flags flying, hunger and prayerful co-operation assured on every hand, scores of prayer meetings in progress in homes of various denominations, a multitude looking forward with earnest anticipation to your coming, trusting that you would enlarge such a work as that of these dear ones who herald your name have done, and all organization complete (as indeed it should be) before the launching of the campaign and sweeping victory crowned the effort; would you not be more than a little prone to say: "WE DID IT, we worked it up, our organization was so complete and the interest and respect justly won because the soundness, wholesomeness and integrity of our co-laborers laid the foundations in sapphire stones, strengthened the bulwarks with gleaming gems and the revival *had* to come, because it had the right start as far as human agency was concerned?"—I wonder!

But if, on the other hand, you found that the Campaign was to be launched, within twenty-four hours of your arrival from a four weeks' journey, and begun under the most terrific handicap any evangelist could possibly be asked to face; if, upon arrival, you discovered that the company by whom your name had been broadcasted for many months were not only small in numbers, but were ostracised and feared by the most earnest ministers and Christian workers, who believed them to be unsound in doctrines and methods; and if, stunned with these assertions coming from every quarter, you investigated and found to your horror that by the leader's own written "Confession" she so differed from the Orthodox Christian teaching that she had declared herself to have been a "fool" to join the Methodist denomination and that by doing this "she had taken the first step toward carnality" and found her views of the Word to be "diametrically opposed to the teaching of the church" on the fundamentals; and if, still, by this one's own written "confession" you found that she had become a convert of Miles Grant's "Conditional Immortality" teaching that God had not created man with an immortal soul, total annihilation, and that because she "was assured that in whatever else they differed, all sects agreed in teaching that man by nature was immortal" her own "denominational bonds" had been "violated," name removed from the class book, weekly prayer meetings disbanded, Sunday classes given up because "she could not teach a book which she was unable to uphold as the infallible Word of God," and if, in her written "Confession," she admitted such unscriptural and psychic demonstrations as "mysterious tappings in her body" until she "thought that the valves of her heart were giving way," "momentary entrances forced and electrical shocks sent through her frame," "wind shaking the floor . . . and rattling the china . . . while the woman's frame was *convulsed* till suddenly, as though shaken from their resting place by the *convulsing spirit,* strange unwonted notes burst from her mouth, cleaving the air in front like living creatures" all of which she had mistakenly represented as the blessed dealings and Baptism of the Holy Ghost (oh, Pentecost, what crimes are perpetrated in Thy name), and that, moreover, these things were generally known, till the whole cause of the Holy Spirit and Divine Healings was in disrepute therefrom and that, hurling defiance at their critics, they had distributed handbills declaring that "No power on earth or in hell could hinder" the revival, and the result was that:

Instead of bands, choirs, ministerial co-operation and confidence, you faced a stone wall of resistance which must be broken down, a mountain of prejudice which must be removed, and a shattered confidence which must be restored, a quagmire of doubt and misgiving about your own doctrinal views along these lines cleared away before you could, by the help of God, build a solid foundation of sound faith and trust for the superstructure of the Campaign to be builded upon; and that if, almost single handed, you opened the Good Book and with a heavy-burdened heart, but unswerving faith, preached the simple Word of the Living God; and if God sent a mighty tidal-wave of revival which in three short weeks removed prejudice, swept over the city, filled the platform to overflowing with clergymen from practically every orthodox, evangelical denomination; and if the very ones who had written, preached warnings and circulated letters against the revival, sat and worked at your side with tear-brimmed eyes, helping pull the nets to land and welcome the hundreds of sinners home and the meeting ended in sweeping victory with ministers, Salvation Army Bands and officers, church choirs, and Christian workers wringing each other's hands, reading a new love in each other's shining eyes, all urging a return visit and promising to keep the fires burning, and if, after the trial, God brought the triumph, wouldn't you be more apt to say:

"Blessed be the God who saveth not with spear or with sword, for the battle is the Lord's. Sing unto Him, oh ye people, for He hath triumphed gloriously, He hath stretched forth His hand and the horse and the rider are cast into the sea. He hath swept back the curtains of the clouds and darkness is utterly consumed from before His face; the mists that veiled His glory are dispelled. NOT MAN BUT GOD hath triumphed?"—I wonder!

At any rate it was the handicap that we faced in Melbourne, but God blessedly rose to the occasion and took the seemingly impossible and made it gloriously possible, throwing the light of His blessed word upon many a hungry heart that had been afore time in bondage and swinging them clear into soul-winning channels. Getting back to fundamental truths concerning the inspiration of the scriptures, the eternal deity of the Lord Jesus Christ, the personality and true Baptism of the Holy Spirit, statements and teaching of doctrines occupied the first few days, then the enemy began to retreat and the Lord to come forth blessedly. Sinners filled the altars from the first meetings and increased in numbers at the penitent form as the Campaign continued. Ministers and laymen from almost every denomination and walk of life volunteered, the most spiritual men and women workers came forward and laughed and wept, sang and shouted the victory together as sinners streamed home to the cross.

A large percentage of the converts were those confessing Christ as Lord and Saviour for the first time in their lives. Drunkards came in under the influence of liquor—a sight we have not witnessed in America for some time—were sobered up and gloriously saved and kept. One man, said to be from one of the best families in Australia and to have spent some twelve hundred pounds in one year's riotous living and drunkenness, was thus sobered at the altar and became an inspiration to all day by day with his changed life, face and wonderful singing. He is expecting to enter the work of Christ as evangelistic singer we are told. Several whole families, one of ten souls, came to Christ, husbands and wives kneeling together. Boys who had not written Mother for years left the altar to wire the news.

There were some precious instances of healing in answer to prayer, but the Lord gave us a very decided check in spirit, that we should not take up this phase of the work in any public or special way, partly because healing had been unduly exploited prior to our arrival as a means of advertising, and this battle, the Lord revealed, must be waged and won on the merits of the Word and the Blood, and partly because there was not as great a general need along this line as along that of soul-winning and teaching regarding the Holy Spirit. Having just so much time and strength to give, we were led to expend this in spiritual upbuilding which was so much the more needed. Other faithful co-laborers were given by the Lord, who, with the "little Mother," lifted much of this work. Several times we were persuaded to break over this invisible restraint and pray for the afflicted (who were comparatively few in number) but each time the Holy Spirit laid a restraining check upon our hands and showed clearly that the mission of this campaign was to clear away the debris, and make straight paths for the feet of the Gospel of His Holy Spirit and of His own dear coming.

The Campaign closed in a burst of glory. The Sunday night announced as the closing meeting four thousand people unanimously began to clap and call and pat their feet on the dance-hall floor till we promised to return on Monday night, and repeat the address on the Second Coming of our Lord. Night after night they would gather about our car as we left the building, and only with the aid of several strong men, could we get through the throngs that blocked the entrance ways to say goodbye and fill our arms with flowers and Australian souvenirs.

Of the final results of the "men's" and "girls'" meetings and of the final service for "converts" etc., I will let the ministers, who kindly wrote their impressions of the revival, speak.

At the final meeting of the advisory committee (which the Lord sent to our help and organized after the meeting had gotten under way), it was suggested by some of the clergymen, who were there to say goodbye, that a photo be taken of the assembled group and this was given in the "Bridal Call." They compose some of the finest clergymen in Melbourne and two laymen, Col. Bjelke Peterson and Brother Denniston, who, as city business men, were on the committee. These are, however, but a portion of the ministers who lent their kindly and efficient help and influence.

A BODILY TEST AND VICTORY

Continual rain and cold drafts of early spring (which comes at time of our early fall) was quite a test to us. The buildings are unheated and we were chilled till sometimes we wondered if we would ever be warm again. In addition to this a large open-air well was located immediately back of the platform. A continuous stream of cold, damp, foul air flowed over the speaker. Every one else could bundle up in warm wraps, but she must stand without a coat for hours.

The Lord gave supernatural strength, but at last a badly ulcerated throat resulted. But after 48 hours of constant chilling the Evangelist was gotten warm and instantly a high fever soared—but, rising from bed in the name of the Lord, she went out and went on with the work. And as she went she was healed—defeat was swallowed up in victory—Praise the Lord.

THE JOYOUS REVIVAL IN ADELAIDE

In order that we might catch the early boat to America,

where the building of the Temple was demanding our early presence, our schedule was revised, and the Adelaide meeting set forward one week. This left but three days to do the advertising for revised dates, but the angel of the Lord went before us opening every door, so that upon the day of our arrival we arranged the printing of several 10x10 posters for the bill-boards, hundreds of day bills, newspaper ads, an electric sign at the corner of the main street, announcement letters to 250 clergymen, the decoration and arrangements of the exhibition building, the large signs to be erected without, and several other matters.

One of the first to respond to the rally call was Dr. Seymore of the Chalmers Presbyterian Church. Coming to the hotel, with a welcoming smile and a hearty handshake he offered his services and prayed for a revival. Within a few minutes the secretary of the local preachers' association, a spiritual dynamo in Melbourne, called, also offering to do all he could. And so they came till within a few hours a minister's meeting was held, and a local committee formed, of which Dr. Seymore was chairman, with other clergymen and representative laymen as aids in every capacity. The finest workers, singers, bands, quartets, fishers, ushers and helpers were brought in. A multitude of now warm friends in Melbourne wrote a multitude of letters to all their friends in Adelaide anxious to smooth our path.

The ministers, who assisted in Melbourne, drew up and signed the following statement of confidence to be distributed to the ministers and workers of Adelaide, and heartily they responded:

TESTIMONIAL OF CLERGYMEN FROM
RECENT MELBOURNE MISSION

We, the undersigned Ministers of various denominations in Melbourne and Suburbs, have great pleasure in testifying to the splendid work which has been done here by Mrs. Aimee Semple McPherson. Personally, we have received a great spiritual uplift and quickening. We have had the joy of seeing hundreds profess decision for Christ, and it has been to our great satisfaction to find that Mrs. McPherson's preaching here has been strictly orthodox and that her methods were extremely wise and effective. She possesses great natural ability, but the outstanding feature is spiritual power and her intense love for souls.

The large Wirth's Olympia has been crowded out even on week nights, and our great regret is, that she cannot remain in our city for a longer period.

We would earnestly commend this Evangelist to the sympathy and co-operation of our Brethren in the other states of Australia, and urge them to use every endeavor to persuade their friends and congregation to attend the meetings.

James Warboys, Baptist Church, Brunswick; David Morgan, Congregational; J. S. A. Warboys, Baptist Church; B. W. Huntsman, Church of Christ; Anthony Lang, United Gospel Mission; Harold B. Robbins, Church of Christ; J. McD. Graham, Colonel, Salvation Army; Adjutant Yee, Salvation Army; J. W. Baker, Evangelist Church of Christ; R. Morrison Bowles, Congregational Church; Edward Tennison Smith, of England, (Prohibition Lecturer); A. B. Carson, Holiness Mission; James A. Gault, Methodist Ex-Chaplain; Walter John Eddy, The Mission to Lepers; T. G. B. Woodfull, Methodist Minister; A. W. A. Roland, Congregational Church; Thomas Williams, Presbyterian Church; R. Green, Presbyterian, Burnley; J. Lloyd Hasham, Methodist; James E. Thomas, Church of Christ, President Conferences of Churches of Christ in Victoria, Secretary Council of Churches in Victoria; Samuel J. Hoban, Wesley Church; James H. Cain, Wesley Church.

From beginning to end, sweet unity and peace settled down upon the whole place, and the crowds grew from a few hundred till they filled the great auditorium to overflowing. Sinners came home to the Christ in each meeting, and Christians were stirred to wait upon the Lord for the infilling of the Holy Spirit and enduement of power. As we left city ministers and members of the interdenominational committee wrung our hands and assured us they would never leave off waiting upon the Lord till they had received power from on high. God bless them and fill each earnest, hungry heart. How our American B. C. readers would have appreciated the S. A. Band, the Norwood Mission Band, the choirs, the singing, the altar calls, the hunger to be filled with the whole fullness of God, the earnestness and the enthusiasm of these precious Australian children of the Lord. Several of them put chairs in the Angelus Temple and the choir donated one chair for the choir in Los Angeles.

HUNGRY HEARTS IN SYDNEY

Upon our return to Sydney, our hearts were stirred by the love and hunger of a multitude of Christian hearts for a revival that should sweep their city. The auditorium was well filled at the first meeting in the afternoon, and overcrowded with people standing at night. The first little invitation to come to the altar and accept the Lord Jesus as Savior, brought an instantaneous response, wherein men and women appeared to rise all over the building, coming from the balcony and the main floor, till they filled the space in front, then overflowed to the platform and crowded that, seeking and finding the Christ.

Expressions of regret that the mission could not be prolonged, and that completion of the Temple and arrangements for its dedication and New Year's convention demanded our immediate return, were expressed on every hand. Ere we sailed a dear brother, known for his beneficent help to God's work in Australia, offered to pay the fare of the Evangelist and party to and from America, if in six or eight months after the opening of Temple we could return for just three weeks' campaign. One of the leading business men took us in his car and showed us the various large auditoriums, Town Hall, Hippodrome, Exhibition Building, etc., so that we would have a working knowledge of same in case it should be possible for us to make a flying visit and complete the work.

Loving friends and Bridal Call subscribers met us at every turn of the way in Australia, and a precious company were at the wharf to see us off. Singing songs of Zion, pressing souvenirs and flowers into our hands, calling invitations to return, promising, many of them, to come to Los Angeles for opening of Temple or soon thereafter, and tossing up to us one end of bolts of brightly colored ribbons, while scores of friends held the other ends and the bolts of ribbon all leading to our hands. Then as the boat pulled from shore, and their songs drifted across the waves, the ribbons kept unwinding in their hands and reached unbelievably far across the waves, a slender thread still uniting loving hands and hearts. A pretty custom, and one that we had not seen before our departure from New Zealand.

And now, sailing through the Fiji Islands and the South Seas, our boat nears the Hawaiian and home shores. Our last port of call was Pago Pago, among the Samoans. We visited their native huts, saw their churches, and the exportation of their great harvests of cocoanuts. The home voyage is filled with hours of prayerful writing, reading, planning for the House which has been built unto the Lord, and with a great longing to be up and at the work which the Master has entrusted to our hands. Busy moments are flying, hungry hearts are calling, soon the Lord of the Harvest is coming; may we make each hour count for God and answer "Here am I, oh Lord, send me."

HONOLULU

On our homeward journey, we had been looking forward to a quiet day in Honolulu and a respite from the heat which had been so oppressive as we crossed the equator. Although we have corresponded with members of our Bridal Call Family residing in Hawaii, yet as we had sent no word of our arrival, it was a happy surprise to find a goodly company of them on the pier to welcome us as the boat came in. So loving, anxious and hungry were they that they were eagerly watching every boat.

The warm-hearted welcome, enthusiasm, rejoicing, sweet hours of fellowship and prayer together could hardly be exaggerated. In addition to lunch of native dishes, and a prayer service in one good Sister's home which was crowded to the doors, and a later gathering in the Seamen's Institute by the pier, our day was brightened by the kindness and courtesy of Brother Richards of the Mission Memorial Bldg., and Sergt. Horning of the U. S. Militia, who took us over the Island in their cars.

WHAT AUSTRALIAN MINISTERS SAY

J. LLOYD HASLAM, M. E. CHURCH
Brunswick, Victoria

THE Revival meetings just conducted in Melbourne by Mrs. Aimee Semple McPherson, have been full of power and inpiration. It has been a rare personal previlege to have heard such an imaginative, deep and inspirational Evangelist.

Mrs. McPherson's meetings present an exceptional advantage to Sunday School Teachers. One whom I know, took the members of her young ladies class to one or two services and five of them were led to Jesus. Mrs. McPherson is God's great gift to the churches in these difficult times of soul-winning.

Church and Sunday School workers will be wisely advised in taking the best advantage of her passing visit.

A. W. A. ROWLAND, CONGREGATIONAL CHURCH
North Richmond, Melbourne

It would be the depth of ingratitude if I were to allow you to leave our shores without expressing my thankfulness for the blessing which God has permitted you to impart to multitudes of people in this city.

Your meetings have been swept by the power of God's Spirit and many have been rescued from the depths of depravity.

I have never heard the Gospel of Jesus Christ preached more simply and lovingly, and the great audiences have been simply captivated by the beautiful picture of the Savior which you held before their eyes.

Your ministry has brought the ministers of all denominations closer together, and all have been led to see the blessing of unity in the service of our Lord.

My own Church has benefited largely through your ministrations and numbers of my young people have made their first decision for Christ while others have had their spiritual life revived.

Your meetings for the healing of the sick have led many of us to think deeply upon the subject of Divine Healing, and many of us deplore that this branch of our work has been so neglected. I trust that ere long the Ministry of Healing will hold its place in the ordinary program of Church work.

Please accept my sincere thanks for the blessing God has permitted you to bring to Australia.

WM. T. WILTSHIRE, M. E. CHURCH
Brompton, South Australia

It has been a great delight to me to have been closely associated with the Mrs. Aimee Semple McPherson Evangelistic Campaign in Adelaide, which took place in Adelaide's largest hall—the Exhibition building—from October 1st to 15th. Our city and suburbs have had their religious life stirred in a rare manner. As the Mission continued the crowds increased, and great enthusiasm prevailed. Thousands can and do testify that their hearts have been "strangely warmed" as the Divinely gifted evangelist delivered the Gospel Message, because she spake the Word of God with boldness, sweetness and with great power, "and great grace was upon them all." Never have I heard the message more winsomely delivered. "The wooing-note" was always present. Prejudices against a woman preaching, prejudices through false statements widely circulated concerning the nature of her work and her attitude to the Churches were swept away. It was a joy to witness the union of Christian forces, the sinking of denominational distinctions, the return of backsliders, and the conversion of sinners in such large numbers. It gladdened our hearts to see old, middle-aged and young respond to the altar calls and literally flock out to the front for salvation. One of our oldest and most highly esteemed Methodist ministers remarked: "Mrs. McPherson is the sanest and finest Evangelist that has visited Australia since California Taylor, who was here over fifty years ago." My memory does not go so far back, but no Evangelist has gripped my soul to a greater extent than our dearly beloved Sister McPherson. It was amazing to see and hear how much of Christ she found in the Old Testament, and through her the huge audiences saw and heard Him there as never before. Though I have charge of an important church in the Brompton suburb, and am busy as the Methodist Industrial Gospel Missioner, in visiting and addressing workshop employees during their lunch hours, I attended most of the meetings, because I could not with comfort be away. Many, very many, thank God for sending our Sister to our city, and we part from her with deep regret, hoping and praying that ere long she will return to us as the Messenger of God. We shall never forget her sweet smile, her pleasant voice, her loving and kindly face, her unique method of presenting the truth, her effective preaching, her wonderful appeals, and best of all the powers of the Holy Spirit that accompanied her Message. We shall follow her with our prayers, and with intense interest. Canada and the United States of America have been richly blessed of God in producing and possessing such a marvelous Gospel Messenger. Her mother's smiling and hearty welcome, and whole-souled devotion to her daughter have in no small measure contributed to the immense success of the Mission.

JAMES A. GAULT, M. E. CHURCH

Brunswick, Australia

I have great pleasure in giving my personal testimony as to Mrs. Aimee McPherson's meetings in Melbourne. Several of our ministers, myself included, rank her the finest of all the Evangelists that have visited Australia. Her methods are thorough—she sees her penitents through. She has a wonderful power of kindling hearts that have grown cold. She is wonderfully loyal to the church and the ministers, and from all that I have seen, and I have seen many of her meetings, I am sure that Melbourne will for many years remember the gracious and blessed personality of this queenly lady who came amongst us.

B. W. HUNTSMAN, BRIGHTON CHURCH OF CHRIST, Melbourne

Wirth's "Olympia"—situated close to the heart of Melbourne, within a few steps of the Central Railroad Station and St. Paul's Anglican Cathedral — built for a circus, but more often used as a dancing pavilion, has just been the scene of a wonderful Revival, for the saving of souls. A little woman from across the seas, Sister Aimee Semple McPherson, came to tell, in her winning and persuasive way, the "four-square" gospel of Jesus the Savior, Jesus the Baptizer with the Holy Spirit, Jesus the Great Physician and Jesus the Coming King. Many had been looking forward to her visit to the sunny land of the Southern Cross, wondering what she would say and do. Hundreds came out of curiosity, but remained to enjoy a great spiritual feast. Some confessed that they came critically, but were immediately won to be ardent and loyal supporters of the Campaign.

As the days passed, the galleries of that barn-like structure, seating several thousand people, began to fill up, until it became a sea of faces eagerly listening to the story of the Gospel. Sister McPherson's opening sentence won its way into the hearts of the people. She referred to the different ones who had been introduced. "Now," she said, "I want to introduce Jesus." This became the keynote of the Campaign, whether the message was from a Bible story, or a great doctrinal theme —it always exalted Christ and was an appeal to surrender our hearts and lives to him. Walking in the garden of the Word, we were led to see the Divine Lover, the Lord Jesus Christ, with his bride, the church. Then these mountain peaks of Gospel Message, "The coming again of our Lord," which had to be repeated at the request of four thousand people; "The loss and restoration of the gifts and peaces of the Holy Spirit;" "The plan of Redemption as seen in one mighty sweep of revelation in the whole word of God;" "The beautiful lessons from the story of Ruth;" "Consecration;" "Soul winning;" "The anointing of a Holy Life;" "The Wedding in the morning," and then the need of more spiritual power in our work, from the story of Elijah, "The God who answers by fire," which led many Christian workers to pray for a deeper experience of prayer, that we might know the same God who answered Elijah's prayer! These and many more uplifting, spiritual messages which we can never forget, and will leave a lasting impression upon our Souls.

During the campaign, while many sick and afflicted were helped, the salvation of souls was kept uppermost. That was always pre-eminent. The "Altar Calls" brought to light many needy souls who were hungry for a Savior and a real friend. What wonderful testimonies were heard from many who had found a Savior from a life of sin. One of the first was a splendid man who had been a slave to drink, but from the time he came to Christ, he has been able to pass the saloons. Then can we ever forget the blind returned soldier, a well-educated man from one of the best families, who was saved from a wasted life? How we loved to hear his testimony and listen to his singing. We had been told of men and women weeping their way to the Cross in other missions conducted by our Sister; here we saw the same thing. How tenderly and affectionately she took girls to her heart and led them to Christ. The mission was a revelation of how many lovely girls there are in a great city, without home ties and real friends. Sister became their friend, they fought for the privilege of her arm, and they will always remember the sweet influence brought into their lives. At the last Sunday evening service, a great company of men and women came to the altar giving themselves to the Savior for the first time, or reconsecrating their lives to Him. All through the meetings Christians received a blessing that cannot be expressed in words; we forgot our denominational ties and lovingly co-operated in the work of saving souls. Cold hearts were warmed with the fire of the old time Gospel; we learned to say "Praise the Lord," "Amen" and we all felt happier for it. It was a glad moment when thousands of people waved their handkerchiefs as they sang, "Shall we gather at the river." It was a sight never to be forgotten.

Australians are warm hearted people. They have only to

know that the one who comes to their shores is genuine and brings a message of love and good-will, then they quickly respond. The campaign began with wonderment, but it grew and grew, not by newspaper support, but by those who came, going out as little missionaries to bring others, until it became a great host. Even visitors from Pertha, Western Australia, two thousand miles away, and from Tasmania and Sydney. It was a feast of good things. The Lord was with us and we were glad. If ever, in the providence of God, Sister McPherson comes again to Australia, she will find in Melbourne a large company of friends eagerly waiting to welcome her.

REV. R. A. GREEN, PRESBYTERIAN CHURCH
Birnley, Australia

Mrs. A. S. McPherson was almost unknown to the people of Melbourne, except readers of the Bridal Call, when on September 3rd, she stepped upon the platform of Wirth's Olympia Circus arena, which served as the auditorium during her revival campaign in the populous city. She faced a fair audience on that opening Sunday afternoon.

People of every denomination were present, although, officially, the churches were not aware of her mission, and certainly the people were not aware of the wonderful spiritual session that was opening in their midst. My own acquaintance with the missioner hitherto had been through reading the Bridal Call. I had been favorably impressed, especially by the accounts of missions opened by prominent ministers in San Francisco and elsewhere. It was a lonely minister that stood on the platform that first afternoon and led the congregation in prayer to the Divine God for His blessing upon the missioner and her mission in the city. I was not alone at the next day's meeting, however, and gradually one and another of the churches became represented until there was no more room on the platform for us.

The opening address proclaimed Jesus; it struck the note that resounded throughout; it revealed the heart of the speaker, and it was a revelation that remained open and transparent throughout the entire mission. Mrs. McPherson proved herself a gifted and gracious herald of the Lord.

The first service made a good beginning, full of promise. The address was mainly to Christian people, but at the end an altar call was given, asking for men and women who would decide for Jesus. The response almost caught away my breath—I believe it caught away my soul for the moment—for some three score filed up the aisles to the altar benches and knelt in penitence and prayer. It was long since I had seen anything like this, and I gained some valuable experience in ministering to the seeking souls.

That sight kept waking me up during the Sunday night watches—the vision of souls surging forward to accept the Lord Jesus. And there was no excitement—there was none throughout the whole campaign—but here and there tears fell silently. I attended as many of the meetings as possible and never left one without a fresh sight of men and women and children coming out to seek Jesus. I have no hesitation in saying that I have never heard anyone preach Jesus so thoroughly, so persistently, so lovingly, so winsomely, as this handmaid of the Lord, Mrs. Aimee S. McPherson.

I spoke with many of those who attended the meetings, and some were from other States of Australia, who had come to Melbourne for the Mission. All were ready to testify to the blessing they were receiving at the services. There were some instances of healing in answer to prayer that came under my notice and I regarded these as a measure of divine certification to the work of the Lord's handmaid. But the chief seals to her ministry were the souls that came to Jesus after hearing her messages. As a minister, I envied Mrs. McPherson the joy she very apparently felt in receiving these men and women. But I had some share after all, as I, too, grasped the hands of the converts. And the missioner pleased me by her loyalty to the churches and ministers of the city, when she asked the converts their church connection and advised them at once to join up with their church, to get into work and to support the House of God. I am happy to say that I received great stimulus and blessing under the ministrations of this gifted and gracious minister of Christ.

The audiences swelled as the days passed until the large auditorium was crowded. The first week of the Mission was so graciously successful that it advertised itself without the aid of the news-press, and the people passed on the invitation to others by warm words of commendation. The churches and prayer meetings of Melbourne have long been praying for a great revival and here almost unrecognized, at first, has come to the city a revival that by God's blessing shall percolate into many a sanctuary. For thousands of Australians, henceforth, Mrs. Aimee S. McPherson will be more than a name—she will be known and honored as a gifted and and gracious messenger of the Savior for whom we will thank God.

DAVID MORGAN, LENNOX STREET CONGREGATIONAL CHURCH

Richmond, Melbourne

The campaign had been in progress for some days before I got into touch with it. Then I went to one of the sessions somewhat prejudiced, I must confess; for certain reports unfavorable to Mrs. McPherson had come under my notice. I was critical. During the first session that I attended, I occupied a seat at some considerable distance from the platform, at the next session I found myself sitting right near the platform. Soon I became convinced that the reports that had come under my notice were false reports. Then prayerfully and sympathetically I entered into the campaign. To me it has been a marvelous campaign. Mrs. McPherson handles the sword of the Spirit which is the Word of God with due reverence, rare skill and very marked ability. It has been my privilege to hear a number of the great preachers in Great Britian prior to my coming to Australia twenty years ago and I have heard during the last twenty years some world famous preachers who were visiting Australia; to me Mrs. McPherson ranks high among them. She is mighty in the scriptures and handles Biblical incidents and passages with wonderfully telling power, absolutely thrilling.

L. S. B. WOODFULL, M. E. CHURCH

Melbourne, Australia

The mission held by Mrs. Aimee Semple McPherson in the Olympia, Melbourne, has been a most gracious spiritual uplift to large numbers of Christian people. Hundreds of backsliders have also been led to reconsecrate their lives to the Lord and many seekers have found Christ and Love entered upon the Christian life.

It is long since Melbourne has had such a gracious visitation. The marked manner in which the Holy Spirit gave wisdom and strength to His Handmaiden was most blessed and convincing. Victory crowned each meeting. The subjects chosen by Mrs. McPherson were practical, searching and scriptural, moving the people greatly by their charm and graciousness, the outstanding feature in each of them being the exaltation of our Lord Jesus. It was this feature, especially, that won the people. It was Jesus always, in His loving, tender power. He was the great *Reality* in all that was said and done. The addresses also evidenced deep insight into the needs, problems and difficulties of present day life and conditions. These were dealt with in such gracious wisdom and faithfulness that many were won to Christ. We could all realize that the wise utterances of Mrs. McPherson were a direct answer to the scornful rationalism that is so prevalent, as well as a direct challenge to the falsities of Christian Science and Spiritualism; they were also a clear alarm call to those professing Christians who were careless and worldly.

Unfortunately, the beginning of the mission was threatened with disaster through the action of some unwise people who created quite a false impression of Mrs. McPherson's work and doctrine, before her arrival. Not only the clergymen, but the people generally, were wrongly influenced. Praise God, these impressions were all swept away by the word of grace that came over the meetings. God, by His Spirit, vindicated his Handmaiden, and we are all rejoicing over the victory won. Foolishness and ignorance have beaten back and confidence took the place of fear.

The ministers of the various denominations, who attended the meetings, have nothing but good to say of what they saw and heard. Prejudices were broken down and joy filled their hearts at the token of grace and glory resting upon all that was done. The work was of God. When the Altar Calls were responded to by such large numbers, the ministers were seen mingling with the penitents, guiding them to Christ. Many of them are carrying the fire into their own churches. We believe that the work of grace begun in Mrs. McPherson's meetings will overflow into their churches with results for good of far-reaching effect.

OLYMPIC THEATRE, MELBOURNE, AUSTRALIA
Where a hard battle was fought and won for "The Four-Square Gospel" during Sister McPherson's campaign

We gladly and most heartily commend Mrs. McPherson to the ministers and people of Australia, believing that she is being graciously used by the Holy Spirit in quickening believers and winning souls to Christ. Our advice to all is go, seer hear. We did this ourselves and our hearts are singing Hallelujah and we are confident your also will say the same —for a joy unspeakable will come to you.

REV. H. L. PARKER, ASCOT VALE CONGREGATIONAL CHURCH

Victoria, Australia

It has been my great privilege to attend many (as many as possible) of your meetings at the Olympia in Melbourne. Last night was the closing session of a wonderful campaign. The great building was packed to its limit, although it was an extra meeting, requested by the audience only on the previous night, and therefore not advertised in any way. Everyone felt deeply the regret of having reached the end of these inspiring meetings, and that you will no longer be with us, including hundreds of bright-faced converts.

You began the Mission under many disabilities of local manufacture, including the indifference or prejudice of the Churches, and lack of adequate preparations for your coming, on their part. But these ministers and other Church-workers who did attend, though at first on our guard, critical and reserved, have been disarmed and won over by the truth the beauty and the power of your message, and by the Spirit of Christ in you. You have proclaimed the living Savior, in the power of the Holy Spirit, and have expounded the Scriptures as only one who is taught of the Spirit could do. You have been entirely free from freakish ideas, sensational methods, or unworthy motives, because you passionately love and adore the Lord Jesus Christ, and love His lost sheep.

I do not write thus to flatter you, but seek to state the simple truth, not only to express our love and gratitude to you, but also, if possible, to prepare the way before you, as you move to other fields, where prejudice or indifference again may hinder your great service to the Churches and to the unsaved.

To all who sincerely love the Lord Jesus Christ and who desire the rousing of the Churches, and the salvation of the perishing, I commend you, His dear servant, that they may welcome and help you, as is meet in the Lord.

If you can make any use of this letter, for sake of the great work, please do so.

COLONEL J. M. GRAHAM OF THE SALVATION ARMY

Orange Grove, Ivanhoe, Melbourne

Jeremiah 1 and 10 has had a modern fulfillment in the city of Melbourne in connection with the visit of Mrs. Aimee Semple McPherson of Canadian and American revivalist fame. They (her mother, Mrs. Kennedy, and herself) landed here in the very midst of cold iron prejudice enough to break the stoutest heart and kill right out any revival flame that might be burning, were it not for a few faithful souls who "sniffed" the enemy, stood to attention, and maintained the honor of Calvary; Christ.

Two weeks passed during which the tide of revival fervor and unction ebbed and flowed, catching up a minister and Christian worker here and there and deluging them in floods of blessing which made them realize that nothing much mattered, if only souls were led to and saved by our living Jesus,and these grand scenes were witnessed in every meeting where the "Altar Call" was given. Then, near half a hundred city and suburban ministers, evangelists and Salvation Army officers met the Evangelist and listened to her sweet, simple story of conversion, induement of the Holy Spirit and subsequent work for God and precious souls in Canada, America, England and China and there, moist eyes, tears, amens and hallelujahs emphasized and endorsed the testimony given and nearly every one jumped into the Revival campaign with both feet. Methodists, Episcopalians, Presbyterians, Baptists, Salvationists, Church of Christ, Quakers, Pentecostals, Jews and others, all uniting in Christian co-operation worthy of HIM, in Whose name we are all one.

Now we begin to realize what Melbourne was missing for want of earlier unity, and ministers and people threw themselves into the campaign to win out. The crowds suddenly swelled and surged to the Olympia day after day, from 12 noon to 10 P. M., until every nook and corner of the spacious building was held by eager, anxious folks, figuratively reaching out their hands for the bread of life. And what a bountiful supply they got! "As much as they would." Hallelujah!

We often sing "the sight that charms us most is a sinner at the cross," and charming indeed has been the nightly scenes we have witnessed of men, women and young people gaining the long aisles and hurrying voluntarily forward to the place of prayer, repentance, pardon and peace. Truly Melbourne has had a Spiritual Oasis in that old Olympia for these three last weeks; and what a splendid gathering of sheaves there was on the last Sunday afternoon, when hundreds of the campaign converts filled the ground floor in front of the platform and afterward filed over the platform to shake Sister McPherson's hand and receive a photo-text card as a reminder of their noble decision to live only for Jesus every day of their lives. I've had long experience as a revivalist, but I never shook hands with so many new converts in one day before, nor sweat over it as on this occasion, and I guess that was the experience of all the ministers who greeted them in like manner, and surely, surely, this is the beginning of better days for the Christian community of Melbourne. We must conserve the fruit already gathered and we must have more fruit that will remain till the great, grand, glorious gathering of blood-washed ones from earth's remotest bounds. There we shall lay all at the feet of our once suffering, crucified Savior Who is now our Advocate, Priest and King, to whom be glory, honor and praise forever and ever.

REV. J. P. H. TILBROOK, B. A., M. E. CHURCH

Goodwood, South Australia

As the missioner said, "The mission is at an end, but the revival will still go on." To those who availed themselves of the meetings there has come a time of blessing and inspiration. Cold print cannot tell what these meetings have been like, for no one can give an adequate description of life. It is a living, bright reality to the man or woman in Christ Jesus.

There are many happy memories of the mission. One feature of help *was the singing. The Christian religion is a singing religion.* The garment of praise is given for the spirit of heaviness. One heard the choruses of childhood sung over again, and his heart was strangely warmed as he listened to strains that brought back the "happy day that fixed his choice."

It was good to hear the men sing and to feel as they sang they meant it. Men do not sing very much when they are sad; but when gladness fills the soul, there is often an outburst of song. It was a happy revival. Everybody who learned to say "Amen" and shake hands with somebody else found a sense of fellowship in the Lord. The mission *was one of prayer.* Prayer was in it all. In the announcements, in the reading of the Word, in the appeal for souls and in the message of song.

There was the prayer of thankfulness when the offering was taken up and the offering became a religious act.

There was the prayer of the penitent at the altar as he or she prayed for strength to guide and power to heal and keep. One felt the spirit of it in the very atmosphere. There was a new vision in prayer and prayer does bring its visions. When Jesus prayed God's glory smote him on the face, when Peter prayed the prison gates were unlocked, when Paul and Silas prayed their chains fell off and all the dungeon flamed with light. We were reminded of the prayer in the upper room, and of the power of Pentecost. Some one has said, "The Church of God advances on its knees." This is true but "how dead and cold if Thou be absent, Lord." There was prayer for the sick and afflicted, and, always, there was the beautiful submission to the will of God and that the answer might indeed be according to His will.

Another feature of the mission was the *reading of the Word of God.* The old stories, parables, prophecies, invitations and warnings of the Bible flamed with fresh light. It was a treat to hear the missioner read. One felt like saying to her as she told us of Jesus, "You know this Jesus, then." There was no mere nodding acquaintance with Him, but many could say, *"He's real to me."*

The Old and New Testaments brought their combined messages and one felt again what a unity there is in the Word of God.

No account of the mission would be complete without reference to the Power of God's spirit and the conviction this gave to many souls. The men and women, boys and girls that decided for Christ, did so with boldness. They stood up and walked out to the altar. They knelt before God. They came from all parts of a building holding its thousands of people. Some of them came alone, some leaned upon the arm of friends. Some came with the story of a new-born resolution shining in their faces, others came with strong crying and tears. Many came for the first public confession of their faith in Christ and to give their hearts to Him. Many who were backsliders came. One young man in the chair gripped my hand. He said, "I am in your brother's church. I have been a backslider, but I am going back to the cross, and going back to teach in the Sunday school."

We have had *a time also of help and uplift to Christians.* Methodist, Presbyterian, Baptist, Salvation Army, Christian, etc., were represented among the workers. It was like a little bit of heaven just to have these times of sweet fellowship and song. To grasp the hands of other warriors in the fight for right, brought strength to one's soul. To kneel by some seeking penitent and to point the way to the Lamb of God that taketh away the sin of the world, was a joy to many a minister and Christian worker.

Let me here pay a tribute to the laymen, local preachers and others. They were a tower of strength, and God used them for His glory. We realize more than ever we are laborers together with God. In closing this brief sketch, let me say it can merely touch some of the salient features of this mission. I have purposely said very little about missioner. One could say very much of deep gratitude for her visit, her help, her sympathy, her work in the Lord. Permit me to commend her as a sister greatly beloved in the Lord. Let us all be up and at work for Christ in winning souls.

"Oh, what joy it will be
When His face we behold,
Living gems at His feet to lay down.
It will sweeten our joy in the City of God,
Should there be any stars in our crown."

REV. A. HARTLETT, M. E. CHURCH

From a recent fortnight's memorable mission in the Adelaide Exhibition Building, S. A., conducted by the Canadian Evangelist, Mrs. Aimee Semple McPherson, we select two subjects and addresses in particular that stand out distinctively in character and influence like mountains lifting their sunlit peaks in majesty and beauty, heavenward—"The second coming of our Lord," and "The dispensation of the Holy Spirit." Truly the deep things of God and life and the soul and Eternity have not lost their old Apostolic charm and power, and adaptation to the deepest wants and longings of the human heart, only a great deal depends on the presentation of the message, and the condition of the messenger.

About the doctrine of the Second Coming there is a peculiar nameless Something that age cannot wither. It never fails to arrest attention, enlist sympathy, awaken special interest and exert commanding influence over the spiritual and devout mind and heart. The danger is of carrying the great truth too far, of viewing it out of relation and proportion to other equally (and even more) important balancing truths and of forcing into it private and personal interpretations. All this Mrs. McPherson studiously avoids. Sound and sane, clear as sunlight, intensely spiritual in beautiful conception and expression, broad and Godlike in vision, abounding with relevant and irresistible proof texts, luminous with apt and homely illustrations, and sparkling with originality and charm of manner; these two addresses created a profound impression on the vast audience that on each occasion listened with unflagging interest for an hour and a half. Thank God there are many faithful ministers in this country who preach the great Cardinal Doctrines of Grace with passion and conviction, and much ability, though with varying interpretations, but for the last fortnight, we are bound to say that we have seen and felt truth *unusually* vivified and active; truth passed through the medium of a pure, surrendered, spirit-filled and most winsome personality; truth on fire of love, burning in the soul like anthracite with a clear, steady, vehement flame, and communicating itself to others in a most remarkable manner. And the secret of it all seems to be that this Evangelist gets her inspiration and perennial freshness first hand and direct, not merely from the great facts and statements about Christ, but from a constant and an ever-deepening communion with the living and unchanging Christ, Himself, through trust and love. And so long as this simplicity and godly sincerity are maintained, will she continue to be used of God to sway great masses of people, and to reach the hidden depths of many a heart with quiet and commanding power that moves to a better life.

A great deal of real and lasting good was wrought by the addresses on "The dispensation of the Holy Spirit." To many it contained nothing new, but it was so marvelously comprehensive and uttered with such a note of certainty and realism and conviction and persuasiveness of love, that it seemed new, and one could feel that the Spiritual life of many was deeply moved and lifted to a higher plane. It brought an added element of power into the mission, moreover, that expressed itself in increasing numbers of penitents at the mercy-seat, and a clearly marked pressure of the people to hear the word of God.

The mission has been a great blessing to this city. Apart from every other consideration we have had the joy—the joy that stands alone—of seeing between three and four hundred souls, ranging in age from seventy years to ten, bowed humbly at the feet of the Blessed Redeemer. Stimulus has come to the churches, hitherto unknown, joy and gladness to many a heart and home, and while we sorrowfully say good-by to our Sister McPherson, we thank God most fervently for her visit and the work accomplished through her here, and will do our best to conserve the results of the mission and to make them more extensive and enduring.

IN DEEP WATERS

SAMUEL BLACKNEY, SEACLIFF PRESBYTERIAN CHURCH
Adelaide, South Australia.

A father and son were leaning on the rail of one of our Jetties one sunny day, when the boy said "Father, what is that blue line out to sea?" "That is where deep water begins, my boy. This light colored water inshore is the shallows where no boat can come, but out there is always deep water where the steamers can ride in safety."

It seems to me that this metaphor can be readily used to describe the effect of the Mission. We have been bumping on the shallows in great danger of being driven on the shoals of "Lost Faith" and "God Forsakenness" but thank God the Wind of the Holy Spirit has blown us clear out into deep waters where we may anchor in safety.

Mrs. McPherson came to Adelaide earlier than she expected and so arrived quite unannounced. A local committee of which I had the honor to be Secretary, was called together in a hurry to assist Mrs. McPherson in her campaign. There was none of the elaborate organization about this Mission that there had been about others that have visited our fair city; but the Holy Spirit was perhaps the more able to work in His own way because He was not hampered by man-made restrictions.

I was present at the first meeting at the Exhibition Building through curiosity as I had read much of Mrs. McPherson in American magazines. The small audience of about 300 or 400 people was there mainly out of curiosity also as the mission had only been advertised for two days. However, the Spirit of God moved mightily even in such an inauspicious beginning and when the Altar Call came the Altar began rapidly to fill.

It was this that to my mind stamped it as a work of God at the outset. There was no working up of emotion, no shouting and raving on the part of the Evangelist, no "come and be saved or you'll go to hell" business.

The preacher simply presented the old message of the infinite Love of Jesus Christ as Savior and Lord with the old-time fervor and in the old-time way, and the Spirit of God moved in the hearts of the people with mighty power. The meetings for the first week were held in the afternoon at Chalmers Presbyterian Church, of which Dr. Seymour is the Pastor. He was also Chairman of the Local Committee for Mrs. McPherson's Campaign. The Exhibition Building was used in the evening. By the end of the first week Chalmers was too small, as the meetings continued to grow steadily. On the second Sunday when Mrs. McPherson gave the story of her life, the building was filled, and continued full right to the end of the Mission.

The time has been all too short; but it has been wonderful how God has blessed us. Not only have numbers of sinners been converted, but backsliders have been restored to faith in the Lord Jesus Christ. Christians have had their hearts warmed and their faith renewed by the wonderfully fresh presentation of the Gospel and the Baptism of the Holy Spirit. As I have had charge of the Fishers in the audience during the Altar Calls, I have had a good opportunity of noting the effect of the message upon the people. Billy Sunday has said, "If you're not stirring up the Devil sometimes you're not on the job." Truly the benign Presence of the Lord was with us in every meeting; but the Evil One was there also as a "roaring Lion seeking whom he might devour." As night after night I pleaded with the most difficult cases of those who were under conviction but who would not, or could not, give their hearts to the Lord Jesus, I looked into faces set as unyielding as iron and saw the Devil look out of eyes as hard as agate. But, praise God, the ancient power of the Atoning Blood of Jesus is as strong as ever it was. For four nights we prayed with one girl under conviction and beheld the wonder of the Miracle that brought her from Death to Life. For seven nights we prayed with another ere she surrendered. We were called another night to an old man who had been away from the Lord for twenty-two years, who yearned to come back but he could not. His face was set in lines of iron. "I want to come back. I know that Jesus is holding out His arms for me to come back; but the Devil has me. I cannot." The next night, another fight, and then he let Jesus come in and oh! the happiness that radiated from his face. We were called up into the gallery where an old man was pleading with two boys and two girls. "These are my two boys," he said, "with their sweethearts." We pleaded and pointed out how wonderful it would be for them to give their hearts to Jesus before they took their marriage vows. When they came to the altar the mother of the girls met them and we all knelt at the altar to thank God for His saving power. I shall never forget the glory on the faces of those young people as they left the building that night. And so the work went on and in the fortnight a work has been commenced which we hope by the grace of God will grow into a mighty nationwide revival. Adelaide has not been so shaken in the last ten years. In closing I would like to give my own testimony. Mrs. McPherson's sermons are true Expository Preaching.

Of all those that I have read and heard they remind me most of Spurgeon. She has taken only the Bible as the basis of her exposition, and no word did she speak that I could not preach from my own pulpit. Especially in the Sermon on the Second Coming, which caused a good deal of controversy here, there was nothing that I could not believe. Her message has given me a closer personal communion with my Savior and opened up treasure troves in God's Word which will be to my lasting benefit. Many of the ministers in the city could duplicate my testimony. We thank God for having sent our Sister across the sea to us, and we ask God's blessing on her work wherever she may be.

BEAUTIFUL ANGELUS TEMPLE AT ECHO PARK

THE CROWNING GLORY OF FOURTEEN YEARS' MINISTRY

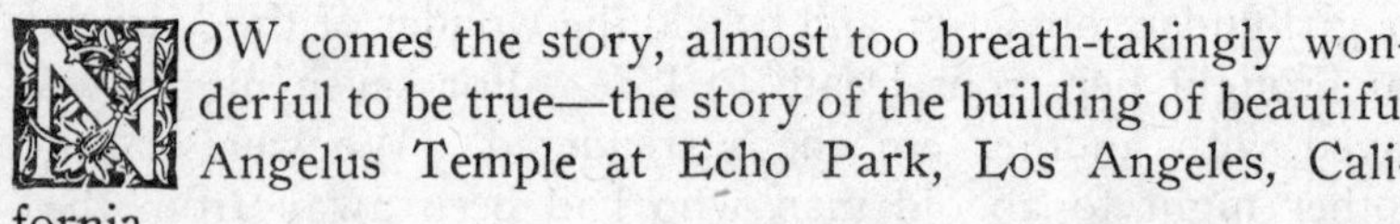

NOW comes the story, almost too breath-takingly wonderful to be true—the story of the building of beautiful Angelus Temple at Echo Park, Los Angeles, California.

You have laughed and cried, rejoiced and sympathized at the story of "The House That God Built," and yet, that little house could be hidden many times beneath the shadow of the great and glorious house which has since been builded in the heart of the salfsame city, and stands as a monument to the power of the living God.

For fourteen years, we had traveled about the world. The last few months had been spent in revival campaigns in Wichita, Kans.; Canton, Ohio; Fresno, Calif.; a return campaign in Denver, Colo.; a campaign in San Francisco, a tent meeting in Oakland, California, a journey to the other side of the world and the holding of a revival campaign in Australia, Melbourne—Adelaide—Sidney, a meeting in New Zealand, Honolulu and our return to America.

During the months of constant traveling across the American continent, our hearts were oft times filled with wonder as to why the Lord had led us to "the little house that God built" and had located the same in the seemingly far-off city of Los Angeles. A meeting in Philadelphia, Washington, Baltimore, and then on the train and away we go back across the desert's burning sands, to the little babes in the Western home. A few hours of visiting, planning, loving and providing for them and then away we would be called, back across those three thousand of miles to plunge into the work in other cities —Rochester, New York, Canton, Ohio, Wichita, Kansas, Oklahoma City, etc., and back again to the "House that God built," e'er setting out again.

"Dear Lord Jesus," we began to ask, "would it not have been better, if you had placed our little home somewhere in the East or in the Middle West, where it would have been more accessible?"

Then it was, that the Lord, most gently, but unquestionably began to reveal to me His will, showing me that there had been a method in the plan of His leading; and that in this City of the Angels, *we were to "Build A House Unto the Lord."*

Little did we dream that this house should be the mighty and glorious Temple, under whose shadow I write these words. Surely it would be a wooden tabernacle, an inexpensive, temporary and very ordinary affair!—Had we ever dreamed of the real plan of God for the present building, the audacity and seeming impossibility of such a gigantic undertaking, we would have been so alarmed as to forbid the very mention of it. During the brief visits in Los Angeles, my Mother and myself went so far as to look at several wooden structures, saying to ourselves—"perhaps this could be built for $10,000—the other for $20,000." How little we know the plans of God, that were to be unfolded in the immediate future.

"Come let us build a house unto the Lord!" So urgently did the words ring in our ears that one day we got in our automobile and set out in search of land. For the Lord had shown us that this "House unto the Lord" was to be builded in the City of Los Angeles whither tourists coming constantly from all parts of the earth, could receive the message, then return like homing pigeons, bearing the message in their hearts.

Reaching Figueroa and Third Streets, where we usually turned into the heart of the city, we were strangely impressed to drive on another block to Second, then turn into Glendale Blvd. We had driven only a few minutes until we came to Echo Park and saw for the first time—for we had never before been in this section of the city—this beautiful park, with its great placid lake, the largest body of water in Los Angeles, its drooping palms, willows and eucalyptus trees; the graceful swan sailing peacefully across the mirrored lake.

Involuntarily, the words burst from my lips, "Why, Mother, this is heaven on earth, the most beautiful spot for the House of the Lord, that I have ever seen! Do you remember, Mother, how in the heart of the great cities, where the building must be emptied between meetings, the people have stood in the hot sun, hour after hour, waiting for admittance? Here they would have the park, the trees, the grass, the benches, the flowing fountain, the picnic tables and here are even the stoves and the wood provided free of charge by the city, upon which to cook their lunches! Here are sand trays for the children, a children's outdoor nursery—here are rest-rooms and every thing that one could desire and yet the whole locality, though so near the heart of the city and on two of the largest car lines, is strangely peaceful and quiet and providing parking spaces for the hundreds of automobiles that would gather—oh, Mother, look!"

We had been driving slowly, and had now come to Park Avenue, the entrance to Echo Park. Lying just before us was a circular piece of property, facing Glendale Blvd., Park Avenue and Lemoyne Street. Something leaped within our hearts saying, *"This is the place."* Never for a moment, in the months that followed, did we doubt that this was the location, or seek another piece of land, nor have we since found its equal, for its beauty of situation.

Just a few doors away, we found a small real estate office and inquired from the elderly gentleman who answered the door, as to the land in question. He replied:

"Certainly, Lady, there is lots of land around this park for sale, but you have picked on the only piece of property that is not in the market. There is an elderly lady named ——, who is wealthy, and has many property holdings, but refuses to part with any of it. Other people have tried to get this land and have offered high prices. To these she answered "No, I am not interested in selling."

"Then, praise the Lord!" we answered. "The Lord has been keeping this property for us, and His word is confirmed."

"Wh—what did you say?" he asked in bewilderment.

We did not repeat our words, for perhaps he would not understand. But *we* knew. Hallelujah!

A few hours later, my mother suddenly felt impressed and stopped in the midst of wrapping and mailing "The Bridal Call," and with a brother, she walked over to the park to look at this property. As they walked my mother was telling this brother of my enthusiasm regarding it, and when they reached the corner, lo and behold! a freshly painted sign stood in the very center of the land, saying "For Sale, Snap this Corner" —a picture of the lot, with the name and address of the owner given below. Quickly the news was brought to me, and later, as we all stood on the lot, I took a lead pencil and sketched upon the sign board—diagram of the lot, the way the "House unto the Lord" should be builded.

"See, Mother, the property is shaped just like a megaphone, the platform and choir will be in this corner—the aisles would run like this—if we put in a balcony it would go here." Rapidly we sketched. We seemed to be able to visualize the floor plan with a flash, almost exactly as it is today, before even the land was ours.

The rest of the story reads almost like a fairy tale. We found our way to the property owner's home. The elderly lady who owned so much land, had suddenly decided that she was land poor, and of all her holdings, this was the one piece that she had decided to part with.

Within a short time, the land was purchased, and oft times, in the middle of the night, we would rise, get in our car and drive eight miles (for the "House that God built" was pretty well out into the country) to stand on the property, to dream and pray for the work which the Lord would have us do. Never were we able to come to the property or to the park without the words bursting from our lips, "This is heaven, heaven below," or without feeling the spirit of the Lord mightily upon us. But how, and where were we to begin? There were just the two little women—my mother and myself. No great board or advisory committees had we, but the Lord was with us.

We decided that the first thing to do was to grade the land, and to this end we hired eleven mules and scrapers and the men to work them and began our task of removing the small hill and preparing for the foundations, still unrealizing the magnitude of the task which the Lord had allotted.

We felt that considering the throngs that had attended the meetings in other cities, we could *not* erect a building with a seating capacity less than five thousand, and were soon informed that our building must be fire proof, if we would hold this many people, and care for them properly. Here the Lord brought into our lives, Mr. Brook Hawkins, builder and contractor, of the Winter Construction Company and into whose competent hands we put the drawings and the erection of the building.

Standing across the street, at the entrance of the park, we said, "It is here that we will build a House unto the Lord," and outlined to him, our plans.

"How much money have you toward it?" was his very natural question.

"About five thousand dollars," was our reply.

"That ought to be enough to dig a good hole for a foundation," he said.

"Well, you excavate and get your steam shovels to work," I replied, "and by that time, we will have the money for the foundations." And so we did.

While they were digging, we were preaching in St. Louis, and there the Lord gave us the means for the foundation.

Proudly, we brought it home, saying, "Now, you put in the foundation, and by the time that is done, we will have enough money for the walls." And so we did—by the loyal help of Denver, Colorado, other cities in which meetings were held, and the rallying round of our old friends in Canada and across the sea.

The building was now being constructed under class "A" rulings, being composed entirely of concrete and steel, and having in addition to the great expanse of its main floor, two balconies and an immense dome, which reared its lofty canopy some hundred and ten feet from the floor, and which is said to be the largest unsupported concrete dome on the American continent. The following is an article written for the "Bridal Call," about this time, which told our feelings during the progress of erection and amid the responsibilities thus entailed. It was written on board the *S. S. Maunganui,* enroute for Australia, as a day dream, over the typewriter, of what the Temple in Los Angeles would be to a dusty, toil-worn sinner:

"HE LOOKETH FORTH AT THE WINDOWS"

Songs of Solomon 2:9.

In fancy I entered a Temple, near a golden, sunset sea; my heart was heavy within me and my feet were dusty and bruised. I had come from life's hedges and highways, and it's din still raged in my ear. Money and greed, worldly sorrows and strife, resentment against the wrongs of my fellow, rose and fell in my disquieted heart till it stormed like a turbulent sea.

Then out of the dust and the strivings I was carried on discontent feet, till I paused by a green and a fragrant place, with waters that mirrored the sky, and trees that bent low, speaking shelter and peace reminding of heaven above. And just through their parted beauty I glimpsed a Temple whose arches and dome, caught my breath with a vision of beauty, and made me rub my hot, tired eyes. Is this earth? Or is it heaven, with it's purity, fragrance and peace, stilling the tempest within my soul and bidding me find sweet rest?

So I crossed the circular, winding street, with its vistas of mirror and green, and I gazed through a door clear as crystal, and there caught a glimpse of cool, clean lobbies and a fountain that sparkled clear: and I read: "Whosoever will, let Him take freely the water of life."—Water! Life! Rest! Cool!—

Ah, how I needed them, craved them, after my bustling, sweating struggle with the world.

My hand I put forth timidly, and touched that crystal door; surely I'd find it bolted 'gainst such a dusty-highway soul! But no, it swung gently inward with only a finger's touch, and I drank of that cool, flowing fountain and wandered on and in through the door of the Temple, where quietly bowing my head, a feeling of reverence stole o'er me—I remembered the prayers of my Mother, snatches of song and of scripture I had not recalled in years.

I seemed alone in the Temple, and drank deep of it's message there. I was conscious first of it's bigness; yet the soft, intimate nearness of it all. Mellow pools of rose, violet, gold, green, crimson and blue bathed altar and floor at my feet. The great hundred-foot dome, sweeping up and away above me held captive the blue of an Arizona sky, while the fleecy clouds of heaven, tinged with the glow of sunrise, nestled here and there. Beneath it, in a broad band of gold, as a wondrous message from the sky, I read: *"Jesus Christ The Same Yesterday, Today and Forever."*

And then, turning about, I forgot all else, and my battered and sin-sick soul was lifted clear out of it's strife and storm and caught up in ethereal calm. I'd forgotten the Temple, the galleries, the dome—except as a setting exquisite—for my eyes had come to rest on a window that swept aside the curtains of time and space. I stood in ancient Bethlehem, where the little Christ Child lay wrapped in swaddling clothes and in a manger, with a halo 'round His head. From the arch above, the cherubs sang, and the light of Bethlehem's star illumined His face, surpassing fair—the light of the world, was He. Mary, His mother, was seated there, and Joseph in the shadows dim. The wise men kneeled, offering gold, frankincense, myrrh; and a lamb lay asleep at His feet. But these eyes of mine, were for but one little face; and His eyes gazed down at me; while the angels sang: "Unto you, O man, is born this day in the City of David, a Savior, which is Christ the Lord" and suddenly there was with the angel a multitude of heavenly host, saying: Glory to God in the highest, and on earth peace, goodwill toward men.

A Savior to *me?* Peace—goodwill to *me?* Could it be true. He was come for *me?* That from out the storm of life with it's heart-break and toils came the voice of the Savior of Peace calling *me?*

Suddenly I found myself before another window, and He looked forth from it's light. I stood by the River Jordan and my Savior was pictured there receiving the Holy Spirit, in form of a heavenly dove; while John and the multitude waiting gazed up at the opened sky, whence the voice of God like thunder introduced to earth His gift: *"This is My Beloved Son"*—How the mountains trembled at His voice, *"In Whom"*—my heart melted before Him, *"I am well pleased."*

And then to ancient Jerusalem, I was swept by the window just next. In the foreground the Lord in a seamless dress, as white as the lilies fair, bended low o'er a woman taken in sin. Her face was flushed from weeping, pearly tear-drops yet wet on her cheek. In her eyes the hurt look of a sore-wounded child was being replaced by a slow, dawning wonder of hope and joy. *"Neither do I condemn thee"*—was ever a voice like that? *"Thy sins which were many, are all forgiven,"* —rushing water, Balm of Gilead, honey in the comb, to what shall I compare His tones? *"Go in peace—and sin no more."*

Peace—peace? Ah, God, how my own heart wanted peace; could it be that there was peace for me; that my sins too could be forgiven. Yea, of this there could be no doubt, for standing there in the mellow light of late afternoon He, my Savior, was "looking forth at the window," in fancies picture. If He could forgive her, could He, would He not also pardon and speak peace to me?

And now I stood by the altar, gazing at the window there depicting the healing of the sick with a touch of His gentle hand. The bedfast were raised; the fevered were cooled, and a little child made to walk. The crooked were straight; the leper was cleansed by the Man Of Galilee. And yonder the evening sun smiled peacefully and slipped 'neath Judean hills. But could He do this for a battered soul of the present day, broken on the wheel of life? Yes, yes, He could, for, lifting my eyes I drank in the message again: "Jesus Christ the same —the *same*—yesterday, today and for aye."

I crossed the altar, soft, carpeted, inviting; and there, on the other side, through a flood of silver and blue I gazed on Gethsemane. "Looking forth at the window" was pictured my Lord; kneeling alone by a cold, shadowy rock, hands clasped resignedly upon it's mossy top, He seemed most wondrous fair. Ferns, lichens and tall lilies swayed toward Him in the breeze. A soft zephyr stilled gently the locks of His uncovered head, and a shaft of silver moonlight fell full upon His pale face and lighted it with startling brilliance midst the gloom. The three disciples sleeping yonder, seemed to remind me that I too had been asleep, rejecting, failing and denying Him—my Lord.

And as I stood, there came someway a strange tug at my heart, as softly I heard His; "Nevertheless, not My will, but Thine be done." I felt I would love to tarry there and watch with Him life's little hour. Why had I never thought of these things during the past busy years of my life! How could I have slept unmindful of such a love as this!

And now, 'twas at the foot of the cross I stood: gazing upon my Lord whose face was marred yet strangely fair as He whispered: "Father, forgive." And my heart just broke within me that my sins had nailed Him there.

But, in a twinkling, my grief was changed to gladness, for I gazed on another scene. 'Twas ascension morning now, and my living, loving, triumphant Lord had risen into the air: hands outstretched in blessing, His words fell in a golden shower: "I go to prepare a place for you; but I will come again."

And now before the last of these eight wonderful windows, as though through curtains that had been swept aside, I gazed on a scene depicting the present-day Lord, Who said "Behold I stand and knock." Yes, there He was pictured in His seamless dress, knocking with nail-pierced hand at the fast closed door of my selfish heart that would not let Him in. No latch was there on the *outer* side; the opening lay with me. "Oh come, dear Lord,"—I cried that day, "teach me how to ope' the door! Come in with Thy Peace, Thy Salvation and Love, and ever abide with me."

The hours had passed in the Temple there, and my cheeks were suffused with tears. I sat me down in a chair and on its arm I read: "Donated, with the prayer that some tired and sin-sick soul, may find rest and peace through the message heard from the depths of this chair tonight." I bowed my head and pondered it seemed not strange but fitting someway that this chair was intended for me.

Suddenly—my thoughts were caught up by music. Some one had entered and taken his place at the console of the organ. A tiny light flashed on and I saw his fingers move silently over the keys of the third manual. With bated breath I listened, as there came drifting down from the Temple Chimes on the outer roof, the glory of the bells:

"Abide with me, fast falls the eventide.
The darkness deepens, Lord with me, abide;
Change and decay, in all around I see,
O Thou Who Changest not—abide with me."

Shaken to the very soul of me, I too cried out in spirit, for this everpresent unchanging Lord of the ages, Whose kindness and power of yesterday had been shown me through "the windows" and whom my bible declared to be just the same today. I suddenly felt very much like a little child that had lost its day in the gathering darkness that shrouded the close of life's short day, and I wanted Him so—how could I find the way?

Then the lights were lit. A multitude of people had filled the Temple now. All eyes were toward the front, from whence the great pipe organ was speaking in thundrous volume of the glory, power, majesty of Him Who loved and washed poor sinners in His own Blood. The very structure seemed to rock and tremble before the stately steppings of His feet. Then the music drifted into a minor strain, speaking of a tender Shepherd, leading His flock into green pastures and causing them to lie down beside the still waters; a Shepherd who carried weak Lambs in His bosom, and Who leaving "the ninety and nine that safely lay in the shelter of His fold" went down the mountainsides to seek the one that had gone astray.

Again the stream of music turned, and now the lights were dimmed. A lighted cross seemed to glow before my eyes as the great organ whispered and somewhere in the dome the echo organ answered it:

"When I survey the wondrous cross,
On which the Prince of Glory died;
My richest gain I count but dross,
And pour contempt on all my pride.

Were the whole realm of nature mine,
That were an offering far too small;
Love so amazing, so divine, demands
My life, my love, my soul, my all."

Unnoticed the chorus had taken its place. The throng was singing. The angels of God seemed hovering near. The sermon and the messenger came to me through a blur of tears; and then an altar-call was given. Gentle nail-pierced hands were lifting, guiding, bearing me to the altar-rail. I kneeled at the Savior's feet, gentle voices were teaching me to pray. The burden of years was gone. I lifted myself up. I straightened my shoulders from which the load had disappeared. I drew a long breath and wiped my eyes of their mistiness—*I was a child of God.* Looking up at the organ, I wondered if this glory could be but the beginning of a new life.

"Ring the bells of heaven, there is joy today;
For a soul returneth from the wild.
See the Father meets Him, out upon the way,
Welcoming His wayward, wandering child."

The bells and the chimes of the Temple organ pealed forth above the glad voices of the singers, thrilling, exultant:

"Glory! glory, how the angels sing!
Glory! glory, how the loud harps ring!
'Tis the ransomed army, like a mighty sea,
Pealing forth the anthems of the free."

The poor, lonely, sin-sick, heavy-laden heart of me was aweary no longer. I was lifted up into heavenly places with Christ Jesus my newfound Lord. New life was before me, new hopes and ambitions, and the pathway like a heavenly ladder with angels ascending and descending thereon, began at my feet.

A bugle is sounded in my ears; a kiss, soft little mothery kiss is planted on the back of my neck; stout little eager hands of my children are tugging at my garments:

"Lunch-time, honey-dear! Are you going to sit there day-dreaming with your head on your typewriter all day long? Put away your work for a little while, my dear, mustn't keep them waiting you know."

I sit up with a start; blink my eyes at the sunlight that glows like molten fire on the waves on the rolling sea and find that instead of being in the completed Angelus Temple at Echo Park planning the wooing and winning of some poor sin-sick fellow and what his feelings would be upon entering that Temple upon which so much of our love and prayers have been expended for the past months, I am still on board the *S. S. Maunganui* sailing the foam-flecked billows of the broad Pacific. The swish of the sea is in my tears. Hurrying feet are pattering lunch-ward along the deck and I suppose that I should go too.

But, vision—prophecy—day dreams or not, the fact remains that the thousands of miles of rolling seas and landless horizons cannot keep in bound the thoughts and prayers of this fond heart of mine. Angelus Temple, Echo Park, the planning of seats and aisles, the organ that shall swell the Savior's praise, the need of the picture-windows which will tell so well the story that e'en a way-farer and deaf and dumb could read and understand the message glowing there as "*He* looketh forth at the windows and showeth Himself through the lattice," the effect of it all upon the tired, rushing thousands of men and women of today, their thoughts and feelings as inspired by the Temple fill my heart and soul and send me a-dreaming 'way back across the billows to that place where today this beautiful Temple of God is rising into the air as concrete mixers churn, bars of steel are lifted, window-frames are being fitted and a house unto the Lord completed.

On anuary the first, 1923, this mighty temple was opened. Since the break of day, surging multitudes had been gathering, filling the streets in every direction, waiting for the doors to open. At 2 o'clock in the afternoon, a scaffolding had been hastily erected in front of the Temple and draped with a great American flag. Loving hands, atremble with eagerness and the excitement of the moment, lifted me to the top of the scaffolding, from which the outside dedication service was held, and from which we read the story of the ancient Temple of Jerusalem and kneeling down, repeated Solomon's prayer. From somewhere within, a clear voice came singing:

"Open the gates of the Temple,
Strew palms on the Conqueror's way,
Open your hearts O ye people
That Jesus may enter today—

Hark, from the sick and the dying,
Leaving their couches of pain,
Voices, glad voices are swelling,
Are swelling, the glad, the glad refrain."

The following is an article written under the glow of the Dedicatory Service:

THE DEDICATION OF ANGELUS TEMPLE

Story from The Bridal Call

Lord God of Israel, there is no God like Thee, in heaven above or on earth beneath, who keepest covenant and mercy with Thy servants that walk before Thee with all their heart. Thou speakest also with Thy mouth, and hast fulfilled it with Thy hand as it is this day.

But will God indeed dwell on the earth? Behold the heaven and the heaven of heavens cannot contain Thee; how much less this house which I have builded?

Yet have Thou respect unto the prayer which Thy servant prayeth before Thee today:

That Thine eyes may be opened toward this house night and day, even toward the place of which Thou hast said, My name shall be there: that Thou mayest hearken unto the prayer which Thy servant shall make toward this place.

And hearken Thou to the supplication of Thy servant, and of Thy people Israel when they shall pray toward this place: and hear Thou in heaven thy dwelling place: and when Thou hearest forgive.

SLOWLY, majestically the old year faded and the new year dawned over the green fragrance and beauty of Echo Park in Los Angeles, California. The booming of the midnight bell had found hundreds of saints with bowed heads wrapped in earnest prayer. Singing and testimony, prayer and bible study had freighted with jewels of silver and gold the passing of the closing hours of 1922. Christian hands had reached out, sought each other, clasped, and clung, in Christian fellowship and good will. With deep emotion and with eager, prayerful anticipation each had waited the coming of the new year that was to be so eventful in each waiting heart and life. Many had crossed the continent or come from abroad for the opening of Angelus Temple, Church of the Four-Square Gospel at Echo Park.

The darkness faded. Night gathered the purple fringed folds of her garments together and lifted them clear of the mountains that surround Los Angeles, California. The day—the day of days —the day we had all waited for with such earnestness of prayer and expectation—the greatest—the crowning day of fifteen years of ministry—the day when the seemingly imposible had become possible, the glorious dream a living fact and the wondrous vision a concrete reality.

Hurry, sun, hurry! Lift your shining, golden face above eastern hills and kiss the fields, the flowers, the trees, the shining lake, the park, the streets to wakefulness, peep through drawn shades, bid every sleeper wake—this is the day of days. But Ah! methinks you will find many another face pressed like mine against the window pane lifted in prayer, eagerly waiting your coming, oh New Year's day of nineteen twenty-three.

Slowly, surely the pearl gray of dawn lights the heavens. Slowly, gloriously, the brush of morning tints the clouds with rose and gold. Slowly, majestically, the palms and cypress, the eucalyptus and the willows of Echo Park begin to be clean cut from the night and stand silhouetted against the glory of the California sky, slanting rays of light come sifting through the foliage of green. The sun is risen, the day — the day is come.

Like the unveiling of a breath-taking beautiful monument it seems, the lifting of the curtain of slumbering night from Angelus Temple. Footsteps can be heard on the pavement without. Motor cars are beginning to draw up at the curbing. Others have come to watch night unveil the Temple and morning clothe it in her radiant glory.

Hold your breath, watchers in the streets below, throw up your shades, draw aside the curtains from your window—all ye houses that line the hill that overlook the city. Does it mean to you, the unveiling of the Temple on its first birthday, what it means to us? See, the sun has kissed the first point of the top of the dome! It is creeping down the rounded sides. See it flash and twinkle, scintillate and glow as though encrusted in gems. Dew, you ask? No, crushed abalone shells from the sea shore have been powdered and sprinkled through the concrete of the dome and now catch the sun and flash, making the beauty which newspaper writers call "the jeweled dome." Ah! now the light has crept lower, bathing the entire Temple in her radiance, the columns and arches, the cornices and the hundreds of window panes all flashing back her shining.

On the two center columns are the granite tablets, veiled, waiting the dedication service.

The footsteps on the pavement increase in number. Other automobiles are drawing up from every side. Happy voices, singing voices, drift up to our windows. The streets are filling with people who are determined to gain admittance when the doors of the Temple swing open, if being early is any advantage over being late. They are assured by workers and attendants that the building does not open till 2:30 in the afternoon. They reply that they are fully aware of the fact and that it does not make the slightest difference. More people are coming, and still more.

We realize that we who wait also are trembling with excitement and the greatness of the day almost frightens us. We turn away and bathe our faces and fully dressed, run to the Temple doors to assure ourselves that all will be in readiness. Yes, there are the workers who have toiled within its gates, armies of them since midnight putting on the finishing touches required for opening. Brooms are sweeping, carpet is being laid, the piano is being brought in, and the golden harp of Miss Carter of Australia is lifted to the platform; Dickey, the little canary bird given to the House that God Built and told of in "This is That," is being carried in and hung by the piano. Quick orders are being given; scores of workmen are almost flying here, there, yonder. Mr. Brook Hawkins, builder-architect, is directing everything, superintending the bringing in of the rubber trees in their boxes, the box woods and the palms. Now he is draping the Stars and Stripes over one rampart and the Canadian flag over the other. This last touch is of his own planning and thoughtfulness. Yonder ushers are drilling and planning as to how they shall handle the crowds.

Outside the sun is climbing higher. A sound of hammers is heard, a temporary platform is being built in front of the Temple and also draped with a huge flag, gift to the Evangelist from the women of the Grand Army of the Republic.

The crowds are growing. Police are becoming anxious. Traffic must be turned into other streets. Officers are struggling to keep the people free of the street car tracks that the cars may pass. The hours creep on—nine, ten, eleven, twelve o'clock; one, two—the crowd is being augmented every moment. It is a wonderful sight, specially wonderful on this New Year's day when hundreds of thousands are in Pasadena to witness the Tournament of Roses, wherein, in a most beautiful and impressive way, California displays to the onlooking world the flowers that God has given her while the rest of the country is buried in winter's ice and snow. But those in Pasadena must know the Temple, too! The whole world, we feel must know! So while at Echo Park, assembled thousands gaze up at the real Temple, in Pasadena other thousands gaze upon the Temple in miniature (yet large enough to cover entirely the largest truck in Los Angeles), made entirely of roses and fragrant dew-kissed flowers. We have a float in the parade advertising the Temple and its opening as the Church of the Four-Square Gospel. And this float being a replica of the real Temple with its choir girls singing like angels to the strains of the organ within, is awarded a prize and bears it home to Angelus Temple triumphantly.

Two-fifteen! How patiently the people have waited. Come, the time of Dedication is here! A door in the front of the Temple is opened. Willing hands are there to assist the Evangelist onto the platform. Won't you come up with me, we ask several timidly. No. Sister, you must go alone, they answer. A final push and we are alone on that improvised platform looking down into that great sea of upturned faces.

And now they are singing, "All Hail the Power of Jesus' Name." Did you ever hear singing like that? Seems as though it would make the very heavens ring. Fleecy clouds of softest white are nestling above in the blue sky and reflected in the shining lake beneath. Can it be that there are angels looking on from heaven on this day of days? And now we are reading to that silent, listening sea of humanity of the building of another Temple in the days of Solomon, of its dedication and of the glory of the Lord that filled it. There is a choke in our voice and a catch at our heart as we come to the prayer of Solomon, wherein he kneeled down upon his knees before all the congregation of Israel and rejoiced in the Lord his God in that He had fulfilled with His hand that which He had promised with His mouth.

Another song, a prayer, and we are lowered to the pavement where a trowel with some mortar is put into our hand and we are completing the laying of the dedicatory stones, and unveiling the tablets with solemn ceremony. We brush the tears from our eyes and look a second time at the inscription thereon. The surging but quiet multitude behind are also straining to see, and there we read:

"Here it is, O Lord," we hear our own voice as though from a great distance, "we lift this Temple in the arms of Faith and give it unto Thee, set it apart, consecrate it wholly unto Thy cause and the preaching of Thine eternal gospel. It seems strange to be giving this Temple unto Thee today, dear Master, for it was Thine before a stone was laid or a trowel full of mortar laid. It was Thine, all Thine, when by faith we saw it afar. But now, O Lord, we give it unto Thee in actuality and lift our hearts and voices unto Thee in thanksgiving and earnest supplication, praying that naught but Thy will shall ever be done within its gates and borders. May thousands of sinners be carried thither upon the streams of prayer and in Thee find Salvation. May the sick in multitude here touch Thy garment and be made whole. May believers here be baptized with the mighty power of the Holy Spirit and go forth as a blazing firebrand for Thee. May consecrated young lives be here trained and consecrated to the preaching of Thy Word and go forth as flaming Evangels who will turn communities upside down for the Lord Jesus. May young men and women here consecrate their lives and be trained for missionary work, then go out to sail the seven seas bearing the message of Jesus of Nazareth to the ends of the earth. May naught but faith in Thy Word, and the ever-present great I AM of the Lord Jehovah's power be preached. May the multitudes of hungry seekers see Jesus Christ revealed before their eyes and know that He is indeed the same yesterday, today and forever. Amen."

Again the people are singing. Hands have drawn us through a doorway into the Temple. We are started up a stairway and on our way to the training school for a moment's quiet before the indoor meeting. As we mount the steps we hear the doors of the Temple flung wide. We hear a murmur of voices like the billows of the sea. And then the crowd surging over the steps and up the aisles, filling the main auditorium, filling the balcony, climbing the balcony, packing each available inch of space, and then the doors are closed.

The choir in shining, white, new uniforms are assembled in a long row across the entire middle aisle of the first balcony. A signal from the piano, and they are singing:

"Holy, holy, holy, Lord God Almighty
Early in the morning our songs
Shall rise to Thee.

Only Thou art Holy, merciful and mighty
God, in three Persons,
Blessed Trinity."

With the second verse they had begun a slow but impressive processional down the balcony steps and dividing their number are flowing along the ramparts that lead to the choir loft above the platform of either side. How beautiful they look, consecrated, bright faces, earnest young people who have volunteered for service and many of whom expect to receive training for the work of Evangelism.

And now, with a coterie of ministers on either side and Mr. Brook Hawkins, Temple builder, taking our arm, we are on our way, also making our way down the rampart and to the platform.

"Don't tremble like that, Sister; keep steady, you mustn't be nervous. The battle is all fought and the victory here now," a voice is saying.

"Oh, it isn't with nervousness, brother, but with joy," we answer. "This, this is the greatest day of our lives save two—the day when I was converted in that lonely country road in Canada, and the day I received my baptism with the blessed Holy Spirit. Oh, how good, good, good, God has been to bring my little family back across the continent safely for the opening. How wonderful it is to see all these dear ministers marching in at my side—Methodist, Baptist, United Brethren, Congregational—and to know they have all been so wonderfully baptized with the Holy Spirit during our revival services in their respective cities and that they are standing solidly for the mighty word of God today and the cause of the Four-Square Gospel. Hallelujah! You wonder I am trembling, but now with this Temple as a mighty monument to God's power and the crowning blessing of fifteen years of humble but adoring ministry, could I but see it endowed, that if Jesus tarry a little longer we would know other hands had caught up the flaming torch and would bear it on and out, I think I could say: "Now, Lord, let thou Thy servant depart in peace, for mine eyes have beheld Thy glory."

The meeting is on. How the volume of their singing fills the Temple. We lift our eyes to the great concrete dome, the largest unsupported concrete dome in America, if not in the world, we are told. We lift our eyes to the azure blue of heaven flecked with bright clouds as of blessing, and again our eyes are suffused with tears. Thousands of friends are about us. They have come from all over America and abroad; they, too, are wiping their eyes as they sing and lift up their dear faces in prayer.

Prayer and short addresses by others; a song, "Open the Gates of the Temple," by Sister Stanley, Temple soloist; a quartet of sweet-voiced singers, and we are on our feet reading from the Book of Ezra the story of the rejoicant people when the foundation of the house of the Lord was laid. How among their number on that far-distant day some shouted with a great voice, some wept aloud for joy till they made such a noise that the prophet declared he could not tell the noise of them that wept from the voice of them that shouted. And their jubilance was only over the foundation being laid, and we had the walls up and the roof on. Glory to Jesus!

Then we are talking out of the fulness of our bursting hearts about the worship of the Lord. Telling how though God is so great the heavens can not contain him and the earth but a stool for His blessed feet. It has been the custom and longing of believing hearts to assemble themselves together to call upon His Name. Starting with the first recorded altar—that of Abel, then the altar of Noah, of Abraham, Isaac and Jacob; on to the days of Moses in the wilderness and on to the magnificent Temple which Solomon did build; the altar fires, whereunto Samuel didst minister; then to the days of the Son of man when He gathered His little flock about Him; the Lord's sermons in the Synagogues and the Temples; the church established by the disciples of the Lord; their ministry in the Temples and Synagogues and from house to house was rapidly sketched. Now we beheld the embers of a lonely altar fire upon Moriah rising heavenward from a night of prayer, and again we gaze upon the glory of Solomon's Temple. Then likewise rapidly we sketch the story of our own life. The calling of Jesus to our own soul from that Canadian farm to preach the Gospel of the crucified, resurrected Savior. The years of toiling, battling wind and rain and weather in tents and open fields; the blessing of the ever-present Lord, the call to build unto Him a house in the city of Los Angeles for the cause of Evangelism and the training of workers.

All over the building people are weeping and praising the Lord. How good He has been; And now we are giving our first altar call in the new Temple. Even though it is the first and the dedication service we feel we must not let the opportunity slip past unheeded. And now they are coming, down this aisle, swarming up yonder passage way; they are coming from the balconies, trooping down the ramparts, coming from the gallery and from every direction. The communion rail is filled, again and again. They are crowding the orchestra with their instruments from before the platform and filling the space reserved for them and yet they come. Thank You, O thank You, dear Jesus, for this token at the first service. We are unworthy, but Thou, Thou art worthy; let them come unto Thee and be saved.

Kneeling at the altar and bringing their arms filled with the most gorgeous floral offerings one could ever imagine come the precious Gypsies. Such baskets of flowers, but no brighter or more gay than their garments of vari-colored hue! They fill our arms; ministers and workers are taking them from us, basket after basket, bouquet after bouquet. More flowers than one ever remembered seeing in one building before. God bless the Gypsies! Some five hundred of them have crossed the continent and some have come from abroad to be converted and blessed at this meeting.

See this beautiful velour curtain just back of the platform? The Gypsies bought it. See this beautiful hand-carved motto that hangs just over our heads: "Jesus Christ; the same Yesterday, Today and Forever," they gave that, and many other things. God bless the Gypsies and make them all evangels to bear the message to their kind throughout the world. They have never owned a Bible nor had even a gospet printed in their language.

IF ANGELUS TEMPLE COULD SPEAK

Story from the Bridal Call

"The Lord is in His Holy Temple, Let all the Earth Keep Silence before Him."

REEN trees sway in the breeze. Tall cypresses point like fingers to the sky as though to pierce their canopy and reach to the clouds above. Palm branches wave 'neath mellow California sunshine. Foliage and flowers breathe their sweet scented perfume, a quiet lake shimmers and glows as a mirror.

Multitudes of homes are built on every side. Street cars and motors go whirling by. In the distance the blue and purple mountains lift their heads and yonder stand Wilson, Lowe and Baldy. Their snow-clad summits glisten and flash across the intervening space.

Below them, broad acres of citrus and orange groves stretch on every hand both in blossom and in fruitage; while just yonder upon the sands of the seashore roll the mighty waters of the broad Pacific.

In the midst of it all, surveying these beauties that are like the vistas of the heavenly land, come down to dwell among the sons of mn, rising like an unbelievedly beauteous jewel from an exquisite setting stand I—a mighty temple—builded by Faith and Hope and Love in the land of the sunset sea.

High from the streets my mighty walls arise; looming, towering up, up and away—then sweeping inward, in soft graceful curves, upholding the awe-inspiring height and enormity of my magnificent dome—the largest, unsupported concrete dome in the continent of America, I am told.

Glistening, gleaming, in their fresh new cleanliness, my walls flash back the brilliant semi-tropic sunshine that comes pouring, cascading over the treetops of neighboring Echo Park.

Brushing wings of sea-gulls, pigeon and dove who have already learned to seek a shelter atop the buttresses and cornice my columns and arches support, glint and throb in the balmy fragrance of the perfume-ladened air.

And below it all the Temple doors are open.

Across the way the pine trees, the palms and eucalyptus are whispering together in the morning breeze.

On the lake shore tiny ripples washing in from quiet mirror depths, murmur and splash.

From above, the confidential cooing of the doves and pigeons in earnest conversation comes adrifting down.

It seems as though they all are whispering together:

"They're open! They're open! The gates of the Temple are open. Oh, let the redeemed come in."

Wonderingly, admiringly, the passerby, the tourist, the multitudes passing afoot and by car lift their eyes and gaze questioningly upon me. Catching up the sunlight, my newly painted walls seem almost to be living, moving, pulsing things as they flash and glow and flash again,—signalling the message to every soul that looks:

It's true! It's true! The dreams, the hopes, the prayers have all come true. And here I stand—the visible answer from the invisible God who still doth live and move and answer prayer.

And down below, standing on the earth by my mighty foundations, the little Evangelist lady, her mother, and immediate friends clasp their hands, lift up their faces and gaze on me through misty tear-dimmed eyes, and say:

"Dear Temple, child of our dreams, our faith, our labors and our prayers. Are you really true? Let us touch you! Let us prove again that this mighty miracle is really standing in our midst; that you are really up and open with shining doors flung wide unto the hungry and needy sons of men; that by your most miraculous erection, it has been proven again unto the world that Faith and Prayer still triumph; that unto her who believeth there shall still be a performance of those things which were told her by the Lord."

"Mighty Temple, glorious Temple, you are no longer merely a vision,—a fondly cherished dream, a shining hope, a flaming desire,—you are a concrete reality.

With you the realization far exceeds the fondest anticipation. Yet, let me whisper it softly, you great, precious crown of our fourteen years of ministry—you were none-the-less real in our hearts when we saw you only through the eyes of Faith and prayed your first materials down from heaven."

"Oh, look! The trees sway forward in the breeze as though the better to see it. The gulls and pigeons pause a moment, suspended on wide wings to gaze upon it. The neighbors stand in their doors and at the windows for the like of the happenings at Echo Park have never been seen before.

Through the doors of my wide set columns and arches a steady stream of humanity flows. Old and young, rich and poor, sinner and saint, sick and well, afoot and by trolley, in purring motor cars and in wheel chairs, with springing, joyous stride and painfully slow on crutches—on, on, they come.

Through my doors they surge, seeking a glimpse of the tender Lord Jesus, Who biddest them all: "Come unto Me."

Within my courts the servants of the most high God minister humbly unto the Lord and to His saints; tending reverently and with all diligence, the revival fires that burn unceasingly upon the sacred altars day and night.

SMILES? YES, BUT TEARS ARE NEAR! AMERICA, WE LOVE YOU! NOW WE ARE ABOARD SHIP SAILING FOR THE OTHER SIDE OF THE WORLD. GOD BE WITH YOU TILL WE MEET AGAIN

FRIENDS AT PIER, SAN FRANCISCO, SINGING SISTER McPHERSON AND FAMILY OFF FOR A MISSIONARY TOUR TO AUSTRALIA, NEW ZEALAND AND HAWAII

It is Sunday night,—in and in, the great sea of humanity sweeps 'till they fill the ground floor of my auditorium, and not an available inch of space is left. Still in they surge over the shining red floors of my lobbies, up the grand stairways, to pack the first and second half of my great balcony, 'till not another seat is left.

Move over, everybody! Mother, would you mind holding your little girl on your lap to make room for this gentleman? Brother, would you mind taking your overcoat off that seat so that this lady might sit there? Yer, yes, you may have the seats which have been reserved for the ushers. None of them will have a moment to be seated tonight. The streets outside are black with people. I will never be able to hold them all.

There, there, ushers, rope off the stairways leading to the first balcony. Throw open the passages leading up through the social foyer to the third floor. Let them pack the galleries now. This way, brother; this way sister; go clear in as far as you can go. Leave the end seats for the newcomers. That's right. Lady, would you mind bringing your baby down to the nursery? This sister will hold your seat for you until you get back. You'll enjoy the meeting much better, and run no risk of the baby disturbing the speaker. Oh, yes, it's a beautiful nursery with a trained nurse in charge, and many assistants. I knew you would like it. See, it says "Baby Bank—Check Your Baby Here." The Evangelist and her mother spent hours selecting these little tables and chairs, these cribs and soft beds, pink, blue, white, grey, ivory—which will you put your baby in, mother? Leave her bottle. We'll make sure that the milk is just the right temperature. Now your baby is Number 43. Take this slip, will you? And sit right in the mother's section, so that we can call you quietly if you are needed. Run right along to the meeting now, and forget all about Helen May. She'll be perfectly happy.

Now, ushers, you had better hold the downstair doors a few moments till I see how many seats I have left. Five, ten, fifteen, twenty,—that's it. Pack in tightly folks. Many are going to be disappointed this Sunday night, who have driven miles to hear the message.

And just to think this has been such a busy day,—from seven o'clock this morning when scores of pilgrims could be seen wending their way through my doors and u pthe steps just as the sun was rising in the East, making their way to the "Hundred and Twenty" or "Upper Room" on this, as on every other morning, for the sunrise Prayer Service and "Tarrying Meeting." Since Sunday School at nine-thirty; preaching services at ten-thirty and again at two-thirty in the afternoon, these multitudes have surged and eddied about my edifice.

But, here! here! while we have been talking, the people have been surging up the stairways, and have overflowed every nook and crannie. They are standing in the lobbies, in the stairways, crowding into the aisles. This will never do. Firemen will not allow it. The people are swarming up the fire-escapes. They have crowded the emergency exits.

Quick, ushers, hold the outside doors, stop this river of people. You *must* hold them back.

You say you are holding the doors? But that you can't hold the door-yard? The fire escape doors must be kept open you say? And if they are open the people are coming up them? Well, do the best you can. Hold a rope across the door, with an usher standing on each side. Only whatever you do, do it quick. Not but that I am built strong enough to hold them all, only the firemen will not permit such overcrowding.

The street is black in front, you say? Why so it is. Looking out through my multitude of lighted eyes, and from my lighted dome I can see the streets parked with cars for more than a half mile in every direction. Must have a man out there to instruct them to park at forty-five degree angles after this.

Poor people! I'm so sorry I can't hold you all, but my arms, my balconies, my multitude of seats are filled to the brim and running over. You have driven many miles, you say, and are so disappointed? I am more sorry than ever, but what can I do? Except bid you come back on the morrow when the midweek crowds will not be quite so heavy, or advise you to come earlier on the next Lord's Day.

"Why, Mr. Temple, it's only seven o'clock," you gasp? "No church in the city opens its doors before quarter of eight and eight," you say?

I know it, but we have been practically full here since six and six-thirty.

In the Five Hundred Room, the choir has assembled; the ladies are all clad in spotless white. Many of them wear choir uniforms most modestly and simply made. The men are all dressed in dark suits. The male section of the chorus is composed almost entirely of business men. Choir rehearsal is over. The singers have all been graded as to voice, size, and number, and are now marching through the center division of the first balcony which spans the whole auditorium from one side to the other. The pianist has taken his place at the Steinway concert grand piano, at the left of the platform. At the signal note the great chorus standing now behind the people in the first balcony drenches the audience in a shower of golden-voiced melody:

"Holy, holy, holy,
Lord, God Almighty"

The people are turning in wonder to see from whence this music springs.

"All thy works shall praise thy name
In earth and sky and sea
Only thou art holy, merciful and mighty,
God in three persons,—the Blessed Trinity."

How gloriously they sing. How perfect the harmony. How magnificent the theme. The astonished congregation look a second time at the beautiful white robed choir girls to make sure whether they are not angels, for the whole scene is indeed a heavenly one—the blue sky and the fleecy clouds o'er head,—the mural painting of the "Coming Christ," the assembled thousands of people—the decorations of the Temple being composed not of swords and shields or anything symbolizing pugnacious warfare, but of angels and bells, typifying a message which is to be joyfully pealed forth and declare a gladness unto the sons of men from—the Temple of the Angels.

And now they're marching—that splendid, soul stirring choir. They are wending their way down the steps of the first balcony to the rampart passage ways which flank my either side. Slowly, impressively, they make their singing, marching way toward the flower-decked platform and to the choir loft, immediately above.

One finds oneself trembling at the beauty of it all.

As they wind their way up the steps and down the aisles of the choir loft, leading in the center from either side, they form a perfect letter "W," seeming to spell "Welcome" to the watching assembly. Each remains standing until the other is seated.

The ministers are on the platform. The Evangelist, Sister McPherson, is in her place. The choir director is standing out on the edge of the platform. With one motion of his hand, the entire sea of people spring to their feet, and almost split my dome with the volume of their song:

"All hail the power of Jesus' name,
Let angels prostrate fall.
Bring forth the royal diadem
And crown Him, Lord of all."

My scores of windows circling the main floor, balcony and gallery are open and the mighty torrent of the song which fills and makes me tremble through the height and breadth of my entirety, flows out and out to the assembled multitude on the streets, and these are but the third and fourth Sundays since my opening. The music can be heard for great distances. In the orchestra cornets, trombones and saxophones vie with the piccolo, flute and violin in making a joyful noise unto the Lord of Hosts, the King of Glory.

"Oh, that with yonder sacred throng,
We at His feet may fall,
We'll join the everlasting song
And crown Him Lord of all."

They are singing with uplifted hands and upturned faces. Singing rapturously and with deepest feeling. And now they stand with bowed heads. The voice of the Evangelist is floating out over the heads of the congregation and up through my vaulted dome to God upon the throne.

"O Lord Jesus, Thou King of earth and glory, look down upon this assembled multitude tonight. Thousands are gathered here in Thy presence and other numbers are shut outside the doors, all hungering and thirsting for Thee, for the Bread of Life and the rivers of blessing, which only Thou canst give.

Dear, glorious Master, mighty and strong to deliver, walk Thou, we pray Thee, upon and down these aisles tonight and through these seats. Lay Thou, Thy gentle pierced hand in benediction and tenderest blessing upon each head. Spread out Thy wings of mercy and love o'er this vast sea of humanity, let golden streams of blessing flow down from every feather, now we pray.

Lift thou the fallen, cheer the faint, heal the afflicted, convict the sinner and draw him to Thyself. Baptize believers with the Holy Ghost.

O, Lord of glory, Prince of Peace, Thou art the great I AM and there is none beside Thee. Surely all Thy people shall praise Thee, for Thy bounteous mercy is from everlasting unto everlasting. Thou art the Alpha and the Omega—the beginning and the end Thou art worthy—worthy of glory and power, dominion and praise, majesty and might, both now and forever more.

We thank Thee for the supreme gift of Thine own dear self—the blood which you shed upon the cruel cross of Calvary—the Redemption which you purchased there—the new and the living way which Thou didst open through the rended veil. O, glory, glory, glory to Thy name, Lord.

We thank Thee for this House unto the Lord which Thou hast given us by Thine own hand, as truly as though Thou hadst picked it up from out the streets of Heaven and set it down within the realms of man. It seemeth to us a building created by faith, a temple builded without hands, a house of worship, whose builder and maker is God. And now, Thou dost fill it with Thy glory and with Thy saving Grace.

Recording angels, Lord of Hosts, have been busy in this place, we know, for in the past three weeks—the opening weeks of this temple more than one thousand men, women and children have wept their way unto these altars crying, 'Lord, be merciful to me a sinner,' and drenching the altar with their repentant tears. The blind have cried aloud that they could see—the deaf, that they'd been made to hear—the lame have leaped for joy, believers have been filled from day to day with the blessed Holy Ghost, even as Thou didst fill the early church in the upper room so long ago.

And here Thou art, tonight, standing in our midst and that to bless—what shall we say, O Lord, wherewith shall we find words to praise Thee? Thy glory hast filled the Temple and Thy love o'erflows our hearts. Praise Him all ye angels, catch up your harps and sing. Flow down before Him, O ye mountains! Shout aloud ye blood washed saints, lift up your voices and declare His glory! Tremble, O ye unbelieving, and ye that have rejected the holy one of Israel. 'The Lord is in His Holy Temple, let all the earth keep silence before Him'."

See how the multitudes are swept beneath the power of the Holy Spirit—Fervent amens and hallelujahs are rising here, there and yonder. And now, still standing, a flood tide of song again rises and swells from the heart of the audience:

"Revive us again,
Fill each heart with Thy love;
May each soul be rekindled,
With fire from above."

They are clapping their hands as they sing the chorus—O, if this is earth, what will heaven be? Hear them singing now:

"There is a land that is fairer than day
And by faith we can see it afar,
For the Father waits over the Way,
To prepare a dwelling place there."

Did you ever in your life, hear anything like the way they are swelling that chorus? The choir immediately behind and above us, sing the first line,

"In the sweet by and by,"

and away up under the dome in the top gallery, sweet voiced singers send showering down upon us, the words that sound as though they came from out the vaulted blue of heaven,

"We shall meet on the beautiful shore."

Then the whole audience takes it up, till my columns of steel and concrete tremble beneath its majesty. To and fro, now in this section—now in that section of the building.

"Shall we gather at the river"

comes the question from the choir behind us—

"Where bright angel feet have trod."

comes floating down from the gallery

"With its crystal tide forever."

the first balcony catches up the refrain, to be followed immediately by the voice and song from the main floor.

"Flowing by the throne of God."

Then thunderously, almost deafeningly, the whole house takes it up—the piano, the orchestra, the voices. Handkerchiefs are waving, thousands of them, till they are like the foam-flecked waves of the mighty, moving sea.

"Yes we will gather at the river
The beautiful, beautiful river,
Gather with the saints at the river,
That flows by the throne of God."

And now the song is finished. There are few dry eyes in the audience. Everyone is turning to shake hands with three people who are standing near, smiling at them and saying "God bless you, brother—God bless you, sister." One can feel the power of the Holy Spirit—His love and fellowship, radiated everywhere.

Hush! the harpist is now running her fingers over the strings. Melody, such as one has dreamed of hearing in heaven, comes floating out in mellow tones and rises to fill the vastness of my dome and shower down upon the people. Now a quartette is singing! Now, the announcements are being made.

The choir is singing during the offering and it is time for the address of the evening. How the people listen—how they sit forward in their seats, drinking in every word! It seems as though the whole world is hungry—hungry to hear the story—the old new story of Jesus and His love. For over an hour, the speaker stands there, pouring out her heart, telling of the Lamb for sinners slain—of His power ever present to comfort, strengthen and guide. It is the "Four-Square Gospel" which is being preached, portraying Jesus Christ the only Saviour, the Baptizer with the Holy Spirit, the Great Physician and the soon Coming King.

Now the altar call is given—standing there with hands outstretched, the evangelist is giving a simple call for sinners and wanderers to come home to the Savior and to be washed in the fountain filled with blood.

And how they come! Pouring down from the galleries—streaming down the ramparts—from the balcony—flowing down the aisles of the main auditorium. It seems that they are coming from every direction at the same time.

Hurry, ushers! Hurry altar workers! Hurry, ministers! Meet them as they come. Guide them in the way. Some of their eyes are blinded with tears. Deal with them tenderly. Show them where to kneel. Some of them have never confessed Christ before in all their lives, as Saviour and Lord. Some of them have never prayed since Mother died and they learned to lisp 'Now, I lay me down to sleep."

Hurry, mother! Come throw your arms around this little, sobbing motherless girl, whose feet had been caught in the pitfalls of a great city. Hurry, brother! pray with this husband and wife, who are kneeling side by side with their four sons at the altar, seeking and finding salvation. Sing softly, O audience—

"I have wandered far away from God
Now I'm coming home,
The paths of sin I long have trod,
Now I'm coming home."

Ah! here they come—up this aisle—down yonder stairway—coming from the right, the left, the gallery, the balcony, the main floor—the rampart.

That is it, brother! That is it, sister! Press your way through the crowd and kneel at Jesus' feet. O, how He loves you! How He loves to save you! Come, come, weary one, and lay down your burdens at the Master's feet—

"There is a fountain filled with blood
Drawn from Emanuel's veins,
And sinners plunged beneath that flood
Lose all their guilty stains."

How they are weeping! Little pools of tears can be seen all along the communion rail. "God be merciful to me a sinner"—the words burst from many lips. These are surely in the grip of sincere repentance—

"The dying thief rejoiced to see,
That fountain in his day
And there may I, as vile as he,
Wash all my sin away."

Now the glory is coming—the Evangelist has led the people in prayer and they repeat it after her, sentence by sentence—that plea for forgiveness, which brought them step by step into the place of absolute faith and confidence wherein they rejoiced in the Lord for deliverance and cleansing by His blood.

See! they are on their feet now, with uplifted hands and tear-choked voices, they are repeating aloud the words:

"Here and now I do accept Jesus Christ as my personal Lord and Saviour and by His grace I will follow Him."

O! hear the song that rises, as the converts are flowing across the platform, that ministers, that members of the official board may grasp their hands and wish them God-speed upon their heavenly journey

"'Tis done, the great transaction's done,
I am my Lord's and He is mine,
He drew me and I followed on,
Charmed to confess His voice divine.
Happy day, Happy day,
When Jesus washed my sins away,—"

O! hear the song that rises, as the convert are flowing across again, but they will be back—many of them, just as the sun is rising on the morrow.

O, yes, I am a Temple—a mighty glorious Temple. Builded by faith, and hope, and love. Erected by prayer and trust and courage in the land of the sunset sea. But I doubt that any other building feels, if buildings can feel, quite so happy as I tonight. My altars have been wet with tears. I can show you proudly some of the pools that dripped upon the rose-taupe carpet that lines my chancel space. My frame has trembled 'neath the shouting of thousands of lifted voices, my dome has reverberated with triumphant songs. Already over a thousand souls have been born again into the Kingdom at my altars, and my Evangelist pastor has patted me on the back and told me that I have paid for myself and been worth my weight in gold and made up to her mother and herself every hour of anxiety and prayer and sacrifice that she had put into me by the souls which have already been won in me. And I have yet before me—if the Lord tarries, many years of faithful service.

That is why I wonder if any other building is quite so happy and contented as I, under the silvery beams of a California moon tonight.

A TYPICAL WEEK-END IN ANGELUS TEMPLE

(Taken from recent Bridal Call)

"The Lord is in His Holy Temple. Let all the earth keep silence before Him."

HE glory of the Lord, like a great golden cloud, has come to rest upon Angelus Temple at Echo Park, Los Angeles, California.

INTERDENOMINATIONALISM—That is the Word, the key to the whole wonderful outpouring. Meeting here, in this mighty Temple, one is made to forget that one is a Baptist and one's neighbor, a Methodist, while yonder is a Presbyterian and over there a Lutheran. Denominational barriers seem to be forgotten, all fences are down and meeting with tear-brimmed eyes at the cross of Calvary, hands instinctively reach out for other hands, clutch and clasp tightly in the love of a common cause, the praises of a common Lord.

Temple membership is swelling by hundreds. Altars are wet with tears of penitents, walls are echoing with the praises of the King, and Oh! while the glory and the wonder of it all is in out hearts it seems to be almost an impossible task to put the story of it in mere words. The workings of the mighty Spirit of God ever beggars description. This week-end is but a sample of the continuous revival.

OLD FOLKS MEETING GOOD FRIDAY AFTERNOON

They wanted to come.

Their friends wanted them to come.

Their sons wanted them to come, saying, "Oh! if my Mother only could!"

But *how could* they come in the crowd? It had been years since daddy had been to the office. It was years since mother had been in active life. Their ears were heavy. Their eyes dim. Their limbs were trembly—not able to bear long standing in the throngs ever pressing their way into the doors of Angelus Temple at Echo Park.

* * * *

There had been a strange stir about the house lately. What did it mean? Nodding in their chairs—had they been dreaming? Snatches of old familiar hymns, which they had not heard for generations, had broken in upon their dreams. Was it real or had they been translated to glory? These were songs such as the angels might sing, or a song with which a well-remembered loved one might greet them on the other shore. Or a song that had been sung in the great revivals of years ago. Years and years since they had been in touch with things like that.

Wakened up by the gentle buzz and prayers in the home, where there had been no family altar, they were almost made to feel as though they were again getting their little ones ready for Sunday School and worship. There seemed to be a new love and interest in the home some way. Loved ones who had always been kind, seemed to take on a new tenderness now. They talked constantly of the great revival that was on.

How they would have loved to go too! But how could they with their weakness and age and rheumatics that must be considered and consulted?

The bringing home of the hymn-book—the imagining of what the meeting must be like—the recalling of the revivals and camp-meetings of their childhood. Wouldn't it be wonderful if they could go? But there—they must not even consider such an undertaking at their time of life.

Then came the day when the children ran into the house—big stalwart sons, and tender daughters with children at their skirts with the announcement that Sister McPherson had sent for them and set aside the most Holy day of the year for "the gentle folk of the silver hair," and that they—the children were going to bundle up mothers and grandmothers, fathers and grandfathers as careful as could be, get the easiest riding car they could find and take them to see the wonderful new Temple and to attend the old folks day.

How this news had gone around the country, and all through Southern California. For weeks this had been announced. For weeks they had been preparing. Now they were being dressed and fussed over like they used to fuss over and dress their children two generations ago.

The coming. The long lines of cars that streamed up and lined Glendale Boulevard, Park Avenue, Lemoyne Street, Echo Park and Sunset Boulevards. The strong arms of manly sons bringing their loved ones in, and seeing to their every comfort. The long rows of old folk who sat leaning on their canes. The meeting of old friends they had not met since school days back over the Rockies. The great sections of seats with heads as white as drifting snow. Each snowy head like the summit of a mountain, Mothers and Fathers of Statesmen, Lawyers, Ministers, Artists, Inventors, Brave Soldiers, people who had made history and fame, old pioneers of church and state, old monarchs of California and the U. S. A. all gathered together in this great interdenominational melting-pot for such a religious gathering of old folks as is seldom seen in these United States of America.

The youngest invited person on the main floor of the great auditorium is 60 years of age. The oldest man, 103. Unique amongst the stately silvered throng was a wrinkled and withered Gypsy, incased in embroidered silken shawls, who is said to be in her 113th year.

One holds one's breath and wipes the mist from one's eyes. Who would have imagined, in one city, so many heads white as the driven snow!

AGED VETERANS FILL PLATFORM

Flanking Sister McPherson, the evangelist, and filling the entire platform, are grouped the aged veterans of the Civil War, smiling, nodding, singing, encouraging. The revival is on.

Song after song is lifted heavenward and supported by the strains of the great Angelus Temple organ.

Twenty of the oldest guests have been invited to name their favorite hymns—hymns which were sung when they were boys and girls. The first number to be requested is, "How Tedious and Tasteless the Hours." Then follows:

"There's a land that is fairer than day,
And by faith we can see it afar,
And the Father waits over the way
To prepare us a dwelling place there."

God bless them! Looking through their eyes one can almost see the lights of that fairer world, and as the last strain, "We shall meet on that beautiful shore" dies out in the distance, we all sit still without speaking or moving for a moment. Every heart in the building must have been visioning that glorious day and the meeting of the multitudinous saints of God upon that happy shore.

With the closing number of the song service, a great wave of power rolls over the entire assemblage. They are on their feet singing. Strong voices—weak voices—firm voices—quavering voices—blending into one sweet melody,

"Shall we gather at the river,
Where bright angel feet have trod
With the crystal tide forever
Flowing by the throne of God?"

Then, with the crash of the organ, every voice in the building seems to have joined the chorus. Younger, surer voices showering down from the upper balconies, swell the song,

"Yes, we'll gather at the river,
The beautiful, beautiful river,
Gather with the saints at the river,
That flows by the throne of God."

An aged minister is praying now. Heads bowed everywhere. Fervent Amens, from every quarter of the building.

Now the testimony meeting is on. Here, there, yonder—dozens are on their feet. Many who testified, declared that they had been walking with the Master for sixty and seventy years. Proudly, they tell of sons and daughters in the ministry and Mission Field; tell of constant "family altars" and the abiding benediction and blessing of the Almighty One who never slumbers nor sleeps.

THE SERMON AND PRAYER

Now, we are preaching the Word. A more attentive audience could not be desired. Leaning forward in their seats—eyes dewy with teardrops—lips moving as though repeating the words we say. Heads nodding—fervent Amens lifted.

Oh, God, bless them! Bless them and give us words to say to their hearts that will make the Savior more real and the "end of the way" more precious!

Hundreds upon hundreds of these are already Christians, but scores are here who have never confessed Christ as Savior. Anxious children and grand-children have plead with us, that we urged upon these older folk, the decision they have never made. Our hearts are moved within us, we realize that this may be the last invitation for a large number of the audience, that never again, this side the River, will all of these aged people meet.

"O, God, our Heavenly Father," we pray, "The feet of hundreds who are here this afternoon are treading the sunset trail. Hundreds are stepping down the gentle decline. Their feet are almost touching the water's edge. A year, perhaps a month from now, many will have crossed the dividing stream and we shall see them no more till we reach the other side.

"O, Master, look down and help us tell to them the story.

"Many there are who are waiting to go. Their shining craft of Faith is ready to lift anchor at a moment's call. The snow white sails of unclouded hope and love are hoisted, waiting for the heavenly breezes. The blood-stained banner of the cross is unfurled to the breeze. The blessed Pilot of Galilee is at the helm. And Faith is at the rudder. We seem to see the reflected lights of the New Jerusalem in their faces and eyes as they look steadfastly toward their Home—almost catch the throbbing of angel wings and hear the heavenly chorus with their harps of gold.

"They are coming, Lord Jesus. They are coming—these older folk, with hoary hairs found in the paths of Righteousness. They are coming with the trusting confidence of little children. Thou has borne for them the sting of death and the grave has lost its victory. Hallelujah! Lord, with open arms Thou waitest to receive them. With gentle hand, Thou shalt support; for as they come, there is no fear within their hearts. Hear them, Master, as they sing—

'Lead me gently home. Savior,
Lead me gently home.
Lest I falter by the wayside
Lead me gently home.'

"But, Oh Blessed Redeemer, not all who are here assembled have this hope within them! Some have lived for 50, 60, 80, one 100 years without the knowledge of Thy saving Grace. Walk through these aisles we pray. Knock once again, with gentle nail-pierced hand, upon the hearts' doors and surely they will let you in.

"Oh, Savior, dear, Thou hast been so good, good! Though they have wandered Thou hast followed close. Though they have been ungrateful and untrue, Thou hast been faithful, true and ever kind and just; sending sunshine and rain, raiment and food, from dawn of life till close.

"And when they kneel at Thy feet today — for they are coming Lord,—only one regret will fill their hearts, that they knew not Thee in the dawn of life, rather than in the afterglow of sunset. Thou, Savior of mankind, truest Friend, and mighty Counselor, tender Shepherd of the sheep—Thou hast been seeking them so long! May this be the hour when Thou shalt find and fold them to Thy heart. Grant that none within this Temple, either young or old, today, shall go away unsaved. In Jesus' Name, and for the Glory of our Lord and Christ, we pray, Amen."

We read to them the Word of the Lord, the old; old story that is ever new—the story of the rugged cross whereon the King of Glory died. For it is about the cross of Calvary our thoughts are centering this Good Friday afternoon. As we speak of His supreme and awful sacrifice, the long, slanting beams of golden light from the "crucifixion" window high above seem to grow brighter and the Form more real that hangs suspended there.

Jesus the Christ in Gethsemane—in Pilate's judgment hall—the Savior at the whipping-post—the man acquainted with sorrow, bearing His cross upon Calvary's hill—the Lamb of God, smitten, rejected, laying down His life upon the tree—the King of Glory, pleading, "Father, forgive them they know not what they do"—the triumphant, resurrected Redeemer alive again and risen from the dead, standing with open arms today, crying, "come unto me and I will give you rest." Rapidly we paint the scenes one by one.

Beholding Him must be to surely love Him. If He be lifted up from the earth He will draw all men unto Himself.

THE ALTAR CALL

The altar call is given. Men and women are rising here and there and yonder. Eyes blinded with tears, are groping their way into the aisles. They are making their way to the front. O look at them coming from every direction! They are filling the communion rail! They are overflowing and filling the chancel-space within! They are kneeling on the steps, everywhere!

Praise, oh praise the Lord, for He has triumphed gloriously!

"That's it, brother, just kneel right here at Jesus' feet."

"That's it, sister." "Come along brother." Suddenly we are on our own knees beside an aged man. His shoulders are heaving with sobs.

"Are you seeking salvation, brother?"

"O yes, Sister, pray for me. I've been a sinner for 89 years. Will He—do you think He will—would He ever forgive me?"

"Why of course He will, brother. He is of great mercy and tender compassion. Call upon Him just now while He is so near, while he is bending over you, waiting to receive."

"But—I've been a sinner all my life! My life is wasted—wasted! I am an old man now, with so little to offer in return. Do you think—are you sure—that He will take me now? It don't seem reasonable somehow!"

"Oh grandpa, I know how you feel and I am sorry for you. But don't you see that it is you yourself that has been the loser, you and your children.—Have you any children, grandpa?"

"Yes, seven sons and twelve grandchildren, and four great-grandchildren."

"Did you ever have a family altar in your home, brother? Have any of those children ever seen you kneel in prayer before or lift your voice to ask God's blessing on them, and His wisdom for your own heart, that you might guide them in His paths?"

"No—No! I've told you before, sister,—I've always been a sinner. My wife used to pray when she was alive but I am afraid I was a discouragement to her."

"Then brother, just begin to pray now. Ask the Saviour to forgive, to pardon, to wash your heart from all sin in His own precious blood. Can you not see that you have no time to spare, if you are going to meet her there, and tell her you have led your sons and grandchildren to the Saviour's feet?"

Oh how he prays—and how the light breaks through at last, like sunlight through the clouds! The memory of his tear-wet face as he makes his way through the audience, in search of his sons, to ask their forgiveness in not having guided their feet in the paths of Righteousness before them; the memory of his face at the water baptismal service on the next Thursday night where he is buried with Christ in baptism; the depth of feeling in his voice, when as being lowered into the water, he exclaimed, "This should have been done eighty years ago! But thank God I am home at last!" lingers with us yet. Yet this dear man was but one, of the long rows of seekers at the altars.

THE HARVEST

Tremulously, earnestly, with up-stretched hands they are singing,

"I've wasted many precious years,
Now I'm coming home;
The paths of sin too long I've trod,
Now I'm coming home."

and now they are on their feet, the power is falling everywhere. Aged husbands and wives are embracing each other—both on the same road at last. Aged veterans are shaking hands saying, "Sister I fought in a great war. I fought under General Lee," or "I fought under General Grant. I thought I fought in a great battle, but this is the greatest warfare—this battle for God and Souls! Yours is the greatest general—General Jesus who never loses the day! This meeting has brought back old times to me. I haven't been so happy in years!"

"Thank God, I have known the Saviour for years! Lift Him up, sister. Preach Him and His salvation as long as He lends you breath, and may you have many souls for your hire."

We find our own eyes brimming with happy tears as we watch our congregation filing out through the doors into the kindly afternoon sunshine, singing softly to the strains of the great organ as they go,

"Yes we'll gather at the river
The beautiful, beautiful river,
Gather with the saints at the river,
That flows by the throne of God."

CRUSADERS' COUNCIL FRIDAY EVENING

Life at Angelus Temple is a constantly changing panorama. It is a great painting in kaleidoscopic colorings, ever changing —picture melting into picture—a slate, filled with beautiful pictures and carefully moulded figures, which is immediately wiped clean and filled with other pictures of still more gorgeous colorings.

No sooner has the tidal-wave of one blest service gone riding far out to sea in triumph, and one's happy tears been brushed aside with the feeling that no other meeting could ever be quite so dear, so precious—than another tidal-wave meets and swallows up the first, leaps completely over it and comes riding in, white plumed and bannered, shouting joyously and breaking upon the shores of the present hour.

Seven-thirty P. M.

Just one hour since the Temple was cleared.

Seven-thirty P. M. Good Friday evening. But now the scene is changed.

The hundreds of seats so recently filled with aged folks who came to worship Christ are now abrim with breath-takingly, enthusiastic young folk between the ages of sixteen and thirty-five.

Our eyes are scarce cleared from the vision of those precious aged folk-feet pressing close to the river Jordan, and the scanning of their sail-unfurled ship. The glory of their white crowned heads is still most vividly enshrined in our minds.

When here, entering the Temple some sixty minutes later, we open our eyes wide and catch our breath with a little start, as we look down now upon these of the younger generation, rising up from the eastern dawn of life's morning, and marching—marching on to take the place of those of yesteryear, and lift the burdens feeble hands must needs lay down.

Clear of eye—strong of limb—clean of heart—bubbling over with vivacity and health—lusty of voice—enthusiastic and indefatigable of spirit—battalion after battalion—rank after rank, they come, marching on through the years to fill their place in life.

It is the weekly meeting of "The Four-Square Gospel Crusaders of Angelus Temple," and of the young folk who are being drawn to the Christ and are consecrating their lives to His service.

THE SPIRITED SONG SERVICE

How different the spirit of the songs tonight to those of this afternoon!

No "tedious and tasteless hours" here! No song with a minor refrain has yet been interwoven through the warp and woof on the looms of their young lives. No resigned tears mingled with their smiles.

"Onward Christian soldiers, marching as to war,
With the cross of Jesus going on before;
Christ the royal Master leads against the foe,
Forward into battle see his banners go.
At the sign of triumph, Satan's host doth flee;
On then Christian soldiers on to victory!
Hell's foundation quiver at the shout of praise,
Forward into battle see His banner go!"

How straightly they stand. How firm their voices. Heads back. Eyes flashing. Consecration fires burning. God bless them, they are singing again—singing as though their whole heart and mind and strength was in the song; lifting it high, exultant as though 'twere thus they would lift the Christ.

"Stand up, stand up for Jesus,
Ye soldiers of the cross,
Lift high His royal banner,
It must not suffer loss."

"Hold the fort for I am coming,
Jesus signals still,
Wave the answer back to heaven,
By Thy grace we will."

Testimony Time!—at the words dozens of young men and women spring to their feet and form a long line that flows over the platform. One after another they pour out, out of the fullness of their hearts, the story of God's dealings with them.

TESTIMONY TIME

"Just one week ago tonight," a clear-cut young business man is speaking first, "I kneeled at that altar, just there, and gave my life to the Lord Jesus Christ. This has been the happiest week I have ever known. I have now humbly offered my life to God's service for any work to which he may see fit to call me. This is the first testimony I have ever given, but please God it will not be the last."

Another steps to the front—a well dressed young lady this time—

"I'm a school teacher and surely the happiest one in the city. Just three weeks ago I was converted from a life of worldliness and coldness toward God. I kneeled at this altar—a clean heart was created within me. I have been singing ever since. The world is new. My work is new. My life is new. I am His to command from this day forth. Praise the Lord!"

"I wish to testify that I was converted one week ago. I have been on the stage for years, but have left the profession and have entered Sister McPherson's Evangelistic Training School, and as soon as I have graduated and been ordained, expect to enter the ministry."

On, on they come, line after line. Short, livewire testimonies, just brimming over with the story of salvation, healing and the baptism of the Holy Spirit. The river of testimony never ceases for a moment, except when interrupted by a ringing chorus.

Then the announcements: "Four-Square Gospel Crusaders will please remember the street meeting of the morrow. Angelus Temple Reapers (Men) and Angelus Temple Gleaners (Ladies) at their posts! Everyone be at your post of duty, also for Sunday service in the choir and at the altar; in the Sunday school and bible class.

Monday morning at 9:30 promptly a special train has been engaged at the Pacific Electric Depot to take the Crusaders and the Evangelistic Students to Long Beach, where the Angelus Temple young people will conduct a prayer meeting on the beach. Tuesday afternoon young people be ready to preach, sing and pray in the chapel at the County Poor Farm, etc.

FOUR MINUTE SERMONS

Now, the sermons. Seven speakers from the Evangelistic and Training Institute are bringing their first sermons. For four or five minutes, each opens the Word of God and breaks the bread to the other hungry hearts. Some speak with fear and trembling His Truth; but the message is all the sweeter and the more effective because of the very humility and utter dependence of that one upon God. Such "First Sermons" are given here every Friday night. Some of them are truly remarkable, and listening, one shuts one's eyes, and dreams of the Ministers, Missionaries and Evangelists, that, if Jesus tarries, shall go forth from this Temple to spread the Four-Square Gospel around the earth. One's heart is made to leap for joy, and one's lips to shout Hosannah!

Simply, unaffectedly they speak. Earnestly they give the altar call. Quickly the long communion rail is filled. Young business men and women; high school students; young married couples from the home, all kneeling together, saying: "Lord be merciful to me a sinner, and make my heart Thine own."

Bright faced, consecrated altar workers are kneeling with them. Songs—prayer—lifted hands—and soon on their feet again they are singing,

"'Tis done, the great transaction's done,
I am my Lord's and He is mine;
He drew me and I followed on,
Charmed to confess His voice divine."

New members are singing the Crusader's covenant. Joining the ranks of them who have already taken up the work. Now they are shaking hands, smiling as they sing:

"Oh you win the one next to you,
And I'll win the one next to me;
We'll all work together, in all sorts of weather,
And see what can be done.

If you win the one next to you,
And I win the one next to me;
We'll have them all in no time at all
So win them, bring them, one by one."

No excuse for young folks now to say that they must go with worldly companions because they are lonely and can find no young Christian friends. Here's work and companionship for all in The Big Sister Crusade, The Big Brother Crusade, The Music Crusade, The Prayer Crusade, The Evangelistic Crusade, The Mission and Charity Crusade; The Hospital and Prison Crusade, The Altar Crusade, The Street Crusade and The Home Fire Crusade.

Something for everyone to do. Whitened harvest-fields waiting. Strong and willing young arms ready to lift and bear the precious sheaves into the heavenly garner.

With the dismissal of the service in the main auditorium, the meeting is by no means over. Scores are trooping their happy way to the Upper Room to reconsecrate their lives to the Master and receive the fullness and power of the Holy Spirit. What a glorious sight to behold! Scores of young men and women on their knees, praying with uplifted hands, praying down revival fires. What a glorious day it has been—a day of fasting and prayer, since early morning, and now that the young people are filing out of the building and the roar of their motor cars is vanishing down the street, the light in the watch tower burns on till morning, for here prayer never dies—women pray by day and men by night.

SATURDAY AFTERNOON'S CHILDREN'S CHURCH

"And once again the scene was changed
The streets no longer rang,
Hushed were the glad Hosannahs;
The little children sang."

It is children's afternoon at the Temple. Hundreds of little tots, between the ages of four and sixteen, fill those self-same seats occupied by the aged, and by the young men and women of yesterday.

What a throng of fresh young faces, upturned like flowers. Eyes shining like stars. Hands and voices eager to serve. Waiting for the old, old story.

A changing panorama did we say? A kaleidoscope of colors! Yes, battalion after battalion; troop after troop—'twould take a word painter indeed to depict the scenes enacted hourly in this place.

Children's Church—held each Saturday afternoon at 2:30.

A little lad, whose name is John, is leading the singing. The grown-ups in the balcony are smiling broadly at the beating of his diminutive hand. But he is doing well. The singers are keeping time.

The children pray, preach and call their school-mates to the altar, where they meet and pray for them as earnestly as grown-ups could ever do.

Three-minute sermons preached by the children now follow each other in quick succession and are indeed a revelation as to the scriptural understanding and beautiful orthodoxy which it is possible for the heart of a child to possess.

The glory, the simplicity, the heart-stirring appeal of their altar call.

CHILDREN'S ALTAR CALL

"Let all the children bow their heads now, boys and girls"—a young "boy preacher" is the speaker now. "Let every one lift your hands who has never definitely accepted the Lord Jesus Christ. You know that we need Him, at school—at home, and play. It takes real courage to be a Christian. Any coward can be a sinner. It takes a brave boy and girl with the grace of God in their heart to be a soldier of the cross. Just lift your hands now and say: 'Pray for me.' Give Him your heart today while you are young and have all your life before you."

Here they come, row after row, boys and girls, all kneeling, surrendering their hearts and lives to the King of Glory. Their treble voices are lifted. Hands clasped. They are following us in prayer.

"O dear Jesus—I'm only a little child—but I kneel at Thy precious feet today—and ask that Thou shouldst save me." Sentence after sentence they repeat the words after us; praying not only with their lips but their hearts. "Make my heart Thine own—Wash me by Thy cleansing blood and make me clean today. Help me to be a brave little soldier of the Cross. Oh, never let my footsteps stray from the paths of Thy righteousness! Amen!"

God bless them!

See their little heads bowed in prayer—brown heads—yellow heads—black and red—braids and curls—boys and girls—all bending their knees at the altar together.

How different the scene of twelve hours ago—when this very spot was filled with aged folk who wept sore because of a long life wasted outside of Jesus Christ! What a contrast between the Alpha and Omega—the beginning and the end of life.

The one with life ahead—its sands unrun—its pathways all untried—their feet and hearts and hands and lives all eager for the fray, marching 'neath the skies—all painted in the blazing glory of the dawn. The other, with the sands all run and sunset fading in the sky!

Bless, oh bless these babies, Lord! Incline their minds, their hearts to Thee that they may never stray down the roads of sin and vice.

There—they are on their feet now—hands lifted,

"I'm so glad that my Father in Heaven,
 Tells of His love in the Book He has given;
Wonderful things in the Bible I see,
 This is the dearest that Jesus loves me."

EASTER PARADE

Now, for the Easter Street Parade. Hundreds of happy children pour from the doors and form four abreast in the streets surrounding the Temple. There they are joined by a brass band, and at the command:

"Mark Time! Left, Left, Right, Left!! Forward March!!! The band is playing. The children are marching, singing of the risen Christ, each carrying an Easter Lily in his or her hand and so marching through the streets while hundreds stop to gaze at the unusual sight of so youthful an army, demonstrating their love for their Lord and Savior.

"Good-bye, children, good-bye," another meeting is waiting and crowds are pouring into the Temple.

SATURDAY EVENING—DIVINE HEALING SERVICE

But a short space of time has elapsed since the children's service—yet a complete transformation has taken place.

Willing hearts and capable hands have seen to the emptying and the cleaning of the building. The task of setting things in order for the next service is accelerated by the frequent word of anxious ushers.

"How soon will we be able to open the doors? The crowds are growing each moment. They have filled the entire space in front of the building now."

At 6:00 P. M. one and a half hours before the service opens the doors are swung wide. It is like the opening of the sluice gates of a mighty dam. The ushers who are standing at their posts are swept aside like matches in the tide. It is a wonderful sight to see men and women fairly running down the aisles to get themselves settled in the front seats of main auditorium and balcony.

As they fill the building, they pack solidly, scanning each row for an empty seat; each seeking to be as far forward as possible.

The main floor and the balcony being well filled, the gallery is next thrown open. A steady stream of humanity is pouring in at every entrance, and flowing down the aisles to fill the 5,000 seats of this the largest auditorium in Southern California.

The thing that many Christian workers said could not be done is being done before our eyes—the House of God, well filled on a Saturday night when the Call of the World is the loudest. Not only is this true of this particular Saturday night, but of every Saturday, month in and month out.

The sweet strains of the Temple organ are pealing forth. The white-robed choir are marching down the balcony and down the ramparts to the choir loft, singing as they go:

"Sweet hour of prayer, sweet hour of prayer,
That calls me from a world of care,
And bids me at the Father's throne,
Make all my wants and wishes known.

In seasons of distress and grief,
My soul has often found relief
And oft escaped the tempter's snare
By thy return, sweet hour of prayer."

How impressive and stately the appearance of the marching choir! How sweetly consecrated and earnest their faces! The song service is opened. The meeting is on:

"I must tell Jesus all of my troubles,
I cannot bear these burdens alone;
In my distress he kindly will help me
He ever loves and cares for His own."

Thousands of voices take up the refrain and lift it high till the great dome seems to swell and quiver with the melody.

"I must tell Jesus, I must tell Jesus"

Thousands of hands are lifted—faces upturned as they sing;

"He is a kind, compassionate friend."

The great Angelus Temple organ is supported by a 14-piece orchestra, which includes a golden harp.

"If I but ask Him He will deliver
Make of my troubles quickly an end."

Dr. Thomas Gale, pastor of the Temple Baptist Church of Oakland, California, is on his feet now, pouring out his soul to God:

"O Lord, we thank Thee for Thy presence here tonight. We are assembled in Thy name, and Thou art in the midst to bless. With outstretched arms Thou standest, waiting—waiting the penitent child to receive. Walk through these aisles we pray. By Thy Holy Spirit's power convict of sin of righteousness and judgment. Be Thou lifted up and exalted that men and women may be drawn unto Thyself. Grant that none shall leave this building unsaved tonight. Comfort the troubled heart, Thou Blessed Balm of Gilead. Lift the fallen, cheer the faint, heal the sick and lead the blind."

"Bless, we pray, the Messenger and the Message. May Thy word accomplish tonight that whereon it is sent. In the Name of our all-conquering Saviour Christ, we ask it, Amen!"

Fervent Amens are heard from every quarter, as the audience—still standing—lift their voices in song:

"I need Thee, oh I need Thee,
Every hour I need Thee,
O bless me now my Saviour,
I come to Thee."

With eyes all misty with unshed tears, the audience is following out instructions of a pretty little custom of the Temple—that of shaking hands with three people, smiling, saying "God bless you, brother, God bless you, sister!" that none may leave the building without a warm handshake and a "God Bless you."

The message of the evening—"The body for the Lord and the Lord for the body."

The power of the Spirit settles upon the place:

"'Seek first the Kingdom of God and His Righteousness and all things shall be added unto you.' Put first things first. Look to the Lamb of God. Turn from your sins. Seek Him with your whole hearts. Seek Him while He may be found. Call upon Him while He is near. Remember that He came not into the world to call the righteous but sinners to repentance. No matter how far you have wandered from the paths of righteousness, He is standing beside you this moment ready to deliver and bring you back 'neath the wings of His love.

"Oh, why should any one stay away from such a Saviour another moment? He is such an incomparable glorious friend and counselor! His is such a practical salvation—not a gospel of mere words and fine sounding theories. His arm is strong to save and mighty to deliver. It is His good pleasure to give you the Kingdom.

"He stands ready, willing to cleanse from all unrighteousness—to lift the heavy end of every cross—to heal the sick and suffering body—to fill with His Holy Spirit—to send you forth into the whitened harvest-field of life with a strength to do His bidding, supplanting your weakness with His might.

"Many there are here tonight who need Divine Healing for your physical bodies, but seek first the blessing of a clean heart—the knowledge of a 'born-again' experience. Many are will ing enough to claim the latter part of our text, 'The Lord for the body,' His strength for our weakness; His healing virtue for our infirmities. But we must remember that there is another part to this message—a part for us to do if we would tip the scales of God's balances toward divine favor, and that is 'The Body for the Lord.'

"Give Him yourself—He will give you Himself.

"Give Him your life—He will give you of His life more abundantly.

"*The body for the Lord*—hands, feet, lips, voice, heart, means, time, talents.

"*And the Lord for the body*—strength, blessing, healing, virtue flowing from Him. Just as the branch is to the vine, I take—He undertakes.

"On, on from the depths of our heart, we are asking Him, to clothe with words the thoughts that He hath given. Every song, every prayer, every word, leads in a direct line to the altar of salvation.

"Every head be bowed and every eye closed. How many here tonight will say, by the lifting of the hand: 'Sister McPherson, I am a sinner' or 'I am a back-slider.' or 'I am not living the life that I should live and I ask you to pray for me that I may become a Christian?'

"Five, ten, twenty, forty, one hundred—hands are going up all over the building—on the main floor—in the balcony—away up yonder in the gallery.

"Now, will all they who lifted their hands for prayers, please rise to their feet."

A general rustle is heard all over the house. Men—fine, clean-cut business men—men, old and young, rich and poor, are standing side by side. Women—mothers—business girls—society women are standing together.

"Just another question—before you come forward, how many of those now standing can praise God for a reasonably well body—signifying that it is not a healing for the body—but simple old-fashioned salvation that you seek?"

Practically every hand is lifted.

"Then come to Jesus as you are,
Weary and worn and sad,
You'll find in Him a resting place,
And He will make you glad."

Streaming down the aisles, they have filled the long altars in a moment—the chancel space within—the platform—the steps—the aisles—the ramparts—and still they come! Workers are streaming down from their posts to meet and pray with the penitents. Quietly and efficiently they work without an unnecessary sound or movement.

The power of God has gripped the place. Scores and hundreds are being constantly converted. Yet the whole meeting is free from fanaticism or excitement. Personal workers are not needed in the aisles to urge people into a decision. This great company, now weeping and praying, "Lord be merciful to me a sinner," have come of their own volition, after making up their own minds, positively to say "I arise and go."

The altar service over, the new converts are on their feet, hands lifted, singing:

> "Where He leads me I will follow
> Where He leads me I will follow
> Where He leads me I will follow
> I'll go with Him, with Him, all the way."

What a large company they are! How radiant their faces —smiles shining through their glistening tears!

Now, they are all back in their seats. The audience is in perfect order again. The altars and platform are cleared for action. The sick folk are coming now for prayers that the Lord may touch and heal their broken bodies.

A call is made for all the clergymen in the audience, who believe in the power of answered prayer for the sick and afflicted to come to the platform and to assist in lifting them to the throne; some fifteen ministers instantly respond and the long line of sick and needy begin to flow over the platform.

Jesus of Nazareth passeth by and unto Him they lift their voices, saying

> "Master, I have put my all, my body, soul and spirit upon the altar of full surrender. I can truthfully say, The body for the Lord and that henceforth for me to live is Christ. If Thou willes' that I should bear this thorn in the flesh, Amen, Thy will not mine be done.—But Lord I feel within me that having surrendered the body to the Lord I may claim the Lord for the body. Strength I seek to do Thy bidding—health to work for Thee."

One by one they are mounting to the platform, pausing for prayer, then the other side shouting Victory! Feeling within themselves that they have been healed.

The Divine Healing testimonies are amazingly convincing and powerful. Several blind folk declare after prayer that they could see—deaf that they can hear—lame that they can now walk, without their canes, braces and crutches—thousands of hearts are lifted in prayer and thanksgiving as the line flows on and on.

At the close of the prayer for the sick, wherein Methodist, Baptist, Presbyterian, Congregational and other ministers, pray as one, a second altar call is given and the altar fills again with others, who are now melted in surrender to the Lord.

It is now 10:30 Saturday night; tomorrow will be a tremendous day. One hour and a half is left before midnight in which to sweep and dust the vast auditorium. Who ever heard of such a thing as opening such a mammoth building on a Saturday night with four strenuous services of the morrow so close at hand!

We tried sometime ago to close the Temple three days a week but hundreds came and camped right at the doors until we were obliged to open, and carry the meetings on every day in the week. Delegates are here from almost every State in the Union and from abroad. There seems to be no stopping of the tide that is rising constantly; nor do we wish to see it halted for a moment.

Service over, the thousands of believers who have stayed to the last stanza of the last song, are filing out, singing softly to the strains of the organ as they go;

> "Oh it is Jesus, oh it is Jesus,
> Oh it is Jesus in my soul;
> For I have touched the hem of His garment
> And His Power has made me whole."

Janitors, cleaners and volunteers are already at work, but we must hasten for we have a long drive ahead of us yet tonight. We are to go to Eagle Rock near Pasadena to preach the sunrise Easter sermon on the mountain top for the multitudes that shall assemble there. These famous Eagle Rock services on Easter morn are among the prettiest customs of Californians and are held in memory of the risen Lord, and the women who went to the tomb early in the morning while it was yet dark so many years ago. We are to preach under the auspices of the Eagle Rock Committee of the Women's Club.

Bundled into a closed car that has been provided for us, our suitcase tucked in at our feet, we are speeding off through the night rejoicing at the blessings of the meetings of today and praying for the four great meetings of the morrow. Six heavy meetings within 36 hours! Lord, we ourselves must needs claim promise,

"The body for the Lord and
The Lord for the Body."

SUNRISE SERVICE ON THE FAMOUS EAGLE ROCK

Sometime between three and four A. M. a tap on our door awakens us. Where are we? What is it? Everything is an inky blackness! Ah, yes! This is Easter morning! We are to dress hastily and make our way by auto through the lines of other machines, who are on a like pilgrimage, up the mountain side as far as a motor can take us, then by foot to the summit of Eagle Rock.

A little pinched look of anxiety is upon many faces for rain has been falling in the night. Will the clouds roll back for the Sunrise Service?

"O Lord we do pray that if it be pleasing in Thy sight, the rain clouds may be driven away for this one day. We know the earth and the farm lands need it, Lord, and that the water in the mountain reservoirs is low—but thousands are planning on this day to worship. If it please Thee hold back the rain, and send it down tonight, when the services of the day are over and the worshipers have gotten safely to their homes."

Thank God for answered prayer, as our car speeds along, we leave the suburbs, and begin to climb the foothills. We are in a few moments righht in the heart of the mountains, still wrapped in the slumbering mantle of the night!

The rain is slacking—stopped! Not another drop falls to our knowledge during the day, but at midnight the storm-clouds gather and the rain comes down in torrents, lasting the better part of several days.

As our car comes to a stop, the headlights reveal lines of other waiting automobiles. Eagle Rock rises sheer and high above us, and in line with scores of other pilgrims we begin to climb the path so lately drenched with rain, to the summit.

How fragrant the grasses, the mosses and clover!

Someone is supporting us on either hand up the rugged steep. Our minds are far away and our eyes dreaming. We are thinking of that other Easter morning of which we read that on "The first day of the week came Mary Magdalene early, when it is yet dark, unto the sepulchre and seeth the stone taken away from the sepulchre."

The marvel of the resurrection—the glory—the thrill—and the power of it all, takes hold upon our minds and hearts.

High on the top of Eagle Rock, startlingly brilliant, and breath-takingly beautiful to the Christian heart, stands the enormous electric-lighted cross.

Scores of pilgrims are climbing beside us. We hear their breathing as they climb. All eyes are turned toward the cross, high and lifted up upon the hill before us. Upturned faces catch the illumination of the cross and shine strangely in the gloom.

There! We have scaled the last rock steep and are on the top of Eagle Rock! We are ushered within a roped enclosure. By the light of the cross we conduct the service and can see the faces of many of our friends from the Temple, smiling and offering wraps and cloaks to protect us from the raw mountain breeze that pours over the summit.

The faint grey of dawn is tinging the sky. Clouds are rolling away—wrapping themselves up and tucking themselves away in the clefts of the mountains before our very eyes. It is going to be a fair day.

We are sitting quietly, clasping our bible tightly, thrilled with the strangeness and the glorious significance of the scene. A great quietness is upon all.

Suddenly, away in the far distance, upon another mountain peak, a trumpeter shivers the silence, and wakes the mountains and the valleys, with the silver tones of the call to worship. As he stands clear-cut, silhouetted, on the mountainside, against the pearl-grey dawn and the rose of the coming sun, one holds one's breath for a moment and thinks of the day when one shall hear the trumpet of the Angel Gabriel declaring the second coming of our glorious Lord. No sooner do the strains of the bugle die away than another sound cleaves the air. 'Tis the chiming melody brought forth by the Bell ringers.

"Christ, the Lord, is risen today,
Hallelujah! Hallelujah!"

The perfume laden morning air is made resonant. Peal after peal ring out over the valleys and climb the hills ascending into the heavens, as these two sisters and three brothers with their bells fling the message far and wide. Fleecy clouds, shell pink and rose, are hovering over the lighted cross—one almost expects to hear the angel bands singing in the midst of them. Surely the hosts of heavens are looking down.

A rich tenor voice is singing now. A full orchestra is accompanying him. And then standing at the foot of the cross as the first light of day begins to dawn, we are preaching—preaching with the glory of the cross upon our hearts and its light athwart our pathway.

"He is not here, He is risen—Why seek the living among the dead? Go tell my disciples and Peter that I ascend unto my Father and your Father; and to My God and your God."

Everyone is singing now as the sermon is finished, and our voice has ceased to ring out over the heads of the assembled company in the valley. Hands have been lifted asking prayers for salvation and blessing. As the benediction is pronounced, a dazzling golden sunbeam breaks through the clouds and points with unerring finger to the cross, bathing it with heaven's glory.

With lightened footsteps and singing hearts we make our way reverently, thoughtfully, down the mountainside. The eyes of friends meet and they gaze into the depths of each other's souls silently, but with a depth of meaning. We feel that we have seen the empty tomb and gazing into the open heavens have glimpsed the risen Lord. Back in the car, with the door shut tight, we are whirling along the road, back to Los Angeles, to the duties of the day, with a strange sense of having been in a far-off country, and having spent an hour in the Garden of Joseph of Arimathaea.

THE SUNDAY SCHOOL—9:30

After the children's demonstration and parade of yesterday, hundreds of children are again pouring out to Sunday-school.

In every room in the Temple classes are in progress—in the main auditorium—in the balcony—the Sunday-school room—

ANGELUS TEMPLE, DEDICATED JAN. 1, 1923, AIMEE SEMPLE McPHERSON, PRESIDENT AND FOUNDER

ADMINISTRATION BUILDING, ECHO PARK EVANGELISTIC ASSOCIATION

the lecture hall—the 500 room—the social foyer—while the young men's Bible class completely fills the 120 room. For the children, there is the Rose Bud Class, The Dainty Dots, The Lamp Lighters, The Soldiers of the Cross, the Cradle Roll, the Nursery Class and the Junior Crusaders. While for adults are Bible Classes, senior and junior.

The Sunday School that began with 136 jumped in ten weeks to 1194, and is increasing steadily. The *Sunday School Times* writes to say that this has broken the record of the U. S. A. No special prizes or inducements of any kind have been offered—they are simply coming because the revival is on—and the fire of God is falling!

OVER THREE THOUSAND PARTICIPATED IN COMMUNION SERVICES

Outside the Temple the streets are filled with the roaring of motor cars. Workers are endeavoring to direct the traffic and have the cars parked at 45 degree angles, to conserve space. The late comers are often obliged to park their cars a half a mile from the Temple, so filled are the streets with automobiles of those attending the services.

Within, a glorious scene is enacted. Thousands of Christians are assembled to hear the Easter message and to participate in the great communion service, which marks the first Sunday of each month. Hundreds have brought basket-lunches which they will eat in Echo Park, just across the street, while scores of cars never move from the curb from morning till night.

All hearts are lifted, happily, expectantly; the glorious light from the stained-glass windows comes streaming down and lies in warm pools of sunshine everywhere.

Chanting the praises of the risen Lord, the choir take their places and the hush falls over the audience. Surely every mind is turning back to the empty tomb and the resurrection morning of our Lord.

The pealing bells of the organ. Then—high from the gallery above—comes floating down the clear soprano voice of Sister Stanley, that might well have been the voice of an angel;

"Lo, in the grave He lay"

and the choir answers, softly,

"Jesus, my Saviour"

And the voice on the gallery goes on;

"Waiting the coming day,
Jesus. my Lord."

With great power and fervor it is caught up everywhere

"Up from the grave He arose
With a mighty triumph o'er His foes,
He arose a victor from death's dark domain
And He lives forever with His saints to reign;
He arose, He arose, Hallelujah, Christ arose!"

The Easter message is brought amidst shouts and tears of rejoicing, as the scenes in and about the garden of Joseph of Arimathaea are painted. The inconsolable grief and longing of Mary. The tempestuous joy and happiness at the discovery that her Lord liveth. The battle between the powers of darkness and the forces of light. The triumph of the right. The defeat of Satan. The vanquishing of night. The gladsome triumph of the risen Lord. The coming forth of the Son of Righteousness with healing in His wings. The shouting of the heavenly hosts. The rejoicing of the children of earth; and the meaning of the resurrection to the world today.

Again and again the power falls, till one must pause a little to let the storm of heavenly praises spend themselves—'ere continuing the message.

Then the serving of the Holy Communion. 3500 saints, solemnly participate in this service—after a thorough heart examination. The glory of the Lord fills the Temple as the elders assisting in the service, pass the bread and the fruit of the vine to the assembled multitude. Heavenly singing and glorious praises fill the Temple like sweet incense at the ancient morning sacrifice.

Where, we wonder on the American continent, or in the world, is such a mammoth communion service being held this day? And where is there a communion set of such proportion as that of Angelus Temple, which contains 2500 glasses, half of which must oftentimes be refilled 'ere all are served. And yet so systematically has the serving been ordered that the entire company, without semblance of haste or confusion, are served in fifteen minutes and thirty seconds.

As the last communion is served the whole audience rise to

their feet, spontaneously, and with uplifted hands burst into singing;

"Holy, holy, holy,
  Lord God Almighty,
Early in the morning
  Our songs shall rise to Thee.

Holy, holy, holy,
  Merciful and mighty,
God in three persons,
  Blessed Trinity."

SUNDAY AFTERNOON AND EVENING

Sunday afternoon and evening may almost be considered as one continuous service—hundreds never leave their seats—but sit tight—to be ready for the evening hour.

The Temple is one sea of faces—hundreds are turned from every door. In order to make more seats for those who would otherwise be sent away disappointed, the little children are invited to come and sit on the floor around us within the altar space and on the platform, filling every available inch of it and then overflowing on the steps, they resemble a beautiful flower garden, with fresh little faces upturned.

The altars, after the afternoon message, are filled with hundreds and a wonderful work is wrought for the Lord of Glory.

The musical hour, which precedes the evangelistic service each Sunday evening, opens at 7:00 o'clock. The English Hand-Bell Ringers, the harpist, the girl buglers, the male quartette, the child soloist, the golden tenor, and others bring gospel messages in music and song. Enthusiasm runs high. The sermon is punctuated again and again by clapping and cheers. At the suggestion of the altar call, aisles are again blocked, and scores finding salvation.

Now, dear reader, the author has only been able to give you a glimpse of one week-end at Angelus Temple. In addition, when we tell you that, counting the Training School, meetings are held on an average of five a day, and that this is the schedule week in and week out, you will better realize how mighty is the revival, which is shaking the community and making its influence felt both far and wide.

JUDGE BEN LINDSEY AT ANGELUS TEMPLE

LIKE a mountain breeze from Pike's Peak, refreshing, inspiring, re-vivifying, came the message and presence of Judge Ben Lindsey, of the Juvenile Court of Denver, Colorado, to Angelus Temple, Sunday morning, April 29th.

With his coming for which we had been looking for days, came trooping a host of happy memories of our two evangelistic campaigns in Denver—"The Mile High City." What happy memories they were! Happiness unalloyed!

From the day the Temple opened, we had longed that Denver, who had so much to do with making the Temple possible, might be officially welcomed and represented at the Temple. So now it has come to pass.

Met at the door, and escorted to the platform by a guard of honor, composed of Angelus Temple boys, he came. What joy it was to welcome him, and to remember the support which he, with Mayor Bailie, of Denver, gave the campaigns in that place.

The message of the morning was brought by Judge Lindsey, to a well-filled house. When 'midst a burst of applause and cheering, he had finished his talk of bringing the love of God and the teaching of Christ into the courts and jails, and the better way of dealing with boys and girls, there was but one chapter to read that most embodied his whole talk and that was the thirteenth chapter of first Corinthians. Then the whole house rose to their feet and sang with new significance:

"Down in the human heart crushed by the Tempter
Feelings lie buried that grace can restore,
Touched by a loving hand, wakened by kindness,
Chords that were broken will vibrate once more."

MAYOR OF LOS ANGELES ON TEMPLE PLATFORM

Following the splendid talk of Judge Hardy, of our Superior Court, a few Sundays previous, Mayor Cryer of Los Angeles, escorted by Police Officer Croft, occupied the seat of honor on Angelus Temple platform, and by his enthusiastic endorsement and commendation of the work of Sister McPherson and the Temple, of which he said the entire city felt the uplift and good, won the hearts of the great multitude.

He said that the influence for good was being felt in ever-widening circles from the Temple and through the city and country, and expressed earnest desire that the good work might go on and on in increasing power and fervor.

REVIVAL TIDE RISING

DURING the first eight months after the Temple was opened, between eight and ten thousand souls kneeled at the altar, seeking the Lord Jesus Christ as their personal Saviour, and hundreds have received the baptism of the Holy Spirit and other scores have been healed of their diseases in answer to believing prayer. Cancers have melted like snow before the sun. Tumors and tubercular bones have been healed and signs and wonders wrought in the Name of the Holy Child, Jesus. For months, the revival has gone, sweeping on and on, day after day, without sign of cessation. The Temple seats still continue to be filled with people, but also with the glory of the Lord.

SUNRISE PRAYER MEETINGS

Just as each new day is breaking and the rising sun is kissing the earth to wakefulness, a little stream of earnest pilgrims can be seen wending their way toward Echo Park and entering the Temple doors.

These are they who are sincerely and devotedly in earnest, waiting upon the Lord for the mighty baptism of the Holy Ghost and of fire. They have not met to visit, one with the other, nor to engage in idle conversation—they have not even met to sing or testify or hear the ministers who bring sermons from the Word, each day. They have come together to pray, definitely and to "tarry until" they are endued with power from on high.

Silently, but with fixed determination, they mount the steps that lead to the upper room, which accommodates just one hundred and twenty. Here they fall upon their knees and pour out their hearts' desire, before the Giver of every good and perfect gift. This beautiful room, upon which is being expended more love and thought and tastefulness in decoration and appointments than any other room in the house, has become indeed, the "Holy of Holies,"—the power house. It is here that workers are being prepared for the field—Christians being baptized with the Holy Ghost and prepared for the ministry. Sometimes a holy stillness pervades the air—sometimes the beams of the upper room tremble and throb with the songs of rejoicing of spirit-filled believers.

Sometimes, the prayer meeting continues until noon—sometimes through almost the entire day. Oh, the radiant faces which we have seen coming out from that room and down into the auditorium filled with the fire and glory and love of God, to point sinners to the foot of the cross and engage in practical, whole-souled labor in the harvest fields of life.

WATCH TOWER

A few weeks after the Temple was formally dedicated and opened to the public, another room—the smallest room in the Temple— was built on the top floor.

This room was named "The Watch Tower" and solemnly dedicated to continuous prayer.

Since February, 1923, and up to the present writing perpetual intercession has been made therein, without ceasing night or day.

Devout sisters pray throughout the day and godly men therein continue to pray throughout the watches of the night.

There are 320 persons on the weekly Watch Tower schedule, and there is not the slightest difficulty in securing enough intercessors to fill the hours. Those praying in the Tower pray in two-hour shifts.

Telegrams, letters, cables, etc., have come from almost all parts of the globe asking prayer. No one ever needs try to start a prayer meeting in Angelus Temple, for there is a continuous fire of intercession burning upon the altars of Almighty God.

Many times we, who dwell close to the Temple, have been awakened in the small hours of the morning by the fervent voices of those interceding for the lost. Needless to say those who come down from the Watch Tower have faces that shine with the light of heaven. Of a truth, prayer moves the Hand that moves the world.

WATER BAPTISMAL SERVICES

Each Thursday evening, since the opening of the Temple, a most impressive water baptismal service has been held and largely attended.

The first Thursday night, as the curtains were swept aside and the lights of the auditorium were dimmed, the audience at first gasped at the beauty of the scene depicting the River Jordan, flowing under stately palms and foliage and then over a miniature waterfall into the snow-white baptistry. As the lights brightened from break of day to mid-noon and the first candidates stepped into the river in their flowing robes of white, the congregation suddenly rose to their feet and began to clap their hands and shout aloud the praises of the Lord. Over eighty were buried with Christ in the waters of baptism, that first night. Dr. Wm. Keeney Towner, of the First Baptist Church, assisting the pastor, Sister McPherson, in the baptistry. In many instances, whole families have been baptized together; in scores of instances husbands and wives have gone down into the waters simultaneously, side by side. Several of the gypsy converts have also been buried with Christ in baptism and the very presence of the Lord and the Holy Spirit, like a brooding dove, has been felt throughout the place.

Week after week, these baptismal services have continued without abatement as new converts have given their hearts to the Master. During the first eight months more than two thousand were immersed.

ANGELUS TEMPLE TRAINING INSTITUTE

An Evangelistic and Missionary Training Institute has also been growing in power and numbers. since February, 1923, wherein students are preparing for the Missionary Field abroad, and for the Evangelistic Field at home. Each day seems to grow deeper, and sweeter, than the day before. Such beauty and love prevails—that this has truly become a heaven below. Multitudes come flowing in over the threshold to hear the story of Jesus and His love, catch up a lighted torch and go streaming out again to all quarters of the land, taking with them the message of "The Four-Square Gospel—Jesus, Only Saviour, Baptizer and Healer, Jesus the Coming King."

CONVERTING THE WORLD BY RADIO

How often we have sung that grand old hymn:

"Give the winds a mighty voice
Jesus saves, Jesus saves.
Let the nations now rejoice
Jesus saves, Jesus saves."

We are singing it with new meaning these days, for in very deed and in truth the winds are to be given a mighty voice.

The preaching of the Gospel—the Four-Square Gospel—is to be broadcasted upon the air to hundreds of thousands of "listeners in". A huge 500-watt sending station installed in the Temple, catching up the preached Word will mount up on the great galvanized steel towers and then be flung far and wide to hungry hearts, in Canada, Mexico, the U. S. A., the islands of the sea and the ships of the ocean.

What a wonderful day we are living in! What an unprecedented opportunity for the preaching of the Gospel to every creatureis now afforded! Years ago a preacher whose voice could be heard for a half a mile was lauded and thought to have accomplished a most remarkable feat. But think of it, seated in the radio studio, or standing in the pulpit of Angelus Temple, we will now be heard for thousands of miles without lifting the voice above that of the ordinary conversation.

The author has already had the privilege of preaching many times over the radio of the newspaper offices in Los Angeles, Denver, Oakland, etc., and has received letters and wires from "listeners in" who heard the message in Oregon and Washington. One lady was healed of a fearful disease and converted through the message that came to her over the air.

The days, weeks and months speed by with almost incredible rapidity. We know not how soon our Lord shall come, though we believe that He is near, even at the door.

"In the meantime, keep us, O, Savior dear, very humble

and lowly at the foot of the cross, adoring and magnifying Thy name, bringing souls into Thy kingdom, with the cry ever ringing in our own adoring hearts—even so, Lord Jesus, come quickly. And grant, O Lord, that if we should fall asleep before you come in the clouds of glory, that people may be able to say of us as they did of Ruth in the days gone by:

"So she gleaned the field until evening, and beat out that she had gleaned, and it was an ephah of barley."

SOME SERMONS AND WRITINGS

of

AIMEE SEMPLE MCPHERSON

on

SALVATION

THE BAPTISM OF THE HOLY SPIRIT

THE SECOND COMING OF JESUS

DEEPER TEACHING

Part II

WHAT SHALL I DO WITH JESUS?

"W*HAT shall I do with Jesus?*" Clear and imperative rang out the voice of Pilate above the clamor of the throng assembled in the Judgment Hall.

"*What shall I do with Jesus?*" The question was flung forth over the mob of frenzied, upturned faces.

Fair and square, demanding an immediate, decisive answer, this question of momentous importance resounded through the court room, and hung suspended in the tense, tragedy-laden air. From the murmuring sea of anger-tossed accusers was born a mighty, unquenchable tempest of howlings and ragings, while dark faces grew darker still with blood-thirsty fury against the still, calm figure standing so meek and sweet in his robes of flowing white.

It was Jesus—this pure, mild Man, standing there friendless and alone in the midst of this howling rabble. How out of place He looked—like a tall, sweet, fragrant lily in the midst of thorns and briers; like a pure little lamb in the midst of a pack of hungry wolves, with bared fangs. Dear Lamb of God, innocent, and unresisting, before the great judgment seat of Pontius Pilate he stood, awaiting the verdict of those arrayed against Him.

"*What shall I do with Jesus?*" What decision would they render upon this question—this momentous question—this greatest and most important question that has ever been decided since the world began? There were only two possible ways of answering—only two courses of action open: there was no neutral ground, for had He not declared that

"*He who is not for Me is against Me*"? Either they must accept Him as the King of Heaven, Jesus, their Saviour, or they must crucify and drive Him away from their hearts. Either they must accept Him as their Messiah, their Redeemer, or they must reject and put Him to an open shame.

Louder, and with ever increasing determination, rose and fell the cry of the people;

"Away with Him! Crucify Him, Crucify Him! We have no King but Caesar." They had rendered their decision, their choice had been made; they had given their irrevocable answer, and had determined to crucify and put their Lord to an open shame.

Harsh hands fell upon the gentle Nazarene, and rushed Him from the court. Mercilessly did they tear His garments from Him, and bared His precious back to the smiters. He meekly bore the cruel lash—to the last, stinging blow—that by His stripes we might be healed. A crown of thorns was thrust down upon His brow; a purple robe put upon Him in mocking derision. He was led to Calvary's Hill, bearing His cross, and crucified by cruel men.

They crucified their Lord; they gave Him vinegar and hyssop to drink; they spurned and rejected Him to the last. And He bowed His head and died—He who would have gathered them to His bosom—He who would have been their King, and have taken them up to reign with Him on His throne.

Pilate's Judgment Hall—the very name calls to memory that shameful scene, and our hearts cry out:

"How cruel, how foolish those Jews were to reject and crucify their Lord—to let Him stand there on trial alone, with no one to accept Him and stand on His side!"

Yet, did you ever stop to realize that the border of Pilate's Judgment Hall has been enlarged and its walls have widened and widened, till today this whole world is a judgment hall—Jesus is still on trial, and the Spirit is echoing and re-echoing the question:

"What will you do with Jesus?"

The whole world is obliged to answer this question, as did the Jews of old. Each living soul, irrespective of race, color or creed, must take sides either for or against Jesus. There are—today as in that day of old—but two courses of action open. Each heart must answer individually and definitely whether he, too, will cry:

"Away with Him! Crucify Him," or whether he will open his heart's door and let Him enter as King and kings and crown Him with love and allegiance.

Perhaps some reader cries out in horror:

"Oh! We would never crucify Jesus—we would never think of driving the nails in His hands!" But consider a moment, dear one. If you have not accepted Him as your Saviour from all sin and unrighteousness, if you have not come to Him in repentance and had the blood applied to your heart, you have done just that—crucified your Lord afresh and put Him to an open shame. Remember he who is not for Him is against Him—neutral you cannot be.

Each time you go out of a meeting unsaved; each time you go to bed unrepentant; each new day the sun rises and finds you unprayerful, unthoughtful of your soul's salvation, you are crying out:

"Away with Him! Away with Him!" O, perhaps you do not say it in words. But actions speak louder than words, and even though your mouth may speak much love, if you have not unconditionally surrendered your heart and life to Him, and permitted Him to rule on the throne of your heart, you are unconsciously answering the question—

"What shall I do with Jesus?" by saying:

"Away with Him! Crucify Him! I have no king but self and the world; I want my own way. Away with Him! Away with Salvation." And another voice is added to the throng rejecting Jesus.

"In what way am I saying 'Away with Him'?" you ask.

Why, can you not realize, dear unsaved soul, that every step you take—every foot-fall that resounds along the corridors of time, apart from Jesus—every step towards worldliness in sin —is crying out, louder than you could ever speak;

"Away with Him; I choose the world; I have no king but self." Each time you put off Salvation and say:

"Not tonight," you are adding another thorn to the crown which you are making of your life and placing it on His dear brow.

We are all making a crown for Jesus out of these daily lives of ours, either a crown of golden, divine love, studded with gems of sacrifice and adoration, or a thorny crown, filled with the cruel briers of unbelief, or selfishness and sin, and placing it upon His brow.

Each new day lived in holiness unto the Lord; each new sacrifice of praise, is just another gem in the royal diadem with which the Christian is constantly crowning the King who sits supreme on the throne of his heart.

Each new day lived in sin and indifference to Jesus is just another thorn, another cruel brier the sinner's life is weaving into the crown he is placing upon the brow of the Friend and King he has rejected and driven away from his heart.

Then they put upon Him a purple robe, crying, "Hail, Jesus, King of the Jews," and smote Him with their hands. Many today are still living lives of hypocrisy, mockery and pretence; many are putting upon Jesus a purple robe of outside formality; they go to church and sing—"All Hail the Power of Jesus' Name," but by their lives they smite Him with their hands.

And He, bearing His cross, went forth unto Golgotha, and there they nailed Him to the cross. The great, rugged cross was stretched upon the ground, and Jesus' dear body stretched upon that cross. O, sinner, behold that man—the Son of God—with the kind, resigned, tender eyes, waiting to be nailed there for your sins. See those rough, heavy hands seize the nails and place them to the palms of Jesus' hands. Hear the great, ringing blows of the hammer, as the nails are driven deep—crunching through flesh and sinew and bones—deep into the wood of the cross for your transgressions. Dear hands—hands that had fed the multitude—hands that had blessed the children, healed the sick, raised the dead—faithful hands that are knocking at your heart's door just now as you are reading these very words—they nailed them to the cross. It was your sins, and my sins that nailed Him there. Are you still pushing His hands away from your life, and piercing them with nails of scorn, and unbelief, and pride?

Then they drove the nails through His feet—the feet that had traveled so many weary miles to bring hope and cheer and light—and He was lifted up high on the cross, up and up, suspended upon those cruel nails till at last the cross sank with a thud into the hole that had been digged for it. And there He hung, the King of glory, between earth and heaven, in shame, alone, for us.

Sinner, dear, how high you have lifted Him in open shame—others have seen you reject Jesus! O, won't you receive Him just now as your Saviour? Will you not love Him who first loved you?

See that beautiful face, more marred than the face of any other man. Hear His cry:

"Lo, I thirst! Give me to drink." They offered Him vinegar and hyssop—the bitterest of their hatred and unbelief. But ah! He thirsts for the sweetness of their love and adoration and acceptance. What are you giving Jesus to drink—sweetness or bitterness?—love or rejection? Our lives are as a sponge, either absorbing vinegar and hyssop from the world and the devil, or sweetness and fragrance and the water of life—from Jesus and His Word.

Jesus is calling anew today:

"Lo, I thirst!" Dear one, what have you to offer Him today from your life—acceptance or rejection?

Jesus cried: *"Father, forgive them; they know not what they do."* Oh, sinner, it does not seem possible that you could have realized what you were doing in refusing to accept Jesus, and persisting in crying:

"Away with Him! Crucify Him!" Perhaps you never quite realized that you were crowning Him with thorns, and crucifying Him afresh, and that he who is not building up for Him is tearing down.

What will you do with Jesus today? How will you answer this eternal question? Jesus is standing before you awaiting the verdict. You must judge; you must render your decision, for or against—Jesus or the World, Life or Death. Judge, and choose ye this day, for soon this whole scene will be changed forever. The sinner will be removed in a hurry from his judgment seat, and Jesus will mount the judgment seat to judge the nations. The graves shall be opened, the sea shall give up its dead, and all the dead, both small and great, will stand before Him whom they have judged.

Everything will then be quite reversed. Instead of it being a question of "What shall I do with Jesus?" the question confronting each sinner will be, *"What will Jesus do with me?"* In that great day those who have accepted Jesus and made

Him ruler in their lives, will be accepted of Him and sit with Him on His throne, but all those who have rejected Him, and cried:

"Away with Him from my life, I have no time for Jesus," will be rejected then by Jesus. He will Himself echo the sinner's own words;

"Away with him; *'depart from Me, I never knew you.'* Depart into the home prepared for the devil and his angels."

Those who gave Him to drink of the sweetness and wine of their love will drink anew with Him the wine of His Father's Kingdom, but those who gave Him naught but rejection, and the gall of bitterness, must drink the cup of their own sin and death to the dregs.

What will you do with Jesus? O, accept Him now; seek Him whilst yet He may be found; *call upon Him while He is near. Put away the evil of your doings; cease to do evil; learn to do well; wash you; make you clean.* Accept Him as your Lord and Saviour just now. He is calling you who are weary and sick with sin; seeking you in tenderness. He is whispering, *Come unto Me all ye who are weary and heavy laden, and I will give you rest. Him that cometh unto Me I will in no wise cast out.* Today is the day of Salvation; tomorrow it may be too late, for He is coming soon to earth again, coming with power and great glory. Get ready to meet Him.

WHICH ROAD?

ONLY TWO ROADS IN LIFE; UPON WHICH ARE YOU?

SEARCH where you may, the wide world over, there are only two roads to be found in this life.

One road leads to Heaven; the other road leads to Hell. The first road leads to everlasting life, the second to everlasting death. The one to joy and peace and eternal day; the other to eternal sorrow and darkest night and destruction.

Every man, woman and child in this world, irrespective of race, color or creed, is at this very moment traveling either the one or the other of these two roads. In other words, every individual living is either on the road to heaven and life. or upon the road that leads to Hell and death.

WHICH WILL YOU CHOOSE?

I am just a plain body, that believes in stating a plain fact in plain words. It is time that preachers stopped sugar-coating and misconstruing God's Word; time they stopped preaching politics and oyster suppers and began to preach these plain facts that are so simple that even a fool need not err therein.

First of all let me give my text, and we will see what the Lord says about these two roads, their destinations, and the pedestrians thereon. Jesus says, *"wide is the gate, and broad is the way that leadeth to destruction, and many there be which go in thereat; because straight is the gate and narrow is the way that leadeth unto life, and few there be that find it."*

This statement, if understood, would surely revolutionize the ideas of a great many so-called broad-minded people, who have always believed that living a moral life or being a church member would be a sufficient passport into Heaven. Being a church member is no longer a despised way, but quite the opposite; it is now considered quite the fashionable and proper thing to do. Many think this is all the Lord requires of us; but upon this erroneous belief falls the Word of God with a startling blow that overthrows all such false security.

Narrow is the way that leads to life and few there be that find it. O, that Christians, as well as sinners, and cold professors, would awaken to the reality of this fact and get one glimpse of the countless millions pouring into eternity every day without God and without hope! They would spring from their beds of ease and rush into the highways and hedges to compel men to come into the narrow way, and get right with God before it is too late.

The Word of God shows us where these two roads start. "*All* were born in sin and shapen in iniquity." "*All* have sinned and come short of the glory of God." We are also reminded that as God "cannot look upon sin with the least degree of allowance," "the soul that sinneth, it shall die." But Jesus took our place, He died in our stead, thereby opening a new and a living way, the narrow way, into the presence of the Father.

O, sinner friend here tonight! O weary, heavy-laden pilgrim! halt a moment and consider. Which road are you on? Are you traveling towards Heaven or Hell? We all entered life by the one and self-same road, that is, we were all born in sin, and shapen in iniquity.

Figure one on the chart shows us just a little of the circle which represents the earth. All having been born under the curse of sin, and having need of the second birth (*"Except a man be born of water and of the Spirit, he cannot enter into the kingdom of God."* (John 3:5), enter the infancy of life on the wide road marked by figure two on the chart.

Many anxious mothers ask the question:

"Sister, what do you think becomes of the little babes, and children who die before the age of accountability?" I answer promptly, and without a moment's hesitancy—

"I believe they are taken to be with the loving and compassionate Jesus, who said: *"Suffer the little children to come unto Me, and forbid them not, for of such is the kingdom of heaven.'"*

But there comes a day, possibly most of you can look backward along the road of time and recall that day for yourself when the little heart and mind began to know the difference between right and wrong. The young pilgrim, after running along carelessly from infancy, suddenly sights in the distance a great, old, rugged sign post, that has stood the storms of many generations, but still stands firm and unmovable. This sign post—the Cross of Calvary—stands just at the parting of the way.

Did you ever notice the peculiar and wonderful shape of the cross? The foot points to the earth and humility, and to the fountain filled with blood, as though it were saying—

"Come, poor, tired, troubled, sin-sick soul. Lay down your burden; plunge into the fountain filled with blood. Here is cleansing for the filthy, pardon for the sinful, rest for the weary, peace for the troubled, relief for the oppressed, freedom for the captive. Just throw yourself down at the feet of Jesus and He will make you whole."

The top of the cross points upward toward the sky and heaven, as though saying—

"Lift up your head, poor, weary pilgrim; lift up your eyes to the heavens above you; lift up the hands that hang down; strengthen the feeble knees; say unto them that are weak, 'be strong and of good courage, for He who died upon the tree has gone up yonder, beyond the clouds of glory, to prepare a place for you, that where He is there you may be also.' "

The two arms of the cross are outstretched as though to gather the whole world into the loving embrace of Him who said:

"Come unto Me, Oh, ye ends of the earth, and be ye saved."

Thank God for such a sign-post to reveal the way of pardon and point out the narrow heaven-bound road to the sin-sick soul.

Figure three on the chart shows us where the two roads divide. Oh, let your feet pause here, dear one, at the parting of the way. Don't make a mistake, for this is the most important decision you will ever be called upon to make in your whole life. Which road will you take? One turns to the left, the other to the right. One leads to heaven, the other to hell.

Look carefully at the two roads as depicted on the chart, and you will notice that the broad road which leads to destruction is a crooked road, so crooked that he who walks upon it is always unable to see just what lies ahead. Each new turn of the road he finds himself committing sins more vile than his conscience would have permitted a month or a year before. Were the road not crooked he would be able to see the flames of hell and hear the weeping and the anguished cries of the lost who call:

"Go back! Go back!" He would run for his life to the refuge of the cross.

"Why is the road crooked?" you ask. Because it is the trail of the serpent. The same serpent that deceived Eve in the garden is deceiving the nations today.

"Why is it crooked?" Why, because it is impossible for a serpent to crawl straight. The devil is crooked and he will deceive you at every turn of the road till at last he has plunged you into destruction.

Now while the trail of the serpent leads into hell, 'tis the way of the cross that leads home to the glorious land of heaven. Oh, 'tis a heaven to go to heaven in when we walk in the shadow of the cross. Hallelujah!

The broad road, that leads to destruction, looks inviting to your feet. It is strewn with flowers and worldly pleasures. The so-called broad-minded man who lives on the broad way can tell you of worldly pleasures, theatres, dance halls, fashion, love of money, popularity, music and sin to be found at every turn of the road.

They could tell you, if they would, of broken hearts, too, of drunkards, and harlots, of empty hearts, and misspent lives. They could whisper, too, with white faces and scared eyes, of ghastly deaths they have witnessed of those who found the wages of sin were death, and went into the presence of their father, the devil, and to the home prepared for him and his imps.

But no, they will not tell you of these true facts, but tell only of the light surface, and the tinseled, varnished side.

THE BROAD WAY

That downward road (figure four) is broad and easy to enter. Just a little disobedience, a little lie, forgetting to pray, wandering from God, whatever it was that came first into your life—you remember it—when you began your downward career on the broad way that leads to destruction. Perhaps you did not really mean to go far on that downward path, but somehow it all seemed so easy. One sin led to a greater one, till soon you were so tangled up and slipping so fast it seemed impossible to stop and go back.

It is so easy to go down to hell and destruction, just a toboggan slide, till at last you shall awaken to find it is too late, unless you listen now to the warning and stop and return to the cross, that dear old weather-beaten sign-post, and weep it all out at Jesus' feet.

THE END THEREOF IS DEATH

It is a dreadful thing to go on to the end of the broad, sinful road. I have gazed with wide, horrified eyes into bleary, sinful eyes and bloated faces. I have marked the lines of sin upon the face and oftener upon the heart. I have seen the great chains of appetite, the prison doors of evil, I have stood at the death beds of those who had rejected Christ, and such a message as you are now hearing, and held their hands with a shudder as they passed out into the dark, without God, to reap their reward. I have heard those who would never seem to sober down and think before, when asked to accept Jesus on their death beds cry out:

"Too late! Too late! I'm lost!" I can tell of weeping and wailing and gnashing of teeth, as they died.

The proud and haughty sinner, the infidel, they who have declared in their learning that there was no God, no hell, no heaven, shall have to pass with the drunkard and the harlot through the jaws of death (figure five) into that awful home prepared for the devil and his angels. There shall be weeping and wailing and gnashing of teeth. Their not having believed there was such a place will not have moved it or taken it away. *"The wages of sin is death."*

DYING WORDS OF THE UNSAVED

Here are some of the dying words of the unsaved:

"Hell is a refuge if it hide me from thy frown."—Altamont.

"I would gladly give thirty thousand pounds to have it proven there is no hell:"—Charteres.

"Give me more laudanum that I may not think of eternity and what is to come."—Mirabeau.

"Oh, my poor soul! what will become of thee? Whither wilt thou go?"—Cardinal Mazarin.

The atheist Hobb's last words were: "I am taking a fearful leap into the dark."

Voltaire was a noted, wealthy infidel, yet his last words were: "I am abandoned by God and man; I shall die and go to hell."

Death in that awful place where the worm dieth not, and the fire is not quenched.

"Oh," you say, "if God is a God of love He would never cast a soul down into hell." No, God will not willingly cast the sinner into destruction, and if he goes to hell he will have to go over the body and blood of Jesus Christ who died to save him; rejecting the love of the Saviour who did all in His power and shed every drop of His blood to redeem him from that place which was built, not for the sinner, but for the devil and his angels.

Those who live in sin, with the devil as their father, in this world, will live with the devil as their father in that home which has been prepared for him; but the children of God who have owned Him as their Father here below, will live with Him in His home in peace and joy for evermore.

THE NARROW ROAD

The other road (figure six), the narrow road, blest road of light and life, begins at the cross. Jesus is the door; there is no way to enter but by Him, and the blood He shed for the remission of our sins. It is a narrow road, there is no room to take earthly things with you; there is just room for Jesus and you. If any man would follow Me, let him deny himself daily, take up his cross and follow Me. It means a right about face. It means being born again and being made a new creature in Christ Jesus, so that the things we once loved we now hate, and, Hallelujah! the things we once hated we now love.

In order to enter this narrow road that leads to heaven you must repent of all sin, make things right, straighten up your back tracks as far as possible, ask Jesus to cleanse you from all sin and unrighteousness, and *"though your sins be as scarlet, they shall be as white as snow; though they be red like crimson, they shall be as wool."*—Isa. 1:18. "For he who cometh unto Him, He will in no wise cast out."

Those who travel upward, for it is a steady climb, can tell you of joys untold. They can tell you of a peace the world can not give nor take away. They can tell you of broken hearts that have been healed, and sad lives made glad. They will testify to you of salvation from all sin, and deliverance from all bondage, of broken chains, and captives made free in Christ Jesus. They can tell of the baptism with the Holy Ghost (Acts 2:4) and the gifts and fruits of the Spirit in their lives.

I have in this road also looked into eyes and faces, but they were filled with the glory and love of God. Instead of evil and avariciousness, they were filled with tenderness and tears of gratitude to the blessed Saviour who grows sweeter as the days go by. Glory! Glory! Glory! Each step you take in this road brings you one step nearer heaven; one foot says "Glory!" and the other says "Hallelujah!" and with a pure heart and a clear conscience you are on your way to heaven. O, sinner, where have you such joy as this?

THE END THEREOF IS LIFE

Here, too, I have stood by death beds and instead of convulsed, fearful faces of sinners, I have seen calm, peaceful faces of those just going to rest in the arms of Jesus. Blessed are those that die in the Lord, and go shouting home to glory.

Here are the dying words of a few of the saved:

"Lord Jesus, receive my spirit."—Stephen.

"I have fought a good fight, I have finished my course, I have kept the faith.

"Henceforth there is laid up for me a crown of righteousness, which the Lord, the righteous judge, shall give me at that day; and not to me only, but unto all them also that love His appearing."—II Tim., 4:7—Paul.

"The best of all, God is with us."—Wesley.

"I am sweeping through the gates, washed in the blood of the Lamb."—Cookman.

"I am in perfect peace, resting alone on the blood of Christ: I find this sufficient to enter the presence of God with."—Trotter.

"The battle is fought, the battle is fought; the victory is won."—Dr. Payson.

The cross-bar of the cross (figure seven), represents the river of death through which so many saintly feet have trod. Oh, what a wonderful thing to have Him bear you up that the floods do not overflow, and to be able to cry with Catherine Booth:

"The waters are rising, but so am I; I am not going under, but over."

Just beyond the waves of death a glorious crown is waiting. Will there be any stars in your crown? Do you not long to be a soul-winner for Jesus? How pitiful it would be in that last day to have lived the most of our lives for the devil, to have given Jesus but the few closing hours of life's little day, and to be obliged to go empty-handed without a single soul with which to greet the Master, not a trophy nor a jewel to adorn the crown that you lay at His feet.

Beyond lies the glorious city of Heaven whose twelve gates are each composed of a solid pearl, whose street is made of pure gold, as it were transparent glass and the foundation of whose wall is garnished with all manner of precious stones. The building of the wall is of jasper, and the city of pure gold like unto clear glass. That land has no need of the sun, neither of the moon to shine in it, for the glory of God doth lighten it, and the Lamb is the light thereof.

Here there shall be no sickness nor crying, no pain nor death nor sorrow, no misunderstandings and no heartaches, and there shall in no wise enter into it anything that defileth or that worketh an abomination or maketh a lie, but they which are written in the Lamb's book of life.

Ah! the toils and thorns of the way are naught to be compared with one glimpse of the glory that awaits us in that beautiful city where Jesus wipes all tears from all faces, and there is no more night. Hallelujah! the very thought of seeing Jesus sets my whole soul on fire.

Who ever heard a sinner saying, "O, I'm so glad that some day this life will be over and I am going to die and go to hell and destruction." NO! You never hear them anxious to talk about death and punishment. But the true child of God loves to think of the day when he shall lay down the cross and receive the crown.

Between heaven and hell is a great gulf fixed. There is no possibility of crossing from one to the other after death. As a tree falls, so shall it lie. Today is the day of salvation—tomorrow may be eternally too late.

Now sinner, stop, and decide just now, which road you are on, and which road you choose to journey on from this time forward; decide which home you will dwell in forever—where the fire is not quenched and the worm dieth not, or where no weeping shall ever be heard, but singing and rejoicing and joy unspeakable forever and forever.

You are a free-will agent; you must decide for yourself. Jesus has opened the way, and He is holding the gate open wide for you just now. O come tonight, dear ones, come just now. Never, never blame Jesus, or say He sent you to hell, for if you refuse to be saved and enter in, you send yourself there; He has done His part. How He will help you and carry you through if you will only let Him. Just now, wherever you are, He is whispering,

"Behold, I stand at your heart's door and knock." Open to Him just now. Say, "I will arise and go unto my Father." Today is the day of salvation. You have no lease of tomorrow. Come just now.

"Angels are lingering near,
Prayers rise from hearts so dear,
O wanderer, come."

BEHOLD, THE MAN!

"Then came Jesus forth wearing the crown of thorns and the purple robe, and Pilate said unto them, Behold the man."—John, 19:5.

JESUS has promised us in His Word that He, if He is lifted up from the earth, will draw all men unto Himself, and before beginning this subject today I cried out to the Lord to help me to sink out of sight and to lift Him up above the earth until you should see no man save Jesus only.

BEHOLD the man! Behold *THE* man! Behold the *MAN!* I would like to repeat it over and over again, until I catch every wandering mind and bring each straying thought into captivity. Behold the man. Just close your eyes to all else for a few moments.

STOP beholding your business—your pleasure—your home—your earthly cares and duties—your neighbor—whatever it may be that has been absorbing your attention, and *Behold the Man, Christ Jesus.*

If you have never stopped long enough before in your busy life to behold the Man, the Lamb of God, the one who loves you more than any earthly friend loves you, I want you to behold Him NOW.

I am sure that if you could only get one glimpse of that face which is the fairest among ten thousand, if you could only catch one cadence of His voice, sweet as the rushing of many waters, if you could only gaze for one moment into the depths of those tender eyes filled with understanding and sympathy and love, the tears of love and gratitude would spring to your eyes, your heart would fill with praise till you would never wish to cease from beholding and adoring and worshiping this Man, Christ Jesus. As the shades of darkness and unbelief are driven back by the light of the sun of righteousness, and as you behold the Man, you will find new beauties, new attributes and graces unfolding themselves before your astonished and adoring eyes each moment you behold, till your heart bursts forth into singing,

"Since mine eyes were fixed on Jesus,
I've lost sight of all beside,
So enhanced my Spirit's vision,
Gazing at the crucified."

As we sweep back the curtains of the centuries and look back through the undimmed corridors of the past, we behold the Man seated with His Father upon his throne. He was with His Father from the beginning—the brightest jewel in heaven, the joy of the Father, the delight of the angels, the light of the temple, the only begotten Son, worthy of praise upon harps of gold, and the angels fell prostrate at His feet as He sat in His kingly robes and splendor in their midst.

Behold the Man, with His Father when He spoke the world into being, and set the sun, the moon and the planets in the sky.

Behold the Man, filled with sorrow on that memorable day when our ancestral parents fell into sin and because of that sin were banished from the sight of God under penalty of death. And when there was no eye to pity, no arm to save, none that could pay the ransom price for their redemption, we

Behold the Man, saying: "Father, send me, I will pay the price. Without the shedding of blood there is no remission of sins; I will shed my blood, Father, I will be the bridge to span the gulf 'twixt man and God." Then we read that *"God so loved the world that He gave His only begotten Son that whosoever believeth in Him should not perish but have everlasting life."*

Behold the Man, standing up to take leave of the Father, leaving the songs and the adoration of the angelic hosts, laying aside His royal robes, His sceptre and His crown, stepping down from the throne and coming all the way from heaven to earth for you and me, that we might not perish but have everlasting life.

Behold the Man, conceived of the Holy Ghost, born of the virgin Mary, coming to a world that found no room for Him in the inn. Behold Him born in a manger amidst the most deplorable and humble surroundings, coming to reach the lowest and the poorest of sinners.

Behold the Man living and growing up with Mary, His mother, and Joseph, in the carpenter shop. Behold Him at the age of thirty, baptized of John in the river Jordan, ready to begin His ministry. Behold the Man rising from a watery grave as the heavens opened and the Holy Spirit descended upon Him and the voice of God spoke aloud saying, *"This is my beloved Son in whom I am well pleased."* Thus He entered upon His ministry with divine authority and the power of the God-head resting upon Him and abiding with Him.

Behold the Man tempted in the wilderness for forty days, tempted in all points like as we, and yet without sin. Behold Him turning the water into wine, preaching the gospel of the Kingdom, healing the sick, cleansing the leper, raising the dead, opening the eyes of the blind, unstopping the deaf ears, feeding the hungry multitudes, calming the troubled sea, weeping over Jerusalem, forgiving the sinner, giving water to the thirsty, healing the broken-hearted.

Behold the Man—the King of Glory—walking in humility upon this earth, footsore and weary. Behold Him praying alone, night after night on the mountain side, praying for you, dear heart, and for a sleeping world that would never appreciate nor understand. The birds had their nests, the foxes their holes, but the Son of Man had no where to lay His head.

Behold the Man, at the last supper when even though His heart was aching, even though He knew the hand that would betray Him, and the disciple that would deny Him, even though He knew that all would forsake Him and flee away, His thoughts were for you and for me when He vowed that He would drink no more of the fruit of the vine until He drank it anew with us in His Father's kingdom, saying:

"As oft as ye do this ye do show forth my death 'till I come."

Oh, glorious bridge that spans the long, silent years *from the day of His death till the day He shall come.*

Behold the Man, praying in the garden alone while His

disciples slumbered and slept. Behold His agony and the travail of His soul as He cried: "*Nevertheless, not my will, but thine, be done. And being in an agony He prayed more earnestly: and His sweat was as it were great drops of blood falling down to the ground.*"

Behold the Man—bending low over His disciples in His sorrow, craving one understanding heart to watch with Him. But He found them sleeping and said unto them: "*Why sleep ye, rise and pray.*" "*And while He yet spake, behold a multitude,*" pressing on through the gray dawn of morning, coming with staves and swords to take this Man—this Jesus of yours, and mine.

Behold the Man, led as a sheep to the slaughter, and as a lamb before his shearers is dumb, so He opened not His mouth. Behold Him despised and rejected of men, a Man of sorrows and acquainted with grief. Behold Him bearing *our* griefs, carrying *our* sorrows, wounded for *our* transgressions, bruised for *our* iniquities. He was taken from prison and from judgment.

Behold the Man, condemned to die by the multitude He loved and longed to gather in His arms. Behold Him, beaten with stripes and nailed to the cross. The crown of thorns was placed upon His brow, the Roman spear pierced His side. But, Oh, beloved, hear Him cry, "*Father, forgive them, they know not what they do!*" Then when the debt had been paid, when He had borne our penalty (death) in His own body on the tree, hear the glad triumphant words that rang through the sky that hour, and still resound through the earth today:

"IT IS FINISHED." Then behold the Man as midst rending rocks and darkening sky, He bowed His head and gave up the ghost.

Behold the Man, lying wrapped in the cold silence of death in the tomb. Then in the early dawn of the third day, as the first *gold* and purple rays of morning rose in glad triumph above the hills of Jerusalem, an angel from heaven spread his great white pinions and, sweeping down from heaven to earth, rolled the great stone away from the mouth of the sepulchre.

Behold the Man resurrected, rising and coming forth again to look upon the world—His world, purchased by His blood.

Behold Him again, living and loving, walking and talking with His people, feeding the hungry, encouraging the downcast.

Behold the Man, leading captivity captive, ascending on high to give gifts unto men, saying: "It is expedient for you that I go away, for if I go not away the Comforter will not come. But if I go away I will not leave you comfortless, I will send another, even the Holy Ghost. If I go away I will come again and take you unto myself that where I am there ye may be also," and the clouds received Him out of their sight.

Behold the Man seated again at the right hand of God the Father. Behold Him standing at your side just now as revealed by the Spirit, hear Him say: "Behold I stand at the door and knock, if any man will open to Me, I will come in and sup with him and he with Me." Let Him in, dear heart, draw nigh to Him and He will draw nigh to you. Receive the Holy Spirit which He has sent to lead you into all truth. Be faithful a little longer. Then soon, yea, very soon, you will *BEHOLD THE MAN,* coming in the clouds of heaven with power and great glory to take you to Himself, where in the midst of joys unbounded as the waves of the ocean, we will behold the Man by the glassy sea, and worship in adoration at His throne, our Redeemer, our Bridegroom forevermore. Open your eyes just now, dear heart, Oh!

BEHOLD THE MAN!

BARABBAS

"And they all cried out at once, saying, 'Away with this man, and release unto us Barabbas.'

Now Barabbas was a robber, who for certain sedition made in the city, and for murder, was cast into prison."—Luke 23:8, 19; John 18:40.

JUST these few vivid, gripping incidents—nothing more is told us of this great Barabbas. The thick shroud of mystery that envelops both the beginning and the ending of his life is undispelled by the light of the scriptures, but these few bright crimson drops, wrung from the very heart of his story, as it were, seem to cry aloud the tale of

Innocence pursued by *Temptation.*

Temptation overtaken by *Sin.*

Sin pounced upon and condemned to die by *The Law.*

Stern Law conquered and its grip loosened by *Jesus, the Substitute* and *Redeemer* who died in the sinner's place.

Such a striking type is Barabbas of the whole human race, and of ourselves individually, that, as we stand looking down upon the incomplete story of his life, it seems like some wondrous, fascinating, unfinished texture stretched upon the loom of life, its riotous colors bespeaking sunshine and shadow, joy and sorrow, tragedy and triumph, threads frayed and hanging from the ending, threads loose and dangling at the beginning, as though inviting the onlooker to pick them up and weave again the history of the whole human race, as embodied in the study of Barabbas.

CHILDHOOD DAYS

About the spring time of every child we love to weave the white threads of innocency, a godly, praying Mother, and the picture of a little white-robed form learning to pray at mother's knee. The home that has robbed its children of a praying mother has deprived them of one of the richest treasures that it is within its power to bestow, a memory which money could never buy, nor time destroy.

Whether Barabbas had a praying mother or not we do not know, but we long to think of her as instructing him in the old laws and the prophets, weeping and praying for him as he wandered into bad company and the paths of temptation. As he grew older we do not know whether or not he was married, but there may have been woven into the loom of his life with golden threads of love, a wife and a beautiful baby boy, but one thing we are certain of, and that is that he was led into sin, ever deeper and deeper, while God was speaking to him and the angels were warning him, saying,

"BARABBAS, BE SURE YOUR SIN WILL FIND YOU OUT"

Doubtless, Barabbas meant to call a halt some time in the near future. He never meant to go so far into sin as to be caught, cast into prison and condemned to die. Every dark cloud of warning that the Lord put into his way was doubtless tinted rosy with promising colors of golden wealth and remuneration by the devil, as he was led on and on from one sin to another, until at last we read that

"BARABBAS WAS A ROBBER"

In all probability his robbing started in some seemingly simple and trivial way, some tiny, childhood theft for which his conscience troubled and accused him. At the second theft, a little larger than the last, his conscience did not seem to trouble him quite so much, and unbelievably soon, his soul was hardened, until he became the leader of a band of robbers and started up insurrection in the city. He may have chuckled to himself and told his colleagues that they were clever enough to evade the law, and that they never would be caught, as many another sinner assures himself. But once more came the last and final warning:

"Repent; be sure your sin will find you out. Whatsoever a man soweth, that shall he also reap. The soul that sinneth, it shall surely die."

(Oh, Barabbas! What a striking type you are of our foreparents who, in the Garden of Eden, when first tempted by this same sin, stole and ate the fruit from the forbidden tree. No doubt Satan, in the form of a serpent, whispered in your ear, as he did in the ear of Eve, saying:

"Eat thereof. Ye shall not surely die." And then, guilty and sinful, you sought to hide yourself behind the trees of deception, and to assure yourself that neither God nor the Law would see nor punish you there.

But just as surely as Adam and Eve, shrinking guiltily behind their covering, heard the firm footfalls of Almighty God, walking through the garden to meet them, in the cool of the day, just as surely as God called out, saying:

"Adam, where art thou?" just as surely as He discovered, condemned, and punished their sin; just so surely did the footsteps of the law seek and overtake you, Oh, Barabbas!)

Cunningly the devil led him on and on until one day he found himself the ringleader of an insurrection made in the city streets. Then, blinded with demoniacal rage, his blood surging in tumultuous riot through his veins, his reason overstepped her bounds, and quick as a flash a heavy blow was struck; the limp body of his victim fell with a sickening thud to the ground; a deep-eyed thread of crimson was shot through the texture upon the loom of life, and

BARABBAS WAS A MURDERER

Swiftly the heavy, relentless hand of the law fell upon the shoulder of the guilty wretch, staring with horror upon the work of his hands. *Escape* was impossible. *Mercy* was out of the question. *The Law* must take its course. Doubtless the trial that followed was fair and square in every respect. Barabbas was G-U-I-L-T-Y. And there were many witnesses to prove his guilt, both as a robber and as a murderer. No power could avert the penalty of the law, nor hinder it from descending upon him.

To and fro, back and forth flew the shuttle of time across the loom of life, now weaving threads that were dark—sombre—mournful. Was it with bated breath and blanching cheeks, or was it with a thin veneer of bravado that he heard the awful sentence pronounced upon him:

"Barabbas, with your two thieves, who conspired to work under your leadership, are condemned to die, and shall be hanged upon three crosses of wood on Calvary's hill till you are dead."

And when, plunged into the blackness of the dark dungeons beneath Pilate's judgment hall, chains clanking upon the damp flagstones as he writhed in the anguished throes of remorse, did he cry aloud?

"Oh, bitter thongs of the law! Oh, bands and chains of justice! Is there no escape from thee, e'en though I see my awful error and now repent?" And did the voice of firm, relentless law, with face like flint, echo from the haunting memory of mother's teaching, *"An eye for an eye, a tooth for a tooth; the Murderer shall surely be put to death."* Sitting there in the darkness of sin, unable to help himself, beyond the help of mortal man, the chains of approaching retribution already biting into the flesh of his body, condemned to die without hope, nothing to look forward to but death, what a picture is Barabbas of the whole human race.

BARABBAS A PICTURE OF THE HUMAN RACE

By Adam sin entered. The first sin recorded was that of theft; Gen. 3:6. The second sin to be recorded was murder. Gen. 4:8. God, in His infinite holiness, could not look upon sin with the least degree of allowance; the soul that sinneth, it

"SPEAK, MY LORD, SPEAK TO ME; SPEAK AND I'LL BE QUICK TO ANSWER, 'LORD, SEND ME'"
Students preparing for Evangelistic and Missionary field at the Training Institute, Angelus Temple, Los Angeles

OUR BOYS AND GIRLS—Evelyn, Louise, Romelda, Sarah, Marguerite, Josephine, Laurea, Helen, Vivian, Consuelo, Woodford, Ruth, Dorothy, Pauline, Grace, Pearl, Lusina, Edwina, Winifred, Eunice, Pauline, Claribel, Miermae, Norman, Charles, Willa Mae, Violet, Edward, Howard, Ernest, Finis, Patrick, Parker, Alfred, Aubrey, Allen, Herbert, Chaster, Olive, Margaret, Onetia. Uldine, Irma, Mary, Genevieve, Jean, Leona, Nyna, Louise, Irene, Afton, Bernice, LaDelle, Walter, Sanford, Cathlyn, Eveline, Harvey, Robert, Frank, Horace, Allen, Everett. Donovan, Rolf, Benny, Ray, Samuel, Thomas, Lee, Angela, Eva, Lena, Ira, Emma, Jeanette, Edna, Esther, Kathryn, Lela. June, Francis, Loretta, Lolite, Alice, Thelma, Maxine, Vine, Charlotte, Vivian, Arline, Julie, Lois, Lavelle, Grace, Virginia, Marjorie, Macia, Wayne, Coney, Agnes, Evon, Gene, Adeline, Roberta, Maude, Naomi, Magnolia, Rebecca, Blanch, Stanley, Jack, Lewis, Max and many others.

must die. Death and eternal despair followed in the wake of sin. A great gulf had been fixed between man and God, the strong arm of the law fell heavily upon the human race, and after a fair trial the verdict, G-U-I-L-T-Y, was brought in. The sentence of "death" was passed, and man was plunged into the dark prison of captivity beneath the judgment hall waiting the hour when judgment should be executed upon him.

Oh! that someone would come to open the prison doors of those who were bound. Oh! for an arm to save, one who would bear the griefs and carry the sorrows of a sin-stricken race, one who would be wounded for the sinner's transgression and pay the sinner's debt!

Who knows the thoughts that throbbed through the aching brain of Barabbas during the days that followed, the stabbings of remorse, memories of other days, and thoughts of what might have been, the sleepless nights, the hopeless days, not one ray of light to pierce the gloom! Did that awful voice that had prounounced the sentence in the judgment hall keep ringing in his ears:

"Thou shalt be hanged upon a cross of wood on Calvary's hill, thou and thy two thieves, till thou art dead?" Did he lose all track of time, till his ears were ever straining to hear his name called and the great door to be swung wide, the hour when the dark silence would be broken, and midst the roaring of the voices of the rabble, and the piercing light of day, he would be led forth to die that shameful and ignominious death? In the silent darkness of his cell, with no other sound than the drip, drip of the sweat drops which came from the ceiling and fell like tears upon the flagstones at his feet, did the vision of the cross, his cross, rise before him, ever drawing nearer and nearer as the hour of his crucifixion approached?

Steadily on and on the shuttle flies across the loom in sombre and desolate colorings.

Oh, what is this! The threads of wild terror and panic are being shot across the loom! Barabbas, sitting stock upright, rigid as though turned to stone, listens with every nerve tense. Hear it? There it is again; it is his name they are crying:

"Barabbas! Barabbas! Release unto us Barabbas. Bring forth Barabbas! Barabbas! B-A-R-A-B-B-A-S!"

'Tis the voice of a multitudinous rabble, ever growing and swelling in volume. But how could he hear it away in this dungeon? The doors must be open. Yes, footsteps are echoing along the stone corridors that lead to his cell, nearer and nearer they sound, swords swinging, keys jangling on their rings, and ever as a blackground, comes the imperative roar of the mob in the judgment hall above, a roar that is now settling into a steady chant brooking no denial.

"Barabbas! Barabbas! Release unto us BARABBAS!!!!"

Louder and plainer comes the tread of the soldiers, until, at the sharp word of command, they halt before the cell. The rattle of the ponderous key in the door, the grating of the lock, the creaking of the heavy door, and then the expected words:

"Come forth, Barabbas, another is to die in your place today. *You* are a free man."

Tell me, O weaver at the loom, did a faint ray of hope dawn in his heart, or did he shrink back and cry, from the anguish of his soul?

"Oh!! Do not laugh at my calamity, and mock when my fear cometh. I know that I have had a fair and square trial. I know that I have been proved guilty and am worthy of death. I will go to my death upon the cross, but Oh! don't, don't mock at my calamity and jeer at my hour of sorrow." And did the keeper reply:

" 'Tis neither jest nor mocking, Barabbas. 'Tis true, thou art a free man. For one named Jesus is to be stretched upon your cross on Calvary's hill, 'twixt the two thieves today. With mine own eyes have I seen Him tied to the whipping-post in the court without, His back bared to the smiters, the blows of the cruel lash raining upon His shoulders. They are now leading Him up the hill to be crucified. Come forth! Barabbas! Come forth! You are free! He shall be bruised for your iniquity, and the chastisement of your peace is to be upon Him. He will die in your stead."

A FREE MAN

Free? FREE?? F-R-E-E??? Surely his ears could not hear aright! Surely this must be some horrible dream rising up to torment him.

"Make haste, Barabbas, come forth!"

Ah! the chains were loose at his feet. His hands were free. The biting iron that had long lacerated his flesh was gone. One trembling step—two—three—and he was almost to the door, but no restraining hand had fallen upon him, no voice had jeered:

"Ah, Barabbas, come forth and pay the price. Thy sin hath found thee out." Four—five—six—he had gained and passed the door. Seven—eight—nine steps. He was groping his way along the corridor, stumbling blindly toward yon distant ray of light. True, the soldiers were marching behind him, but they were making no effort to seize him. What did it all mean? Surely they would seize upon him at the last moment. But, no, they are turning off in another direction and he is left alone, walking into the ever-growing light that pierces his unaccustomed eyes.

When at last, reaching the yawning doorway, clinging to its portals with one trembling hand, and shading his eyes with the other, what were his thoughts as he gazed once more upon the sunlight, and once more heard the singing of the birds, and the voices of children round about him? Were the golden threads of hope and new resolution already being woven into the texture, even amidst his bewilderment?

Oh, these dangling threads that hang loose from the end of the texture, tell me, just how was the story finished? Did Barabbas catch sight of the throng wending their way to Calvary's hill? Did he hear the hissings and the jeerings of the multitude, and see yon lonely Man, in robes of white, fall beneath the burden of the cross. Did he run, perhaps, to the old cottage home, and clasping his amazed wife and little boy by the hand, cry:

"Oh, come with me, and let us go and see the man that is dying in my place. Today was the day set for my execution. Today I was to be hanged upon the cross and die a felon's death, but another man, an innocent man, is dying, dying for me. Oh, come and let us go and look upon His face that we may fathom the mystery of such love."

LET US GO AND SEE THE MAN

And did they push their way together through the throng

and up the hill, ne'er stopping till they reached the foot of the cross, where sobbing women mourned the grief of Him who bore our sorrows? And as Barabbas gazed into that face most fair, and saw the nails, and the blood drops streaming down from brow and hands and feet, as he looked into those eyes of deep, unutterable love, and heard the words:

"Father, forgive," falling from those anguished lips, did he cry:

"Oh, Jesus, thy love has won my heart! Yonder are the two thieves, one on the right, one on the left, but there is the middle cross, the cross upon which I should have died." And stooping down, did he take his little son up in his arms, and pointing to the cross did he sob in his ear:

"Oh, Sonny, look, that is the cross your Papa should have died upon; that is the place where I should have hung, the death I should have died, but yon lonely Man, whom they call Jesus, is dying in Papa's place. Oh, wife and son and Oh, my heart, let us ever love and live and work for this Jesus who gave Himself for me?"

As Barabbas gazed steadfast into the eyes of Jesus, did the face of the Lord turn toward him? Did their eyes meet, and was there a look of understanding exchanged between the two that broke Barabbas' heart and held him captive by the chains of love forever? Did he fall upon his knees, crying: "Jesus, how can I ever thank you?

"Drops of grief could ne'er repay
The debt of love I owe;
Here, Lord, I give myself to Thee,
'Tis all that I can do."

Was he there when the mangled body of Jesus was lowered from the cross and laid within the tomb? Was he there upon the morning when Jesus appeared to His people and ascended up in the clouds into His Father's throne? Was he among the hundred and twenty on the Day of Pentecost who received the gift of the Holy Ghost and went forth proclaiming the message of Jesus and His power to save?

We know not of a certainty, but one thing we do know, and that is, that when this whole world of ours was wrapped in darkness and imprisoned by sin and death, the Spirit of the Lord was upon Jesus, anointing Him to preach the gospel to the poor, to heal the broken-hearted, to preach deliverance to the captives, recovering of sight to the blind, to set at liberty them that are bruised, and to preach the acceptable year of the Lord. We do know that Barabbas was no greater sinner, nor more devoid of hope than this whole world of lost sinners, and that Jesus came and was wounded for our transgressions, bruised for our iniquities, the chastisement of our peace was upon Him, and by His stripes we were healed; that when we like sheep had gone astray, and had turned every one to our own ways, the Lord laid upon Him the iniquity of us all. *He was oppressed and He was afflicted, yet He opened not His mouth. He was taken from prison and from judgment. He was cut off from the land of the living. For the transgression of the people was He stricken. He made His grave with the wicked and with the rich in His death, yet He had done no violence, neither was there any deceit in His mouth. He was numbered with the transgressors, and He bare the sin of many and made intercession for the transgressors.*

MANKIND, IN THE DUNGEON OF DESPAIR, AWAITS DEATH

By one man sin entered into the world, and death by sin; and so death passed upon all men, for all have sinned. Rom. 5:12.

What a hopeless, miserable dungeon, man had placed himself in by his sin, and disobedience to God. No matter how he might search, there was no way out. The great, massive *DOOR OF MERCY* was the only hope. The Law, stern jailer that he was, refused to open that. Because of one man's sin Death reigned supreme upon his throne from Adam to Moses. (Rom. 5:14.)

Sitting there within the prison cell of despair, there came the day when *the people which sat in darkness saw a great light, and to them which sat in the region and shadow of death, light sprang up.* (Mat. 4:16.)

The footfalls of *Deliverance* were heard coming along the corridors of time, *Grace* (heaven-sent turnkey) bore the key of divine, sacrificial love that turned the lock of condemnation and swung wide the ponderous door of mercy.

Mercy and Love (inseparable pair) stepped within the prison cell, and, loosening the bands of Despair, and breaking the power of Sin's strong chains, called to all mankind:

"COME FORTH"

"You are free men; another has died in your place, one named Jesus has borne your cross and paid the price of your redemption. Come forth, come forth. Oh! trembling souls, why sit longer in the valley and in the shadow of death? Can you not understand? The door is open, the chains are broken. Barabbas, BARRABBAS, COME forth!" What would you have thought of Barabbas, had he refused to leave the dungeon, choosing chains and darkness rather than liberty and light? What opinion would you have had of Barabbas had he been such an ingrate, so void of appreciation and gratitude that he did not even take the trouble to climb blest Calvary's hill to see and thank this Jesus who died for him?

Jesus died for you; your prison door stands WIDE, the Spirit calls: "Come forth, the sunlight of God's love and mercy awaits you, pardon and peace are yours for the taking. Will you turn just now to Calvary, wend your way to the cross and gaze into the face of your Saviour, that face which was more marred than the face of any other man?"

There are your two old companions, Sin and Death, hanging upon the two crosses beside your Lord; for the first thief, sin, there can be no allowance, no excuse—sin must die to you and you to sin. *For how can we that are dead to sin live any longer therein?*

As for the second thief, at the eleventh hour his pardon came, when death was swallowed up in victory. For the sting of death is sin, and when our old companion, sin, is dead, then it is that the sting is taken out of death, and the ransomed soul can cry: *"Oh! death, where is thy sting?"* Whether the body sleeps or wakes matters not. To be absent from the body is to be present with the Lord. *Verily, I say unto you, this day shalt thou be in Paradise with Me.*

Yes, dear sinner, Jesus paid it all, all to Him you owe. Turn to Him just now. Thank Him for His great love and for the shedding of His precious blood, and as you gaze upon

Him your heart will be melted, the tears will fall from your eyes, and you will break forth into singing:

"My Jesus, I love thee, I know Thou art mine;
For Thee all the follies of sin I resign;
My gracious Redeemer, my Saviour art Thou;
If ever I love Thee, my Jesus, 'tis now.

A CERTAIN MAN WENT DOWN.

Luke 10:30-35.

THE message which the Lord has laid upon my heart to bring to you, whilst directed to all sinners, is intended more especially for the backslider.

Oh, there are so many backsliders in the world, so many who once walked with the Lord, but have someway or other let go of His hand and have wandered far away. There is not a man or woman on the face of this earth more miserable than a poor backslider, who, once having walked in the presence and joy of the Lord, feasting upon the dainties from His bountiful hand, goes down into sin and seeks to drown the achings of his longing heart in the swirl of this world's gaudy, tinseled pleasure.

It would be impossible for one who had never been a backslider to fully understand or sympathize with the mute agony, shame, and longing in the backslider's heart. *I* was a poor, discouraged backslider just once since my conversion, and I know the miserable yearning and crying of the heart to be back in the sunlight of His dear smile—and leaking out—the trying to cover up our backslidden condition from those round about us—the plunge into the world to try to stifle and satisfy the restless longing that *nothing but Himself can satisfy.*

How desperately I longed for someone who could enter in and sympathize with and help me, and had there been someone to make a real effort to reach out and help me back to victory and the security of His Love, I would have escaped much suffering and buffeting at the hand of the enemy.

And so tonight my whole heart goes out to the backslider, and I long to reach your hand and help you back to Jesus and the city of Jerusalem.

The first step toward getting back to Jesus is made by realizing and frankly admitting that you *are* a backslider.

We are going to read tonight about a certain man who went down, and I want each of you to watch, as we follow him in his journey, and see whether his case is not very similar in every respect to your own. First of all let us refresh our memory by reading the whole story. It is found in the tenth chapter of Luke, beginning at the thirtieth verse:

"And Jesus said, A certain man went down from Jerusalem to Jericho and fell among thieves, which stripped him of his raiment, and wounded him, and passed by on the other side.

"And by chance there came down a certain priest that way; and when he saw him, he passed by on the other side.

"And likewise a Levite, when he was at the place, came and looked on him, and passed by on the other side.

"But a certain Samaritan, as he journeyed, came where he was; and set him on his own beast, and brought him to an inn, and took care of him.

"And on the morrow when he departed, he took out two pence, and gave them to the host, and said unto him, 'Take care of him; and whatsoever thou spendest more, when I come again, I will repay thee'."

Now as we go through it word by word, and follow the picture on the chart, let every backslider and sinner put themselves in the place of the "certain man" and find their location in this picture. There are many of the certain men—and women—who have been "going down," here in this room tonight, but let each forget the other—forget that there is another "certain man" in the room, and narrow the words down to his own individual case.

Oh, "certain man" here tonight, you who have been wandering away from God, how easy it is *to go down.* The road to destruction and eternal sorrow of hell is just one long, swift toboggan slide. There is nothing to boast about in being a sinner or a backslider. Anybody could go down, any coward could become a sinner, but it takes the real courage and grace of God, and every spark of manhood and womanhood there is in you to go up the steep incline to heaven. A dead fish can *float down* the stream, but it takes a live one to *swim up* against the current. Any poor, spiritually dead soul can float down to destruction; it does not require any swimming or resistance. Nothing but the divine life and power of the Lord, however, can take him up again.

Went down! Oh, the depths of the precipices and pits of sin that are conveyed by that one word d-o-w-n.

FROM JERUSALEM TO JERICHO

Let *Jerusalem,* on the chart, stand for all that is holy and pure and Christ-like, for all that is embodied in the New Jerusalem that is soon coming down from God out of Heaven, and *Jericho* for all that is sinful and profane and ungodly.

How you, dear certain man, ever came to pass out through the gate of Jerusalem and start on your long downward journey, I do not know. Perhaps it was lack of prayer—it may have been a failure to read God's Word (you can not dwell in the presence of the Lord without prayer and the Word any more than you could live without breathing. When you pray you are talking to God—when you read the Word He is talking to you)—it may have been that you allowed the cares of this life to press heavily upon you.

With me it was the taking away of the dear one who had led me to Jesus, and upon whose strength I had ever leaned instead of allowing the Lord to teach me to grow in Him and be able to stand the storms. When my earthly support was suddenly transplanted to Heaven's garden, I was left like an ivy, stripped from the oak to which it had clung. Oh, what a poor little, fallen, tumbled heap I was! But now, bless His dear name, I have learned to cling to and lean upon Jesus—a support that will never die nor leave me alone.

Be the primary cause what it may, the fact remains that the certain man went down from Jerusalem to Jericho.

AND FELL—

Oh, you cannot walk one single step without Jesus, no matter how strong you are, or how many years you have been a Christian; the moment you let go of His dear hand, that moment you will cease to stand, and you will fall

AMONG THIEVES.

It is not long after the backslider has begun his downward journey that he discovers that he, too, has fallen among thieves.

These thieves that we are reading about did two things to the certain man before they left him:

I. THEY STRIPPED HIM OF HIS RAIMENT.

II. THEY WOUNDED HIM AND DEPARTED, LEAVING HIM HALF DEAD.

And that is exactly what the thieves have been doing to you.

Did you ever stop to realize just what constituted the raiment which used to clothe you in Jerusalem (the city of salvation)—this priceless raiment and attire of which the enemy has stripped you?

Let us look at the chart and see what sort of raiment the holy life in Jerusalem stands for, and what you have lost.

Those who walk and live in the presence of the pure and holy Son of God must be attired in the raiment clean and white—which is the righteousness of the saints.

Each individual that goes into the marriage supper of the Lamb must have on the wedding robe Jesus has prepared—worldly garments and the cloak of self-righteousness and morality will not suffice but will vanish before His gaze.

J stands for JESUS: When we walk with Him He clothes us with Himself, and the garments of His righteousness. (Rev. 3:18.)

E stands for ENJOYMENT: His presence is fullness of joy. (Ps. 16:11.) He has poured the oil of everlasting joy upon the heads of His people. (Isa. 35:10.)

R stands for REST: In the presence of Him who said: "Come unto Me and I will give you rest." (Matt. 11:28.) "The weary find rest for their souls." (Jer. 6:16.)

U stands for USEFULNESS: Those who walk with the Saviour, who said: "Work while yet 'tis day, for the night cometh when no man can work," will long to be soul-winners and wear the cloak of service.

S stands for SALVATION: Ah, dear backslider, do you not remember how you used to go forth, glad in the beautiful garments of salvation, which had been put upon you by Him who was *"your light and your salvation"?* (Ps. 27:1.)

A stands for ADORATION: Where is there a soul that could behold his glorious Redeemer without bowing at His feet in adoration and praise? Did you not feel a great loss when the thieves stripped from you the garments of adoration and worship?

L stands for LOVE: When we dwell with the GOD who IS LOVE (I John 4:8), and He *"hath set His love upon us"* (Ps. 91:14), we will imbibe and partake of His nature until the first fruit of the Spirit, LOVE (Gal. 5:22), shall spring forth from our lives.

E stands for ENRICHMENT: No mortal tongue can tell the great, inexhaustible store of riches to be found in the Christ who became poor that we by His poverty might be made rich.

M stands for MERCY: The child of God who abides beneath the blood is covered with the MERCY (as a garment) that is "great above the heavens" (Ps. 108:4), and TRUTH (the girdle which fastens the garment about him) of (Ps. 85:10), these meeting together to form His raiment.

What a dreadful loss it was when the thieves stripped YOU of YOUR raiment. It was impossible to go without the secure walls of the city of His love and to begin your downward journey toward Jericho without losing those beautiful garments. It was indeed a sad day when you were stipped of your robes of Christlikeness. Gone was your **J**esus; gone your **E**njoyment, your **R**est. Taken away was your **U**sefulness, your robes of **S**alvation, your **A**doration, **L**ove, **E**nrichment, and **M**ercy.

The first stroke of the enemy which left you denuded of such garments was bad enough, but, Oh, the second thing that happened to the "certain man" was far, far more sad, if that were possible, for—

T-H-E-Y W-O-U-N-D-E-D H-I-M, and departed, leaving him half dead.

What wounds the devil and his imps (the thieves who rob you of salvation, rest and happiness in this world and the world to come) can inflict upon the backslider and the sinner! When the garments which Jesus purchased for Him by his blood are taken away there is nothing left to protect the sinner from the blows rained upon him by the enemy.

The backslider, wandering far from God, who has been thus stripped and wounded, is in a critical condition indeed. The wicked old thieves nod and wink to one another as they pick up their booty and DEPART, LEAVING HIM HALF DEAD.

The mile-posts by the way now point toward JERICHO, and each mile-post the "certain man" reaches on his downward way mean just another wound to burn and sear its way into his very soul.

Let us look again at the chart and see what these mile-posts that lead to Jericho stand for—First:

J stands for JOLLIFICATION. "Not a serious wound," you say, "just a little amusement, no serious harm in that, a little gossip, an idle jest, the theatre, novel or a game of pool." "Young folks must have entertainment," says the enemy. Who hearkens will find that jollification has left a wound and hastened him to the second mile-post—

E which stands for EVIL. I have seen the serious wound reflected in the sinner's eyes, in the lines of his face, and have heard the words of profanity rise from his heart—but O, the eyes of God look right down into the depths of that soul, and from Him there is nothing hid.

R stands for RESTLESSNESS. Instead of rest which was once his, when he loved the quiet hours of prayer "alone with God," there is now a driving, irritating restlessness that goads him day and night. Anything to get away from his own thoughts is a welcome diversion.

I stands for INDIFFERENCE. The heart that once responded to His every leading and sprang to obey His call, is now indifferent to His voice.

C stands for CALLOUSNESS. The indifferent heart soon becomes calloused and hard. Once so tender that he melted in contrition before the Lord, he now listens to the tender story of the Crucifixion, the warning thunder of coming wrath unmoved.

H stands for HATRED. When the devil has gotten his victim into the place where he hates the Spirit, who endeavors to rouse him into sense of his peril, hates good and loves evil (Mic. 3:2,), he rubs his evil hands and a smile of demoniac joy twists his countenance as the poor, duped soul draws near the city of eternal Woe.

O stands for OBSTINACY. When one receives this wound he obstinately refuses to be warned of his danger or flee from the wrath to come. He walks out of the meeting, goes home and to bed, hard, unyielding, obstinate.

What a deceitful old traitor the devil is! He smiles and tricks and fools the soul along while it has life and strength and means, but when it is down and out, helpless, dying and alone, the devil does not even take the trouble to pretend that he is his friend.

Half dead—thank God he is not altogether dead, for whilst there is life there is hope! Helpless, unable to drag himself one painful step toward the city of salvation, the sin-sick soul is left lying in the road. *"The whole head is sick and the whole heart faint; from the sole of the foot even unto the head there is no soundness in it, but wounds and bruises and putrifying sores; they hove not been closed, neither bound up, neither mollified with ointment."* Isa. 1:5, 6.

What a picture, not only of the individual, but of the whole human race, that wandered from God.—

"THERE CAME DOWN A CERTAIN PRIEST THAT WAY"

Surely this priest, who typifies the L-A-W, will be able to lift, heal and restore the sin-sick soul. But no, there is nothing to hope for from him, for,

"HE PASSED BY ON THE OTHER SIDE"

And Paul explains to us that *"The law made nothing perfect."* Heb. 7:19. Moreover the law entered that offenses might abound.

"And likewise a Levite, when he was at the place, came and looked on him." Surely one would be justified in expecting help from the Levite who is filled with his good works and self-righteousness, but no, the Word tells us that all our righteousness is but *"filthy rags"* (Isa. 64:6), and that *"a man is not justified by the works of the law"* (Gal. 2:16). Turning over a new leaf or signing your name to a pledge can never lift you nor heal the wounds of your sinful soul, and thus we read of the Levite: "And he passed by on the other side."

In what a deplorable, perilous condition humanity found itself. Is it any wonder that the helpless soul should cry aloud:

"Oh, wretched man that I am, who shall deliver me from the body of this death?" Rom. 7:24. Is there no arm to save? Is there no eye to pity? Ah, yes, glory to Jesus, there is one who sees and approaches from the distance.

"BUT A CERTAIN SAMARITAN"—

Who could it be but Jesus—this good Samaritan—filled with compassion and tender love for lost, wretched humanity, groveling in the dust of humiliation and despair?

"AS HE JOURNEYED"—

Oh, what a journey Jesus took in order to reach poor, fallen souls who lie bruised and bleeding on the road to destruction. What a journey! All the way from heaven to earth He came; all the way from the manger to the cross He went, and from the tomb to His Father's throne.

"As He journeyed"—no distance was too great to go, no soul too far out of the way for Jesus to reach him with His love and proffered help—

"CAME WHERE HE WAS"—

Yes, this good Samaritan who was none other than the King of Glory, never rested, once He had seen the fallen condition of the world, until He had laid aside His crown, divested Himself of His kingly raiment, taken upon Him the form of man—was not contented even with standing by the sinner's side, but must come where he was, taking his place, and hanging upon his cross, paying his penalty, and dying his death.

"For what the law could not do, in that it was weak through the flesh, God, sending His own Son in the likeness of sinful flesh and for sin, condemned sin in the flesh:

That the righteousness of the law might be fulfilled in us, who walk not after the flesh but after the Spirit." Rom. 8:3, 4.

Was ever such love, such mercy as this known in this universe of ours? *"Came where he was."* Why, dear sinner, dear backslider, there is not one of you who has wandered so far away whose wounds are so obnoxious and horrible but Jesus has come where you are.

Was humanity poor? Jesus became poorer than they all.

Were any despised? He was more despised than they.

Was there any friendless and alone? He prayed on the mountain-side, sweat great drops of blood in the garden alone, and groaned upon the tree.

Was any filled with sin and laden with iniquity? He bore their sins and their sickness in His own body on the tree.

Oh, how I love those words, love to repeat them over and over:

"As He journeyed, He came where he was." Why, sinner, look! Can you not see Him just now? He is standing right beside you. If you put out your hand you can touch Him and feel His nearness. *"They should seek the Lord, if haply they might feel after Him, and find Him, though He be not far from every one of us."* Acts 17:27.

Just the faintest little cry for help, uttered or unexpressed, and He will reach down His great arms and place them about you. Praise His name!

"And it shall come to pass, that whosoever shall call on the name of the Lord shall be delivered: for in Mount Zion and in Jerusalem shall be deliverance, as the Lord hath said, and in the remnant whom the Lord shall call." Joel 2:32.

"Call unto me, and I will answer thee, and show thee great and mighty things which thou knowest not." Jer. 33:3.

"AND WHEN HE SAW HIM"—

What an awful and yet what a wonderful thing it is to know that Jesus sees right down into the depths of the heart, and the intents of the human mind—that nothing is concealed from Him—that everything is laid bare and open in His sight.

Oh, what will this good Samaritan do when He looks down into your heart? Will He shake His head and walk away when you confess your awful sins? Why, no, the Word tells us that when He saw him

"HE HAD COMPASSION ON HIM"—

No matter what your mistakes, your failures; no matter how vile your sins have been; if you will but truly repent and obey the Word of the Lord He will have compassion upon you. If

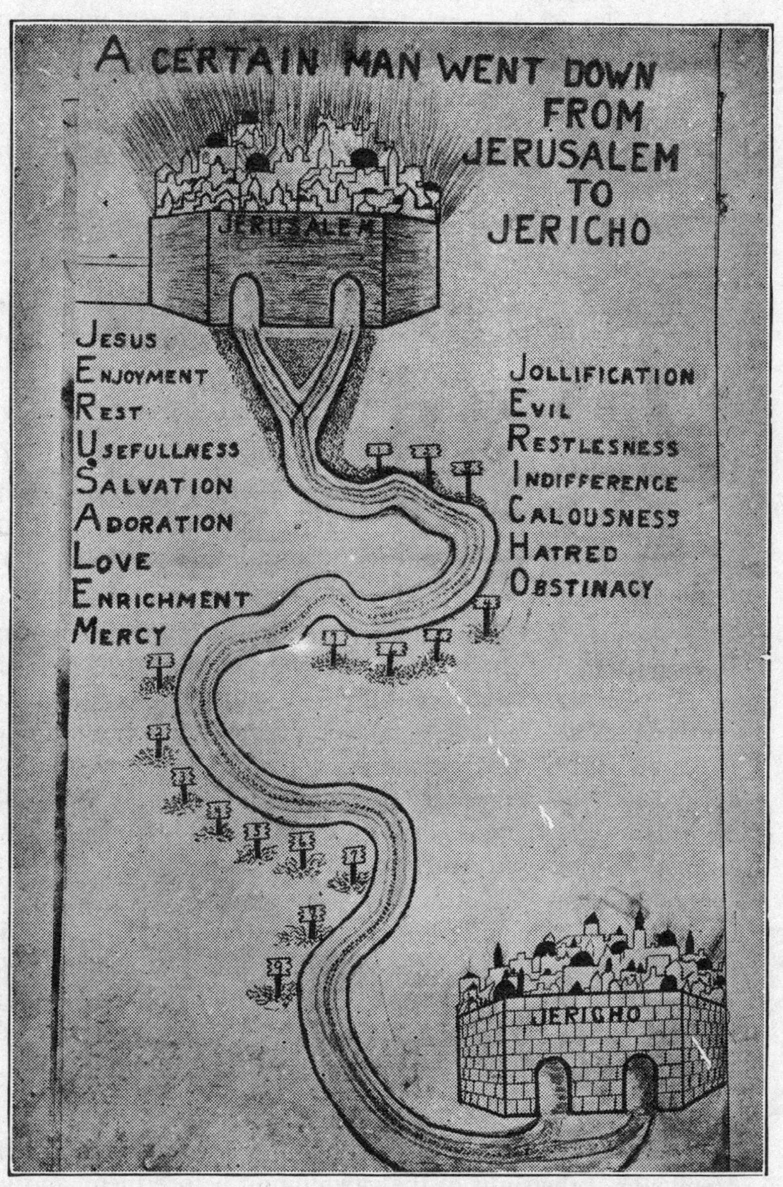

HAVE YOU TAKEN THIS JOURNEY?

man were your judge there would be very little to hope for or to expect but punishment, but His heart is filled with compassion. He knows the many times that you have wept upon your pillow; He knows the heartaches and the longing; He remembers the weakness of your frame, and pities you as a Father pitieth His children. It was that great heart full of compassion that caused Him to weep over Jerusalem and cry upon the cross:

"Father, forgive them; they know not what they do."

"AND WENT TO HIM"—

Jesus has come to meet you, not half way, not three-quarters of the way, but all the way. He has come to you just now with pleadings and tender mercy. Just one word and He is right at your side with hope and succor.

"AND BOUND UP HIS WOUNDS."

Yes, those painful, cankerous wounds are the first thing that demand His attention. All infection must be cut away and sin destroyed. He can bind every heart-bruise so gently, pouring in oil and wine.

"But, oh!" you say, "I don't seem to have the feeling and the tender desire for the Saviour which I should have. My heart seems hard, and my conscience dulled." Yes, I know; that is because of those dreadful wounds—indifference, callousness, and obstinacy, but do not let this discourage you from calling upon the Lord, for when He comes He will bring with Him his cruse of oil and will soften every hardened wound, making your heart tender, and flooding your soul with the old-time love.

"Oh, but I do not seem to have any strength. My spiritual energy seems to be so faint and at such a low ebb." Well, praise the Lord! He brings His wine with Him also. He will revive and bring back life and strength by the quickening of His Spirit.

"AND SET HIM ON HIS OWN BEAST."

How many poor, timid souls, halting between two opinions, trembling at the sight of the yawning pit before them, and yet fearful to trust themselves to the Lord's tender hands, say:

"Oh, I do so long to be a Christian, but I am afraid I could not hold out. I am afraid I could not hang on to my profession." Why, Hallelujah! I have such good news to tell you. This is a salvation you do not need to hang on to—it will hang on to you. This is a Saviour that you do not have to uphold and keep from falling; He will uphold and keep you if you will but put your trust in Him.

"They that trust in the Lord shall be as Mount Zion, which cannot be removed, but abideth forever." Ps. 125:1

What would you have thought of this good Samaritan had He turned to the wounded man and said:

"Now come, my man; I have bound up your wounds. I have poured in oil and wine. Here beside you stands the little beast (salvation), the sure-footed little animal that can climb the most rugged mountain without slipping or making a misstep. I want you to pick up this beast, put it on your poor, bruised back, walk back all the many weary miles to Jerusalem with this burden upon your shoulder and mind you do not let it fall."

Was this what he said? NO, Never! He did not ask the man to carry the beast, but He brought the beast to carry the man. Therefore He set him on His own beast—

"AND BROUGHT HIM TO AN INN"—

The inn is the place of shelter and security where his wounds shall be ministered unto—in other words, the church of God. It was the good Samaritan Himself who brought him to the inn; not by his own struggles and weak efforts, was he carried thither. Put your case in the hands of Jesus and He will bring you forth by His own hand and lead you in a way you know not of. Mountains that seemed impassable in your own strength will be surmounted, and you will be borne up upon wings as of an eagle over every difficulty.

"AND TOOK CARE OF HIM"

Have you ever sung that chorus:

"God will take care of you,
Through all the day, o'er all the way
He will take care of you.
Be not dismayed, whate'er betide;
God will take care of you;
Within His arms of love abide;
God will take care of you."

The tender, loving solicitude and care of the good Shepherd over His little lambs—of the good Samaritan over the wounded soul, can never be described. His patience and His love are boundless. He will supply every need of body, soul and Spirit.

"ON THE MORROW WHEN HE DEPARTED"—

Yes, there came the day when, after Jesus had journeyed all the way from heaven to earth, and from the manger to the cross; after He had fed the multitudes and healed the sick, and comforted the broken-hearted, and taken the sinner's place, and shed every drop of His blood for the redemption of a lost world, conquered death and the grave, He fulfilled the word which He had spoken to His disciples, saying:

"Ye have heard how I said unto you, I go away and come again unto you. If ye loved me ye would rejoice because I said, I go unto the Father, for my Father is greater than I." John 14:28.

"It is expedient for you that I go away; for if I go not away, the Comforter will not come unto you; but if I 'DEPART' I will send Him unto you." John 16:7. And thus it was that on the morrow, *"while they beheld, He was taken up and a cloud received Him out of their sight."* But before He departed the thoughtful Saviour, who was ever providing for our good,

"TOOK OUT TWO PENCE"—

(Salvation and the Baptism of the Holy Ghost.) Two pence was a day's wages at that time; so He has left enough to supply the need for this entire day. Praise His name.

"AND GAVE THEM TO THE HOST"

Has the host of your inn, the preacher of your church, been faithfully spending and preaching these two pence, dispensing all that they provide for your comfort? Many hosts hold back one penny and feel that when they have preached salvation and repentance they have given the man all that he has need of, and is for his good. If this is what your preacher has been doing you should go up to him and ask him what he has done with that other penny, why he is not preaching the baptism of the Holy Ghost according to Acts 2:4.

Peter, who acted as host to the three thousand on the day of Pentecost, dispensed the two pennies freely as he said:

"Repent, and be baptized, every one of you, in the name of Jesus Christ, for the remission of sins"—penny number one;

"And you shall receive the gift of the Holy Ghost"—penny number two. Acts 2:38.

"AND SAID TAKE CARE OF HIM"

Stewards, hosts, and pastors, you are responsible to God for the way you preach the Word. There is power enough, encouragement and grace enough in the Word of God to take care of and support all them who come beneath your teaching, if you preach the Word in its entirety, and they will but obey.

"WHATSOEVER THOU SPENDEST MORE:"

These words open to us such a vista of glories, such unlimited acres of promised land, with the fruits of the Spirit, the luscious grapes, and the land that flows with milk and honey, such a boundless and fathomless ocean of blessing, such heights and depths, such lengths and breadths in the great unsearchable love of God, that we cry out—

"The half has never yet been told."

"Whatsoever thou spendest more"; why, dear heart, salvation and the baptism of the Holy Spirit are just the beginning —just the first few toddling steps of the new-born child into the realm of the Spirit—just the a, b, c's of the gospel. To live without salvation through the blood of Jesus and the baptism of the Holy Spirit according to Acts 2:4, is to live in an abnormal condition nowhere recorded in the Word of God. Ahead of you are the gifts and the fruits and the graces of the Spirit, and a life that He longs to change from glory into glory until He has brought us unto perfection and can present us to the Father faultless, without spot or wrinkle.

"WHEN I COME AGAIN"—

Why, beloved! He is coming again!! Did not He whose promises are known never to fail say:

"If I go, I will come again, and receive you unto Myself"? John 14:3. And when the disciples had watched Him until the clouds had received Him out of their sight, did not the

two men who stood beside him, clothed in white apparel, say:

"Ye men of Galilee, why stand ye gazing up into heaven? This same Jesus, which is taken up from you into heaven, shall so come in like manner as ye have seen Him go into heaven." Acts 1:11.

Did not the apostle Paul declare that

"The Lord Himself shall descend from heaven with a shout, with the voice of the archangel, and with the trump of God: and the dead in Christ shall rise first:

"Then we which are alive and remain shall be caught up together with them in the clouds, to meet the Lord in the air: and so shall we ever be with the Lord." I Thess. 4:16, 17. Did He not tell us to comfort one another with these words? Did not the Lord, speaking through John on the Isle of Patmos, say:

"Surely, I come quickly." And is not the Spirit speaking today throughout the whole world, through yielded vessels:

"Behold, Jesus is coming soon; get ready to meet Him"?

"When I come again"—Oh, what a glorious day that will be when we shall gaze with open face upon the beauty of the good Samaritan, our Redeemer and Saviour divine. *"And when I come again—*

"I WILL REPAY THEE"

Why! Just one glimpse of His beautiful face—fairer than the lilies, brighter than the sun—just one smile from His tender eyes—just one "well done," and we would be a million times repaid for any little labor of love that is naught but our reasonable service when all is said and done.

Oh, dear backslider, and Oh, dear sinner, will you not speak the word just now:

"Lord save me." He is standing right beside you. He will hear the faintest cry; His glorious salvation is ready to carry you to the safe refuge of the inn. He is waiting to care for and watch over you, and at last, when He comes again, to take you to dwell with Him forever.

"Come, weary soul, by sin oppressed,
There's mercy with the Lord;
And He will surely give you rest,
By trusting in His Word.

"Only trust Him; only trust Him;
Only trust Him now.
He will save you; He will save you;
He will save you now."

THE TWO HOUSES

THE HOUSE ON THE SAND AND THE HOUSE ON THE ROCK

EVERY man, woman and child throughout this world is erecting a building. *"Except the Lord built the house, they labor in vain that build it."* Ps. 127:1.

The great army of house-builders is divided into two classes, namely, the sinner and the saint. (Right here let us make it plain, that each individual is either a sinner or a saint. It is impossible to be both; it is impossible to be neutral; there is no half-way business in God. Either you are the child of the Lord or you are serving the devil—there is no middle territory.)

Just as there are only two classes of house-builders, just so there are but two foundations, the sandy foundation of sin and unrighteousness, which lies in the devil's domain, and the solid Rock, which is Jesus Christ.

THE MAN ON THE SAND GATHERS HIS MATERIAL

The sinner is building day by day. His mind is not troubled by the lack of foundation. He does not deem it at all necessary to dig deep, but begins erecting the edifice of his life by bringing up the stones of unrepentance, and wilfulness; the stones of sin and unbelief; and piling them, moment by moment, hour by hour, day by day, year by year, one upon another, on the sands of this life.

The stones of evil thoughts and distrustfulness are piled up day by day. The stones of pride, selfishness and hardness of heart toward God take their places in the building, which is growing moment by moment into a life and structure which will surely fall in the great day, when God's judgments are poured out upon the world.

THE MAN ON THE ROCK DIGS A FOUNDATION AND GATHERS HIS BUILDING MATERIAL

While in New York City some time ago, I was very much impressed with the great world-famed sky-scrapers. For many weeks, yes, months, I saw a high board fence built around a certain lot. Behind this board fence, and above it, I could see great cranes and derricks, and hear the steel drills.

Dozens of men were working there, drilling and digging, and blasting down into the solid rock; down, and down, and down they went, digging a foundation for the great steel sky-scraper which was soon to be erected, and one of the men assured me that the higher the building was to be the deeper the foundation must be sunk into the solid rock.

After having been away for a short visit and returning again to the city, my eyes opened wide with surprise as I saw the steel building so quickly taking shape, and towering with imposing grandeur above its neighbors. Why, it really seemed that it took longer to build the foundation than to put the steel frame-work of the building together.

This is a very apt illustration, it seems to me, of the Christian's life, as he prepares to build upon the solid Rock, Christ Jesus.

First of all he digs a deep foundation of repentance, and goes down in humility into Jesus, his Lord. He plunges into the fountain filled with the blood. He falls prostrate at the dear, pierced feet of his Master; for indeed the way down is the way up, in our spiritual life. *"He that humbleth himself shall be exalted."*

THE FOUNDATION

His neighbors may laugh at him and tell him this digging deep, this weeping and mourning over his sins is not at all necessary; but the work goes on. The great boulders of hindrance must be blasted by the love and power of God. Every obstacle must be removed, and a solid, settled, foundation made. He must dig deep into the atoning work of Jesus, before the building of his Christian life can be constructed. *"But let every man take heed how he buildeth thereon, for other foundation can no man lay than that is laid, which is Jesus Christ."*

The foundation having been laid, the building begins to take shape. Upon the stones of repentance and godly fear, are laid the stones of mercy and divine tenderness. The boundless grace and love of Jesus Christ, the stones of sincerity and truth, the stones of thanksgiving and glorious praises to the Lord of his salvation, are added to the building. Love, joy, peace, long-suffering, gentleness, goodness, faith, meekness and temperance are piled moment by moment, day by day, year by year, one upon another.

The stones of love and unselfishness, a longing for souls, and a yielding to the will of God, a desire to live like Him and abide in His presence are added again to these; and so the work goes on by each word, and deed and thought, here a little and there a little, precept upon precept, line upon line, tier upon tier.

"Jesus Christ being the chief corner stone, the building is fitly framed together, and groweth into a holy temple in the Lord, for a habitation of God through the Spirit."

Next in importance in the house comes the door through which admission is gained into the house. As for the sinner who builds upon the sand—*"Sin lieth at the door"*—the devil, who is the controlling agent of his will-power, is the door-keeper; thus the door swings on its hinges to admit the worldliness, and sin, and evil thoughts and companions, who occupy the rooms within.

THE DOORS

The door is ever shut and locked against God as He is manifested through the great love of Christ—ever shut and barred to the wooings of the Spirit and the rappings of that gentle hand. His ears are closed to the voice that is saying, *"Behold, I stand at the door, and knock; if any will open, I will come in and sup with him and he with Me"*—closed to the warnings of the Saviour who would plead with him to leave this sandy foundation, and this perishable building, which can never stand the storm, and to the invitation to him to come over and build upon the solid Rock, Christ Jesus.

WHERE ARE YOU BUILDING—ON THE SHIFTING SANDS OR THE ROCK OF AGES?

The door of the child of God who builds upon the rock is not so; but righteousness, through the power of the Spirit, standeth as doorkeeper. The blood of the slain Lamb is sprinkled upon the door-posts and the lintels. The door is ever open to admit the leadings of the Lord, the dealings of His Spirit, His righteousness, and all His blessed will, and swings shut to bar out the things of the world, the flesh and the devil, which are displeasing to the Lord, his Maker. Thus his rooms are occupied by faith, and hope and love.

Next in importance come the windows in the two houses. The windows of the sinner are darkened with the things of this world, and his vision impaired. He can not realize his own danger, and his viewpoint is distorted. He cannot foresee the awful storm of wrath which is soon to break. *"When the keepers of the house shall tremble, and the strong men shall bow themselves, and the grinders cease because they are few, and those that look out of the windows be darkened."*

THE WINDOWS

The windows of the saint are illuminated with the glory of God, as revealed by the Spirit. His view is clear as he gazes into the future and beholds that—

"There's a land that is fairer than day,
And by faith he can see it afar,
For the Father waits over the way,
To prepare him a dwelling-place there."

Those who stand without his walls see the light of the Lord shining through, for—

"Behold, he standeth behind our wall, He looketh forth at the windows, showing himself through the lattice." Song of Sol. 2:9.

In his dining-room the sinful man who is building upon the sand, is feasting upon the things of this world; he says to his soul: *"Soul, thou hast much goods laid up for many years; take thine ease, eat, drink and be merry."* But God is saying unto him: *"Thou fool! This night thy soul shall be required of thee; then whose shall those things be which thou hast provided."* Luke 12:19-20. He feasts upon things that can never satisfy

DINING ROOMS

the hunger of the soul that is craving after God. He is as one that *"dreameth, and behold, he eateth; but he awaketh and his soul is empty."* Isa. 29:8.

In his dining-room, the child of God is feasting on the milk, and the honey and the wine. The fruits of Canaan are spread before him. The bread of life is his, and for him the glorious crystal waters flow from the throne of God. The voice of the Bridegroom is heard speaking:

"I am come unto my garden, my sister, my spouse; I have gathered my myrrh with my spice; I have eaten my honeycomb with my honey; I have drunk my wine with my milk: eat, O friends; drink yea, drink abundantly, O beloved." Song of Sol. 5:1.

While the sinner is feasting upon the applause of his fellowmen, and the treasures of this world, the children of the Most High are dining at the table of the Lord—dining upon his righteousness and love; upon the joys and fruits of the Spirit, and their souls are filled to overflowing, as He leadeth them through the green pastures of His Word.

DANCING HALLS

The inmates of the house which is builded upon sand are dancing to the tunes of this world and its applause—dancing to the strains of earthly popularity, and self-centered aims. Outside, threatening storm-clouds of death's dark night are gathering, and the rolling thunders seem to cry aloud in warning. The wrath of God is soon to be poured out, but unheedingly they dance on and on, ever nearing the brink of destruction and hell.

The inmates of the house on the rock are dancing, too. You remember as the brother of the prodigal son approachd his father's house, he heard the sound of music and dancing. Some folks seem to think the devil has a monopoly on all the dancing and joy; but dancing and joy really belong to God, and as the devil cannot steal it he has tried to counterfeit it.

Within the heart of him whose hopes are built upon the solid foundation of Christ and His righteousness, there is joy unspeakable and full of glory, for: *"His mourning has been turned into dancing,"* Ps. 30:11, and *"There the virgins rejoice in the dance, both old and young together."* Jer. 31:13.

They *"Praise Him with the timbrel and dance,"* Ps. 150:4, and cry: *"Let them praise His name in the dance."* Ps. 149:3.

> "For the children of the Lord have a right to shout and sing,
> For the way is growing bright, and our souls are on the wing,
> We are going bye and bye to the palace of the King.
> Glory to Go, Hallelujah!"

As for the sinner—*"his bed is so short that he cannot stretch himself upon it, and the covering so narrow that he cannot wrap himself in it."* Isa. 28:29. When he lies down at night there is an unrest in his heart, for he is unprepared to meet his God; his conscience is troubled as the Spirit of God strives with him, assuring him that *"Whatsoever a man soweth that shall he also reap,"* and his covering of self-righteousness and excuses cannot cover or conceal him from the eye of God.

BED CHAMBERS

As for the child of God, his rest is sweet in the Lord. He hears the voice of the Psalmist ringing down through the ages: *"I remember Thee upon my bed, and meditate on Thee in the night watches."* Ps. 63:6. Let *"the saints be joyful in glory. Let them sing aloud upon their beds."* Ps. 149:5.

O, the peace that belongeth unto the child of God, to know that if his eyes never open again, *"to be absent from the body is to be present with the Lord,"* and *"to live is Christ, and to die is gain."*

The Word tells us that *"Where your treasure is, there will your heart be also."* The worldly man is storing up treasures of this world's goods, heaping to himself riches, houses and lands. He tears down his barns and builds greater, and there bestows his fruits and goods. He bids his soul take its ease, because he has much goods laid up for many years. But God is speaking to him through His word, saying: *"Thou fool, this night thy soul shall be required of thee: then whose shall those things be, which thou hast provided?"* He has laid up treasure for himself, but is not rich toward God. *"For what shall it profit a man if he gain the whole world. and lose his own soul?"*

TREASURE ROOMS

The worldly man takes no thought of the great tomorrow, and does not seem to realize that he cannot take one penny away with him. Born into this world naked and without a penny, he will have to enter into the next world in the same condition.

The child of God is laying up treasure above *"where moth and rust do not corrupt, and where thieves do not break through nor steal."* The poorest child of God, who lives in the humblest cottage in the dell, and has laid up treasure in the world beyond is richer than an ungodly king that sits upon his throne, with all his splendor, for his riches are laid away in Heaven, and will not pass throughout the endless ages of eternity.

The Lookout Tower of the sinner, and the Lookout Tower of the saint are totally different. Both look out upon life, but from very different viewpoints. The Search-light of the sinner's vision goes through all the earth, searching for earthly possession, earthly treasure, earthly pleasures and popularity. From his lookout tower, the search-light of the sinner's eye is ever turning expectantly and inquiringly, from one end of the land to the other—Searching, *searching,* SEARCHING, ever searching for new amusement, new pleasure or gain, ever seeking something to still that gnawing hunger that is eating into his heart; ever endeavoring to satisfy the longing in his soul, which, if he but knew it, nothing but God can satisfy.

LOOKOUT TOWER AND SEARCH-LIGHT

DARK CLOUDS APPROACHING STORM—GOD'S WRATH

The dark clouds of the approaching storm of God's wrath are filling the sky above the sinner's head. He refuses to see them, for he has eyes only for earthly things. Then, though the thunders crash with deafening roar about him in these last days of war and tribulation—though the lightnings flash and strike round about him—he refuses to believe that this is more than a passing shower, and his search-light still continues to wander restlessly throughout the earth for new achievements and honors.

The wise man, who has built his house upon the rock has his search-light constantly turned upward toward the Heavens. God is his high tower, in which he is safe from the enemy. He has set the watchmen of Vigilance and Prayer upon his walls, of whom he is ever enquiring: *"Watchman, what of the night?"* Is. 21:11. The watchman's answering voice can be heard saying: "The dark night of God's wrath is breaking over the whole world. The hour of storm and tribulation is at hand; the great ocean of God's love, which has floated on, calm as a river and deep as the sea, through the many centuries of sin and unbelief, is now being churned into a mighty storm of wrath."

The storm signals are all set, the danger signals are up, and woe to that man whose house is built upon the sand. Everything that can be shaken, will be shaken, and only those things that cannot be shaken will remain.

"Watchman, what of the night?" and again the answer comes:

"Wars and rumors of wars, plagues and pestilence, blood and fire and vapor and smoke." The storm is raging, but the children of the Lord are preparing for the coming of their Redeemer.

Upward, ever upward, turns the search-light of the child of God, searching, ever searching. In each new cloud that brings sorrow to the sinner, he sees another sign of the coming of the Lord, for has he not said: *"When ye shall see these things come to pass, rejoice, for the coming of the Master draweth nigh"?*

THE RAIN IS FALLING

The rain is falling—falling upon the just and the unjust. The rain increases to a downpour. Unto the man whose house is built upon the sand the rain brings terror and destruction, and the beginning of the wrath of God; but to the man whose house stands on the rock, it brings floods of blessing. It is to him the Latter Rain falling on the earth, and "his heart is filled with song, and praise and mirth."

The clouds of darkness that are gathering over the sinner are bright clouds to the saint. He is looking for Jesus to come in the clouds, and fully expects to be caught up in the clouds to meet Him.

The lightning of God's wrath which brings sure and certain

destruction to the sinner, brings power and glory to the child of God. *God sitteth on His throne. Out of the east proceedeth forth thunder and lightning.* The sinner quails beneath this power, but the man whose house is built upon the rock sings aloud:

"O Lord, send the power just now,
And fill us, every one."

And through all the storm the child of God is in his watch-tower of prayer and vigilance, his search-light ever gazing above:

"He is looking for Jesus from glory to come,
That Jesus who died on the tree,
A cloud of bright angels to carry him home,
To that glorious eternity."

He seeks to warn the man who has long been building upon the sand, but the latter refuses to take warning. Ah, if he could but see already the great billows that are sweeping over this earth today, lashing at the stones of his shaky foundation, causing even kingdoms and thrones to totter and fall!

Each sinner, both small and great—each soul who has rejected God, and failed to build upon the solid rock, Christ Jesus—shall surely fall in ignominious shame and death, and the place wherein he stood shall know him no more, but throughout the endless ages of eternity he will mourn his disastrous folly in neglecting to build upon the solid rock: *"For what shall it profit a man if he gain the whole world and lose his own soul?"*

HOUSE ON THE ROCK STANDS ETERNALLY SECURE

And though winds may blow and the storm may beat upon that house, it will not fall, for it was founded upon a rock:

"All they that put their trust in God
Can never be removed,
They stand secure like Zion's mount,
By many ages proved.

Though fierce the storm in fury beat,
And awful thunders roar,
The children of the Mighty God
Are safe forevermore."

While the sinner's house sinks down to the lowest pits of hell, the house of righteousness, founded upon the rock, will stand eternally in the Heavens, in that land where storms never come and tears never flow.

TARRY UNTIL

ALTHOUGH there were but twelve apostles, the Lord whilst here on earth had many disciples and followers. These disciples He commanded to go into all the world and preach the Gospel, but bade them *tarry* first in Jerusalem until they should be endued with power from on high.

Appearing to many after his resurrection, and He reiterated His Command:

"Go, but tarry until you receive the Holy Spirit whom I shall send you from My Father above."

Just how many heard His command we know not. There were at least five hundred, but we do know that out of even that five hundred, three hundred and eighty knew a better way. Had they not walked with Jesus? Had they not seen the sick healed and miracles wrought? Their experience was good enough for them—why should they go up to Jerusalem and tarry ten days for this promised power?

There were a faithful few, however, about one hundred and twenty in number, who were simple enough to believe the Lord implicitly, take Him at His word, and make haste to Jerusalem, there to tarry until the Comforter should come.

Have you ever tried to picture that little company hurrying along the streets toward the upper room, looking neither to the right nor to the left; filled with but one idea, one longing —to receive the Holy Spirit as their Lord had commanded.

Can you not close your eyes and picture Peter hurrying around the corner, a light of expectancy and hope in his eyes. Someone may have stopped him and said:

"Peter, where are you going in such a hurry?"

"I am on my way to the upper room, to tarry until I receive the gift of the Holy Spirit."

"Why, Peter, you don't mean to say that *you* need the Holy Spirit?" Have not the great miracles been wrought at your hands? Did you not preach throughout the land for Jesus? Were not the sick brought unto you, and did not the demons go forth at your command? Surely you are mistaken. You do not need the Holy Spirit. Then, too, you might lose your standing if people see you down seeking some new experience; they will think you are backslidden." But I seem to hear Peter reply:

"Oh, yes, I do, I do need the power of the Holy Ghost. There is such a lack in my life. Did you not hear how I denied the Lord? Failed in the most crucial testing hour. Hinder me not; I must be on my way. I need the Holy Spirit." And up the stairs He goes to "Tarry Until"—

Before long other footsteps are heard, and 'round the corner comes Thomas.

"Thomas, where are you going in such a hurry this morning?"

"Going to the upper room, there to receive the Holy Spirit. My Lord has ascended unto His Father that He might pour Him out upon us."

"But, Thomas, surely you do not think that an old doubter like you could ever receive such an experience."

"Yes, Glory to Jesus. The promise is unto me. The past is all under the blood. This is just the power that I need to banish doubts forever from my heart and mind," and on he hurries, down the street until he turns in at the upper room stairway.

Before he has more than vanished from sight, two soft, earnest voices are heard, and round the corner in their long, flowing robes, come Mary and Martha. By the light in their eyes and the tenderness of their voices it is easy to know they are talking about their beloved Jesus.

"Pardon me a moment, Sisters, Mary and Martha, but where are you going this morning?"

"We have come to Jerusalem, there to meet and wait with other hungry hearts in obedience to our Lord's command, until we have received the Comforter whom He shall surely send from on high."

"Oh, Mary," someone expostulates, "surely you do not mean to admit that you who have lived so close to Jesus, you who have sat at His feet and learned of Him, need to tarry for another experience. Now if it was Martha, I might understand, but *you,* Mary!"

"Ah, yes, Brother, every fiber of my being cries out the need of this promised gift of the Father. 'Tis more than an experience, it is the incoming of the Holy Spirit who shall lead and guide into all truth, who shall pray through us with groanings that cannot be uttered, who shall take the things of Jesus and reveal them unto us, show us things to come and endue us with power from on high.

"Kindly pardon our haste, but we have no time to lose. Come, Martha, we must away."

What a procession they must have made, that little hundred and twenty! Yonder goes Mary Magdalene. From the other direction comes James and John. There is Andrew and Philip, Bartholomew and Matthew, James and Judas—but hark. Again I hear voices and the tread of feet upon the pavement, and round the corner comes Mary the Mother of Jesus, leaning upon the arms of His brethren. Though her head is bent a little and the lines in her pale face reveal the suffering and the sword which had lately pierced her heart, there is a new light and glorious hope shining in her eyes.

"Be not downcast, nor discouraged, my sons, for Jesus, your brother and my Son, hath plainly declared that He would not leave us comfortless but that if He went away He would send another, even the Holy Ghost and that when He was come He would lead us into all truth."

"Why, Mary, thou pure virgin, surely Y-O-U do not need the Holy Spirit, you who were so consecrated and abandoned to the will of God that you could look up into the face of the angel—in the face of misunderstanding, reproach, persecution, and the likelihood of being taken into the market square and stoned to death, as was the custom—and say:

" 'Behold the handmaiden of the Lord. Be it done unto me even according to thy word.' "

"You who have been sanctified through suffering and the death of your Lord, Mary, do you really mean to say that you feel the need of this baptism of the Holy Spirit?"

"Ah, yes, never did I feel the need of the Comforter as now that Jesus is gone unto His Father. But even outside of my feeling the need of the Spirit, the command of my Lord would be enough for me. He said that I needed the Spirit; He commanded us to tarry until He came; and surely Jesus knew best." With a gracious bow they move on and e'er long lift their voices with those of the others in prayer and supplication in the upper room. (Acts 1:14.)

Who can describe or picture the heart-searching, the humbling, the crying out to be made conformable to the will of God's dear Son, that took place in the ten days that followed His ascension? We read that they continued with one accord, Peter not pointing to the failures of Thomas, nor do we read that any pointed the finger of accusation at Peter, saying:

"You have no business up here, you denied the Lord."

The past is all under the blood; past failures have been acknowledged, confessed and forgiven; earthly cares and the duties and the stress of the busy world outside have been shut out. With open hearts they simply and humbly wait before the Lord with prayers and supplications, knowing that His Word cannot fail—and that they that ask shall surely receive.

"And when the day of Pentecost was fully come, they were all with one accord in one place.

"And suddenly there came a sound from heaven as of a rushing, mighty wind, and it filled all the house where they were sitting. And there appeared unto them cloven tongues like as of fire, and it sat upon each of them.

"And they were all filled with the Holy Ghost, and began to speak with other tongues, as the Spirit gave them utterance." (Acts 2:1-4.)

They had met the conditions—the Lord had kept His Word —the Comforter had come.

Believer, are you tarrying before the Lord for the promise of Father today? Have you come to the end of yourself, empty, cleansed, humble, low under the precious blood of Jesus? Are you waiting with prayer and supplication as did those Bible saints of old? If so, the Lord will meet you quickly. God's time is now. It is not His will that you should wait until some vague tomorrow for His Spirit. In the day you seek Him with your whole heart He will be found of you.

Have you failed in the past? Have you at times denied your Lord just when you should have stood most true? Have you been a doubting Thomas? And do you feel your need of strength and power? Does your soul cry out for a greater revelation of Jesus and His Word, for a greater vision and a broader horizon? Then TARRY UNTIL you are endued with power from on high.

Believer, have you been used mightily in the past in soul-winning? Have the sick been healed and demons cast out in answer to your prayer? Have you, like Mary of old, sat learning at the feet of Jesus? Has the joy of salvation and the presence of the Spirit abiding with you, and at times anointing with gladness until your soul o'erflowed with joy, seemed precious?

If so, thank God, but you, too, like Peter and John, Thomas and Bartholomew, with all the other apostles, and with Mary the Mother of Jesus, and the other women with their brethren, need the Holy Spirit. Oh, how you need Him. Doors are opening just before you. The land of Canaan—a new land, a land of power and glory, lies just beyond. Jesus is coming soon. The message must be spread broadcast, and souls gathered in before His appearing.

He is calling you to go, preach the Gospel, witness to all about you—GO, BUT TARRY UNTIL the Holy Spirit has come in to abide—go, but tarry first in Jerusalem until you have been endued with power from on high.

THE INQUIRER AND THE WORD TALK TOGETHER OF HIS COMING

"If ye will enquire, enquire ye." Isa. 21:12.

INQUIRER: I have heard it said that you have made many statements and contain much teaching regarding the literal return of our Lord to this earth again. Is this report true?

THE WORD. Absolutely true. Within the 260 chapters of my New Testament alone there are 318 references to the coming of the Lord, i. e., practically one out of every twenty-five verses.

INQ. Speak to my heart, O Word of God, some simple word of the Master, whereby I may know that He is really coming.

THE WORD. "If I go away . . . I will come again." These were the words of Jesus to His disciples. (John 14:3). Did He go away?

INQ. Yes. "While they beheld He was taken up and a cloud received Him out of their sight." (Acts 1:9.)

THE WORD. Then He is coming again.

INQ. But does this not mean that Jesus is here now—first in our hearts as revealed by the Holy Spirit? Second in our midst wherever two or three are gathered together in His name? and thirdly, refer to His coming for us at death?

THE WORD. No, Jesus, who is soon to come in the clouds of glory, is now at the right hand of the Father. (Rom. 8:34.) 'Tis the Holy Spirit who has come to reveal Jesus during His absence and prepare us for His coming. He reveals Jesus in the heart (Jn. 14:23), in the midst of the congregation (I Cor. 14), and lifts us, when life and death are over, into His presence (Rom. 8:11). Speaking of the Holy Spirit, Jesus said: "I will not leave you comfortless." (Jn. 14:16.) "But when the Comforter is come, whom I will send you from the Father . . . He shall testify of Me." (Jn. 15:26.) Then, too, He plainly said: "It is expedient for you that I go away, for if I go not away the Comforter will not come to you, but if I depart I will send Him unto you." (Jn. 16:7.)

These scriptures make it plain that it is the Spirit who is with us today, while if you will turn my pages to I Thess., the 4th chapter, 16th and 17th verses, you will plainly see that "the Lord Himself shall descend from heaven with a shout and with the voice of an archangel, and with the trump of God; and the dead in Christ shall rise first; then we which are alive and remain shall be caught up together with them in the clouds, to meet the Lord in the air." We read also (Mat. 24:30) that we "shall see the Son of man coming in the clouds of heaven with power and great glory."

INQ. Yes, yes. Your teachings have made it plain to me that this Jesus who ascended to the Father and poured out the Holy Spirit (the Comforter who was to abide during His absence) is to come again. But what will be the manner of His coming? You surely do not mean, as some have understood you to say—that He will come back in the body—the same, real, tangible Jesus who went away?

THE WORD. Yes, I mean just that. This *same* Jesus who was taken up from you into heaven *shall so come,* in *like manner as ye have seen Him go* into heaven. (Acts 1:11.)

THIS SAME JESUS who was taken up—not another Jesus whose body was destroyed, and who is naught but spirit, as many suppose, but the *same* Jesus, the one who, after His resurrection, said: "Handle me and see" (Lu. 24:39), who talked and walked with His disciples, and who did take a piece of a broiled fish and honey-comb and did eat before them. (Lu. 24:15, 42, 43.) This same Jesus, who shall drink anew with us the wine in His Father's Kingdom, the real, literal Jesus who was taken up from you into heaven,

SHALL SO COME. He who said, "I am the Lord, I change not," will be seen by His ready, waiting people just as He was when He went away.

IN LIKE MANNER—When the company of faithful disciples who watched His ascension into heaven, hear the trump of God and rise from their tombs (I Thess. 4:16) their eyes shall behold the same Lord descending in the same form as that in which they did see Him go.

INQ. You say that we will not know the day nor the hour, coming?

THE WORD. No, not at this time. Those who are ready shall rise to meet Him in the clouds. (I Thess. 4:17.) He shall return later bringing His saints with Him. (Jude 14.) Then shall appear the sign of the Son of man in heaven, and then shall all the tribes of the earth mourn, and they shall see the Son of man coming in the clouds of heaven with power and great glory. Then shall His feet touch upon the top of the Mount of Olives (Zech. 14:4) and it "shall cleave in the midst thereof toward the east and toward the west, and there shall be a very great valley."

INQ. What of the sinful people of the earth and those who are unprepared, will they see Jesus at His next coming when He appears in the clouds of glory?

THE WORD. No, only those who are ready, and watching. He shall come as a thief in the night. (Mat. 24:43.) "Two women shall be grinding at the mill, one shall be taken and the other left, two shall be sleeping in one bed, one shall be taken and the other left." (Mat. 24:40, 41.)

It is at His final return, when He comes to set up His kingdom and reign a thousand years (Rev. 20:4) that every eye shall see Him. (Rev. 1:7.)

INQ. Is it possible to know the day and the hour of His return?

THE WORD. Of that day and hour knoweth no man, no not the angels of Heaven, but the Father only. For as in the days that were before the flood, they were eating and drinking, and marrying and giving in marriage, until the day that Noah took them all away, so shall also the coming of the Son of man be. (Mat. 24:38, 39.)

INQ. You say that we will not know the day nor the hour, but is it not given to us to know the seasons?

THE WORD. Yes. "Of the times and the seasons . . . ye have no need that I write unto you," for "ye are not in darkness, that that day should overtake you as a thief." (I Thess. 5:1, 4.) There are manifold signs given through my pages, whereby ye may know when the season is nigh.

INQ. Tell me, Oh, thou light unto my path, thou blest lamp unto my feet, when shall these things be and what shall be the sign of thy coming?

THE WORD. Many shall come, saying, I am Christ, and shall deceive many. Ye shall hear of wars and rumors of wars. Nation shall rise against nation, kingdom against kingdom; there shall be blood and fire and vapor of smoke. (Joel 2:30, 31.)

There shall be famines and pestilences and earthquakes in divers places. When they cry peace and safety, then shall sudden destruction come upon them.

Iniquity shall abound, the love of many shall wax cold. Then shall arise false Christs and false prophets, and shall show great signs and wonders insomuch that if it were possible they should deceive the very elect.

Then, too, when the fig tree putteth forth her leaves ye know that summer is nigh, so likewise, when ye see these things come to pass, ye know that the kingdom of God is now nigh at hand (Lu. 21:31). In the last days, saith God, I will pour out My Spirit upon all flesh! your sons and your daughters shall prophesy.

INQ. Why! these are the very things that are taking place today—wars and rumors of wars, blood, fire, vapors of smoke, are covering the earth as the fog covers a ship at sea. Six million have been swept into their graves during the past few years of warfare and plague. Almost every home has been entered by death. Never so many homes in America in all its history have been entered by the death angel as in the past five years.

Cries of peace and safety, sudden destruction, coming plagues, pestilences at home and abroad—the fig tree putteth forth her leaf, and the Jews are today, for the first time in centuries, free to return to Jerusalem and rebuild their temple. Chariots, automobiles and cars run like the lightnings and jostle each other, because of their very numbers, in the broad ways. (Nah. 2:4.)

All about me I see the love of many waxing cold. Forms and ceremonies are taking the place of power. So-called Christian Science and Spiritualism has flooded the land with false Christs and false prophets. Then, too, in these days the Holy Spirit is being poured out upon all flesh, and in every land a spiritual company are preparing for the rapture. Surely,

surely, according to your words, and the signs of the times, the coming of the Lord must be near at hand, yea, even at our very doors.

With all these signs being fulfilled and thy word so plain, why is it that the people of today are so stupid and dull that they do not realize this truth?

THE WORD. For the same reason that the Jews did not recognize the signs attending His first coming or discover that the Slain Lamb of Isa. 53 and their crucified Lord were one and the same. Their eyes are holden by sin. They slumber and are drunken with the intoxication of the world.

INQ. I thank you for making it plain to me that the Lord Jesus Christ is soon to come, and in view of this truth I see that we should acquit ourselves like men and stand with our loins girded about with truth, our sandals upon our feet, with oil in our vessels, with our lamps, ourselves filled with love and robed with praise, transformed daily by the Spirit's power into the likeness of God's dear Son, watching earnestly unto the coming of our Lord, insomuch that I shall be enabled to pray the last prayer recorded in the Bible: "Even so, Lord Jesus, come quickly."

MY WONDERFUL VISION

IT HAD been a hot and wearisome day at camp meeting. My duties had been long and strenuous. Now the last sermon had been preached, the last seeking soul faithfully prayed for, but I still knelt on the altar. The hour was so late, and I was so tired and empty. I felt I must ask the Lord to touch and bless me before I retired.

"O, Jesus dear, precious Saviour, will you please lay your hand upon my head and bless even me? Let me see Thy beautiful face, and hear Thy tender voice; strengthen, encourage and comfort me before I go."

Almost immediately my prayer was answered. A sweet tranquillity descended upon my spirit like a mantle from the skies, wrapping me in its holy stillness. How calm, rested

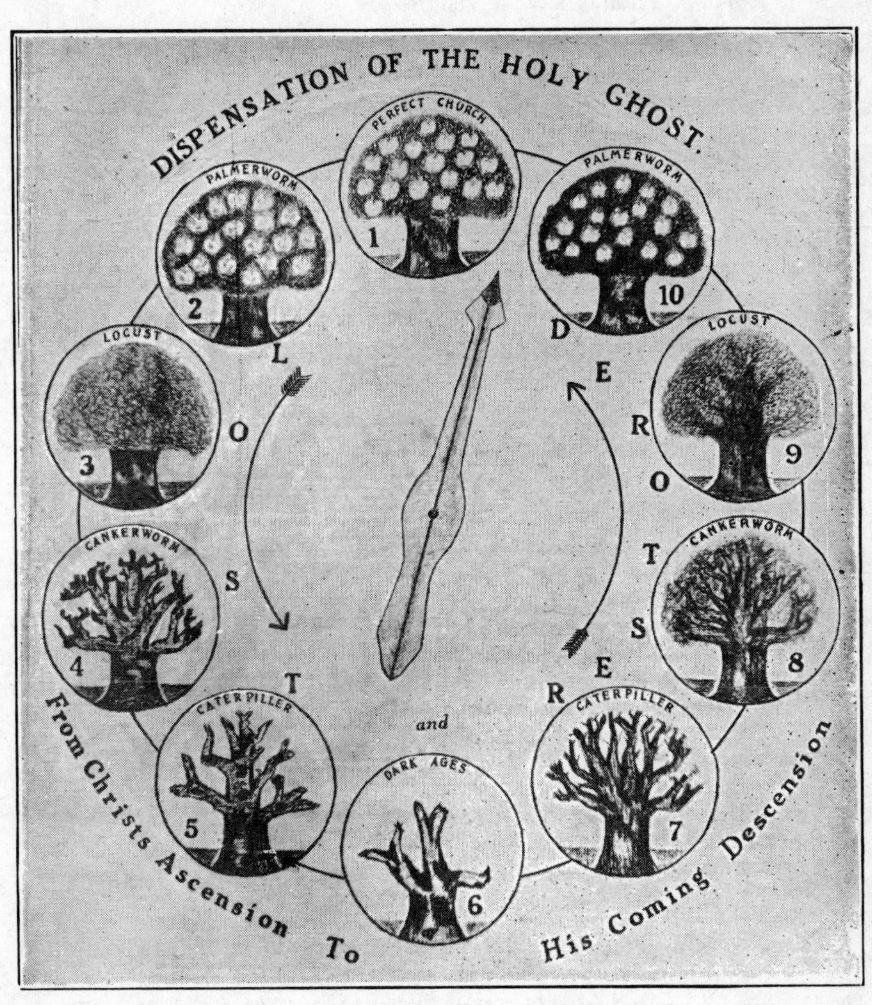

AS I SAW IT IN MY VISION

and detached from my surroundings I felt. My body slipped to the floor before the altar, but I made no move to prevent it lest I disturb this "shut-in-ness" in the presence of the Lord. Then I saw a vision—

The whole world was wrapped in darkness. One could not see an arm's length through the blackness of the night.

But, hark! out of the gloom there came a sound of voices sweetly singing:—

"O Lord Jesus, how long, how long
Ere we shout the glad song?
Christ returneth, Hallelujah!
Hallelujah! A-M-E-N."

At the sound of that great "Amen" a streak of lightning tore its way through the heavens, from the east unto the west, rending them in twain. As I looked, the skies began to roll apart as smoothly as folding doors upon their hinges. Shafts of heavenly light came streaming down through the opening, piercing the gloom of earth and illuminating it with wondrous radiance. Through the aperture I saw descending, first the pierced feet, then the garments white as snow, then the extended hands, then the beautiful face and head of Jesus Christ, My Lord. He was surrounded by an innumerable company of angels. In fact, quickly as a flash of lightning the entire heavens were filled with seraphic heavenly hosts, cherubim and seraphim, angels and archangels—surrounding the Christ of God—they were coming down, down, down in a beauty that beggars description. I thought of those great sky-rockets bursting in the air in multi-colored glories and coming down in silent grandeur through the night. I know of nothing else with which to compare their wonderful descent.

Every angel carried a musical instrument. Many there were having harps of various shapes and sizes. They were different from any that I have ever seen upon earth, and of marvelous workmanship. There were those who carried long silver trumpets and other musical instruments, the like of which I had never seen before. The first part of their glorious descent was made in silence. Then, suddenly, the Lord put His hand to His mouth and gave a shout, calling and awakening His people. At the sound of His voice, every angel struck his harp of gold and sounded upon the silver trumpets. (For years people have talked about the lost chord, but oh, surely there had never been a chord of such melodious, wondrous beauty as this.) As they struck their harps, it seemed that the very stars of the morning broke forth into singing, and trembled beneath its majesty. The earth began to vibrate, and the dead arose from their graves. They came from the East, from the West, from the North, and from the South, and ascended through the air in beautiful white garments that seemed to float about them; their faces were turned upward and their hands extended to the resplendent heavens.

They were rising higher and higher into the air to meet the central figure of the Lord as He came down with His host of of angels. As the resurrected dead rose through the air, they seemed to gather in toward the center of the heavens, taking their places as though by prearrangement in a shape that began to resemble a body.

Then the Lord gave a second shout, and, at the sound of His voice, the angels again swept their golden harps and sounded upon their instruments—holding the chord until the very stars shook, the earth rocked and the mountains trembled. At that second shout, those who were living and remained upon the earth—whose garments were washed white, and whose hearts were looking for the coming of the Lord—were caught up together with those resurrected from the graves to meet Him in the air. They came from every direction—from mountains, valleys, plains, and from the islands of the sea, to take their places in the Body. Some were in the head, some in the shoulders, some in the arms of the Body, some in the feet; for though there are many members, there is but one Body. (See I Cor. 12.) What a picture! They were going up, and the Lord was coming down. Soon they would meet in the air, and what a meeting that would be! As I gazed upon this scene, I was overwhelmed, and my heart burst forth into the cry:

"Oh, dear Jesus, aren't you going to take me? Jesus, you know I love you; I have been waiting and looking for you so long. O Jesus, surely you are not going to forget me. O Lord, take me!"

Suddenly, I found myself running up a steep and rugged hill as fast as my feet could take me. Once I stumbled and fell (that must have been the time I almost backslid, and got out of the Lord's work, running from Ninevah to Tarshish), but I arose and started to run again. Up and up I ran, and this time, praise the Lord, I did not stumble—up and up I went, until at last I had reached the top of the hill, but instead of going down the other side I went right on up, hallelujah!

The Bride was still rising to meet the Bridegroom, and I was rising too. What a wonderful sensation—sweeping through the air! All weights and fetters laid aside—rising to meet the Lord. As I went up, however, I began to weep again, crying:

"O Lord, is there no place for me in the Body? It looks as though 'twere completed without me?"

But as I drew near, I saw that there was a little place unfilled in the foot. I slipped in and just fitted there. Glory to Jesus! When the Lord gives us a vision, He does not tell us how high and important we will be, but shows us our place at His precious feet. It may be that the Lord will permit me to be a part of the foot of the glorious running, soul-winning Bride, until He shall appear to take us to Himself forevermore.

With the Body completed, I seemed to be standing at a distance again. I saw the Bride and Bridegroom meet. Her arms were extended up to Him; His arms reached out and clasped her to His bosom. Oh, that embrace! Oh, that meeting in the air! How can I describe it? The angels were playing softly now upon their harps. How wonderful the music was! They talk about Mendelssohn's "Wedding March," but ah, you wait until you hear our wedding march at the meeting in the air. The Bride, however, seemed to be listening to nothing but the voice of the Bridegroom. I saw Him wiping the tears from her eyes, and saying:

"There shall be no more death, neither sorrow, nor crying, neither shall there by any more pain; for the former things are passed away."

Now they were going up together—higher and higher they rose, melting through the starry floor of heaven, disappearing in the distance as the heavens rolled together again. Upon the earth there descended a deep, thick darkness—a hundred times blacker than it had been before. 'Twas a famine for the Word of God. But up in heaven a light was shining brighter than the noon-day sun. Oh, how bright and glorious it was—the mellow, golden light of a new-born sunrise seemed to rest upon everything, tinting each spire and dome with a border of gold and crimson. Here all was life, music and movement. The greatest day ever known in heaven or upon earth had dawned. The wedding day had come!

The angels had formed a great, long aisle leading from the heavenly gates to the Throne of pearl, upon which sat One so wonderful, so dazzlingly glorious, that my eyes could not gaze upon Him. Line upon line, row upon row, tier upon tier—the angels stood or were suspended in midair at either side of the aisle thus formed. Above this aisle the little cherubim formed an arch singing sweetly and playing upon tiny harps.

As they played the wedding march, down the aisle came the Bride and Bridegroom. She was leaning upon His arm and looking up into His face. Oh, the love, the joy, the hopes fulfilled that were written upon her fair and lovely countenance. 'Twas as though she were saying:

"Thou beautiful Bridegroom, Thou Prince of Peace, Thou Pearl of Great Price, Thou Rose of Sharon and Lily of the Valley—I love Thee, oh, I love Thee! How long I have been looking forward to this day, how I have yearned to see Thy face, to hear Thy voice. True, I have seen Thee through a glass darkly, but now, oh now, my Saviour, slain Lamb of Calvary, I see Thee face to face! Oh, Jesus, to think that I shall live with Thee forever and forever! I will never leave Thee more, but I shall lean upon Thine arm, rest upon Thy bosom, sit upon Thy Throne, and praise Thee while the endless ages roll."

As the Bride looked into His face, Jesus, the Bridegroom, was looking down and smiling upon her clad in her white robes with her misty veil floating about her. Oh, that look in His eyes, that tender expression upon His face. 'Twas as though He were saying:

"Oh, my love, my dove, my undefiled, thou art fair; there is no spot in thee. Before you loved Me I loved you. Yea, I have loved you with an everlasting love. I loved you when you were deep in sin; I loved you when you were far away. I loved you enough to leave My Father's home to go forth to seek to save, to rescue, to draw you to Myself. I loved you so much that I died for you—I died to redeem you, and to fill you with My Spirit. Oh, my Bride, you have been faithful. Coming out of great tribulation you have washed your robes and made them white in the blood of the Lamb. You have endured hardness as a good soldier, and now through Me you are more than conqueror. How long, how long, I have waited for this day when you should be caught up unto my side.

"Oft have your feet been pierced with thorns, but here the streets are paved with gold. Oft the way was rugged and steep and your tears have flowed unbidden but now behold, the last enemy, even death, is conquered. Nevermore shall a shadow fall across your pathway nor a tear-drop dim your eye. Forever and forever you shall dwell with Me in the presence of My Father and the holy angels—My Bride, My Wife forevermore."

As they made their way up the aisle and neared the Throne, the angels broke forth into soft, sweet singing:

"Let us be glad and rejoice, and give honor to Him; for the marriage of the Lamb is come, and His wife hath made herself ready. And to her was granted that she should be arrayed in fine linen, clean and white: for the linen is the righteousness of the saints."

As they walked into the brilliant light that sat upon the Throne, my eyes were blinded with the glory, and the vision faded from my sight, but it is indelibly stamped upon my mind.

Oh, I am looking forward to His coming, His glorious coming, and the day wherein the Bride shall be presented to the Bridegroom. Are you preparing for His coming? Would you be ready if the clouds roll apart and the heavens cleave in twain, and you should hear Him descending with a shout just now? If not, come to His feet today, fall upon your knees in contrition before Him, and cry:

"Oh, Lamb of God, I come. Help me to yield my life completely to Thee; make me all that Thou wouldst have me to be; cleanse my heart; fill me with Thy Spirit; fill my vessel with oil. Help me to bring others with me that, when Thou shalt appear, I shall see Thee and be as Thou art."

Then rising from your knees with heart made pure and garments clean, your voice will be added to the swelling chorus:

"Even so, come quickly, Lord Jesus, come quickly! Thy Bride is waiting and longing for Thee."

THE PLAN OF REDEMPTION

IN order to make the great Plan of Redemption simple and plain to a certain audience, and that the eye might assist the ear and the understanding of many who knew little or nothing about God's Word, or of the combined efforts of the Triune God to save a sinful race, I conceived the idea of drawing "The Plan of Redemption" chart. It sets forth in a simple, panoramic form the chain of events from creation and the fall to the final restoration of all things.

The first three divisions in this chain, as you will see, represent the dispensation of the Father, the dispensation of the Son, and the dispensation of the Holy Ghost, as linked together in their combined efforts to redeem sinful humanity.

FATHER

Over the first circle is placed a coffin, representing the sin and death that reigned from the time of Adam to Moses, and from Moses on to Christ.

Satan, who had been cast out of heaven, tempted our forefathers (the first inhabitants of the earth), led them into disobedience and sin, thus causing the downfall of the whole human race. God, in His holiness, could not look upon sin with the least degree of allowance, *"wherefore, as by one man, sin entered into the world, and death by sin, death passed upon all men for that all have sinned."*

The first chapter of Genesis opens with life and creation pulsing everywhere; the last verse of the last chapter of Genesis ends with a dead man embalmed and buried in a coffin in Egypt. *"The soul that sinneth, it shall die,"* was the verdict that God had given, and His word could not be broken; thus the whole human family had gotten themselves into a box, a coffin that they could not get out of.

The human race began with a perfect man and woman, fashioned in the likeness of God's own self, walking together with Him in life and purity beneath the fruitful trees of the garden of Eden—and ended in a coffin, the sentence of death passed upon the seed of woman.

God, in His plan of Redemption, reversed the whole order of things.

He began with a man (Jesus Christ whose blood was shed for sinners) lying in a tomb, still and cold in death, and ends with a perfect man and woman (Christ and His bride) walking with God beneath the never-fading trees of the New Jerusalem in eternal life and purity.

Just as Eve was deceived by the fair words of the serpent, and just as Adam was not deceived, but took willingly and knowingly of the forbidden fruit, so it was that when the whole human race was deluded and deceived by the tempter and condemned to death, Jesus, our second Adam, willingly and knowingly came down and partook of the fruits of death and stood by the sinner's side that he might take the sinner's place, bear the sinner's banishment, die the sinner's death, and lift him from the fall.

In that fall from grace, mankind fell so low and descended to such depths, that nothing short of the combined efforts of the Triune God could lift him up or reinstate him in the presence of the Father blameless, without spot or wrinkle or any such thing. During the dispensation of the Father, as recorded from Genesis to Malachi, God had repeatedly promised that in the fulness of time He would bestow a love gift upon this sinful world—that gift was to be Jesus, His only begotten Son. He, Jesus, was to bruise the serpent's head, and by His own precious blood on the cross bridge the gulf 'twixt man and God, rend the veil, and open a new and a living way into the Holy of Holies.

Through the centuries recorded in the Old Testament, and divided into periods—Creation and Adam—sin enters—flood—Moses leads the children of Israel forth—Canaan land—minor prophets—a faithful people had been looking *forward* to the cross and the day when Jesus would shed His blood (see types and shadows—shedding of blood of bulls, goats and lambs), just as we who live in the dispensation of the Holy

Ghost today look *back* to the cross and the blood shed thereupon.

True to His promise, in the fullness of time, *"God so loved the world that He gave His only begotten Son, that whosoever believeth in Him should not perish, but have everlasting life."*

SON

The second dispensation (that of the Son), is recorded in the four Gospels of the New Testament. It is overshadowed on the chart by the cross, even as the old dispensation had been overshadowed by the coffin (sin and death), and is joined to the first dispensation by the small preparatory link—the preaching of John the Baptist.

In delivering his two great messages—"Repent" and "Behold the Lamb of God," John the Baptist prophesies the coming of the dispensation of the Holy Ghost. *"There cometh One after me, the latchet of whose shoe I am not worthy to unloose. He, when He is come, will baptize you with the Holy Ghost and fire."* It is as though John looked right straight through this circle upon the chart—the work of the Son—and saw the end from the beginning. There are many things he might have said about Jesus.

He, when He is come, will heal the sick; He, when He is come, will raise the dead, feed the hungry multitudes, cleanse the lepers, shed His blood, and be resurrected the third day; but looking through all of these things, wonderful as they were, with the clear vision of the Spirit, John looks ahead and cries:

"He, when He is come, will baptize you with the Holy Ghost and fire."

The second dispensation, the life of Jesus, taking in the birth of Christ—boyhood—baptism in Jordan—ministry—last supper and garden—crucifixion and burial—and the resurrection of our Lord, while completely spanning the gulf between God and man, and bringing salvation from sin through His precious blood, still needed the work and dispensation of the Holy Spirit, third person of the Trinity, to complete the plan of redemption in its fullest sense. Jesus plainly declares:

"It is expedient for you that I go away; for if I go not away, the Comforter will not come." There must needs be a third

PLAN OF REDEMPTION

story to the ark, in which the sin-cursed multitude might take refuge to escape the flood of judgment which must fall upon the iniquities of earth.

HOLY GHOST

Just as the Father bestowed the gift of Jesus Christ, His Son, as a love gift to the sinner, so now in turn, Jesus bestowed the Holy Ghost, the promise of the Father, His love gift to the believer.

The link which joins the dispensation of the Spirit to that of the Son is the ten days between the ascension of the Lord and the outpouring of the Holy Spirit, wherein the one hundred and twenty tarried for the promised Comforter. 'Tis as though the Father joined hands with the Son and the Son with the Holy Spirit, that by their unity and oneness of purpose, the plan of redemption might be wrought out.

Just as sin and death overshadowed in circle one and the work of the cross rises high aloft above any other event in circle two, so now the Holy Spirit, as a dove, broods over and o'ershadows the dispensation of the Holy Ghost.

The dispensation of the Holy Ghost, which began on the day of Pentecost, we are still living in, and will be living in, in fact, until Jesus sweeps back the billowy clouds which curtain earth from heaven, and takes His bride unto Himself.

Today we live in the closing hours of the dispensation of the Holy Spirit. Looking back through the centuries which it embraces, since the day of Pentecost, we see first, the church filled with power—signs and wonders wrought under the downpour of the former rain which accompanied the first seed-sowing days—loss of the gifts and power—loss of the teaching of the Holy Ghost—the days when the curtains of the dark ages obscured the light of justification by faith—then restoration begins, and the teaching of the Holy Ghost and latter rain is flung broadcast.

We stand today on the verge of the coming of the Lord. Through the power of the Spirit the church is being restored to the full standard of Pentecostal power and perfection. A little band of despised overcomers is coming through blood and fire, triumphant, purged and made white through the blood of the Lamb. With uplifted faces and stretched-out arms, its members are yearning for the coming of the Lord—the bright and morning star—the Son of righteousness who shall arise with healing in His wings.

"For the Lord Himself shall descend from Heaven with a shout . . . the dead in Christ shall be raised first; then those that are alive and remain shall be caught up together with them to meet the Lord in the air, and so shall we ever be with the Lord."

SON

While the resurrected and translated saints are caught up in the rapture to the wedding and marriage supper of the Lamb, like three, the tribulation, sorrow and punishment such as was never known, leads on to the day in which the Lord shall descend with His saints, and the government shall be upon His shoulders. *"For He must reign till He hath put all enemies under His feet."*

The dragon, that old serpent, which is the Devil and Satan, shall be bound a thousand years and cast into the bottomless pit, where an angel shall shut him up and set a seal upon him that he deceive the nations no more till the thousand years shall be fulfilled, and after that he must be loosed for a little season.

Then shall be fulfilled the prayer of our Lord—*"Thy kingdom come; Thy will be done on earth as it is in Heaven."* The saints, who have overcome, who have neither worshipped the beast nor His image, who have refused to receive his mark upon their forehead, or in their hand, shall *"live and reign with Christ a thousand years."*—Rev. 20:4.

Read Rev. 20 (1 to 15). When the thousand years have expired Satan shall be loosed out of his prison for a little season, and shall go to deceive the nations, inasmuch that they shall gather round the beloved city and compass the camp of the saints, but fire shall come down from God out of Heaven and devour them. The devil that deceived them shall be cast not into the bottomless pit again, but this time into the lake of fire and brimstone, where the beast and the false prophet are, and shall be tormented day and night forever and ever.

FATHER

Then comes the great white throne judgment, when the

dead, both small and great, shall be called to stand before God, before the face of whom earth and heaven flee away.

The book of life shall be opened and the dead shall be judged out of those things which are written in the books, according to their works. The sea shall give up the dead which are in it; death and hell shall deliver up their dead and they shall be judged, every man according to his works. Then it is that Jesus *"shall have delivered up the kingdom to God, even the Father"* and *"shall be subject unto Him that put all things under Him, that God may be all in all"*—I. Cor. 24, 28. Thus the Lord, having subdued His enemies, places the reins again in the hands of the Father, the plan of redemption completed.

Read the chart from left to right — Father, Son, Holy Ghost, Son, Father. Now read it from right to left—it is the same.

The circle has been closed, but the work of redemption is not complete until the vision seen by John on the Isle of Patmos has materialized and again the perfect man and the perfect woman —Christ and His bride—walk beneath the ever-verdant trees, whose leaves shall not fade, and whose fruit shall not decay. The final overthrow of the devil and his power shall be brought about: sin shall never enter there.

Oh, the infinite love and patience—the sweat drops of blood —the thought—the labors—the toils of the Triune God to redeem a fallen world and bring back unbroken communion with Father, Son and Holy Ghost!

THE BRIDE IN HER VEIL OF TYPES AND SHADOWS

"Come hither, I will shew thee the Bride, the Lamb's Wife."—Rev. 21:9.

THE great Wedding of the King of kings is soon to take place. The most colossal preparations are being made, both in Heaven and in earth. In the angelic hosts above, and in the Bridal Company on earth, harps are being tuned and the first superb strains of the New Song—the Wedding Song—are flowing forth from love-filled hearts in liquid streams of praise.

Every Spirit-filled child of God—each member of the Bridal Body, is wide awake and on tip-toe now, looking for the coming forth of the Bridegroom who is soon to appear in the clouds of glory. Mortal mind cannot picture nor conceive the stupendous glory and beauty that will flood the heavens at His appearance.

Have you ever stood, spell-bound, in the rosy glow of early morning, as the rising sun threw back the shades of night, touching and illuminating each snowy cloud and transforming them into flaming, livid beauty, until the whole sky seemed filled with angels' wings of gold and fire and crimson?

Have you ever wondered, if the earthly sun could rise with such attendant glory, what the coming of the Son of Righteousness, who shall rise with healing in His wings, will be?

Yes, the Marriage of the Lamb is at hand. The Bridegroom, who has gone to prepare a place for His Bride, is soon to appear.

On earth the Bride is making the final preparations: the last finishing touch is being put upon her trousseau. The days of her purification with oil of myrrh and with sweet odors are almost accomplished; the day when she shall be brought forth unto the King has come.

Even in the natural, a bride is ever an object of interest and a whispered—

"Here comes the bride," is enough to arouse the instant attention and smiling interest of an hundred pair of eyes.

In the spiritual the interest in the Bride is intensified a thousand fold, and surely this interest is begotten by the Spirit, for just as the angel spoke unto the beloved disciple on the Isle of Patmos, saying:

"Come hither, I will shew thee the Bride, the Lamb's wife," and caught him away in the Spirit to a great and high mountain, there to reveal her glories to him, so the Holy Spirit today speaks to the children of God, saying:

"Come hither (to the Word of God) and I will show thee the Bride, the Lamb's wife."

Once He has caught us up unto the mountain, and has begun to unfold the Word before our wondering eyes, we gaze into its pages and see the Bride in almost every picture.

We see her in the PAST, wrapped in a mist of types and shadows.

We see her in the PRESENT, emerging from the types and shadows, coming forth a living, visible, Spirit-filled, Spirit-led people, humble and lowly, yet walking with the dignity and majesty of her coming Lord.

We see her in the FUTURE, reigning with her Bridegroom upon the everlasting throne, in that glorious City, where the streets are all pure gold, the gates are a solid pearl, and where joy and praises forever echo through His courts.

THE BRIDE—A RIB COMPANY—BROUGHT FORTH FROM THE WOUNDED SIDE OF THE BRIDEGROOM. GEN. 2:21

Looking into the past where the Word is filled with types and shadows of the Bride and her coming forth to meet the Bridegroom, one of the first types that the Spirit shows us is that of Adam and Eve.

It was a man and a woman (Adam and Eve) who first brought sin and death into the world, and

It will be a man and a woman (Christ and His Church) who will go forth together, hand in hand, ruling and reigning, when the last grim foe of sin and death is conquered. Bless the Lord.

For the FIRST ADAM *"there was not found an helpmeet"* (Gen. 2:20), in all the beautiful Garden of Eden wherein he dwelt. *"And the Lord God caused a deep sleep to fall upon Adam"* (Gen. 2:21), and while he slept He took out one of his ribs, and of the *"rib which He had taken from man made He a woman and brought her unto the man."* (Gen. 2:22.) Here immediately we see a beautiful type of

The SECOND ADAM—for whom, amongst all the seraphic hosts of heaven there was not found an helpmeet. Then came the deep sleep of death which the Lord God allowed to come upon Him, and as He slept, there on the cross, His side was opened wide and—

Hallelujah! From the wounded side of Jesus, our Second Adam, a rib company is being formed today and will soon be brought to the man Christ Jesus, to be His wife and His helpmeet forever.

CLOTHING OF THE BRIDE MUST BE BLOOD-BOUGHT. GEN. 3:21.

Then comes the day when Adam and Eve realized their need of clothing. By their own efforts an apron of fig-leaves was made—but not approved of by God. Man by his own works and by garments of his own self-righteous making, can never please the Father. His covering must needs be bought at the price of blood, therefore was the blood of an innocent creature shed and the Lord God did make coats of skins (skins typifying the covering and righteousness of Jesus), and clothed them.

OFFERING OF THE BRIDE MUST BE MADE BY BLOOD. GEN 4:4, 5

Though CAIN brought the best fruits of the *ground*—the best results his own works and labors could make—unto his offering the Lord had no respect.

But when ABEL brought the firstlings of his *flock,* the slain lamb, and God saw the blood, He had respect unto this offering.

Good works and man-made efforts can never win the respect of God, but when the humblest saint, upon his knees, comes with an offering made through the blood of Calvary's Lamb, he, through that blood, commands the respect and approval of all Heaven.

PREPARATION OF ARK—SEPARATION AND OBEDIENCE,
GEN. 6, 7, 8

"Come hither and I will show thee the Bride, the Lamb's wife," cries the living Word, as we turn our eyes upon the Ark, the Noahic Covenant, and the flood of waters that covered the earth.

The Holy Spirit catches up the searchlight of Matt. 27:37-39, and turns its blazing light full upon the mists and shadows that before so shrouded this Genesis 6th, 7th and 8th chapters as to make it seem nothing more than a history of bygone days. The illuminating words of Jesus:

"AS IT WAS, in the days of Noah—

So SHALL IT BE," reach out and draw aside the outer veil and reveal the inner depths, until the pages seem alive again, peopled with the surging, sinful masses of today. Again the wickedness of man is great—the earth—filled with corruption and violence. Again through raging storm, through war and plague and pestilence, we hear the warning voice of God:

"My Spirit shall not always strive with man . . . I will destroy them with the earth." Again we see God's little remnant, His infinitely precious few—His Noahs, the just and perfect ones, who with their households, walk with God. Again we see the faithful, whose ears are open to the call of God, whose eyes have discerned the darkening sky, o'ercast with threatening clouds. Then in their midst there looms the three-storied Ark, with its one door—set within the side, and the one window, in the top. At the words:

"AS IT WAS . . . SO SHALL IT BE," the three-storied Ark blazes forth throughout obscurity, and we perceive that its three stories are composed of none other material than the combined, united, three-fold efforts of a loving, Triune God. The dispensation of the SON was builded upon the sure foundation of the Father's love (John 3:16); the dispensation of the Holy Spirit was built upon that of the Son (John 16:7).

The OPEN DOOR within the side that seemed but commonplace before, now fills our hearts with love—our eyes with tears, for the Spirit whispers:

"The Door? Who could it be but Jesus, through whose wounded side a new and living way was opened, leading through Himself unto the depths of the Father's love and the heights of the Spirit's power?"

Again we hear the call ring in our ears:

"Come, *thou,* and all *thy* house, in to the Ark"—we see the Bridal Company passing through the Door—separated and shut away from the outside world, within the staunch and storm-proof vessel of the Triune God that will weather every gale.

In the CLOSING OF THE DOOR we see the closing of the day of mercy.

IN THE FALLING OF THE RAIN—the raging of the seas—the rising of the floods that envelop the earth and all that therein is (Rev. 16), we see the coming tribulation and dire sorrow soon to burst upon this world.

The RISING OF THE ARK, surmounting every wave, shielding the little, chosen, faithful few from wind and rain, is Father,

Son and Holy Spirit, enveloping, catching up the Bride, and holding her on high above the turmoil of coming tribulation's waves.

THE WARNING, HASTY FLIGHT AND ESCAPE. GEN. 19:17-30

The Bride—small in number (Matt. 7:14)—despised of men—beloved of God—how she rises from each Spirit-filled page, as the Spirit takes the things of Christ and reveals them unto us.

We turn our eyes upon the destruction of Sodom and Gomorrah, and again, as the Spirit's hand sweeps back the curtain, we find ourselves gazing into the living, surging throngs of today—the vain, sin-filled earth—the coming tribulation—the escape of the obedient few and the falling of God's fiery wrath.

In that wicked city, Sodom, we see our lands today, wherein wickedness has waxed worse and worse.

In the humble, obedient Lot, we see the Bride dwelling in the midst of a perverse and crooked generation, in the world and yet not of it.

In the coming of the two angels at even, and their warning cry at midnight, we recognize the "SPIRIT AND THE WORD"; warning of the coming tribulation and urging instant flight. As soon as the two angels had warned Lot, he, in turn, hastened to warn his sons-in-law, crying:

"Up, get you out of this place, for the Lord will destroy this city." This is the cry of the CHURCH today as she prepares to leave this earth.

In the mocking and unbelief of the sons-in-law we see mirrored the attitude of the world at large today when warned of the impending wrath of God.

As they lingered, the two angels laid hold upon the hands of Lot, his wife and his two daughters, and brought them forth and set them without the city. The Spirit and the Word are today laying hold upon the hands of God's little children and bringing them forth and setting them without the city in a life of real separation unto the Lord.

The cry—*"Escape for thy life, look not behind thee, neither stay thee in all the plain—escape to the mountain lest thou be consumed,"* is the cry of the Spirit and the Word to God's little family today. *"Escape for thy life, destruction is coming, no time to look back now; neither stay thou in all the plain,"* for the Lord is calling a called-out, out of a called-out, out of a called-out people who will escape to the mountains (rise up into the heights of God).

At the hesitation of Lot, the cry of *"Haste thee, for I cannot do anything until thou be come hither,"* we find mingled with the cry of an angel ascending from the east in Rev. 7 :2-3, *"hurt not the earth, neither the sea, nor the trees, until we have sealed the servants of our God in their foreheads."*

In the looking back and the turning to a pillar of salt of Lot's wife, we see the condition of back-sliding churches and individuals today, standing, stiff and frozen, at the very point where they first looked back. This is no time for looking back, 'tis a time to go forth quickly, Bless the Lord.

In the *"raining upon Sodom and Gomorrah of brimstone and fire from the Lord out of heaven—the overthrow of the cities and all the inhabitants of the cities, and that which grew upon the ground"* we recognize the fiery wrath and indignation and judgment of God, the great tribulation foretold in Revelation.

Lot and his daughters took refuge in a cave in the mountain. The Cave in which we hide is Christ; the Cave is in the Mountain—God. (Dan. 2 :45.)

In the safe refuge of Lot and his daughters in the cave in the mountains we see the faithful children of the Lord whose lives are *hidden* away with *Christ in God,* far above the fiery indignation poured upon the earth.

THE SPIRIT ABIDES WITH AND GUIDES THE BRIDE TO THE ARMS OF THE BRIDEGROOM. GEN. 24

Turning the pages we open at the story of Rebecca, the bride chosen for Isaac by Eliezer, the servant of Abraham.

Again the Spirit holds aloft the light of Revelation, and again the printed page, with its history of what seemed at first glance but an interesting account of the romance and love of an earthly Isaac and Rebecca, fades away.

We find ourselves gazing into the mirror of yesterday, which throws back the reflection of today.

REBECCA RISES with a new dignity—the dignity of the Bride of Christ—

AND COMING OUT—(separation)—

To THE WELL—(salvation)
GOES DOWN—(humility)
AND FILLS HER PITCHER—(*with joy shall ye draw waters from the wells of salvation*)—
AND COMES UP—(the way down is the way up—"*he who humbleth himself shall be exalted.*")

As the servant runs to meet her; tells her of the glorious Bridegroom far away, and opens the door to bridehood, the light of understanding falls upon him, and we recognize at once the blessed Holy Spirit—sent to guide us into all truth. (John 16 :13.)

RUNNING to meet the pure in heart at salvation's well—

REVEALING the beauties and attributes of the Heavenly Bridegroom, and—

INVITING all who are willing to bid farewell to earth's dearest relations and ties, to mount the bumpy camel of daily tests and trials (knowing that when we are tried we shall come forth as pure gold)—

LED BY the Spirit, and go forth to meet the Bridegroom. (Mat. 25 :6.)

In Isaac's walking forth in the field to meet Rebecca at eventide, we see in type our Bridegroom Jesus coming forth in the clouds to meet His Bride at the end of her pilgrim journey.

And when Rebecca, lifting up her eyes, beholds Isaac, and alights from off her camel, our hearts leap within us at the vision of the day when the Bride's lifted eyes shall behold her Redeemer. Then shall she alight forever from the camel of tests and trials and hardships, and all her tears shall be wiped away.

In the veil with which she covered herself we behold the Bride at His coming, completely shut off and obscured from the sight of the world.

The closing words: "And HE LOVED HER" flood our souls and overwhelms us with holy joy and rapture. If, when we were yet sinners, He loved us enough to shed His blood for us; if He loved us at the cross enough to wash our sins away; if He loved us enough to fill us with His Spirit and put the finely embroidered wedding gown upon us, what mortal pen can be enough inspired—the boundaries of what human mind can be enough enlarged to depict the LOVE that will be lavished upon the Bride when she becomes—(O, holy, sacred word) —*His wife!*

CONSECRATION UNTO LIFE OR DEATH—GLEANING—HUMILITY, AND REWARD OF THE BRIDE. RUTH 1, 2, 3, 4,

Turning to the book of Ruth we again behold the Bride.

Chapter One, LEAVING HER NATIVE COUNTRY, following the God of Naomi, and making her consecration, which was to be unto life or death.

Chapter Two, GLEANING in the fields, from the beginning to the end of the harvest—gathering sheaves—watched over and fed by the Bridegroom, Boaz.

In Chapter Three, we behold her LOVE FOR THE BRIDEGROOM, and her desire to be his bride, and the deeper consecration that caused her (verse 3) to

WASH HERSELF (from all her works and labors)

ANOINT HERSELF WITH OIL (the anointing that abides—the oil of the Spirit)

PUT HER RAIMENT UPON HER (the fine linen, clean and white, which is the righteousness of the saints, Rev. 19 :8, embroidered with the fine needlework and wrought gold of Psalms 45:13-14),

AND GET HER DOWN TO THE FLOOR (in lowliness and humility to lie at the feet and mercy of the Bridegroom, covered with the skirt of his garment (verse 13) "till the morning" breaks and the shadows flee away.)

In Chapter Four we behold RUTH THE BRIDE, who, though shut out by her nearest kin—the Law—who was unable to redeem her (Deut. 23 :3), was admitted by Grace when wedded to Boaz, who became at once her Redeemer and her Bridegroom. What a picture! Bless the Lord!

THE BRIDE, TRUE IN THE MIDST OF FIERY TRIAL, PROTECTED FROM ITS BLAST. DAN. 3 :21.

The pages turn again. This time we gaze upon the three Hebrew children, Shadrach, Meshach and Abed-nego.

Firmly do they refuse to bend the knee in worship or in compromise to the gods of this world.

Fearlessly, their words ring out, declaring unswerving faith and allegiance to Jehovah, the one true God.

Breathlessly, we watch them bound in their coats, hosen, hats and other garments; cast into the midst of the burning, fiery furnace, protected, preserved, and delivered from the heat of the flame.

Then, all at once, we opened our eyes in amazed recognition and look again to find, as the burning flame penetrates the mists of types and shadows, that these THREE (with the Son of God in their midst) are none other than the BRIDE herself, BODY, SOUL and SPIRIT, protected and preserved amidst the raging flames. (*I pray God your whole spirit and soul and body be preserved blameless unto the coming of our Lord, Jesus Christ*—I Thess. 5 :23.)

Walking unharmed in the midst of temptation and fiery trial, without the smell of scorching, we catch a glimpse of the glorious Bride who is being prepared by the Spirit to abide the "day of His coming" (Mal. 3 :2), and to dwell with our God, who is a consuming fire.

Suddenly the furnace door swings wide, and the voice of the King is heard crying:

"Ye servants of the Most High God, 'COME FORTH' and 'COME HITHER'!" and with eyes of faith and hope we see a doorway opening in the heavens, leading from the furnace of this world into the presence of the King, and hear the voice of the Kingly Bridegroom saying:

"Well done, good and faithful servants, 'COME UP,' higher 'OUT OF' the *'FIERY FURNACE'* and *'TRIALS OF EARTH,'* and be thou promoted in My provinces, even to My throne to reign with Me."

THE PRAYING BRIDE DWELLS THROUGH THE NIGHT WITH LOCK-JAWED LIONS, AND IS LIFTED AT BREAK OF DAY. DAN. 6:10-23

Next we catch a glimpse of the praying bride as revealed through the prophet Daniel.

His eyes of discernment are open wide (Dan. 5 :25-28.)

The windows of his chamber (the eyes of his soul) are open toward Jerusalem (the coming of the Lord—Rev. 21 :2.)

Neither threat nor cunning of the enemy could stop this valiant, earnest soul who, down in the depths of the lions' den, watched and prayed while the angel of the Lord held and locked the lions' jaws.

At break of day the stone was rolled away from the mouth of the den, and the voice of the King was heard saying:

"It is enough, come up unto me," and Daniel was lifted from the lions' den, and stood upon his feet beside the King.

The BRIDE of King Jesus, though shut in by the dark night of this world, and surrounded by raging lions—demons and men, who would gladly gnash upon her and rend her with their teeth—is protected by the Holy Spirit (the angel of the Lord), who shuts the mouths of all who would destroy her.

Watchfully, trustfully, she lifts her eyes, clear, undimmed, luminous with the light of faith, and fixes them upon the door in momentary expectancy.

Well does she know that He who will come, will come and not tarry. Well does she know that the long night will soon be over and that at break of day the King's voice will be heard calling her from above, as He rolls back the clouds and opens a door in Heaven through which He will lift her forever from the lions' den of this world into His own glorious presence, in that land where no ravenous beast can come.

In verse 24 we behold the wicked ones who had cast her into the den of trials and persecutions, themselves cast into the midst of the furious, ravenous beasts. No angel's hand will be there to stay their fury; all their bones shall be broken and they shall be utterly consumed.

Here again is the tribulation which immediately follows the catching up of the Bride into the presence of the King.

THE SLAIN LAMB MUST HAVE A SLAIN BRIDE—THE RESURRECTED BRIDEGROOM A RESURRECTED BRIDE

On and on through the long, heaven-canopied corridors of the Word, the Spirit leads, until at last a hush enwraps our souls, as we are brought to a manger, and our reverent eyes looking down into its depth, behold the Christ-child cradled in its soft embrace.

The Holy Spirit—Christ-revealing Guide—softly whispers in our ear:

"As He was in the world, so shall you be . . . that when He shall appear ye shall be like Him and see Him as He is."

Looking still upon the tiny form, the Christ-child fades from our vision; and in its place we see the Christ-life of the Bride, conceived and brought forth from a pure and virgin life, o'er-shadowed by the Holy Spirit's power. (Luke 1 :35.)

As the child in stature grows (Eph. 4 :15) from milk to meat (Heb. 5 :13-14), we see him walking ever in the shadow and the glory of the Cross. (Mat. 16 :24.)

Knowing Him in the fellowship of His sufferings, the Bride dies out to earth and self, until she cries aloud with Paul:

"I am crucified with Christ; nevertheless I live: yet not I, but Christ liveth in me; and the life that I now live in the flesh, I live by the faith of the Son of God; who loved me, and gave Himself for me." (Gal. 2 :20.)

Thus we behold the Bride—the Lamb's wife, knowing Him not only in the fellowship of His sufferings, but also in the power of His resurrection; yielding herself as one who is alive from the dead—one who is risen with Him and shall, therefore, reign with Him forevermore. Just as resurrection power preceded the translation of our Lord, so the Bride, now rising up and coming forth in resurrected glory, shall soon receive the translation power of Acts 1:9, I Thess. 4:17, and rise in mid-air, to meet her Lord.

These are but a few of the many mist-wrapt types unveiled before our eyes—a few of the erstwhile concealing shadows now dispersed by the illumination of the Spirit as He reveals the Bride before our wondering eyes. (John 14:26, John 16 :13-14.)

We might continue our search of the hidden treasures revealed through Esther, the Songs of Solomon, the ten virgins with their lamps, and many others.

We might press on and gaze through the eyes of "John the Beloved" from Patmos, the blest and sea-bound isle, at the glorious, REIGNING BRIDE, seated with her royal Bridegroom upon His throne.

We might gaze upon the regal power and splendor with which the King hath clothed her—upon the Heavenly Jerusalem in which she dwells, with its streets of gold, its jeweled walls, its gates of pearl, its flowers that never fade, and the fruits that ne'er decay, its sea of glass, its ransomed throng with harps of gold, and its light that never shall grow dim.

The time for this afternoon talk is gone, however, before our subject is well begun. But get your Bibles down when you go home, open wide its pages, take the lighted lamp of Psalms 119:105 in your one hand, place the other in the hand of the Holy Spirit, and let Him guide you through the long, begemmed, heaven-lit corridors of God's eternal Word, that stretch in an unbroken line from the first verse of Genesis to the last verse of Revelation.

Then quicken your step, beloved, fasten your girdle tightly about you; bind your sandals securely upon your feet; and with spotless robes and glowing heart, go quickly forth to meet your Lord, for He is coming soon.

ISAAC AND REBECCA

A REMARKABLE TYPE OF CHRIST AND HIS BRIDE

THERE are many beautiful types of Christ and His Bride in the Old Testament. One of the most precious and striking of these types is that of Isaac and Rebecca.

Just as in the Word of God, the whole story and plan of Redemption circle around a company of four—namely, the Father, the Son, the Holy Spirit and the Bride—so, in this type, the story is woven around the four central figures of

Abraham, who is a type of God, the Father,

Isaac, who is a type of Jesus, the Son,

Eliezer, the servant, who is a type of the Holy Spirit, sent from God to search for and bring the Bride, and

Rebecca, who is a type of the Bridal Body being called forth to meet the Bridegroom.

ISAAC AND JESUS, BOTH LONG LOOKED FOR, COME AS A FULFILLMENT OF PROMISE

For many long years Sarah had looked forward with intense longing for the coming of Isaac, the birth of the manchild who was to take away her shame. Sometimes hoping, sometimes despairing, she waited 'till finally God spoke out of the long silence, and Isaac came as a fulfillment of promise.

For centuries humanity had waited and looked for the coming of Jesus the Son, who was to redeem and bear away the shame of each sinner who put his trust in Him. Then God spoke, by His Spirit, to Mary, and Jesus came as a fulfillment of the promise of the Father, and a sacrificial offering to every one that believes.

Who can describe or fathom the flood of love that must have filled the heart of Abraham, as he looked upon his son, his only son, Isaac, the son of promise. As the lad grew, he was the pride of Abraham's heart; he was the treasure of his house. But much as Abraham loved Isaac, he loved God more.

The *greatest test of Love is Sacrifice,* and to sound the depths of Abraham's love God put him to the test, by saying to him:

"Take now thy son, thine only son, Isaac, whom thou lovest, and get thee unto the land of Moriah; and offer him there for a burnt offering." (Gen. 22:2.) How similar is this verse to John 3:16, which says: *"God so loved the world that He gave His only begotten Son."*

Abraham stood the test, and rising up early in the morning, he saddled his ass, and taking with him two young men and his son, he clave the wood for the burnt offering, and rose up, and went to the place God had told him. Then came the long journey, but though his heart was bleeding with love for his only son, the steps of the father never faltered, but he went on and on, surmounting every hill of difficulty, till he saw the place afar off.

Bless His dear Name. How far God our Father journeyed to offer His Son Jesus! He surmounted every hill; He climbed the mount of Sinai; He never faltered; but though it meant giving the richest treasure of heaven, the Son of His bosom, He came on and on till at last He saw the place, and Calvary's hill came into view. Still, without a moment's hesitation, He journeyed on. *"For God so loved the world that He gave His only begotten Son, that whosoever believeth in Him should not perish, but have everlasting life."*

ISAAC BEARS THE WOOD TO HILL OF MORIAH, JESUS BEARS CROSS TO TOP OF CALVARY'S HILL

"And Abraham took the wood for the burnt offering, and

laid it upon Isaac his son; and he took the fire in his hand, and the knife; and they went, both of them together." It was Abraham's own hand that placed the wood upon him whom he was to have offered, upon the shoulders of Isaac, as he ascended Mount Moriah. It was God's own hand which willingly suffered the cross of wood to be laid upon the bleeding back of Jesus, as He bore it up Calvary's hill.

"Then Isaac spake unto Abraham his father, and said, 'MY FATHER'" (O, the great heartfelt cry of Jesus—*"MY FATHER, My God, why hast Thou forsaken Me?"*) Isaac said:

"My father, here is the fire; here is the wood; but where is the lamb for the offering?" And Abraham said:

"My son, God will provide Himself a Lamb." Ah! What a Lamb, what a bleeding, spotless Lamb God did provide when He gave Jesus as a propitiation for our sins!

A RAM TAKES THE PLACE OF ISAAC, NONE COULD TAKE THE PLACE OF JESUS

At last the top of the hill had been reached; the altar was completed; the wood had been laid in order, and Abraham had bound Isaac his son, and laid him on the wood on the altar. Then, just as Abraham stretched forth his hand and took the knife to slay his son, the angel of the Lord called to him out of heaven (Why, I believe every angel in Heaven was looking down to see this wonderful exhibition of faith and obedient love to God), and the angel said:

"Lay not thine hand upon the child, for now I know that thou fearest God, seeing that thou hast not withheld thy son, thine only son, from me." (Gen. 22 :12.)

"And Abraham lifted up his eyes, and behold, behind him was a ram, caught in a thicket by his horns. And Abraham took the ram and offered him for a burnt offering INSTEAD OF HIS SON." A ram was able to substitute for Isaac, but none could ever substitute or fill the place of Jesus. He was led up Calvary's hill, bearing His cross of wood. He was laid like Isaac upon the wood, the hand with the knife (the hand with the spear, in Jesus' case) was raised for the blow, but even though the Father Himself had to turn away His face, no angel cried from heaven to stay the blow. It fell, and

the blood of Jesus flowed forth with the healing of the nations in its crimson flood. Jesus, the Lamb of God, slain from the foundation of the world, had paid the price; by His sacrifice brought redemption to all who should come beneath the cleansing blood forever.

ABRAHAM SENDS HIS ELDEST SERVANT BACK INTO HIS COUNTRY TO SEARCH OUT A BRIDE FOR HIS SON ISAAC.—GOD SENDS THE HOLY SPIRIT BACK TO THIS WORLD TO SEARCH OUT AND BRING A BRIDE FOR HIS SON JESUS

Skipping lightly over the intervening years, we come, in the 24th Chapter of Genesis, to the day when Abraham called his eldest servant to him and commissioned him solemnly to go back into his own country to choose a wife for his son Isaac. Abraham made the servant swear he would not choose a wife from amongst the Canaanites, where he then dwelt, but commanded him thus:

"Go unto my country, and to my kindred, and take a wife unto my son Isaac."

How far beyond our feeble minds is this great love of God! How the magnitude of His abounding grace o'erwhelms us when we remember that He did not permit a bride to be chosen from amongst any of the angelic hosts of the heavenly Canaan, but sent the Comforter, the Holy Spirit, back into this world, which indeed is His country, to His kindred—brought nigh through the blood of His Son—to call out a people who would follow Him to the great marriage of the Lamb, not only as a guest, but as the Bride, without spot or blemish, Hallelujah!

"And the servant said unto him: 'Peradventure the woman will not be willing to follow me unto this land: must I needs bring thy son again into the land from whence thou camest'?"

"And Abraham said unto him: 'Beware that thou bring not my son thither again. If the woman will not be willing to follow thee, then thou shalt be clear of this my oath; only bring not my son thither again'."

I can never read those words of the servant, *"Peradventure the woman will not be willing to follow me,"* without tears springing to my eyes. O the gentle, pleading, wooing drawings of the Holy Spirit, as He walks up and down these aisles tonight, enquiring: "Will you go?" There is no conscription in this Bridal procession—only freewill enlistment. But whether the woman says yes or no; whether she is willing to go to meet the Heavenly Isaac who shall soon appear, or chooses to remain where she now abides, the Son of God will never be brought here again to plead His cause other than by the Spirit sent down by the Father. Jesus has made the sacrifice; His dear feet trod this earth to be rewarded only by unbelief and spittings and death. He will never come again to be beaten, rejected, and nailed to the tree; the next time He comes it will be with power and great glory. His kingly robes will be upon Him; His sceptre will be in His hand. Whether you will be willing to follow the leadings of the Spirit who has come to guide you into all truth, or not, must rest with you tonight. What have you decided to reply to this invitation?

Each man, woman and child in the world, irrespective of earthly standing, color or creed, is invited to accept the leadings of the Spirit and follow Him to meet Jesus, the heavenly Bridegroom. If you would find this heavenly guide I will tell you where to find Him—at the well of Salvation.

ELIEZER WAITS FOR REBECCA AT THE WELL OF WATER. —THE HOLY SPIRIT MEETS AND CHOOSES THE BRIDE AT THE WELL OF SALVATION

As Abraham's servant journeys he comes to the well, where the daughters were wont to bring their pitchers for water. There he prays, and waits for the coming of the bride, saying:

"Behold, I stand here by the well of water." Dear child of God, you who have drawn with joy from the wells of Salvation, lift up your eyes tonight and behold the Spirit, open your ears and hear Him say:

"Behold, here I stand, waiting to baptize you and lead you on to meet your Jesus."

"And it came to pass, before He had done speaking, that Rebecca came out." How similar is this instance to that recorded in Acts 10:44. *"While Peter yet spake these words, the Holy Spirit fell on all them which heard the Word!"* He is speaking to you now; will you receive Him?

"Behold, Rebecca came out" (He is calling a come out

people these days, a called-out, separated people) *"with her pitcher upon her shoulder. And the damsel was very fair to look upon, a virgin, neither had any man known her; and she went down to the well, and filled her pitcher and came up."*

As I look over your faces it seems I can almost pick out the Rebeccas who have come here tonight with their pitchers on their shoulders, empty pitchers, clean pitchers, ready to go down in humility to draw from this inexhaustible well of Salvation. If your pitchers—or heads—are filled with learning or earthly wisdom, you must empty them out in order to be filled at this well. No matter how big or great you may be you must all alike get down in humility to draw with joy from these waters. Rebecca *went down and filled her pitcher, and came up!* The way up is down, bless God.

We read that the servant ran to meet her, just as the Spirit is running to meet you tonight. At his invitation she gave him to drink, and all his camels did she draw for also. The Word says: *"She hasted, and emptied her pitcher into the trough, and ran again unto the well to draw water for his camels."* Dear ones, is your pitcher empty enough, are you down low enough, to have this abundant supply that not only satisfies the demand of your own soul, but hastens to draw and empty for others about you, knowing, with unbroken confidence, that you can run again to the well and draw again and again from the hidden source that never runs dry?

She was fair to look upon. Can the Lord look down into the depths of your soul and say: *"Thou art fair, My love, there is no spot in thee"?* Are you a virgin, pure in heart, that knows not the old man of sin and worldliness? Then the Spirit is calling you to be a member of the Bridal Body. Earrings, and bracelets and precious gifts were given to Rebecca, and she returned with the servant to her parents' house, and there the servant brought forth jewels of silver (which represents Atonement), jewels of gold (or the Divine nature of Jesus), and raiment (which typifies the Righteousness of Jesus), and the marriage robe. These he gave to Rebecca. Then to the brother and the mother he also gave precious things to be given to those who do not go all the way through to the perfection of full sacrifice, the Bride receives the best and most beautiful gifts. There is no comparison to be made between the two.

Then before eating or drinking, the servant told his message, and of the wonderful Isaac, and his beautiful home, far away, and of his desire to take Rebecca to this home to be the son's Bride.

"And they said, *'We will call the damsel and enquire at her mouth.' And they called Rebecca, and said unto her*:

" 'Wilt thou go with this man?' and she said: 'I will go'."

This is the great question of today, the question now facing each one of you, "Wilt thou go with this man?" Each individual must answer it for himself and herself. Oh, can you say, as Rebecca of old, *" 'I will go!'* Where He leads me I will follow"? Trust yourself in His hands, and He will never leave you till you are safe in the arms of Jesus.

As Rebecca journeyed through the wilderness she did not lose her way; she did not have to run about inquiring of every passerby which road to take; the Servant had come to guide, lead, yea, and carry her, all the way to Isaac's house. What tales he told her by the way, how her heart was gladdened and lifted above all earthly things, as she listened to his glowing description of her Bridegroom and his home awaiting her. I am sure she forgot the bumpy camels, and the dusty road, and the blazing sun, as she pressed on toward the longed-for moment when she should see him face to face.

Just so is the Holy Spirit leading and guiding all who will receive Him and follow Him, over every obstacle, surmounting every hill of difficulty, taking the things of Jesus and revealing them unto us as we journey, till we cry out in longing:

"O Lord Jesus, how long till we shall see Your blessed face?" Our hearts swell with love and gratitude, and unutterable longing, as the Spirit speaks, *"not of Himself"* but of Jesus, our Bridegroom, and lover divine.

At last, after long days of traveling we read of that wonderful meeting.

ISAAC MET REBECCA IN THE FIELD.—JESUS TO MEET HIS BRIDE IN THE AIR

"As Isaac went out to meditate in the field at eventide, he lifted up his eyes, and behold, the camels were coming!" O Jesus! Jesus! He is lifting up His eyes just now, this very eventide, and He sees, and beholds the camels are coming. Are

you amongst that little company that is swiftly coming up the road to meet Him? Steadily, surely, we are drawing near the glorious day, dear pilgrims, when the consummation of our journey will arrive and we, as Rebecca, will lift up our eyes and see our Bridegroom; and even now, as we see in faith our Bridegroom from afar, we should take the vail of greater separation, and cover ourselves, that we shall indeed be a separated people unto Him.

We read of Isaac that he *"brought her into his mother's tent and took Rebecca, and she became his wife, and He loved her."* Soon our Saviour shall come for His Bride who has set out to meet Him, come for those who have heard and answered the call:

"Behold, the Bridegroom cometh, go ye out to meet Him." Soon the great song will resound. "Let us be glad and rejoice, for the marriage of the Lamb hath come, and the wife has made herself ready." The tables are being spread, the marriage is at hand. Beloved, will you go, will you receive the Holy Spirit and let Him guide you to the wedding of the Lamb?

If you have not yet found the well of Salvation, empty that pitcher you carry upon your shoulder, and get you *down* in haste to the wells of Salvation, for it is there you will meet and receive the Holy Spirit, who, if you will follow Him, will lead you on over the hills and through the valleys till you meet your Bridegroom in the air.

THE LIFE AND GROWTH OF PETER

IT is not only God's will, but it is absolutely necessary and essential that every child of God should grow in grace and enlarge in love daily. When I was a little girl my Mother used to stand me up at the door once in so often and take a pencil and make a little mark just at the top of my head on the frame of the door. After a few more weeks she would again put another mark above the last one to measure and see how much I had grown since the last mark was made. It is a good thing for Christians to measure themselves carefully and frequently, not by one another, but by the Word of God. God's Word is a true measuring rod, also the life of Paul, of Peter, and many others. Let us take the latter, the life and growth of Peter, today, and see whether we have grown as quickly and as much as he; if not, let us press on, for God is no respector of persons, and what He has done for Peter He is not only able but anxious to do for us.

Peter's first sight of Jesus came unexpectedly, one day as he was about to cast his net into the sea. Jesus saw Peter, and went and spoke to him, saying:

"Follow me and I will make you a fisher of men." Peter straightway left his net and followed Jesus. Dear one, do you remember the day when first your eyes were opened to the lovely form of Jesus walking along the shores of time to your heart, when first you heard that dear voice, sweet as the sound of rushing water, bidding you to leave your nets of worldly cares and your sinful life and follow Him? Praise His name, just one sight of that lovely face and all other faces lost their attraction and power to satisfy; just one cadence of His voice, and earthly voices lost their charm. Hallelujah! No wonder Peter left his old, worn-out fishing nets and followed: no wonder we left our unrighteousness and accepted His righteousness.

Straightway Peter left his nets and followed Him. How eagerly he promised to follow, and how little he understood just where the following would lead him. No shadow of the cross did he see, no whisperings of a dark night when he would deny his Lord, the future with its train of joys and sorrows, its victories and defeats, its honor and dishonor; no visions of a cross where he himself should hang, were forseen as he eagerly and joyfully promised to follow all the way.

How little did we realize the mountain tops of transfiguration and the valleys of trial we should pass when our hearts said yes to Jesus and promised to follow all the way. The main and most important thing is to say an eternal Yes to Jesus, and whether it is weal or whether it is woe, the Jesus who took Peter through will bring us forth triumphant if we trust and follow all the way.

Through the many days that followed, wonderful days lived in the presence of Jesus, precious days of submitting to

His leadings and dealings, Peter learned the meaning of faith and trust. He had seen his wife's mother instantly healed of the fever; he had witnessed the healings of many sick, and the raising of the dead; he had beheld and assisted in the feeding of the multitudes; and now in the 14th chapter of Matthew, we find him in the ship with the other disciples, tossed and driven by the tempestuous waves of the sea.

Dimly through the darkness of the night, then clearer and more distinctly, they saw a calm figure in white raiment walking to meet them on the waves, and in fear they cried out: "It is a spirit." O, faint heart, tempest-tossed in your frail craft of faith, have you ever found your Lord walking to meet you over the roughest wave of trial, surmounting the highest crest of difficulty and tests? Did you, like Peter, fail to recognize Jesus as you were passing through the storm? Or have you learned to see Jesus in every test walking forth to reveal Himself to you in some new attribute, in greater beauty and power than you have yet known Him? And when all around you seemed turmoil and strife, and you saw nothing but circumstances and trials, did you ever hear His voice saying: "It is I; be not afraid"? Cease to see waves and tests and turmoil, and recognize the Jesus that walks to meet us on their billows.

Have you ever, like dear Peter, had your faith inspired and encouraged by that word, "Come," till you swung your feet over the side of your small craft, and yourself began to walk in naked faith, with all material and earthly foundations removed from beneath your feet, to meet the Lord on top of the waves that so lately threatened to engulf you? Perhaps you, too, got your eyes on the wind and the waves, saw people and conditions and cirucumstances instead of Jesus, and began to sink. But Jesus' ear was open to Peter's cry, and is open to the cry of every follower. *"Lord, save me,"* Peter cried, and immediately Jesus put out His hand and caught him, chiding him for his lack of faith.

More blessed days of growing and learning passed and Peter is found still following Jesus. He is called blessed by the Lord, for recognizing the divinity of the Son of God. We find him rebuked in the same chapter for trying to persuade Jesus from going to suffer that shameful and ignominious death upon the cross. Dear Jesus, how quick He has been with Peter and with each one of us to praise and encourage that which savoreth of faith and sacrifice, and to rebuke and chasten that which savoreth of the human and selfishness.

"And after six days, Jesus taketh Peter and James and John and bringeth them up into an high mountain apart, and was transfigured before them, and His face did shine as the sun, and His raiment was white as the light." Beloved, how about that measuring rod? Are you measuring up so far to Peter's experience? Have you been upon the Mount of Transfiguration, and seen Jesus revealed and transfigured in His beauty and loveliness before your amazed and adoring eyes?

Soon after we find Peter receiving another lesson in faith, when he was sent to the sea to take the first fish he caught, and in its mouth to find the needed money to pay the tribute or tax, for himself and his Lord.

Through the many, but swiftly passing days of Peter's walk with Jesus, he grows in faith and wisdom, he hears the preaching and sees the life of his Master, he sees miracles wrought, sick healed and demons cast out, and even sees the sick healed and demons depart through his own prayer and faith. But now, with ever increasing emphasis, Jesus informs and seeks to impress upon the minds of His little flock, that soon He is to lay down His life, to be resurrected again and ascend unto His Father. Moreover, He tells them again and again that although He departs He will not leave them comfortless, but will send another Comforter, even the Holy Ghost, to lead them into all truth, and endue them with power from on high.

Again we find Peter seated with his Lord at the last supper, declaring that though all men should be offended because of Jesus, yet would he never be offended. Upon hearing the warning of the Lord that he would deny Him, we hear his impassioned denial:

"Though I should die with Thee, yet will I not deny Thee." How we, too, have promised the Lord in those precious hours of feasting and communion, that we would never again deny Him in any way! Truly the Spirit was willing, and the flesh weak.

Then Jesus took His disciples, and went forth to the garden of Gethsemane to pray through the great depression and sorrowful heaviness, he felt pressing down upon Him. Leaving the rest behind with the injunction to *"sit here while I go and pray yonder,"* Jesus took with Him Peter and the two sons of Zebedee, and said to them: *"My soul is exceeding sorrowful, even unto death: tarry ye here and watch with me."* Jesus went a little further, and falling down upon His face, travailed in prayer. O, the yearning of His soul to have some one to watch and pray with Him, but coming to His disciples and finding them asleep, He did not address the others, but said unto Peter: *"What! could ye not watch with me one hour?"* Again He prayed, and upon returning a second and a third time, found them sleeping.

O, beloved, have you, too, failed Jesus miserably on this same line of prayer? Now, in this last short hour before the door of mercy is forever closed, and intercessors are needed as never before, have we, too, been guilty of sleeping at our post? Have we also been overcome with the slothfulness that has wrapped us in slumbering blindness to the face of Jesus bending over us, beseeching us to rise and pray, not only for others but that we ourselves enter not into temptation? Jesus knew that Peter was going to be specially tempted and singled him out with a command to pray. What dismay it would bring us to hear Him say:

"Sleep on now, and take your rest. The souls you might have prayed through to salvation are lost forever, the brand you might have plucked from the burning is now in hell. Your opportunity for prayer and intercession is past. Sleep on."

Peter sprang to his feet, wide awake now. His Lord was grieved, his beloved Lord. What could he do to show his love? With zeal he smote off the ear of the high priest's servant. He would just prove his love and zeal. But, ah! Peter, *"obedience is better than sacrifice, and to hearken than the fat of rams."* The ear was restored by Jesus, and the little procession of captors and captive moved on to the judgment hall, Jesus was taken inside to be tried, but Peter remained outside and began to warm his hands by the fire. Ah! it is a dangerous place to go to warm your hands by the fire of this world; and as Peter sat there a damsel declared that Peter had been with Jesus. But Peter indignantly denied it before them all, and was ashamed of Jesus.

Peter moved off to the porch, but could not escape the notice of the people, for if we have been with Jesus and walked with Him the world will know it. Another maid asked him if he had not been with Jesus, and soon yet more standersby asked him if he were not "one of them." But Peter began to curse and swear, saying, *"I know not the man."*

O Peter, how our hearts have ached for you and the shameful thing you did in denying your Lord! Yet, dear ones, how many of us have denied Him? Just the time we should have been true and witnessed from the house tops that He was our Saviour, how many times we sat silent just too long. We must either deny ourselves or deny our Lord, deny the flesh or deny the Spirit. Surely something was radically wrong with Peter, something was missing that was much needed. O, it was surely the Holy Ghost that Jesus said would endue them with power.

Then followed those agonized hours and days of suffering for Peter, reproach and conviction over his failure, the crucifixion of his Lord, the burial, and days of utter loneliness and despair. His Lord was gone, the tender voice was hushed, the face he loved was still in death. And there was a great, big empty void everywhere that none could fill. Then out of that black, vacant void came the swift, breathless messenger, Mary, with the message that Jesus was risen. Jesus' first words and thought were of Peter, and now we see him arising, running, out-stripping the others, stooping down before the sepulchre, looking, wondering in himself.

Again we find Peter fishing, still discouraged, for he knew not where his Lord had gone, leaping from the boat and rushing to the shore at the first glimpse of Jesus. We see him eating of the bread and fish upon the fire, hear him declaring his love for Jesus, hear His commission, *"Feed My sheep, feed My lambs."* Then came the day of departure, when Jesus was to leave for His Father's throne, and we hear Him still impressing upon the disciples the necessity of obeying His command to tarry in Jerusalem until they were filled with the Holy Ghost saying: *"You shall receive power after that the Holy Ghost is come upon you."*

After Jesus had been caught up, we find Peter hastening to the upper room, tarrying until the Holy Ghost was poured out on the day of Pentecost. We picture him filled with the Holy Ghost, Acts 2:4, speaking with other tongues as the Spirit gave him utterance, so filled with the Spirit that onlookers thought him drunken with wine. Hear the shouts and praises of the hundred and twenty, see the multitude come running together, astonished, amazed, in doubt, crying, *"What meaneth this?"* O, it meant that the Holy Ghost had come, that the hundred and twenty, and Peter, had been endued with power from on high, and were now able to stand up and witness with holy boldness of Jesus the crucified. It meant that out of their innermost being now flowed rivers of the Spirit that none could check nor gainsay.

What meaneth this? cried some. Others, mocking said: *"'These are filled with new wine.' But Peter, standing up, said, 'These are not drunk with wine, but this is that, which was spoken by the prophet Joel'."*

Peter standing up! O, what a change from the cringing, cowardly, denying Peter! This new Peter had received the Holy Ghost and now, instead of fearing a little maid, he stood boldly before this scoffing, doubting multitude of Jews, and boldly preached in the Holy Ghost, of Jesus, while multitudes turned to the Lord and accepted Him as their Saviour.

Are you measuring yourself by the measuring rod as we go on, dear ones? If you have left all to follow Jesus, have you received the Holy Ghost since you believed, with the Bible evidence? Have you felt your lack of power to testify and your heart has been dismayed when you denied Him or failed in prayer, or lacked in power? Then what you need is the Holy Ghost. Or have you perhaps been on the mountain top, and beheld Him transfigured before you? Have you been as Peter, used in praying for the sick and casting out demons? Have you mistaken these experiences for the baptism of the Holy Ghost? Then measure up today; compare your experience with the Bible evidence of the incoming of the Spirit.

If you have measured up so far and have received the Holy Ghost evidenced by the speaking in tongues, as Peter of old, don't stop there. This is just beginning the preparation for further advancement and growth, for when "He, the Spirit of truth is come, He will lead you on into all truth."

Behold Peter's life after Pentecost, where he received the Holy Ghost. See him at the beautiful gate saying to the lame man,

"Silver and gold have I none, but such as I have give I thee. Rise up and walk." See the sick being brought out from all the villages and towns round about, as recorded in the 5th chapter of Acts, and when even the shadow of Peter fell upon them they were healed, every one.

Behold Peter at Samaria, and at Caesarea, laying hands upon the believers in the one instance and while he was yet preaching, in the other, they received the Holy Ghost as had the hundred and twenty in the beginning. Follow Peter through his imprisonments, his beatings, and scourgings, his shame and reproach. Follow him through his courage and faith, his love and life of power. Follow him to his death on the cross, crucified head downward because he felt unworthy to be crucified as his Lord. O, dear ones, I fear that e'er now the measuring rod, upon being applied to our lives, will find us all far short. But God is no respecter of persons, and He who took Peter through from his first eternal *"I WILL"* at the sea of Galilee to the cross where he laid down his life, will take us through if we will follow Him.

"Follow thou Me?" The future all unknown and trusted in His hands. Dear Peters, weak in yourselves, He will make you strong in Him. Follow Him to the cross, to the grave, through the resurrection, to the upper room and the reception of the Holy Ghost, on to the gifts and fruits of the Spirit, perfect development and identification with Him in His death on the cross, and on to meet Him in the air.

Let us then press on and follow all the way. Do not stop short of God's best and perfection.

"Following Jesus day by day,
Nothing can harm while He leads the way,
Sunshine or darkness, what e'er befall,
Jesus, my Saviour, is my all in all."

IS JESUS CHRIST THE GREAT "I AM" OR IS HE THE GREAT "I WAS"?

SHUT in my closet of prayer today, with my Bible and the Spirit, my Guide, I muse a while o'er its pages, then pray for the world with its throngs who, in teeming millions, walk through this life in need of "The Great I AM."

As I ponder and pray in the stillness, I dream as a dreamer of dreams. A steepled church stands before me—a church with open doors. Within it I see the preacher stand; hear his voice in earnest call. But 'tis the throng that flows through the street outside that holds my anxious gaze.

"Pit-a-pat! Pit-a-pat!"—say the hundreds and thousands of feet, surging by the church doors of our land.

"Pat! Pat! Pit-a-pat!"—hurrying multitudes, on business and pleasure bent.

From out the church door floats the voice of Pastor and Evangelist in an effort to halt the down-rushing throng in their headlong race toward destruction and attract their attention to the Christ.

"Stop! Stop! Giddy throng, surging by like a river, take your eyes from the bright lights of the gilded way," they cry. "Leave the paths of death, enter our open door and listen while we tell you the sweet though ancient story of 'The Great I WAS.'

"Eloquently, instructively, we will tell you of the wonderful power Christ *'used'* to have, the miracles He *'used'* to perform, the sick He *'used'* to heal. 'Tis a graphic and blessed history of those things which Jesus did almost 1900 years before you were born. They happened far, far away across the sea which you have never sailed, in a country which you have never seen, among people you have never known.

"Wonderful, marvelous, was the power that *'used'* to flow from 'The Great I WAS.' He *'used'* to open the blind eyes, unstop the deaf ears, and make the lame to walk. He *'used'* to show forth such mighty works, and even manifest them through His followers that the attention of the multitudes was arrested and gripped in such an irresistible way that thousands were brought storming at His door of mercy, to receive blessing and healing at His hand.

"Of course, these mighty works Christ *'used'* to do are done no longer,—for some reason. Perhaps Jesus is too far away, or is too busy making intercession at the Father's throne to be bothered with such little things as the physical infirmities of His children, else His ear may have grown heavy or His arm be short, or maybe these mighty works were only done to convince the doubters in that day, and since we have no doubters (?) in this civilized day and age, the miraculous has passed away and is no longer necessary.

"At any rate the fact remains that the signs and wonders which He once declared should accompany His preached Word (Mark 16) are seen no longer. The power He once displayed, till the glory of His majesty and love in coming to destroy the works of the devil, flashed and played through the gloom like the lightnings around Mount Sinai, is now dark, cold, dead. And, as for the visible manifestation of His power, we are left desolate as though the light which once shone in the darkness had gone out.

"Come, come to this attractive feast, unheeding sinners. Turn now from your Sunday golf, fishing, theatres and novels. Come enter our doors that I may tell you the story of 'The Great I WAS,' and the power that *'used'* to be." But—

"Pit-a-pat! Pit-a-pat!"—On go the thousands of feet; on to the movie and on to the dance; on to the office, the club and the bank.

"Pat! Pat! Pit-a-pat!" "Why don't you stop your wayward feet? Do you not know that you are headed for sorrow? Why is it that the theatre is o'erflowing whilst our pews are empty and bare?"

"Pat! Pat! Pat! Pit-a-pat!" "Oh, stop a moment, the maddening, ceaseless, pattering of multitudinous feet and tell me why you take such interest in the world about you and show such lethargy, carelessness and lack of active interest in my story of 'The Great I WAS,' and the power He *'used'* to have and the deeds He *'used'* to do? Why is it that people grow enthusiastic over the ball-game, the boxing-ring, the movies and the dance, while we see no revival of interest or turning to the Christ?"

On and on they go, paying no heed, neither turning their eyes from the glittering baubles beyond.

"Why is it, dear Spirit of God," I ask, "they do not listen to that dear Brother's call? They do not seem interested in the power Christ *'used'* to have. In a steady stream they pass by the church and on into the world of grim realities and the problems which they must face."

"Pat! Pat! Pit-a-pat!"—there are young feet, old feet, light feet, heavy feet, glad feet, sad feet; joyous feet, tired, discouraged feet; tripping feet, lonely, groping feet; straight feet, sick and crippled feet; eager, searching feet; disillusioned, disappointed feet; and, as they pass, a message is somehow tangled up in their pattering, which rises from the cobblestones like a mighty throbbing from the heart of the world.

"'Tis not so much what Christ used to do for the world in answer to prayer in bygone days," they seem to say, "but where is His power NOW? And what can He do TODAY?"

"Ah, yes!" sigh the crippled feet from the pavement, "we are not so vitally interested in the sick He *'used'* to heal, the limbs He *'used'* to make straight and strong. (Of course, we are glad to know that somewhere, sometime, in the distant past Christ healed the sick in far off lands). But we live in *the great today*—and Ah me!! We are very worn and weary! We yearn for healing, hope and strength *today*. We stand in need of succor NOW. But you say these mighty provisions for the healing of the body (as well as the soul), which Christ promised in Psalms 103, Isaiah 53, Matt. 8, Mark 16, Jas. 5, were not at all lasting, but were mainly for the Jews who lived in other days. And in reality your teaching says Christ's healing of the sick, when He walked this earth, was not so much for the demonstration of the tender Saviour's love and sake of relieving the sufferers' pain and a pity for the sick themselves, as to build up His own cause and make the world believe and, accomplishing this, He withdrew the lifeline of hope and coiled it up again. So, as the church cannot supply my need, I must pass on in further search of help from another source."

"And we," say the tired, discouraged feet, "are also glad that in a far off land, He gave the weary rest; and they, who had well nigh lost the faith and trust in their fellowman, found truth and grace in Him.

"But you say He is afar off now? That we live in a different dispensation? His promises were largely for the Jewish people anyway? Then there's not much for us here, so we walk past your door seeking elsewhere a haven of rest and hope."

"And we," the glad, young, joyous feet, send up a rippling echo from the pavement, "we are in search of something that can give us joy and happiness *today*. You say God *'used'* to make His little ones so happy that they danced and shouted for joy. We, too, want joy! Not the joy that *'used'* to be but joy of heart *today*. As it is taken away from the church, we seek it in the world."

"And we," say the heavy, groping, lonely feet, "are bereaved and seek comfort and rest. For us the shades of night are falling. The knowledge that Christ *'once'* dried tears and bare the heavy load is blest indeed, but Oh! *we* of *today* need succor *now*. Preaching 'The Great I WAS' can never satisfy our longings, WE NEED 'THE GREAT I AM.' "

"The Great I AM"—why yes! That's it exactly! That's what this old world needs. A Christ who lives and loves and answers prayers today. A Christ who changeth not but is the same *today* as He was yesterday, and will be evermore. A Christ whose power knows neither lack nor cessation. A Lord whose Name is "I AM" forever, even unto all generations.

When the Lord bade Moses go, call the children of Israel from the flesh pots and bondage, sin and sickness of Egypt, Moses inquired of Him, "When they shall ask who sent me? and *What is His Name? what shall I say unto them?" and He said, "Thus shalt thou say unto the children of Israel, I AM hath sent me unto you.* This is my Name *forever,* and this is my memorial *unto all generations."*

Oh, what a wonderful Name! What a wonderful promise! Glory! Glory to God!

Moses did not need to go about apologetically and say, " 'The Great I WAS' hath sent me unto you; His name is 'I WAS' because He *'used'* to do great things—long ago. He expended the last of His power in creating the heavens and the earth and all that in them is. He is quite far off now and the necessity for this miraculous manifestation of His power is no longer needed, seeing that all things have now been created. He does not do mighty works today but please come, follow and obey the message of 'The Great I WAS.' "

Why, I doubt whether they would have followed such a call. The message which Moses bore rang clear and firm—"I AM hath sent me." He walked with assurance. The solid rock was under his feet. His God was a living God—a miracle-working God. Moses knew his business was to preach and deliver the message God had given him. "The Great I AM" had contracted to back up that message with signs following. "I AM—I AM—I AM!" rang in the ears of Moses every step he took.

Ah! It gives a servant of God some heart to know that "I AM" hath sent him. No more apologizing. No more hanging the head and resorting to earthly means; no more trembling and fear of failure, no dread now that the crowds will not follow! Head erect, footsteps firm and full of assurance, earthly temple clad with a robe of the majesty and tenderness of the Father, hands pointing unhesitatingly to the way, voice ringing clear and authoritative—"I AM, *I AM* hath sent me unto you!"

" 'I AM' lives today. He will tabernacle in our midst. 'I AM' will deliver us from our enemies. He will guide us by His hand. 'I AM' will feed us with the bread from the heavens and give us water from the rock. 'I AM' will deliver us from the sickness and the diseases of the Egyptians, saying, 'If you will walk in My ways and keep My statutes none of the diseases which have been put upon the Egyptians shall come nigh you. 'I AM' will lead us into the promised land—"

Oh, the blessed assurance, the authority, the majestic glory of the name "I AM!" No wonder the children of Israel left the flesh-pots and the bands that bound them. No wonder the weary eyes of the toiler looked up with new interest and hope. No wonder that hands which had hung down were lifted and the feeble knees made strong when Moses could promise them that when the Lord said unto those which were weak, "Be strong and of good courage, for the Lord will do great things," He meant just what He said. He did not have to say, "The Lord *'used'* to do great things," but could triumphantly declare, "The Lord *'will'* do great things; for He is 'The Great I AM', and though heaven is His home, the earth is His footstool where He answers the prayers of His people."

During Moses' ministry, the sick were healed, the lepers cleansed, the plague stayed.

Oh, Moses—how we envy you, the great commission, GO! call my people out of bondage into liberty; out of darkness into light; out of sin into holiness; out of sickness into health! But tell us, just when did the day of supernatural, miraculous manifestation of the power of God end?—When did "I AM" become "I WAS?"

Why, little children, "I AM" hath never changed! His power is just the same in this thy day as it was in the days of yore. Did He not say, "This is My Name forever—even unto ALL generations?" They who have faith shall see the lightnings of His glory flash in power of answered prayer today, as in the days of old. Elijah and Elisha lived in a day when doubters said the miraculous had passed away and "I AM" had become "I WAS." But through faith and prayer they proved His name to be "I AM" unto their generations. After the ascension of the Only Begotten of the Father, Jesus Christ, the disciples proved that "He who was dead is alive forevermore"—the Great I AM, who saves and heals and baptizes with the Spirit's power.

On and on through the centuries, though surrounded by unbelief and skepticism, there have always been the Elijahs and the Peters who have proved that "I AM" is His Name even unto *their* generation. John Wesley believed that Christ was not only to save but to heal the sick in *his* day. In his biography he tells of the lame made to walk, cancers which melted away and even a lame horse made whole through answered prayer; thus proving "I AM" to be the Lord's Name even unto *his* generation.

Then surely He has not changed at this late hour! Surely, He is the same today. Elijah, Peter, John Wesley and an army of others who had heard and obeyed the message, "Thus shall you say—I AM hath sent me," were ridiculed and persecuted by those they loved the best. Even so today, though it means being despised and misunderstood, get alone in the wilderness of quiet and stillness before God. Seek His face till your soul is kindled with the flame of love from the burning bush. Get your authority from God. Inquire of Him,

"When they shall ask who sent me and what is his name? what shall I say unto them?" Hear His reply, "Thus shalt thou say unto them, 'I AM' hath sent me" and let it ring in your soul forever, louder, clearer, more wonderful in its revelation of the ever-living Christ with each new step and turn of the way. Victory is assured and the only solution to the problem of drawing the multitude is to lift up, not the dead, but the living Christ; not the Great "I WAS" but the Great "I AM."

Thanks! Thanks! for that message, dear Lord. The clouds of uncertainty are dispelled—the shades of night rolled back. We see Thee in a new and glorious light, even as the Sun of Righteousness with healing in Thy wings. "I AM" is Thy Name today and shall be evermore!

"*I AM* the Lord, I change not."

"*I AM* the Lord that hath chosen thee and called thee by thy name."

"*I AM* come down to deliver thee and to bring thee up into a good land and a large; unto a land flowing with milk and honey."

"*I AM* (not I WAS but I AM) the Lord that *healeth thee.*"

"*I AM* He who was dead but am alive forevermore."

"*I AM* Alpha and Omega, the beginning and the end, the first and the last."

How the "I AMS" of the Lord come rolling in, like the billows of a full, o'erflowing sea, whose tide rises higher toward down-bending heavens.

Glory! Glory! My own poor heart is running over like a tiny cup that would seek to hold the ocean! God is speaking in my ears, "I AM THAT I AM." The earth resounds with His voice. The eternal hills and the mountains swell the song, *"I AM shall be My Name forevermore."* And away up yonder the glorious stars of the heaven echo back again—*"Even unto all generations this shall be my Name."* Angels and cherubim bend low over heaven's balustrade and sing a new song of inspiration—"Go forth, my child, and this thy cry shall be, *'I AM, I AM hath sent me unto thee'.*"

Again, I see the steepled church,—But now the scene is changed.

"Pat! Pat! Pit-a-pat"—The street that lies before it is still with people filled. But they are no longer passing *"by"*—the crowds are passing *"in."* They fill the pews and the galleries. They stand in the aisles and climb to the window sills. They pack the doorways and stand on the stairs. The streets and the lanes are filled. The Gospel nets are full to the bursting and there is no more room to contain the multitudes that throng the place.

And out o'er the heads of the people I hear the message ring:

"Awake! thou that sleepest, arise from the dead! The Lord still lives today. His power has never abated. His Word has never changed. The things He did in Bible days, He still lives to do today. Not a burden is there He cannot bear nor a fetter He cannot break.

"Here bring your sins, He'll wash them away. Here bring your sicknesses, He'll heal you today. We serve not a dead but a *living God*—not 'I WAS,' but 'The Great I AM.'

"Come young, come old; come sad, come glad; come weary and faltering of step; come sick, come well! come one, come all unto 'The Great I AM.' There is food for the hungry, there is strength for the faint; there is hope for the hopeless, and sight for the blind."

"Pit-a-pat! Pit-a-pat!" Faster and faster they come! The church is o'erflowing; they are filling the streets. Their faces are shining; in their eyes the light of hope has been kindled by the taper of faith through the preaching of "The Great I AM."

They are reaching out their hands for forgiveness, for the healing of the crippled and sick. They are thirsting for the joy of salvation; hungering for the Bread of Life. They are seeking the power of the Holy Ghost and something practical which can meet the immediate and pressing need of the great today, and fit them for the morrow. And they have found the source of sure supply *in the church*—the house of God—from under whose altar and o'er whose threshold runs the ever deepening stream of life. They seek no further, through the briers of the world—they have found "The Great I AM" and sing:

"Wisdom, righteousness and power,
Holiness forevermore—
My redemption full and sure,
Christ is all I need."

Burdens are lifted, tearful weeping eyes are dried, the sick are healed, the crooked made straight. Sin-guilty hearts are cleansed and made holy. Empty water-pots are filled with wine. And the cold, worldly church has risen from the dust in garments glistening, white. With oil in their lamps and sheaves in their arms—they worship "The Great I AM."

THE BAPTISM OF THE HOLY SPIRIT

THE NEED OF THE CHURCH TODAY

HE crying need of the church today is a real baptism of the Holy Spirit. The hearts of earnest pastors are crying out to God, as they kneel in the study, over the lack of power, the indifference and absence of the young people, the cold materialism and unbelief of those that remain and the lack of revival fires.

The remedy for this ailment, the solution of this problem, is a real baptism of the Holy Ghost and fire upon the church.

With the outgoing of godliness and the power and demonstration of the Holy Ghost came the entrance of worldliness and "forms of godliness" that deny the power thereof, and the cooling off of the white heated love for God and souls. Many have turned to socials, suppers, community uplift, moving pictures in parish house and compromise that professes to "fight fire with fire" and brings the world into the church in order to draw the people from the world, arguing that if they are to have it anyway they might better have it in the church than without.

This, however, will never prove a satisfactory solution of the problem. There is one sure way back to power, back to the old time glory, back to Pentecostal conviction, soul winning and sweeping revivals—one way back to the old time welling, praiseful hallelujahs and glory that will draw the thronging multitudes from the haunts of sin, help us arrest their attention and fix their eyes upon Christ. This *one way* is plainly described by Jesus:

"Tarry ye in the city of Jerusalem until ye be endued with power from on high. . . . Ye shall receive power after that the Holy Ghost is come upon you. . . . Receive ye the Holy Ghost."

Just as the flowers, with drooping heads, who have been bathed in the bright sunlight every day need the refreshing showers of rain from heaven—so the church of today having found and basked in the warmth of the Saviour's love needs the outpouring of the Holy Spirit to refresh, invigorate and cause its drooping head to lift with strength and courage new.

Just as the electric light bulb in the finest chandelier in the White House, despite the splendor of its setting, must be connected without a break clear to the distant power house if it would give light—so the pastor and the church of Jesus Christ, though they be in the finest cathedral in the land, must have an unobstructed line and a solid connection with the power house of the Holy Spirit if they would shine and draw perishing multitudes from the darkness of unbelief and worldliness of today.

Just as the finest automobile, in spite of its satin finish, its cord tires, its properly lubricated and well tuned motor must have gasoline in its tank in order to cover ground and to make real headway—so the clergy, the laymen, and christian hearts the whole world over need the power of the Holy Ghost. No matter how much shining polish, lubrication and well tuned machinery we may have, if the *power* of the Holy Spirit is missing, it is pretty hard to push the church automobile up the hill of real revivals.

Just as——, but there! We all know that that which we need above all else is a real genuine baptism of the Holy Ghost! *Not* just the theory, the "take-it-by-faith-believe-you-have-it-and-go-on-experience." We have tried this substitute too long. *Not* a wild fire excitement that runs to fanaticism, emotionalism, or side issues that causes the recipient to fight and argue and boast more as to the manner in which the Holy Ghost enters into His temple than of the real, practical power and soul-winning efficiency, which His dear incoming brings. *Not* an experience which causes one to strut about and plume oneself with an "I-am-holier-than-thou, for-I-have-had-an-experience-which-you-do-not-possess" air. *Not* an experience that boasts only of its own joys and transporting moments of transfiguration, its attendant signs and evidences (though, thank God, these will attend that incoming), but real, sane, practical, level-headed, mighty baptism of the Holy Ghost and fire, such as the hundred and twenty received on the day of Pentecost. Such a baptism will equip the recipient for service, endue him with power as a winner of souls, fill him with a love and passion for the lost akin to that in the heart of the Father and will help him lift up the crucified Lamb of God to a dying world.

Oh, yes, dear Lord—with all our hearts we long to see our church of today tarry until she receives THE GENUINE BAPTISM AND POWER OF THE HOLY GHOST. We do not want anything that is foolish, unscriptural, or impractical, but that which is genuine, Biblical and applicable to the business of preaching the gospel in the power and demonstration of the Holy Ghost, with the same methods and results that attended Thy work in the Apostolic days of old.

We yearn not for the spirit of fear, but of *"love* and of *power* and of a *sound mind."* That love which will draw multitudes to the cross of Christ—that power which can cleanse away sin and heal those that are oppressed—the sound mind of the genuine Holy Spirit who has come to guide us into all truth, to take the things of Jesus and reveal them unto us.

A mountain top experience is of value only as it equips and fits us for practical service in the valley. The Power of Pentecost, with its rushing wind and tongues of flame, was of value in that they who received the Spirit became his temple thenceforth to glorify the Christ and win the multitudes unto the Lord.

And hallelujah, this power is to be had today. God's store is not run short. The gift and power of Peter's time are for us yet today. Let us cease beating ourselves against the stone wall of coldness, formality and unbelief in our own feeble strength; let us set our faces one and all to seek the power the disciples found on the Day of Pentecost.

Let us open our hearts to the searchlight of heaven and cry unto Him: Strip us, Lord, of everything, of the world and self and sin. Empty, cleanse, purify these cold hearts of ours. Melt us in humble contrition at Thine own crucified feet. Take doubts and fears away, dear Lord. Help us to forget the giants in the land, to forget the hypocrites who have professed to have had this great experience, but have become like vain children, playing with and boasting of a toy which they knew not how to use.

Help us to fix our eyes upon the Bible—the dear Word of God—the promised power—the pattern given—the definite, practical results that lead therefrom, and then,—Oh, precious Lord, help our poor faltering feet to find the lowest step and mount the stair that leads us to "The Upper Room."

Baptize us with Thy power, endue us with Thy might. Give us, Master, nothing short of the mighty power of Acts 2:4; not for our own sake, but for Thy Name's sake that as a flaming torch we may be held within Thine hand to point the way to others, to lead the lost to Calvary, the Christian to The Upper Room and the Spirit filled believer to the harvest fields to glean and work for Thee.

Then will we see the sinners saved, the sick made whole, believers filled with Thy power; then will our altars overflow, our churches be too small. The world is starving for the gospel of power that will meet the crying need of body, soul and spirit. There is but one way to meet that need—there is but one solution to the problem, one glorious path of Victory open—'tis the baptism and the power of the blessed Holy Ghost.

BRINGING BACK THE ARK

"So David arose, and went with all the people that were with him from Baale to Judah, to bring up from thence the ark of the Lord, whose name is called by the name of the Lord of Hosts that dwelleth between the cherubims . . . So David and all the house of Israel brought up the ark of the Lord with shouting, and with the sound of the trumpet." (2 Sam. 6:2, 15.)

"When David danced before the Lord,
The ark was coming up the road.
His wife despised him in her heart,
But the ark was coming up the road.

And it's coming—Hallelujah!
The ark is coming up the road.
It's coming, Hallelujah!
The ark is coming up the road."

O brother, sister, have your eyes seen the vision? Has your heart caught the flame? Have your ears heard the sound of the shouting, the music and the tabrets? Do you realize that even in this our day the ark is coming up the road?

For years, we had sang the above verse and chorus, and each time they were repeated the power of God fell in the meetings and our hearts were strangely stirred within us. We knew vaguely that the coming of the ark stood for the coming of a revival and the power and presence of the Holy Spirit. But it has only been during the past few months that the real vision and understanding of the significance of the return of the ark has been dawning upon us, as (the Davidic company) the church of Jesus Christ is everywhere waking up to their need, demanding the return of the old time power and glory, and rising up to go forth and bring back the ark—the Shekina glory and presence of God's Holy Spirit to the Temple wherein it rightfully belongs.

When King David ascended the throne, the ark of the covenant was missing. There was in the tabernacle a strangely vacant spot that nothing else could ever fill. The mighty presence of God's Holy Spirit, and Shekina glory was absent and nothing else could ever take its place.

For many years the children of Israel had talked and dreamed of those early days of Moses, when their forefathers had been led through their wilderness journey toward the Promised Land. How the glory of the Lord had rested like a cloud o'er the tabernacle and above the Mercy Seat! What miraculous, supernatural power had been manifested in their midst! But alas, the glory had departed through disobedience and sin, the ark had been lost to their hosts and captured by the enemy. Thus it was that there was in the tabernacle an empty, vacant spot that no superficial, man-made substitute could ever fill, and the glory gone which no artificial light could ever replace. The Philistines had taken the ark, slaughtered thirty thousand footmen, broken the heart of Eli, slain his sons, and caused the dying wife of Phinehas to cry: *The glory is departed from Israel: for the ark of God is taken.* (1 Sam. 4:22).

Now throughout the reign of Saul (type of those who have lost the anointing) little or nothing had been said about the ark, and no effort was made to fetch it again unto its place. It is doubtful whether Saul had even enough spirituality to seriously miss its loss, and it must have seemed at times as though the place thereof would know it no more.

WE TOO HAD LOST THE ARK

And thus has it been in our own day. For generations, we have talked and read with bated breath of the olden days of our forefathers when the presence and power of the Holy Spirit rested upon the church in the Apostolic day. What supernatural, miraculous manifestations of the glory of God rested upon the tabernacle and above the Mercy Seat! Ah, blissful, blessed years, wherein the power and demonstration of the Shekina glory had filled the house with rushing wind and tongues of flame, and shaken the place wherein they were assembled! What mattered then the whippings and stonings! What mattered then damp prisons and chains! Was not the Lord in His holy temple, and the Spirit dwelling within His people?

But alas, through sin and disobedience, there came a day when the ark of His presence in the power of the Holy Ghost was taken by the enemy, and carried away by the Philistines and many were slaughtered in that dark day. Not that the Philistines went unpunished—ah, no! their gods fell down with broken necks and the true God was triumphant even in the darkest of the dark ages. But Oh! His people had lost the vision, the glory had departed from the church, and the ark of the Lord was taken.

Many a Saul who has lost the anointing and the vision of what it means to see God dwelling in power and demonstration of the Holy Spirit in the midst of His people, have never mentioned or proposed a real, united going out to bring back the ark. Many have declared that it can not be had today. But, praise the Lord, David is coming to the throne, with the real anointing and the zeal and faith of God unspoiled in His heart, and the first cry of His heart after coming into power is that the ark should be brought back and established in its rightful place—the tabernacle of the Most High.

DAVID AND ALL ISRAEL GO OUT TO BRING BACK THE ARK

No sooner had David ascended the throne, than his heart, ever tuned to the praise of God, was filled with longing for the return of the Ark of the Covenant. He declared not only his conviction, that the Ark *could* be brought back to its rightful place in the tabernacle, but his determination to go and get it and bring it back with dancing and music. To this end a call was sent forth, and the people were gathered together unto the City of David from whence they set forth in a body to fetch the Ark from the house of Abinadab.

But instead of bringing out the Ark in the old fashioned way, bearing it upon their shoulders, thus making their bodies the conveyance of the Ark, they were persuaded that the more modern, up-to-date, Philistine way of carrying the Ark upon a *new* cart, drawn by milch-kine was just as good and perhaps even better. Surely God was not tied to one pattern. The methods He used and His way of doing things so long ago must surely have been revised and modernized to fit the new age, they reasoned. Surely we can bring up the wheels of the cart in the grooves of our own chariot ruts and reach our city with greater ease.

The result, you all remember. When the Ark came to the Threshing Floor—the sifting, testing place—the Ark began to shake so violently that Uzzia felt duty bound to steady it and hold it down a bit with a restraining hand.

God's displeasure fell upon him like a bolt of lightning from the sky and he fell dead by the way. David was filled with fear and anger to think that when they were truly seeking to bring about the return of the glory of the Lord, that this shocking, humiliating reproach should be brought upon their work.

Leaving the Ark right there, he assayed to take it no further along the road toward Jerusalem, but returned to his city chagrined, humiliated and hurt.

The Ark turned aside into the humble home of Obed-Edom and found a welcome there. Prosperity, joy and blessing filled his household from the moment the Ark entered his open door. Such blessing and power were his, that the news thereof reached even unto the ears of the King in his palace. So David said: "We will go out and bring up the Ark to the City of David with gladness."

THE CHURCH OF CHRIST SETS OUT TO BRING BACK THE OLD TIME POWER

So with the Church of Jesus Christ, while they who have lost the anointing and spirituality, may not even miss the old time power of the Spirit and be contented with the superficial imitation of a card-signing, hand-shaking, oyster-suppering, moving-picturing religion, the Lord's Davids, who have the anointing and are in real touch of Heaven, realize the lack of power in her midst and are filled with determination to bring back the Ark and put it in its rightful place.

And so it was, that some fourteen years ago at the beginning of the "Latter Rain," great numbers of churches and people throughout the land began to cry mightily for the return of the Spirit. All-night prayer meetings were held in hundreds of churches. Thousands of letters, praying for a revival, were written; each one who received a letter was directed to write ten other letters and address them to as many Christian friends. Saints fell upon their faces and prayed:

"Lord send the old time power,
The Pentecostal power.
The flood gates of glory,
Upon us open wide.
Lord send the old time power,
The Pentecostal power,
Let sinners be converted,
And Thy Name glorified."

But though thousands prayed for the return of the old time power and outpouring of the Holy Spirit, few indeed were there who really expected Him to come, just as He came in the days of our forefathers.

Surely, we were living in a different age, they reasoned, and more modern, dignified and conservative methods might be employed in the bringing back of the Ark!

But some way, the new cart, whose wheels we attempted to keep in the grooves and ruts, which the wheels of our theological chariot wheels had carved, began to be violently shaken too, just as we came to the threshing floor. Disaster and even spiritual death smote those who would try to hold and restrain the movings of the Ark.

Shocked and troubled, the company returned, each man to his own house, leaving the Ark to turn aside into the humble (of-times dilapidated) house of Obed-Edom—the same often being a lowly cottage prayer meeting, or Mission Hall. Here 'twas met with open arms of welcome and thanksgiving.

Now the house of Obed-Edom, by the threshing floor, was not the intended resting place of the Ark, whose presence would be a gracious honor and benediction in the finest tabernacle, cathedral, or temple in the land.

The Ark has indeed rested by the threshing floor and there has been lots of chaff and dust of fanaticism and earthiness, which almost blinded and severely tried the more deeply thinking, spiritual and consecrated Christians in this humble abode. But no one could deny that the Ark was in the midst, or that the Glory of the Lord and the Holy Spirit of God hovered above the Mercy Seat. And, because the Ark was there and the real truth of the Spirit, many remained in the house of Obed-Edom and put up with the dust and chaff, because of its presence there.

Undoubtedly, hundreds were being saved, healed and filled with the Spirit in the old time Bible way and the Lord blessed the household till it came to the ears of hungry churches and godly pastors and they said: "Let us go forth to seek and bring back the old time power into the Tabernacle of the Most High."

And, bless God! There is a great stirring, a great move under foot to gather the people together in prayer, consecration, the study of the Word and then clad in the white linen, which is the righteousness of Jesus Christ, to go forth with singing, music, tabrets and shouting to bring back the Ark of the Lord, the power of the Holy Spirit and the Shekina Glory of the days of our forefathers.

Thus, having learned our lesson, we are going forth, washed in the blood of Jesus, having clean hands and a pure heart, taking the Word for our pattern and guide, that we may bring back the Ark of the Lord; not in the *new* cart, with Philistine methods, in our own ruts and grooves, but bearing it according to God's direction and pattern, making our bodies the resting place and conveyance of the blessed Holy Spirit.

Every church in the land, every tabernacle and temple, be it great or small, needs the power of the Holy Spirit and the glory of God today. The Ark can be caused to rest again in the midst of the people if we will go out in the right way to bring about its return. The church and the temple is its rightful habitation. It was not given for the house of Obed-Edom alone, but for the honored place in the midst of the hosts of Israel.

Today, a great company of ministering brethren and high priests, with their congregations of the righteous are going out with singing and shouting and "The Ark is coming up the road!"

O, can you not see it coming, brother? Can you not hear the shouting, sister? "And it shall come to pass in the last days," saith God, "I will pour out My Spirit upon *A-L-L* flesh." Not only upon Obed-Edom—but upon *all flesh.*

The great revival is coming. The first waves of glory are already here. The Ark is coming up the road. The Davids, who have the anointing, are yearning and stretching out their hands in prayer for the old time power. People everywhere are waking up to the need; the amen corner must take the place of pride and formality—the old "on-fire" testimony meeting, the place of the cantata and charade—the old glorious prayer meetings, the place of the oyster suppers and moving pictures. Unbelief must go and faith take its place. New fangled carts and methods must give way to the old time baptism of the Holy Ghost in the old time way.

It *must* come! It *is* coming! The advance guards of blessing, moving before the returning Ark are here already. Jesus is coming soon and he must find the Shekina glory of the Spirit of God resting in the tabernacle in old time power when He appears.

SOME WILL RIDICULE AND CRITICISE

But surely you don't believe that all churches—the proud, stiff, unrelenting churches, many of whom deny the very fundamentals of the Gospel and the virgin birth of Christ—surely you don't mean that they *all* will go out to bring back the Ark? Someone cries incredulously.

Alas, no! There will always be the David's wife class, who like Michael in the days of old, will remain in the house of formality and reserve, behind closed windows looking out upon the lively enthusiasm of the multitude, who sing, shout and cheer as David clad in a linen Ephod dances for joy before the returning Ark, and standing there looking out upon the scene, they themselves are not participating in, will despise the rejoicing company, in their hearts.

Poor Michael! Surely, in a way, she was to be pitied! To stand on the "other side" of a closed window, where no music can penetrate, or be wafted on the breeze—to see only the dance and seemingly foolish antics and *not* to hear the music—to have an incomplete contorted understanding of the whole proceeding—surely, these are grounds for pity.

But not only did Michael (type of those who will not believe and humbly go out to bring back the Ark) refuse to go herself, and not only did she despise David and his hosts in her heart, whom she considered to be extremists and fanatics, but she persecuted and ridiculed the whole thing, and said:

"How glorious is the King of Israel today, in the eyes of the handmaids of his servants, as one of the vain fellows!" In other words, "You made a pretty show of yourself out there before all the people singing, shouting yourself hoarse and dancing in a linen ephod! You must be proud of yourself, I must say! etc."

And so say the Michaels, who stand behind the windows today. Poor dears! Without hearing the music, they only see the "antics" of those overjoyed with the return of the Ark.

"The idea!" say they, "of this revival excitement! The idea of men and women trembling with conviction and running to the altars, and weeping penitent tears! The idea of this rising and shouting with joy, crying 'Hallelujah!' and 'Praise the Lord!' with a loud voice! What a display they are making of themselves! Why, it is not being done in this conservative day! The idea of people being healed, and baptized with the Spirit as they were in the Bible days. Preacher and people are you not ashamed?"

"Well, David, what about it? Were you ashamed?"

"And David said unto Michael, 'It was before the Lord, which chose me before thy father . . . therefore, will I play before the Lord. And I will yet be more vile than thus, and will be base in mine own sight: and of the maid-servants, which thou has spoken of, of them shall I be had in honor.' "

No! Walk in the Spirit of love, and of power, and of a sound mind, in the deep consciousness and leading of the Holy Spirit. Live the Spirit-filled life at home and in the secret place behind the scenes as well as in the throng and there is naught for which to be ashamed. "I will do this and more." This is only the beginning and the end is not yet, praise the Lord!

But in the coming days, even though the glory of God rested upon her husband, David, the criticising, scornful Michael was stricken barren till the day of her death. So today, those who ridicule and scoffingly reject the returning glory and power of the Spirit are stricken barren. Their altars are deserted, their amen corner gone, and the glory departed from their midst.

Yes, O yes! THE ARK IS COMING UP THE ROAD! It is even now on its way to many a temple and tabernacle. Oh, saints, can you see it coming? Then shout for joy! And as for you, dear Obed-Edom, don't be jealous, as you see it entering the temple, for you may come right along too as a spirit-filled doorkeeper and rejoice in the triumph of the Lord.

GOD'S DAVID.

"Now the Philistines gathered together their armies to battle, and stood on the mountain on one side. And Saul and the men of Israel stood on the other side and set the battle in array against the Philistines . . . and there was a valley between them. And there went out a champion, out of the camp of the Philistines, named Goliath of Gath. And he stood and cried I defy the armies of Israel this day—Give me a man that we can fight together. And when Saul and all Israel heard these words, they were dismayed and when they saw the man, they fled from him and were sore afraid." 1 Sam. 17.

I AM GAZING into the mirror of the Old Testament page tonight; and a battle is fought before me. Soldiers struggle and shout as I write. Army against army, line against line, the battle is set in array — in the types of the old are reflected the new, and I see the Church of today.

On the mountains of sin, the Satanic host stand, and their champion, Goliath of Gath, is the "Love of the World" who comes daily to stand to mock at the church and to laugh, saying:

"I've taken your young, and I've taken your old in my dance halls and theatres gay. Through my haunts of amusement, money-making and sin, I've emptied your altars today. I'm greater than God or His armies, I draw, I conquer and break. As a great looming menace, I tower o'er the church till its morale and courage I shake. And now I defy your armies—dare you to come and fight! You've lost your old time power, 'amen corner' and glory and light."

And as the "World" is defying the church taking captive its strength and its youth, I gaze on the hosts of Israel, who stand on the mountain of truth. Money and churches and armour, swords and helmets of brass have they, but the old time power is missing—faith and power have fled away. Their knees are smiting together. In dismay they stand helpless and weak, as the world walks deliberately into the church other captives and youths to seek.

But in the fields, God's preparing His David—type of the Spirit-filled few; making him daily victorious o'er the bear and the lion too. Making him faithful o'er "those few sheep," and in doing the little things, ere He brings him for great things into the camp, to honor His name before Kings. *God's David—Lord make US "God's Davids" as we gaze on this sweet yielded life, bringing food to the brethren and hope to the faint, and victory in the strife!*

* * * *

Only a slender lad he was, but over the mountains he sped; in his heart the Father's message, in his arms the life-giving bread prepared by the Father's loving hand, and sent to his sons at war.

"Bear them my message of comfort," said he, "and see how the battle goes. Inquire if they're gaining the victory, over their deadly foes. Fresh from the Father's table, bear this bread from my bountiful store, to my children who stand and fight today where battles rage and roar."

Lifting fearless eyes to the circling hills, for guidance and strength he prayed. Thus, into the camp at last he came where the battle was arrayed; to enquire of his elder brethren the victories they'd wrought for the King; to lift his voice with theirs to shout and make God's praises ring.

But he found them alas, with downcast heads and faces as black as a cloud. Defeat, not victory, had crowned their toil. They were giving, not gaining, ground.

"Child, what dost thou here?" they ungraciously ask. "With whom left you those few sheep? Thou art too weak and little, positions of trust to keep."

"I come at my Father's bidding—I come in my Father's name, He bade me bring you food and drink, and for this cause

I came. I come for news of victory—to see how the battle goes, and bear Him word that your chariot wheels pass over your deadly foes. But—where are the shouts of victory? And where the dance of praise? And where is the laurel that ought to crown the smiles of a victor's face? Why look ye so dejected? Why stand your armies still? Why do ye not rise and forward go, and scale the enemies' hill?"

"Ha! List to the stripling!" his brethren cry. "He does not understand, and would chide us, in his ignorance, for our fear of the Philistine's hand. He knows not the long days and nights racked with fear, nor how even hourly defeat draweth near.

"Look, child—see yon mount clad with Philistine's tents? Their armies in thousands against us are sent! They care not for God—they boast of their strength. They take our youths captive, and taunt us at length. And into that valley 'twixt their camp and ours, comes a giant before whom the strongest man cowers. His name is Goliath, and daily his cry:

"'Ha! Hosts of Israel, your power I defy! Where is your strength and where is your God and where is the man I can fight? I've taken your young and captured your lambs and broken their will in the palms of my hands. I've filled you with terror, till your knees quake with fear. If there's a man left among you, then let him now draw near.'

"Look, David—listen! There he stands even now. Before him the knees of the strongest man bow." His voice like a lion, his armour of brass, he towers o'er his fellows and could mow them like grass. The roar of his voice in the valley and hill, cause faces to blanch, hearts with terror to chill.

"Where is thy God? And where is His power? Why does He not fight for thee in this hour? Preach if you like but your power is fled. Pray if you will but your God is dead. Or—if He is living, then where is He now? Send a man who can cause me before Him to bow."

Straight, flushed and quivering at the insult to his God, stands David of Bethlemite, the seed of Jesse's rod. Righteous wrath falls on him, transforming the childish face with a look of stately grandeur and the calm of a soldier's grace.

"Who is this uncircumcised Philistine, that the armies of God he defies? To God he's but a grasshopper, with foolish chirps and cries. My God is a God of power, whom the heavens can not contain—this man but puny boaster whose heart is deceitful and vain.

"My God can break him asunder, as a twig is snapped from a tree. A breath from His nostrils, a word from His mouth can set His people free. Why do ye not go and kill him? Why cumbereth he the ground?"

Hearing the sound of the clear, young voice a multitude gather round, and word is taken by messenger and carried to Saul the King:

"What! Thinkest the lad that he hath power deliverance to bring? Go—fetch him at once before my face, I'm weary of tremblings and fear. If there's one with courage and strength and faith, then let him be brought me here. The enemy has gotten us beaten. Our young are led captive away. Our knees are smiting together in defeat and shame today. If this lad has a solution to the problem that baffles our hearts, let us humble ourselves and listen, as the knowledge he imparts. Sometimes, God uses the weak things, and the small to confound the wise, and those upon whom the Spirit dwells to work wonders before our eyes."

And, thus it was that before King Saul stood the little keeper of sheep, with the power of God upon him and a confidence strong and deep.

"Let no man's heart fail within him, because of this Philistine. Greater, stronger and wiser than he is this wonderful God of mine. Thy servant will go and fight him and cleave off his head in the fray, and still the voice that mocks and scorns and defies our God today."

"But child! Thou are not able—a youth art thou in years! What giveth thee this confidence and dissipates thy fears?"

"My confidence is in God, O King, and not in strength of mine, for I know that He is able to conquer this foe of thine. With vigilance and with tenderness, I've guarded my Father's sheep, and slain the lion and the bear that assayed on the flock to leap. I have walked before God and overcome in the secret place each day. 'Tis victories in the life at home that make victors in the fray. I've proven my God in the little things—my Lord hath never failed. Nor will He fail to deliver me from this boaster who mocks and rails."

"Then go, little lad, in the strength of your God. But put *our* armour on. Our helmet and sword, restrictions and creeds you now shall quickly don. Organization, ceremonies and forms, red-tape, regulations and rules, then go forth and fight for the King today, equipped with our man-made tools."

But God's David was lost in the great coat of mail, the sword hanging down to the ground. The helmet of brass bowed his head with its weight. In an armour of chain he was bound.

And he cried out: "O King—let me put these away. Let those who have proved them wear them today. Their weight and size my soul oppress, my footsteps they retard. The helmet is too great for my head. My freedom of vision is marred.

"Just as I am in my shepherd's dress, my staff and sling with me, O King I beseech thee let me go, in my simplicity. The Lord saveth not with sword or spear, for the battle is the Lord's. He giveth strength, not to the proud, but to them who trust His Word. If armour and ceremony were enough to win the day, long since we'd have been victorious and conquered in the fray."

So down in the valley went the shepherd lad and there in the lowly place, he took five smooth stones from the songful brook—faith, hope, love, prayer, and praise. And putting a stone in his "Word of God" sling he drew near the Philistine, crying:

"Come! Thou defier of God and His Word. Come, pit thy strength against mine. Come and see the end today of these proud words of thine!"

"What! What!" roared the giant. "Insignificant child! Am I a dog to be whipped with a stave? Thy body I'll cast to the fowls of the air and the beasts of the field and cave."

"Nay, but THY flesh shall be riven, till all the assembly shall know, that the Lord saveth not with the sword and with spear but the victory to *Him* we owe. Not by might nor by power is the battle won, but by My Spirit alone saith the Lord. Thou comest to me with a great coat of mail, with a spear, a shield and a sword; I come to thee in the Name of the Lord, the God thou hast dared to defy, with prayer and with faith, with assurance and power and Jehovah close by my side.

"Thou art great, O Goliath, and great is thy sway, as you challenge us in this hour. But the armies of God even now shall arise and return to their old time power. No more shalt thou stand crying: Where is thy God, and the power of yesterday. For a revival of faith will sweep our camps, in the dust of defeat thou shalt lay! Then *'God is with us'* shall be our cry, and, 'His power is on us *today*.' Not compromise, or worldly display, but His Spirit shall win in the fray."

And so he drew near—the mighty one, a type of the conquering 'World'—proudly defying the armies of God who stood with banners furled. And walking to meet him came David—type of the Spirit-filled few, baptized with the Spirit, endued with the power God's perfect will to do.

So they met in the valley of Elah in that decisive hour; the great man trusting in his strength, the lad in Jehovah's power. Suddenly through the sunlight whirled the little shepherd's sling. Through the air sped the stone like an arrow, sure as a bird on the wing till it sank deep in the Philistine's forehead, and he fell on his face to the ground. There David cut off his head with the giant's great sword which in his own sheath was found.

Then a mighty cheer from Israel's hosts cleft the air with its deafening roar—the God of their fathers still lived today, and the giant was no more. Confidence lending them wings of faith, down the hills with new courage they sped. When the Philistines saw that their champion was dead, they turned to a man and fled.

And the men of Israel and Judah pursued them and shouted that day, till they came to the gates of Elkron, unto Gath and the Shaaraim way. Their tents were despoiled, their power overthrown and God was the Victor supreme, and David returned to the City of God, with the head of the Philistine.

With dancing and singing and tabrets of joy the conquerers return was led. Women played joyful music and sang as they played, for the hosts that oppressed them were fled. "Saul hath slain his thousands; David his tens of thousands hath slain."

*But the song of the women displeased King Saul, for his heart was jealous and vain. And the next day he threw a javelin saying: "I will smite him to the wall." He was afraid —for the Lord was with David,—departed out of Saul.

†But God's David twice avoided the spear, its sharp point went astray. Within the palace and without, he behaved wisely every day. And all Israel and Judah loved David as they saw his wise daily life. And Saul set him over a thousand, and gave him his daughter to wife.

* * * *

The hours have come, the hours have gone—dawn floods the skies as I write. Through my window I see the rising sun kissing the hills with light. Another day has been ushered in with Philistines to kill, for the church of God and the powers of sin are encamped on either hill. The world again is defying the church—the church that's lacking power. *Lord, make US 'God's Davids'—God's Spirit-filled Davids, to fight for Thee in this hour.*

---

*"Saul hath slain his thousands, and David his **tens** of thousands." In other words, David with the anointing of God, was ninety per cent more efficient than Saul, who had lost the anointing and power. Is it possible that they who have the anointing—the baptism of the Holy Ghost—can be made ninety per cent more efficient today than they who have lost the old time power and glory?

How sad, therefore, that Saul did not repent, seek anew the face of the Lord and the old time power instead of allowing himself to be jealous because of the anointing of God's little David and throwing pointed javelins at him.

†O that we, as God's spirit-filled children, may like David of old deport ourselves daily with such wisdom and righteousness that even the critical "Sauls" may find us "safe and sane"—so deep in the love and power of God that they have no fault to find.

SOUL WINNING.

THE moment we have given our hearts to the Lord Jesus Christ we should become soul winners. "Follow Me and I will make you fishers of men."

Oh, the moment I gave my heart to Jesus—how that day stands out as the high light of my whole life!—there came into my very being a yearning to win souls for Him. It was a longing of such intensity, such white heat, such earnestness I had never known anything like it before. I wanted to be a soul winner. 'Twas the Lord that kindled that desire in my heart, for I never could have put it there myself. But it seemed a discouraging outlook. Who was I? Nothing but a little country girl, a farmer's daughter. How could I be a soul winner? But oh, I did want to win souls so very much for Jesus and even though I was nothing I just determined that I would give that little nothing to the Lord Jesus Christ who has promised to take the things that are naught to confound the things that are. And I cried, "Jesus, make me a soul winner."

Sometimes almost discouraged, it seemed as though I never could be one because I was so far away in Canada, so far out on the farm, I did not know where to begin. But oh, if I only could! There would sweep over me sometimes in prayer the fear I would never be a soul winner. I thought that would be the most terrible calamity that could ever befall a Christian and used to sing that song,

"Must I go and empty handed,
Thus my dear Redeemer meet,
Not one soul with which to greet Him,
Lay no trophies at His feet?"

As I prayed I seemed to picture the harvest day, that great, grand day when the gates of the beautiful city would be opened. I pictured Jesus standing at the gate of that celestial city, the Saviour with whom I had fallen in love, the Master to whom I had given my heart. I used to picture Him standing there welcoming the soul-winners home, the angels grouped behind Him ready to crown them with crowns set with many stars, souls they had won for Jesus. And yonder was the Victory Way leading up to the gate. Oh, I could see the warriors coming, Hallelujah! Every one of them was coming with rejoicing, bringing in the sheaves. I thought that I would feel so very badly, my heart would be hurt with a hurt that would never heal should I go to heaven empty-handed, not a soul with which to greet Him, no one that I had won for Jesus while all these other folk were cheering and bringing in their trophies. I feared that should I be empty-handed on the day when the saints come marching in, that I would draw back almost ashamed to go through the gates, and how troubled I would be, and that when He gazed questioningly upon me I would have to say:

"Dear Jesus, I love You. Jesus, I have been serving You, oh, really I have, Lord. I love You better than anything in all the world but I have not won a soul for You. My life has been wasted as far as soul-winning is concerned." I determined then and there by His grace to be a soul-winner. I never expected to preach, did not expect to do the great things. Oh, if I could but do the little things! I was so in earnest that I remember telling the Lord I would willingly go across the continent from Atlantic to Pacific and say to one sinner, "Jesus loves you," and to lead him to Christ. Oh, thank God that in a little measure at least He has made me a winner of souls.

I think that being a winner of souls is the most blessed calling, the most sacred calling, the highest vocation, the most honorable occupation a man or woman could follow. Have you ever won a soul for Jesus? If not, it is not too late. You can begin right now, praise the Lord!

As I was coming to this meeting this afternoon the chauffeur who is kindly driving for me, said, "Oh, sister, it was wonderful to see those people going to the altar last night. I was standing at the back of this building and I saw a young man there, under conviction. When you asked everyone who wanted to be a Christian to lift their hands he lifted both hands. But when you asked them to come forward he sat down." "Why didn't you go to him?" I asked. "I did not have a chance," he replied. "He was clear across the building. Several times he tried to get up, then sat down, but before I could reach him he unbuttoned his overcoat, took it off, threw it across the seat, got to his feet and fairly ran to the altar."

Praise the Lord, Hallelujah! You have wonderful opportunities in this meeting to become a soul-winner. There is somebody sitting next to you now, I wonder if they are a Christian. Have you tried to find out? Somebody sitting right behind you, somebody sitting right in front of you. You can win souls this afternoon for the Lord Jesus Christ.

When we set out to be a soul-winner so very often we look away on yonder somewhere in the future. Distant fields always look more green. But right here, now, the waters are troubled, seasons of refreshing are coming from the presence of the Lord. A mighty flood tide of revival is rolling over our heads.

"He that winneth souls is wise." Thank God for the opportunity of being a soul-winner! It is a wonderful thing to be an artist. It is a wonderful thing to be able to paint great, beautiful pictures on canvas, but it is a much more wonderful thing to be a brave soldier in the army, to be a captain that leads his troops forward into victory, to catch up the flag from the hand of some fallen comrade and plunge forward in the fray winning great victories for one's country. But it is a still more wonderful thing to be a victor for the Lord Jesus Christ, going into the enemy's ranks, taking captive soldiers from its ranks and leading them as love slaves of the Lord Jesus Christ. I would rather be a winner of souls, a brave soldier for Jesus, than I would to win the greatest earthly conquest and receive great medals.

Oh, dear hearts, have you ever won a soul for Jesus? Have you ever really led anyone to the feet of the Saviour? If not, praise God, now is your opportunity. The Lord wants to help you. "He that winneth souls is wise."

THE UNWISE BARBER

If you want to be a soul-winner you are going to need skill and wisdom. You are going to need the faith and the power and the help of the Lord Jesus Christ. You have all heard the story of the barber who wanted to be a soul-winner. He was converted at the meeting so happily. They said, "Now Brother, you have been saved but you are not saved to yourself alone, go out and win other people for Jesus." "Oh, I hope I can," said the man. "Of course you can," they replied. "You have a barber shop and people will be in there all day long. When shaving a man you have a wonderful opportunity to tell him to prepare to meet his God." "All right," he said; "I will certainly do so."

The next morning a man sat in the barber's chair. All the time his heart was going thumpety thump, jumpety jump. How was he to talk to that man about Jesus, what should he say? He took his barber's brush and stirred up the lather, and all the time he was thinking. "What can I say to that man, how can I get up my courage? Here is a man whose soul is worth more than all the silver, all the gold, all the rubies in the world put into one. Lord, give me courage to say something." But he had the man all lathered, had not thought what to say. He took up his razor and began to strop that, getting it sharper and sharper. "What in the world can I say to that man?"

Finally he drew a long breath, straightened himself, and determined to make a plunge before his courage waned.

He went over to the man with two leaps and a bound and, waving the razor over his head, cried: "Brother, are you prepared to die?" The poor man was so alarmed he leaped to his feet and ran out the door with the lather on his face, thinking the man was intending to kill him.

Now, we cannot go at it like that. If we want to be a winner of souls we must be wise, we must have skill, tact. Oh, yes, it takes skill to be a winner of souls, it takes tact, it takes wisdom, praise the Lord! But it takes more than any of these, more than skill and wisdom and tact.

THE SILVER NET OF LOVE

One of the greatest things you need in order to be a soul-winner is love. If you want really to be a soul-winner for the Lord Jesus Christ you need to have on a robe of love that will cover you from head to foot—the love of the Lord Jesus Christ. You must first of all have given your heart to the Lord Jesus Christ and have put your hand in the hand of the Master. You must have sought His face, not only singing it but meaning, "Draw me nearer, nearer to Thy blessed bleeding heart." Oh, it is when we get close to that bleeding heart, that heart divine, broken for mankind, that, Hallelujah, some of the love that overflows from the heart divine comes atrickling down and fills these little hearts of ours, and praise God, ere long, they are running over.

Oh, we need to get close to the Lord Jesus Christ, we need such a baptism of love for souls as Jesus had. Then we should see through the eyes of Jesus and feel through the heart of Jesus. You say people would not know it? Yes, they will. Love bears a message all its own. The greatest secret of soul-winning is that of having the real love of God and the love of souls upon our hearts.

I know so many precious ministers winning souls for Jesus who have the baptism of love. I know other dear Christian workers who have not or they have effectively concealed it if they have. We may have our training, our theology and we need it, praise the Lord. True, we have training in the Bible, true, we may be just as straight as a die. Our teaching, our doctrine, may have the ring of solid gold: We may stand for the fundamentals of the Gospel, for the inspiration of Scripture, the virgin birth of Jesus Christ, the Atonement, the resurrection and our Lord's return; we may preach it right from the shoulder. If we just make our preaching theology, even though our theory is absolutely correct, and have not the love, some way we do not get the results.

You can tell if you have that love when you are winning souls for Jesus. It seems to me sometimes when preaching I have not the love I ought to have. I do want more. I am nothing, I am not setting myself up as an example. Jesus is the example. Yet with that little love that He has given me it seems to me sometimes when I am preaching to sinners my heart is bleeding for them, I am trying to blink back the tears, trying to keep on smiling at them, yet my heart is breaking with longing to see them come to Jesus while I am talking about Him and His goodness, glory, mercy, and love. I feel while I am speaking in the Spirit as though a beautiful, shimmering silver net was going out, out, out. Then at a certain time in my sermon, I see the shimmering, silver love net dropping and going around the people, then at altar call fairly feel the tugging of nets full to the bursting as strong and willing hands help me pull these souls to land.

If you want to be a soul winner get the love of the Lord Jesus in your heart. But Sister, how will I get it if I don't feel it? Just come close to Jesus, seek His face, put your all upon the altar, ask Him to draw you so very close to His heart that that love of His just fills your heart for a lost and a dying world. And oh, when He fills you with His Holy Spirit you know the first fruit of the Spirit is love. It doesn't matter what other gifts we have, speak with tongues, heal the sick, raise the dead, perform every miracle, if we haven't love we are nothing. Oh, Lord, give us a love like Thine. Have you that love, Sister? Have you that love, Brother? If not, let us come and get it. It is the love of Jesus, the Christ.

If you want to be a soul winner for Jesus don't start with a hammer or club. Don't start talking against churches and ministers. Refuse to see anybody or anything but the Lord Jesus Christ. "I know, but so many are against me," you say. Never mind. If God is for us who can be against us?

THE MIDDLE OF THE ROAD

If we want to be a soul winner we will have to be a middle of the roader, glory to Jesus. Especially when we come into a city-wide revival campaign lots of us have our own ideas, theories, particular side line of doctrine. If you want to win souls in the greatest, widest sense of the word drop everything for a little while, just fix your eyes upon Jesus, the crucified Lamb of God, bleeding, dying, hanging on the tree, saying, "Come unto Me all the ends of the earth and be ye saved."

How I long to stick to the Bible—close to Jesus Christ. One time a man was going to a certain place and was in a great hurry to get there, rather late train, about ready to pull out. He got a ticket, saw the first car, got on it. It was packed full of people, and many were hanging on to straps. He looked at the car and said, "This is no place for me." He went through and the last car was empty, not a soul in it. "I am smart to find this out." He congratulated himself and patted himself on his chest, for here he had elbow room and could spread himself out—a private car all to himself. He waited for a while for the train to go. Waited for twenty minutes, looked at his watch. Ten minutes more. To his amazement the rest of the train had gone and he had a private car all to himself. Indignantly calling to a railroad official he demanded an explanation as to why he was left behind.

THE PRIVATE CAR

"Why," explained the man, "that car was not going with the rest of the train. It had been placed there so that if there was too big an overflow from the other cars they could hook it on at a moment's notice. You thought you were better than the rest, wanted to have elbow room and a private car. You have it now and you can sit in it for three hours and wait for the next train."

So many of us want to have a private car, teach our own little doctrine, non-essential feasts, sabbaths, forms. We can have a nice big private car all to ourselves and sit around till the next revival comes. If you want to be with the moving train, keep in the crush, praise the Lord. Keep with those who believe in Jesus Christ, the Saviour who died to cleanse us from sin. Lift up this bleeding, dying Lamb of Calvary, this resurrected Lord. Make the cross the theme and the blood the test of fellowship and nothing else, Hallelujah! Oh, then, glory to Jesus, we are going to see souls saved, people washed in the blood of Jesus and brought to Him. But let us make souls the great important thing all of the time. If we want to win souls for Jesus I believe we need to be filled with the Holy Spirit to equip us for service and endue us with power from above.

POWER FROM ON HIGH

"Mrs. McPherson, do I understand you to mean by that I should not attempt to win souls till I have received this enduement of power?" Not at all. The moment you become a Christian that moment turn around and help bring the one next to you to the Lord Jesus Christ. Don't wait for anything, become a soul winner right there and then. But oh, how this blessed incoming of the Holy Spirit will strengthen you, guide you, fill you with wisdom and love and holy zeal to lead men and women to Jesus. I believe the filling of the Holy Spirit ought to be intensely practical, glory to Jesus. Ought to be something to make us more level-headed, sound, sane, wholesome soul winners for the Lord Jesus Christ than ever in our lives before; not something to put us up on a pedestal where we say, "I thank God I am not as other men! I thank my Lord I am holier than others! I have been filled with the Spirit." No, that is not the idea. When we come to Jesus under the blood with open hearts praying, "Breathe upon me, Holy Spirit, with Thy love my heart inspire," and are filled with the Holy Spirit, praise God, then we are going back down amongst the people, not making ourselves holier than they because we have gone a little further, but we will return to practical soul winning for the Lord Jesus Christ.

You remember the three disciples, Peter, James and John, how they had been closer to Jesus than the other nine. We read that Jesus took them up into a high mountain apart. They had been climbing hour after hour. At last they had reached the summit: There you know what happened. Jesus was transfigured before them and oh, His face did shine as the sun and His raiment was white as the light. They were so blessed that all of them fell down under the power and God the Father spake saying, "This is My beloved Son, hear ye Him." Peter was so delighted.

"Oh, Lord, this is a grand experience, the most wonderful place! Jesus, do you know what I would like to do?" "No, Peter." "I would like to build three Tabernacles up here, one for Yourself and two for your heavenly visitors. Oh, Lord, let us stay up here on the mountain. This is a grand place."

"No, Peter, you are wrong. I have not brought you up the mountain of blessing, Peter, for you to stay up here, and hug yourself, and consider what a grand fellow you are, and separate yourself from the throng. That is not the idea, Peter. I have brought you up here, glorifying Myself before your eyes to make you a more practical, level-headed winner of souls down in the valley. Peter come here a moment." "What is it, Lord?" "What do you see down there, Peter?" "I see a valley deep and wide." "Look closer. What do you see in the valley?" "Lord, I see a great multitude of people in the valley." "For whom are they waiting, Peter?" "They are hungry for You, Jesus, Thou blessed bread of Life." "For what are they thirsting, Peter?" "For the water of salvation, Jesus, which only You can give."

"Look, Peter, who is at the front of that great audience?"

"Why, there is a man with a little demon-possessed son in his arms. Poor man, his son is bound by the devil. Oh, Jesus, isn't that too bad?" "Yes, it is, Peter, but who is able to set him free?" "Only You, Jesus." "Whom else do you see, Peter?" "A mother with the dearest little girl in her arms, whose face is flushed with fever, her eyes bright as two little stars." "Who can heal her, Peter? Can the doctors do it, Peter?" "No, Lord, they are able to do lots of things but are not able to help that little girl." "Who can do it, Peter?" "You can, Jesus, for unto You is given all power in heaven and in earth."

"What else do you see, Peter?" "Oh, such a lot of folks, Lord, all bowed down with burdens, some people with a great big load of sin more than they can bear, some that are motherless, fatherless, friendless, discouraged, just on the brink of giving up. Jesus, don't let us stay here any longer. Come, let us go back into the valley and bring them the message of Jesus the mighty to save, able to deliver, able and willing to break every chain of the devil and set the prisoner free."

They went their way on down from the top of the mountain into the valley. They did not boast, "We have got to pull out from you people and start a new place because we have this deeper experience. You have not been up on the mountain as we have. We cannot associate with you any longer."

No—but let us go back to our various posts of duty when this campaign is over so filled with the Spirit that the fires of the Lord's altars will be revived, people saved, healed and demons cast out, and those taken captive by the devil delivered. Don't you want to be a soul winner, dear? Then you had better come up on this mountain, you had better take time to pray, to seek the face of the Lord till He is just glorified before you, for it is only when Jesus is glorified in our own eyes that we are able to make Him glorious to others. We must ourselves have had the vision before we can make the vision real to others. We must have the glory in our heart before we can give it to others. You know it is not out of your head the waters flow that really bring souls to Jesus. It is when we have been filled until out of our innermost being there flows rivers of living water and "this spake He of the Spirit."

IN THE HUMBLE PLACE

Dear little children, it does not matter who you are. You may not have a great education, you may not have the great opportunities, but if you are only a farmer's daughter or son, if you are even a coal miner like Evan Roberts; just a baseball player like Billy Sunday; a poor common laborer sweeping the streets; a wife whose babies come at eventide and put their paddies up and pray, "Now I lay me down to sleep," there is an opportunity for you to be a soul winner, praise the Lord.

"Mrs. McPherson, you make me feel so sad. I wish that I could be a soul winner, but Sister, I am a mother. I have my children to care for. I haven't time to go out and hold meetings." Of course you haven't. But you can work for Jesus right in your homes, right in your church, right in the Sunday School and right among those darling children. Some time ago a minister went to call on a certain mother who was mourning, "Oh, pastor, I feel so discouraged!"

"Why, my dear sister, you have always been so happy, what makes you discouraged now?"

"Because it seems to me as though I have never had to do anything for the Lord. I did want to be a soul winner, pastor. But all my life has been taken up with sewing, washing the dishes, sweeping the floor and tending the family. Now I am old, my hair as white as snow. Soon I'll be laying my head upon my pillow for that last long sleep. Oh, pastor, I wish I could have done something for Jesus."

"Wait a minute, my dear Sister," replied the kindly old minister. "Where is your oldest son, George, now?"

"Why, you know where he is, pastor. He's on the Yunan River in China as a missionary."

"And where is your next son, Benny?"

"Why, you know where he is, Pastor, he just sailed eight months ago to go to China to be with my eldest son. Why, Pastor, you must be forgetting."

"Umhum, and let's see now, where is Sammy today?"

"Sammy went to Africa, out there in the midst of those people in darkest heathendom, teaching them about the Light of the world, that is Jesus."

"Yes, and where is your youngest son, your little boy you have loved so?"

"Why, Pastor, you know where he is. He is right here at home with me. He said to me the other day, 'Mother, I want to tell you something, I think it will make you happier before you go, mother. I am never going to leave the little old home with the roses climbing over it until the Lord has taken you home. I am going to stay here and look after you. The other three boys have gone, mother, but I think you need me. I have always been your baby, mother. But I thought it might make you happy to know that when you are gone, mother, I am going over to Africa and work with Samuel. I am going over there and stand with him because he says he is alone and needs more help and I am going to help him.' All of my boys are doing well, but I wish I could do something."

"But mother, don't you realize those boys are winning souls every day? They have had a family altar, they have felt the caress of a mother's hand, they have heard you pray, they have seen your tears and now your children have gone out to do the work of God. Oh mother, don't you realize you are to share their reward? God bless you."

She clasped her dear old wrinkled hands together, on her face was that beautiful look of peace, that peace that passeth understanding, the joy that only a soul winner knows. She thought that she had given nothing, but she had given everything to be a real soul winner. Even as Christ gave His life for us, so we must give our all for Him. You cannot have a selfish heart and be a real successful soul winner. Give your all to Him and He will give His all for you.

TWO MEN WHO GAVE

Some time ago a minister, whose daughter was called to go to China, felt as though his heart were torn and desolate, he could scarcely bear it. He tried to be brave, but his friends saw his heart bled. At last the beautiful daughter, his only child that had filled the home with smiles, music and joy, was leaving for China. Next day when the friend went to visit him he found the father smiling and happy. "What has happened?" he asked. "When I was here before you looked so downcast. I almost feared to come today."

"I will tell you," he replied, "when I went down to the big ocean liner this morning to see my daughter set sail for China, a man came along. Both of us stood watching the boat go out. The man stood there with his hands in his pockets whistling. His face lit up with a smile. He must have some one he loved on that boat, too. 'Brother,' I asked, 'whom have you on that boat that is going to China?' 'Why, don't you know? I have just given $100,000 to send to the missionaries over there. Going to build mission stations, help them spread out their borders, win many souls. Yes, sir, I gave $100,000 and it's all on that boat.' "

The other man said, "I did not have a hundred thousand dollars to give, sir, but I have given my daughter, that little ewe lamb I loved so and cherished close to my heart. She is going to China."

"Oh," said the other man, "I thought I had given something, but sir, I have given nothing. My hundred thousand dollars is not as much as your daughter's little finger. It is you who have given all." Oh, if we want to be soul winners we must be willing to give our all to Jesus, to make a whole hearted surrender, body, soul and spirit.

I remember when Jesus had called me first to go and preach the Gospel, my darling little mother has always stood back of me, God bless her. Isn't it a wonderful thing to have a praying mother? When I was going out into the work mother said, "Aimee," (I was just to be married to the Evangelist, under whom I had been converted), "Aimee, who is going to buy your things? You know Robert hasn't any salary."

"Mother, I know it."

"Who is going to buy your shoes, your dresses, and look after you?"

"I don't know, but I will ask the Lord about it." I prayed before my open Bible; Jesus spake from the pages, "Child, take no thought of what you shall eat, drink or put on. The Lord knows you have need of these things. Consider the lilies, they toil not, neither do they spin, and yet Solomon in all his glory was not arrayed like one of these."

I said, "Oh, thank you, Jesus." And from that day to this I have never worried one second about what I had to eat, drink and wear. Many a time we have gotten down to the last 5-cent piece, then given that away. For two years I lived in a tent, without a board floor under my feet. Oftentimes I would get up and put on my clothing wet with the dews and rain. But Hallelujah, Jesus always protected and supplied. It is glorious to be a Christian, glorious to be a soul winner. Oh, if I could just take a little bit out of my heart this afternoon and sow the seed in your hearts, my dears, kindle the flame of love and zeal for souls during this revival, till from the altar of every life exultant flames would leap high into the open heaven, how happy I would be.

O Jesus, speak to every heart this afternoon and burn this text upon every mind. Let us repeat it aloud together: "He that winneth souls is wise."

THE DESCENDING MANTLE

THERE was a prophet in the land! The fame of His doings had gone broadcast through the country. A prophet sent from Jehovah was he, whose torch had been fired at the altars of the living God. The pitch black midnight of unbelief closing in like some impregnable smothering pall, succeeded not in extinguishing or diminishing that light, but in making it shine the brighter. The lashing winds of doubt and idolatry but fanned and scattered it abroad till other torches caught the flame and the schools of the prophets were formed.

A Prophet of God was in the land. And because of the darkness of unbelief that shrouded the sky, and because of his faith in El Shaddai, he loomed as a great central character, radiating light, and trust and firm unshaken confidence in the everlasting, omnipresent power of the great I AM. As flashes lightning through the gloom, so flashed the miracles and the fulfilled prophecies of this man of faith. His every word and gesture was a burning rebuke to a backsliding, idolatrous nation, which called upon gods of stone and clay. His very name, Elijah, was a challenge meaning, "Jehovah — He is God."

His prediction of the drought, his preservation and the miraculous manner in which he was fed by the brook Cherith, his raising of the widow's son to life, his rebuilding of the altar and calling down fire from heaven on Mount Carmel, his confounding of the worshippers of Baal, his praying down the abundance of rain on the parched fields, his fearless denunciation of Ahab and Ahaziah, and his consistent, valiant stand for Jehovah, flashed and glowed through the darkness, and were enough, it would seem, to attract and convince the whole nation; but he was like as unto the Master Himself as "the light that shineth in the darkness; and the darkness comprehendeth it not."

For a wonderful type of the Christ is Elijah, of the Christ whom men called a mighty Prophet sent from God, as they listened to His burning messages and gazed upon His miracles, but who was in deed and in truth the very Son of God, the only begotten of the Father. How it towers—that wonderful life of the Lord of glory—towers as a light, a hope, a beacon, bidding men look up from their groveling in the darkness and the mire of sin's unbelieving night, arise and loose them from the bands and burdens of despair—look and believe, ask and receive, and then leave all to follow Him up the shining road that leads to Home and Glory. O, blind of eye, and slow of heart, why could they not believe?

There were those, however, who believed on Elijah, even as there were many who believed upon Christ of whom he is so wonderful a type, and became disciples studying in the school of the Prophets at Bethel and at Jericho.

THE CALL AND CONSECRATION OF ELISHA

There were others, also, who believed, and but waited for his call, and such an one was Elisha, the son of Shaphat, who was plowing in the field. Long, straight furrows lay behind, skillfully and with straight eye he guided his twelve yoke of oxen which went before, when suddenly, a man passed by—the very man methinks, who occupied his thoughts—and cast his mantle o'er the shoulders of this tiller of the soil.

Turning and catching a glimpse of Elijah's face, the heart of Elisha must have leaped for joy for the words that burst from his lips were these:

"Let me, I pray thee, kiss my father and my mother, and then I will follow thee."

Ah, how sacred memories stir within our breast as we read of Elisha's call! How the tears spring to our eyes unbidden, and we feel a tug at our hearts as we remember the day—O, happy day of days—when our Elijah, Jesus Christ, the King of heaven, passed through the field of life in which we toiled and cast His own dear mantle o'er our lives. And that face! O, brother, say, do you remember how it shone fairer than the morning, brighter than the dawn? And that voice sweeter than the rushing waters, and His smile! O, sister, do you remember how our hearts melted and brake, when He said, "Follow Me!" And how we cried out: "Goodbye, dwelling place of unbelief and sin—Goodbye, land of doubts and haunts of pleasure—Farewell, seat of the scornful and counsel of ungodly men—Farewell, bright lights and empty tinsel—gaiety of sin's delusive path! I've seen the face of Jesus, the heaven-lit face of the wondrous Son of Man; I've seen His smile, I've heard His voice, and my being thrilled as He cast o'er me His mantle of mercy, love and power—henceforth will I follow Him!

"Oh, tarry just a moment, Master dear, till I bid adieu to every earthly tie, for I love Thee more than father, or mother, or houses, or lands, or money, or rubies, or honor, or fame, and by Thy grace I will follow Thee!

"Let me love Thee, Jesus,
Take my life forever,
Nothing but Thy service,
My soul can satisfy."

Quick farewells were said to home and kindred; farewell to the new plowed fields and broad meadows that had been the border of his horizon; and he was ready to follow the stranger with the light of heaven on his face, and the peace of God in his eyes.

But wait! One thing more—every bridge must be burned behind him, the consecration complete.

"And he returned back from him, and took a yoke of oxen, and slew them, and boiled their flesh with the instruments of the oxen, and gave unto the people, and they did eat."

Elisha did not leave the gateway of the past ajar. He closed it tightly and destroyed the key. No half heartedness here, but a mighty determination to follow all the way! No arranging to leave the plow handy by the fence and the oxen in the stall, so that if he regretted the step or failed he could return and be none the loser! Oh no, he slew the oxen and boiled their flesh upon the flames of the burning plow handles, harness and instruments of the oxen. No prevarication here! No playing with the past! No turning back now, praise the Lord! And he *"gave unto the people, and they did eat."* There will always be food and strengthening for the people to be rendered from a hundred per cent consecration such as that of Elisha.

HIS DISCIPLESHIP AND TRAINING

"Then he arose, and went after Elijah, and ministered unto him."

Why, these very words might be written over the lives of

Peter and John, and Matthew, and Paul, and you and me, and any other follower of the meek and lowly Jesus!

"Then he arose." Thank God that we did too!

"And went after him." Yes, "since mine eyes were fixed on Jesus, I've lost sight of all beside; so enchained my spirit's vision, gazing on the Crucified."

"And ministered unto him." Precious life art, O ministering life—ministry of prayer, and praise, and service, love and devotion, strength, time, talents, loving words, self-sacrificing deeds, living the life, treading in the Master's footsteps, sharing the cross, drinking the cup, fellowshipping His sufferings, tasting the power of His resurrection—a life that pays an hundredfold both in this world and in the world to come!

O'er mountain peaks of transfiguration glory; down deep into valleys where the shadows lie; o'er fertile fields; o'er deserts bare and waste, Elisha, the disciple, pressed hard after Elijah the Master—even as the disciples of Jesus followed daily the footsteps of their Lord, gazing into His face, drinking in His words, inscribing His teaching upon the tablets of their hearts, beholding His miracles, imbibing His faith and power, and receiving commandments and instructions as to the carrying on of the work when He should be caught up unto His Father's throne.

But at last, the ministry of Elijah, even as the ministry of Christ Himself, was to come to a close, but His work was not to end, for another, even Elisha, was being fitted to take up his ministry where he had laid it down, and go out and go on with the work even as the disciples had been taught and fitted by the Lord Jesus Christ to take up His ministry and carry the glorious Gospel to the ends of the earth.

The knowledge of his master's coming ascension was not kept secret from Elisha but was revealed to him, even as the message of Christ's coming glorification and ascension was made known to the disciples. And the same great longing filled his heart which filled that of the adoring disciples and fills the heart of every true follower of the Lord Jesus:

"Oh, to be like Thee! Oh, to be like Thee!
Blessed Redeemer—Pure as Thou art!
Come in Thy sweetness, Come in Thy fulness,
Stamp Thine own image deep on my heart."

And so as the Master departed from Gilgal and made His way to Bethel and Jericho, there to give final instructions and comfort to the members of the school of the prophets which he had formed, Elisha pressed hard after him. Oh, methinks I can see that set determination to go all the way, written upon that strong, spiritual face. Talking little but following hard; heart aching at the loss he was soon to sustain, but pressing on with that quiet, unswerving purpose that none could dissuade and none could move; lips firmly set with his fixed resolution to press on to the very end. But though from his lips there come few words, the cry in his heart is as a great shouting that rises from between the lines of this second chapter of II Kings, and fills the heavens, and sets the hills to echoing—

"If I have been chosen to do my master's work, I must have my Master's power! If I am to carry on His ministry, I must keep my eyes fixed upon Him till I see Him go and His mantle falls upon me!"

O dear heart, you and I, even as was the early Church, are called to carry on the ministry of our Lord and Master, Jesus Christ, of whom Elijah is such a glorious type. But if we would do His works we must needs have the same power by which the Lord and the disciples wrought them—the power of the Holy Ghost. There is but one way to receive, and Elisha surmounting every difficulty, true in every test, unfalteringly took that way.

FROM GILGAL TO BETHEL

The first test came when Elijah said unto Elisha: *"Tarry here, I pray thee, for the Lord hath sent me to Bethel."* Methinks I hear the enemy whisper: "Stay here, and take things easy, Elisha. Let down a little on your praying, and seeking, and following hard upon the footsteps of the Master. Would you not rather consult your own feelings and the desires of the flesh a little, Elisha? You know one must look out for one's self not to overdo. The day has been hot, the journey long. Would you not like to take back just a little of the consecration vow you made o'er the burning plow handles and boiling oxen where you pledged body, soul and spirit in unstinted giving and discipleship?"

But no! In the cry that is wrung from the lips of Elisha,

is poured forth the determination and the longing that is surging and filling his heart to the bursting:

"As the Lord liveth, and as thy soul liveth, I will not leave thee."

Oh, can you say it, Brother, Sister? Is this same cry in your heart?

> "Jesus, I my cross have taken,
> All to leave and follow Thee;
> Perish every fond ambition,
> By Thy grace I'll follow Thee!"

It matters not that the world fails to understand; it matters not that to them the cross is but a reproach; it matters not that I am leaving ease, public opinion, worldly standing, fleshly desires and earthly store behind—As the Lord liveth, I will not leave Thee! I am going on to Bethel, which means the "House of God."

And the sons of the prophets that were at Bethel came forth to Elisha and said unto him: 'Knowest thou that the Lord will take away thy master from thy head today?' And he said: 'Yea, I know it; hold ye your peace.'"

Oh, I see that white, set determination of his face grow stronger—"Yea, I know it, sons of the prophets, I know it! And my heart is aching with the sense of loss I shall soon sustain. But do not talk about it, and do not ask me to come in and talk with you. I desire not to talk and visit, or even hold friendly conversation. My soul is burning with earnest prayer—Hold your peace—Do not distract my thoughts from my petition, or take mine eyes from off my master till I receive of His power, and His mantle descends upon me."

BETHEL TO JERICHO

The second test came when Elijah said unto him:

"Elisha, tarry here, I pray thee; for the Lord hath sent me to Jericho."

Has the test ever come to you, dear child of God? "You have done well, you have turned your back upon sin, and have followed the Lord to Bethel—the house 'of God.' He knows that you love Him, you are a Christian and doing your duty. 'Tarry here,' and go no further up the hot and dusty road of heart-searching, and earnest petitioning. Here is a cool and restful place. The other sons of the prophets are here—if they are content to here abide, and do not follow further, why can you not do the same? Tarry here and sleep a little."

And have you cried out, as did Elisha, the second time: "As the Lord liveth, and as thy soul liveth, I will not leave thee!"

"I'd rather walk with Jesus alone,
And have for my pillow, like Jacob, a stone;
Living each moment with His face in view,
Than turn from my pathway, and fail to go through."

Then it can be said of you as of Elijah and Elisha: *"So they came to Jericho"*—which means "a fragrant place." Be willing to go through with Jesus o'er the hot and dusty highway, and you will find yourself in the shadow of His great love—in a fragrant place. Fragrant? Ah yes! With such fragrance as only the Rose of Sharon, and the Lily of the Valley can give forth! Fragrant—with new vines which put forth dewy leaves and tender grapes, as He leads you through the garden of His grace and there gives you of His loves, mandrakes, pomegranates, apples, and shows us at our gates, all manner of pleasant fruits both new and old, laid up for His beloved, His overcoming Bride.

So they came to Jericho—a fragrant place. And oh, it is only they who really go through and press on with the Lord, with hearts that pant like the hart after the water brooks, that really reach the fragrant place, wherein our own lives are made as "a garden inclosed, a spring shut up, a fountain sealed; where the plants are an orchard of pomegranates, with pleasant fruits; camphire, with spikenard, Spikenard and saffron; calamus and cinnamon, with all trees of frankincense; myrrh and aloes, with all the chief spices."

And it is of such persevering, consecrated overcomers that the Lord can say, "I am come into My garden, My sister, My spouse: I have gathered My myrrh with My spice"—you have shared with Me the myrrh and bitterness of My sufferings and known of Me in the spices and frankincense of My resurrection. O precious place of fragrance, how sweet is thy reward! O blessed, blessed Jesus, all along life's pilgrim journey, let me ever walk with Thee.

"And the sons of the prophets that were at Jericho came to Elisha, and said unto him, Knowest thou that the Lord will

take away thy master from thy head today? And he answered, Yea, I know it; hold ye your peace."

It is as though they had said, "There is no need of your going further, Elisha. Your master has now completed his ministry, his miracle working days are o'er, the clouds will soon receive him out of your sight, and you would be left away out there in the wilderness somewhere, all alone. Better stay with us, Elisha, for our master is going down, down to the chilly waters of the Jordan, you know, and this will be the greatest test of all."

TWIXT JERICHO AND JORDAN

"Tarry, I pray thee, here," added Elijah, *"for the Lord hath sent me to Jordan."*

And for the third and last time Elisha settled the question, stood the test, and steadfastly declared,

"As the Lord liveth, and as thy soul liveth, I will not leave thee."

Oh, how the next five words thrill our beings, set themselves to music, and make our hearts to sing!—

—*"AND THEY TWO WENT ON."*

Let the rest of the world take their ease in peaceful habitations—but *"they two ment on!"*

Let the sons of the prophets fail to follow to the end of the way and "stand afar off"—but "they two went on!"

Let those whom He loved, criticise, misunderstand, and declare that his white-heated zeal was fanaticism—but "they two went on!"

And oh, the unspeakable joy of sacred companionship, as they traveled that road together, hand in hand, heart of master and disciple throbbing as one! Who can lift the veil of fathom the depth of love and confidences exchanged between Jericho and Jordan? Who can tell the intimate glimpses into the soul of the prophet which Elisha caught; the final words of instruction and advice which he received; or how his heart burned within him as they walked by the way, even as the hearts of the disciples burned on Emmaus' way, when their Master, Jesus Christ, walked and talked with them, before His ascension into the clouds of heaven?

"And fifty men of the sons of the prophets went, and stood to view afar off: and they two stood by Jordan."

Brother, Sister, in which company are you? With which of the three groups do you stand?

I. Far away lie the worldly, sinful, unbelieving masses in home and field; busily occupied with the things that are of the earth, earthly; totally unaware, uncaring, and unappreciative of the opportunity to walk with the Master.

II. Separated from the world by their faith and love of the Master, are the sons of the prophets. They are students of the prophetic Word. They know and cherish the law of the Lord, and worship the God of Abraham, Isaac and Jacob. Yet, instead of pressing close, and following hard,—they "stand to view afar off." And not only do they stand afar off themselves, but they sometimes seek to discourage and dissuade Elisha from going on.

How many do we know today who "stand to view afar off?" —stand back and say, "Well, I am going to watch this thing, and see which way the matter will fall, and then get in on the winning side." Are you one who stands to view afar off, as a mere spectator, and an onlooker upon those who teach and seek a deeper life of consecration, and the descending mantle of the Master?

III. Or are you in the third company, of whom we read, that while the sons of the prophets "stood to view afar off— they two stood by Jordan."

Multitudes in the world—fifty devoted lives standing afar— but only two that pressed on to the Jordan. And ah, my dear hearts, they who go through and receive the mantle of power, will find that as they press on there will be many a time that the company will be narrowed down to two—"My Lord and I."

> "Walk Thou with me, nor let my footsteps stray
> Apart from Thee, throughout life's threat'ning way;
> Be Thou my Guide! the path I cannot see;
> Close to Thy side, Lord, let me walk with Thee."

The number who press on all the way are ofttimes pathetically few:

—But one Noah, just and devout, when the floods came down!

—But one Lot in Sodom, and even his wife turned back!

—But one interceding Abraham, to whom God could reveal this coming catastrophe, and who could pray for the city's deliverance!

—But one Joseph in Egypt, who stood for the true God, and there declared His Word!

—But one Moses to lead the children of Israel forth!

—But one Daniel in the kingdom, who dared stand for the right, and be true to the courage of his convictions!

Thanks be to God, however, the number need never be lessened to *"one!"* We need never walk alone, for even they who view from afar off, will ever see "they two" going to the Jordan.

GOING DOWN

Jordan means "going down," and there will ever be a "going down" before the "going through," and the receiving of the mantle of power. But no matter how precipitous the descent, or how lowly and humble the pathway through which our Lord may lead, let us ever remember that it is the pathway of humility that leads us to the place of power; the "going down" that leads to the "going up"—the going down into the realization of our own need, and that emptying out of self that brings down the mantle of power, and the filling with the Spirit of Elijah—the Holy Ghost. Falter not, beloved, and if the depths affright, just

"Ask the Saviour to help you,
Comfort, strengthen, and keep you;
He is willing to aid you,
He will carry you through."

"And Elijah took his mantle, and wrapped it together, and smote the waters, and they were divided hither and thither, so that they two went over on dry ground."

Elisha could not take himself through the Jordan; Elijah, the master, parted the waves and took him through. Just so, we cannot take ourselves through into the Spirit-filled land, or fill ourselves with the Spirit, but He will take us through.

There are two waters the Christian pilgrims must cross, which must needs be miraculously opened by the Lord. The first is the Red Sea, so blessed a type of the river side, the rent veil, the crimson blood of Jesus, opened for our salvation. The Jordan also which leads to the Promised Land whose boughs hang low with an abundance of fruitage of the Spirit-filled life, must be divinely opened for us.

"Take, take me through, Jesus,
Take, take me through;
You know the way better than others do,
Whate'er the cost, whate'er the test,
I'll keep close to Jesus,
And He'll do the rest."

"And it came to pass, when they were gone over, that Elijah said unto Elisha, Ask what I shall do for thee, before I be taken away from thee."

So spake the Master to His little ones ere He went away: "Ask what ye will, and it shall be done unto you. . . . Hitherto have ye asked nothing in My Name: ask, and ye shall receive, that your joy may be full."

Oh, if Jesus could stand before us in the flesh today, and speak again these words, I wonder what our petition would be? Would we ask riches, fame, popularity, higher earthly standing? I wonder!

THE PETITION OF ELISHA

Elisha had but one petition that burned his heart, and fired his soul, and glowed within his eyes! Surely he must have been rehearsing that petition o'er and o'er in his heart, for his request was right on the tip of his tongue as soon as the question was asked:

"And Elisha said, I pray thee, let a double portion of thy spirit be upon me."

Elisha was to take up his master's work—he must needs possess his master's power. Even so, the disciples of Jesus were to take up the ministry of evangelizing the world and preaching the Gospel to every creature, just where Jesus laid it down. And they must needs have His power, even the Holy Spirit, who dwelt within the Master, and by whose power He did His mighty acts, and of which He spake saying, "The works that I do I do not of Myself. He that dwelleth in Me, He doeth the works."

Small wonder Elisha pressed on across the Jordan with his cry, "Let a double portion of thy spirit be upon me!" Small wonder that the disciples pressed on a Sabbath day's journey to Jerusalem, and climbed the steps to the upper room, with the fixed determination to "tarry until" they be endued with the power from on High and the mantle of Jesus should descend upon the waiting Church. Tossed and driven, helpless and needy, hardly daring to meet together for fear of the Jews who had smitten the Chief Shepherd, and would fain have scattered the sheep abroad, realizing that soon their Elijah, Jesus, the tender and glorious Lord, would be taken away and they would be left alone to carry on the work, they knew that they simply must have the Spirit, be endued with power from on High, and that they would receive this power after the Holy Spirit was come upon them. And their waiting hearts were throbbing,

> "Breathe upon us, Holy Spirit,
> Bathe each trembling heart and brow,
> Fill us with Thy hallowed Presence,
> Come, oh come, and fill us now."

"And he said, Thou hast asked a hard thing: nevertheless, if thou see me when I am taken from thee, it shall be so."

"A hard thing?"—Some think it a very light and easy matter to receive this holy mantle of power. "Just take it by faith, and try to believe you have it," say some "and you have it." "You received all there was for you at conversion and did not know it. Every Christian has this mantle," say others. But ah, 'twas only the Elisha who pressed on all the way, who really received in Elijah's day. 'Twas only the hundred and twenty that pressed on to the upper room who received the baptism of power. Not the fifty sons of the prophets standing to view afar off who received the mantle of Elijah!—not unto the three hundred and eighty who, out of the five hundred disciples to whom Jesus appeared, yet who stood afar off, but unto the hundred and twenty who pressed on and followed hard, came the rushing wind and tongues of flame.

It means something to receive this mantle of spiritual power and you will know it when you have received. Why, if one could receive the mantle and never know it, one could lose it and never miss it.

"Thou hast asked a hard thing." It is going to mean self-denial, self-sacrifice, heart-searching, a fullness of consecration and abandonment to the will of God of which you never dreamed; a dying out to the opinions of the people, and the desire to go with the crowd; a willingness to go on with the Master alone, and a crossing of the Jordan—"Nevertheless, if thou see me when I am taken from thee, it shall be so unto thee; but if not, it shall not be so."

The sons of the prophets, standing afar, saw not the ascension. They doubted the report and thought to find Elijah in the mountains, and received not the mantle. Elisha saw him go and the spirit of Elijah fell upon him.

Many there are today who wonder why they have not the power of the Spirit to sweep communities, and bring revival fires. It is often because they have not seen the Savior go, His resurrection, His ascension, His aliveness from the dead has never really been revealed to their dear hearts. They worship the dead and not the living Christ—the great I was, and not the great I AM. They fail to realize that this Jesus hath God raised up, whereof we are all witnesses, and hath shed forth this, which ye now see and hear—fail to understand that He hath ascended on High, leading captivity captive, and giving gifts unto men.

And praise the Lord, even as Elisha saw Elijah go, so the believers saw Jesus go and received of His Spirit.

THE FIERY CHARIOT

"And it came to pass, as they still went on, and talked, that, behold, there appeared a chariot of fire, and horses of fire, and parted them both asunder; and Elijah went up by a whirlwind into heaven. And Elisha saw it, and he cried, My father, my father, the chariot of Israel, and the horsemen thereof."

Up, up into the opening heavens, ascended Elijah, as Elisha, the disciple, stedfastly beheld till the billowing clouds unfolded him and he saw him no more.

Such a sight had never been witnessed! The air fanned with angels' wings, the rushing of fiery steeds, the farewell words of Elijah, the ascension and the disappearing flame of attendant glory, must have swept over and ravished the soul and body of Elisha as though a tornado had passed o'er him, and thundered by into the distant horizon leaving him prone in the desert in that strange hush that always succeeds the passing of a swift moving storm.

Tears and laughter and shouting must have filled his heart.

Trembling must have laid hold upon his very bones. Excitement, joy, sorrow, wonder, loneliness, responsibility, need, expectancy—he must have run the entire gamut of emotions to behold such a sight and live. But though he cried, *"My father, my father, the chariot of Israel, and the horsemen thereof,"* and though his heart must have pounded, and the wind of the chariot wheels have sang in his ears, that one great cry was still in his soul, "Let a double portion of thy spirit fall on me."

Hands upstretched, face lifted to the heavens, lips moving in earnest prayer, eyes devouring every movement of that departing form in the ery chariot—he is looking, he is waiting for but one thing. He is believing and expecting it to descend upon him at any moment, for was it not the promise of the Master, was he not to take up the Master's work and must he not needs have the Master's power?

Ah, there he goes! The fiery chariot is disappearing through the gateway of the clouds, and heaven drops her misty curtains o'er the opened sky.

He is gone! Elisha, your master has taken his departure, and you are left alone *without* the power.

THE DESCENDING MANTLE

But wait a moment—what is that? The fixed unwavering eyes of Elisha are shining now. The uplifted hands reach higher, his face is illuminated and, following his upward gaze, we see it too—a little speck in the distance first—and then, unfolding, fluttering, down, down, down from out the heavens, light, confident, sure—as though 'twere the pinions of a dove, descends the mantle of Elijah and comes to repose at the feet of Elisha where all he must needs do is to put out his hand and take it.

Oh, what did you do, Elisha? Did you impulsively reach out your hand in faith, seize the mantle and throw it on over your own garments?

No, indeed! We read that before he clothed himself with the mantle: *"He took hold of his own clothes, and rent them in two pieces."* Then—*"He took up also the mantle of Elijah that fell from him, and went back, and stood by the bank of Jordan."*

What a picture! What a type of the ascension of the Lord

Jesus Christ, and the descension of his mantle, even the power of the Holy Ghost upon the early Church and all who will press on to the Jordan and receive the Spirit.

In the last verses of the last chapter of Luke we read of the Lord Jesus that: *"He led them out as far as to Bethany, and He lifted up His hands, and blessed them."* His last words being, according to St. Luke: *"And, behold, I send the promise of My Father upon you: but tarry ye in the city of Jerusalem, until ye be endued with power from on high."* (v. 49). *"And it came to pass, while He blessed them, He was PARTED from them, and carried up into heaven. And they worshipped Him, and returned to Jerusalem with great joy."* (vs. 51, 52). Note the striking similarity of this verse to that of 2 Kings 2:11, "And it came to pass, as they still went on, and talked, that, behold, there appeared a chariot of fire, and horses of fire, and "PARTED" them both asunder; and Elijah went up by a whirlwind into heaven."

In the first chapter of Acts we also read of the words spoken by our Lord just before His translation when He promised the mantle of His power to the Church, saying: *"Ye shall receive power, after that the Holy Ghost is come upon you: and ye shall be witnesses unto Me both in Jerusalem, and in all Judaea, and in Samaria, and unto the uttermost part of the earth. And when He had spoken these things, while they beheld, He was taken up; and a cloud received Him out of their sight."* And as they looked steadfastly toward heaven as He went up, they were reminded by heavenly visitors that the Lord would someday come again; they bethought themselves of the work to be done ere His return, and hastened to Jerusalem, there to receive the mantle of His power before taking up the ministry He had entrusted to their hands.

With rushing wind and tongues of flame, descended the Holy Ghost upon the hundred and twenty on the day of Pentecost, and filled them with His Spirit. They had seen the ascending Christ, they had received the descending Holy Spirit. The mantle of power which had descended from God out of heaven, and fallen upon Jesus in the Jordan, had now descended upon, and did abide upon the believers who were to carry on His work.

Even as it was necessary for Elijah to be caught up before his mantle could fall on Elisha, so it was necessary with our Lord and Master who said: "It is expedient for you that I go away: for if I go not away, the Comforter will not come unto you; but if I depart, I will send Him unto you."

The perserverance, going-through, and expectancy of Elisha were rewarded.

The obedience, prayer, and ten days' waiting of the disciples in the upper room were also rewarded as will be the earnest following after the fulness of the Spirit, by every truly consecrated child of God.

FAREWELL, MY WAY—WELCOME, THY WAY

But before Elisha put on the mantle of Elijah, he rent his own clothes in two pieces. And the only way in which we as a Church or an individual can successfully put on the wonder-working mantle of the Holy Spirit, is to first rend our own garments, our own plans and methods, ideas, desires and schemes, red tape regulations and rules, in two pieces, and strip them away, and then put on the mantle of power which our Lord has sent down and which lies within the reach of all who will pay the price and go all the way with Jesus.

As we rend our robes in two pieces, we cry, Goodbye, to our own man-made plannings and ponderings, our futile efforts of the flesh, our forming of committees to get up concerts, entertainments and suppers to bring the people to Church, our thinking and scheming as to how to get sensational subjects to hold the crowds; Goodbye to man-made strivings to work up a revival in our own strength and, as we take up the mantle of power and are clothed with the Spirit, we cry: Welcome, Holy Spirit of God! Have Thine own way and wield Thine own dear sceptor o'er my life! Be Thou my guide, my wisdom and my strength! Plan Thou each hour and lead the way! Speak through my lips and fire my tongue with praise! Burn in my heart with white heat, oh faith and love, till self and dross be burned away, my plans and wishes, ashes on the altar of Thy holy will! Come, Holy Spirit, mantle sent from the Christ of God—Oh, let a double portion of Thy Spirit fall on me, that all the world may see 'tis no more I but Christ that lives in me, and seeing Him, may love Him, and the old time power descend.

Clothe me, fill me, o'erflow—not that I may strut, or boast, or live within the mantle's joy alone, but that I may return to a world of sin, suffering, and grim realities, to tell that world of Christ, my living Lord.

True, there may be those who will despise, and forsake you, but they left the Savior, too. True, the enemy may fight and bitterly contest each step of the journey, but lift your eyes to Him who "always causeth us to triumph," and sing,

"Go, then, earthly fame and treasure!
Come, disaster, scorn and pain!
In Thy service, pain is pleasure;
With Thy favor, loss is gain.
I have called Thee, 'Abba Father,'
I have stayed my heart on Thee;
Stormy clouds may o'er me gather,
All must work for good to me."

The Lord caused to descend on Elisha the mantle of Elijah, not for his own pleasure or joy but for practical service and ministry, and we read that:

"He took up also the mantle of Elijah that fell from him, AND WENT BACK."

What a message to the believer who has attained unto great spiritual heights, is contained in those last three words, *"And went back."*

ELISHA'S RETURN

Though this spot by the Jordan must have been the most hallowed spot on the face of the earth to Elisha, he did not set up his abode on the scene of his transporting, rapturous experience. He did not say, "Well, I have journeyed farther than any of the others, and will now exclude myself from their company, and give myself to deeper teaching and feeding my own soul upon the riches of my experience. They would not understand me anyway." No! He *went back,*—back to the brethren who stood afar off—back to a world of need and aching hearts, a world that dwelt in the darkness of unbelief and hunger—back to a sphere of practical service in the commonplace dwellings of life. But oh! He took the mantle of power with him as he went! And so should we ever return from the highest heights of transfiguration glory to the valley of upstretched hands and needy lives.

We read of *the shepherds* to whom the host of angels appeared, announcing the birth of the Savior, that "they came with haste, and found Mary and Joseph, and the Babe lying in a manger." It had been to them a day of transporting glory. Their souls had been swept into heavenly places by the rhapsody of praise which the angels sang. They had run swiftly and beheld the face of the infant Messiah, but the Word is careful to state that, *"The shepherds returned, glorifying and praising God for all the things that they had heard and seen"*—returned to testify and "made known abroad that which was told them concerning this Child."

The Wise Men followed the star and found the Babe and rejoiced with exceeding great joy, as they opened their treasures, and presented unto Him gifts; gold, and frankincense, and myrrh, and fell down, and worshipped Him. But they arose and *departed into their own country,* witnessing of the Christ.

The One Hundred and Twenty were filled with the Holy Spirit in the upper room. 'Twas a place of unspeakable blessedness and joy, where they might have closeted themselves for many days, and feasted on manna from above, but they *went back* down the stairs from the upper room, back to the thronged streets and busy marts of life to *"noise abroad" the story of the risen Lord, and win the hearts of multitudes unto the Christ.*

Elisha *"went back, and stood."* Thank God, it is a wonderful thing to go back and "stand."

"By the Bank of the Jordan"—How that Jordan, which means "going down," is mixed up and interwoven through the deepest Christian experience!

"He took up also the mantle of Elijah that fell from him, and smote the waters, and said, WHERE IS THE LORD GOD OF ELIJAH?"

Elijah was gone but Elijah's God still lived. Elijah, the worker of miracles, was gone, but the day of miracles was not passed.

Elijah was gone but there were still rivers to cross and hearts to gladden and lives to cheer, lepers to cleanse, hungry to feed, and chains to be broken.

THE CHALLENGE

So, standing there by the river's edge, he cried, "Where—Is—The—Lord—God—Of—Elijah?"

O Elisha, prophet of God, your lips have been long since silent, but how your words keep ringing and ringing, echoing and re-echoing across the waters of Jordan, and on across the sands of life, "Where—Is—The—God—Of—Elijah?"—words which span the gulf of time and pierce to the depths of our being, clear, keen, insistent, demanding an answer and are as a two edged sword that searches our innermost heart with a double message:

The first being that of rebuke that we have so far lost sight of the fact that Elijah's God still lives today, with power as unlimited and unchanged as in the days of yore,

And the second, an exhortation that we lift up our faces unto the heavens even now and believe right this moment in the living, loving, resurrected Lord, and in the God of Elijah.

"Where—Is—The—Lord—God—Of—Elijah?" Well, indeed, may we stop and ask ourselves the question today! Where are His miracles? Where is His power? And where the glorified Jesus who declared Himself to be the same yesterday, and today, and forever? If these prophets of old saw such mighty miracles wrought by faith before the coming of the Messiah, the opening of the new and living way, the outpouring of Pentecostal power, and the birth of the Church, why should we not stand by the river of Humility and see them through faith today?

"And when he also had smitten the waters, they parted hither and thither: and Elisha went over."

How eloquent in the verse just quoted is the word *"also"*—like the opening for a moment of a gate that gives a comprehensive glimpse of the vistas of similitude between the ministry, pathway and life of servant and master; the following in His footsteps; the doing of His works. Elijah had parted those waters before, so Elisha smote them "also" for he had become the recipient of the master's mantle and was to carry on the master's work.

And how it calls to mind another "also" used by Jesus ere He went away—*"The works that I do shall ye do ALSO."*

There were those in Elisha's day who would have rebuked him for thus stepping in his master's footprints and doing as he had seen Elijah do,—but the Lord did not rebuke him.

There were those in Peter's day who rebuked him for leaping out of the boat and walking on the waves as he saw the Savior do, but the Lord, instead of rebuking him, reached out His hands and spake just one word—"Come."

There are those today who would rebuke those who would seek to claim the promises the Savior gave, and follow close in the steps of His ministry—but the Savior smiles and answers, Come:

"There is a Guide that never falters,
And when He leads I cannot stray,
For step by step, He goes before me,
And marks my path, He knows the way."

"And Elisha went over." After all, that is what real overcoming is—a going over—not under, or around, but abundantly and triumphantly over.

"And when the sons of the prophets which were to view at Jericho saw him, they said, The spirit of Elijah doth rest on Elisha."

Ah, would to God the world could say this of the Church today!

And would to God that the ministering brethren from the schools of the prophets, (or theological seminaries), many of whom are standing to view afar off those who are seeking the power of the Holy Ghost, might see the Spirit-filled Elisha's return to the field of practical whole-hearted, soul-winning, with such transforming glory that they would be forced to cry: "The spirit of Elijah doth rest on Elisha." The same Holy Spirit who descended in bodily form as of a dove, and abode upon the matchless Son of God, the Only Begotten of the Father; the same Spirit that filled the one hundred and twenty on the day of Pentecost doth rest upon this Elisha company, causing them to show forth, not the spirit of fear; but of love, and of power, and of a sound mind. And they would cry,

"Lord, send the old-time pow'r, The Pentecostal pow'r!
Thy flood gates of blessing on us throw open wide!
Lord, send the old-time pow'r, The Pentecostal pow'r,
That sinners be converted and Thy Name glorified!"

"And they came to meet him, and bowed themselves to the ground before him."

Many there be who are fearful of going all the way with Jesus lest they be shut out of the presence of their brethren and be put out of the synagogues;. loving the praise of men more than the praise of God. But when Elisha returned with the mantle and the spirit of Elijah, his brethren recognized that spirit and ran to meet him. Why, there are thousands, yes, hundreds of thousands of brethren in the world today, who are just starving for the old-time power, yearning for some solution of the problem that will meet the needs of a cold, backslidden worldly-minded Church, bring them back to God, make the desert bloom and the barren field to yield her increase; thousands who will run to meet and welcome those who are really filled with the Spirit, and can help solve the needs of the hour, as did Elisha of old.

He was now qualified for service and following in his master's steps. His plow and oxen burned upon the altar, his consecration complete, he had followed all the way to Jordan, received the spirit and mantle of Elijah, and returned for practical service. His first act was to heal with salt the waters which had caused to be barren the land of his people, and oh, God's spiritual children are the salt of the earth, and when they are plunged into the brackish waters whose spirituality has been lost, there must be a revival and a healing of the spring from whose fountain head will flow forth streams of blessing that will cause the desert to blossom, and the words of Elisha at the spring to be re-echoed, *"Thus saith the Lord, I have healed these waters; there shall not be from thence any more death or barren land."*

True, there may be children who will come forth by the way to mock and scorn, but the bears shall devour them, and the victor go on his way unharmed.

The first task in the ministry of Elisha was as the first duty in the ministry of the Church, the healing of the waters and causing the barren land to yield.

The second task in the ministry of Elisha was that of filling the empty vessels with oil—even as the next duty in the ministry of the Church is the preaching of the necessity of the virgins having their vessels filled with the oil of the Holy Spirit.

His raising of the Shunommite's son; his curing the death in the pot, his feeding of the one hundred men with twenty loaves; the healing of Naaman's leprosy; the causing of the iron to swim; the Syrians to be struck blind; his prophecy of plenty in Samaria when besieged by the foe; his anointing of Jehu; his death and the miracle of his bones in the sepulchre causing the dead man to live and stand up on his feet, are all blessed types of the ministry of the Church which should be as much a reflection of the life of Christ as was the ministry of Elisha, or that of Elijah.

Come, dear hearts, let us leave all and follow Jesus, the Lamb of God. He is calling us from the fields of sin and selfishness; He is passing by this very hour, so close you can put out your hand in simple faith and touch His seamless robe, His nail-pierced hand. See! He is holding His mantle of mercy, and love, and power, ready to cast it o'er each surrendered and consecrated life. Oh, why should we tarry a moment longer? Will you not look up into the down-bending face of Jesus just now and say: "Let me kiss my father and my mother goodbye, and I will follow Thee! Let me burn the oxen upon the handles of the plow, and give my neighbors to eat of the fruitage of my yielded life! Then take me with Thee to Bethel, Jericho, and beyond the Jordan! Let my life be lost in Thee, and a double portion of Thy Spirit descend upon me, that I may do Thy bidding and glorify Thy Name!"

"Savior, 'tis a full surrender,
All I leave to follow Thee;
Thou my Leader and Defender
From this hour shalt ever be.

No withholding—full confession;
Pleasures, riches, all must flee;
Holy Spirit, take possession!
I no more, but Thou in me.

Oh, the joy of full salvation!
Oh, the peace of love divine!
Oh, the bliss of consecration!
I am His, and He is mine."

THEY HAVE TAKEN AWAY MY LORD

THE Garden of Gethsemane was past. Golgotha with its agony of soul and body was over. The throbbing, rending rocks were still at last. The storm-swept heaven was clear, and the morning star shone down benignly. The day had not yet begun to dawn, and the Sacred City was wrapped in slumber. The frightened guards had taken their departure, and there was silence in the Garden of Joseph of Arimathaea.

Silence did I say? But no—what is that sound? 'Tis more than the whispering of the olive trees; more than the moan of the wind through the sycamores. 'Tis a sound that strikes a chill through the heart of the listener—the sound of a woman weeping—heart brokenly, inconsolably, and repeating over and over again in hopeless tones:

"They have taken away my Lord! They have taken away my Lord, and I know not where they have lain Him!"

"Oh Jesus—where are You? Oh Jesus I want You! All the world is dark and drear, and my heart is gripped with loneliness without You. Jesus, Jesus of Nazareth, Jesus of the Tender Heart—where are You? Don't You hear the cry of the needy, the sinful, the sick, the broken-hearted? Oh! He will not answer me! The tomb is empty! They have taken away, they—have—taken—away—my—Lord!"

There is a lump in our throat and a catch in our heart as we gaze upon that poor little disconsolate figure clad with the garments of grief, rocking herself to and fro, repeating over and over: "They have taken away—they have taken away my Lord."

Oh how her heart must have throbbed, as she sat rocking herself in her grief, in that hour which is ever darkest just before the dawn. What scenes must have lived themselves over again in her mind!

"Jesus," I can hear her say. "Jesus who was born in Bethlehem, and whose birth the angels did announce. Jesus the light that did shine in the darkness e'en though the darkness comprehended it not. Jesus, Thou Tender Shepherd of the sheep, who did forgive the vilest sinner of his sins; who healed the sick and cooled the fevered brow; who cast out demons, raised the dead, set the captive free. Jesus, who did feed the hungry and calm the storm-swept billows of the sea—how—how am I ever going to live without You? Who now will cleanse the sinner? Who now will heal the sick, and lift the burdens of those that are sore oppressed? Who now will meet our need with such miraculous power—none—none but Thee, Lord, wert ever able to give this poor old sorrow-stricken world beauty for ashes, and the oil of joy, for the spirit of heaviness. But now—you are gone! They have taken away, they have taken away my Lord."

Poor Mary! Dear Mary, forgiven much, loving much, her heart was well nigh broken as she sat weeping at the empty tomb.

Yet hundreds and thousands who today sit at an empty tomb—a powerless, revival-less, church, devoid of the miraculous, prayer-answering Christ of the long ago, Jesus the great I Am wrapped in the slumber of worldliness and unbelief; higher criticism and formality, might well take up the cry of Mary: "They have taken away — they have taken away my Lord; taken away the Lord of the Bible—taken away the Great I Am, who is the same yesterday, today, forever; taken away the Deity of my Lord and Master—taken away the inspiration of the Scriptures that declare atonement through the precious blood,—taken away the preaching of the old time born-again experience, and of the victorious life above the world and sin—taken away the old-time altar-calls—taken away the old all-night prayer meetings where saints of God were wont to lie upon their faces in prayer till a revival came down which swept the entire community—taken away the warmth, and fire, and faith, and fervor which they have now come to call emotionalism, and in its place they have left an empty tomb—my Lord they have taken away!

"O miracle-working, prayer-answering Jesus, where are You? I need You—want You so! Thou of whom the Word doth speak as healer of soul and body, where art Thou? Once You walked among the sons of men, once Thou wert all in all unto Thy people for body, soul and spirit. Jesus, who once said: Go in peace, thy faith hath made thee whole, oh don't you know—can't you see—we of today need You—need You just as much as those who lived nineteen hundred years ago?

"But now men say that You have changed, Jesus dear, that You are far away beyond that dome of blue; that You are no longer the miracle-working healing Christ of the Bible—and they have taken You away, dear Lord, and I know not where they have lain You."

God only knows the number of Marys who today have been sitting before the empty tomb, mourning their departed Lord—mourning the need of a revival of the old-time power and the preaching of a Christ who is not dead but risen. Oh, why have men limited the Holy One of Israel? Why have they taken away the Lord of the Bible?

Weeping, yearning, longing for the return of the old-time glory of a Christ who lives and moves in the midst of His people, thousands have wept and prayed inconsolably. Moving pictures in the parish-house, chicken suppers, festivities, preaching of psychology, community uplift and social reform—none of these have been able to fill the empty void nor still the heart-broken cry: "They have taken away my Lord. Oh, I want Him! I want to hear His voice! I want to feel the touch of His hand on mine! I want to feel the warmth of His fires burning on the altars of the church! I want to see Him heal the sick and break the captives' chains."

But hark! Through the gloom comes a clear, sweet voice like a shower of golden melody. It is the voice of the angels, speaking to the troubled heart.

"Woman, why weepest thou? Mary, why do you not enter into the spirit of the world round about you? Why are you not contented with the forms and ceremonies in the Temple, even though they do deny the power thereof? Why are you weeping, crying and praying so?"

"Why am I weeping? Why am I crying? Why can I not be satisfied with the empty, foolish things that can never take the place for a moment of the old-time power? Oh, how can you ask the question! 'Tis like feeding of the husks the swine do eat, after once I have tasted the heavenly ambrosia of His fulness. Oh why—why have you taken away my Lord?"

"But see, even as Mary is speaking, the day is beginning to dawn, a new day indeed. The mountains round about Jerusalem are touched with fire. Pink and gold are lighting up the clouds.

that just a little while ago seemed so dark and black as though they never could shine again. And through the scattering gloom and through the chill of the morning, a white-clad form in a seamless dress is coming. His face is lighted with an inner radiance, and His voice like rushing waters on the fragrant hillsides. Look, Mary dear, is there not something familiar about that form?"

But no—her eyes are too blurred with tears, her ears too dull from the agony of her aching heart, as she turns herself back from the empty tomb.

"Woman, why weepest thou? Whom seekest thou?" Something about the tone and the loving solicitation of the voice, pierces the gloom a little and something of the quiet, efficient power of this Man of Galilee made itself felt to Mary even though she could not see Him clearly through the blur of tears.

How the heart of that Man must have throbbed as the strangled, little choking voice of Mary made answer: "Sir, if thou hast borne Him hence tell me where thou hast laid Him, and I will take Him away."

"I can't—I can't go on without Him! I must find Him! And, though I'm only a woman, my love shall make me strong and in these two arms of mine I shall take Him away. I need Him; the world needs Him; the sinful, the sick, the suffering, the hungry—we all need Him. Seems as though He must hear us calling, seems as though He must see our tears and as though the prayers and anguish of our hearts would bring Him back. O Sir, hast thou borne Him hence? Have you seen my Lord?"

"What—what is happening to Mary? A peace like the dawning of a glorious day, after a night of storm and fury, is coming over her face. The mist of tears is clearing away, and some way the agony of her heart seems eased a little, and through the garden a soft, small morning breeze is playing, stirring into wakefulness which seem to open their hearts and send forth the sweetness of their perfumes to that Stranger of Galilee. The lilies are swaying toward Him; and He is fairer than them all. The roses are bending in the breeze as though to kiss His feet. A still sweet calm like the calm of heaven itself, is stealing through the garden, and wrapping itself like a restful, quiet mantle o'er that erstwhile broken-hearted weeper at the tomb. A bird springs from the tree tops yonder into the air, and showers the waking earth with his morning song. Surely the garden of Joseph of Arimathaea was never so beautiful before! Mary's grief-torn, sorrow-stricken heart seemed hushed and lifted. Then through the Garden rang one word:

"Mary." Oh, the sweetness of that voice! The birds must have paused mid-wing to listen. The flowers and the leaves of the trees have ceased their swaying whispers to listen. As for Mary, the clouds of her comprehension were riven now, and she turned herself about.

"Mary!"

No one in all the world could speak that name with such melting tenderness except the Lord.

"Mary!" What memories that sweetest of voices carried to her soul!

"Mary," and she turned and fell upon her knees, clasping her arms about that form, lifting her tear-drenched face, now transfused with a joy celestial, and cried:

"Master!"

"Oh Jesus! Jesus! Is it really You? Oh Jesus! Master, Lord, they said that You were dead, that You would never live again, that the day of miracles and power and glory was over forever, but Oh, dear Lord, I needed You so! My heart was so lonely, and Oh Jesus, the whole world groaneth together in travail needing You.

"Jesus, are You really alive? Oh Jesus, speak to me again—touch me—lay Your hand upon my head—tell me that it is really You—that You are not changed—that You are the same as You were in the days gone by."

"Yes, Mary—it is really I. Be not afraid. Yes, Mary, he who was dead is alive forevermore, and because I live you shall live also. I have carried your sins, the sickness, suffering, the curse of the whole world in my body on the tree and now I have conquered the last enemy, death, and am alive forevermore. Yesterday, today and forever my power is just the same. I wait to save, to bless, to heal, to comfort just as in the days of yore.

"Dry your tears, Mary, mourn no longer the dead Christ; but rejoice in the living Lord. Hark, the birds are singing. The flowers are breathing forth their fragrance, the sun is rising o'er the hill tops. Darkness and night and death have fled away. The angels of heaven are singing around the great white throne. Be of good cheer, Mary—I am not dead but living."

Oh, that the Marys of the Church today could turn themselves about, turn their backs upon the empty tomb and face the risen Lord, who comes to meet them, in shining robes of light!

Can you not see Him, Sister?

Can you not hear His gentle footfalls, Brother?

Oh see, He is coming to meet you. Methinks I see Him now through the dim light of the early dawn, walking through the garden of the Church, coming in response to the weeping disconsolate Marys, who have mourned the loss of His power, mourned the lack of the preaching of the living, loving, miracle-working Christ. Such love and seeking, as that of Mary, will ever bring the Master to our side.

And oh, methinks I see His face grow brighter, fairer; and His voice like honey in the comb as He is calling to His Church—His Marys—His faithful hearts who have waited patiently for Him, speaking that same message that He spake to Mary in that day of yore:

"Go to my disciples, and say unto them, I ascend to my Father, and to your Father; and to my God and your God—Death is conquered; night is at an end. The things which I did in that hallowed yesterday, which you have come to hold so dear, I live to do today.

"Go Mary—go and tell the story. Bid the weeping one rejoice, bid the heavy laden come, and I will give them rest. Bid the hungry come and dine; the sinful plunge into the fountain opened in the house of David for sin and uncleanliness; the sick and the suffering touch the hem of My garment and be made whole."

To the awakened Marys of the Church today, the Lord is speaking the self-same message, bidding them run swift-footed to bear to His brethren the self-same message, the sweetest message that could be brought by man or angel—"I have seen the Lord."

"No longer need we have for our church or place of worship an empty tomb! No longer need we be barren of revivals, altar calls, soul-winning, amen corners and the miraculous, supernatural joyous presence of the Lord Jehovah! I have seen the Lord. He is able to save, able to heal, able to baptize with the Holy Spirit. He is not dead, He is risen and in the midst to bless."

Doubting Thomases may be skeptical of the message and of the power of Jesus to do the same things which He did yesterday. Yet, nevertheless, 'tis true, 'tis true, for I have seen the Lord.

Oh, that the churches of Christ could see the Lord today! Oh, that they could brush the tears of sorrow from their eyes, and shake the dust of the tomb off their garments, and rise up with open arms with faith to meet the living Lord.

"Mary, My Church company, can you not see Me? I am coming to meet you. To send you with a message of hope and comfort to the world that needs me so."

Sing ye angels of Heaven! Sing ye cherubims around the throne! Sing ye birds of the morning! Clap your hands ye trees, and sing His praise, ye hilltops! Speed, ye Marys, on the swift pinions of love and joy, and cry to all men everywhere:

"He lives! He lives! He lives! And I have seen the Lord!"

THE VALLEY OF DRY BONES

Ezekiel 37:(1:14).

LET us begin this wonderful chapter with the first words of the first verse and go down into this valley and its experiences step by step with the Prophet Ezekiel.

THE HAND OF THE LORD WAS UPON ME:

What a wonderful thing it is for an individual to know that the hand of the Lord is upon him! Away down in Florida, when we were preaching to the dear colored people, they used to love to sing this verse:

"Chil'en, Ah knows de Lawd,
Chil'en, Ah knows de Lawd,
Ah knows de Lawd,
Dun got His han' on me."

and O, this afternoon I am so conscious of the hand of the Lord resting upon me. Praise His name.

THE HAND OF THE LORD WAS UPON ME, AND CARRIED ME OUT IN THE SPIRIT OF THE LORD:

This was by no means the first time the hand of the Lord had been upon Ezekiel. Had he not been caught up unto mountain tops of Revelation? Had he not seen the four living creatures, the cherubim and the Ark? Had he not beheld the glory of the Lord? and the mighty movings of His power? Ezek. 1:28 and 10:4.

Doubtless, when the hand of the Lord came down upon him and carried him out in the Spirit, Ezekiel longed to be lifted again to some ethereal height of glory. The Lord was moving him out; what wonders was the Lord about to show him now? Have you ever wondered what Ezekiel's feelings must have been when he opened his eyes and discovered that the Lord had

SET HIM DOWN IN THE MIDST OF A VALLEY.

Being set suddenly down in a valley after a hill-top experience is bad enough, but that was not the worst of it, this was a valley

WHICH WAS FULL OF BONES.

I think that perhaps some of us know in a little measure how to appreciate and understand what the feelings of Ezekiel were. We, too, have felt the hand of the Lord upon us. We, too, have, at many times, beheld His glory and dwelt in the midst of light and power. We, too, have had the Spirit of the Lord *set us down* in a certain assembly, home, neighborhood or city, wherein we have opened our eyes to discover, with a start, that we have been deposited right in the *"midst"* of a valley which is literally *"full"* of bones.

AND HE CAUSED ME TO PASS BY THEM ROUND ABOUT; AND BEHOLD THERE WERE VERY MANY IN THE OPEN VALLEY, AND THEY WERE VERY DRY.

Behold, there were *very many.* Oh, the pity of it! Were there only a few it would not seem so terrible, but the great number of these dry bones is staggering. There are so many precious Christians in so many churches, in so many climes, that are down in the valley, no spiritual strength or meat to cover their frames of profession, nothing but bones—bones—bones.

IN THE OPEN VALLEY.

You need neither a spade nor a pickaxe to find the kind of bones that I am speaking of. They are in the open valley. Why, I would not be surprised if you could turn round and find some of them sitting right in the seat beside you at this moment.

AND THEY WERE VERY DRY.

So dry they can not say "Amen" or "Hallelujah"—so dry they have not said "Praise the Lord" since they entered this building—so dry that they can neither shout nor clap their hands themselves, and would like to stop everybody else shouting and rejoicing if they could. (They are almost like the dog in the manger who could not eat the hay himself and would not allow the horse to eat it)—so dry that there is no real victory in their lives or ring to their testimony, or sterling worth to their profession. Dry! Dry! Dry! You can almost hear the bones rattle beneath their cloak of profession whenever they preach or testify or move.

AND HE SAID UNTO ME, SON OF MAN, CAN THESE BONES LIVE?

What a staggering question it was with which the Lord confronted Ezekiel—a question which would at once stop his murmuring over the dried-up condition of affairs in the bone-yard, and require unlimited hope and faith in the resurrected, life-giving power of the Lord.

Have you been placed in a valley (be it home or assembly or neighborhood or workshop) that is full of dry bones? Is your minister dry? your congregation, etc.? Then God is confronting you today with the same question that faced Ezekiel away back yonder.

"Son of man, have you a faith that can cause these dry bones to live?" It is one thing to find fault with and lament over deplorable conditions of dearth and barrenness; it is quite another thing to have the prayer and faith and confidence in God which will bring life and strength and better conditions round about you.

If you have discovered that you are in the midst of a valley of dry bones, stop lamenting and complaining because you are there and wishing you had been placed in a different environment on the hilltop where revival fires are burning and live armies are marching. Thank God that YOU are alive and that GOD is alive, and that as you believe and pray life will banish death in those round about you today as surely as it did in the day of Ezekiel. Your being placed in that hard, dry, difficult place was not an accident, not an oversight or a mistake on the part of God. Just as surely as the hand of the Lord set Ezekiel down in that valley of dryness and death, so surely has the hand of your loving Father set you down in that valley, or position, or home or parish.

"All things work together for good to them that love God, to them who are the called according to His purpose."

And now, having placed you there, He has confronted you with the same question with which He confronted Ezekiel:

"Have you faith to believe and to lay hold upon Me, the Life Giver, and claim that life for these dry bones?"

AND EZEKIEL ANSWERED, OH, LORD, THOU KNOWEST.

Here again many can heartily sympathize with the hesitancy of Ezekiel, for many children of the Lord, I fear, have often answered the challenge to faith in the same way:

"Oh, Lord God, Thou knowest! They are a pretty dried-up lot of people. There does not seem to be a spark of life, or even a longing for it. It hardly seems possible that this church or these people ever could be brought to a real live spiritual place. But, Oh, Jesus, increase my faith. Help mine unbelief, for I long to see them live, Oh, Lord."

THEN HE SAID UNTO ME, PROPHESY UPON THESE BONES AND SAY UNTO THEM: OH, YOU DRY BONES, HEAR THE WORD OF THE LORD GOD, BEHOLD, I WILL CAUSE BREATH TO ENTER INTO YOU, AND YOU SHALL LIVE.

Poor, dried-up lifeless professor, there is hope for even you. You dear ones that do not believe in noise and shouting, you who do not believe in so much earnest prayer and praise to the Lamb, He will cause breath to enter into even you (and you know that Psalm 150 says "Let everything that hath breath praise the Lord"), and you shall live.

SO I PROPHESIED AS I WAS COMMANDED.

Ah! there was the secret of the power and success of Ezekiel's prophecy in the valley. Do you see it? A-s I w-a-s c-o-m-m-a-n-d-e-d, not with enticing words of man's wisdom, which seemed wise and plausible to himself—not words—to please and lull his audience into a false security, nor yet a self-righteous tirade of condemnation that merely showed them their condition and dryness; but a prophecy that was according to the commandment of the Lord.

Hallelujah! *"The entrance of His Word giveth light,"* and life and liberty. Oh, for more Ezekiels today who would prophesy according to the commandment of the Lord instead of bringing in side issues and divisions and strifes—then would we see more shaking in the valley of dry bones, and the wind of the Spirit should blow, bringing life to those that sleep.

AND AS I PROPHESIED THERE WAS A NOISE.

God grant that even as, whilst Ezekiel prophesied, there was a noise, and as whilst Peter yet spake the Holy Ghost fell (Acts 10), that while I am yet speaking, the power may fall upon you just now. Oh, that our words may be so in accord with the commandments of God that whilst we are yet speaking we, too, will hear a *"noise"* of men and women crying out:

"What shall I do to inherit eternal life, and to receive the Holy Spirit?" the noise of praise and intercession, the sound of an abundance of rain, the sound of His chariot wheels upon the mountains, and the stirring in the tops of the mulberry trees.

AND AS I PROPHESIED THERE WAS A NOISE, AND BEHOLD, A SHAKING, AND THE BONES CAME TOGETHER, BONE TO HIS BONE.

You notice that as Ezekiel prophesied there were three distinct things that took place in the valley of dry bones—three periods that they passed through. Firstly, the noise: Secondly, the shaking: Thirdly, the bones came together.

FIRST, THE NOISE

When the latter rain began to fall in copious showers in 1907, the Spirit moved mightily in answer to prayer the whole world over, awakening and bringing to life innumerable valleys of dry bones—there was a noise. Sinners wept their way to Jesus and cried aloud:

"What shall I do to be saved?" Believers were filled with the Spirit, shouted, and often talked for hours at a time in other tongues (Acts 2:4) as the Spirit gave utterance. The noise of their joyous praises filled the sky. The glimpse which believers caught of the body and of the plan of God to restore the church to her full Pentecostal power and life caused them to shout aloud before the glorious vision, and well, it is putting it very moderately to say:

"There was a noise."

But stop! Listen! What is this—this remarkable shaking as of an earthquake, which immediately follows—surely and inevitably everywhere—behind the first noise of the Spirit's outpouring? If you but open your eyes and look about you throughout this movement the world over, you too will see, *"and behold a shaking."*

SECOND, THE SHAKING

Has your assembly or the company with which you have been wont to worship, been going through a shaking? Have you personally been subjected to a severe shaking? Has your heart ached? and have you, too, asked a continual Why? Why? and wherefore? when you have seen brothers, that were bosom friends and comrades in the battle, separate and drift apart, assemblies split in two, or half a dozen factions, as the case may be. Have you wondered why this one doesn't come back, and that one compromised, and those two couldn't agree and were so widely divided? I will tell you why it was. It was because of the shaking which followed the noise. It is following in the life of every assembly. It is following in the life of every believer. A mighty shaking-time is on.

Just as God shook out of Gideon's army until there were but three hundred left that could not be shaken (Judges 7) so the Holy Spirit is today sifting, purging and shaking, for *He "whose voice then shook the earth . . . hath promised saying, yet once more I shake not the earth only, but also Heaven, and this word 'yet once more' signifieth the removing of those things that are shaken . . . that those things which cannot be shaken may remain. Wherefore, we, receiving a kingdom which cannot be moved . . . may serve God acceptably."*—Heb. 12:26-28.

When first one sees the shaking, the splits and divisions amongst those whom we know should be bound together in love, it is heart-rending, but when we begin to see the plan of

God as revealed in His Word, we enter into a place of rest, and when we read the next clause:

AND THE BONES CAME TOGETHER, BONE TO HIS BONE,

we lift our hands and shout for joy.

There is going to be a coming together after the shaking, some of these days, dear hearts, and those that come together will be bound by such cords of unity and love that nothing can separate them again, and moreover when the body comes together it will be "BONE TO HIS BONE."

This is nō patched-up affair, no man-made peace, no temporary armistice, but a unity that shall remain.

"Bone to his bone." When man in his own wisdom tries to fix the body up by choosing and ordaining, pastors, teachers, evangelists, prophets, helps, governments, etc., he is almost sure to pick the wrong bones or else put the right bones in the wrong places. That is why so many man-made organizations have the ear where the eye ought to be, or the foot where the hand ought to be.

THIRD, THE COMING TOGETHER

Aren't you glad that God sets His own church in order and that HE sets some in the church, first apostles, secondly prophets, thirdly teachers, etc. (I Cor. 12:28), and that when He has shaken out all that can be shaken and tossed about by every wind that blows, and has gathered together the firm, true, uncompromising, unshakable bones, He will Himself put them in their appointed places in the body, bone to his bone. *"For as the body is one, and hath many members, and all the members of that one body, being many, are one body, so also is Christ, for by one Spirit are we all baptized into one body" . . . and "now hath God set the members every one of them in the body as it hath pleased Him . . . now ye are the body of Christ and members in particular."*

We will not see the body come together in an entirety which will be apparent to the human eye, before the coming of the Lord. This movement, please God, will never be one great *organization,* but rather an *Organism.* We *are* expecting, however, a unity amongst the different members of the body (such as we have never seen before) to develop right down here in this old world.

One member of the body is made up of many joints which are in one accord and work harmoniously, one in connection with the other, joined together by the cords of love. The members of the body (that is the assemblies or communities) are moved and controlled not by their own wisdom or the orders of one another, but by the Head, which is Christ. And as each member, moved by the Head, obeys His will, there will be unity and harmony and a coming together. Each member is made up of many smaller members. In the arm there are the fingers, the hand, the bones of the wrist, of the forearm, and the shoulder. Today is the day that the smaller bones and joints are taking their place in forming the members. When Jesus shall appear the many members of the body shall be gathered, and the final great coming together will take place in the air. Hallelujah!

AND WHEN I BEHELD, LO, THE SINEWS AND THE FLESH CAME UP UPON THEM, AND THE SKIN COVERED THEM ABOVE; BUT THERE WAS NO BREATH IN THEM. THEN SAID HE UNTO ME, PROPHESY UNTO THE WIND, PROPHESY, SON OF MAN, AND SAY TO THE WIND, THUS SAITH THE LORD GOD, COME FROM THE FOUR WINDS, O BREATH, AND BREATHE UPON THESE SLAIN, THAT THEY MAY LIVE.

SO I PROPHESIED AS HE COMMANDED ME, AND THE BREATH CAME INTO THEM, AND THEY LIVED, AND STOOD UPON THEIR FEET, AN EXCEEDING GREAT ARMY.

Oh, if there is a soul here tonight who was once as a dried-up skeleton, has now been redeemed and has been covered with the sinews and flesh and skin (the covering of grace and salvation), and you have been slain by the mighty sword of His power, what you need now is the baptism of the Holy Spirit. The same Holy Spirit that filled the house with the sound as of a rushing, mighty wind on the day of Pentecost, shall come upon you, endue you with power, stand you upon your feet, and join you to this exceeding great army. (Rev. 7:9).

Sinner, backslider, luke-warm professor, whosoever and wherever you are, you do not need to remain in the grave or the valley of dry bones any longer. The Lord is waiting to bring you up out of your graves of coldness and death, and cause you to know Him in salvation, to fill you with His Spirit and lead you to Canaan's land. Read the 12th, 13th and 14th verses of this 37th chapter of Ezekiel.

"Behold My people, I will open your graves and cause you to come up out of your graves" (sin), *"and bring you into the land of Israel"* (salvation). *"And ye shall KNOW that I am the Lord when I have opened your graves, Oh, My people, and brought you up out of your graves."* (Notice He says you will KNOW—there will be no "think so" about your salvation. You will have a definite knowledge that you have passed from death unto life).

The 13th verse is glorious. Do not stop there, however, but go on into the 14th, *"and shall put My Spirit in you and ye shall live; and I shall place you in your OWN land; then shall ye know that I, the Lord, have spoken it and proclaimed it, saith the Lord."*

Here is another definite experience you will know about. He does not say you will guess I have performed it—My promise to fill you with the Spirit—or you will take it by faith, but *you will KNOW I have performed it.* Then praise the Lord. When He saves you you know it, for He has brought you into the Land of Israel, and when He baptizes you in the Holy Spirit and speaks through you with other tongues you will know it, and He will bring you into your own land, the land of fruitfulness and victory which He has made as a promised land to those who will obey Him.

And you, dear child of God, no matter how dead and dry the bones in your particular valley may be, do not be discouraged or question the divine wisdom that set you down, just where you are, but respond to the call of faith the Lord is sending you, and prophesy as His Word commands, and if you, hidden behind the cross, lift Jesus up, He will shine down into the cold, benighted hearts round about you, bringing healing and life and filling with His Spirit until from that valley of dry bones a transformed, triumphant army shall rise and march forth to join the great body (for now are they many members, yet but one body.—I Cor. 12:20).

The great, final coming-together day when the many members of the same body shall be united, and when the body shall be united to the Head, is at hand. What a wonderful day it will be when Jesus speaks from the heavens—the NOISE of

His triumphant shout shall be heard (I Thess. 4:16); the graves shall be SHAKEN wide, fetters of mortality shall be shaken loose; and from the four quarters of the earth, from the dead and from the living, each bone, each member of the body SHALL COME TOGETHER and rise to fill its allotted place in that body, bone to his bone.

The time is short now, dear ones. Each setting sun brings us just one day nearer the catching-up of this triumphant body who shall rise to meet the Lord in the air. 'Twill be a body of overcomers, a band of people who have been tested, shaken, and proved—who have washed their robes in the blood of the Lamb and come up out of great tribulation. Will you yield yourselves as never before to the dealings of the Lord, and instead of murmuring at His shakings in your life, cry unto Him:

"Strip me, Lord, of everything,
Of this world and self, and sin,
That I may see the coming King,
And a crown of glory win."

"DEATH IN THE POT."

"And Elisha came again to Gilgal: and there was a dearth in the land; and the sons of the prophets were sitting before him: and he said unto his servant, Set on the great pot, and see the pottage for the sons of the prophets.

And one went out into the field to gather herbs, and found a wild vine, and gathered thereof wild gourds his lap full, and came and shred them into the pot of pottage: for they knew them not.

So they poured out for the men to eat: and it came to pass, as they were eating of the pottage, that they cried out, and said, O thou man of God, there is DEATH IN THE POT. And they could not eat thereof.

But he said, Then bring meal. And he cast it into the pot; and he said, Pour out for the people, that they may eat. And there was no harm in the pot."—II. Kings 4:38-41.

ELISHA came to Gilgal and there was a dearth in the land"—There had not always been a dearth in Gilgal:

Gilgal had once been wondrously blessed of God. Blessing and bounty had walked its streets hand in hand. Had they not echoed and resounded with shouting and rejoicing and the marching feet of four thousand men of war, as the priests, led by Joshua, had borne the ark of the covenant of the Lord thither?

After they had pitched camp and set up their twelve stones as a monument of Jordan's parted waters (Jos. 4:3 and 20), and kept the Passover, had they not eaten of the old corn of the land and the fruit of the land of Canaan? The long-looked-for promised land had been reached. No more need for wilderness wanderings, *"and the manna ceased on the morrow after they had eaten of the old corn of the land; neither had the children of Israel manna any more, but they did eat the fruit of the land of Canaan that year."* (Jos. 5:11, 12).

Was it not at Gilgal that, after the Lord had appeared as Captain of the host (Jos. 5:14), and Joshua had fallen on his face to the earth, the Lord said unto him:

"Loose thy shoe from off thy foot; for the place whereon thou standest is holy?"

And after Samuel had anointed Saul, did he not send him unto Gilgal to *"tarry until"* the *"Spirit of the Lord"* should *"come upon"* him with *"signs"* following, that should give him *"another heart"* and turn him *"into a new man?"* (Read I Sam. 10:6-9). What a wonderful type of Pentecost! Later Samuel said to the people:

"Come, let us go to GILGAL and renew the kingdom there," even as the early apostles had returned to Jerusalem for fresh anointings of the Spirit.

"A DEARTH IN THE LAND."

But behold, now, something has happened. The children of the Lord have become cold, lukewarm, backslidden. Such a great dearth has come to Gilgal and the surrounding countries that they have *"cleanness of teeth and want of bread."* (Amos 4:6). *"Transgressions have been multiplied,"* but in Hosea 4:16, the Lord promises Israel (who, in her iniquity, He has likened to a backsliding heifer and forbidden to enter Gilgal), that if they will follow Him He will feed them as a lamb in a large place.

During the former rain outpouring of the Holy Spirit, which began on the day of Pentecost (Acts 2:4), the ark containing the glory of the Lord (spiritually speaking), rested in Jerusalem as in Gilgal of old. Even as Saul had been sent to Gilgal to tarry till the Spirit of the Lord was come upon him and till the signs came to pass, so the hundred and twenty had been commanded to tarry in Jerusalem until the Holy Spirit should come upon them with signs following.

The long-looked-for, long-prophesied (Isaiah 28:11, 2:13; Joel 2:23 and 28; Zech. 10:1; Mat. 3:11; Luke 24:49; John 14, 15, 16; Acts 1:5 and 8) promised land had been reached. True, God had kept them whilst in the wilderness, and manna had come upon them, as the inspired words fell from the mouths of the holy prophets of old as they were moved by the Holy Spirit—true, the words of Jesus had been as manna from heaven, whilst He walked this earth in the fleshly body, but now—*now*—the Holy Spirit had come—*N-O-W—they* had entered Canaan's land, and instead of the manna which had been taken away, and fell no more upon them (Jesus being returned to the Father and His voice being heard no more), they had corn and oil and wine (Joel 2:19), as the Spirit spoke through them of Jesus and His coming kingdom. *"And they did eat the old CORN of the land"* (Jos. 5:11, 12) *"neither had they manna any more, but they did eat the fruit of the land of Canaan."* (See fruits of the Spirit, Gal. 5:22).

Jerusalem (as Gilgal of old) rang with the praises of the Lord, and with the marching feet of new converts, new men of war, who went forth to follow the Captain of the host. On the day of Pentecost three thousand souls were added to the church; with pure hearts o'erflowing with joy, and with unshod feet, His people walked softly before Him and fell upon their faces in adoration. Just as the twelve tribes erected their monument of twelve stones, so the twelve disciples stood as a monument of the mighty power of the great and holy One who had parted the waters of the Red Sea—*"Salvation"*—and parted the waters of Jordan to bring them to Canaan's land—*"The Baptism of the Holy Ghost."* Each time did the Lord Himself have to part the waters before His children could cross over into the new experience.

Humanity could neither swim nor ford *the Red Sea*—The Lord Himself miraculously *opened,* through His blood, a path—salvation—which meant at once deliverance and *Life* to repentant believers—and *Death* to unrepentant unbelievers.

Mankind could not cross the judgment of *old Jordan's* waves, nor make themselves worthy to enter Canaan and, again through *parted* waters (His GRACE and His WORTHINESS, which towered on either side) He led His people forth to the promised land, and filled them with the Spirit. Here are two experiences—Salvation and the Baptism of the Holy Spirit—which we could not have brought ourselves into, therefore did He part the waters each time. Bless His name.

"ELISHA CAME AGAIN TO GILGAL."

After the disciples and apostles had fallen asleep in the Lord, and the many years of blessing wherein the power and glory of the Holy Spirit had been manifested, came the gradual falling away of the spirituality of the church. The apostasy and dark ages followed, but holy, inspired prophecy had said:

"He who sent the former rain moderately shall send you the rain, both the former and the latter rain together in one month," and "It shall come to pass in the last days, saith God, I will pour out My Spirit upon all flesh," etc.

"AND ELISHA CAME AGAIN TO GILGAL," Hallelujah! The time for the latter rain outpouring of the Spirit which was to take place in the last days had come, and Elisha (who stands for the visual manifestation of the power of God in signs and wonders) came A-G-A-I-N to Gilgal.

And when he came he found that *"THERE WAS A GREAT DEARTH IN THE LAND."*

Ah, yes! What a dearth there was in the land! What a crying out for food, and pottage, and bread and lentils in and just prior to the years 1905 and 1906.

How many churches and saints cried to Heaven:

"Oh, for the old-time power! Oh, for another Pentecost!" The Methodist church, the Salvation Army, the Holiness church, and many others sang and prayed these words over and over (but Oh, how few really recognized the answer when it came, "wrapped in swaddling clothes and in a manger"). Nevertheless the Word of God said:

When you call upon Me I will answer, and *in the day that you seek Me with your whole heart I will be found of you; turn unto the Lord with weeping and mourning, and . . . "He will return and repent and leave a blessing behind Him, even a meat offering and a drink offering."*

"SET ON THE GREAT POT."

Therefore, when Elisha came again to Gilgal, that is when the Holy Spirit, at the specified time for the latter rain, found the hungry saints sitting before Him with one accord and one desire, even as the hundred and twenty had sat in waiting expectation of old, *"He said unto his servant":*

"Set on the great pot and seethe the pottage for the sons of the prophets." "Blessed are they that do hunger and thirst, for they shall be filled."

Oh, glory to Jesus! I can just close my eyes as I write, here before my open Bible tonight, and see the great Pentecostal pot (the entire Pentecostal movement), being brought out and set upon the fire—the Holy Spirit is, of course, the fire—our prayer, and praises are the WOOD (and Oh, it takes good dry wood, full of pitch, to make a real red hot fire—water-soaked, rotten wood of worldliness and unbelief will only smoke and smudge and hinder).

Once suspended over the fire of the Holy Spirit, the Pentecostal pot soon began to boil and simmer, as hungry saints came together, each bringing a contribution of carefully tilled vegetables in their hands as an offering.

What a mixture, what a conglomeration came together in that pot!

Perhaps there is not another movement on earth made up of such a varied assortment of teachings, creeds and organizations, yet all melt and blend into one when put into the WATER of the Word, and boiled over the fire of the Holy Spirit.

It was as though myriad streams, coming from myriad fountain-heads, had met and mingled together, and NOW flowed on in ONE great stream as though they had never been divided.

Its fire was as that of a great burning pile of WOOD, hewn and gathered from many sources—from varied kinds of trees —from widely separated forests, *now* leaping heavenward in one great flame of love and devotion.

It was as many VEGETABLES, planted, watered, cultivated, tilled and brought from many fields, put into one pot, and now forming, with the strong meat of the Word, and the water of the Spirit of life, a rich, nourishing food, whose appetizing and inviting fragrance was wafted to all about upon the vapor of praise and testimony which arises from the dancing, joyful mixture within.

With lightning rapidity the Pentecostal revival has encircled the world; thousands and thousands of hungry souls have been filled with the Spirit.

Wait a moment! You who are investigating, or gazing curiously into the lively, bubbling, dancing Pentecostal pot. Let us halt and examine some of the people—the endless procession of people who are coming to contribute some edible to the movement. Let us begin with this man hurrying along toward the pot, laden with vegetables and bread of the first fruits, and see what he has to say.

THE METHODIST.

Q. "Halt! *Who* goes there? From whence do you come?"

A. "I am a METHODIST. I come from a church founded upon the sound doctrines of Justification and Faith in the present Power of God, as revealed to John Wesley—a church where the power of the Holy Spirit used to fall in bygone years, until *saints shouted,* and *sinners wept,* and the *joyful* danced before the Lord."

Q. "O? And what bring you in your hand?"

A. "I bring with me carefully tilled vegetables and bread of the first fruits, from a grand old field—a little sparsely *'sprinkled,'* and—well—a little *'short of water'*—nevertheless, diligently cultivated by watchfulness and the Word of God."

"Our harvests come from various gardens and are tilled by different gardeners, some of which are known as 'The Epworth League,' 'The Free Methodists,' 'The Ranters,' 'The Shaking Methodists,' etc., yet 'tis the same sun of righteousness which, from the lofty heavens, shines upon one and all."

"Coming out from the parent field I bring with me an appetite whetted by the cherished memories of how God once did work in the old-time Methodist church; for, alas! Dearth and formality came into our field, and many therein were an hungered."

"Kindly excuse me, and allow me to pass, for in these last days (Acts 2:17) the great pot of blessing has been set upon the fire of the Spirit, and thither do I hasten that I may find this old-time power increased an hundred fold."

(There! He is gone! I would that I could have detained and conversed with him a little longer. Let not our hearts be troubled, however, for lo, one goeth, and behold, another cometh.)

THE BAPTIST.

Q. "Halt! Who goes there? And whence come you?"

A. "I am a BAPTIST. I come from a garden whose original plan of gardening (as recorded in our book of instructions) was patterned by the Word of God, the planting and springing up of the seeds required Justification and a Change of Heart. The young plants were well watered, too—in fact, *'completely immersed'* in the beginning of their growth, but as the plants grew and developed, and had need of the wind of the Spirit and the falling of the latter rain for developing the harvest, Alas! between the high, well-guarded fence of *'close communion'* and the heavy overhead trellis of theology and forms and ceremonies, neither wind nor rain could reach the garden."

"Consequently, many of our gardeners, realizing that the fruit of their labors was exceedingly *'hard shelled,'* and that some life and breaking of the dry stiffness was needed, tried an artificial irrigation process of worldliness and structural magnificence. Lectures, concerts and amusements were recommended and tried as fertilizers. The spiritual life of the plants, however, did not thrive well under this method, and many withered and pined away, and there was a dearth in the land."

"Coming forth from behind our *'close communion'* fence, I am hastening toward yonder brightly burning fire, for I do both 'see and hear' that the great pot has been set upon the flame. Hark! Can you not hear its dancing and bubbling, and see the vapors of praise rising, even from here?"

Q. "And what bring you in your hand to contribute to the Pentecostal pot?"

A. "I bring with me, as bread of the first fruits, the knowledge of the scriptures, sound doctrine, and a firm stand on Water Baptism as set forth by our forefathers. I bring with me a hunger for the real, tangible power of God."

"But, Ah! I catch the fragrant odors rising from yonder steaming caldron."

"Please allow me to pass, that I may receive my portion from the great pot."

THE SALVATIONIST.

Q. "Halt! Who goes there? From *whence* come you, and *why* do you come?"

A. "I come from the SALVATION ARMY, that, in obedience to the call of God, marched fearlessly beneath their banner of 'Blood and Fire,' into the very heart of the enemy's territory, taking captives and making love-prisoners for King Jesus."

"I come from a people who in their extensive gardening found labor for both the 'servant and the maid,' a body of people who were once deeply spiritual and prayerful, and entirely separated from the world and its earthly lore."

"True, amidst persecution and trial, they sowed the seed and gathered the harvest—not behind fenced enclosures, but in the streets and market-place, the slums and the hovels."

"I come from a people that used to stand for the manifestation of the Spirit, and many there were among them who shouted and danced, and fell prostrate under the power, and saw visions of the glory of God."

"Why do I leave? Why, because *there is a dearth in our land*—the old-time power is sadly lacking today, times and business are so pressing, pressing, popularity—our war work in the great world contest—never-ending financial needs—new barns for the extended harvest fields—have been as quick-growing weeds that have sadly choked and crowded out the old spirituality and whole-hearted abandonment and humble dependence upon God."

"Seeking and hungry for the old-time power, I come for food to the great pot which has been set over the fire of this Holy Ghost movement."

Q. "And what bring you in your hand?"

A. "I bring with me the first fruits of our labors. Our field of vegetables had a wonderful beginning; the planting was beyond criticism, and if our field had been watered according to the instructions of Chief Gardener Jesus, none should have excelled it. Our under gardeners, however, felt neither the prescribed water baptism nor the latter rain outpouring

(The Baptism of the Holy Spirit, as recorded in Acts 2:4) to be necessary.

"Our vegetables were not even sprinkled. Nevertheless they contain a real zeal for souls and a courage to go after them. I bring in my hands the old *'Amen Corner'* and the ringing Hallelujahs, singing and music, and a faith and perseverance that sow beside all waters."

On and on they come!

They are flocking in from every direction, each bringing some contribution to the Pentecostal Pot. Here comes the staunch

PRESBYTERIAN—the old Scotch COVENANTER—the HUGENOT, and the staid EPISCOPALIAN follows after—pride and formality forgotten.

One breath from the fragrant, boiling Revival on the fire brings back a rush of memories that recall the Faith and Power which rested in *their* midst in days of yore, when steadfast, persecuted forefathers fell upon their knees in caves and dens and dungeons, where plush and padded prayer-cushions were unknown—memories of old-time power and glorious blessing that followed in the days when "they who lived godly suffered persecution"—memories of long nights spent in prayer—the sincere unaffected heart's devotion of the Saviour and His love.

Ah, no! Neither gilded dome, nor frescoed arch, nor rolling tones that throb and thunder in the organ loft, nor surpliced choir, nor e'en the college-moulded, eloquent 'divine' (?) who speaks in modulated tones from flower-embowered canopy, can still the longing for the old-time power that glorified the sacrifice, surrender, prayer and faith of the Pilgrim Fathers' day.

Devoted saints come from the HOLINESS church, bringing the message of *Heart-Purity* and the *Coming of the Lord,* and wonderfully blessed of God, as fruitage needing but one thing—the latter rain.

The ADVENTIST adds his teachings on the *Coming of the Lord,* deep study of the *Prophetic Word,* teachings of *Holiness* and *Freedom* from *Worldliness.*

The QUAKER hastens up—deep wells of joyous recollections rising in his soul—eyes alight, beneath his broad-brimmed hat, with the memories of how HIS church, once shaken and controlled by the Spirit's power (before the dearth), had walked so close to God. Glowing coals within his heart, long banked and smouldering, now burst forth in flames again as he hastens to the Holy Spirit's fire and the great Pentecostal pot suspended thereupon. He adds the fruitage from his field—*'sterling qualities of truth,' 'unswerving faith,* and *'yieldedness to the movings of the Spirit.'*

And, would you believe it, here comes the ROMAN CATHOLIC—not one, but many of them, leaving the old church, many have come to the Saviour, have been redeemed, filled with the Spirit, and bring with them a *Holy Reverence* and *Obedience* and *deep appreciation of this new-found reality* and *life in Jesus* to add to the happy mixture bubbling in the pot.

So many come from every quarter that it is impossible to halt and question them all. Then comes THE SINNER—Yes, what lines and lines of them. Attracted by the reality and the mighty moving of the Spirit, they bring with them the Fruits of Repentance and First Love.

"And Elisha said:

SET ON THE GREAT POT, AND SEETHE POTTAGE FOR THE SONS OF THE PROPHETS."

Oh, what a glorious feast we are going to have! What wonderful pottage!

Lift up the cover and peep in at the dancing, joyous mixture. See how, when boiled over the great *FIRE OF THE SPIRIT* and with the *WATER OF LIFE,* with the *MEAT OF THE WORD* and the *SALT* which has never lost its savor, a great change comes to all the viands within the pot; the fruits of the fields, the vegetables and the barley, lose their "hard shells," slip out of their walls of *differences, creeds* and *forms*—forget they came from widely separated gardens and were tilled by gardeners who never could agree as to methods, and soon they burst with praise as their innermost hearts flow forth in love.

Then, as the fire burns on, they melt—and melt—and M-E-L-T until the pottage is but one united, savory mixture.

Outside walls crumble and fall away, for vegetables must be peeled before entering the pot (that is barriers of organizations and differences must be left outside; peelings do not make good pottage). Then, as the fire still continues to burn and the pot to boil, each vegetable and fruit, in melting, has lost its own identity and has so united and merged itself into the other broken, melting hearts round about it, that 'tis hard to realize they ever were divided.

THE MAN WITH THE LAPFUL OF GOURDS.

Many eyes and many footsteps were turned eagerly toward this Pentecostal movement; brethren patted each other on the back and said:

"No more need of hunger or separation or dearth. Here is unity everlasting with nothing to mar."

Hungrily, servants and handmaidens alike drew near with clean plates and shining spoons. "What a wonderful feast we are going to have," they said.

But stop! Who is that man, slipping in so stealthily behind the others, carrying something in his garment? Let us question him.

Q. Halt! Who goes there? From whence do Y-O-U come?

A. "Me? Oh, I come from no particular garden. I am the 'ONE WHO WENT OUT IN THE FIELD TO GATHER HERBS.' "

Q. "And what sort of vegetables do you bring in your lap?"

A. "Why—er—that is, I—It is not vegetables I bring. Vegetables must be most carefully planted in prepared ground, tilled and cultivated (study to show thyself approved unto God, a workman that needeth not to be ashamed). Whilst wandering yonder I found a wild vine full of nice, fat *gourds,* no trouble to till them at all. They were there already, and all I had to do was to pluck the wild gourds in passing. See? I have a good big lapful here. Fine looking specimens, are they not?"

Q. "Good specimens of 'gourds,' yes, but I am not so sure of their being good to eat, or being a desirable addition to yonder feast. I fear that they are poisonous?'"

Ah. "Oh, no, they are not poisonous, I assure you."

Q. "Well, what are the names of these different gourds?"

A. "Why—a—This one is called *'False Teaching'*; this one is called *'Error'*; whilst this prickly one is known as *'Doctrinal Issues'*. This puffy fat one is *'Lover of Power and Recognition'*. Then there is *'Self-Righteousness'*, *'Formality'*, *'Preconceived Ideas and Teaching'*, *'Fear of Manifestations'*, *'Flesh'* and *'Fanaticism'*. There are many other gourds, and amongst their number are *'Lack of Brotherly Love'*, *'False Reports'*, *'Harsh Criticism'* and *'Tale Bearing'*."

Q. "Why, Man! You would never think of bringing such things into the midst of a Pentecostal gathering!

"You are wrong, and the gourds are poisonous. They will destroy unity and curdle love and make endless confusion and trouble.

"Surely you do not realize what you are doing?"

A. "Oh, yes I do. The Lord (?) revealed this thing to me and I know this new idea is the only right one. I know these gourds are perfectly all right and you can't teach me anything about them. Kindly allow me to pass."

Q. "Wait, wait, come back! There, he is gone—he worms his way into the inner circle, gets close to the pot, lifts his lapful of gourds, and in they go, the whole lot of them, into the pottage. On-lookers innocently allowed the gourds at first to pass them, and even—

Shred them into the pot of pottage, *"for they knew them not."* So they poured out for men to eat; and it came to pass as they were eating of the pottage that they cried out and said: OH, THOU MAN OF GOD, THERE IS DEATH IN THE POT, and they could not eat thereof."

Amidst the many who come with good contributions to the pot, here and there steals up a man or woman with a lapful of gourds, which they have plucked from some wild vine as they journeyed, and they are thrown, sometimes ignorantly, sometimes knowingly, into the great pot upon the fire.

"Oh, what a distressingly large lapful of poisonous gourds!" exclaims the on-looker who had been approaching with his empty dish and spoon, ready to dine, and who now draws back in fear.

"Horrors—the whole thing is spoiled!"

There is false teaching and error in that movement, and I am afraid to have anything to do with it.

There is "So and So," who did "such and such" a thing and if *that's Pentecost,* or if *that's the Baptism of the Holy Ghost,* I for one, don't want it. There's Mr. "So and So" in our assembly, and there's that one who professed to be a Holy Ghost preacher—did you hear what he did?

Did you hear of the gourd that he brought and dumped into this movement?

No, Sir! The whole pot is contaminated and poisoned. I tell you there's DEATH in the pot," and they are in a straight between two, whether to try to overturn the whole pot or to walk away and leave it, warning others as they go.

Some say, "Come on, let's fight this movement. Let's write some tracts against it and do what we can to overturn the whole thing." Others who walk away, warn everyone they meet by saying:

"Did you hear the news about that Pentecostal movement down there? Why, 'So and So' has just brought the most distressing lapful of gourds and dropped them into Pentecost; unity is disrupted; love is curdled, the people are made sick at their very hearts. Don't you go near that place."

Perlexity and confusion falls upon many an on-looker, some stay to criticize; others to wring their hands and weep.

What shall YOU and I do? We know that the movement is ninety-nine per cent pure, but Oh, that lapful of gourds has brought so much trouble! Of course we know that *"WHEN THE SONS OF GOD CAME TOGETHER THE DEVIL CAME ALSO,"* and that there never was a movement but where some one came in to bring reproach, and that even amongst the twelve disciples one was a Judas. We also know how one who does not measure up to the standard is singled out from the ninety-nine others and enlarged upon until the "ninety and nine just ones" are forgotten in pointing to and discussing him who went astray.

"Well, we know the thing is not right anyway, as it is, and I guess we better go away. Too bad, isn't it?"

"But wait a moment—

"Who is this so swiftly approaching with a well-filled sack clasped tightly in his arms?"

Q. "Who goes there, and what do you bring in your hands?"

A. "I am the man with the sack of meal. The meal is the Word of God. I go to cast it into the pot. This meal will simmer down to the bottom of the whole affair and settle all disturbances. It shall cry aloud:

" 'What saith the scriptures? Bring forth the plumb line. Let God be true and every man a liar. Prove all things. Abhor that which is evil; cleave to that which is good. Be not overcome of evil, but overcome evil with good.' "

This word is quick and powerful and shall not fail, if cast into the pot, to purify and bring order out of confusion.

"And Elisha said, bring meal, and he cast it into the pot; and he said, pour out for the people that they may eat, and there was no harm in the pot."

Oh, hallelujah! The Word of God is being poured into this movement and His Word is accomplishing that whereunto it has been sent. The Holy Spirit today is calling as did Elisha of old:

"POUR OUT FOR THE PEOPLE THAT THEY MAY EAT."

I can seem to see the surrounding circle of empty plates and see the hungry faces of the dear ones as they are partaking themselves and calling to others to come, "taste and see that the Lord is good."

"POUR OUT TO THE PEOPLE THAT THEY MAY EAT." Oh, yes, that is the greatest mission of the hour. Give unto the people that they may eat.

If you have discovered something somewhere in your vicinity or in the movement at large, which looks to you like a gourd, instead of turning your back and your judgment and wholesale condemnation upon the whole thing, go bring the meal (II Kings 4:41), get the Word of God and find out what saith the scriptures. *"If this work be of men it will come to naught; but if it be of God, ye cannot overthrow it, lest haply ye be found even to fight against God."* (Acts 5:38-39.)

Get out the meal—if you see this Baptism of the Holy Spirit with the Bible evidence, speaking in tongues, in the WORD, with the accompanying gifts and fruits of the Spirit, believe God and come boldly to receive this Bible experience even though every one round about you seems to be in error or falls below the standard.

INSTEAD OF BEING THE ONE WHO CRIES "THERE IS DEATH IN THE POT," BE AN ELISHA WITH A SACK OF MEAL; receive YE the Holy Ghost; let God make YOU to measure up to the Word. All your criticizing or scolding or telling where the trouble is or even trying to fix it, can never help. The Meal of the Word will alone avail.

Pour out for the people that they may eat. Dear worker, what are you feeding your hungry people on? Are you telling them and repeating over, meeting after meeting, every story and incident that has come to your knowledge where gourds have been put into the pot? If so, you are guilty and putting gourds of doubts and discouragement in the pot yourself.

When you set the table for your guests that hunger all about you, do not frighten people away by bringing up from your cellar the poorest potatoes or the mouldy preserves, or the mildewed bread from your larder—*THEY DO NOT WANT TO HEAR ABOUT MAN'S WORST; THEY WANT TO HEAR ABOUT GOD'S BEST.* What are you feeding your people on? Relating the worst things you ever heard of man doing or the best things you ever heard of God doing? The former makes poor fighting food—the latter makes firm spiritual muscles and makes strong, developed, matured men and women who grow quickly under such teaching *"unto a perfect man, unto the measure of the stature of the fulness of Christ."* Eph. 4:13.)

Remember that by relating past wrongs, etc., you are as guilty as those who committed them, and are only frightening people away by crying: "There's death in the pot." Go bring the meal: preach the Word. Lift up the pure standard and God will vindicate and honor His Word.

Does it seem sometimes that you have very little to set before the people, and do you feel your own lack and insufficiency? Remember that the servant felt it that day, too, when he said:

(II Kings 4:43): *"What, should I set this before an hundred men?* And Elisha said: *"Give the people that they may eat; for thus saith the Lord, they shall eat, and shall leave thereof. So he set it before them, and they did eat, and left thereof, according to the word of the Lord."*

The Word of God rights every wrong, dispels all darkness, removes all impurities, settles all misunderstandings, and whether is dissolves or eliminates all the gourds or just what becomes of them I cannot exactly say, but at any rate I know that after the meal was cast into the midst *"THERE WAS NO HARM IN THE POT."*

If you have been standing afar off in doubt and are an hungered, hesitate no longer but bring your meal with you and come and dine, for there is no harm in the pot.

With all the gourds (and indeed they are comparatively few in number, considering that this movement has enveloped the entire globe, and into it have come streams of people from every creed and clime and color), this great pot set upon the fire, this Holy Spirit movement is the best thing in the world and contains the best food on earth.

PRAISING THE LORD.

PRAISING the Lord has ever been to me one of the most inspiring and exalting of themes. Oh! how I love to praise Him and hear Him praised.

It has been my privilege, on several occasions, to witness the never-to-be-forgotten scene of one thousand saints standing on their feet with uplifted hands, and tears streaming down their radiant faces, praising the Lord with all their might and soul and voice, with one accord, till the great volume of thunderous praises blended into a sound as of rushing mighty waters as it rolled majestically heavenward. It went up as *one* voice, of *one people* who were *one* in heart and adoration of the Most High God and His Glorious Son, Jesus Christ.

It is when praising the Lord thus, as at no other time, my spirit catches the greatest revelation—the greatest vision of the mighty, omnipotent King of the Ages, *high and lifted up*. 'Tis then that the very atmosphere seems electric, charged with the mighty power of the great God, and I catch the sound of His chariot wheels leaping o'er the mountains, ever coming nearer as His saints continue to adore Him, till I hear the stately steppings of the King in the midst of His holy tabernacle—then, as the cloud of glorious adoration still rises from the hearts of the people, I see Him robed with Honor, crowned with Glory, seated upon a jewelled throne of adoration which His people have builded for Him by their praises.

The Lord inhabiteth the praises of His people. Where real praise is, there God is.

It is impossible to over-estimate the power, victory, blessing, healing, encouragement and inspiration embodied in this wonderful secret of praising the Lord.

PRAISE THE LORD AT ALL TIMES.

"Oh! but you know that I could never put anything on, I never could praise the Lord unless I f-e-e-l like it," someone exclaims.

Unless you feel like it! Oh! Is that the gauge by which you measure your offerings of praise? Is that the foundation upon which your Christian experience is based? My dear Brother, Sister, feelings are a poor and a very uncertain guide upon which to rely when it comes to praising the Lord, or any other Christian experience. Only one man in the Bible that I know of went by feeling; that was dear old Isaac, and you remember how he f-e-l-t the hands and arms of Jacob, his son, and how deceived he was. Oh, hear hearts, praise Him,

NOT BECAUSE YOU HAPPEN TO FEEL LIKE IT,

but praise Him at "all times," and let His praise "be continually in your mouth,"

BECAUSE HE IS WORTHY.

Begin to praise Him whether you feel like it or not, and you soon *will* feel like it. Why, it is impossible for me to lift up my hands and begin to praise and adore my Master without a downpour of His blessing that is as rain to the thirsty fields and flowers, or as the anointing-oil upon my head, running down to the borders of my garments.

"Let everything that hath breath praise the Lord." Why, acording to David, the only excuse you have got for not praising the Lord is being out of breath!

"Oh, Sister, I praise Him in my heart. I could never shout aloud or be demonstrative. It is not my make-up or disposition."

Beloved, when you have put on your beautiful garments of praise (for no matter how homely you may be to the natural eye, you are beautiful to the Lord when you have put on praise as a garment), you are lifted above your own "make-up" and "disposition" and swing far out into the realm of the Spirit. As for praising the Lord in your heart, why, your heart is no different from anyone else's. When it gets just so full of glorious praises and adoration and He becomes so real, so fair as to be altogether lovely, the chiefest of ten thousand to your soul, your heart will run over and you will shout His praises, and your voice will be blended with the voices of all the other redeemed ones and soar upward to the Lamb that sitteth upon the throne.

I was much impressed recently, while in New York, by the notices posted on the subway and elevated trains and in other prominent public places, warning the people of the severe penalty awaiting anyone who should try in any way to break the morale of the soldiers by talking of possible defeat, or failure, or by lauding the strength of the enemy. This should be a warning to Christians also.

DO NOT BREAK THE MORALE OF THE CHRISTIAN ARMY.

Two saints attend the same meeting. Probably you have these two saints in your assembly (for almost every assembly has them).

One enters with a long face, takes her seat, looks solemnly about, and if the meetings seem a little stiff or in need of a blessing, or lacking in praise, or "tied up," this dear one, meaning well enough, begins to be burdened and sigh, to pray aloud, or exclaim in this manner:

"Oh, Lord, what is the matter here? Oh, there is such a binding spirit, such a power of darkness. It seems as though the room were filled with demons. Lord, help," etc. Immediately every eye and every thought is directed to the devil, to darkness and binding spirits, and of course (like Peter when he got his eye on the waves), when we get our eyes on the devil we have them off Jesus.

When we advertise and meditate upon the greatness and strength of the devil, and show fear, we underestimate the power of the great *I AM*, the Mighty Conqueror who never lost a battle. Such despondency and burdened agonizing is contagious and soon everyone is moaning and crying and miserable, and it is not until someone begins "seeing and praising Jesus" that the cloud lifts.

The other saint enters the same meeting, where it seems that not one breath of Heavenly gales is stirring, feels the same pressure upon the meeting, and refusing to look at or recognize the enemy, says:

"This is the time to praise our Jesus. This is the time to see our God arise and scatter His enemies. He has told us that He will do great and mighty things if we will but praise Him, and we know that the enemy cannot lodge or abide in an atmosphere that is filled with the praises of the Lord." This saint straightway begins to shout:

"Hallelujah! We rejoice in Thee! We glory in Thy might, Oh, our King! Victory and honor ever attend Thy troops. Power and dominion envelop Thee. Thy glory and presence fill the heavens and the earth. It fills my heart just now. It overflows and fills the room. Why, glory to Jesus! Beloved, the Lord is in our midst. Do you not feel Him? Why, this atmosphere is just like Heaven!"

Such faith and praise is contagious. The fire of unwavering confidence in God that burns within this temple soon leaps over its parapets, spreads first to those in the seats nearby, then on to the farthest corner of the room, inspiring, encouraging, lifting up drooping heads, strengthening feeble knees, and in a moment every eye is fixed on Jesus, His praises fill the tabernacle, souls are blessed, vessels are filled to overflowing, the Latter Rain is heard pattering on the roofs, running down the troughs, overflowing the rain-barrels, the dry ground is saturated and the wilderness and the desert places are blossoming as the rose!

What was the difference in the two saints? The one recognized and saw only the power of the devil, and straightway began to bemoan the sad state of affairs, depressing everyone who listened, while the other saw only Jesus in His all-conquering, invincible might and splendor, riding on to sure and certain victory.

MY VISION OF THE DEMONS AND THE ANGELS.

The Lord taught me a wonderful lesson sometime ago, demonstrating the majesty and power of praise. I was seated on the rostrum in my tent during the evening meeting. Not only was every seat in the big tabernacle filled and crowds standing in the aisles, but all about the outside of the tent hundreds and hundreds stood closely packed together. It was the early days of the meeting and conviction had not yet taken the place of curiosity. Therefore, as a great many of the onlookers were Roman Catholics, and the balance unused to any demonstration of the power of God, the very air was filled with unbelief, skepticism, scoffing and ridicule. The people would listen as long as we sang (or was it because that drowned their murmurings?) But as soon as anyone endeavored to speak, the whisperings and the murmurings would begin until another song was started.

As I stood there on the platform, with my eyes closed, I saw the entire tent surrounded with great black demons, with huge, bat-like wings. Each demon seemed to stand about ten feet tall, and as they stood in a circle, completely surrounding the tent, they were so close together that their wings touched, tip to tip. They stood close to the border of the tent, and with my eyes still closed, my heart began to cry out:

"Oh, Lord, what shall I do?" And He spoke to me in such a real way, in that calm, undisturbed voice which those who love the Prince of Peace know so well:

"Just begin to praise Me. I will do the fighting. You do the praising." So I began to praise Him.

"Praise the Lord!" The first time I said it I noticed the demons seemed to tremble.

"Praise the Lord!" The second time I shouted it. I am sure my voice was heard above every other sound, and I saw each demon take one step backwards, away from the tent.

"Praise the Lord! Praise the Lord!! Praise the Lord!!!" Each time I said "Praise the Lord" the demons took another step backward, until I lost all sight of them in the distance.

"Praise the Lord!" The next time I said it I saw in the distance a circular band of angels standing around the tent.

"Praise the Lord! P-R-A-I-S-E T-H-E L-O-R-D!" Each time I praised Him they took one step nearer, another step nearer, still another step nearer, till at last they stood at the very border of the tent, such tall, wonderful-looking angels, with their beautiful white wings spread so wide that the wings of each touched, tip to tip, the ones of the next angel on the right and on the left. Father had sent one of His legions of angels to guard the tent.

Perhaps not another person in the tent saw the vision of this great shining band of angels, yet everyone inside and out must have sensed the presence of the divine, for not only did a great peace steal over my soul, but the whole audience was hushed. When I opened my eyes I could see only the people looking with rapt attention, but closing my eyes again I could see the angels just as plainly as I could see the people.

Is it any wonder that I believe that

THE POWER OF PRAISE DRIVES BACK THE ENEMY AND BRINGS DOWN THE BLESSING.

Jesus says: *"What things soever you desire when ye pray, believe that ye receive them, and ye shall have them."* Now, if we ask God to give us a certain answer to prayer, and we then proceed to believe we have it, it is only polite to begin to thank Him for it, in other words, shoot upward through the prayer zone into the praise zone, and thank God beforehand that, according to His word, it is done.

When contending with sickness, trouble, misunderstanding, discouragement or depression, begin to see Jesus. Praise Him with all your heart, and the upward flight of His praises will lift you as with the wings of a great eagle, above the woes of this earth till sorrow and sighing are lost sight of and consolation and joy unspeakable fill their place as you exalt and magnify the Lamb for sinners slain.

PRAISING HIM IN THE FLESH.

"But I do not want to praise Him in the flesh," says someone. Ah, but we walk no more *"after the flesh, but after the Spirit,"* and all this poor flesh of mine is fit for anyway is to praise

Jesus, and if you never do anything worse in the flesh than to praise the Lord you will never be displeasing in His sight.

When the Comforter abides and has His way, it is so easy to praise Jesus, for *"He, when He has come, will glorify Me,"* and *"out of your innermost being shall flow rivers of living water."*

BRING THE OFFER OF FRANKINCENSE.

You may have but little gold or silver—a little of this world's goods to offer—but there is no excuse for being sparing or miserly with His praises.

Heap up His praises upon the glowing altar of your soul, and pile His adoration atop of that, crown Him with glory, laud and magnify His name until His burning praises rise in precious frankincense, as a sweet-smelling savor to be caught in the golden censer of the angel who offers unto the Lord much incense (praise), with the prayers of all saints upon the golden altar which is before the throne. Rev. 8:3.

IN TUNE.

Let your heart be tuned up until it shall be as a harp of a thousand strings swept with melody by the fingers of the Holy Spirit.

If you have hung your harp on the willow-tree, if the rust of coldness or self or formality has formed upon the strings, or if they are broken or out of tune,

GO GET YOUR HARP!

Take it down from the willows, clean away the rust which has gathered from long disuse, let the Holy Spirit tune up each string until again the music will spring forth at His slightest touch. Remember it takes but a slight jar to put the most costly harp out of tune; walk softly, dear heart, with unshod feet before Him.